ENDANGERED SPECIES: NEW RESEARCH

ENDANGERED SPECIES: NEW RESEARCH

ALEXANDRA M. COLUMBUS
AND
LUKE KUZNETSOV
EDITORS

Nova Science Publishers, Inc.
New York

LIBRARY OF CONGRESS CATALOGING-IN-PUBLICATION DATA

Columbus, Alexandra.
Endangered species : new research / Alexandra M. Columbus and Luke Kuznetsov.
p. cm.
ISBN 978-1-60692-241-5 (hardcover)
1. Endangered species--Research. I. Kuznetsov, Luke. II. Title.
QH84.C63 2009
333.95'22--dc22 2008041178

Published by Nova Science Publishers, Inc. ✦ New York

CONTENTS

PREFACE

Endangered species can be defined as a group of animals or plants in danger of becoming extinct. This book presents an overview of such species as a result of certain factors such as climate change, extensive urbanization, overgrazing, and agricultural expansion.

Endangered species can be defined as a group of animals or plants in danger of becoming extinct. This book presents an overview of such species as a result of certain factors such as climate change, extensive urbanization, overgrazing, and agricultural expansion.

Short Communication - The Yangtze finless porpoise (*Neophocaena phocaenoides asiaeorientalis*) is the only freshwater subspecies of finless porpoise (*Neophocaena phocaenoides*), living only in the middle and lower reaches of the Yangtze River. It has been declared to be endangered under the Red Data List criteria (C2b), by the International Union for the Conservation of Nature and Natural Resources (IUCN) in 2004. As well as other odontocetes, Yangtze finless porpoise possesses of sophisticated echolocation systems. Recent researches demonstrated excellent capabilities of high-frequency sound production and reception in this species. The animal produces one sonar click train per 5 s in average with inter-click interval changing typically between 10–70 ms. The click signals hold the characteristics of "typical" high-frequency, narrow-band, and short-time duration phocoenid echolocation sounds. The means of peak frequency of clicks are about 125 kHz, and the means of time duration are shorter than 70 μs. Careful scanning and acoustical auto focusing behavior in porpoises was also observed in free-ranging conditions by using biologging techniques. Hearing capability research by using evoked potential technique indicated that the range of greatest hearing sensitivity of Yangtze finless porpoise covered frequencies from 45 to 139 kHz, and the lowest thresholds of less than 50 dB re: 1 μPa were found at a frequency of 54 kHz. Frequent biosonar production by this subspecies allowed effective passive acoustical survey. These several years, density and distribution of Yangtze finless porpoises are being surveyed acoustically along its habitat.

Chapter 1 - This chapter describes China's experience in attempting to protect its rare, threatened, and endangered species and their natural habitats. Because China is a mega-diversity country, with 10-11 percent of world species, its record is of international importance.

The chapter describes the distribution of endangered species, and the recent progression of biodiversity loss. It identifies the root causes of species loss, focusing on consequences of rapid economic development. In response, the state has developed a complex regulatory regime, including China's participation in international environmental conventions, national law and policy, and national and provincial regulations. Although three central agencies have most management responsibility, nearly a dozen are involved altogether, which the State Council has coordinated through several means. Proposed revisions to the regulatory regime indicate a maturation in thinking about species protection issues.

The protected area (PA) system is at the heart of China's efforts to avert biodiversity loss, and the chapter recounts the evolution of this system, the distribution and structure of PAs, and their management. Then, the chapter turns to agents of civil society—the media, scientists, and non-governmental organizations (NGOs)—which together are of increasing importance in alerting government officials to problems in biodiversity conservation.

Like other developing nations, China's regulatory regime has "implementation deficits." These are explained in the context of the administration of policy in PAs, focusing on limitations to the structural framework, administrative coordination, finance, personnel training, and community conflicts. The chapter concludes with a summary of the argument and both comparative and temporal observations.

Chapter 2 - The Mediterranean Basin is widely recognized as one of the main plant biodiversity hotspots of the world. In its western part, the Catalan Countries, which represent the eastern section of the Iberian Peninsula, is one of the areas with the highest floristic diversity of the basin, containing more than 4,500 taxa, and showing a rate of endemism of about 5%. At the same time, this region is one of the most fragmented and man-modified of the basin. Here the authors present a synthesis of the literature concerning allozyme genetic diversity in plant taxa occurring in the Catalan Countries. From 36 taxa examined, which are mostly rare and/or threatened, relatively high levels of genetic variability have been detected (P = 28.85%, A = 1.46, and H_e = 0.112 for diploid taxa), although with a substantial percentage (around 6%) of rare alleles per population, high rates of imbreeding (F_{IS} = 0.245), and a considerable genetic divergence among populations (G_{ST} = 0.248). The causes of such patterns, together with their relationship with different biological and ecological traits of the studied taxa, have been analyzed in detail. Such information has significant conservation implications, and may provide guidelines for setting up management and recovery plans of the Mediterranean endangered flora.

Chapter 3 - Abundance estimation of marine benthic fauna is usually conducted with surveys using commercial fishing gear such as trawls or dredges. These estimates are often unreliable due to low and variable efficiency and are inappropriate when dealing with rare or endangered species. At shallow depths, direct visual surveys through SCUBA diving are advantageous when compared to fishing surveys, as the records are not dependent on catch efficiency and visual surveys are not destructive, which is of concern when dealing with protected species or habitats. Distance sampling is a widely used set of methods for estimating abundance and/or density of biological populations and has been extensively used in terrestrial ecology and for marine mammals. The main distance sampling methods are line transects and point transects. A standardized survey is conducted along a series of lines (in line transects) or points (in point transects) searching for the animals of interest. For each animal detected, the distance from the line or point is recorded. A detection function is fitted from the set of recorded distances and is used to estimate detection probability, i.e., the probability of detecting the presence of an individual within some area. Failure to properly account for the detection probability leads to biased estimates of population status and trends, which may lead to false management decisions. Distance sampling is the standard method for abundance estimations for many endangered species. However, it has only rarely been used for underwater surveys of benthic fauna. As population assessment and monitoring is absent for most endangered marine benthic species, distance sampling through SCUBA diving may prove to be a valuable management tool, at least for shallow water benthic animals. As an example, the abundance of the endangered bivalve *Pinna nobilis* was estimated in a marine lake using distance sampling techniques. Two different methodologies were applied: classical distance sampling with line transects, and a density surface modeling approach using survey data from line transects, integrated with a Geographic Information System (GIS).

Chapter 4 - The Middle East is characterized by a high diversity of flora including a large number of medicinal plants. This region has one of the oldest and richest traditions of medicinal plant use. However, these plants are becoming increasingly rare and facing extinction due to a number of threats. Agricultural expansion, extensive urbanization, desertification, unsustainable harvesting, destruction of natural habitat, overgrazing, increasing demands of drugs and climatic changes have resulted in the loss or the endangerment of many of these plant species.

In view of this alarming situation, many efforts have been attempted during the past few decades in the Middle East region to conserve these plants and the traditional knowledge related to them. Such efforts are conducted by governmental and non- governmental organizations, academic institutes and research centers.

This chapter will review the status and causes of medicinal species endangerment in the Middle East as well as conservation measures to protect and preserve them from extinction. Conservation strategies include protected areas, cultivation, tissue culture, seed banks and botanical gardens. Some suggestions will be put forward for the efficient protection of these valuable natural resources of the region.

Chapter 5 - Pine marten (*Martes martes*) is a palaearctic species having a broad diffusion in central and north-eastern Europe, while it is localized or absent in southern and western Europe. British and Mediterranean insular populations are well developed and widespread. In Italy pine marten is diffused in the main islands, while it is rare and has a fragmented distribution in the peninsula. Its conservation state is poorly known; in addition, incidental killings, forest reduction and habitat fragmentation caused populations decrease in recent years. The conservation state of pine marten is defined by the III Appendix of Berna's International Convention and by the V Annexed of the Habitat Directive 92/43/CEE that defined this species as under risk.

One of the major criticisms concerning the management and conservation of this species is the difficulty to distinguish it from a "twin species", the beech marten (*Martes foina*); in several European regions the two species are in simpatry and seem to share the same trophic niche. Ecological competition between the two *Martes* species, with the supremacy of the more widespread and abundant beech marten, can be postulated. Thus the opportunity of a correct taxonomic identification of these congeneric species, and the status of genetic variability of pine marten, is fundamental for any management and future conservation program. Morphometric and molecular methodologies are an important tool for the study of wild fauna and, particularly, to distinguish pine and beech marten. The molecular approach, in fact, allows the unambiguous assignment of the studied samples, as well as phylogeographic and population genetics analyses. The application of molecular markers, furthermore, minimizes the impact on analyzed samples.

In fact, the animal manipulation is greatly reduced or absent when using non-invasive molecular methodologies for DNA extraction from hairs and faeces.

The aim of this chapter is to review the knowledge on molecular and morphological approaches that can be employed on this species in Europe, particularly concerning its conservation state.

Chapter 6 - The systematics of the family Esocidae is essentially based on morphological characters. It points to the existence of five species distributed in Eurasia and North America. Only northern pike (*Esox lucius* Linnaeus, 1758) is present in Europe with a broad geographical and environmental distribution, including most of the northern temperate zones, above 40° latitude up to the Arctic zone, and Italy, Greece and Turkey. Northern pike is one of the most important freshwater fish for recreational and commercial fisheries. In addition, being a big, edible, freshwater top predator, it is a key species for the conservation and management of lakes and rivers ecosystems. Although recent reports indicate a decline in most North American and European populations, northern pike is not yet considered an endangered species and does not appear in the IUNC Red List of Threatened Species (2007 IUNC: www.redlist.org). The effects of overfishing, habitat reduction and fragmentation, anthropic perturbations, climate changes and competition with newly introduced species, have a detrimental impact on northern pike. Furthermore, recent genetic investigations strongly indicate a very low polymorphism in all the populations studied, suggesting a high evolutionary risk for this species. With the aim to manage southern European population, in the last decades of the twentieth century this species was artificially repopulated using fries of unknown origin. This practice has probably introduced new genotypes which, besides polluting autochthonous populations, were not fully adaptable to the environment of destination. Furthermore a great effort should be spent to ensure that these genotypes are not used in artificial repopulation practice based on autochthonous breeders. This chapter describes the actual conservation and management state of this species in Europe comparing genetic and molecular ecology data obtained for European and North American populations.

Chapter 7 - Predation critically threatens many rare species, with the deleterious impacts of predation losses compounded by habitat loss. Predators of endangered species are frequently invasive species or artificially over-abundant native species. Often, predation is most damaging to a species' ability to reproduce. The authors use examples from the tropics to the tundra with which they have been involved to demonstrate how predator management can be a highly effective and economically efficient means to protect populations of rare species and enhance their reproduction.

Management of predators, like all wildlife management, must be carried out within finite fiscal and human resources. Examination of the predator populations in response to management actions only provides an indicator of success. The true measure of success is improvement of the endangered species as a result of the management action. Moreover, a vital means to establish the success of an endangered species protection program is to demonstrate that the benefits to the protected species exceed the cost of the program. To this end, methods to monetarily value rare species allow species improvement to be assessed in the same metric as the costs for the protection.

Predator management to aid conservation of rare species requires is much more likely to succeed if: 1) applied by skilled/trained personnel able to focus on the task, 2) management efforts are timed so the most favorable impact can be achieved, 3) the effort is applied with sufficient intensity that the desired effect can be achieved, 4) predator population information is used for optimizing the timing, distribution and intensity of management efforts, and 5) adaptive management strategies are applied to changing circumstances through time. If predator management is not being applied effectively, then predator management is not taking place. It would be a disservice to a species in need of protection to discount predator management as useful because it was ineffectively applied.

Chapter 8 - The role of cryobanks in preservation of genetic material has been growing at an exponential rate. Practically all semen that is nowadays used in cattle industry in the developed countries is cryopreserved. However, collection (retrieval) of spermatozoa of wild animals has been a formidable task: it is expensive, time consuming and even sometime harmful both for the animal and for the collector. From this standpoint, collection of the mortem (cadaveric, posthumous) sperm of recently died animal (Postmortem Semen Cryopreservation, PMSCP) for rare and endangered species can be a substantial addition, and sometime the method of choice in preservation of reproductive cells, both in wild and at Zoos and & national parks.

This work addresses the cadaver sperm cryopreservation. A comprehensive review of the state of the art with the main emphasizes on the team's own achievements is presented and discussed in details. Special attention is given to the following aspects of PMSCP: 1) Epididymal sperm as the source for artificial insemination and *in vitro* fertilization in general. 2) Comparison of quality and viability of epididymal sperm *vs.* electroejaculated semen. 3) Brief summary of a 4-yr work in the Moscow Zoological Park (one of the largest Zoos in the World) in collaboration with ICB and Celltronix (CTX). The Chapter is focused on the use of mammalian post-mortem sperm; however, a similar approach can be applied to other higher terrestrial vertebrates.

Finally, in the Discussion underscores the importance of PMSCP, its achievements, pitfalls, ways of improvement and future directions.

Chapter 9 - During the last centuries, many wild avian species have suffered a steep decline in numbers and range. They are now rare and steel decreasing due to human activities affecting natural habitats and food supplies. In some species immatures and juveniles do not show sex-linked morphology and Authors do not agree upon the development of an unambiguous sexual dimorphism. Nevertheless, a discrimination between male and female is possible based on some discernible plumage traits. However, the knowledge of the sex of young individuals in a population greatly facilitates the study of behaviour, evolutionary ecology, conservation strategies, breeding system, and genetics. Therefore, the development of an objective test would undoubtedly facilitate the species management. In recent years, DNA-based tests have became available and have been applied for the detection of sex in some species of birds. In these tests the determination sex chromosomes specific markers have been used. A crucial point in any kind of studies of free ranging animals is sampling, that must be sample, not stressing, and non-invasive. In this respect, hair and faecies have been proved to be suitable materials in mammals, wile bird feathers increasingly used. Different approaches are compared and discussed.

Chapter 10 – The authors used ecological niche modeling and place prioritization procedures to identify areas for conservation and restoration for the Neotropical river otter, *Lontra longicaudis annectens* Major 1897, in central Mexico. This species is highly sensible to fluvial ecosystem degradation, and large areas of the Apatlaco-Tembembe basin fluvial ecosystems have been highly transformed. The authors selected ecological indicators (EI) from literature and own field work to determine variables best describing the fluvial ecosystem degradation, relating them to the species' presence or absence. Field data of EI, species records, and digital thematic information of hydrology, geomorphology and climate were used in ResNet Place Prioritization algorithm for the selection of potential conservation and restoration areas. The authors generated a spatial model considering a hierarchy of key areas based on river otter's ecological niche requirements and habitat *ad hoc* conditions for the species permanence. This allowed identifying areas to be included in landscape management plans for conservation and restoration. The sequential integration of species′ potential distribution and place prioritization modeling allows merging biodiversity conservation and ecological restoration strategies at different ecological scales, helping adaptive management in land planning to be more flexible and feasible.

Chapter 11 - Deforestation is one of the main factors negatively affecting the conservation of biological diversity. The authors assess the impact of deforestation on biodiversity in Mexico by quantifying its effect on (1) mammal species' distributions, (2) delineation of biogeographical regionalization, (3) the effectiveness of conservation area networks to prevent biologically deleterious land use/land cover change, and (4) area prioritization for biodiversity conservation. Deforestation has a significant impact on species' distributions with habitat loss ranging from 10-90%, leading in some cases to high risks of extinction. Significant changes also occur in the delineation of biogeographical provinces (bioregionalization) due to deforestation because several areas with unique fauna show high rates of natural habitat reduction, leading to potential ecological and biogeographical changes in species interactions and distributions. A variety of decreed natural protected areas now show increasing pressures due to potential land use conversion from natural habitat to agriculture and urban settlements which threatens their biodiversity content. Area prioritization for biodiversity conservation is seriously negatively affected by deforestation because a significantly increased total area is required to conserve endemic mammals as compared to what would have been adequate 30 years ago before significant loss of forest cover. These trends urge immediate collaborative actions between academic, governmental, and NGO sectors to prevent and reduce further deforestation nationwide.

Chapter 12 - The chapter challenges the assumption that humans generally treat all animal species equally according to their need of conservation. The authors reviewed recent studies suggesting that humans show strong preferences toward particular animal species/taxa and are willing to protect them more than others. Such understanding of human preferences is an important part of conservation strategies.

The main body of the chapter is based on original data analyses performed separately for main reptile, bird and mammalian taxa. The representation of animal taxa in zoos and sizes of zoo populations are reviewed. Human preferences to particular species and/or families were examined directly by presenting their picture to the respondents. The results showed that factors affecting human aesthetic preferences toward particular species differ among higher taxonomic groups. The authors concluded that animal attractiveness (both body size and beauty itself) influences human effort devoted to ex situ breeding projects more than inclusion in Red book lists. Special attention has to be paid to less preferred, but endangered species. Fortunately, the highly preferred species are present in almost every family and also among threatened species. Thus, the zoos can replace preferred but common species by endangered one that reaches both, conservation as well as visitor's aesthetic criteria.

Chapter 13 - Felidae have had long and uneasy relationships with humans. Many of the world's wild cats are or becoming endangered species and one of the reasons is the use for traditional medicinal purposes. The present work provides an overview of the global usage of felines in traditional folk medicine around the world and the implications for its conservation.

The results demonstrated that at least 27 felines are used in traditional medicine worldwide. Of the felines recorded, 24 are included on the IUCN Red List of Threatened Species (with 7 species classified as vulnerable and 3 as endangered) and all is listed in the CITES. This evidenciates the importance of understanding such medicinal uses regarding animal conservation as well as the need for considering socio-cultural factors when establishing management plans concerning the sustainable use of these mammals.

In: Endangered Species: New Research
Editors: A. Columbus and L. Kuznetsov
ISBN 978-1-60692-241-5

Short Communication

BIOSONAR AND AUDITORY SYSTEM OF THE YANGTZE FINLESS PORPOISE

Songhai Li[1], Ding Wang[1,*], Kexiong Wang[1], Tomonari Akamatsu[2], Alexander Ya. Supin[3] and Vladimir V. Popov[3]

[1]Institute of Hydrobiology, The Chinese Academy of Sciences, China
[2]National Research Institute of Fisheries Engineering, Fisheries Research Agency, Japan
[3]Institute of Ecology and Evolution, the Russian Academy of Sciences, Russia

ABSTRACT

The Yangtze finless porpoise (*Neophocaena phocaenoides asiaeorientalis*) is the only freshwater subspecies of finless porpoise (*Neophocaena phocaenoides*), living only in the middle and lower reaches of the Yangtze River. It has been declared to be endangered under the Red Data List criteria (C2b), by the International Union for the Conservation of Nature and Natural Resources (IUCN) in 2004. As well as other odontocetes, Yangtze finless porpoise possesses of sophisticated echolocation systems. Recent researches demonstrated excellent capabilities of high-frequency sound production and reception in this species. The animal produces one sonar click train per 5 s in average with inter-click interval changing typically between 10–70 ms. The click signals hold the characteristics of "typical" high-frequency, narrow-band, and short-time duration phocoenid echolocation sounds. The means of peak frequency of clicks are about 125 kHz, and the means of time duration are shorter than 70 μs. Careful scanning and acoustical auto focusing behavior in porpoises was also observed in free-ranging conditions by using biologging techniques. Hearing capability research by using evoked potential technique indicated that the range of greatest hearing sensitivity of Yangtze finless porpoise covered frequencies from 45 to 139 kHz, and the lowest thresholds of less than 50 dB re: 1 μPa were found at a frequency of 54 kHz. Frequent biosonar production by this subspecies allowed effective passive acoustical survey. These several years, density and distribution of Yangtze finless porpoises are being surveyed acoustically along its habitat.

* Correspondence should be addressed: wangd@ihb.ac.cn

INTRODUCTION

Despite research on biosonar in bats can be traced back to the work of the Italian scientist Lazzaro Spallanzani in the 1770s (Au, 1993), the discovery of biosonar in odontocetes started at the end of 1940s. In 1947, American Arthur McBride observed that Atlantic bottlenose dolphin (*Tursiops truncatus*) could avoid fine mesh nets, and could go over nets where the cork lines were pulled below the water, at night in the turbid waters. He supposed that *T. truncatus* may detect objects underwater by echolocation (McBride, 1956). During the 1950s many investigators suspected echolocation in dolphins (Kellogg & Kohler, 1952; Kellogg et al., 1953; Wood, 1952, 1953; Schevill & Lawrence, 1953a, b, 1956; Kellogg, 1958), such as *Tursiops* and *Stenella plagiodon*. However, unequivocal demonstration of echolocation in dolphins was firstly performed by Norris and his colleagues in 1960 (Norris et al., 1961).

The finless porpoise (*Neophocaena phocaenoides*) is one of the smallest odontocetes and a member of *Phocoenidae*, living widely in Asian coastal waters (Reeves et al., 1997; Kasuya, 1999). Research on biosonar of this species had not been launched until the end of 1960s. The first description of underwater sounds from *N. phocaenoides* was reported by Mizue et al. (1968). They investigated underwater vocalizations of some animals captured from Japanese coastal waters in captivity with a system limited in response above 20 kHz. As far as the present knowledge of odontocete biosonar is concerned, the frequency of underwater sound produced by *N. phocaenoides* could range up to some 150 kHz. The information presented in Mizue et al. (1968) was much restricted. Extensive description on detailed nature of the sonar sounds from *N. phocaenoides* was firstly done by Kamminga et al. (1986) with animals in captivity at the Toba Aquarium in Japan. By using recording system with a bandwidth of 150 kHz and an accompanying signal-to-noise ratio of 42 dB, Kamminga et al. (1986) indicated the dominant frequencies of echolocation-type pulses produced by *N. phocaenoides* are 128 kHz, the time duration of a click waveform ranges from 40 to 80 μs with a number of cycles of 5 to 10.

The Yangtze finless porpoise (*N. p. asiaeorientalis*) is the unique freshwater subspecies of *N. phocaenoides* (Wang, 1992; Gao and Zhou, 1993, 1995). It shares the same habitat with Yangtze River dolphin, locally called baiji (*Lipotes vexillifer*), which has been declared to be functionally extinct (Turvey et al., 2007), living historically in main stream and tributaries of the middle and lower reaches (Yichang to Shanghai reach) of the Yangtze River and its conjoint large lakes, such as Poyang Lake and Dongting Lake (Fig. 1). Due to overloaded human activities, such as fishery, transportation, pollution, dam construction, and so on, biodiversity in the Yangtze River System has suffered a serious threat. *N. p. asiaeorientalis*, which is one of the key species of the River, has been declining in population size and reducing in distribution ranges sharply in the past thirty years. It was listed as endangered species by IUCN in 2004. In November and December 2006, an intensive six-week visual and acoustic survey (Yangtze Freshwater Dolphin Expedition 2006, YFDE 2006) to find baiji and document status of finless porpoise was carried out by Institute of Hydrobiology, Chinese Academy of Sciences (IHB) and Baiji.org Foundation (Swiss organization). The survey covered the entire historical distribution range of baiji and finless porpoise in the main stream of the Yangtze River and part area of Poyang Lake. Although there was no visual or acoustical finding of baiji (Turvey et al. 2007), the results showed the population of porpoise in the main stream of the Yangtze River is less than 1200 (Zhao et al., 2008), which is less than half of its population in the early 1990s (Zhang et al., 1993). The whole population size of porpoise in the Yangtze River System was estimated below 1800 (Zhao et al., 2008). The porpoises are disappearing in some of their original habitats and tending to concentrate onto only a few specific sections (Zhao et al., 2008).

Since the end of 1970s, biological researches on the Yangtze finless porpoise, including researches on its ecology, molecular genetics, behavior, reproductive biology, and so on, have been widely deployed by both Chinese and international scientists. Biosonar research on this subspecies started at 1990s. In 1992, research on echolocation signals of a Yangtze finless porpoise, captured from the lower reach of the Yangtze River, was firstly reported by Hua and Zhou (Hua & Zhou, 1992). Recent years, scientists conducted a series of research on biosonar of Yangtze finless porpoise, including sound production (Wang, 1996; Akamatsu et al., 1998, 2005a, b, 2007a, b; Wang & Wang, 1999; Li et al., 2005a, b, 2006, 2007, 2008), hearing (Popov et al., 2005, 2006), and new survey methodology using sonar sounds (Akamatsu et al., 2001, 2008; Wang et al., 2005; Kimura et al., 2007).

Figure 1. Distribution of the Yangtze finless porpoise in the Yangtze River System, China, including main stream and tributaries of the middle and lower reaches (Yichang to Shanghai reach) of the Yangtze River and its conjoint large lakes, Poyang Lake and Dongting Lake (gray solid line).

Sound Production

Up to date, all investigated odontocetes were revealed to produce high-frequency pulsed sounds (clicks) with energy extending into the ultrasonic region. The clicks were considered to be used mainly for echolocation (Au, 1993). By using sound recording and analyzing system with frequency response up to 147 kHz, Li et al (2005a) indicated the free-ranging Yangtze finless porpoise in wild produces "typical" high-frequency, narrow-band clicks, which are produced by phocoenid family. The peak frequencies of the typical clicks range from 87 to 145 kHz with an average of 125 ±6.92 kHz. The durations range from 30 to 122 μs with an average of 68±14.12 μs. The waveforms and frequency spectra of typical clicks emitted by Yangtze finless porpoise in the free-ranging environment were given in Figure 2.

Histograms of the signal duration, the peak frequency, and the 3-dB bandwidth of the signals used by the free-ranging Yangtze finless porpoise were reported by Li et al (2005a) and are reproduced here in Figure 3.

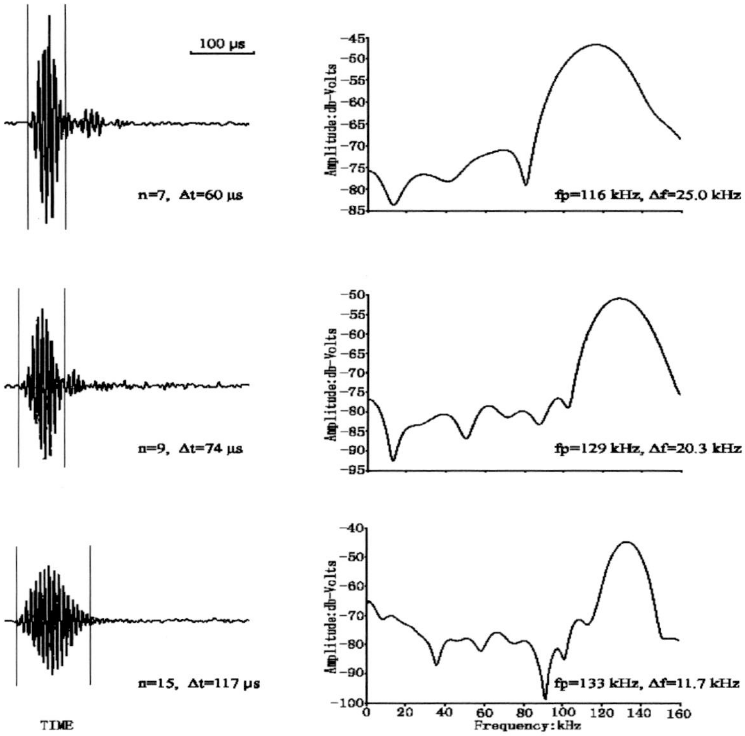

Figure 2. Waveforms and frequency spectra of three typical types of clicks emitted by the free-ranging Yangtze finless porpoise. "*n*" represents the number of cycles in one click, "Δt" represents the time between two points at which the click oscillations rose from the background noise and descended into the background noise or inflexion formed by reverberation, "f_p" represents the frequency of maximum energy, and "Δf" represents the width of the frequency band between the two points that are 3 dB lower than the maximum amplitude of a spectrum (From Li et al., 2005a).

The signal duration histograms indicate that over 75% of the analyzed clicks have signal durations between 50 and 80 μs, less than 3% of the signals have durations longer than 100 μs and only 0.55% have durations less than 40 μs. The most common signal duration for this species is between 60–70 μs. The peak frequency histograms indicate that more than 90% of the clicks have peak frequencies between 115 and 135 kHz. Less than 4% have peak frequencies over 135 kHz, and only 2% of signals have peak frequencies lower than 100 kHz. The animals tend to produce sonar signals with peak frequency range between 125 and 135 kHz. The 3-dB bandwidth histograms indicate that about 80% of the signals have a bandwidth between 15 and 25 kHz, and only 0.18% and 0.73% of the signals have bandwidths narrower than 10 and wider than 35 kHz, respectively.

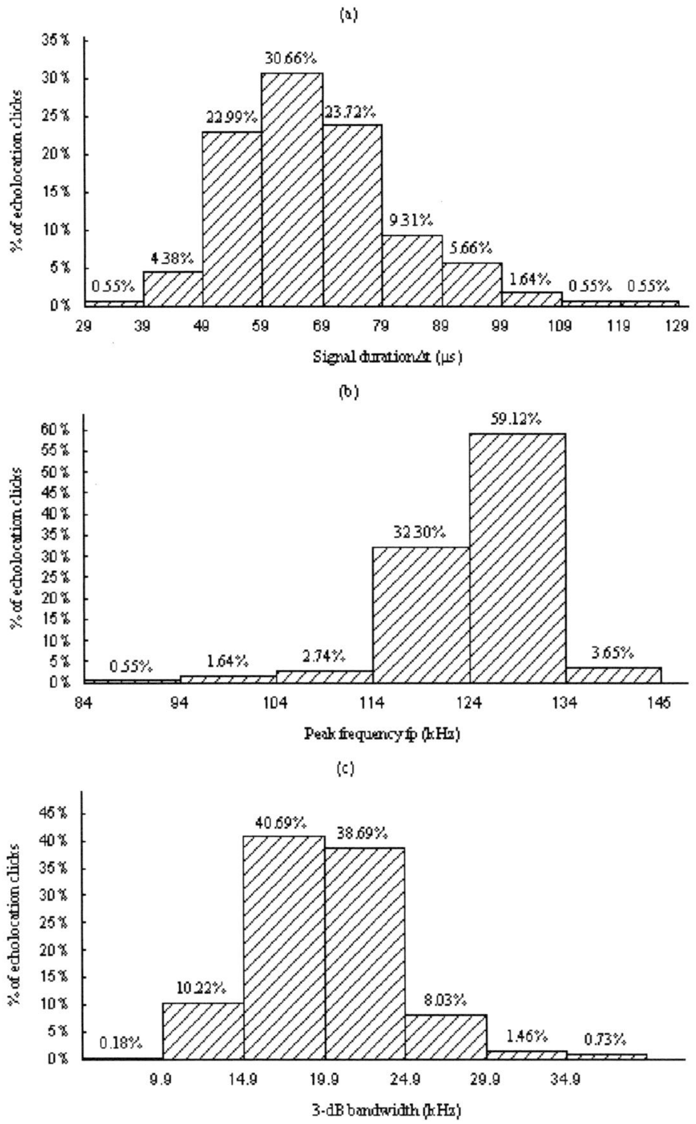

Figure 3. Histograms of signal duration Δt (a), peak frequency f_p (b), and 3-dB bandwidth Δf (c) of clicks of the free-ranging Yangtze finless porpoise (From Li et al., 2005a).

The back-calculated source levels, acquired by Li et al (2006) in a water channel with 1.6 km in length and 80–220 m in width, ranged from 163.7 to 185.6 dB (p-p) re: 1 μPa @ 1 m. The source levels are highly range-dependent and varied approximately as a function of the one-way transmission loss (20log$R$) for signals traveling from the animals to the hydrophone (Fig. 4).

Clear double- and multi-pulse waveform structures of the clicks were presented by Li et al (2005a). However, as the waveforms and inter-pulse intervals in the double- and multi-pulse waveform structures depended on the animal-hydrophone geometry, Li et al (2005b) confirmed that the double- and multi-pulse structure of clicks in Yangtze finless porpoise is not caused by the phonating porpoise itself, but by the multipath propagation of the signal.

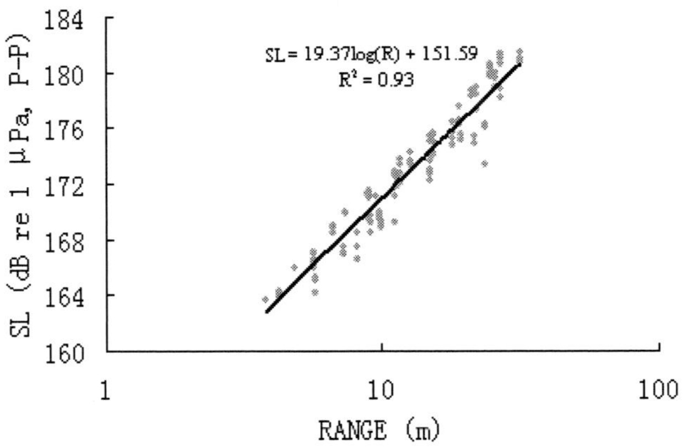

Figure 4. Source levels SLs in dB (p-p) *re*: 1 μPa as a function of range R (m). The SLs increase with the log of ranges (SL = 19.37log$R$ + 151.59, r^2= 0.93), which is approximate to the one-way transmission loss (20log$R$) (From Li et al., 2006).

When navigating or searching for distant targets, dolphins and porpoises often emit series of clicks normally referred to as a click train. Click interval studies on Yangtze finless porpoise in both captivity and free-ranging environment have been performed by Akamatsu et al. (1998). The results indicated that there is a large difference on inter-click interval in a click train between in captivity and free-ranging environments. In free-ranging environment a wide variety of click intervals of up to 100–200 ms was observed, while in captivity environment the click intervals present frequently between 8–10 ms. In recent years, the structure of click train and sonar behavior of Yangtze finless porpoise was also studied widely by using acoustic data loggers (W20-AS, Little Leonardo, Japan), which were attached on free-ranging animals to record their underwater high-frequency phonation events (Akamatsu et al., 2005a, b, 2007a, b). These studies indicated that the inter-click intervals depend on the distance of interest and the animals focused their sonar on the target. The animals inspect the area ahead of them by sonar click train before swimming silently into it. The inspected distances of porpoises, which were estimated according to the inter-click intervals, could be up to 77 m, whereas their swimming distance without using sonar was less than 20 m. The inspection distance was long enough to ensure a wide safety margin before the animals facing interested targets. Once a potential prey was detected, porpoises would adjust their inspection distance from the remote target throughout their approach (Akamatsu et al., 2005b, 2007a).

Researches on ontogeny of echolocation in Yangtze finless porpoises, showed that neonatal porpoises produce clear low-frequency (2–3 kHz) pulsed signals frequently without distinct high-frequency energy just after birth, and can produce both low- (2–3 kHz) and high-frequency (over 100 kHz) pulsed signals simultaneously at latest after about twenty days postnatal (Li et al., 2008). The high-frequency pulsed clicks produced by neonatal porpoises are indistinguishable from adult echolocation clicks both in temporal and frequency domains (Li et al., 2007). A similarity between neonatal high-frequency pulsed sound and adult echolocation click was shown in Figure 5. However, before 100 days postnatal, calf high-frequency click trains were found to decrease in maximum click-repetition rate, duration, and number of clicks per train with age while the minimum click-repetition rate remained more consistent (Li et al., 2007).

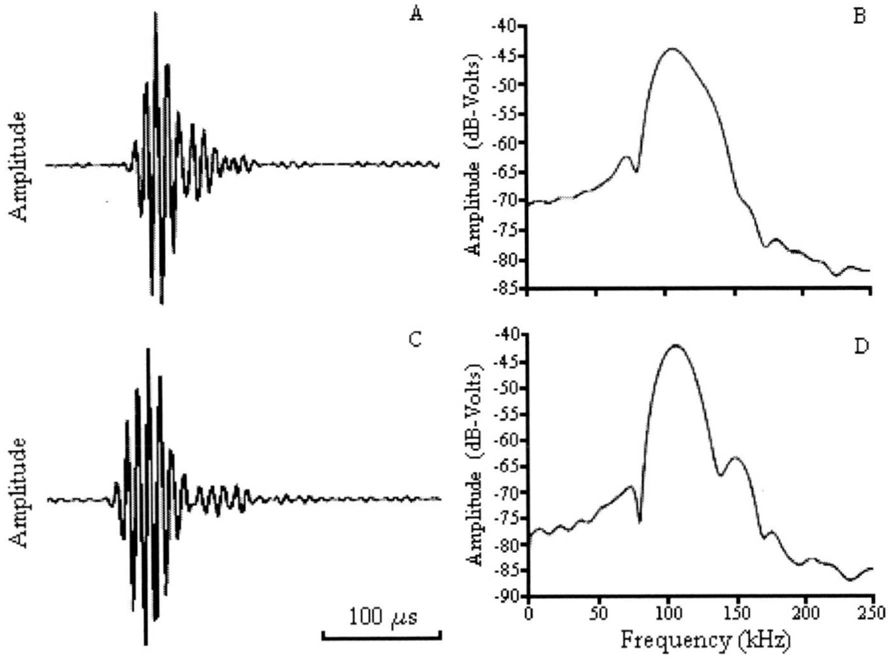

Figure 5 (a) Waveform of a representative click from the earliest recorded calf click train, at 22 days postnatal; (b) Power spectrum of the click depicted in (a); (c) and (d): Comparison examples of click waveform and spectrum from the mother porpoise in the same tank (From Li et al., 2007).

Hearing

Hearing capabilities studies on two adult Yangtze finless porpoises (one male and one female) were performed by Popov et al. (2005, 2006), using evoked-potential method, in facilities of Institute of Hydrobiology of the Chinese Academy of Sciences (IHB). The studies indicated that the range of greatest hearing sensitivity of Yangtze finless porpoises covered frequencies from 45 to 139 kHz. Two high-sensitivity regions of 45–54 and 90–108 kHz with a dip between them were observed in the audiograms of both the investigated individuals. A lowest threshold of 47.2 and 48.5 dB re: 1 μPa was found at a frequency of 54 kHz in the two subjects, respectively. The audiograms of the two investigated animals along with their mean audiogram were shown in Figure 6. Popov et al. (2006) found, in the auditory system of Yangtze finless porpoise, the equivalent rectangular quality Q_{ERB} of the obtained tuning curves varied from 8.3–8.6 at lower probe frequencies (22.5–32 kHz) to 44.8–47.4 at high frequencies (128–140 kHz). The Q_{ERB} dependence on probe frequency could be approximated by regression lines with a slope of about 0.85 in log-log scale, which corresponded to almost frequency-proportional quality and almost constant bandwidth of 3–4 kHz. Thus, the frequency representation in the finless porpoise auditory system is much closer to a constant-bandwidth rather that to a constant-quality manner, different from that in other mammals and humans, where the auditory system is closer to a constant-quality manner. Frequency-tuning quality (Q) dependence on frequency in two finless porpoise subjects were given in Figure 7.

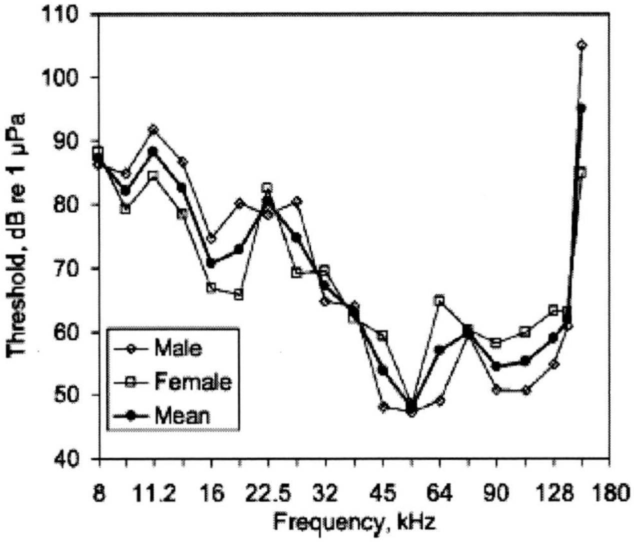

Figure 6. Audiograms of the two investigated Yangtze finless porpoises and the mean of them (From Popov et al., 2005).

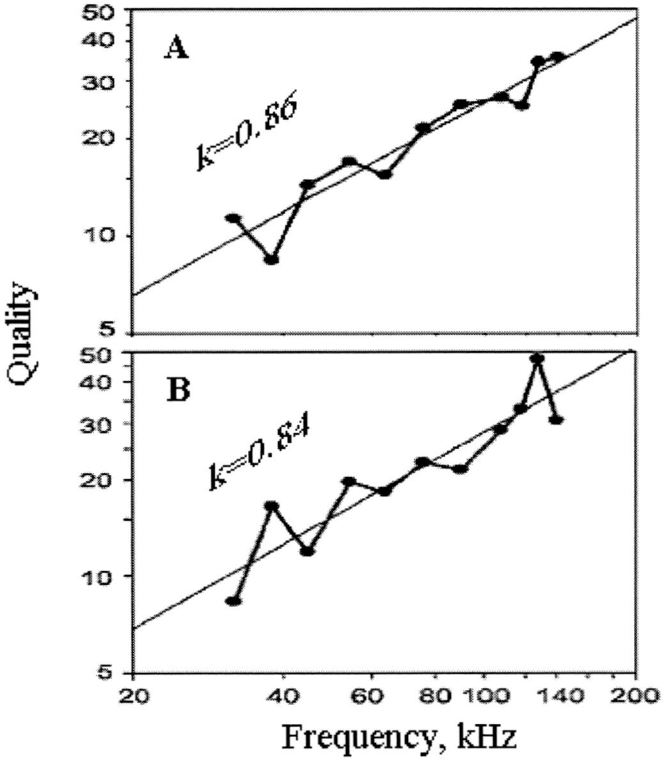

Figure 7. Frequency-tuning quality (*Q*) dependence on frequency in two Yangtze finless porpoises: porpoise female (A), and porpoise male (B). Solid lines—experimental data, thin straight lines—approximating regression lines. k is indicated for each regression line (Revised from Popov et al., 2006).

Application for the Passive Acoustic Monitoring

Yangtze finless porpoise is increasingly getting popular in Chinese public. This species is recognized as the top predators in food-chain of the Yangtze River ecosystem. Its population size has been decreasing remarkably with the reduction of fish resources in the Yangtze River. The concern on the information of population dynamics of this subspecies is increasing. Documenting long-term population changing trend of this subspecies, frequent monitoring of entire habitat is necessary. Traditional visual survey for porpoise is difficult to detect animals, both due to the brief appearances of animals without a dorsal fin at the surface when breathing, and limitation of visual observation by weather condition, circadian pattern, and unintentional variation of efforts among observers. In addition, as visual surveys are typically performed using a small number of observation points, one or a few vessels, and for a few weeks to a few months of the year, the results can be highly variable.

As described above, the Yangtze finless porpoises produce high-frequency pulse signals frequently. This characteristic is useful for passive acoustic survey which monitors sound from porpoises. By monitoring the underwater sound production of Yangtze finless porpoise using B&K 8103 hydrophones, concurrent with visual observations, Akamatsu et al. (2001) indicated, porpoises could be detected reliably within 300 m of the hydrophone with a threshold level of 133 dB *re* 1 μPa, and suggested the high-frequency acoustical observation is an effective method for field surveys of porpoises. Wang et al. (2005) tested the validity of the acoustic data loggers (W20-AS, Little Leonardo, Japan) being used as a stationary passive acoustic observation method in detecting the presence of porpoises and in estimating the group size. In recent years, the acoustic data loggers have been widely used for Yangtze finless porpoise observation in wild in both stationary and mobile platforms. In a joint visual-acoustic survey performed in 2006 in the natural distribution area of Yangtze finless porpoise, the detection probability using acoustic method was calculated to be approximately twice that of visual detection (Akamatsu et al., 2008).

Conclusion and Prospect

Yangtze finless porpoise, as well as other odontocetes, possesses highly developed sonar signals production and reception systems. Frequent biosonar production by this subspcies allowed effective passive acoustical survey of the animal along its habitat. While great progress has been made on the biosonar research of this subspecies in the last ten years, there are still many scientific questions open to investigation. These include mechanisms of sound production and transmission, mechanisms of sound reception and hearing, and so on.

Mechanisms of Sound Production and Transmission

Although experimental evidences indicate that odontocetes do not produce sounds in the larynx but in the nasal passages above the larynx (Ridgway et al., 1980; Mackay and Liaw, 1981), the specific organs and specific physical mechanisms involved are not clear (Au, 1993). Further more, finless porpoise was generally considered as non-whistling species, the organs and mechanisms for sound production in this species might be different with those of whistling dolphins. Recently, Li et al. (2008) found the neonatal finless porpoises were able to produce both low- (2–3 kHz) and high-frequency (>100 kHz) pulse signals simultaneously, which suggested neonatal finless porpoises may possess at least two different sound production mechanisms. However, how is high-frequency signal produced? How and where is low-frequency signal produced? Does adult porpoise produce any form of low-frequency signals? What is the function of the low-frequency signals? How does the sonar beam transmit in front of the head of porpoise? Can the animal control the sonar beam consciously? These are just small part of questions concerning the sound production and transmission of finless porpoise.

Mechanisms of Sound Reception and Hearing

Concerning the mechanisms of sound reception and hearing of finless porpoise, there are many unknowns including some basic knowledge. Such as what is the anatomy and model of finless porpoise ears? Only one experiment has been performed on hearing research of finless porpoise, in which noninvasive electrophysiological techniques was used (Popov et al., 2005, 2006). However, the animals were restrained in a small woody container. How does the acoustic environments in such experiment affect the results is unclear. In addition, how does the hearing capability of finless porpoise change in frequency range below 10 kHz? How does the audiogram change in noisy environments? Are there any different acoustic channels between low- and high-frequency sound receptions? All the questions need to be answered to understand the auditory system of finless porpoise.

ACKNOWLEDGEMENT

This work was supported by the National Basic Research Program of China (2007CB411600), the Chinese National Natural Science Foundation (30730018), the President's Fund of the Chinese Academy of Sciences, Special Funds for Presidential Scholarships of the Chinese Academy of Sciences (082Z01), Research and Development Program for New Bio-industry Initiatives of Japan, Grant-in-Aid for Scientific Research (B) of Japan (19405005), Russian Foundation for Basic Research (02-04-39017, 03-04-48117), and Russian Ministry of Science and Education (NSh-2152.2003.4).

REFERENCES

Akamatsu, T., Wang, D., Nakamura, K., & Wang, K. (1998). Echolocation range of captive and free-ranging baiji (*Lipotes vexillifer*), finless porpoise (*Neophocaena phocaenoides*) and bottlenose dolphin (*Tursiops truncatus*). Journal of the Acoustical Society of America, 104, 2511–2516.

Akamatsu, T., Wang, D., Wang, K., & Wei, Z. (2001). Comparison between visual and passive acoustic detection of finless porpoises in the Yangtze River, China. Journal of the Acoustical Society of America, 109, 1723–1727.

Akamatsu, T., Wang, D., & Wang, K. (2005a). Off-axis sonar beam pattern of free-ranging finless porpoises measured by a stereo pulse event data logger. Journal of the Acoustical Society of America, 117, 3325–3330.

Akamatsu, T., Wang, D., Wang, K., & Naito, Y. (2005b). Biosonar behaviour of free-ranging porpoises. Proceedings of the Royal Society B-Biological Sciences, 272, 797–801.

Akamatsu, T., Wang, D., Wang, K., & Naito, Y. (2007a), Underwater acoustical sensing behavior of porpoises. In N. Kato, & S. Kamimura (Eds.), Bio-mechanisms of Swimming and Flying (pp.117–127). Springer-Japan.

Akamatsu, T., Teilmann, J., Miller, L.A., Tougaard, J., Dietz, R., Wang, D., Wang, K., Siebert, U., & Naito, Y. (2007b). Comparison of echolocation behaviour between coastal and riverine porpoises, Deep-Sea Research II, 54, 290–297.

Akamatsu, T., Wang, D., Wang, K., Li, S., Dong, S., Zhao, X., Barlow, J., Stewart, B. S., & Richlen, M. (2008). Estimation of the detection probability for Yangtze finless porpoises (*Neophocoena phocoenoides asiaeorientalis*) with a passive acoustic method. Journal of the Acoustical Society of America, 123, 4403–4411.

Au, W. W. L. (1993). The Sonar of Dolphins. New York: Springer-Verlag.

Gao, A., & Zhou, K. (1995). Geographical variation of external measurements and three subspecies of *Neophocaena phocaenoides* in Chinese waters. Acta Theriologica Sinica, 15, 81–92.

Goold, J. C., & Jefferson, T. A. (2002). Acoustic signals from free-ranging finless porpoises (*Neophocaena phocaenoides*) in the waters around Hong Kong. Raffles Bulletin of Zoology, Supplement, 10, 131–139.

Hua, M., & Zhou, K. (1992). Statistical measurement of frequency spectrum of echolocation signals of the finless porpoise, *Neophocaena phocaenoides*. 14th International Congress on Acoustics Proceedings, Volume/Band 4 I4–3. Beijing, China.

Kamminga, C., Kataoka, T., & Engelsma, F. J. (1986). Investigations on cetacean sonar VII: Underwater sounds of *Neophocaena phocaenoides* of the Japanese coastal population. Aquatic Mammals, 12, 52–60.

Kasuya, T. (1999). Finless porpoise *Neophocaena phocaenoides* (G. Cuvier, 1829). In S. H. Ridgway, & R. Harrison (Eds.), Handbook of marine mammals, Volume 6: The second book of dolphins and the porpoises (pp. 411–442). San Diego, California: Academic.

Kellogg, W. N. (1958). Echo ranging in the porpoise. Science, 128, 982–988.

Kellogg, W. N., & Kohler, R. (1952). Responses of the porpoise to ultrasonic frequencies. Science, 116, 250–252.

Kellogg, W. N., Kohler, R., & Morris, H. N. (1953). Porpoise sounds as sonar signals. Science, 117, 239–243.

Kimura, S., Akamatsu, T., Wang, D., Wang, K., & Li, S. (2007). Monitoring local migration of Yangtze finless porpoises by acoustic gate. Journal of Marine Acoustic Society of Japan, 34, 40–45.

Li, S., Wang, K., Wang, D., & Akamatsu, T. (2005a). Echolocation signals of the free-ranging Yangtze finless porpoise (*Neophocaena phocaenoides asiaeorientalis*). Journal of the Acoustical Society of America, 117, 3288–3296.

Li, S., Wang, K., Wang, D., & Akamatsu, T. (2005b). Origin of the double- and multi-pulse structure of echolocation signals in Yangtze finless porpoise (*Neophocaena phocaenoides asiaeorientalis*). Journal of the Acoustical Society of America, 118, 3934–3940.

Li, S., Wang, D., Wang, K., & Akamatsu, T. (2006). Sonar gain control in echolocating finless porpoises (*Neophocaena phocaenoides*) in an open water. Journal of the Acoustical Society of America, 120, 1803–1806.

Li, S., Wang, D., Wang, K., Xiao, J., & Akamatsu, T. (2007). The ontogeny of echolocation in the Yangtze Finless porpoise (*Neophocaena phocaenoides asiaeorientalis*). Journal of the Acoustical Society of America, 122, 715–718.

Li, S., Wang, K., Dong, S., Wang, D., & Akamatsu, T. (2008). Simultaneous production of low- and high-frequency sounds in neonatal finless porpoises. Journal of the Acoustical Socicty of America, 124,716–718.

Mackay, R. S., & Liaw, C. (1981). Dolphin vocalization mechanisms. Science, 212, 676–678.

McBride, A. F. (1956). Evidence for echolocation by cetaceans. Deep-Sea Research, 3, 153–154.

Mizue, K., Takemura, A., & Nakasai, K. (1968). Underwater sound of the Chinese finless porpoise caught in the Japanese coastal sea. Bulletin of Faculty of Fisheries, Nagasaki University, 25, 25–33.

Norris, K. S., Prescott, J. H., Asa-Dorian, P. V., & Perkins, P. (1961). An experimental demonstration of echolocation behavior in the porpoise, *Tursiops truncatus* (Montagu). Biology Bulletin, 120, 163–176.

Popov, V. V., Supin, A. Y., Wang, D., Wang, K., Xiao, J., & Li, S. (2005). Evoked-potential audiogram of the Yangtze finless porpoise Neophocaena phocaenoides asiaeorientalis. Journal of the Acoustical Society of America, 117, 2728–2731.

Popov, V. V., Supin, A. Y., Wang, D., & Wang, K. (2006). Nonconstant quality of auditory filters in the porpoises, *Phocoena phocoena* and *Neophocaena phocaenoides* (Cetacea, Phocoenidae). Journal of the Acoustical Society of America, 119, 3173–3180.

Reeves, R. R., Wang, J. Y., & Leatherwood, S. (1997). The finless porpoise, *Neophocaena phocaenoides* (G. Cuvier, 1829): a summary of current knowledge and recommendations for conservation action. Asian Marine Biology, 14, 111–143.

Ridgway, S. H., Carder, D. A., Green, R. F., Gaunt, A. S., Gaunt, S. L. L., & Evans, W. E. (1980). In R.-G. Busnel & J. F. Fish (eds.), Animal Sonar Systems, Electromyographic and pressure events in the nasolaryngeal system of dolphins during sound production (pp. 239–250). New York: Plenum.

Schevill, W. E., & Lawrence, B. (1953a). Auditory response of a bottle-nosed porpoise, *Tursiops truncatus*, to frequencies above 100 kc. Journal of Experimental Zoology, 124, 147–165.

Schevill, W. E., & Lawrence, B. (1953b). High-frequency auditory response of a bottlenosed dolphin, *Tursiops truncatus* (Montagu). Journal of the Acoustical Society of America, 24, 1016–1017.

Schevill, W. E., & Lawrence, B. (1956). Food-finding by a captive porpoise (*Tursiops truncatus*). Breviora (Mus. Comp. Zool., Harvard), 53, 1–15.

Turvey, S. T., Pitman, R. L., Taylor, B. L., Barlow, J., Akamatsu, T., Barrett, L. A., Zhao, X., Reeves, R. R., Stevart, B. S., Wang, K., Wei, Z., Zhang, X., Pusser, L. T., Richlen, M., Brandon, J. R., & Wang, D. (2007). First human-caust extinction of a cetacean species? Biology Letters, 3, 537–540.

Wang, D. (1996). A Preliminary study on sound and scoustic behavior of the Yangtze River finless porpoise, *Neophocaena phocaenoides*. Acta Hydrobiology Sinica, 20, 127–133.

Wang, P. (1992). The morphological characters and the problem of subspecies identification of the finless porpoise. Fisheries Science, 11, 4–9.

Wang, K., & Wang, D. (1999). Characteristics and functions of sound of the Yangtze finless porpoise (*Neophocaena phocaenoides*) in captivity. Acoustic Technology, 18, 9–12.

Wang, K., Wang, D., Akamatsu, T., Li, S., & Xiao, J. (2005). A passive acoustic monitoring method applied to observation and group size estimation of finless porpoises. Journal of the Acoustical Society of America, 118, 1180–1185.

Wood, F. G., Jr. (1952). Porpoise sounds. Underwater sounds made by *Tursiops truncatus* and *Stenella plagiodon*. (phonograph record). Marineland Research Laboratory, Florida.

Wood, F. G., Jr. (1953). Underwater sound production and concurrent behavior of captive porpoises *Tursiops truncatus* and *Stenella plagiodon*. Bulletin of Marine Science of the Gulf and Caribbean, 3, 120–133.

Zhang, X., Liu, R., Zhao, Q., Zhang, G., Wei, Z., Wang, X. & Yang, J. (1993). The population of finless porpoise in the middle and lower reaches of Yangtze River (in Chinese with English abstract). Acta Theriologica Sinica, 16, 490–496.

Zhao, X., Barlow, J., Taylor, B. L., Pitman, R. L., Wang, K., Wei, Z., Stewart, B. S., Turvey, S. T., Akamatsu, T., Reeves, R. R. & Wang, D. (2008). Abundance and conservation status of the Yangtze finless porpoise in the Yangtze River, China. Biological Conservation, (In press, doi: 10.1016/j.biocon.2008.09.005).

RESEARCH AND REVIEW

In: Endangered Species: New Research
Editors: A. Columbus and L. Kuznetsov
ISBN 978-1-60692-241-5

Chapter 1

ENDANGERED SPECIES PROTECTION IN CHINA

Jerry McBeath and Bo Wang

ABSTRACT

This chapter describes China's experience in attempting to protect its rare, threatened, and endangered species and their natural habitats. Because China is a mega-diversity country, with 10-11 percent of world species, its record is of international importance.

The chapter describes the distribution of endangered species, and the recent progression of biodiversity loss. It identifies the root causes of species loss, focusing on consequences of rapid economic development. In response, the state has developed a complex regulatory regime, including China's participation in international environmental conventions, national law and policy, and national and provincial regulations. Although three central agencies have most management responsibility, nearly a dozen are involved altogether, which the State Council has coordinated through several means. Proposed revisions to the regulatory regime indicate a maturation in thinking about species protection issues.

The protected area (PA) system is at the heart of China's efforts to avert biodiversity loss, and the chapter recounts the evolution of this system, the distribution and structure of PAs, and their management. Then, the chapter turns to agents of civil society—the media, scientists, and non-governmental organizations (NGOs)—which together are of increasing importance in alerting government officials to problems in biodiversity conservation.

Like other developing nations, China's regulatory regime has "implementation deficits." These are explained in the context of the administration of policy in PAs, focusing on limitations to the structural framework, administrative coordination, finance, personnel training, and community conflicts. The chapter concludes with a summary of the argument and both comparative and temporal observations.

Introduction

China is the world's third greatest mega-diversity county, and has about 10-11 percent of globally threatened species; yet protecting rare and endangered species is a relatively recent objective of the Chinese government. Like other environmental issues, it has received sustained attention from central authorities only since the late 1980s. This chapter examines the endangered species problem based on the available scientific literature (in Chinese and English) and our interviews in China with government officials, scientists, and representatives of non-governmental organizations (NGOs), from 2004 to the present (2008).

We first treat the nature of the endangered species problem in China, by considering the spread of biodiversity, including progression of species endangerment, and also examine the causes of biodiversity loss. Then, we introduce the elements of China's regulatory regime to conserve biodiversity: the international treaties and conventions to which China is a party, national laws and policies on species protection, and national and provincial regulations. In this section we also discuss the ministries most responsible for species protection and coordination of these authorities.

Because protection of the natural habitat of species is essential to their survival, we analyze at some length the system of protected areas that China has developed. Next, we turn to civil society—the roles that media, scientists, and non-governmental organizations play in species protection. In the final substantive section, we evaluate the implementation deficits in species protection, arising from the nature of China's governmental system, the limited resources China has been able to allocate toward species protection, and the vast area over which protective efforts must be staged. The chapter concludes with a brief comparison of the nature of China's approach to species protection, to other developing nation-states and to those of economically developed states.

The Endangered Species Problem

To gain a sense of the problem in preserving threatened and endangered species, we begin by reviewing the distribution and current status of species. Then we examine the direct and indirect causes of biodiversity loss. Much of this treatment follows the discussion in *Governance of Biodiversity Conservation in China and Taiwan.*[1]

Distribution and Current Status of Endangered Species

China is the world's third largest country, almost as large as all of Europe, and is first in population size (1.3 billion in 2008). It covers 9.6 million square kilometers, which is 6.5 percent of the area of the planet. Its large number of rare and endangered species is not, as one might expect, distributed evenly. The most economically developed region of China is along the long-settled East Coast, which has few endemic species and few that could be considered rare. In the northern, southern and western peripheral regions, one finds a very large number of endemic species and a high degree of biodiversity.

In *A Biodiversity Review of China*[2], Mackinnon et al. identify seven biogeographical regions of China, which expresses the high degree of ecological diversity:

1. Northeast China: forested hills and the Changbai and Da Xing'an Mountains;
2. North China: plains and low hills (with deciduous forests) of the heavily populated regions north of the Yangtze River;
3. Inner Mongolia-Xinjiang: the northern third of China, including steppes and deserts north of the Tibetan Plateau and also the Tianshan and Altai mountain systems;
4. The Tibetan Plateau and Himalayan highlands;
5. Southwest China: transitional mountains from the eastern Himalayas to the Sichuan and Yunnan plateaus, including deep river gorges that impede movement of species;
6. Central China: divided into the Guizhou plateau, the Sichuan basin, and southeastern provinces; and
7. Tropical South China: including the South China rain forest, Hainan Island, and Taiwan.

The team of researchers summarized China's significance to global biodiversity in these terms:

> China is one of the world's richest countries in terms of biodiversity. It owes its great natural richness to its large size, great physical range of conditions and the fact that it contains ancient centers of evolution and dispersion together with the fact that many areas served as Pleistocene refugia during the temperate species decimations of the Ice Ages.[3]

Table 1. Comparison of China's Species to World Total

Category	Species in China	World Total	Percentage (%)
Mammals	581	4170	13.93
Birds	1244	9198	13.53
Reptiles	376	6300	5.97
Amphibians	284	4148	6.79
Fish	3864	19056	20.28
Freshwater Algae	9000	26900	33.46
Lichens	2000	20000	10.00
Moss	2200	23000	9.57
Pteridophyta	2600	12000	21.67
Gymnosperm	250	850	29.41
Angiosperm	30000	260000	11.54

Source: National Environmental Protection Agency of China (1998), *China's National Report on Implementation of the Convention on Biological Diversity*, Beijing: China Environmental Science Press, 9.

China's varied land ecosystems include forest, shrub, grassland, meadows, desert, mountain tundra, and agricultural regions. Each ecosystem also varies by climatic conditions and categories of species. Forests, for example, include coniferous, mixed, and broad-leaf types. Deserts include dwarf-tree, shrub, semi-shrub, and mat semi-shrub vegetation.[4]

Marine ecosystems include inter-tidal belts, estuaries, saline marshes, mangrove forests, coastal ports, seaweed beds, coral reefs, continental shelf, and open oceans and islands.[5]

Table 1 indicates the significance of China's species as compared to estimates of those found globally.

Within the last 20 years, China's scientists have made great efforts to identify threatened and endangered species. Below we discuss the 1989 Wildlife Protection Law (WPL), which establishes two categories of protection, I and II, listing "key" (*zhongdian*) species. In the early twenty-first century, these two categories have about 1,300 listed species, most of which are mammals. This listing process involved numerous scientific experts, and tended to emphasize species with economic significance (as well as the mega-charismatic fauna, included in most countries' lists of rare and endangered species).

At the recommendation of the Biodiversity Working Group of the China Council for International Cooperation on Environment and Development (CCICED),[6] China adopted the Red List of Endangered Species. This was based on research of the International Union for the Conservation of Nature (IUCN, now called the World Conservation Union [WCU]).[7] Nearly 100 Chinese scientists and conservation experts, representing all of the biological sciences and some non-Chinese authorities, contributed to this project over three and a half years. They applied the Red List criteria, the categories for threatened and endangered species, to more than 10,000 species in the animal and plant kingdoms. The listings presented findings up to 2004 of virtually all species of mammals, birds, amphibians, reptiles, fish, and a select group of insects, mollusks and vascular plants.[8] Based on this work, Wang and Xie estimated that 40 percent of mammals, 7 percent of birds, 28 percent of reptiles, 40 percent of amphibians, and 3 percent of fish were at risk, and a greater percentage of endemic than non-endemic species appeared in the threatened column.[9]

Continued analysis of Red List data by Xie and Sung suggests a more pessimistic prognosis. Based on a more comprehensive evaluation, they find the percentage of species listed in the threatened categories (including critically endangered, endangered, and vulnerable) for invertebrates to be 34.75 percent, for vertebrates 35.92 percent, for gymnosperms 69.91 percent, and for angiosperms 86.63 percent.[10] The percentage of endangered plant species greatly exceeded previous estimates. Xie and Sung list the following percentages of fully evaluated taxa:

- All species of hermatypic corals
- 12.8 percent of butterfly species
- 39.9 percent of amphibian species
- 27.52 percent of reptile species
- 17.4 percent of bird species
- 39.8 percent of mammal species
- 55.44 percent of ericaceous species, and
- 78.26 percent of orchid species.[11]

Moreover, groups such as fish, mammals and gymnosperms confront far higher levels of threat in China than they do globally. Overall, the most recent studies indicate a greater threat to biodiversity in China than previously estimated.

Causes of Biodiversity Loss

Three interrelated factors are the direct source of pressure on the natural habitat of species in China: population, urbanization, and economic development. China's huge population, which is now expected to peak at 1.6 billion in 2030,[12] has put immense pressure on natural habitats of threatened and endangered species. Increase in China's population brings a corresponding increase in use of land for housing and human settlements.

Urbanization is a related factor. Although China's rural population has peaked at about 750 million in the early twenty-first century, the urban population continues to grow. As cities become more populous, they expand into the countryside, putting new pressure on fragile species. Further, urban residents have more disposable income than most rural residents, and they expect to use their leisure time in recreational activities. Many areas near cities and towns have been converted into golf courses, parks, and other recreational uses, which threaten natural habitats of species as well.

Finally, economic reforms unfolding since 1978 have spurred economic development in all parts of China, at the cost of natural habitats. Factories, office buildings, hotels and resorts, and shopping centers consume space in China's cities, suburbs, and countryside. Of equal importance, the pressure for rapid economic development has increased exploitation of China's natural resources—for example, its forests, minerals, and many species considered to have economic value such as fish.

These socioeconomic changes have led to serious degradation of land and of water, with quite deleterious impacts on endangered species and their critical habitats. Reports in recent years point out the serious extent of land degradation. The Ministry of Water Resources stated in 2006 that 37 percent of China's total territory suffered from land degradation. This despoliation included soil erosion, deforestation, salinity, reduced fertility and sand storms, affecting 3.56 million square kilometers.[13] The study *Chinese Ecological Protection,* issued by the State Environmental Protection Administration (SEPA) in 2006, reported continued deterioration of China's ecology. Major problems included excessive logging, degradation of natural pasture land, shrinking wetlands, and overuse of pesticides and fertilizers in farmland and contaminated coastal areas. The study reported these specific findings:

- The ecology of 60 percent of China's territory was considered fragile;
- About 90 percent of natural pasture land (accounting for more than 40 percent of China's territory) faced degradation and desertification; desertified pastures had become major sources of sand and dust storms;
- Only about 40 percent of China's wetlands were under effective protection.[14]

A study of habitat loss in two counties of China's southwest points out the role that agricultural expansion and commercial logging have played in destroying habitat of endangered pandas and snub-nosed monkeys.[15] While the central government has undertaken massive reforestation and afforestation programs, these have replaced natural forests and have "altered the variety, quality and the pattern of delivery of plant and wildlife habitats that had been provided previously."[16]

Also destructive of natural habitats are several types of pollution: industrial plant waste, mining operations, and use of chemical fertilizers and pesticides. Similarly, air pollution has had destructive impacts on plant and animal life. In 2005, one third of China's land mass was affected by acid rain; in some regions of the nation, all rainfall was acidic. For example, with 26 million tons of sulfur dioxide discharged in 2005—27 percent greater than in 2000—China became the world's largest sulfur dioxide polluter.[17]

Degradation of water, in the view of many observers, has reached crisis proportions. An obvious indicator is that 16 of the world's 20 most polluted rivers are in China. The three major sources of water pollution are industrial contaminants spewed into rivers and lakes, chemical pesticide and insecticide run-off from crop fields, and human waste and garbage disposed into waterways. Rivers of north China are perhaps the most polluted, but in recent years, pollution levels have increased enormously in the Yangtze River, which (including its tributaries) accounts for about one-third of China's total fresh water resources. High levels of pollution have led to a shrinking of fish catch and threatened endangered species.[18]

Both the Yangtze and Pearl River estuaries were listed as "dead zones" in a study released in late 2006 by the United Nations Environment Programme (UNEP).[19] Dead zones are water areas where nutrients from fertilizer runoff, sewage, human and animal waste and the burning of fossil fuels trigger algae blooms. The blooms require oxygen and remove it from the water, a condition called eutrophication, which endangers all water life. The number of deoxygenated areas has increased each decade since the late 1970s, and they are a major threat to fragile species.

Finally, species whose habitat is in the ocean are threatened by overfishing, destructive fishing methods, pollution, and the reclamation of coastal lands. The loss of coastal wetlands to agriculture, aquaculture, and reclamation projects has devastated both wildlife and marine resources. Several species already have become extinct: sea cows, species of kelp, and the habitat of sea turtles has been threatened.

These deleterious effects on natural habitats are the consequence of wide ranging socioeconomic changes. In addition, species of economic significance have been appropriated by humans, often illegally (for example, through poaching of mega-charismatic fauna), to which we refer specifically below.

China's Regulatory Regime to Protect Species and Their Habitats

By regulatory regime, we mean the complex of treaties, laws, regulations, and policies, as well as the agencies of government implementing laws, which are designed for the purpose of protecting endangered and threatened species and their critical habitats. We examine three sets of authorities for endangered species protection in China—international treaties and conventions, national law and policy, and national/provincial regulations. Then we review the institutions involved in implementing law and policy and proposals to revise the regime.

International Treaties and Conventions

China's involvement in international environmental conferences and agreements began, haltingly, in the early 1970s.[20] Two multilateral environmental agreements (MEAs) to which China is a party are of great importance in biodiversity conservation, the Convention on the International Trade in Endangered Species of Flora and Fauna (CITES) and the Convention on Biodiversity (CBD).

In 1981, China joined CITES, which pledged it to ban the import and export of endangered species listed in the CITES annexes.[21] This trade became especially problematical as economic development and rising affluence increased the demand for wild plants and animals. International criticism of China's trade in internationally threatened species, such as the use of tiger and rhino parts in traditional Chinese medicine, caused the state to ban sales in 1993,[22] but as we note below, the problem of illegal trade remains.

China was one of the first developing nations to ratify the Convention on Biodiversity. The CBD acknowledges sovereign equality of nations and their rights to biological resources within their territories, while it urges nations to conserve biodiversity.[23] An important component of the convention is the recognition of aboriginal and community use of biological resources, and the emphasis on traditional, as well as modern, forms of ecosystem knowledge (Articles 8[j], 10[c], 17[2], and 18[4]. Article 6 of the CBD calls for planning and the development of measures in each country to reduce threats to biodiversity. Under this requirement of the CBD, China files a "biodiversity action plan."[24] Related to the CBD is the Cartageña Protocol on Biosafety, which China ratified in 2005. This subsidiary convention affects China as it is one of the largest importers of genetically modified organisms (GMOs). Also, the treaty is of importance to China as it provides protection for China's diverse plant species, used in traditional Chinese medicine, and of interest to international pharmaceutical companies.[25]

A number of other conventions add international dimensions to China's regulatory regime. For example, China joined the International Convention for the Regulation of Whaling in 1980, the Convention Concerning the Protection of the World Cultural and Natural Heritage in 1985, and acceded to the International Tropical Timber Agreement in 1986. In 1992, China joined the Ramsur Convention, the Convention on Wetlands of International Importance Especially as Waterfowl Habitat. China also participates in the Convention to Combat Desertification and the United Nations Convention on the Law of the Seas (UNCLOS), which are also relevant for preservation of rare and endangered species and the sustainable use of biological diversity.

National Law and Policy

China's latest constitution (1982) provides a cachet of legitimacy for species preservation:

> The state protects and improves the environment in which people live and the ecological environment. It prevents and controls pollution and other public hazards. The state organizes and encourages afforestation and the protection of forests.[26]

More than a dozen laws address aspects of species protection. Laws offer a relatively strong degree of protection. They are enacted by the National People's Congress, China's supreme legislative body, on the recommendation of the State Council. Chinese law, as compared to that in western nations, is quite broad and often resembles more closely policy statements than statutes, but laws are transparent and enforceable. General laws, such as the

Environmental Protection Law, adopted in 1979 (and amended in 1989), and the new Environmental Impact Assessment (EIA) Law provide for impacts of development projects on rare and endangered species. Pollution laws, such as the Water Pollution Prevention Law of 1984 (revised in 1996), the Solid Waste Pollution Prevention Law of 1995, and the Air Pollution Prevention Law of 1987 (revised in 1995) speak to the growing threat that pollution represents to biodiversity in China. Here we focus on laws specifically targeting ecosystems and species.

Early laws concerning natural habitats were developed in the 1980s, and pertained to protection of China's forests. The first forest legislation was enacted in 1985.[27] This Forest Law made formal the division of forests between state ownership and that of collectives (*jiti*). The law articulated principles for forest management, established a timber harvest quota system, and required that permits be obtained in order to ship timber. Article 20 of the law specifies that forest administrative sectors at national and provincial levels should set up nature reserves to protect typical ("representative") forests, habitats of rare and endangered animals and plants, and other forests with special conservation values. Yet the Forest Law did little to protect natural (old-growth) forests in the process of rapid deforestation.[28] (The Forest Law underwent revision in 1998, which clarified market use of forest resources and ownership, leaseholds, and management. However, the revisions did not provide additional protection to natural forests.[29]) In 1985, the Grassland Law was enacted, followed by additional legislation on the marine environment, fisheries, water and soil conservation, and land management.

The most comprehensive species protection legislation—the Wildlife Protection Law (WPL)—was not enacted by the National People's Congress until 1988; it was promulgated the following year. This legislation instructs the state to insure the protection of wild animals and their habitats, organize regular field surveys of wildlife resources, and to improve ecological impact assessment for construction projects. As mentioned, the law established two key categories of protection for endangered or valuable species. Furthermore, the law imposed penalties for killing or trading in banned species. The maximum penalties included long prison terms and even execution. Sayer and Sun point out that "more than 30 people have been executed for killing or trading in parts of elephants and giant pandas."[30]

Altogether, the body of law on species protection is large, but it lacks comprehensiveness.[31] The forest and marine environments are protected legally, however, wetlands are not, and there is considerable interest in their protection.[32] Although the WPL mentions natural habitat of rare and endangered species, it does not provide explicit protection for it. Coral reefs in China's territorial waters are not protected from coastal industrial development and over-fishing.[33] In the opinion of plant scientists, plant species are devalued in the sense that there is no plant protection law (but plants receive protection via regulations). Species without apparent economic value, such as insects, are devalued as well. Parenthetically, in the absence of national legislation, some provinces and municipalities have crafted local laws, for example, in order to protect mangrove forests.[34]

Policy statements and action plans are not quite laws, yet they reveal the intention and pledge action of the state to species conservation goals. In the last 15 years, China has announced a large number of action plans, for example the forestry action plan for China's Agenda 21 (1995), plan for the centralized conservation of urban rare flora species (1996), and biodiversity protection and sustainable use of wetlands (2000-04). For instance, China's commitment to biodiversity conservation encouraged the Minister of Construction to tell cities and towns to develop biodiversity plans. In planting trees, he advised that they should use different varieties instead of single species. Too, he advised them to submit plans on how to stop invasive pests.[35]

National and Provincial Regulations

Regulations (in Chinese, *fagui*) provide a less authoritative basis for action than legislation. They do not undergo a public review process, as occurs increasingly for proposed legislation through the National People's Congress. State Council regulations of 2008, however, state that official documents of the state, which includes regulations, are to be publicly available, which greatly increases their transparency. Regulations reflect negotiations among affected bureaucratic interests. They are issued by China's paramount administrative body, the State Council.

Three sets of regulations implement the WPL. Regulations on "Terrestrial Wild Animal Conservation," issued in 1992, include specific stipulations on the protection of wild animals, management of wild animal hunting, and the domestication, reproduction, and other utilization of wild animals. Regulations on "Aquatic Wild Animal Conservation" were issued in 1993. These regulations prohibit fishing, killing, and the sale and purchase of key national protected aquatic wild animals, and they institute a permit system for their domestication. Regulations on "Wild Plant Conservation," issued in 1996, prohibit the collection, sale, or purchase of key wild plant species. They also outline rescue measures for endangered plants and recovery of their habitats.

Recently, the State Council has issued regulations on the protection in China of endangered species listed in CITES annexes. These attempt to reconcile the difference between the WPL categories on endangered species and the CITES strictures on import and export of endangered wildlife.[36] Too, provincial governments and governments of directly-administered municipalities (Beijing, Tianjing, Shanghai, and Chongqing) issue regulations on wildlife protection.[37]

Regulations address some topics on which the law is silent, such as wetlands and protected areas (discussed in the following section). The first mention of protected areas (PAs) in planning documents was in 1979. Regulations were promulgated for them in 1985. Revisions to these rules were endorsed by the State Council in 1994. As we note below, currently draft legislation is being written for a new law on protected areas.

Institutions and Coordination Mechanisms

Three central agencies have most responsibility for management of China's endangered species—the Ministry of Environmental Protection (MEP), the State Forestry Administration (SFA), and the Ministry of Agriculture (MOA).

China developed an environmental ministry, then called the National Environmental Protection Administration, in 1988. In 1998, the name of the agency changed to the State Environmental Protection Administration (SEPA). SEPA had broad responsibility for each of China's major environmental problems, and thus its attention was diffused to issues of air, water, and land pollution, acid rain, and climate change. In the area of biodiversity conservation, it has a small department of nature conservation and division of nature reserves and species management; too, it has general responsibility for developing and maintaining the biodiversity data management and information system. In early 2008, the State Council elevated SEPA to ministerial status as part of a reform to improve government efficiency, and it is now called the Ministry of Environmental Protection (MEP). Nevertheless, it remains a relatively small agency, with about one-twentieth the personnel of the US EPA, but with a far more expansive mandate. In 2008, the agency requested a large increase in budget and personnel to assist its performance of monitoring responsibilities.[38]

Most of China's endangered and threatened species are located in forested areas and thus the SFA has large administrative responsibilities for their preservation. The SFA also is a relatively small agency, with fewer than 300 Beijing office employees. Since the reorganization of central government agencies in 1998, its status has declined to the sub-ministerial level. (In 2008, there was spirited discussion of combining SFA with the Ministry of Agriculture, or dissolving it and attaching its environmental protection functions to the MEP and its timber production functions to the Ministry of Commerce.[39]) The SFA is the primary agency for implementation of the WPL and the Forestry Law. It is responsible for 70 to 75 percent of China's protected areas. The SFA has compliance powers and a network of permit and security (or police) officers to enforce laws and regulations pertaining to endangered species and ecosystems.

The third agency involved in protection of species and critical habitats is the Ministry of Agriculture. This department was once housed together with forestry, but they have been independent since the mid-1980s. The MOA has an office for endangered and threatened species and administers a small number of protected areas, about 3 percent of the total. The MOA has primary responsibility for plant species and fisheries: the national protection list assigns aquatic species to MOA and all other terrestrial species to SFA. This framework of the WPL does not account well for amphibians and reptiles, which has led to disputes between MOA and SFA as to which agency regulates what species.

Other central government agencies also have some responsibilities for species protection. The Ministry of Construction supervises national parks registered with the UNESCO natural heritage sites. It also regulates the Chinese zoo system, and all city zoos belong to it. The State Oceans Administration is responsible for marine reserves and all endangered and threatened marine species, but identification of such species is least well-advanced among the categories of protected species.[40] This agency administers a small number of marine protected areas, but lacks compliance powers. The Chinese Academy of Sciences is one of the earliest institutions to promote biodiversity research and protection in China. It has founded new institutes to expand biodiversity research and organized large field studies of biological resources.

Finally, a number of other agencies are involved less directly in biodiversity conservation. The Ministry of Foreign Affairs is responsible for international conventions in which China participates, and it heads delegations at international environmental conferences. The Ministry of Commerce has duties with respect to certain environmental treaties, such as CITES. The Ministry of Education has training functions with respect to environmental education. And the Ministry of Finance has responsibilities regarding environmental assessments.

The large number of agencies involved in species conservation work puts a premium on coordination and linkage mechanisms, and we discuss several. First, the State Council establishes coordinating bodies and mechanisms. It authorized the work of the Biodiversity Working Group of CCICED, the *China Red List* and the report on protected areas discussed below. In response to the requirements of the CBD, the State Council established a Coordinating Group for Implementation of CBD, with a membership of 20 departments and a technical support system.[41]

The State Council also monitors law enforcement, and in 1993 promulgated a "Notice on Strengthening Investigation on Enforcement of Environmental Laws and Punishing Illegal Activities." Within one year (1993-94), it increased by 50 percent the areas of investigation, which turned up around 100,000 cases of violations concerning wild animals, forests, grasslands, and mining development. By 1996, investigation reached 29 provinces or regions.[42]

China has adopted Agenda 21 and sustainable development planning, which is pursued under State Council aegis. Beginning in 2004, sustainable development entered economic planning as SEPA and the National Bureau of Statistics worked to create a "green GDP measure," which would subtract resource depletion and other environmental externalities from the GDP in order to illustrate the relationships between the environment and the economy.[43] A related concept, the "circular economy," focused on low energy consumption, low pollution and high efficiency. Both potentially may help raise the value of environmental protection activity and increase integration.

Second, the central government has the largest budget in China, approximately 6.2 percent of GDP.[44] As explored below, the central government has leveraged its fiscal power to improve management and protective capabilities of nature reserves. Too, it effectively manages all foreign financial assistance China receives to protect its endangered species and ecosystems. As foreign financial assistance is such a large component of China's overall spending on biodiversity conservation, the center influences directions taken by provinces and local areas.

Third, some integration of policy is attained through the use of national campaigns. Although mobilization campaigns have been explicitly repudiated as a method of rule,[45] a compulsory national tree-planting campaign, which began in 1981, has been a main factor in the success of China's afforestation program.[46]

In short, the State Government has the capability to integrate protection of China's rare and endangered species and ecosystems, but this competes with all the other conflicts and issues it must resolve.

Revisions to the Regulatory Regime

While China's participation in international conventions has intensified the focus on species protection, the existing body of legislation and regulations is under revision, and this reflects a maturing in the attitude of the state toward species and habitat preservation. Revision focuses on the WPL and management of China's PA system.

The premier legislation on rare and endangered species, the Wildlife Protection Law of 1989, underwent revision in 2003-04. The SFA wrote a draft and submitted it to the State Council, but the severe acute respiratory syndrome (SARS) epidemic in 2004 (reportedly initiated by the eating of wild civet cats in Guangzhou) intervened and delayed the process.

Revisions focused on five areas, showing important changes in thinking about species protection in China.[47]

1. Ownership and use of wildlife—whether species domesticated in China could be sold by the enterprises raising them;
2. Management fees in wildlife areas—a proposed reduction or elimination of fees for using PAs;
3. Wildlife classification system—a clear distinction in legislation between endangered species and all other vulnerable (and valued) species;
4. Critical habitat provisions—a strengthening of provisions protecting natural habitat of species and including habitats for migratory species; and
5. Compensation for wildlife damage—a rationalization of the current scheme that relies on local governments (which often lack financial resources), to increase the likelihood that those whose crops or livestock are damaged by wild animals will receive compensation.

The overall impact of revisions would be to increase the comprehensiveness of species protection while enhancing flexibility. However, changes in administrative configuration (specifically, the elevation of SEPA to ministerial status), and disagreement among implementing agencies, have delayed the development of consensus on these reform proposals.[48]

A second area of reform concerns China's protected areas, currently managed under regulation and not law. One of the recommendations of the Protected Area Task Force was that China develop an authoritative basis in law for the administration of its protected areas. A second recommendation was that a single agency be put in charge of management, instead of the myriad agencies presently involved. A proposed law on PAs has now been developed in draft form. However, the recommendation that a single agency manage the more than 2,000 PAs in China met opposition from SFA and MOA. These two agencies claimed they alone had the trained staff needed to manage PAs currently under their jurisdiction; they saw little value to another agency's replacing their supervisory authority.[49]

Protected Areas and Species Protection

The primary means through which China seeks to preserve threatened and endangered species and their critical habitats is the protected area system. We review the evolution of the system, its distribution and structure, and the current administrative apparatus.

Growth of the Protected Area System

China's system of protected areas evolved in four stages (see Table 2). In the earliest stage (from 1956 to 1966), the state established a small number of reserves, with the first, Dinghushan Nature Reserve, founded in Guangdong Province in 1956. At this time, the State Council did not issue regulations for the management of PAs, but the Ministry of Forestry proposed targets, methods, and areas for the delimitation of reserves. By 1965, 19 protected areas had been set up.[50]

Table 2. Development of China's Nature Reserves

Year	Number	Hectares (in thousands)	Land Territory Percentage (%)
1956	1	1	0.00
1965	19	649.	0.07
1978	45	1,265.	0.13
1982	106	3,990.	0.40
1987	400	20,000.	2.10
1989	460	24,000.	2.50
1991	638	55,050.	5.73
1993	763	66,184.	6.84
1995	799	71,850.	7.20
1998	926	76,979.	7.64
2000	1,276	123,000.	12.4
2001	1,551	123,840.	12.9
2002	1,757	126,720.	13.2
2003	1,999	143,980.	14.3
2004	2,194	148,226.	14.8
2005	2,349	149,949.	15.0
2006	2,395	151,535.	15.2

Source: Editorial Committee, *China's Strategy for Plant Conservation*, Guangzhou: Guangdong Science & Technology Press, 2008, 51.

In the second stage, from 1966 to about 1978, political conditions delayed the expansion of protected areas. The Cultural Revolution was especially destructive, as the decline of effective governmental control led to the hunting of wild animals, felling of timber, and other appropriation of the resources in existing nature reserves. Yet at this time, during China's first national environmental conference in 1973, provisional regulations on nature reserves were discussed. By the end of 1978, altogether 45 nature reserves had been formed.

The third stage (1979 to about 1995) was a period of rapid expansion in number of PAs. At the onset of China's economic reform policies and opening up to the world, the State Council and National People's Congress laid the legislative foundation for biodiversity protection, as discussed in the previous section. Both the Forest Law and WPL called for establishment of nature reserves. At the start of this period, several ministries jointly released the "Notice of Strengthening Management, Planning and Scientific Investigations in Nature Reserves," followed in 1992 by SEPA's formation of an evaluation committee for national nature reserves. In 1994, the State Council issued regulations on protected areas.[51] By the close of the period, China had approximately 800 PAs.

The fourth stage (1995-96 to 2006) was a period of continued expansion in number of PAs, with attempts at rationalization of the overall system. PAs were included within China's Biodiversity Action Plan, and in 1995 the Global Environmental Facility pledged US$18 million to improve management of nature reserves. Two other factors led to an exponential increase in nature reserves: natural disasters and regional economic development projects.

Professor Xie Yan reports that PAs increased at an average of 160 sub-national and 16 national-level reserves every year after 1997, with a peak of 350 in 2000 and another peak in 2003.[52]

By 2006, China had about 2,400 nature reserves covering more than 15 percent of its total land area.[53] In addition, there are about 1,400 forest parks, 800 scenic landscape and historical sites, 50 geological parks, 50 water conservation scenic areas, and at least 1,000 small conservation and agricultural reserves.[54]

The number and expanse of PAs in China exceeds the global average, including that for post-industrial states.

Distribution and Structure of Protected Areas

Each province or autonomous region has protected areas, but the greatest expanse lies in the western provinces, which have relatively low human population density. Nineteen nature reserves are larger than 10,000 square kilometers (most are in the West); collectively, they comprise about 66 percent of the total nature reserve area.[55].

The largest nature reserve in China is the Sanjiangyuan (Three Rivers' Source) in Qinghai Province.[56] In eight provinces—Tibet, Xinjiang, Qinghai, Inner Mongolia, Sichuan, Gansu, Yunnan and Heilongjiang—nature reserves cover approximately 20 percent of the area, and the population density is 32 people per square kilometer. In the other provinces, nature reserves extend to only about 5 percent of the land area, while the population density is 393 people per square kilometer.[57]

The western and southwestern provinces of China have the highest levels of biodiversity, explaining the large spaces allocated to nature reserves. Low-altitude regions with high population density and concentrated biodiversity are not adequately covered.[58] The exclusion of economic activities except tourism would make it quite difficult to add populated, low-altitude regions to the system of protected areas.

Nature reserves in China are organized into three types: natural ecosystem, wildlife, and natural monuments. Of the areas included in natural ecosystems, ocean and coastal ecosystems tend to be poorly covered, less than 1 percent of the total (yet the number of protected areas had doubled to 80 by 2008). Some 18 percent of natural ecosystem types are forest; 15 percent desert; and 67 percent inner wetlands.[59] As indicated previously, in the wildlife ecosystems, there are few PAs for plants as compared to animals.

By regulation, the protected areas include three separate management zones:

> (Core) area with no use, habitation or interference permitted, apart from limited scientific research; buffer zone where some collection, measurements, management and scientific research is permitted (but which is not really a buffer zone in the usual international meaning of that term); and experimental zone where scientific investigation, public education, tourism and raising of rare and endangered wild species are permitted.[60]

This zonation system is uniform throughout all nature reserves. As we discuss at greater length below, this structure to the PAs creates difficulties for populations living within nature reserves.

Management of Protected Areas

Protected areas fall under either the central government or sub-national authorities. Just about 10 percent (some 300 or so) PAs are national nature reserves. The remainder effectively are controlled by provinces (or autonomous areas), municipalities, or counties. Since 1979, the state has used four criteria to evaluate applications from regions for the formation of nature reserves:

- Whether they have typical natural ecosystems, representing different natural zones;
- Whether it is an important survival and breeding area for national first grade protected animals, for rare plant species or for other wildlife with special protective value;
- Whether natural ecosystems or species have been damaged, but are of high value and should be restored or replaced; and
- Whether the region has natural and historic relics, important water catchments such as geological sections, glacier relics, lava, hot springs, or fossil locations with special protective value.[61]

Those seeking provincial, municipal, or county-level reserve status apply to the relevant local government for approval, and the report is forwarded to the supervising national ministry or agency for recording purposes. Those seeking the status of a national-level reserve for a region undergo special review by the Evaluation Committee of the National Nature Reserves chaired by the MEP. Additional criteria for this designation include national and international representative characteristics of the area, scientific importance, and specific research value.[62]

Although the largest number of nature reserves is found at the sub-national level, they occupy just one-third of the total protected land area—about 22 percent for PAs at the provincial level, and 11 percent for municipal and county-level nature reserves. The national nature reserves occupy more land than the others, some two-thirds of the total. Moreover, they have what could be called "more valuable" biodiversity resources, and they are much better funded. This explains the great pressure to upgrade PAs from sub-national to national status.

As mentioned, the majority of PAs, about 75 percent, fall under SFA control. The MEP controls approximately 11 percent, and the MOA about 3-4 percent. Other ministries—water conservation, land resources, oceans, construction etc.—control the remaining 10 percent.

For reasons discussed below, the national PAs tend to be the best managed and offer greatest protection to habitats and endangered species. Many of the sub-national PAs could be called "paper parks," with serious problems of finance and management, to which we turn momentarily.

Civil Society and Species Protection

Civil society refers to the network of institutions, social groups and organizations operating at some distance from the state, and enjoying a degree of autonomy in their operations. The concept is of recent relevance to China, as authoritarian states, and especially communist ones, typically do not allow the formation of autonomous groups, which might pose a challenge to the party-state. Nevertheless, since economic reforms began in the late 1970s, China has undergone a degree of political liberalization, and this has entailed a loosening of state controls over the media, over scientists, and over the formation of environmental groups. We discuss each of these new forces in turn.

The Media

Increasingly, the media in China have raised awareness on environmental issues broadly and species protection concerns specifically. The first environmental newspaper in China was the *China Environmental News*, sponsored by SEPA and initiated in 1984. During the 1980s it was the primary voice on environmental issues.[63] By 2000, China's 2,000 newspapers carried 47,000 articles on environment-related issues.[64] The central television station CCTV has produced a number of programs on the environment. A 2001 opinion survey found that 79 percent of respondents relied on television and radio as the primary source of news on environmental issues; for 42 percent of respondents, publicity produced by the government was the second source of information.[65]

These media are subject to censorship, and they do not report all dissidence concerning environmental protests. Yet environmental concerns are less sensitive than issues such as labor protest and human rights, and for this reason journalists report on the environment frequently. In addition to the more than 2,000 newspapers, there are 8,135 magazines, 1,210 broadcasting stations, 1,000 TV stations, and 2,400 cable networks,[66]

More than 220 million Chinese, the largest number in the world, are connected to the internet,[67] and the usage rate has grown exponentially since the 1990s. The internet accommodates a number of blogs on biodiversity conservation issues, yet this usage is supervised. While it can be said that species preservation is a government objective, to the present awareness is limited beyond the elite. A scientist pointed out the difficulty:

> To protect a painting is simple; you put it in a room and guard it. To protect an ecosystem is hard. You can't put it in a room. It shouldn't only be government. There is a generational problem too, especially with farmers and workers, and for remote areas and forests. That is the greatest challenge to environmental conservation, not money.[68]

Thus, while media are an emerging force in Chinese civil society, consciousness raising on endangered species protection is evolving slowly.

Scientists

Most of the data on China's species and ecosystems have been collected by biological scientists and ecologists, working in research institutes and universities. The Chinese Academy of Sciences (CAS) is the center for research institutes, organized largely by discipline. The institutes have played a large role in policy recommendations, which we noted above in the development of the China Red List and the report on protected areas.

Several of the biological science disciplines have professional associations. However, these associations have limited contact with foreign scientific organizations, and they do not take political positions. Nevertheless, individual scientists have worked with international and domestic NGOs. Some have taken positions on adverse environmental consequences of large-scale construction projects, such as the Three Gorges dam, dams on the upper reaches of the Yangtze River, and the Nujiang dam. Sometimes, government authorities have made modifications in project designs to meet scientists' environmental objections. Thus, while scientists do not form pressure groups on issues of concern, they too are a sign of the growing importance of civil society in China.

Non-Governmental Organizations (NGOs): Domestic

Political liberalization accompanying economic reforms has made it possible for social organizations to form in the environmental area, and today they are a vibrant part of society. They perform a variety of functions of benefit to the state, such as environmental education. They play a role in the dissemination of state policy and to some extent play a role in the resolution of social conflict. However, the Chinese party-state remains intolerant of fully autonomous social groups and organizations.

International NGOs occupy a special place in Chinese civil society, because they provide an interface for communication with other countries. Too, they are an indispensable vehicle to trap economic assistance from foreign governments and international financial organizations such as the World Bank. Domestic NGOs in the environmental area are far more numerous than international groups, but they fall under the increased scrutiny of the state. Since 1989, the state has established regulations for social associations, requiring that they be sponsored by an agency of the state and meet requirements pertaining to their membership and financing. In 1998, new and tighter regulations issued from the Ministry of Civil Affairs.[69] The regulations prohibited social associations from registering as business affiliates; they limited membership to 50 and required demonstration of fiscal responsibility. Additionally, groups needed to seek separate registration in each place they operated, and permitted only one association to register in the same area for a specific activity, such as environmental protection. These regulations and the crackdown on the *Falungong* in 1989 seemed to have a chilling effect on formation of social associations, yet as we note below, in 2008 both domestic and international NGOs in the environmental area seem to be thriving.

A large number of domestic NGOs, as many as 350, are government-organized, called GONGOs. Examples include the China Wildlife Conservation Association, which engages in education on biodiversity conservation issues and serves as a liaison for China on international conservation issues; the Chinese National Committee for Man and the Biosphere, which implements China's membership in the UNESCO MAB program; and the China Environmental Protection Foundation, which gives annual wildlife conservation awards. Some of the GONGOs have a considerable amount of autonomy from the state and may be evolving into important elements of civil society.

There are about 50 national-level NGOs headquartered in Beijing that play important roles in species protection. Best known is Friends of Nature (FON), established in 1994 by Liang Congjie (member of the Chinese Political Consultative Conference and grandson of the Republican China luminary Liang Qichao). It has the largest membership, around 2,000, of any NGO in China. The main activity of this NGO is environmental education, including publication of a newsletter and operating a mobile environmental educations van outside Beijing. It has worked with community groups to resist siting of incinerators and landfills in their residential compounds, and it has played an active role in endangered species problems. In the late 1990s, it was successful in urging the government to established a PA for the snub-nosed monkey in Yunnan Province.[70]

A second Beijing-based NGO is the Global Village of Beijing, established in 1996 by environmental activist Liao Xiaoyi. It has an active environmental education program and emphasizes women's role in environmental change. It has hosted a back-to-nature training base near Beijing and sponsored recycling programs.[71]

A third type of domestic NGO is composed of student groups at university campuses throughout China. Many colleges and universities have student organizations focusing on environmental issues. One example is the Green Camp Volunteers, which formed in 1996. It has organized camps in areas of endangered species and their natural habitat. Students write reports on their experiences, capture the locales in photos which they exhibit on campuses, and make public presentations.[72]

Finally, the most numerous NGOs are those operating at the grassroots level in cities, towns, and villages. Their membership probably numbers in the tens of thousands. In many cases, they form in opposition to ecological disturbances happening in their vicinity. One example is the Upper Yangtze Organization, established in the western part of Qinghai Province in 1998. It formed because of concerns about poaching of wild yaks in the region, but developed into an ecological protection committee for several endangered species. It too promoted environmental education, and partnered with several external agencies sharing its preservationist objectives.[73]

International NGOs

The richest environmental NGOs operating in China are those with headquarters in North America or Europe, which focus on problems of global significance. Although most are not registered with the Ministry of Civil Affairs, they typically have developed memoranda of agreement with central government agencies such as the MEP or SFA.

The World Wildlife Fund (WWF) has been involved in conservation activities in China for nearly 30 years. It assisted the government in establishing the Wolong Giant Panda Reserve in 1979, and continues panda preservation programs in the Minshan region, in the Qinling Panda Focal Project (Shaanxi Province) and supports surveys and studies on pandas and their habitats. Too, it has assisted in restoration of wetlands in the Yangtze, Lancang and Heilongjiang river basins, and in 2001 launched a China species preservation program.[74] It has new programs on forest and ocean conservation, climate change, poverty alleviation, and sustainability.

The Trade Records Analysis of Fauna and Flora in Commerce (TRAFFIC) has an office in the WWF complex in Beijing, and is the foremost NGO involved in monitoring and investigating illegal wildlife trade, and providing information to the CITES Management Authority in SFA on violations. In recent years, it has focused on trade in rhino and tiger parts and smuggling of African elephant ivory to China (where it is carved and then smuggled to North America and Europe).[75] Recently, it has sought to have the pangolin, a second category species of concern, raised to category I under the WPL.

The Nature Conservancy (TNC), entered China only in 1998 but now is engaged in 15 projects in the northwest Yunnan Province, one of the most biologically diverse temperate ecosystems on the planet. TNC representatives have worked to establish nature reserves in this region, develop enterprises generating economic benefits for local communities, and enhance the capacity of local governments, communities and NGOs for sustainable conservation.[76]

Other NGOs are more specialized in their work to preserve ecosystems and endangered species. The International Fund for Animal Welfare (IFAW) has monitored Asian elephants, Tibetan antelopes, and illegal trade in wild and captive-bred tigers. In Yunnan Province it has helped communities develop enterprises and alter crops grown to reduce conflict with resident endangered species.[77] Conservational International (CI) has mapped sacred sites, assessed biodiversity values, and documented and gathered indigenous knowledge in the mountains of southwest China hotspot. The International Crane Foundation (ICF) specializes in bird species conservation and preservation of wetlands, while the China program of the World Conservation Society pays attention to China's diminishing population of wild tigers, alligators, and environmental education in this area.[78]

Although China's civil society is less robust than those of democratic developing states, such as the Philippines and India, it nonetheless is far more resilient than at the start of economic reforms in the late 1970s. Wood et al. suggest "The role of civil society in promoting, implementing and monitoring the conservation of biodiversity needs to be recognized and supported by national governments and international institutions."[79] The Chinese government has warmed to the positive role that NGOs play in biodiversity conservation, but does not yet "support" them.

THE IMPLEMENTATION DEFICIT IN SPECIES PROTECTION

Protected areas are the primary element in China's strategy to conserve biodiversity. The SFA estimates that PAs cover about 80-85 percent of China's endangered and rare wildlife species.[80] The explosion in numbers of protected areas, as well as problems of law, finance, staffing, and management spurred focused study. In 2003, the China Council for International Cooperation on Environment and Development (CCICED) formed the Protected Area Task Force (PATF), to continue earlier work done by the Biodiversity Working Group; its 2004 report to the State Council, *China's Protected Areas*, made comprehensive recommendations for reform of the PA. We report on five areas covered by the report: the architecture of nature reserves, horizontal and vertical administration, financial resources and incentives, human resources and training, and community-level conflicts.

Structural Framework

The structural framework of the protected area system lacks a basis in law, and for this reason, the PATF recommended "a comprehensive legal framework for an advanced system of protected areas based on the full range of protected area objectives."[81] The task force justified the recommendation by pointing to this pattern: PAs throughout China have been superimposed on "a mosaic of land uses that are often in severe conflict" with PA regulations.[82] In some areas, PA boundaries overlapped priority development projects; in others, they overlapped areas of traditional community use. Complicating the state's control over PAs is the fact that collectives, operating under the "responsibility system," control about 40 percent of the land in nature reserves. As mentioned, there are problems of gaps in the coverage of endangered and rare species and ecosystems. Finally, the three-part system of management zones is rigid and inflexible. For this reason, the PATF recommended that China adopt the international standards of the World Conservation Union, which would introduce greater flexibility into the zonation system. For example, a large number of PAs in China would fit more easily into the second IUCN management category (national parks) or as protected landscape/seascape. The PATF opined that the current system:

> Faces a lack of flexibility to adjust to local conditions and solve conflicts between conservation and development objectives. This is the biggest reason for the poor management of China's NRs. China needs to develop a PA system suited to Chinese conditions and the six-category scheme of IUCN will be the most important reference.[83]

The draft law on PAs is now under review, and it addresses several of these criticisms.

Administration

Administrative problems also adversely affect management. At the central government level, protective functions are divided among a large number of agencies, each with different missions. The problem of vertical integration is much more intractable, and mirrors the difficulty China has faced in devolving economic development activities from the center to provinces and local governments. One aspect to this problem is the system of divided loyalties, with provincial and municipal environmental and forestry bureaus responding to both national and sub-national masters. A second problem is having different systems of incentives and values. An NGO representative who frequently visited PAs pointed out the dilemmas local government officials, who "look at economic development needs first (as they) . . . have only 4-5 years to get promotions" and can attain them more easily by constructing roads and dams than by protecting natural habitats.[84]

When there are strong pressures to develop an industry that may impinge on a critical habitat or fragile ecosystem, the contradiction between central and local control becomes most clear. Many of the recent stories of habitat degradation in China feature a provincial or local government, seeking to develop the local economy, in conflict with a national law and environmental office. Even scientists well-known for their efforts to preserve biodiversity acknowledge the priority of economic development concerns. Asked why national policy on biodiversity conservation was often not effective at local levels, a biologist commented:

> Although China has a strong government, it cannot control everything. It is not like the U.S. or other western countries. Distant places can get away with a lot. Second, places which have many threatened species and ecosystems are also very poor. Economic development is more important to them. Local governments look to people's needs.[85]

The relevant phrase in Chinese is *Shangyou zhengce; shiayou duice*, which roughly translates as "officials set policy, subordinates alter policy."

Finance

Funding problems beset most of China's PAs. Although foreign government and foundation funding contributes to training and management of nature reserves, much of this funding is one-time-only. It tends to emphasize capacity building, resource investigation, and environmental education efforts, but is unsustainable over the long-term.

The central government's primary contribution to funding has been to pay for infrastructure—construction of buildings such as offices, rescue centers, tourist facilities, roads, and sometimes zoos or botanical gardens. However, one of our respondents opined that insufficient funds were available to buy out leaseholders and collectives in areas of greatest species endangerment. Instead, the government issued orders to preserve species, but did not resettle residents, whose livelihoods were threatened by establishment of PAs.[86]

Central government funding is the chief factor explaining why sub-national governments have sought to elevate the status of their PAs. Most domestic funding of nature reserves, however, comes from provincial and county sources, and this funding is insufficient. A 2004 study reports major funding shortages for "staff salaries and benefits, maintenance and running costs of equipment and infrastructure, travel, compensation for animal damage . . . communications, publicity and meetings with local stakeholders."[87] In response, cash-starved managers of provincial and municipal-level PAs then become entrepreneurial. Managers of areas with charismatic fauna, or other aesthetic values, emphasize eco-tourism. Staff in reserves with exploitable resources began to develop them. This increases revenues for administration while adversely affecting the ecosystem and species being protected.

In 2008, China allocates approximately 1.5 percent of GDP to environmental protection work, less than the average of 2.5 percent of GDP spent by economically developed states. One can hope that the emphasis on "scientific" and balanced development, announced by party chairman (and state president) Hu Jintao at the Seventeenth Congress of the Communist Party of China in October 2007, will lead to increased funding for environmental protection.

Training

The education and training of PA staff also are problematical. The PATF criticizes drawing directors from the local civil service without qualifications to manage nature reserves; the absence of a formal career structure that would enhance morale; and staff ignorance of ecological approaches to management.[88] With respect to provincial, municipality, and county-level PAs, appointments to positions often were made on patronage grounds until recently. Protected area staff were ill-educated; they lacked knowledge of the life sciences, could not easily distinguish the species they were employed to protect, and had no incentive to increase their knowledge or capability.

This observation applies across the board to China's efforts to protect rare and endangered species. Harris notes that by mid-2006, only one Chinese university offered wildlife biology as an academic discipline, compared to offerings at 106 American universities.[89] Yet much attention has focused on the development of management capacity in China's nature reserves of late, involving foreign funding agencies and international NGOs such as WWF, TNC, and CI. In addition, at least five colleges/universities in China have developed specialized degree programs in the management of nature reserves, such as at Beijing Forestry University and Northeast Forestry University.

Even with increased training and funding, however, there remains the problem of lack of a protective ethic. A renowned scientist called the State Forestry Administration a "great obstacle to preservation of China's rare and endangered species." She noted:

> Their people aren't really concerned about endangered species. It's just a job for them. While they say "Don't break the law," they don't take an environmental perspective. There's an attitude problem. They use their regulatory authority as a power base only.[90]

Community Conflicts

Finally, pressures of local communities—for access to land and resources of nature reserves, for participation in decisions of PA authorities directly affecting their lives, and for recognition of the value of their local culture—contribute much tension to the development and management of conservation units. Most of China's threatened endemic species are located in China's poorer regions, and in those with substantial numbers of minorities. In the competition between hungry humans and threatened non-human species, the former have won out consistently. As our respondents often opined: "If people don't have enough to eat, you can't expect them to protect the environment."[91]

Raising awareness about endangered species and ecosystems of farmers and other rural residents, in the view of our respondents, was the "greatest challenge." In addition, there is no incentive for communities to preserve species upon which they rely for survival. Harris argues that a wildlife conservation system for western China would need to include "a larger component of consumptive use of truly wild resources" than now possible.[92] This is one example of a policy shift that would reduce community conflict.

Of course, these problems in the governance of protected areas are not unique to China. They occur also in other developing nations, which lack resources to allocate to environmental protection. They are magnified in China because of its huge territory, and the very large number of endemic species and critical habitats to protect.

Conclusion

China's experience in the protection of threatened and endangered species is of importance to all who are concerned about the rapid loss of biodiversity internationally. China has about 10-11 percent of globally threatened species, and recent scientific studies indicate that the rate of extinction is higher than the global average. The state developed an articulated set of laws, policies, and regulations to address biodiversity threats only in the 1980s. This regulatory regime is relatively broad, and a large number of agencies at the central, provincial, and local levels are charged with its administration. The central element of protection policy is China's vast system of protected areas. In 2008, some 2,400 nature reserves cover over 15 percent of Chinese territory—the largest such expanse in the world.

Since the economic reforms and political liberalization began in the late 1970s, a network of groups and organizations has taken interest in environmental protection. Media help raise consciousness, scientists point out problems in the evolution of policy, and a host of environmental NGOs—international, national, student, and grassroots—mobilize resources and work on concrete problems. Both scientists and global NGOs have brought the best available knowledge on endangered species protection to China. Notwithstanding the framework of laws and regulations, and a growing civil society starting to focus public attention on endangered species problems, there are serious implementation deficits. These can be attributed to the design of nature reserves, problems of administrative coordination, finance and personnel training, and conflicts between preservation goals and survival instincts of communities included within natural habitat areas of threatened and endangered species.

Although China now has the world's most rapidly developing economy, its per capita income is lower than that of economically developed states. The conflict between state goals of economic development—necessary to alleviate poverty—and environmental protection is especially heated, as it is in other developing nations. Much of China's implementation deficit is explained by economic factors. As the Chinese economy grows, more resources likely will be allocated to financing biodiversity conservation work, to training personnel, and to increasing environmental awareness. Politically, China remains under the control of a single party, and party leaders have been less responsive to species conservation interests than leaders in many (but not all) liberal democracies. Yet in 2007-08, China's premier leaders have directed attention to environmental issues and called for "scientific" development, which presumably will not sacrifice major environmental values to open-ended economic growth plans.

Because there tends to be a lag between a nation's economic development and the institution of effective environmental protection (called the "environmental Kuznets curve"), we cannot expect a resolution to endangered species and critical habitat exigencies in the near-term. This means that a number of species (especially those without established economic value) will be lost as their natural habitats are destroyed. Also, unlike all other mega-diversity states, China is territorially vast, and the range of problems does not lend itself to resolution through a uniform, top-down protective strategy. Yet, we are heartened by the attention that many scientists, national leaders, and grassroots organizations are now giving to the issues of endangered species protection, which, we hope, will lead to an increased awareness of the critical importance of biodiversity conservation in coming generations.

References

[1] McBeath, Gerald A. and Tse-Kang Leng, *Governance of Biodiversity Conservation in China and Taiwan*, Cheltenham, UK: Edward Elgar Publishing, 2006. McBeath wrote the China sections of the volume.

[2] Mackinnon, John, Mang Sha, Catherine Cheung, Geoff Carey, Zhu Xiang and David Melville (1999), *A Biodiversity Review of China*, Hong Kong: World Wide Fund for Nature (WWF) International, 39.

[3] Ibid., 21.

[4] National Environmental Protection Agency of China (1998), *China's National Report on Implementation of the Convention on Biological Diversity,* Beijing: China Environmental Science press, 7-8.

[5] Also see National Environmental Protection Administration (1998), "National Research Report on China's Biological Diversity" (in Chinese), Beijing: Beijing Environmental Science Publishing Co., 23-27.

[6] The CCICED was established in 1992 as a high-level non-governmental advisory body of China's State Council. Working groups under CCICED made annual reports to the Council based on investigations and studies, including action recommendations. Of eight working groups, the Biodiversity Working Group (BWG) dealt with living resources including species, ecosystems, and genetic diversity. See BWG/CCICED, "Introduction to Biodiversity Working Group, China Council for International Cooperation on Environment and Development, no date.

[7] The Red List includes these ranges of endangered species: extinct, extinct in the wild, regionally extinct, critically endangered, endangered, vulnerable, and near threatened, to those of least concern. The English version of the IUCN Red List Categories and Criteria can be found at: http:www.iucn.org/themes/ssc/redlists/rlcategories2000 html.

[8] John MacKinnon, in the preface to Wang Sung and Xie Yan (eds) (2004), BWG of China Council for International Cooperation in Environment and Development, *China Species Red List*, Vol. I, Beijing: Higher Education Press, ii.

[9] Ibid., 5-7.

[10] Xie Yan and Wang Sung, "Conservation Status of Chinese Species: (I) Overview," *Integrative Zoology* (2007), Vol. 1, 29, 32.

[11] Ibid., 32.

[12] This is an estimate only. Several sources predict that population will not peak at the 1.6 billion level until 2050.

[13] Siaofeng Guan, "Experts Discuss Answers to Land Degradation," *China Daily*, August 28, 2006, 2.

[14] Fangchao Li, "Ecological Degradation Continuing," *China Daily*, June 5, 2006, 1.

[15] See Wood, Alexander, Pamela Stedman-Edwards & Johanna Mang, *The Root Causes of Biodiversity Loss*, London: Earthscan, 2000, 153-82.

[16] Scott Rozelle, Jikun Huang, and Vince Benziger, "Forest Exploitation and Protection in Reform China," in Hyde, William F., Brian Belcher, and Jintao Xu (eds) (2003), *China's Forests: Global Lessons from Market Reforms*, Washington, DC: Resources for the Future, 20.

[17] Li Liu, "One Third of Nation Hit by Acid Rain," *China Daily*, August 28, 2006, 2.

[18] The white-fin dolphin, with a history of 20 million years along the Yangtze, has practically died out because of pollution and over-fishing. See Liu Xiao, "Swift Action Needed to Save Yangtze, Forum Says," *China Daily* September 18, 2007, 3.

[19] Xinhua News Service, "SEPA to Get Tough on Gov't Violations," *China Daily*, March 2, 2007, 3.

[20] For a review of China's involvement in environmental treaties, see Jerry McBeath and Bo Wang, "China's Environmental Diplomacy," *American Journal of Chinese Studies*, Vol. 15, no. 1 (April 2008), 1-16.

[21] Parties signatory to CITES are obliged to regulate international trade in species listed in its appendices. Appendix I includes species threatened with extinction by international trade, such as tigers and rhinoceroses. These species are strictly regulated and are not allowed to be commercially traded internationally. Appendix II includes all species which may become extinct if their trade is not regulated. CITES permits are required for any deviations to the prohibitions on trade. See Rosalind Reeve, *Policing International Trade in Endangered Species: The CITES Treaty and Compliance*, London, Earthscan, 2002.

[22] Reeves, 2002, 191.

[23] For example, Article 8 calls for countries to establish representative systems of protected areas; Article 17 obliges countries to share such information globally.

[24] See, for example, National Environmental Protection Administration of China (1998), *China's National Report on Implementation of the Convention of Biological Diversity,* Beijing: China Environmental Sciences Press; State Environmental Protection Administration (2001), *China's Second National Report on Implementation of the Convention on Biological Diversity,* Beijing: China Environmental Sciences Press; and State Environmental Protection Administration (2005), *China's Third National Report on Implementation of the Convention on Biological Diversity*, Beijing: China Environmental Sciences Press.

[25] See Li Jing, "World Biosafety Standard Adopted," *China Daily*, May 30 2005, 2. China sends large delegations to the Conference of Parties (COP), including specialists on endemic plants used in TCM. Personal interview with Chinese scientist and delegation member, Beijing, May 15, 2008.

[26] Constitution of the People's Republic of China, Article 26.

[27] For a brief history of the protection and management of wildlife resources, see *Forty Years of Chinese Forestry: 1949-99* (in Chinese), Beijing: State Forestry Publishing, 1999, 193-99.

[28] Lan Xiaoci (2004), "Study on Natural Forest Protection Legislation" (in Chinese), Northeast Forestry University, MS thesis. Also see Zhang Zhiping (2001), "Improvement of Forestry Law and Sustainable Development," *Journal of Nanjing Forestry University*, Vol. 1, no. 4 (December), 33-37.

[29] Zheng Zhengrong (2004), "Study of Essential System of Forest Law of China," (in Chinese), Northeast Forestry University, MS thesis.

[30] Sayer, Jeffrey A. and Changjin Sun, "Impacts of Policy Reforms on Forest Environments and Biodiversity," in William F. Hyde, Brian Belcher and Jintao Xu (eds) (2003), *China's Forests: Global Lessons from Market Reforms,* Washington, DC: Resources for the Future, 181.

[31] Li Zheng (2003) compares the WPL to the American Endangered Species Act in "Consideration from US Endangered Species Act (1973) to China's Wild Animal Protective Act (1988)," *Yunnan Environmental Science*, Vol. 22, no. 2 (June), 38-41 (in Chinese with English abstract).

[32] See Qin Yu-feng (2004), "Legislative Necessity for Wetland Protection in Our Country," *Academic Exchange*, Vol. 124, no. 7 (July), 29-32 (in Chinese with English abstract); Wang Yue-xian and Gang Wang (2004), "On the Necessity and Possibility to Establish China's Wetland Resources Conservation Law," *Journal of Heilongjiang Administrative Cadre Institute of Politics and Law*, Vol. 43, no. 4 (April), 26-28 (in

Chinese with English abstract); and Wetlands International (2004), "Summary on Implementation of the State Council Notice and National Wetlands Conservation and Management," *Newsletter for Wetlands,* Vol. 5, nos 2-3 (in Chinese and English).

[33] Chen Zhiyong, *China Daily*, March 15, 2005, 13.

[34] Lu Zhou-li (2004), "Discussion of the Protection of the Mangrove by Local Legislation," *Journal of Guangxi Administrative Cadre Institute of Politics and Law*, Vol. 19, no. 6 (November), 43-45 (in Chinese with English abstract).

[35] Personal interview with manager, Office of Biosafety and Biodiversity Conservation, SEPA, Beijing, May 21, 2005.

[36] See *TRAFFIC Newsletter*, "Regulation in China on the Import and Export of Endangered Wildlife," May 18, 2006, 45-47.

[37] See, for example, the "Protection Rules for Wild Animals in Tianjing," *TRAFFIC Newsletter*, January, 2007, 45-7.

[38] Personal interview with director, Ministry of Environmental Protection, Beijing, May 21, 2008.

[39] Personal interviews with MOA, SFA, and MEP officials, Beijing, May 18-22, 25-29, 2008.

[40] Personal interview with official of the State Oceanic Administration, January 1, 2005.

[41] See SEPA (1997), "Biodiversity Action in China," *The Newsletter of Biodiversity Conservation and Implementing of the Convention on Biological Diversity, no. 1, August 30, 1997.*

[42] National Environmental Protection Agency (1998), *China's National Report on Implementation of the Convention on Biological Diversity*, Beijing: China Environmental Science Press, 39-40.

[43] Qin Chuan, "Highlighting Green Factor in Economy," *China Daily*, July 20, 2004, 7.

[44] Saich, Tony (2001), *Governance and Politics of China*, New York: Palgrave, 155.

[45] Lieberthal, Kenneth (1995), *Governing China: From Revolution through Reform,*, New York: W.W. Norton, 199.

[46] See Zhang Zhida (ed.) (1999), *Ten National Ecological Forest Projects* (in Chinese), Beijing: China Forestry Press, and Harkness, James (1998), "Recent Trends in Forestry and Conservation of Biodiversity in China," *China Quarterly*, no. 156 (December), 911-34.

[47] This analysis summarizes interviews held at the SFA, June 28, 2004, May 20, 2005, and May 29, 2008, with managers in the SFA Division of Wildlife Management and the Institute of Economic Research and Development.

[48] One observer of the negotiations claimed that turf battles, the interest of each agency in protecting its existing jurisdiction, made resolution of conflict difficult. Personal interview with consultant to the SFA, Beijing, May 23, 2008

[49] Interviews with officials of MEP, MOA, and SFA, Beijing, May 21, 23, 25, 28, 29, 2008.

[50] Division of Wildlife Protection, SFA (2003), *Study on China's Nature Reserves Policies* (in Chinese and English), Beijing: China Forestry Publishing Co., 237.

[51] Xie Yan, "Review on the Management System of China's Nature Reserves," in Xie Yan, Wang Sung and Peter Schei, (2004), *China's Protected Areas*, Beijing: Tsinghua University Press, 317.

[52] Ibid., 317-18.

[53] The phrase "nearly 2,000 nature reserves" is reported in the 2004 publication edited by Xie, Wang, and Schlei (2004), ibid., 281. Government sources list several numbers, with the variance explained by time of publication and whether the source includes the most recent figures from provinces and special administrative regions. Respondents to our interviews in 2005, 2006, and 2007 all mentioned "more than 2,000" protected areas. A section chief of the new MEP, in May 2008, reported that by this year, China had more than 3,000 PAs.

[54] Xie et al., 281.

[55] Xie Yan and Li Lishu (2004), "Gap Analysis on Nature Reserve System in China," in Xie et al. (2004), 518.

[56] See Wang Zuoguan, Wang Zuolong, and Zhang Li (2002), Research into Legal Countermeasures of Nature Preservation Zone of Three River Sources'" (in Chinese), *Journal of Qinghai Nationalities Institute,* Vol. 28, no. 2 (April), 82-89.

[57] Ibid., 518-19.

[58] Ibid., 519.

[59] Editorial Committee, *China's Strategy for Plant Protection*, 2008, 9.

[60] Xie, Wang, and Schei, 2004, 283.

[61] Xie Yan, in Xie et al. (2004), 322.

[62] Ibid.

[63] Personal interview with first editor, *China Environment News*, Beijing, January 11, 2005.

[64] Wen Bo (1998), *Greening the Chinese Media*, China Environment Series, no. 2, Washington, DC: Woodrow Wilson Center Press, 39.

[65] Economy, Elizabeth (2004, *The River Runs Black: The Environmental Challenge to China's Future*, Ithaca, NY: Cornell University Press, 163.

[66] Hu Kanping and Yu Xiaogang (2005),"Bridge over Troubled Waters," in Jennifer Turner (ed), *Promoting Sustainable River Basin Governance*, Tokyo: IDE-JETO, 129.

[67] Xinhua, "China Internet Users Surpass the U.S.," *China Daily*, May 8, 2008.

[68] Personal interview with forestry professor, Beijing, January 10, 2005. This remark was repeated by most of the intellectuals we interviewed. Said an official in MOA: "It is very difficult to raise the awareness of farmers about issues concerning threatened and endangered species and ecosystems. They are antagonistic toward them, because they don't understand their significance or value;" Beijing, May 17, 2008.

[69] See Schwartz, Jonathan (2000), "Environmental NGOs in China: Roles and Limits," *Pacific Affairs*, Vol. 77, no. 1 (Spring), 38.

[70] Personal interview with program director, FON, Beijing, May 26, 2008.

[71] Personal interview with GVB representatives, Beijing, May 18, 2005.

[72] Personal interview with Green Camp activist, Tsinghua University, Beijing, May 25, 2005.

[73] Foggin, J. Marc, "Highland Encounters," Innovative Community Initiative, September 2003.

[74] Personal interview with WWF representatives, Beijing, July 1, 2004 and May 20, 2008. Also see *WWF China Programme Annual Report*, Beijing, 2007.

[75] Personal interview with TRAFFIC representatives, Beijing, May 15 and 20, 2008. TRAFFIC publishes occasional newsletters on endangered wildlife in China and

changes in the regulatory regime. Also, it prints special reports, for example: *The State of Wildlife Trade in China* (2006), *Taming the Tiger Trade* (2007), and *Trade and Conservation of Taxus in China* (2007).

[76] Personal interview with TNC Staff Director, Kunming, May 27, 2005.

[77] Personal interview with IFAW representatives, Beijing, May 19, 2008. See *International Fund for Animal Welfare in China* (2004) and special reports, for example, *Made in China: Farming Tigers to Extinction* (2007).

[78] Personal interviews with IFAW, CI, WCS representatives, Beijing, May 18-20, 2008.

[79] Wood et al., 2000, 82.

[80] Personal interviews with officials, State Forestry Administration, Beijing, May 20, 2005, May 27, 2008.

[81] Xie et al. (2004), 274.

[82] Ibid., 283.

[83] Ibid , 338.

[84] Personal interview with NGO representative, Beijing, June 11, 2004.

[85] Personal interview with CAS biologist, Beijing, April 13, 2004.

[86] Personal interview with division director, SFA, Beijing, May 28, 2008.

[87] Xie et al. (2004), 288, and Wen Yeli (2003), *Economic Analysis of China Biodiversity Protection Policy* (in Chinese), Beijing Forestry University, PhD thesis.

[88] Xie Yan et al. (2004), 290.

[89] Richard B. Harris, *Wildlife Conservation in China*, Armonk, NY: M.E. Sharpe, 2008, 234.

[90] Personal interview with CAS scientist, Beijing, May 21, 2008.

[91] Personal interviews with officials in each year of study, 2004-08.

[92] Harris, 2008, 211.

In: Endangered Species: New Research
Editors: A. Columbus and L. Kuznetsov
ISBN 978-1-60692-241-5

Chapter 2

PATTERNS OF GENETIC DIVERSITY IN THE HIGHLY THREATENED VASCULAR FLORA OF THE MEDITERRANEAN BASIN

Jordi López-Pujol[1,*], Maria Bosch[2], Joan Simon[2] and César Blanché[2]

[1]GReB, Botanic Institute of Barcelona (CSIC-ICUB), Passeig del Migdia s/n, 08038 Barcelona, Spain
[2]GReB, Laboratori de Botànica, Facultat de Farmàcia, Universitat de Barcelona, Avda. Joan XXIII s/n, 08028 Barcelona, Spain

ABSTRACT

The Mediterranean Basin is widely recognized as one of the main plant biodiversity hotspots of the world. In its western part, the Catalan Countries, which represent the eastern section of the Iberian Peninsula, is one of the areas with the highest floristic diversity of the basin, containing more than 4,500 taxa, and showing a rate of endemism of about 5%. At the same time, this region is one of the most fragmented and man-modified of the basin. Here we present a synthesis of the literature concerning allozyme genetic diversity in plant taxa occurring in the Catalan Countries. From 36 taxa examined, which are mostly rare and/or threatened, relatively high levels of genetic variability have been detected (P = 28.85%, A = 1.46, and H_e = 0.112 for diploid taxa), although with a substantial percentage (around 6%) of rare alleles per population, high rates of imbreeding (F_{IS} = 0.245), and a considerable genetic divergence among populations (G_{ST} = 0.248). The causes of such patterns, together with their relationship with different biological and ecological traits of the studied taxa, have been analyzed in detail. Such information has significant conservation implications, and may provide guidelines for setting up management and recovery plans of the Mediterranean endangered flora.

* Author for correspondence

Introduction: Background of this Study - Patterns of Genetic Diversity in Relation to Ecology and Evolutionary Traits

In the last 25 years, numerous studies addressed to determine the existence of relationships between genetic diversity of vascular plants and their biological, ecological and geographical features have been published. These surveys were aimed to search –based on the available bibliography– certain characteristics of plant species which allow to make predictions on the levels and distribution of genetic variability of plant populations, given the impossibility to perform genetic studies in all the endangered species or at least in a significant fraction of them (Ellstrand & Elam, 1993; Hamrick & Godt, 1996a). On the other hand, the present biodiversity crisis requircs, in many occasions, to take decisions rapidly to ensure the species conservation without having to wait to obtain the corresponding genetic data (Spielman et al., 2004).

The first of these reviews was a collection of genetic (levels of diversity at population scale) and ecological data (from 12 different traits) of a total of 113 plant taxa (Hamrick et al., 1979). Some years later, this study was expanded up to 124 taxa and 14 ecological traits (Loveless & Hamrick, 1984). The most comprehensive one is, however, Hamrick & Godt's review (1990), extensively cited in plant biology, which included genetic data from 449 taxa at species level, at population level and among populations within the same species, and their relationships with 8 large ecological categories. Later, the same authors (Hamrick & Godt, 1996b) performed an analysis with genetic data of approximately 1.500 entries (not necessarily taxa, given that most of them were represented by more than one entry), and comparing among several combinations of two ecological characteristics.

From all these studies, a series of conclusions with relevant implications for species conservation were proposed. Despite the genetic variability depend on a network of ecological, biological and also historical factors, usually intimately linked, there are two characteristics that emerge over the remaining, because they explain a substantial part of the variation of the genetic diversity of vascular plants: the geographical range and the breeding system. Thus, species with narrow geographical ranges (endemic and/or rare species) often present lower genetic diversity levels than those widespread, both at population and at species scale, although there are not significant differences in the distribution of this diversity among populations (Hamrick et al., 1979; Loveless & Hamrick, 1984; Hamrick & Godt, 1990). In relation to the breeding system, the outcrossing species harbor more genetic variability than the selfing ones, although the latter often exhibit a higher level of genetic differentiation among populations (Loveless & Hamrick, 1984; Hamrick & Godt, 1990).

All these reviews have been criticized for the absence of a congruent statistical approach (Karron, 1987; Gitzendanner & Soltis, 2000; Cole, 2003), given that the included taxa in those analyses are considered as statistically independent data, ignoring their phylogenetic relationships. This fact drives to a "pseudo-replication" phenomenon and to a lost of statistical power of the analysis (Felsenstein, 1985; Silvertown & Dodd, 1996; Gitzendanner & Soltis, 2000; Aguinagalde et al., 2005). For these authors, the best procedure is, in the absence of phylogenetic approaches, limiting the comparisons to congeneric taxa, because this will allow us to control the effects of phylogenetic inertia for the different ecological and biological traits. An additional problem of these reviews of multiple species is the difficulty of standardization of the genetic data (such as different number of studied loci, different interpretation of obtained phenotypes, different used programs for the calculation of genetic variability parameters), a flaw that can be avoided in congeneric comparisons because data from compared taxa usually come from the same publication (Gitzendanner & Soltis, 2000). However, congeneric analyses exhibit the remarkably handicap that genetic data for only a few pairs of congeneric taxa is available, limiting thus the power of this kind of approach. Conversely, the classical compilations of multi-species genetic diversity allow the inclusion of all genetic data available from literature, providing a more global approach to the patterns of genetic diversity of plant species.

In the context of the comparisons between congeneric taxa, Karron (1987) was the first to compare 11 pairs of rare and widespread congeneric plants in relation to their genetic diversity and outcrossing rates; whereas he found that rare taxa showed lower levels of genetic diversity than widespread ones, no significant differences were observed concerning the outcrossing rates. More recently, Gitzendanner & Soltis (2000) performed a similar study with a larger sample size (34 genera representing 102 taxa), comparing both the levels (at species scale and at within population scale) and the distribution of genetic diversity, obtaining a lower diversity for rare species but almost the same distribution of diversity among populations. Lately, Cole (2003) included in his analysis a total of 247 plant species in 57 different comparisons of the genetic diversity between rare and common congeneric species, with close results than those reported by Gitzendanner & Soltis (2000), in addition to the finding of a lower genetic variability for the selfing species. Frankham (1995) was the first in trying to correlate the threat degree of a given species and its levels of genetic diversity. In his study, he compared the levels of genetic variation in 38 threatened/non-threatened pair species (taxonomically related but not necessarily congeneric); in most of the cases (32 pairs), the threatened species showed a lower genetic diversity, although only 6 of 38 pairs were plant species. In a more recent paper, Spielman et al. (2004) compared the heterozygosity in 170 pairs of taxa (also taxonomically close) threatened/non-threatened, from which 36 were plant species. From these, in 27 pairs the threatened taxa presented lower heterozygosity than the non-threatened ones.

The studies consisting of comparisons of different characteristics among populations belonging to the same taxon, such as population size or if they are insular or mainland populations, are much more common. However, and despite these comparisons are reported in numerous studies of genetic diversity of plant species, few are the approaches trying to find a common pattern for plants and not only describing what occurs in a certain species. In the review of Ellstrand & Elam (1993) concerning the genetic consequences of small population size, from a list of 10 species, in 7 they reported a positive correlation between population size and levels of genetic diversity. Analogously, Frankham (1996) found a positive relationship between these two variables in 15 of 16 studied plant species. In a second work from the same author (Frankham, 1997), mainland populations showed a significantly higher genetic variation than insular ones in 8 of the 9 plant species included in the analysis.

The Catalan Countries: A Representative Sample of the Mediterranean Hotspot of Plant Biodiversity

The Mediterranean Basin is regarded as one of the 25 world hotspots of biodiversity because of its enormous floristic richness (it harbors ca. 10% of the total amount of the higher plants of the world in an area which accounts for only 1.6% of its surface) and exceptional rates of endemism (13,000 of the 25,000 plant species occurring in the basin are endemics; Médail & Quézel, 1997; Myers et al., 2000). These figures, which acquire special significance when considering that the Mediterranean Basin is one of the most degraded regions of the Earth (it retains less than 5% of its primary vegetation, Myers et al., 2000, and the total number of threatened species is over 4,200; Greuter, 1991), have been attributed to a complicated geological, climatic and biogeographical history (the basin is considered not only a region of refuge and speciation, but also of floristic exchange) and to the large ecological, geological and geographical heterogeneity of the basin (Verlaque et al., 1997; Médail & Quézel, 1997; 1999; Blondel & Aronson, 1999; Thompson, 2005). The Mediterranean does not constitute, however, a homogeneous centre of plant diversity; up to 10 smaller hotpots (areas rich in species abundance and endemism) can be identified within the basin (Médail & Quézel, 1997; 1999).

The 'Catalan Countries' is a geographical entity of ca. 70,000 km^2 defined by those territories in which the Catalan is the mother tongue, and is composed by one sovereign country (Andorra), three autonomous regions of Spain (Catalonia, Valencia and Balearic Islands), portions of a fourth one (Aragon), and the Department of Eastern Pyrenees, in France (Fig. 1). It is a floristically very well studied territory, with regional floras published as early as the second half of the 19th century (Costa, 1864; 1877; Barceló, 1879-1881), and a flora for the whole territory completed in recent times (Bolòs & Vigo, 1984-2001). The Catalan Countries, which account for only 2.9% of the land surface of the Mediterranean Basin, contain 3,586 species or 4,604 taxa (including species, subspecies and varieties; Bolòs et al., 2005), which represent ca. 15% of the floristic richness of this world hotspot (14.34% at species level and 15.34% at taxon level). Thus, this European region is undoubtedly one of the richest areas of the Mediterranean Basin in terms of vascular plant diversity. The mean rate of endemism is, however, relatively low (around 5%), although several areas of the Catalan Countries are included within some of the 10 Mediterranean 'mini' hotspots (see Médail & Quézel, 1997), with rates of endemism close or even larger than 20% (Fig. 2). In addition to their large taxonomic richness, the Catalan Countries also show a great diversity of habitats and ecosystems, from coastal sand dunes and marshes to alpine meadows and nival vegetation. In agreement with these data, the Catalan Countries should be considered as a representative sample of the Mediterranean hotspots. A significant fraction of their plant diversity is, however, currently threatened: although there is not a global figure for the Catalan Countries, red lists available for several areas of this region (Laguna et al., 1998; Sáez & Rosselló, 2001; Sáez et al., 2008) let us to think that the number of threatened taxa may exceed 500.

The present work is aimed to explore the patterns of genetic diversity in vascular plants from the Catalan Countries and, by extension, the Mediterranean Basin, with the following specific goals: (i) to analyze the genetic data available from the literature concerning plant species occurring in the considered geographic area (including those published by our team during the last decade); (ii) to explore the relationships between several biological and ecological traits and the levels and distribution of genetic diversity; and (iii) to determine, on one hand, if geological and climatic history (such as Messinian Salinity Crisis or Pleistocene glaciations), and, on the other hand, if the continued impact of the human activities (especially intense during the last century) have contributed, at least in some extent, to the genetic diversity patterns found for this region.

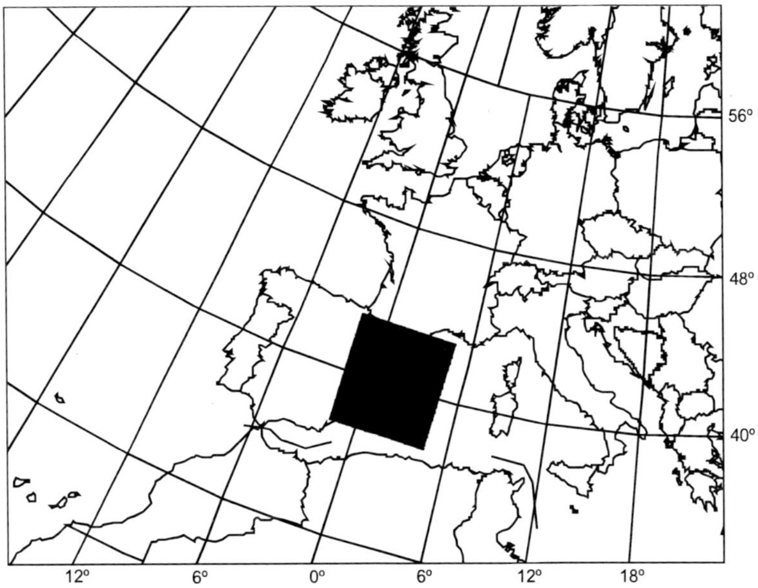

Figure 1. Location of the Catalan Countries, in bold.

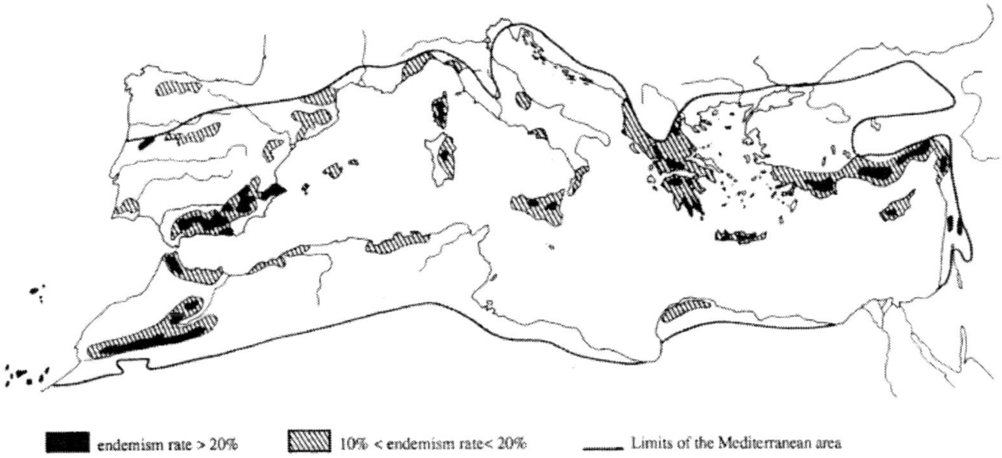

Figure 2. Centres of endemism in the Mediterranean Basin (Médail & Quézel, 1997). Several areas in the Catalan Countries exhibit high rates of endemics, such as the Pyrenean and Pre-Pyrenean ranges, the Catalonian interior ranges, the Balearic Archipelago, and Dianic ranges (the latter with taxes of endemism over 20%). Reproduced from Médail & Quézel (1997) with permission.

Material and Methods

Allozymes as Genetic Diversity Markers

Until the 1960s, the determination of genetic diversity in plant species relied on the measure of morphometric traits. Studies based on these features presented several disadvantages, such as these traits had quantitative variation (they were not discrete phenotypic classes), they showed polygenic inheritance (i.e., the individual loci could not be identified), their expression depended enormously on the environmental conditions, and controlled crossings under homogeneous environmental conditions were required to determine the inheritance mechanism of the studied traits (Allard et al., 1968; Berg & Hamrick, 1997). Since the second half of the 1960, biochemical and molecular techniques began to develop, which allowed, for the first time, the identification of alleles (i.e, qualitative traits and not quantitative ones) in a relatively large sample of genetic loci. The basic assumption in the use of these molecular markers consist in that genetic structure measured with neutral or almost neutral genes (and subsequently independent on the environment) may reflect evolving processes (e.g. inbreeding, genetic drift and gene flow) that affect the entire genome (Bataillon et al., 1996; Hamrick & Godt, 1996a; Petit et al., 1998). The first monogenic markers used were allozymes, still profusely employed nowadays. At the beginning of the 1990s, with the development of the PCR technique (Polymerase chain reaction), which allow the amplification of DNA fragments, a wide array of new types of markers emerged, such as RFLPs, SNPs, AFLPs, ISSR and microsatellites.

Despite the development of all these new molecular techniques, allozymes still continue being one of the most used markers in the detection of genetic diversity (Hogbin et al., 2000; Ridgway, 2005) and possibly constitute the first election in conservation genetics (R. Frankham, pers. com.) due to a series of advantages: technological (an optimum ratio cost-effectiveness, the lack of necessity to have a previous knowledge of the genome, and the simplicity of the technique), genetic (their inheritance is co-dominant, which allow to discriminate phenotypically homozygotes from heterozygotes, and they are products of the expression of coding regions of the genome, which permit a straightforward interpretation of the obtained band patterns in genetic terms –alleles and loci–), and, as well, practical (there is a large body of allozymic literature that, obviously, eases to perform comparisons). However, they present some drawbacks compared to other molecular markers, such as the need of samples coming from living tissues, the impossibility of automatization of the experimental procedure, and the low level of polymorphism obtained, although often it is enough to detect the genetic diversity at population scale (e.g. Crawford et al., 2001a; Ridgway, 2005). Allozymes, therefore, continue being a perfectly valid research tool to study population genetics of plant species, and they have been the selected marker to characterize the genetic variability of the wild vascular flora from the Catalan Countries, that we present in this work.

Table 1. Genetic and ecological data for each of the 36 taxa included in the study

Taxon	*Number of populations* ***	*Number of loci*	*% rare alleles per population***	*P*	*A*	H_o	H_e	F_{IS}	*% private alleles per population*	$F_{ST}{}^{a}$ or $G_{ST}{}^{b}$	*1*	*2*	*3*	*4*	*5*	*6*	*7*	*8*	*9*	*Reference*
DIPLOID TAXA																				
1. *Abies alba*	23 (1)	10	0	40.0	1.40	—	0.063	—	—	—	G	W	IM	LP	S	O	LD	F	NT	Fady et al. (1999)
2. *Aconitum lycoctonum*	19 (1)	10	—	29.0	1.50	0.093	0.100	0.066	—	—	D	W	M	SP	S	O	G	F	NT	Utelli et al. (1999)
3. *Antirrhinum pertegasii*	4 (4)	14	—	17.3	1.21	0.050	0.080	—	—	0.060^{b}	D	E	M	SP	S	O	G	R	T (VU)*	Mateu-Andrés (2004)
4. *Antirrhinum valentinum*	5 (5)	21	—	23.8	1.33	0.184	0.075	—	—	0.480^{b}	D	E	M	SP	S	O	G	R	T (VU)*	Mateu-Andrés & Segarra-Moragues (2000)
5. *Borderea chouardii*	1 (1)	21	4.17	9.5	1.14	0.078	0.046	-0.461	—	—	D	E	M	LP	S	O	G	R	T (CR)	Segarra-Moragues & Catalán (2002)
6. *Borderea pyrenaica*	6 (1)	21	0	19.0	1.24	0.135	0.085	-0.500	—	—	D	E	M	LP	S	O	G	R	NT	Segarra-Moragues & Catalán (2002)
7. *Brassica montana*	5 (3)	11	6.71	36.4	1.88	—	0.184	—	6.41	0.181^{b}	D	W	M	SP	—	M	G	R	NT	Lázaro & Aguinagalde (1998)
8. *Cheirolopus intybaceus*	5 (4)	10	1.92	15.8	1.18	—	0.247	—	5.05	0.293^{b}	D	W	IM	SP	—	O	—	MS	NT	Garnatje et al. (1998)
9. *Cyclamen balearicum*	28 (19)	9	0.87	24.2	1.30	0.006	0.062	0.948	1.01	0.112^{a}	D	W	IM	LP	S	M	LD	F	NT	Affre et al. (1997)
10. *Delphinium bolosii*	3 (3)	15	1.82	28.9	1.40	0.107	0.104	0.019	7.73	0.252^{a}	D	E	M	SP	AS	M	G	MS	T (EN)	Orellana et al. (2007)
11. *Delphinium gracile*	3 (3)	11	10.02	45.5	1.77	0.198	0.159	0.039	18.46	0.073^{a}	D	W	M	A	S	M	G	MG	NT	Bosch (1999)
12. *Delphinium pentagynum* subsp. *formenteranum*	1 (1)	9	6.25	40.7	1.60	0.125	0.180	0.358	—	—	D	E	I	SP	AS	O	G	MS	T (CR)	López-Pujol et al. (2003a)
13. *Delphinium verdunense*	2 (2)	11	16.11	40.9	2.15	0.154	0.205	0.451	17.31	0.028^{a}	D	W	M	A	—	M	G	OT	NT	Bosch (1999)
14. *Erodium rupestre*	5 (5)	14	0	7.1	1.07	0.009	0.025	0.613	1.25	0.372^{a}	D	E	M	LP	S	O	G	R	NT	López-Pujol et al. (2006)

Table 1. Continued

Taxon	*Number of populations ****	*Number of loci*	*% rare alleles per population***	*P*	*A*	H_o	H_e	F_{IS}	*% private alleles per population*	$F_{ST}{}^{a}$ *or* $G_{ST}{}^{b}$	*1*	*2*	*3*	*4*	*5*	*6*	*7*	*8*	*9*	*Reference*
15. *Hippocrepis balearica*	1 (1)	15	6.25	6.7	1.10	0.011	0.010	—	—	—	D	E	I	LP	S	O	G	R	NT	González-Candelas & Montolío (2000)
16. *Hippocrepis grosii*	1 (1)	15	6.25	20.0	1.30	0.122	0.101	—	—	—	D	E	I	LP	S	O	G	MC	T (EN)	González-Candelas & Montolío (2000)
17. *Hippocrepis valentina*	12 (12)	15	5.78	24.4	1.27	0.099	0.085	-0.179	3.35	0.171[a]	D	E	M	LP	S	O	G	R	NT	González-Candelas & Montolío (2000)
18. *Juglans regia*	15 (1)	15	3.85	53.3	1.73	0.331	0.365	0.091	—	—	D	W	IM	LP	S	O	LD	F	NT	Fornari et al. (1999)
19. *Lolium rigidum*	10 (2)	5	—	—	3.90	0.408	0.514	—	—	—	M	W	IM	A	—	O	G	OT	NT	Oliveira & López (1999)
20. *Petrocoptis montsicciana*	4 (4)	16	15.06	70.3	2.20	0.121	0.239	0.486	6.30	0.376[b]	D	E	M	LP	S	O	G	R	NT	López-Pujol et al. (2001)
21. *Petrocoptis pardoi*	3 (3)	16	11.76	56.3	1.90	0.072	0.192	0.620	8.56	0.354[b]	D	E	M	LP	S	O	G	R	T (VU)	López-Pujol et al. (2001)
22. *Pinus halepensis*	6 (3)	15	5.26	26.7	1.27	0.059	0.064	0.068	0	0.031[b]	G	W	IM	LP	S	O	LD	F	NT	Agúndez et al. (1997)
23. *Pinus halepensis*	15 (6)	5	—	—	—	0.262	0.228	0.128	—	—	G	W	IM	LP	S	O	LD	F	NT	Agúndez et al. (1999)
24. *Pinus pinaster*	12 (2)	18	—	41.7	2.00	—	0.159	—	—	—	G	W	IM	LP	S	O	LD	F	NT	Salvador et al. (2000)
25. *Pinus pinaster*	32 (7)	14	—	51.4	1.71	—	0.103	0.038	—	—	G	W	IM	LP	S	O	LD	F	NT	González-Martínez et al. (2005)
26. *Pinus sylvestris*	23 (1)	11	28.57	72.7	2.54	0.316	0.334	0.056	—	—	G	W	IM	LP	S	O	LD	F	NT	Prus-Glowacki & Stephan (1994)
27. *Quercus suber*	18 (2)	14	—	32.1	—	0.135	0.145	0.123	—	—	D	W	IM	LP	S	O	LD	F	NT	Jiménez et al. (1999)
28. *Quercus suber*	7 (1)	13	8.33	61.5	1.85	0.189	0.229	—	—	—	D	W	IM	LP	S	O	LD	F	NT	Elena-Rosselló & Cabrera (1996)
29. *Seseli farrenyi*	3 (3)	14	31.09	83.3	3.00	0.120	0.297	0.592	4.41	0.041[b]	D	E	M	SP	S	O	LD	MC	T (EN)	López-Pujol et al. (2002)

TAXON	Number of populations ***	Number of loci	% rare alleles per population**	P	A	Ho	He	FIS	% private alleles per population	FSTa or GSTb	1	2	3	4	5	6	7	8	9	Reference
30. *Silene diclinis*	2 (2)	26	3.45	5.8	1.11	—	0.023	—	3.33	0.048^b	D	E	M	SP	S	O	G	MG	T (EN)	Prentice (1984)
31. *Silene hifacensis*	8 (8)	12	0.89	7.3	1.08	—	0.085	—	0.96	0.575^b	D	E	IM	SP	S	O	—	MC	T (VU)*	Prentice et al. (2003)
32. *Silene sennenii*	5 (5)	21	7.90	20.9	1.31	0.049	0.063	0.253	0	0.271^a	D	E	M	SP	AS	—	LD	MG	T (EN)	López-Pujol et al. (2007a)
33. *Stachys maritima*	5 (5)	20	2.72	14.0	1.16	0.065	0.066	-0.102	0.95	0.316^b	D	W	M	SP	AS	O	G	OT	T (CR)	López-Pujol et al. (2003b)
POLYPLOID TAXA																				
34. *Delphinium montanum*	7 (7)	15	12.78	23.8	1.48	0.075	0.082	0.089	2.51	0.135^b	D	E	M	SP	S	O	G	OT	T (VU)	López-Pujol et al. (2007b)
35. *Medicago sativa* (wild)	9 (2)	5	—	90.0	3.10	—	0.255	—	—	—	D	W	M	SP	—	O	—	MG	NT	Jenczewski et al. (1999)
36. *Thymus loscosii*	8 (6)	5	18.40	83.3	2.94	0.474	0.423	-0.125	1.04	0.025^b	D	W	M	SP	AS	O	G	MS	NT	López-Pujol et al. (2004)

1. **Taxonomic group**: G: gymnosperms; D: dicots; M: monocots.
2. **Geographical range**: E: endemic (present in less than 50 localities or in an area lower than 10,000 km^2); W: widespread (widespread in the Catalan Countries and even extending to nearby territories).
3. **Insularity**: I: only insular distribution (of analyzed populations); M: only mainland distribution; IM: insular + mainland distribution.
4. **Life strategy**: A: annual plants (include the biannual ones); SP: short-lived perennials (usually < 10 years); LP: long-lived perennials (usually >10 years).
5. **Mode of reproduction**: AS: plants with clonal capacity (asexual + sexual reproduction); S: sexual.
6. **Breeding system**: O: outcrossing; M: mixed strategy (outcrossing + selfing).
7. **Seed dispersal mechanism**: G: gravity (short distance); LD: long distance strategies (epizoocory, endozoocory, anemocory, hydrocory and others).
8. **Habitat**: MC: maritime cliffs; MS: Mediterranean-type shubland; MG: meadows and grasslands; R: inland cliffs and rock exposures; F: forests; OT: others.
9. **Threat status**: T: threatened (listed in one of the IUCN categories); NT: non-threatened. The assignment of threat categories has been done using the most recent criteria of IUCN (2001).

*1994 IUCN categories.

** For the calculation only the populations with N>10 have been considered, given that populations with smaller size cannot contain alleles with a frequency lower than 0.05.

*** In parenthesis, number of populations located in the Catalan Countries.

Compilation of Allozyme Studies in Taxa of the Vascular Flora from Catalan Countries

In order to characterize the genetic diversity of the wild vascular flora from the Catalan Countries, a search of the available literature on allozymic diversity of taxa (species or subspecies) located totally or at least partially in this geographic area (Fig. 1) has been carried out. The available genetic data of the collected plant taxa has been used to build a database, to which the body of data on the genetic variation obtained by our research team during the last decade has been added.

Some of the included taxa, such as *Pinus halepensis*, *Pinus pinaster* and *Quercus suber*, are object of more than one study. In these cases, and following Hamrick & Godt's (1996b) recommendations, they should be considered as independent entries and, thus, calculating the means of the genetic parameters for each species with multiple entries should be avoided. The population size, the number of populations and the number of assayed loci are traits that often vary substantially depending on the research team that carry out the investigation, and sometimes, each work represents a different region of the distribution area of a given taxon. Thus, in these cases we should consider that each entry reports a unique information and, given the multi-taxon database size (three cases of 36 entries in total; Table 1), the redundancy –consequence of the multiple entries for certain taxa–, has a negligible effect in the mean values of the different genetic parameters (*cf.* Hamrick & Godt, 1996b). We only have taken into account data from wild flora species; this fact explains the no inclusion, for instance, of the flagship Mediterranean endemics *Lysimachia minoricensis* (at present extinct in the wild), because all the individuals analyzed electrophoretically had their origin in botanical gardens (Ibáñez et al., 1999).

In addition, we have only considered the surveys which included the genetic interpretation of the electrophoretic band patterns. In the taxa in which monomorphic as well as polymorphic loci were obtained (or only polymorphic), we extracted (or calculated in the case of taxa for which one or more parameters lacked, provided always the raw genetic data, i.e. genotypic and/or allelic frequency matrices, were available) the parameters that describe the intrapopulation genetic diversity levels: A (the mean number of alleles per locus), P (the percentage of polymorphic loci when the most common allele had a frequency below 0.95), H_o (the observed heterozygosity), H_e (the expected panmictic heterozygosity), and F_{IS} (the inbreeding coefficient). When the allelic frequencies were available, we also calculated the percentage of rare alleles (those in proportions lower than 0.05) per population, and the percentage of private alleles per population. We also extracted (or calculated) one indicator of the distribution of genetic variability between populations: F_{ST} (the fixation index) or, alternatively, G_{ST} (the coefficient of genetic differentiation), considering that both are equivalent (in fact they show the same value when there are two alleles per locus; Hartl & Clark, 1989) in order to increase the sample size. For all the cases in which the calculation of one or more genetic parameters has been required, two of the commonest computer programs in population genetics were used: BIOSYS-1 (Swofford & Selander, 1989) and GENESTAT-PC (Whitkus, 1988).

Summarizing, we have built a database with the values of the different genetic polymorphism parameters at population level for 36 plant taxa (Table 1). Nevertheless, the number of existing studies on allozyme diversity of vascular flora from the Catalan Countries is slightly higher. The plant taxa for which genetic diversity parameters at population level (or, alternatively, the raw genetic data necessary for their calculation) were neither provided in the original publications nor obtained by direct request from the authors, were not taken into account for this work. Consequently, these were not included in the database and are the following: *Antirrhinum intermedium*, *A. latifolium*, *A. litigiosum*, and *A. majus* (Mateu-Andrés & de Paco, 2005), *Quercus ilex* (Michaud et al., 1995; Toumi & Lumaret, 2001), and *Q. coccifera* (Toumi & Lumaret, 2001).

Allozymic Diversity and Biological and Ecological Traits of the Collected Taxa

Taking into account the reviews published until the present moment (Hamrick et al., 1979; Loveless & Hamrick, 1984; Hamrick & Godt, 1990, 1996b), we selected several biological and ecological traits with a significant influence in the levels and distribution of the genetic diversity. All plant taxa from the multi-taxon database have been classified in one of the following categories for each ecological trait: (1) the large taxonomic group (gymnosperms, dicotyledons or monocotyledons); (2) the geographical range (endemic or widespread); (3) the insularity (only insular distribution, only mainland distribution or both insular and mainland distribution); (4) the life strategy (annuals, short-lived perennials or long-lived perennials); (5) mode of reproduction (a mixed asexual and sexual strategy or only sexual); (6) the breeding system (outcrossing or mixed strategy), (7) the seed dispersal mechanism (by gravity or a long distance mechanism), (8) the habitat (maritime cliffs, Mediterranean-type shrubland, meadows and grasslands, inland cliffs and rock exposures, forests and others); and (9) the threat status (threatened or non-threatened). A last trait has been added, the ploidy level (10), which allow the comparison of genetic variability between diploid and polyploid species. The criteria for including the collected plant taxa within each category for the different ecological traits as well as the meaning of the used abbreviations are detailed in the footnote of Table 1. The information used to classify each taxon in the corresponding categories has been obtained from the original publications (i.e. genetic diversity surveys), other papers focused in other aspects of these taxa (for instance, the breeding systems), several local floras (such as *Flora dels Països Catalans*; Bolòs & Vigo, 1984-2001), red books or other types of publications. For all the taxa included in the multi-taxon database, we calculated the means (weighted by the product of the number of loci analyzed and the number of studied populations) and standard deviations of the different genetic parameters (A, P, H_o, H_e, F_{IT}, F_{ST} or G_{ST}, the percentage of rare alleles per population and the percentage of private alleles per population) for each category of the different ecological traits abovementioned. To check the differences among the different categories of each ecological trait we used the non parametric test of Kruskal-Wallis, given that in many parameters the values were not normally distributed.

Secondly and when it was possible, we have also performed comparisons between congeneric taxa, as suggested by Karron (1987), Gitzendanner & Soltis (2000) and Cole (2003). Nevertheless, given the small sample sizes, we were not able to use any of the proper statistical tests to develop this kind of analyses (paired-data tests), and comparisons are thus only qualitative. We have only carried out comparisons with a selection of ecological traits (geographical range, insularity, threat status and ploidy level) because the congeneric taxa in our dataset often belong to the same category for most of the traits. Finally, we have completed the study with the comparison among populations within the same taxon: from our multi-taxon database, we have selected all the taxa which have populations belonging to different categories for certain traits (insularity and threat status). All statistical calculations have been performed with STATGRAPHICS Plus 5.0 program.

RESULTS AND DISCUSSION

Levels and Distribution of Genetic Diversity in Vascular Plant Species from the Catalan Countries

In Table 1 is compiled allozyme data of vascular flora from the Catalan Countries which, together with the data reported by the authors of the present contribution, consist of a total of 137 populations, belonging to 33 diploid taxa and 3 polyploid ones. One general conclusion derived from this analysis is that mean values of genetic diversity for diploid vascular plants from the Catalan Countries are apparently poor at population level (P = 28.85%, A = 1.46, H_e = 0.112; Table 2) when comparing with the results from other reviews of genetic diversity. For example, in the first compilation of genetic variability data done by Hamrick et al. (1979), values of genetic diversity computed from a pool of 113 taxa were higher (P = 36.8%, A = 1.69, H_e = 0.156) than those presented here. However, in a posterior review with a larger sample size (653 entries representing 449 species), Hamrick & Godt (1990) reported somewhat lower values (P = 34.2%, A = 1.53, H_e = 0.113), close to the obtained values in this study. The value of expected heterozygosity, the parameter which better describes the genetic variability (Berg & Hamrick, 1997), is almost the same in this analysis than in Hamrick & Godt's (1990) one. Moreover, a series of considerations concerning these results should be taken into account: (i) the taxa included in our analysis represent a very limited geographical area –the Catalan Countries– in comparison to the aforementioned reviews, in which taxa from all latitudes were considered; (ii) an important part of the species collected here (about half of the total) were originally studied, precisely, because of its endemic and/or threatened character (conditions that usually implies a lack of genetic variability of these taxa; Gitzendanner & Soltis, 2000; Cole, 2003; Spielman et al., 2004); (iii) we have only selected the populations of species located geographically within the Catalan Countries boundary; thus, for some of the collected taxa only one population is included in our analysis, cases which are usually not considered in the general reviews; and (iv) the number of both gymnosperms and monocots in this compilation is very small, despite these are taxonomical groups often exhibiting high levels of genetic diversity (see Hamrick & Godt, 1990). Therefore, it may be more proper to talk of levels of moderate or relatively high genetic diversity in the studied vascular plants from the Catalan Countries, as expected in a region which should have acted as a biological diversity reservoir or refuge (for both species and genetic diversity) during the Quaternary glacial periods (Hewitt, 1996; 1999; Taberlet et al., 1998; Thompson, 2005), but which also suffered a drastic transformation of its original ecosystems since the Holocene (Blondel & Aronson, 1999; Thompson, 2005).

The levels of genetic diversity for the studied taxa by our research team during the last 10 years show a great variability (Table 1): from very high values, such as those unexpectedly found in *Seseli farrenyi* (P = 83.3%, A = 3.00, H_e = 0.297; Fig. 3), a narrow endemic species with only three small subpopulations amounting only about 2,000 individuals (López-Pujol et al., 2002), or the tetraploid *Thymus loscosii* (P = 85.0%, A = 3.00, H_e = 0.422), to extremely low levels of variability, such as those obtained in *Stachys maritima* (P = 14.00%, A = 1.16, H_e = 0.066; Fig. 3) and in *Erodium rupestre* (P = 7.1%, A = 1.07, H_e = 0.025; Fig. 3). Nevertheless, these reported values fall well within the range found for the reviewed plant taxa from the Catalan Countries: P vary from 90.0% in *Medicago sativa* to 5.8% in *Silene diclinis*; the interval of A is from 3.90 in *Lolium rigidum* to only 1.08 in another species of *Silene*, *S. hifacensis*; and last but not least, the range of expected heterozygosity (H_e) is also wide: from 0.514 in *Lolium rigidum* to 0.010 in *Hippocrepis balearica*. This large disparity of values for the different basic parameters of diversity in the vascular plants from the Catalan Countries is not surprising given the large variability in the autoecologic traits and phylogenetic origins of the different taxa included in this review. In addition, the very complicated geological and biogeographic history of this Mediterranean region, as well as occurred throughout the basin, has no doubt involved the existence of many different evolutionary paths and processes (Thompson, 2005) giving place to a wide array of genetic diversity patterns for vascular plant species.

Table 2. Genetic diversity parameters for the different categories of each ecological trait of the plant taxa included in this study

Category	*Number of taxa*	*% rare alleles per population*[1]	P	A	H_o	H_e	F_{IS}	*% private alleles per population*	F_{ST}^{a} or G_{ST}^{b}
(1) Taxonomic group									
		NS	*NS*	*NS*	*NS*	*NS*	*NS*	—	—
Gymnosperms	6	8.34	44.70	1.69	0.163	0.130	0.061	0	0.031
		(15.20)	(19.48)	(0.57)	(0.182)	(0.106)	(0.015)		
Monocots	1	—	—	3.90	0.408	0.514	—	—	—
Dicots	26	5.74	26.60	1.44	0.085	0.109	0.280	3.61	0.255
		(7.04)	(20.79)	(0.46)	(0.074)	(0.091)	(0.394)	(5.63)	(0.165)
(2) Geographical range									
		NS	*	*	*	*	*NS*	*NS*	*NS*
Endemic	16	6.87	26.40	1.41	0.090	0.100	0.212	3.28	0.291
		(8.11)	(23.52)	(0.52)	(0.049)	(0.081)	(0.389)	(3.03)	(0.179)
Widespread	17	4.30	30.93	1.62	0.098	0.131	0.319	3.76	0.164
		(8.35)	(16.35)	(0.69)	(0.124)	(0.124)	(0.289)	(7.78)	(0.119)
(3) Insularity									
		NS	*NS*	*NS*	*NS*	*NS*	*NS*	*NS*	*NS*
Insular	3	6.25	19.66	1.29	0.080	0.084	0.358	—	—
		(0.00)	(17.13)	(0.25)	(0.065)	(0.085)			
Insular + mainland	13	2.56	30.03	1.47	0.094	0.126	0.448	1.33	0.248
		(9.45)	(19.92)	(0.81)	(0.140)	(0.139)	(0.328)	(2.24)	(0.241)
Mainland	17	7.45	28.54	1.46	0.093	0.105	0.138	4.42	0.247
		(8.50)	(22.26)	(0.52)	(0.053)	(0.080)	(0.402)	(5.97)	(0.154)
(4) Life strategy									
		NS	*NS*	*NS*	*NS*	*NS*	*NS*	*NS*	*NS*
Annual	3	12.45	43.66	2.23	0.215	0.229	0.204	18.00	0.055
		(4.31)	(3.25)	(1.14)	(0.136)	(0.193)	(0.291)	(0.81)	(0.032)
Short-lived perennial	12	5.95	22.15	1.37	0.097	0.102	0.148	2.55	0.300
		(9.37)	(20.73)	(0.53)	(0.045)	(0.083)	(0.254)	(2.80)	(0.180)
Long-lived perennial	18	3.97	33.29	1.48	0.080	0.112	0.286	2.90	0.205
		(7.66)	(21.63)	(0.44)	(0.104)	(0.104)	(0.420)	(3.37)	(0.151)

Table 2. Continued

Category	Number of taxa	% rare alleles per population[1]	*P*	*A*	H_o	H_e	F_{IS}	% private alleles per population	F_{ST}^{a} or G_{ST}^{b}
(5) Mode of reproduction									
		NS	*NS*	*NS*	*NS*	*NS*	*NS*	*NS*	*NS*
Asexual +	4	2.56	21.70	1.28	0.068	0.075	0.079	1.77	0.285
sexual		(2.88)	(11.47)	(0.18)	(0.035)	(0.054)	(0.211)	(4.21)	(0.033)
Sexual	25	5.95	30.62	1.47	0.095	0.109	0.289	3.42	0.243
		(9.25)	(22.55)	(0.51)	(0.094)	(0.098)	(0.394)	(5.81)	(0.195)
(6) Breeding system									
		NS	*NS*	*NS*	*NS*	*NS*	*NS*	*NS*	*NS*
Outcrossing	27	6.38	29.32	1.47	0.108	0.119	0.108	3.05	0.285
		(8.81)	(22.90)	(0.68)	(0.105)	(0.121)	(0.357)	(2.73)	(0.186)
Mixed strategy	5	3.74	29.74	1.49	0.065	0.102	0.643	5.66	0.130
		(6.25)	(8.67)	(0.35)	(0.082)	(0.059)	(0.437)	(7.48)	(0.089)
(7) Seed dispersal mechanism									
		NS	*	*NS*	*NS*	*NS*	*NS*	*	*NS*
Gravity (short	19	5.69	26.49	1.44	0.101	0.105	0.092	5.13	0.255
distance)		(4.94)	(17.99)	(0.66)	(0.091)	(0.114)	(0.390)	(6.11)	(0.154)
Other	12	7.28	37.03	1.60	0.079	0.119	0.421	0.99	0.140
mechanisms		(12.17)	(20.38)	(0.57)	(0.119)	(0.112)	(0.311)	(2.09)	(0.111)
(long distance)									
(8) Habitat									
		NS	*NS*	*NS*	*NS*	*NS*	*NS*	*NS*	*NS*
Maritime cliffs	3	9.75	29.41	1.63	0.120	0.145	0.592	2.01	0.412
		(16.11)	(40.71)	(1.05)	(0.001)	(0.118)		(2.44)	(0.377)
Mediterranean-	3	2.29	22.10	1.20	0.110	0.155	0.075	5.79	0.243
type shrubland		(2.53)	(12.45)	(0.21)	(0.013)	(0.071)	(0.240)	(1.89)	(0.029)
Meadows and	3	7.05	21.04	1.33	0.085	0.069	0.202	4.12	0.175
grasslands		(3.35)	(20.04)	(0.34)	(0.105)	(0.070)	(0.151)	(9.84)	(0.122)
Inland cliffs	10	6.57	28.40	1.36	0.092	0.104	0.127	4.34	0.283
		(5.22)	(21.37)	(0.40)	(0.057)	(0.077)	(0.536)	(2.87)	(0.149)
Forests	11	3.27	36.30	1.53	0.084	0.115	0.438	0.80	0.095
		(10.61)	(16.14)	(0.40)	(0.121)	(0.108)	(0.308)	(0.71)	(0.057)
Others	4	5.13	18.85	1.42	0.106	0.123	-0.002	3.90	0.264
		(9.47)	(19.02)	(1.39)	(0.178)	(0.229)	(0.391)	(11.57)	(0.204)
(9) Threat status									
		NS	*NS*	*NS*	*NS*	*NS*	*NS*	*NS*	*NS*
Non-	21	5.31	32.77	1.52	0.092	0.126	0.277	4.06	0.183
threatened		(7.78)	(19.26)	(0.67)	(0.120)	(0.124)	(0.354)	(6.82)	(0.137)
Threatened	12	6.67	23.68	1.49	0.095	0.094	0.177	2.67	0.310
		(8.84)	(22.81)	(0.54)	(0.042)	(0.077)	(0.391)	(3.40)	(0.191)
(10) Ploidy level									
		NS	*NS*	*NS*	*NS*	*NS*	*NS*	*NS*	*NS*
Diploid	33	5.88	28.85	1.46	0.094	0.112	0.245	3.47	0.248
		(8.04)	(20.86)	(0.63)	(0.101)	(0.112)	(0.357)	(5.62)	(0.159)
Tetraploid	3	14.03	40.67	1.89	0.164	0.164	0.041	2.18	0.110
		(3.97)	(36.44)	(0.89)	(0.282)	(0.170)	(0.151)	(1.04)	(0.078)

[1]For the calculation only the populations with *N*>10 have been considered, given that populations with smaller size cannot contain alleles with a frequency lower than 0.05.

* $p < 0.05$; ** $p < 0.01$; *** $p < 0.001$; *NS*: non-significant, according to Kruskal-Wallis test.

In parenthesis, standard deviation.

One of the parameters poorly considered in the extant reviews of genetic diversity is the percentage of rare alleles (i.e. those present in very small proportion, lower than 0.05%) per population. Rare alleles are of notably importance in conservation genetics, especially for the management strategies (both *in-situ* and *ex-situ*) of rare and endangered plant species, because these alleles may have a significant adaptative or evolutive value (Caujapé-Castells & Pedrola-Monfort, 2004; Gapare et al., 2005). This parameter can give an idea of the effect of genetic drift within the plant populations (for example, a population that does not contain rare alleles probably could have suffered the eroding effects of genetic drift), and might be used as an indicator of the real threat that a population is facing (e.g. a high percentage of rare alleles means that a considerable fraction of the genetic variability of that population can be lost in few generations in the case of reductions in its size, fragmentation or significant demographic fluctuations). In the populations of diploid vascular plants from the Catalan Countries, nearly 6% of the total number of alleles are rare (Table 2), which indicates that a non-negligible amount of the genetic variation is facing a great and imminent risk of loss. Thus, populations highlighting for their large amount of rare alleles should be targeted for special attention by the biodiversity management administrations, probably constituting conservation units (CUs) and thus meriting specific monitoring. It is remarkably the case of some species, such as *Pinus sylvestris* and *Seseli farrenyi*, where almost the third part of all their alleles are in frequencies lower than 0.05 (see Fig. 4).

Figure 3. Some of the studied endemic and/or threatened plant taxa from the Catalan Countries. a. *Petrocoptis montsicciana*; b. *Delphinium montanum*; c. *Erodium rupestre*; d. *Stachys maritima*; e. *Seseli farrenyi*.

[Pictures: a., b. and d., Jordi López-Pujol, c. Joan Simon, e. Maria Bosch]

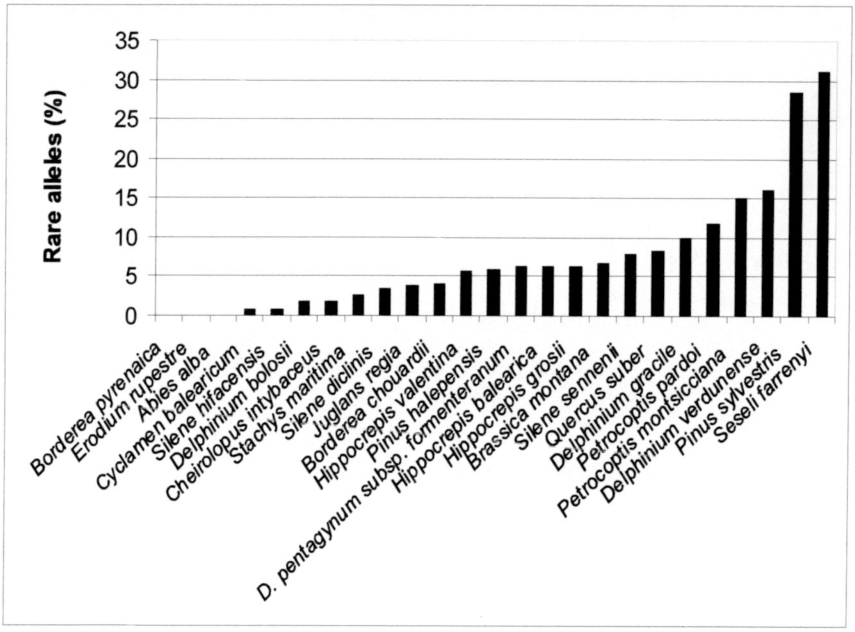

Figure 4. Percentage of rare alleles per population in the species from the Catalan Countries included in the study.

The second of the processes that drive to a genetic diversity erosion, together with genetic drift, is the increase of consanguinity or inbreeding rates, phenomenon that usually occurs when the size of populations decreases. The most used parameter in population genetics to measure the increase of consanguinity is the inbreeding coefficient (F_{IS}; Wright, 1951), which measures the deviation from Hardy-Weinberg equilibrium (i.e. the effects of non-random mating) within populations by comparing observed and expected heterozygosity. For the vascular plants from the Catalan Countries, the value obtained for this parameter was significantly different of zero and positive (F_{IS} = 0.245; Table 2), which indicates that the populations of the studied plants are relatively inbred. The small population sizes reported for many of the plant taxa included in this review (sometimes under the minimum viable population [MVP] size requirements) and the subsequent forced biparental inbreeding may account for this. Habitat degradation, in terms of fragmentation and reduction of the population sizes, or in terms of decrease of the quality and quantity of the pollinator services, has also probably contributed to the levels of consanguinity detected in the plant species from the Catalan Countries.

A significant fraction of genetic diversity of the studied taxa from this Mediterranean region is due to differences among populations: the interpopulation genetic divergence is considerable (G_{ST} = 0.248; Table 2), slightly higher than that reported by Hamrick & Godt (1990; G_{ST} = 0.224). Moreover, the Catalan plant taxa also exhibit a noticeable amount of private alleles in their populations (ca. 3.5%; Table 2), which also indicates divergence among populations. Patterns of marked genetic differentiation have been reported for species with populations located in different glacial refugia of Southern Europe (Iberian Peninsula, Italy and the Balkans), and they have been attributed to the isolation of populations in these favorable places during the Quaternary glacial cycles (e.g. Hewitt, 1996; 1999; 2000; Petit et al., 2003; 2005; Thompson, 2005). This isolation associated with climatic oscillations even produced speciation events in the Mediterranean basin, such as those described for the genus *Senecio* to be occurred during the last 1 My (Comes & Abbott, 2001). However, as evidenced in phylogeographical studies performed in recent years (e.g. Olalde et al., 2002; Gómez et al., 2005; López de Heredia, 2007; Dubreuil et al., 2008), species also exhibit a high degree of interpopulation genetic differentiation within the large proposed refugia (i.e. a pattern of 'refugia-within-refugia'; see Gómez & Lunt, 2007, for a complete review for the case of the Iberian Peninsula). The very high levels of genetic divergence found in several species included in the present review, such as *Erodium rupestre* and the two *Petrocoptis* species (ca. 40%; Table 1 and Fig. 3) may respond to this pattern. These Tertiary taxa are today restricted to several rocky massifs, locations which probably served as isolated (allopatric) refugia during the Pleistocene glacial cycles (Fig. 5).

Figure 5. In the Mediterranean Basin, rocky habitats contain many endemics, partly due to their role as refugia during the Quaternary. On the left, schistose maritime cliff in Cape Creus (NE Catalonia); on the right, limestone cliffs in the Pre-Pyrenean ranges (N Catalonia).
[Pictures: Núria Membrives (left) and Maria Bosch (right)]

Intraspecific (among populations) genetic divergence, however, might also predate the onset of the Ice Ages (see Taberlet et al., 1998; Hewitt, 2000; Petit et al., 2005; Gómez & Lunt, 2007; Magri et al., 2007) in the case of the relict species such as the above examples. Thus, other previous major geological events occurred in the Mediterranean and entirely affecting the Catalan Countries, such as the Messinian Salinity Crisis (occurred during the Late Miocene), the Mediterranean microplate movements (from Late Oligocene to Pliocene) or even the Alpine orogeny (back to Oligocene) cannot be discarded as factors shaping current patterns of genetic structure of populations.

A much more recent episode, however, might have contributed to the remarkable genetic differentiation of plant populations in the Catalan Countries: the destruction and fragmentation of habitats taken place in this region as consequence of human activities. These processes may have several genetic consequences on the plant populations, such as genetic drift and inbreeding, which imply a reduction of intrapopulational genetic variation, and the interruption of gene flow, that drives to an increase of divergence among populations (Young et al., 1996; Oostermeijer et al., 2003). Despite reliable data on fragmentation are not available for the Catalan Countries, its effects are evident in the littoral and peri-urban areas (Fig. 6). As an illustrative example, *Stachys maritima*, a species growing in coastal dunes, has lost more than 90% of its original habitat (López-Pujol et al., 2003b; Fig. 3) due to urbanization. From the observation of herbarium specimens, it can be deduced that this species had a more o less continuous distribution along the coast at the beginning of the twentieth century; today, the remaining patches are genetically very divergent (above 30%; Table 1). Fragmentation is, however, more moderated in the interior of the territory, where even in some zones an increase of patch connectivity is occurring due to abandonment of plenty of agriculture lands during recent decades, phenomenon also detected in France (Lavergne et al., 2006).

Figure 6. Changes in land use in tourist locations in the Catalan Countries have driven to extensive habitat destruction and fragmentation (mainly due to building and urbanization in previously natural zones) in the last century. As a consequence, many sensitive plant species (such as those growing in sand dune habitats) have become rarer and threatened, loosing some of their genetic diversity. Beach of the village of Pals (Girona province, Catalonia): on the left, before transformation (1910); on the right, in recent times (2003), where the threatened species *Stachys maritima* (Lamiaceae) is found. [Pictures: Cèsar Blanche personal archive (left) and Cèsar Blanché (right)]

Genetic Diversity and Ecological Characteristics

1. Taxonomic group. In the present review, the basic parameters of diversity give higher values for monocots, followed by gymnosperms and, finally, dicots (Table 2). The dicotyledons from the Catalan Countries (26 taxa in total) contain levels of diversity (P = 26.60%, A = 1.44, H_e = 0.109) very close or even higher than those found for dicots in the survey of Hamrick & Godt (1990; P = 29.0%, A = 1.44, H_e = 0.096) which –as previously stated– suggest an overall high genetic variation for the plant species of this Mediterranean region. The genetic divergence between populations for dicots from the Catalan Countries is also noticeable (25.5%), of the same order than in the review of Hamrick & Godt (1990; 27.3%).

2. Geographical range. It has been postulated that genetic variability is higher in species with broad distribution areas than in geographically restricted species. Several papers comparing values of genetic diversity between endemic and widespread distributed species found significant differences for parameters A, P, H_o, and H_e (Karron, 1987; Hamrick & Godt, 1990; Gitzendanner & Soltis, 2000; Cole, 2003). In contrast, there are no differences between endemics and widespread species for inbreeding coefficient (Cole, 2003) or genetic differentiation among populations (Hamrick & Godt, 1990; Gitzendanner & Soltis, 2000). In the present survey, endemic species exhibit lower levels of genetic diversity than widespread ones, with significant differences for all the analyzed descriptors of genetic variability (A, P,

H_o, and H_e, see Table 2). It should be noted that the endemic species from the Catalan Countries show a higher proportion of rare alleles per population and a higher divergence between populations (G_{ST} = 0.291 vs. 0.164, Table 2) than those which are widespread, although, in such cases, differences are not significant.

Table 3. Genetic diversity parameters for the two categories of each ecological trait in congeneric taxa. References for each taxon can be found in Table 1

Taxon	*Category*	*% rare alleles per population**	*P*	*A*	H_o	H_e	F_{IS}	*% private alleles per population*	F_{ST}^{a} or G_{ST}^{b}
(1) GEOGRAPHICAL RANGE									
Delphinium bolosii	Endemic	1.82	28.9	1.40	0.107	0.104	0.019	7.73	0.252[a]
Delphinium pentagynum subsp. *formenteranum*	Endemic	6.25	40.7	1.60	0.125	0.180	0.358	—	—
Mean (endemic)		**2.71**	**30.9**	**1.43**	**0.110**	**0.117**	**0.075**	**7.73**	**0.252**
Delphinium gracile	Widespread	10.02	45.5	1.77	0.198	0.159	0.039	18.46	0.073[a]
Delphinium verdunense	Widespread	16.11	40.9	2.15	0.154	0.205	0.451	17.31	0.028[a]
Mean (widespread)		**12.46**	**43.7**	**1.92**	**0.180**	**0.177**	**0.204**	**18.00**	**0.055**
(2) INSULARITY									
Delphinium pentagynum subsp. *formenteranum*	Insular	**6.25**	**40.7**	**1.60**	**0.125**	**0.180**	**0.358**	—	—
Delphinium bolosii	Mainland	1.82	28.9	1.40	0.107	0.104	0.019	7.73	0.252[a]
Delphinium gracile	Mainland	10.02	45.5	1.77	0.198	0.159	0.039	18.46	0.073[a]
Delphinium verdunense	Mainland	16.11	40.9	2.15	0.154	0.205	0.451	17.31	0.028[a]
Mean (mainland)		**7.67**	**37.0**	**1.69**	**0.147**	**0.144**	**0.121**	**13.38**	**0.144**
Hippocrepis balearica	Insular	6.25	6.7	1.10	0.011	0.010	—	—	—
Hippocrepis grosii	Insular	6.25	20.0	1.30	0.122	0.101	—	—	—
Mean (insular)		**6.25**	**13.3**	**1.20**	**0.066**	**0.055**	—	—	—
Hippocrepis valentina	Mainland	**5.78**	**24.4**	**1.27**	**0.099**	**0.085**	**-0.179**	**3.35**	**0.171[a]**
(3) THREAT STATUS									
Borderea chouardii	Threatened	**4.17**	**9.5**	**1.14**	**0.078**	**0.046**	**-0.461**	—	—
Borderea pyrenaica	Non- threatened	**0**	**19.05**	**1.24**	**0.135**	**0.085**	**-0.500**	—	—
Delphinium bolosii	Threatened	1.82	28.9	1.40	0.107	0.104	0.019	7.73	0.252[a]
Delphinium pentagynum subsp. *formenteranum*	Threatened	6.25	40.7	1.60	0.125	0.180	0.358	—	—
Mean (threatened)		**2.71**	**30.9**	**1.43**	**0.110**	**0.117**	**0.075**	**7.73**	**0.252**
Delphinium gracile	Non-threatened	10.02	45.5	1.77	0.198	0.159	0.039	18.46	0.073[a]
Delphinium verdunense	Non- threatened	16.11	40.9	2.15	0.154	0.205	0.451	17.31	0.028[a]
Mean (no threatened)		**12.46**	**43.7**	**1.92**	**0.180**	**0.177**	**0.204**	**18.00**	**0.055**
Hippocrepis grosii	Threatened	**6.25**	**20.0**	**1.30**	**0.122**	**0.101**	—	—	—
Hippocrepis balearica	Non-threatened	6.25	6.7	1.10	0.011	0.010	—	—	—
Hippocrepis valentina	Non-threatened	5.78	24.4	1.27	0.099	0.085	-0.179	3.35	0.171[a]
Mean (no threatened)		**5.82**	**23.0**	**1.26**	**0.092**	**0.079**	**-0.179**	**3.35**	**0.171[a]**
Petrocoptis pardoi	Threatened	**11.76**	**56.3**	**1.90**	**0.072**	**0.192**	**0.620**	**8.56**	**0.354[b]**
Petrocoptis montsicciana	Non-threatened	**15.06**	**70.3**	**2.20**	**0.121**	**0.239**	**0.486**	**6.30**	**0.376[b]**

Table 3. Continued

Taxon	Category	% rare alleles per population*	P	A	H_o	H_e	F_{IS}	% private alleles per population	F_{ST}[a] or G_{ST}[b]
(4) Ploidy level									
Delphinium bolosii	Diploid	1.82	28.9	1.40	0.107	0.104	0.019	7.73	0.252[a]
Delphinium gracile	Diploid	10.02	45.5	1.77	0.198	0.159	0.039	18.46	0.073[a]
Delphinium pentagynum subsp. *formenteranum*	Diploid	6.25	40.7	1.60	0.125	0.180	0.358	—	—
Delphinium verdunense	Diploid	16.11	40.9	2.15	0.154	0.205	0.451	17.31	0.028[a]
Mean (diploid)		**7.55**	**37.3**	**1.68**	**0.145**	**0.147**	**0.134**	**13.38**	**0.144**
Delphinium montanum	Tetraploid	**12.78**	**23.8**	**1.48**	**0.075**	**0.082**	**0.089**	**2.51**	**0.135**[b]

*For the calculation only the populations with N>10 have been considered, given that populations with smaller size cannot contain alleles with a frequency lower than 0.05.

The fact that endemic species showed rates of genetic divergence higher than those of more widespread distribution can be due to the typology of endemicity in the Mediterranean Basin (and, by inclusion, in the Catalan Countries). Following Lavergne et al. (2004), Mediterranean endemic species, in contrast with those of broad distribution, produce fewer flowers and these are smaller, they show a reduced separation between stigmas and anthers, a reduced P/O ratio and a lower seed production. This reduced pollen and seed transfer capabilities may limit the opportunities of gene flow, thus favoring a higher genetic differentiation between populations of endemic species. In fact, values of genetic divergence for endemic species from the Catalan Countries (G_{ST} = 0.291) are higher than those reported for rare/endemic species in other reviews of genetic diversity (0.206 in Gitzendanner & Soltis, 2000; 0.212 in Cole, 2003). Regarding congeneric taxa comparisons, the only genus with available data coming from both endemic and widespread species is *Delphinium*, showing higher values of genetic variability for species of broad distribution (Table 3).

3. Insularity. Insularity is widely considered as a factor with an important influence on levels and distribution of genetic diversity of vascular plants because of two biogeographic characteristics shared by islands: a restricted geographic area and their isolation (Rieseberg & Swensen, 1996). Plants inhabiting in islands usually show, in general, a noticeable genetic depauperation caused by several factors: i) bottlenecks associated to founder effects; ii) small population size of island populations, favoring genetic drift and inbreeding, and iii) adaptation to island ecosystems, that can imply a loss of dispersal ability and a reduced resistance to predators and diseases (Frankham, 1998, Crawford et al., 2001b).

Levels of genetic variability for exclusively insular taxa from the Catalan Countries, that is, those from Balearic Islands (P = 19.66%, A = 1.29, H_e = 0.084) are lower than those for mainland taxa (P = 28.54%, A = 1.46, H_e = 0.105) and than those with both insular and mainland populations (P = 30.03%, A = 1.47, H_e = 0.126), although these differences are not significant, and we should take into account the small sample size of the insular taxa (N = 3) in our database (Table 2). For the species of exclusively Balearic distribution, these values are slightly higher than those found for plant taxa from other archipelagos: Hawaii (P = 25.00%, A =1.32; H_e = 0.064; DeJoode & Wendel, 1992) and Juan Fernández (P = 21.00%, H_e = 0.044; Crawford et al., 2001b), but not for the Canary Islands (H_e = 0.137; Francisco-Ortega et al., 2000, see Fig. 7). The recognized role as glacial refugium for the Balearic Islands

(López de Heredia, 2005; Médail, 2007) may provide an explanation for the not very depauperate levels of genetic variation found in the plant taxa of this archipelago. Unfortunately, data on interpopulational divergence for exclusively Balearic taxa are not available. Concerning congeneric comparisons, while for *Hippocrepis* insular species show lower diversity, for *Delphinium* the results are the opposite (Table 3). At population level, island populations of *Cheirolophus intybaceus* and *Pinus halepensis* contain lower genetic variability than mainland populations. In contrast, and contrary to the expected rule, island populations of *Silene hifacensis* display higher diversity than mainland ones (Table 4), a result which can be interpreted as a consequence of the severe degradation of its habitat and excessive herborization by botanists in the Alacant seashore, in the mailand (Prentice et al., 2003).

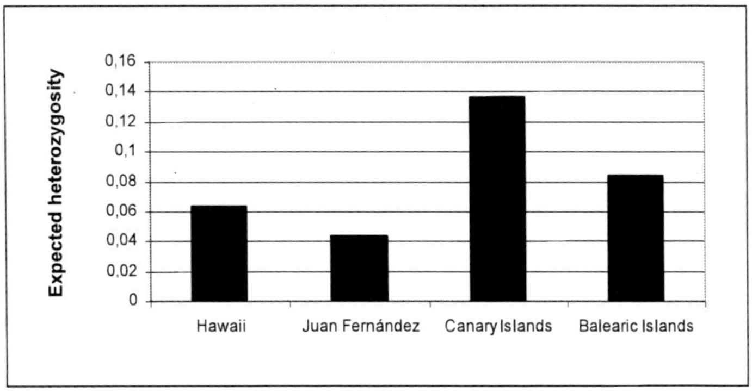

Figure 7. Expected heterozygosis levels (H_e) for the insular species from different archipelagos.

4. Life strategy. The vascular plants from Catalan Countries showing the highest levels of genetic diversity are annuals, with values (expressed as percentage of polymorphic loci, mean number of alleles per locus and observed and expected heterozygosity) higher than those for perennial taxa, either long-lived or short-lived (see Table 2); however, differences are not statistically significant. These results could be surprising, if compared with those reported by Hamrick et al. (1979), in which long-lived perennials showed the highest levels of genetic diversity. Moreover, annual plants from the Catalan Countries show lower levels of genetic divergence among populations than in perennials, the contrary of the results given by Hamrick and collaborators (Loveless & Hamrick, 1984; Hamrick & Godt, 1990). For these authors, long-lived perennial species show the highest intrapopulation genetic diversity levels because they usually display a combination of ecological characteristics favoring the maintenance of genetic variability: cross-pollination, high fecundity and a higher dispersal capability both for pollen and seeds, factors which, in addition, limit the genetic divergence among populations (Hamrick & al., 1979; Loveless & Hamrick, 1984). The small sample size of the annuals in our database (N = 3), besides the fact that these all have a widespread distribution, may have determined these unexpected results for the Catalan plant taxa.

Table 4. Genetic diversity parameters for the two categories of each ecological trait in populations of one taxon. The values of the genetic parameters are population means. References for each taxon can be found in Table 1

Taxon	*Category*	*Number of loci*	*Number of populations*	*% rare alleles per population**	*P*	*A*	H_o	H_e
(1) Insularity								
Silene hifacensis	Insular populations	12	6	1.19	9.7	1.11	—	—
	Mainland populations	12	2	0	0	1.00	—	—
Cheirolophus intybaceus	Insular populations	12	1	0	10.0	1.10	—	0.346
	Mainland populations	10	3	2.56	17.8	1.24	—	0.213
Pinus halepensis	Insular populations	15	1	10.53	13.3	1.27	0.056	0.055
	Mainland populations	15	2	2.63	23.3	1.27	0.061	0.069
Pinus halepensis	Insular populations	5	1	—	—	—	0.196	0.199
	Mainland populations	5	5	—	—	—	0.234	0.275
(2) Threat status								
Delphinium bolosii	Threatened populations	15	2	4.54	26.7	1.40	0.095	0.097
	Non-threatened populations	15	1	0	33.3	1.30	0.115	0.117
Delphinium montanum	Threatened populations	15	3	13.67	20.0	1.44	0.064	0.075
	Non-threatened populations	15	4	12.21	25.0	1.48	0.083	0.087
Erodium rupestre	Threatened populations	14	3	0	7.1	1.07	0.013	0.019
	Non-threatened populations	14	2	0	7.1	1.07	0.003	0.034
Petrocoptis montsicciana	Threatened populations	16	2	7.99	65.6	1.95	0.136	0.232
	Non-threatened populations	16	2	22.13	75.0	2.40	0.105	0.246
Seseli farrenyii	Threatened populations	14	1	22.22	78.6	2.60	0.124	0.285
	Non-threatened populations	14	2	35.52	85.7	3.20	0.118	0.303
Silene sennenii	Threatened populations	21	3	9.33	19.0	1.32	0.046	0.055
	Non-threatened populations	21	2	3.33	23.8	1.31	0.055	0.095
Thymus loscosii	Threatened populations	5	3	19.23	93.3	3.16	0.481	0.441
	Non-threatened populations	5	5	20.16	80.0	2.90	0.466	0.410

*For the calculation only the populations with N>10 have been considered, given that populations with smaller size cannot contain alleles with a frequency lower than 0.05.

5, 6, and 7. Mode of reproduction, breeding system and seed dispersal mechanism. The reproduction systems *sensu lato* as well as the geographical range have been postulated as major determinants of both levels and distribution of genetic diversity in vascular plants (Hamrick & Godt, 1990; Hamrick & Godt, 1996b). The mode of reproduction (sexual or sexual + asexual), however, does not have a significant effect on the patterns of genetic variation in plants (Hamrick & Godt, 1990). For the Catalan species, the taxa with clonal capacity (i.e. those combining asexual and asexual strategies) show genetic diversity levels slightly lower than those exclusively sexual, although these differences have no statistical significance (Table 2).

Breeding systems, in contrast, have a marked effect on the levels and distribution of genetic diversity in plants. Selfing plants are characterized by a much lower amount of intrapopulation genetic diversity and much more pronounced interpopulation divergence than outcrossing (Hamrick & Godt, 1990; Hamrick & Godt, 1996b). In the present survey on genetic diversity of the Catalan Countries, we do not have allozyme data on strictly selfing species, and the comparison between mixed strategy species (combining rates of selfing and outcrossing) and strictly outcrossing show that these latter have somewhat higher intrapopulation genetic diversity, although differences are not significant (Table 2). In relation to the genetic divergence among populations, outcrossing taxa exhibit unexpectedly a higher value, although differences, again, are not statistically significant.

Concerning the seed dispersal mechanism, species dispersing their seeds by gravity (i.e. seeds are deposited close to the parental plants) usually exhibit a lower intrapopulational diversity and a higher interpopulational divergence compared to species dispersing seeds by wind, water or animals (Loveless & Hamrick, 1984; Hamrick & Godt, 1990). In the vascular plants from the Catalan Countries, taxa dispersing seeds by gravity displayed, as expected, lower levels of intrapopulational genetic diversity and higher levels of interpopulational divergence than those with long-distance dispersal systems, although differences were only significant for the percentage of polymorphic loci and for the percentage of private alleles per population (Table 2).

8. Habitat. According to Lavergne et al. (2004), Mediterranean endemic species are often characterized by growing in sites with high rock cover, pronounced slopes, low-stature open vegetation, and few coexisting species. In fact, more than 70% of the endemic species reviewed in this study (12 of 17, see Table 1) grow in rocky habitats (Fig. 5), in most cases corresponding to calcareous rocky outcrops of middle altitude/high mountain ranges (e.g. *Erodium rupestre* and *Petrocoptis* spp.; Fig. 3), whereas some of the endemic taxa are located in maritime cliffs, such as *Silene hifacensis* or *Seseli farrenyi* (Fig. 3). Only a single species growing in rocky habitats reviewed in this survey have a widespread distribution (*Brassica montana*). This close relationship between rocky habitat and endemicity is not new to science: it has already been proven not only for several areas of the Catalan Countries, such as Catalonia (a recent review of Catalan endemisms revealed that c. 70% of endemic species from this area grow in rocky habitats; Sáez et al., 2008), Valencia (Laguna et al., 1998), and the Balearic Archipelago (Alomar et al., 1997), but also for other regions of the Mediterranean Basin, e.g. Corsica (Médail & Verlaque, 1997), SE France (Médail & Verlaque, 1997; Lavergne et al., 2004), Italian Maritime Alps (Casazza et al., 2005), the Balkans (Stevanović et al., 2003), and Greece (Strid & Papanicolaou, 1985), and even in other latitudes (e.g. Simmons et al., 1998; Wolf, 2001; Clements et al., 2006).

Species from both types of rocky habitats, especially seashore cliffs, show relatively high levels of genetic diversity, but, at the same time, very high genetic divergence among populations (Table 2). The flora growing in meadows and grasslands is the poorest genetically, whereas taxa growing in forests show the lowest rates of variability distributed among populations. The relatively high levels of genetic variation and the large genetic divergence among populations detected in the plant taxa growing in rocky habitats may respond to the widely recognized role of cliffs (especially those maritime and those calcareous with a southern exposure) as glacial refugia (see the previous section of the Discussion), which enabled both the survival of Tertiary lineages and episodes of population differentiation and speciation, due to their relatively environmental stability and topographical diversity (Küpfer, 1974; Chytrý et al., 2003; Riba et al., 2003; Lavergne et al., 2004; Thompson, 2005). Many rocky endemics from the Catalan Countries show a high persistence ability driven by their biological characteristics (high longevity, low recruitment levels and poor long-distance dispersal), such as the taxa belonging to the genera *Borderea* and *Petrocoptis*. These traits would have allowed the conservation of, at least, a substantial part of their original genetic variability and maintained the strong population genetic structure shaped by the Pleistocene climatic oscillations.

9. Threat status. Theoretically, it is expected that threatened species will present lower levels of genetic variability than non-threatened species, because of the negative effects of threats (in particular of anthropogenic origin) on plant populations, mainly consisting in the reduction of population size and/or their fragmentation, which drive to a loss of allelic richness and to increased rates of inbreeding (Ellstrand & Ellam, 1993; Frankham, 1995; Oostermeijer et al., 2003). In the present survey, although differences are not statistically significant (see Table 2), the mean values for the different parameters of genetic diversity are higher in the non-threatened taxa than in the threatened ones (considering threatened those listed in any of the three risk categories established by the IUCN: CR, EN or VU). Looking at data of congeneric comparisons, for three of the four genera for which data are available, threatened taxa exhibit less genetic variability than those non-threatened (see Table 3). Regarding the distribution of genetic diversity among populations, differences are also detected: threatened species show higher interpopulation genetic divergence than those non-threatened. It seems reasonable to suppose that habitat fragmentation (one of the main effects derived from human activities in the Catalan Countries in recent times) have had some influence in such figure, as fragmentation has a clear effect of gene flow disruption among populations.

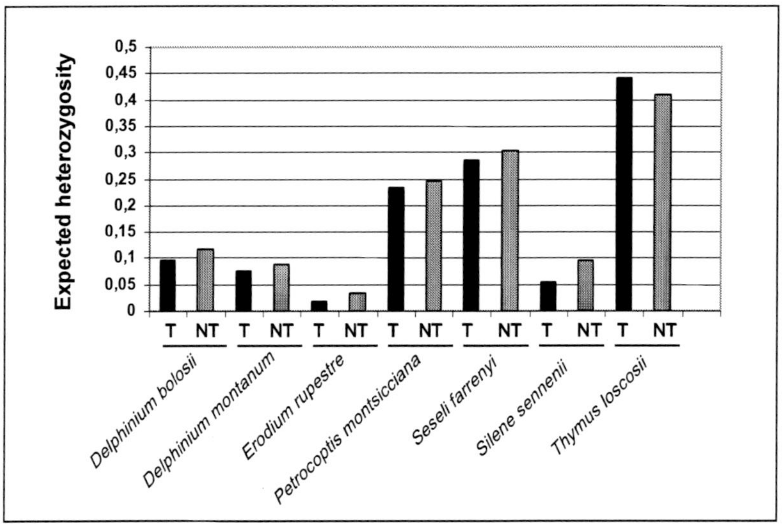

Figure 8. Comparison of the expected heterozygosity levels between threatened and non-threatened populations of different taxa included in the study.

At population level comparisons, from the 7 species in which the threat status for each studied population is known, in 6 species threatened populations show lower genetic diversity levels than non-threatened populations (see Fig. 8 and Table 4). Only for *Thymus loscosii*, a polyploid species, diversity levels for threatened populations are higher than those non-threatened. Therefore, from the overall results it can be hypothesized that the threats affecting plant species in the Catalan Countries could be responsible, at least in part, of a loss of genetic variation in their natural populations (in the same way as reported by Spielman et al., 2004) but also of an increase of their genetic divergence.

10. Ploidy level. The last biological characteristic analyzed here, ploidy level, has usually a significant effect on genetic variability of vascular plants (Soltis & Soltis, 1989). Diploid taxa from the Catalan Countries, as expected, show lower genetic diversity than polyploid taxa: fewer polymorphic loci, fewer alleles per locus, and lower heterozygosity (both observed and expected), but higher degree of inbreeding and higher genetic divergence among populations (Table 2). Polysomic inheritance of polyploids has an effect of reduction of the negative effects of bottlenecks and genetic drift, and is responsible as well of the high heterozygosity levels currently detected in polyploids (Soltis & Soltis, 2000; López-Pujol et al., 2004), which buffers the effects of inbreeding. The observed differences here on the interpopulation genetic differentiation between diploids and polyploids (the latter exhibit lower genetic divergence among populations) have a more uncertain explanation. The perennial habit, a high incidence of vegetative propagation, and a better colonizing ability respect to diploids, phenomena strongly linked to the ecological success of polyploids, could be responsible in part of this finding.

CONCLUSION

Patterns of Genetic Diversity in the Flora from the Catalan Countries

The data compiled in the present study review the knowledge on allozyme diversity of the wild flora from the Catalan Countries since the middle of the 1980s (the first published genetic survey of a plant species native to this region corresponds to *Silene diclinis*; Prentice, 1984) up to the present time. The present work, of course, is not the only source of data available for genetic diversity of plant species in this geographical area (those surveys using PCR-based molecular markers are not included here), but the relatively large body of allozymic literature (not still available for other genetic markers) allow for approaches to the patterns of diversity and their possible causes, based in numerical comparisons. Using the current available knowledge, thus, we are making a first evaluation of the levels and distribution of genetic diversity of this Mediterranean region, which is the primary objective of this work.

In relation to the levels of genetic variability, the values found for diploid taxa are comparable to those reported at global scale (Hamrick & Godt, 1990). Considering the methodological aspects previously stated (see the previous section), levels of diversity should be considered as moderate or relatively high, which are explained, among other reasons, by the role played by this region as a glacial refuge of flora. Nevertheless, nearly 6% of the total number of alleles within populations occur in frequencies lower than 0.05, suggesting that a significant part of genetic variability can be lost in few generations at the present rate of habitat loss and fragmentation. The inbreeding levels for the taxa reviewed are relatively high, partly also attributable to fragmentation and reduction of population sizes. Genetic divergence between populations is also high, a common feature for plant species inhabiting Mediterranean glacial refuges, but which could have been enhanced by the human-induced habitat destruction and fragmentation.

When comparing levels and distribution of genetic variation among different categories of the biological and ecological studied traits, it should be pointed out that endemic species show a lower genetic variability but a higher divergence among populations than widespread ones; that strictly insular species exhibit some degree of genetic depauperation; that outcrossing species present higher genetic diversity than those with mixed strategies; that species with gravity dispersed seeds display lower diversity but more divergence among populations than those with long-distance dispersal mechanisms; that rupicolous species show levels of genetic diversity relatively high, but their populations are very divergent, and, finally, that diploids have lower polymorphism than polyploids. One of the new contributions of this work is that, altogether with the 'classic' ecological traits, the threat status is presented as a predictive factor of genetic variability of vascular plants. Threatened taxa are less diverse genetically but, at the same time, more divergent (among populations) than those non-threatened, giving support to the hypothesis of Spielman et al. (2004) of a true and verifiable genetic impact of threats on plant species.

However, the low statistical significance in many of the comparisons presented in this study recommends the need to add new data of genetic diversity for a higher number of species, which will enable further advances in understanding the genetic variability and their distribution in the vascular flora from the Catalan Countries. A higher sample size for certain categories should allow to check some anomalous results obtained in this analysis (e.g. that annual species showed higher genetic variability than perennials). The incorporation of new taxa should make possible, on the other hand, to perform new comparisons, both congeneric and intraspecific (among populations), for a higher number of biological and ecological traits. In the framework of pair comparisons (species and populations), it should be useful to include genetic data from other molecular markers different of allozymes (AFLP, RFLP, microsatellites, and so on). In this sense, we confidently expect the full launching of the SAGE software developed by Caujapé-Castells (2007) for genotype analysis, which runs with distinct molecular marker data sources. Finally, it is convenient to note that the study of additional biological characteristics could provide new points of view useful for interpreting patterns of genetic variability in plant taxa. The determination of the absolute age of a given taxon (that is, if it is relict or of recent origin), in addition to explore its effect on the levels and distribution of genetic diversity, can be used for the delimitation of endemicity centers, understood as glacial refuge of flora (with high concentrations of paleoendemisms) or as centers of differentiation of flora (amounting many neoendemisms).

Conservation Implications

Some recent diagnosis on the conservation status of the vascular plants from the Catalan Countries reviewed under the scope of the present contribution (Laguna et al., 1998; Sáez & Rosselló, 2001; Bañares et al., 2003; Carrillo et al., 2008; Sáez et al., 2008) advised about the endangered situation of an important part of this flora, a worrisome situation also occurring in other Mediterranean regions (e.g. Raimondo et al., 1994; Montmollin & Iatrou, 1995; Fennane & Ibn Tattou, 1999; Jeanmonod et al., 2001; Çakan et al., 2005). Changes in land use, overexploitation and urbanization activities mainly associated to tourism development have lead to a continous habitat loss and/or fragmentation, increasing the number and level of threatened species. As showed in the previous paragraphs, a moderate but detectable genetic diversity loss begins to emerge as a feature both for endemic as well as for widespread species growing in the Mediterranean Basin.

Together with new efforts to carry out new research on genetic diversity markers, the existing recorded diversity can be applied directly to drive actions oriented to the conservation and/or recovery of endangered species and populations (Avise & Hamrick,

1996; Frankham et al., 2002). Among the main indications of the genetic diversity surveys, these constitute essential tools in the sampling strategy and conservation priorities of *ex-situ* initiatives, as well as in the monitoring of translocation or population reinforcement practices (Young & Murray, 2000; Schoen & Brown, 2001; Schaal & Leverich, 2004; Schwartz et al., 2006; Liu et al., 2006). The absence of data concerning genetic variability and population structure have lead in the past to unsuccessful conservation and restoration actions (although expensive), such as that reported for *Lysimachia minoricensis*. This species endemic to the Catalan Countries (restricted to the island of Menorca, in the Balearic Archipelago), was reintroduced in the wild from botanical garden materials but with no genetic diversity (Ibáñez et al., 1999), which probably produced the complete loss of all transplanted individuals. The detailed study of the genetic diversity (with allozymes or other molecular markers) constitutes, fortunately, the backbone of many conservation plans (both *in-situ* and *ex-situ*) launched in recent times in the Catalan Countries. Examples include the reintroduction plan of *Delphinium bolosii* in a location extinct in 1912, with the goal of reproducing the genetic structure of an extant population (Blanché et al., 2004), and a seed collection plan for the endangered and protected flora of Catalonia (oriented to capture up to 95% of their genetic diversity; Membrives & del Hoyo, 2008), both actions sponsored by the Catalonia's autonomous government.

ACKNOWLEDGMENTS

We wish to especially thank the collaboration, both as data supplying as well as suggestions, of the following researchers: Maria Renée Orellana, Ana Rovira and Julián Molero (University of Barcelona), Gabriel Segarra-Moragues (Centro de Investigaciones sobre Desertificación, CSIC), and José M. Iriondo (Universidad Rey Juan Carlos). The present study has been carried out in the framework of the Research Grants REN2000-0829/ GLO, REN2003-01815 and CGL2007-60475/BOS (Ministerio de Educación y Ciencia), and FBG 301022 (UB-Departament de Medi Ambient, Generalitat de Catalunya). Dr. Jordi López-Pujol has benefited from two MEC fellowships (AP2000-1410 and EX2005-0922), whereas Dr. Maria Bosch had a UB research contract of the "Ramón y Cajal" Program (MEC).

REFERENCES

Affre, L., Thompson, J. D. & Debussche, M. (1997). Genetic structure of continental and island populations of the Mediterranean endemic *Cyclamen balearicum* (Primulaceae). *American Journal of Botany*, 84: 437-451.

Aguinagalde, I., Hampe, A., Mohanty, A., Martín, J. P., Duminil, J. & Petit, R. J. (2005). Effects of life-history traits and species distribution on genetic structure at maternally inherited markers in European trees and shrubs. *Journal of Biogeography*, 32: 329-339.

Agúndez, D., Degen, B., von Wuehlisch, G. & Alía, A. (1997). Genetic variation of Aleppo pine (*Pinus halepensis* Mill.) in Spain. *Forest Genetics*, 4: 201-209.

Agúndez, D., Degen, B., von Wuehlisch, G. & Alía, A. (1999). Multilocus analysis of *Pinus halepensis* Mill. from Spain: genetic diversity and clinal variation. *Silvae Genetica*, 48: 173-178.

Allard, R. W., Jain, S. K. & Workman, P. L. (1968). The genetics of inbreeding populations. *Advances in Genetics*, 14: 55-131.

Avise, J. C. & Hamrick J. L. (Eds.) (1996). *Conservation genetics – Case studies from nature*. New York: Chapman & Hall.

Bañares, A., Blanca, G., Güemes, J., Moreno, J. C. & Ortiz, S. (2003). *Atlas y Libro Rojo de la Flora Vascular Amenazada de España. Táxones Prioritarios*. Madrid, Spain: Dirección General de Conservación de la Naturaleza (In Spanish).

Barceló, F. (1879-1881). *Flora de las Islas Baleares*. Palma de Mallorca, Spain (In Spanish).

Bataillon, T. M., David, J. L. & Schoen, D. J. (1996). Neutral genetic markers and conservation genetics: simulated germplasm collections. *Genetics*, 144: 409-417.

Berg, E. E. & Hamrick, J. L. (1997). Quantification of genetic diversity at allozyme loci. *Canadian Journal of Forest Research*, 27: 415-424.

Blanché, C., Molero, J., Rovira, A., Simon, J., Bosch, M., López-Pujol, J., Orellana, M.R. & Orejuela, L. 2004. *Implementació del Pla de recuperació de Delphinium bolosii. Memòria del projecte*. Barcelona, Spain: University of Barcelona (unpublished, in Catalan).

Blondel, J. & Aronson, J. (1999). *Biology and wildlife of the Mediterranean region*. Oxford, UK: Oxford University Press.

Bolòs, O. & Vigo, J. (1984-2001). *Flora dels Països Catalans*. 4 Volumes. Barcelona, Spain: Barcino (In Catalan).

Bolòs, O., Vigo, J., Masalles, R. M. & Ninot, J. M. (2005). *Flora manual dels Països Catalans*. Barcelona, Spain: Pòrtic (In Catalan).

Bosch, M. (1999). *Biologia de la reproducció de la tribu Delphinieae a la Mediterrània occidental*. Arxius de la Secció de Ciències 120. Barcelona, Spain: Institut d'Estudis Catalans (In Catalan).

Çakan, H., Yilmaz, T. & Düzenli, A. (2005). First comprehensive assessment of the conservation status of the flora of the Çukurova Deltas, southern Turkey. *Oryx*, 39: 17-21.

Carrillo, E., Mercadé, A., Ninot, J. M., Carreras, J., Ferré, A. & Font, X. (2008). Check-list i Llista Vermella de la Flora d'Andorra. In: *Abstracts book* (pp. 30). First Meeting on Flora Conservation of Catalonia, 2-3/07/2008, Blanes, Spain.

Casazza, G., Barberis, G. & Minuto L. (2005). Ecological characteristics and rarity of endemic plants of the Italian Maritime Alps. *Biological Conservation*, 123: 361-371.

Caujapé-Castells, J. (2007). *SAGE: Transformer-based database for the storage and analyis of genotypes*. Las Palmas de Gran Canaria, Spain: Departamento de Biodiversidad Molecular Jardín Botánico Canario "Viera y Clavijo". URL: http://www.exegen.org/sage/index.php

Caujapé-Castells, J. & Pedrola-Monfort, J. (2004). Designing ex-situ conservation strategies through the assessment of neutral genetic markers: Application to the endangered *Androcymbium gramineum*. *Conservation Genetics*, 5: 131-144.

Chytrý, M., Tichý, L. & Roleček, J. (2003). Local and regional patterns of species richness in central European vegetation types along the pH/calcium gradient. *Folia Geobotanica*, 38: 429-442.

Clements, R., Sodhi, N. S., Schilthuizen, M. & Ng, P. K. L. (2006). Limestone karts of Southeast Asia: imperiled arks of biodiversity. *BioScience*, 56: 733-742.

Cole, C.T. (2003). Genetic variation in rare and common plants. *Annual Review of Ecology, Evolution and Systematics*, 34: 213-237.

Comes, H. P & Abbott, R. J. (2001). Molecular phylogeography, reticulation, and lineage sorting in Mediterranean *Senecio* sect. *Senecio* (Asteraceae). *Evolution*, 55: 1943-1962.

Costa, A. C. (1864). *Introducción a la Flora de Cataluña. Catálogo razonado de las plantas observadas en esta región*. Barcelona, Spain (In Spanish).

Costa, A. C. (1877). *Suplemento al catálogo razonado de las plantas vasculares de Cataluña*. Barcelona, Spain (In Spanish).

Crawford, D. J., Landolt, E., Les, D. H. & Kimball, R. T. (2001a). Allozyme studies in *Lemnaceae*: variation and relationships in *Lemna* sections *Alatae* and *Biformes*. *Taxon*, 50: 987-999.

Crawford, D. J., Ruiz, E., Stuessy, T. F., Tepe, E., Aqueveque, P., Gonzalez, F., Jensen, R. J., Anderson, G. J., Bernardello, G., Baeza, C. M., Swenson, U. & Silva, O. M. (2001b). Allozyme diversity in the endemic flowering plant species of the Juan Fernandez Archipelago, Chile: ecological and historical factors with implications for conservation. *American Journal of Botany*, 88: 2195-2203.

DeJoode, D. R. & Wendel, J. F. (1992). Genetic diversity and origin of the Hawaiian island cotton, *Gossypium tomentosum*. *American Journal of Botany*, 79: 1311-1319.

Dubreuil, M., Riba, M. & Mayol, M. (2008). Genetic structure and diversity in *Ramonda myconi* (Gesneriaceae): effects of historical climate change on a preglacial relict species. *American Journal of Botany*, 95: 577-587.

Elena-Rosselló, J. A. & Cabrera, E. (1996). Isozyme variation in natural populations of cork-oak (*Quercus suber* L.). *Silvae Genetica*, 45: 229-235.

Ellstrand, N. C. & Elam, D. R. (1993). Population genetic consequences of small population size: Implications for plant conservation. *Annual Review of Ecology and Systematics*, 24: 217-242.

Fady, B., Forest, I., Hochu, I., Ribiollet, A., de Beaulieu, J.-L. & Pastuszka, P. (1999). Genetic differentiation in *Abies alba* Mill. populations from southeastern France. *Forest Genetics*, 6: 129-138.

Felsenstein, J. (1985). Phylogenies and the comparative method. *The American Naturalist*, 125: 1-15.

Fennane, M. & Ibn Tattou, M. (1999). Observations sur la flore vasculaire endémique, rare ou menacée du Maroc. *Flora Mediterranea*, 9: 113-124 (In French).

Fornari, B., Cannata, F., Spada, M. & Malvolti, M. E. (1999). Allozyme analysis of genetic diversity and differentiation in european and asiatic walnut (*Juglans regia* L.) populations. *Forest Genetics*, 6: 115-127.

Francisco-Ortega, J., Santos-Guerra, A., Seung-Chul, K. & Crawford, D. J. (2000). Plant genetic diversity in the Canary Islands: a conservation perspective. *American Journal of Botany*, 87: 909-919.

Frankham, R. (1995). Conservation genetics. *Annual Review of Genetics*, 29: 305-327.

Frankham, R. (1996). Relationships of genetic variation to population size in wildlife. *Conservation Biology*, 10: 1500-1508.

Frankham, R. (1997). Do island populations have lower genetic variation than mainland populations? *Heredity*, 78: 311-327.

Frankham, R. (1998). Inbreeding and extinction: island populations. *Conservation Biology*, 12: 665-675.

Frankham, R., Ballou, J. D. & Briscoe, D. A. (2002). *Introduction to conservation genetics*. Cambridge (United Kingdom): Cambridge University Press.

Gapare, W. J., Aitken, S. N. & Ritland, C. E. (2005). Genetic diversity of core and peripheral Sitka spruce (*Picea sitchensis* (Bong.) Carr) populations: implications for conservation of widespread species. *Biological Conservation*, 123: 113-123.

Garnatje, T., Susanna, A. & Messeguer, R. (1998). Isozyme studies in the genus *Cheirolophus* (Asteraceae: *Cardueae-Centaureinae*) in the Iberian Peninsula, North Africa and the Canary Islands. *Plant Systematics and Evolution*, 213: 57-70.

Gitzendanner, M. A. & Soltis, P. M. (2000). Patterns of genetic variation in rare and widespread plant congeners. *American Journal of Botany*, 87: 783-792.

Gómez, A. & Lunt, D. H. (2007). Refugia within refugia: patterns of phylogeographic concordance in the Iberian Peninsula. In: S. Weiss & N. Ferrand (Eds.), *Phylogeography of Southern European Refugia* (pp. 155-188). Dordrecht, The Netherlands: Springer.

Gómez, A., Vendramin, G. G., González-Martínez, S. C. & Alía R. (2005). Genetic diversity and differentiation of two Mediterranean pines (*Pinus halepensis* Mill. and *Pinus pinaster* Ait.) along a latitudinal cline using chloroplast microsatellite markers. *Diversity and Distributions*, 11: 257-263.

González-Candelas, F. & Montolío, A. (2000). Genetic differentiation and structure of *Hippocrepis valentina* (Leguminosae) populations. *The Journal of Heredity*, 91: 131-141.

González-Martínez, S. C., Gil, L. & Alía, R. (2005). Genetic diversity estimates of *Pinus pinaster* in the Iberian Peninsula: a comparison of allozymes and quantitative traits. *Investigación Agraria: Sistemas y Recursos Forestales*, 14: 3-12.

Greuter, W. (1991). Extinctions in Mediterranean areas. *Philosophical Transactions of the Royal Society of London, Series B*, 344: 41-46.

Hamrick, J. L. & Godt, M. J. W. (1990). Allozyme diversity in plant species. In: A. H. D. Brown, M. T. Clegg, A. L. Kahler & B. S. Weir (Eds.), *Plant population genetics, breeding and genetic resources* (pp. 43-63). Sunderland, MA, USA: Sinauer Associates.

Hamrick, J. L. & Godt, M. J. W. (1996a). Conservation genetics of endemic plant species. In: J. C. Avise & J. L. Hamrick. (Eds.), *Conservation genetics* (pp. 281-304). New York, USA: Chapman and Hall.

Hamrick, J. L. & Godt, M. J. W. (1996b). Effects of life history traits on genetic diversity in plant species. *Philosophical Transactions of the Royal Society of London, Series B*, 351: 1291-1298.

Hamrick, J. L., Linhart, Y. B. & Mitton, J. B. (1979). Relationships between life history characteristics and electrophoretically detectable genetic variation in plants. *Annual Review of Ecology and Systematics*, 10: 173-200.

Hartl, D. L. & Clark, A. G. (1989). *Principles of Population Genetics*. Sunderland, MA, USA: Sinauer.

Hewitt, G. M. (1996). Some genetic consequences of ice ages, and their role in divergence and speciation. *Biological Journal of the Linnean Society*, 58: 247-276.

Hewitt, G. M. (1999). Post-glacial re-colonization of European biota. *Biological Journal of the Linnean Society*, 68: 87-112.

Hewitt, G. M. (2000). The genetic legacy of the Quaternary ice ages. *Nature*, 405: 907-913.

Hogbin, P. M., Peakall, R. & Sydes, M. A. (2000). Achieving practical outcomes from genetic studies of rare Australian plants. *Australian Journal of Botany*, 48: 375-382.

Ibáñez, O., Calero, C., Mayol, M. & Rosselló, J. A. (1999). Isozyme uniformity in a wild extinct insular plant, *Lysimachia minoricensis* J.J. Rodr. (Primulaceae). *Molecular Ecology*, 8: 813-817.

Jeanmonod, D., Guyot, I. & Aboucaya, A. (2001). Conservation de la diversité vegétale en Corse. *Bocconea*, 13: 65-79 (In French).

Jenczewski, E., Prosperi, J.-M. & Ronfort, J. (1999). Evidence for gene flow between wild and cultivated *Medicago sativa* (Leguminosae) based on allozyme markers and quantitative traits. *American Journal of Botany*, 86: 677-687.

Jiménez, P., Agúndez, D., Alía, R. & Gil, L. (1999). Genetic variation in central and marginal populations of *Quercus suber* L. *Silvae Genetica*, 48: 278-284.

Karron, J. D. (1987). A comparison of levels of genetic polymorphism and self-compatibility in geographically restricted and widespread plant congeners. *Evolutionary Ecology*, 1: 47-58.

Küpfer, P. (1974). Recherches sur les liens de parenté entre la flore orophile des Alpes et celle des Pyrenées. *Boissiera*, 23: 1-322 (In French).

Laguna, E., Crespo, M. B., Mateo, G., López, S., Fabregat, C., Serra, L., Herrero-Borgoñón, J. J., Carretero, J. L., Aguilella, A. & Figuerola, R. (1998). *Flora endémica, rara o amenazada de la Comunidad Valenciana*. València, Spain: Conselleria de Medi Ambient, Generalitat Valenciana (In Spanish).

Lavergne, S., Molina, J. & Debussche, M. (2006). Fingerprints of environmental change on the rare mediterranean flora: a 115-year study. *Global Change Biology*, 12: 1466-1478.

Lavergne, S., Thompson, J. D., Garnier, E. & Debussche, M. (2004). The biology and ecology of narrow endemic and widespread plants: a comparative study of trait variation in 20 congeneric pairs. *Oikos*, 107: 505-518.

Lázaro, A. & Aguinagalde, I. (1998). Genetic diversity in *Brassica oleracea* L. (Cruciferae) and wild relatives (2n = 18) using isozymes. *Annals of Botany*, 82: 821-828.

Liu, Y., Wang, Y. & Huang, H. (2006). High interpopulation genetic differentiation and unidirectional linear migration patterns in *Myricaria laxiflora* (Tamaricaceae), an endemic riparian plant in the Three Gorges Valley of the Yangtze River. *American Journal of Botany*, 93: 206-215.

López de Heredia, U., Carrión, J. S., Jiménez, P., Collada, C. & Gil, L. (2007). Molecular and palaeoecological evidence for multiple glacial refugia for evergreen oaks on the Iberian Peninsula. *Journal of Biogeography*, 34: 1505-1517.

López de Heredia, U., Jiménez, P., Díaz-Fernández, P. & Gil, L. (2005). The Balearic Islands: a reservoir of cpDNA genetic variation for evergreen oaks. *Journal of Biogeography*, 32: 939-949.

López-Pujol, J., Álvarez, N., Bosch, M., Simon, J. & Blanché, C. (2006). Allozyme variation and taxonomical implications of the endemic rocky plant *Erodium rupestre* (Geraniaceae). *Biochemical Systematics and Ecology*, 34: 219-230.

López-Pujol, J., Bosch, M., Simon, J. & Blanché, C. (2001). Allozyme diversity of two endemic *Petrocoptis* species: *P. montsicciana* and its close relative *P. pardoi* (Caryophyllaceae). *Canadian Journal of Botany*, 79: 1379-1389.

López-Pujol, J., Bosch, M., Simon, J. & Blanché, C. (2002). Allozyme variation and population structure of the very narrow endemic *Seseli farrenyi* (Apiaceae). *Botanical Journal of the Linnean Society*, 138: 305-314.

López-Pujol, J., Bosch, M., Simon, J. & Blanché, C. (2003a). Population genetics and conservation priorities for the critically endangered island endemic *Delphinium pentagynum* subsp. *formenteranum* (Ranunculaceae). *Biodiversity and Conservation*, 12: 1937-1951.

López-Pujol, J., Bosch, M., Simon, J. & Blanché, C. (2004). Allozyme diversity in the tetraploid endemic *Thymus loscosii* (Lamiaceae). *Annals of Botany*, 93: 323-332.

López-Pujol, J., Font, J., Simon, J. & Blanché, C. (2007a). Can the preservation of historical relicts permit the conservation of endangered plant species? The case of *Silene sennenii* (Caryophyllaceae). *Conservation Genetics*, 8: 903-912.

López-Pujol, J., Orellana, M. R., Bosch, M., Simon, J. & Blanché, C. (2003b). Effects of habitat fragmentation on allozyme diversity and conservation status of the coastal sand dune plant *Stachys maritima* (Lamiaceace) in the Iberian Peninsula. *Plant Biology*, 5: 504-512.

López-Pujol, J., Orellana, M. R., Bosch, M., Simon, J. & Blanché, C. (2007b). Low genetic diversity and allozymic evidence for autopolyploidy in the tetraploid Pyrenean endemic larkspur *Delphinium montanum* (Ranunculaceae). *Botanical Journal of the Linnean Society*, 155: 211-222.

Loveless, M. D. & Hamrick, J. L. (1984). Ecological determinants of genetic structure in plant populations. *Annual Review of Ecology and Systematics*, 15: 65-95.

Magri, D., Fineschi, S., Bellarosa, R., Buonamici, A., Sebastiani, F., Schirone, B., Simeone, M. C. & Vendramin, G. G. (2007). The distribution of *Quercus suber* chloroplast haplotypes matches the palaeogeographical history of the western Mediterranean. *Molecular Ecology*, 16: 5259-5266.

Mateu-Andrés, I. (2004). Low levels of allozyme variability in the threatened species *Antirrhinum subbaeticum* and *A. pertegasii* (Scrophulariaceae): implications for conservation of the species. *Annals of Botany*, 94: 707-804.

Mateu-Andrés, I. & De Paco, L. (2005). Allozymic differentiation of the *Antirrhinum majus* and *A. siculum* species groups. *Annals of Botany*, 95: 465-473.

Mateu-Andrés, I. & Segarra-Moragues, J. G. (2000). Population subdivision and genetic diversity in two narrow endemics of *Antirrhinum* L. *Molecular Ecology*, 9: 2081-2087.

Médail, F. (2007). La biodiversité végétale méditerranéenne: una évolution en crise. *Echos Science*, 5: 13-15 (In French).

Médail, F. & Quézel, P. (1997). Hot-spots analysis for conservation of plant biodiversity in the Mediterranean Basin. *Annals of the Missouri Botanical Garden*, 84: 112-127.

Médail, F. & Quézel, P. (1999). Biodiversity hotspots in the Mediterranean Basin: Setting global conservation priorities. *Conservation Biology*, 13: 1510-1513.

Médail, F. & Verlaque, R. (1997). Ecological characteristics and rarity of endemic plants from southeast France and Corsica: implications for biodiversity conservation. *Biological Conservation*, 80: 269-281.

Membrives, N. & del Hoyo, A. (2008). El Jardí Botànic Marimurtra i la contribució a la conservació vegetal. In: *Abstracts book* (pp. 44), First Meeting on Flora Conservation of Catalonia, 2-3/07/2008, Blanes, Spain.

Michaud, H., Toumi, L., Lumaret, R., Li, T. X., Romane, F. & Di Giusto, F. (1995). Effect of geographical discontinuity on genetic variation in *Quercus ilex* L. (holm oak). Evidence from enzyme polymorphism. *Heredity*, 74: 590-606.

Montmollin, B. de & Iatrou, G. A. (1995). Connaissance et conservation de la flore de l'île de Crète. *Ecologia Mediterranea*, 21: 173-184 (in French).

Myers, N., Mittermeier, R. A., Mittermeier, C. G., da Fonseca, G. A. B. & Kent, J. (2000). Biodiversity hotspots for conservation priorities. *Nature*, 403: 853-858.

Olalde, M., Herrán, A., Espinel, S. & Goicoechea, P. G. (2002). White oaks phylogeography in the Iberian Peninsula. *Forest Ecology and Management*, 156: 89-102.

Oliveira, J. A. & López, J. E. (1999). Caracterización de poblaciones españolas de *Lolium rigidum* Gaud., para caracteres agro-morfológicos e isoenzimáticos. *Investigación Agraria: Producción y Protección Vegetales*, 14: 453-463 (In Spanish).

Oostermeijer, J. G. B., Luijten, S. H. & den Nijs, J. C. M. (2003). Integrating demographic and genetic approaches in plant conservation. *Biological Conservation*, 113: 389-398.

Orellana, M.R., López-Pujol, J., Blanché, C. & Bosch, M. (2007). Genetic diversity in the endangered dysploid larkspur *Delphinium bolosii* and its close diploid relatives in the series *Fissa* of the Western Mediterranean area. *Biological Journal of the Linnean Society*, 92: 773-784.

Petit, R. J., Aguinagalde, I., de Beaulieu, J.-L., Bittkau, C., Brewer, S., Cheddadi, R., Ennos, R., Fineschi, S., Grivet, D., Lascoux, M., Mohanty, A., Müller-Starck, G., Demesure-Musch, B., Palmé, A., Martín, J. P., Rendell, S. & Vendramin, G. (2003). Glacial refugia: hotspots but not melting pots of genetic diversity. *Science*, 300: 1563-1565.

Petit, R. J., El Mousadik, A. & Pons, O. (1998). Identifying populations for conservation on the basis of genetic markers. *Conservation Biology*, 12: 844-855.

Petit, R. J., Hampe, H. & Cheddadi, R. (2005). Climate changes and tree phylogeography in the Mediterranean. *Taxon*, 54: 877-885.

Prentice, H. C. (1984). Enzyme polymorphism, morphometric variation and population structure in a restricted endemic, *Silene diclinis* (Caryophyllaceae). *Biological Journal of the Linnean Society*, 22: 125-143.

Prentice, H. C., Malm, J. U., Mateu-Andrés, I. & Segarra-Moragues, J. G. (2003). Allozyme and chloroplast DNA variation in island and mainland populations of the rare Spanish endemic, *Silene hifacensis* (Caryophyllaceae). *Conservation Genetics*, 4: 543-555.

Prus-Glowacki, W. & Stephan, B. R. (1994). Genetic variation of *Pinus sylvestris* from Spain in relation to other european populations. *Silvae Genetica*, 43: 7-14.

Raimondo, F., Gianguzzi, L. & Ilardi, V. (1994). Inventaria delle specie "a rischio" nella flora vascolare native della Sicilia. *Quadernario Botanica Ambientale e Applicata*, 3: 65-132 (In Italian).

Riba, M., Picó, F. X. & Mayol, M. (2003). Effects of regional climate and small-scale habitat quality on performance in the relict species *Ramonda myconi*. *Journal of Vegetation Science*, 13: 259-268.

Ridgway, T. (2005). Allozyme electrophoresis still represents a powerful technique in the management of coral reefs. *Biodiversity and Conservation*, 14: 135-149.

Rieseberg, L. H. & Swensen, S. M. (1996). Conservation genetics of endangered island plants. In: J. C. Avise & J. L. Hamrick (Eds.), *Conservation genetics: case histories from nature* (pp. 305-334). New York, USA: Chapman and Hall.

Sáez, L., Aymerich, P., Blanché, C., Font, J. & Vigo, J. (2008). Llibre vermell de plantes vasculars endèmiques i amenaçades de Catalunya. In: *Abstracts book* (pp. 35), First Meeting on Flora Conservation of Catalonia, 2-3/07/2008, Blanes, Spain.

Salvador, L., Alía, R., Agúndez, D. & Gil, L. (2000). Genetic variation and migration pathways of maritime pine (*Pinus pinaster* Ait) in the Iberian Peninsula. *Theoretical and Applied Genetics*, 100: 89-95.

Schaal, B. & Leverich, W. J. (2004). Population genetic issues in ex situ plant conservation. In: E. O. Guerrant Jr., K. Havens & M. Maunder (Eds.), *Ex situ plant conservation* (pp. 267-285).Washington, USA: Island Press.

Schoen, D. J. & Brown, A. H. D. (2001). The conservation of wild plant species in seed banks. *BioScience*, 51: 960-966.

Schwartz, M. K., Luikart, G. & Waples, R. S. (2006). Genetic monitoring as a promising tool for conservation and management. *Trends in Ecology and Evolution*, 22: 25-33.

Segarra-Moragues, J. G. & Catalán, P. (2002). Low allozyme variability in the critically endangered *Borderea chouardii* and its congener *Borderea pyrenaica* (Dioscoreaceae), two paleoendemic relicts from the central Pyrenees. *International Journal of Plant Sciences*, 163: 159-166.

Silvertown, J. & Dodd, M. (1996). Comparing plants and connecting traits. *Philosophical Transactions of the Royal Society of London, Series B*, 351: 1233-1239.

Simmons, R. E., Griffin, M., Griffin, R. E., Marais, E. & Kolberg, H. (1998). Endemism in Namibia: patterns, processes and predictions. *Biodiversity and Conservation*, 7: 513-530.

Soltis, D. E. & Soltis, P. S. (1989). Genetic consequences of autopolyploidy in *Tolmiea* (Saxifragaceae). *Evolution*, 43: 586-594.

Soltis, P. S. & Soltis, D. E. (2000). The role of genetic and genomic attributes in the success of polyploids. *Proceedings of the National Academy of Sciences of the United States of America*, 97: 7051-7057.

Spielman, D., Brook, B. W. & Frankham, R. (2004). Most species are not driven to extinction before genetic factors impact them. *Proceedings of the National Academy of Sciences of the United States of America*, 101: 15261-15264.

Stevanović, V., Tan, K. & Iatrou, G. (2003). Distribution of the endemic Balkan flora on serpentine I. – obligate serpentine endemics. *Plant Systematics and Evolution*, 242: 149-170.

Strid, A. & Papanicolaou, K. (1985). *The Greek mountains*. In: C. Gómez-Campo (Ed.), *Plant conservation in the Mediterranean area* (pp. 89-111). Dordrecht, The Netherlands: Dr. W. Junk Publishers.

Swofford, D. L. & Selander, R. B. (1989). *Biosys-1: release 1.7. A computer program for the analysis of allelic variation in genetics. User's Manual.* Urbana-Champaign, IL, USA: Department of Genetics and Development, University of Illinois.

Taberlet, P., Fumagalli, L., Wust-Saucy, A.-G. & Cosson, J.-F. (1998). Comparative phylogeography and postglacial colonization routes in Europe. *Molecular Ecology*, 7: 453-464.

Thompson, J. D. (2005). *Plant evolution in the Mediterranean*. New York, USA: Oxford University Press.

Toumi, L. & Lumaret, R. (2001). Allozyme characterisation of four Mediterranean evergreen oak species. *Biochemical Systematics and Ecology*, 29: 799-817.

Utelli, A.-B., Roy, B. A. & Baltisberger, M. (1999). History can be more important than 'pollination syndrome' in determining the genetic structure of plant populations: the case of *Aconitum lycoctonum* (Ranunculaceae). *Heredity*, 82: 574-584.

Verlaque, R., Médail, F., Quézel, P. & Babinot, J.-F. (1997). Endémisme végétal et paléogéographie dans le bassin Méditerranéen. *Geobios*, 21: 159-166 (In French).

Whitkus, R. (1988). Modified version of GENESTAT: a program for computing genetic statistics from allele frequency. *Plant Genetics Newsletter*, 4: 10.

Wolf, A. (2001). Conservation of endemic plants in serpentine landscapes. *Biological Conservation*, 100: 35-44.

Wright, S. (1951). The genetic structure of populations. *Annals of Eugenetics*, 15: 323-354.

Young, A. G. & Murray, B. G. (2000). Genetic bottlenecks and dysgenic gene flow into re-established populations of the grassland daisy, *Rutidosis leptorrhynchoides*. *Australian Journal of Botany*, 48: 409-416.

Young, A., Boyle, T. & Brown, T. (1996). The population genetic consequences of habitat fragmentation for plants. *Trends in Ecology and Evolution*, 11: 413-418.

In: Endangered Species: New Research
Editors: A. Columbus and L. Kuznetsov
ISBN 978-1-60692-241-5

Chapter 3

ESTIMATING ABUNDANCE OF ENDANGERED MARINE BENTHIC SPECIES USING DISTANCE SAMPLING THROUGH SCUBA DIVING: THE *PINNA NOBILIS* (MOLLUSCA: BIVALVIA) EXAMPLE

Stelios Katsanevakis*
Hellenic Centre for Marine Research, Institute of Marine Biological Resources,
P.O. Box 712, 19013 Anavissos, Attica, Greece

ABSTRACT

Abundance estimation of marine benthic fauna is usually conducted with surveys using commercial fishing gear such as trawls or dredges. These estimates are often unreliable due to low and variable efficiency and are inappropriate when dealing with rare or endangered species. At shallow depths, direct visual surveys through SCUBA diving are advantageous when compared to fishing surveys, as the records are not dependent on catch efficiency and visual surveys are not destructive, which is of concern when dealing with protected species or habitats. Distance sampling is a widely used set of methods for estimating abundance and/or density of biological populations and has been extensively used in terrestrial ecology and for marine mammals. The main distance sampling methods are line transects and point transects. A standardized survey is conducted along a series of lines (in line transects) or points (in point transects) searching for the animals of interest. For each animal detected, the distance from the line or point is recorded. A detection function is fitted from the set of recorded distances and is used to estimate detection probability, i.e., the probability of detecting the presence of an individual within some area. Failure to properly account for the detection probability leads to biased estimates of population status and trends, which may lead to false management decisions. Distance sampling is the standard method for abundance estimations for many endangered species. However, it has only rarely been used for underwater surveys of benthic fauna. As population assessment and monitoring is absent

* e-mail: stelios@katsanevakis.com; skatsan@ath.hcmr.gr

for most endangered marine benthic species, distance sampling through SCUBA diving may prove to be a valuable management tool, at least for shallow water benthic animals. As an example, the abundance of the endangered bivalve *Pinna nobilis* was estimated in a marine lake using distance sampling techniques. Two different methodologies were applied: classical distance sampling with line transects, and a density surface modeling approach using survey data from line transects, integrated with a Geographic Information System (GIS).

1. Introduction

Ecology (from Greek: oikos, i.e., "household", and logos, i.e., "knowledge") is the scientific study of the distribution and abundance of life and the interactions between organisms and their environment. The central questions of ecology are "where are organisms found?", "how many occur there?", and "why?" Thus, methods for estimating population density (*D*) or abundance (*N*) and the trends in these parameters over space or time for a species or an assemblage of organisms are vital in ecological studies.

Endangered species research and conservation focus on species whose existence is threatened. Abundance estimations of endangered populations are essential to assess population status, reveal population trends, and evaluate the effectiveness of protection measures. However, for many endangered species, reliable abundance estimations are lacking for two reasons. First of all, the forces that incite human intentions for protecting nature are mostly egocentric and concentrate on maximizing and sustaining the exploitation of nature for the human benefit (Kinne, 2006). National and international financing of ecological research focuses on the management, stock assessment and conservation of commercially important species, whereas funding of research on endangered species is limited. Second, appropriate cost-effective, unbiased and precise methodologies for estimating abundance of many endangered species are missing or wildlife managers are not familiar with existing techniques. The main aim of this chapter is to present a useful and effective technique, i.e., distance sampling with SCUBA, to estimate the abundance of marine benthic species in shallow areas (such as coral reefs, sea grass meadows, lagoons, coastal rocky reefs, muddy or sandy habitats). Distance sampling with SCUBA is a non-destructive method suitable for endangered species and protected habitats.

The endangered fan mussel *Pinna nobilis* is used in this chapter as an example species to illustrate the proposed methodology. The fan mussel is endemic to the Mediterranean Sea. It is the largest Mediterranean bivalve and one of the largest in the world, attaining lengths up to 120 cm. It occurs at depths between 0.5 and 60 m, in soft-bottom areas overgrown by seagrass (mostly *Posidonia oceanica* and *Cymodocea nodosa* meadows) but also in unvegetated sandy bottoms (Katsanevakis, 2006; 2007a). *P. nobilis* is long-lived and may live over 20 years (Galinou-Mitsoudi et al., 2006). Fan mussels live partially buried by the anterior portion of the shell and attached by their byssus threads to the substratum. Reproduction of *P. nobilis* takes place by means of external fertilization and its success depends on the proximity of other individuals spawning synchronously. When a population becomes sparse (as is the case for most fan mussel populations in the Mediterranean) failure of fertilization becomes a critical issue for the survival of the species. The planktonic period is short, hence populations (especially those in closed embayments) that are relatively isolated are not easily recolonised if depleted. Natural mortality is strikingly size dependent; *P. nobilis* suffers high natural mortality during the first year of life, but the probability of death by natural causes quickly diminishes as the fan mussels grow in size (Katsanevakis, 2007b).

From ancient times until early in the 20th century, *P. nobilis* was exploited for its byssus, from which an extremely fine and valuable fabric was produced, called 'sea silk'. *P. nobilis* has also been extensively exploited for human consumption and for the use of its shell for decorative purposes. The global population of *P. nobilis* has been greatly reduced over the last few decades as a result of recreational and commercial fishing and incidental killing by trawlers, bottom nets, and anchoring. Consequently, it has been listed as an endangered species in the Mediterranean and is under strict protection according to the European Council Directive 92/43/EEC (Annex IV) and the Protocol for Specially Protected Areas and Biological Diversity in the Mediterranean of the Barcelona Convention (Annex II). However, it is still illegally exploited, and in certain areas, fishing mortality greatly exceeds natural mortality and is a critical determinant of the spatial distribution of the species (Katsanevakis, 2007b).

2. A Need for Non-Fishing Methods to Estimate Abundance

Short-term[1] density or abundance estimation of marine benthic fauna is commonly conducted with surveys using commercial fishing gear such as dredges or trawls. However, catch efficiency and size selectivity issues with trawls and dredges are well documented. The major problem with fishing surveys is estimating the proportion of the individuals captured by the gear. Trawl and dredge surveys normally take the area swept by the gear and expand the catches by the proportion of the study area that was surveyed (Hilborn and Walters, 1992). In this way it is assumed that all individuals present in the swept area are captured, i.e., there is a 100% catch rate, which is far from reality. Catch rates of trawls and dredges may be quite low and variable (e.g., Shafee, 1979; Giguere and Brulotte, 1994; Tuck et al., 1997; Hall-Spencer et al., 1999). Catch rates may depend on several factors such as trawling speed, characteristics of the gear, the substrate, the behavior and life history of the target species, the size of the individuals, the duration of the haul, the time of the day, and the season.

Katsanevakis and Verriopoulos (2004a) compared mean reported octopus (*Octopus vulgaris*) densities between a visual census study and various trawl surveys and found that the densities reported by trawl surveys were much lower than those estimated by visual census. This difference was attributed to a possible low catch efficiency of trawls with respect to the common octopus. A large percentage of *O.vulgaris* live in 'wells' (i.e., vertical burrows) in the soft sediment (Katsanevakis and Verriopoulos, 2004b) and individuals remaining deep in their den are probably invulnerable to the trawling gear. Hence, octopus abundance is probably underestimated with trawl surveys due to low catch efficiency. Furthermore, catch efficiency is not constant and is expected to depend on various factors such as, e.g., the type of the substrate, the sex and maturity of the octopus (mature females that have laid their eggs

1 Abundance estimation is also a by-product of several of the standard analytic fisheries stock assessment techniques, such as catch-at-age analysis, virtual population analysis, and depletion methods. However, these techniques rely on a time history of exploitation of the stock to determine abundance and may not provide short-term abundance estimations (Hilborn and Walters, 1992).

remain in their den caring for the egg masses and are thus more difficult to capture by the trawler) or the time of day (the time octopuses spent out of their den is not uniformly distributed throughout the day). Hence, in the case of the octopus, catch data from trawlers may be inadequate even as a relative measure of abundance, i.e., for population density comparisons among different areas.

Similar conclusions have been made regarding the Norway lobster *Nephrops norvegicus* (mud-burrowing decapod), whose catching efficiency by trawls is greatly dependent on the time of the day, the season (Chapman, 1980) and other environmental factors. A survey by Tuck et al. (1997) found that the trawling catch efficiency of *N. norvegicus* varied between 10.5% and 59.3%. Trawl surveys are generally regarded as an unreliable method for assessing Norway lobster stocks due to low and variable catch efficiency (Bailey et al., 1993).

Dredges have been extensively used to survey benthic populations such as scallops; however, efficiency and size selectivity problems of dredges are well documented. Hall-Spencer et al. (1999) filmed benthic dredges in action, targeting *P. jacobaeus* in the Gulf of Venice, and studied the selectivity and efficiency of the gear. They found an average 44% catch rate for the scallop *P. jacobaeus* and reported that catch efficiency depended on several factors (like trawling speed or the smoothness of the bottom) and diminished with time as the teeth of the trawl became clogged with debris or other organisms. Mcloughlin et al. (1991) found that the efficiency of Australian mud dredges, targeting in the scallop *Pecten fumatus*, depended on scallop size. Shafee (1979) reported that, for the black scallop *Chlamys varia* in the Bay of Brest, dredge efficiency varied with respect to the duration of hauls; the dredge efficiencies of 100 m, 600 m, and 900 m hauls were 28.3%, 8.4% and 6.8% respectively. Giguere and Brulotte (1994) compared the methods of video and dredge sampling in estimating shell height distribution and density in a population of the scallop *Placopecten magellanicus* south of Iles-de-la-Madeleine. They reported that the relative efficiency of the dredge compared to video varied between 15 and 78% for scallops $\leq$85 mm and between 8 and 19% for scallops >85 mm; the corresponding shell height distributions for the two techniques were statistically different. Caddy (1968; 1989) concluded that, for the scallop *Placopecten magellanicus*, size selectivity and efficiency of offshore dredges varied substantially with bottom type and called dredges a "semiquantitative tool" for the study of population density and abundance of scallops.

Trawls and dredges are not appropriate on rocky or coral reefs. Several other techniques have been used to study the abundance of reef populations, such as nets, traps, spears, explosives, and ichtyocides. All of these techniques should be considered qualitative rather than quantitative. Relative abundance might be reported with such techniques, although variability in catch efficiency among sampling sites is quite likely to give questionable results. Furthermore, these techniques are destructive (especially explosives and ichthyocides) and are rarely used for ecological studies because of their adverse impact on the study assemblages.

With the low and variable catch rate of fishing-related methods, in many cases it is rather risky to reach conclusions regarding absolute or relative abundance and spatial distribution of benthic species based exclusively on such data. At shallow depths, direct visual surveys with SCUBA diving (or even swim transects for very shallow waters) are advantageous compared to fishing surveys, as the estimations are not dependent on catch efficiency. In addition, direct visual surveys are non-destructive, which should be of concern, especially when dealing with endangered species or protected habitats such as seagrass meadows or coral reefs.

3. Plot Sampling

The most commonly used method to conduct underwater visual surveys for estimating density and/or abundance of benthic populations is plot sampling. The key idea of plot sampling is to "scale up" the counts of animals from the covered (surveyed) area to the study area (Borchers et al., 2004). There are many different types of plot sampling that vary based on the shape of the plot, which is usually a square, a strip, or a circle, but they are all identical from a statistical point of view.

Underwater visual surveys with plot sampling, and especially strip transects, have been used extensively to estimate density and/or abundance mainly for neretic fish (e.g., Chabanet et al., 1995; Edgar and Barrett, 1997; Ackerman and Bellwood, 2000; Tuya et al., 2000; De Girolamo and Mazzoldi, 2001; Guidetti et al., 2002; Pet-Soede et al., 2001; Denny and Babcock, 2004; Katsanevakis, 2005a), but also for invertebrates (e.g., Edgar and Barrett, 1997; Tuya et al., 2000; Katsanevakis and Verriopoulos, 2004a). Underwater plot sampling is particularly popular for assessing reef fish populations in tropical areas. The two most common forms of plot sampling that are applied for benthic populations are strip transects and point counts.

In strip transects, the plots are long, narrow strips and the observer travels along the center line searching for the animal of interest and counting all individuals within the strip. The survey design comprises k randomly positioned strips or a grid of k systematically spaced strips randomly superimposed on the study area, each of width $2w$ and length l_i. If we denote the total length $\sum_{i=1}^{k} l_i = L$, then the mean population density is estimated by $\hat{D} = \frac{n}{A_c} = \frac{n}{2wL}$, where n is the number of detected individuals and $A_c = 2wL$ is the surface area covered by the survey. Abundance in the study area A is estimated by $\hat{N} = \frac{nA}{A_c} = \frac{nA}{2wL} = \frac{n}{P_c}$, where $P_c = \frac{A_c}{A}$ is the fraction of the study area that was covered by the survey. P_c is called 'coverage probability' because in a survey where strip transects are located randomly and independently of animals, any given animal would fall in the covered region A_c with probability P_c.

In point counts all animals within a circle of radius w about a fixed point are counted. The survey design comprises k randomly positioned points or a grid of k systematically spaced points randomly superimposed on the study area. The total surface area covered by the survey is $A_c = k\pi w^2$ and mean population density is estimated by $\hat{D} = \frac{n}{A_c} = \frac{n}{k\pi w^2}$, where n is the number of detected individuals within the k circular plots. Abundance in the study area A is estimated by $\hat{N} = \frac{nA}{A_c} = \frac{nA}{k\pi w^2} = \frac{n}{P_c}$.

In plot sampling, the critical assumption is that all individuals present in the surveyed areas A_c are detected. However, this assumption cannot be tested using the survey data, and to ensure that it holds to a good approximation in all habitats and environmental conditions, it may be necessary to use narrow strips, i.e., small w, which is problematic for scarce species

(Burnham and Anderson, 1984; Buckland et al., 2001) and increases the variance of density estimators (Kulbicki and Sarramégna, 1999; Buckland et al., 2001). A major problem in strip transects is how to select the appropriate width so that detection is certain. Kulbicki and Sarramégma (1999) found that the maximum width that assures detection of all individuals may vary even for closely related fish species and may even change for a given species at various habitats. When designing a strip transect survey, there is no way to estimate the maximum strip width for certain detection of the target species. If the assumption that all individuals present in the surveyed areas are detected is not met, there is underestimation of abundance, which is not uncommon in underwater surveys especially when counting small taxa or cryptic species (Ackerman and Bellwood, 2000; Willis, 2001) or even for the juveniles of large taxa (Katsanevakis, 2006). Failure to properly account for detection probability (i.e., probability of detecting the presence of an individual within a plot) leads to negatively biased estimates of population density or abundance by a factor equal to the probability that an animal in the covered region is detected.

4. Distance Sampling: An Overview

One of the most active areas of biometric and wildlife research is the development of methods and models to properly account for detection probability, and this is reflected in the recent proliferation of books describing these approaches (e.g., Thompson et al., 1998; Buckland et al., 2001; Williams et al., 2002; Borchers et al., 2004; Thompson, 2004; Buckland et al., 2008). One such widely used method that properly accounts for detection probability is distance sampling, which is an extension of plot sampling.

Distance sampling (Buckland et al., 2001; 2008) is actually a group of methods for estimating the abundance and/or density of biological populations. It has been used extensively in terrestrial ecology (mostly for birds and terrestrial mammals) and for marine mammals, as the standard method for abundance estimations of many species, but it has only rarely been used for underwater surveys of benthic fauna. Up to now, distance sampling has been used to study populations of marine bivalves (Katsanevakis, 2005b; 2006; 2007a), sea anemones (Katsanevakis & Thessalou-Legaki, 2007), marine reef fish (Thresher and Gunn, 1986; Letourner et al., 1998; Kulbicki and Sarramegna, 1999), and freshwater fish (Ensign et al., 1995; Pink et al., 2007).

The main distance sampling methods are line transects and point transects (the analogues of strip transects and point counts, respectively). A standardized survey is conducted along a series of lines (in line transects) or points (in point transects) searching for the animals of interest. For each animal detected, the distance from the line or point is recorded. A detection function is fitted from the set of recorded distances, which is used to estimate the proportion of animals missed by the survey and hence estimate abundance. When the detection of individuals is difficult, a distance sampling method is typically more efficient than a simple strip transect or point count sampling. This is because densities are corrected with the use of the detection function and the sample size is larger for the same amount of effort as all detected individuals may be recorded regardless of how far they are from the line or point.

In distance sampling surveys, it is acceptable that we fail to detect some of the individuals that are in the covered region. The probability that any particular individual that is in the covered region is detected, i.e., the 'detection probability', is denoted by P_a. If n animals were detected in a distance sampling survey, then an estimation of the mean density and the total number of animals in the study area is given by $\hat{D} = \frac{n}{A_c P_a}$ and $\hat{N} = \frac{n}{P_c P_a}$ respectively. It has been assumed that the probability that an animal is in the covered region and the probability that an animal in the covered region is actually detected are independent and common for all individuals.

The main task of the analysis of distance sampling data is to estimate the detection probability P_a (P_c is usually known by design). This is done by modeling the detection function $g(y)$, i.e., the probability of detecting an individual that is at distance y from the line or point. Hereafter, I focus on line transects, which are most often used in underwater surveys; more details on point transects may be found in Buckland et al. (2001).

The standard software for distance sampling is DISTANCE (Thomas et al., 2006). DISTANCE is a Windows-based freeware computer package that allows the researcher to design and analyze distance sampling surveys, aiming to estimate the density and abundance of a biological population. The survey methodologies covered include line transects, point transects, cue counts and trapping webs. All examples of this chapter were analyzed with DISTANCE v.6.0.

Two books have become the standard literature of distance sampling, the introductory book by Buckland et al. (2001) in which conventional distance sampling methods are described in detail and aspects of survey design are covered with several examples, and the 'advanced distance sampling' book by Buckland et al. (2008), where automated survey design, multiple-covariate distance sampling, density surface modeling, mark recapture distance sampling and other advanced topics are covered.

5. Line Transects: Concepts, Assumptions, Models and Estimators

5.1. Conventional Distance Sampling

In line transect surveys, there are k randomly positioned lines or a grid of k systematically spaced lines randomly superimposed on the study area (preferably $k > 20$), each of width $2w$ (w is the maximum distance up to which individuals are detected) and length l_i. For each individual detected its perpendicular distance y_i from the line is recorded. If we denote the total length $\sum_{i=1}^{k} l_i = L$, then the surveyed area will be $A_c = 2wL$. Population density and abundance will be estimated by $\hat{D} = \frac{n}{2wL\hat{P}_a}$ and $\hat{N} = \frac{nA}{2wL\hat{P}_a}$ respectively. Thus, to estimate population density or abundance, $\hat{P}_a$ is needed.

The idea behind the estimation of $\hat{P}_a$ from the distance data is quite simple. If all objects were detected, we would expect, on average, the histogram of the recorded distances y_i to be uniform (Figure 1A), provided that the lines are randomly placed. Any decline in the numbers of recorded individuals with increasing distance reflects a decline in the probability of an individual being detected (Figure 1B). The proportion of individuals detected may be estimated as the unlined area of Figure 1C divided by the total area under the horizontal line; the curve could be estimated by fitting with least squares the midpoints of each histogram class. When standardized (i.e., divided by its value at $y = 0$), this curve is actually the detection function $g(y)$.

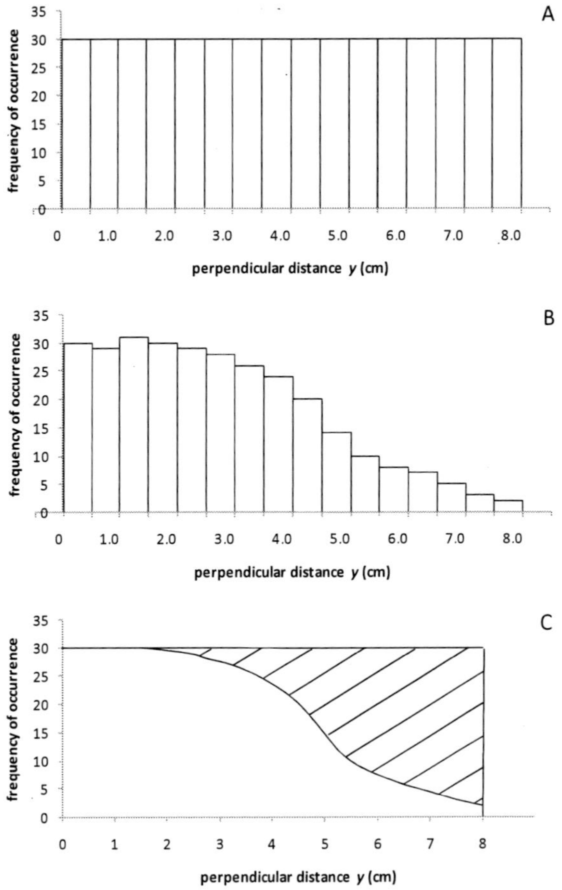

Figure 1. (A) The expected average histogram of recorded distances, when no individuals are left undetected (or else the expected actual distribution of distances) in a line transect survey; (B) real histogram of distances, where a tendency to detect fewer individuals at greater distances is obvious; (C) a model of the distribution of distances of figure B; the lined area is proportional to the number of individuals that remained undetected.

The detection probability is given by $\hat{P}_a = \frac{\int_0^w \hat{g}(y)dy}{w}$. The integral $\mu = \int_0^w g(y)dy$ is called 'effective strip half-width' and represents the half-width of the strip extending either side of a transect centerline such that as many objects are detected outside the strip as remain undetected within it. Thus, an alternative form of the density estimator is $\hat{D} = \frac{n}{2L\hat{\mu}}$. Noting that the probability density function of the distance data *f(y)* is simply the rescaled detection function *g(y)* so that it integrates to unity, it is implied that $f(y) = g(y)/\mu$, and thus $f(0) = 1/\mu$ (because g(0) = 1, i.e., detection probability of an individual that is on the line is assumed to be 1). Hence, $\hat{D} = \frac{n\hat{f}(0)}{2L}$. Such a density estimator, expressed in terms of a probability density function, is convenient due to the large existing literature on fitting probability density functions (Buckland et al., 2001).

There are three main desired properties for models of *g(y)*: model robustness, a shape criterion, and efficiency (Buckland et al., 2001). Model robustness means (1) that the model is general and flexible that can take a variety of plausible shapes, and (2) that data can be pooled over many factors that affect detection probability and still yield a reliable estimate of density or abundance (pooling robustness concept). The desired shape criterion of the detection function *g(y)* is that there is a 'shoulder' near zero distance, which means that detection remains nearly certain at small distances from the line. This is expressed as $g'(0) = 0$. For models that are model robust and have a shoulder near zero distance, efficiency is a desired property, i.e., selecting a model that provides relatively precise estimates (i.e., with small variance).

The function *g(y)* is estimated from the distance data with a semi-parametric approach, as described in detail by Buckland et al. (2001). The proposed models have the desired properties of model robustness, shape criterion, and efficiency. Specifically, the detection function is modeled in the general form $g(y) = \frac{key(y)[1 + series(y)]}{key(0)[1 + series(0)]}$, where *key(y)* is the key function and *series(y)* is a series expansion used to adjust the key function. The uniform function $key(y) = 1/w$ (0 parameters), the one-parameter half-normal function $key(y) = \exp\left(-y^2/2\sigma^2\right)$ and the two-parameter hazard-rate function $key(y) = 1 - \exp\left[-\left(y/\sigma\right)^{-b}\right]$ are usually considered as key functions, while the cosine series $\sum_{j=1}^{m} a_j \cos\left(j\pi y/w\right)$, simple polynomials of the form $\sum_{j=1}^{m} a_j \left(y/w\right)^{2j}$, and Hermite polynomials of the form $\sum_{j=2}^{m} a_j H_{2j}\left(y/\sigma\right)$ are considered as series adjustments, where σ (scale term) and a_j are best fit parameters (Buckland et al., 2001). Some generally useful models are the uniform key function with a cosine or a simple polynomial series expansion, the half-normal key function with a cosine or a Hermite polynomial series expansion, and the Hazard-rate key function with a cosine or a simple polynomial series expansion. These series-expansion models are nonparametric in the sense that the number of parameters used is data-dependent (Buckland et al., 2001). Typically, an adequate model for *g(y)* will include no more than three parameters and quite often the key function will be adequate with no need for a series expansion.

For each dataset, several models should be considered. Model selection may be based on the information theory approach (Burnham and Anderson, 2002) and Akaike's Information

Criterion (AIC) (Akaike, 1973; Burnham and Anderson, 2002). For small samples (when the ratio of the sample size to the number of model parameters is < 20), the small-sample, bias-corrected form AIC_c (Hurvich and Tsai, 1989) of Akaike's criterion might be considered. The number j of parameters in each series expansion may also be defined using AIC or AIC_c between models of increasing order.

When one model is clearly superior to the other models of the candidate set, it is often best to base inference on this single model. However, quite often more than one model is supported by the data. Selecting only the best model incurs substantial costs in terms of reliable inferences, because uncertainty in model selection is assumed to be zero. If model selection uncertainty is ignored, precision is likely to be overestimated, estimated confidence intervals of the parameters are often below the nominal level, and predictions may be less accurate than expected. When the data support evidence of more than one model, model averaging the predicted detection function or the estimated parameters (e.g., P_a or μ) across models is advantageous in reaching a robust inference that is not conditional on a single model. This procedure is termed multi-model inference (MMI) and has several theoretical and practical advantages (Buckland et al., 1997; Burnham and Anderson, 2002). The information-theory approach and MMI are described in detail in Burnham and Anderson (2002). An example of applying information theory and the MMI approach in line transect data is given in Katsanevakis and Thessalou-Legaki (2007).

The variance of the estimated population density is well approximated using the delta method (Seber 1982: 7–9) by the equation $\hat{\mathrm{var}}(\hat{D}) = \hat{D}^2\left[\frac{\hat{\mathrm{var}}(n)}{n^2} + \frac{\hat{\mathrm{var}}(\hat{P}_a)}{\hat{P}_a^2}\right]$. The $\hat{\mathrm{var}}(n)$ is generally estimated from the sample variance of the encounter rates n_i/l_i, weighted by the line lengths l_i. When $f(0)$ is estimated by maximum likelihood, its variance is estimated by evaluating the Fisher information matrix (Buckland et al., 2001). Bootstrapping (Efron and Tibshirani, 1993) is a good alternative for variance and confidence interval estimations. The simplest procedure is to sample with replacement from the replicate line transects using the nonparametric bootstrap. A model selection criterion (such as AIC) may be used to select the best model among a set of candidate models for each resample and in this way incorporate model selection uncertainty into the estimate of precision, as an alternative to the model-averaging approach proposed by Burnham and Anderson (2002).

The key assumption in line transect sampling is that all animals that are located on the line are detected with certainty, i.e., $g(0) = 1$. In practice, detection on or near the line should be nearly certain and survey design must consider ways to assure that this assumption is met (Buckland et al., 2001). Detection probability $g(y)$ is assumed to fall off in a smooth manner out to some distance $y = w$ from the line. When the '$g(0) = 1$' assumption is violated, estimates of abundance are negatively biased in proportion to $g(0)$, e.g., if $g(0) = 0.75$, estimated abundance will be on average 75% of true abundance.

Another important assumption is that individuals are detected at their original location, prior to any movement (this is particularly important when surveying bentho-pelagic fish or other highly mobile animals). Random movement of animals (independently of the observer) might cause a (usually small) bias of the estimated abundance upwards because moving animals are more likely to be detected when they are close to the line, biasing detection distances down. Movement in response to the observer can cause a large bias in abundance estimation, which will be positive if the animals are attracted by the observer, and negative if the observer is avoided. If there is undetected movement ahead of the observer and the same animal is recorded several times while traversing a single transect, bias can be quite large.

Distances are assumed to be measured accurately. Although line transect estimators are fairly robust to random measurement errors, they are sensitive to systematic bias in distance measurement such as rounding to zero distance (Buckland et al., 2001; Borchers et al., 2004).

Example 1: Species-Dependent Detectability

Detectability and the shape of the detection function in an underwater benthic survey may depend on various factors such as habitat type, water turbidity, weather conditions, sun position, the ability of the surveyor, the target species and its brightness, contrast, age, sex, or size. To illustrate how detectability may differ by species, four different species (the fan mussel *Pinna nobilis*, the Mediterranean scallop *Pecten jacobaeus*, the purple sea urchin *Sphaerechinus granularis*, and a sea cucumber *Holothuria* sp.) were surveyed with line transects in the same site (Lake Vouliagmeni, Korinthiakos Gulf, Greece) in the summer of 2004. Habitat, water conditions, and the observer were the same and thus the differences in the detection function may be mainly attributed to the species characteristics. Six models (uniform key function with a cosine or a simple polynomial series expansion, half-normal key function with a cosine or a Hermite polynomial series expansion, and Hazard-rate key function with a cosine or a simple polynomial series expansion) were fitted to the distance data and inference was based on the best model for each species. There was great variability in detection functions (Table 1, Figure 2), and detection probability P_a ranged between 0.444 for the Mediterranean scallop and 0.862 for the purple sea urchin. The Mediterranean scallop has similar coloration as the sediment and is semi-buried in the sand, making its detection difficult, whereas in contrast, the purple sea urchin is epibenthic and its dark color contrasts with the light-colored sediment, making its detection rather easy. However, even for the sea urchin, high turbidity in the lake reduced detectability at distances > 5m (Figure 2).

Table 1: *Example 1*: Best models for detection functions and estimations of detection probability P_a and effective strip half-width □, for four benthic species surveyed with line transect sampling in Lake Vouliagmeni (Korinthiakos Gulf, Greece). Confidence intervals are conditional on the best model and model selection uncertainty has been ignored. *w*: strip half-width, CI: confidence interval

	Pinna nobilis	*Pecten jacobaeus*	*Sphaerechinus granularis*	*Holothuria sp.*
sample size	70	228	81	347
w (cm)	800	400	800	800
Key function	uniform	half-normal	Hazard rate	Hazard rate
Series adjustment	polynomial	-	-	-
No of parameters	1	1	2	2
P_a (estimate)	0.588	0.444	0.862	0.679
P_a (95% CI)	0.537 - 0.643	0.404 - 0.488	0.755 - 0.985	0.615 - 0.7491
μ (estimate)	470	178	690	543
μ (95% CI)	430 - 514	162 - 195	604 - 788	492 - 599

It is clear that detectability is species-dependent and a detection function depends on several characteristics of the species such as size, behavior, color, contrast with the environment, and mobility. Buckland et al. (2001) recommended a minimum sample size of 60-80 detections for reliable estimation of the detection function. However, especially for endangered, rare, or cryptic species, it is possible that this sample size will not be achieved in a survey. If the rare species has a similar size and provides similar visual cues as a more abundant species, then their detections could be pooled to estimate a common detection function and detection probability. This would give increased precision to the estimated detection function, conditional on the assumption of equal detectability, which should be tested and supported by the data. Detectability might differ even for quite similar species, and the assumption of equal detectability should be made with great care.

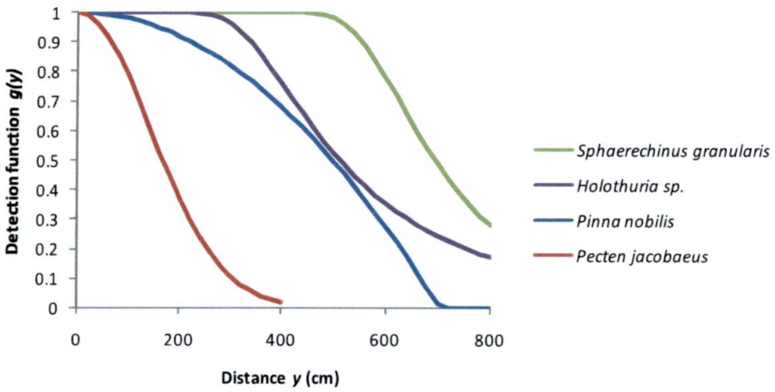

Figure 2. *Example 1*: Variability of the detection functions of four benthic species as estimated by surveys conducted with line transects. Surveys were conducted in the same location (Lake Vouliagmeni) at the same time (summer 2004).

Example 2: Multi-Model Inference (Information Theory Approach)

A population of the endangered fan mussel *P. nobilis* in Souda Bay (NW Crete, Greece) was surveyed by line transects with SCUBA diving during August 2007. A total of 169 individuals were recorded in 41 line transects with $w = 400$ cm.

Six models g_i were considered for the detection function: uniform key with cosine or simple polynomial series expansions, half-normal key with cosine or Hermite polynomial series expansions, and hazard-rate key with cosine or simple polynomial series expansions, as proposed by Buckland et al. (2001).

Model selection was based on the information theory approach (Burnham and Anderson, 2002). Akaike's Information Criterion (AIC) (Akaike, 1973; Burnham and Anderson, 2002) was used for model selection. The number j of parameters in each series expansion was also defined using AIC between models of increasing order. The model with the smallest AIC value (AIC_{min}) was selected as the 'best' among the models tested.

To obtain more robust inferences, the final results were based on model averaging rather than on simply the 'best' model (Burnham and Anderson, 2002). The AIC differences, $\Delta_i = AIC_i - AIC_{min}$, were computed over all candidate models g_i. To quantify the plausibility of each model, given the data and the set of six models, the 'Akaike weight' w_i of each model was calculated, where $w_i = \dfrac{\exp(-0.5\Delta_i)}{\sum_{j=1}^{6}\exp(-0.5\Delta_j)}$. The 'Akaike weight' is considered as the weight of evidence in favor of model g_i being the actual best model of the available set of models (Akaike, 1983; Buckland et al., 1997; Burnham and Anderson, 2002).

Model averaged estimates of P_a and μ were calculated by the formula $\hat{\bar{\theta}} = \sum_i w_i \hat{\theta}_i$, where $\hat{\bar{\theta}}$ denotes a model averaged estimate of parameter θ. The unconditional standard error of θ was estimated as (Burnham and Anderson, 2002) $\text{se}(\hat{\bar{\theta}}) = \sum_i w_i \left(\text{var}(\hat{\theta}_i \mid g_i) + (\hat{\theta}_i - \hat{\bar{\theta}})^2 \right)^{1/2}$, where $\text{var}(\hat{\theta}_i \mid g_i)$ is the variance of θ according to model g_i, conditional on the model.

No adjustment term was selected (according to AIC) with the hazard-rate function, thus models g_5 and g_6 were identical. To avoid model redundancy when model averaging (Burnham and Anderson, 2002), the redundant model was excluded from the calculation of the Akaike weights and of the model-averaged estimates of P_a and μ.

Depending on the model, P_a ranged between 0.356 and 0.568 and μ between 142.3 and 227.3 (Table 2). However, the two models (g_2 and g_4) that gave high values for P_a and μ did not have substantial support by the data. The Hazard-rate model with no adjustment term (model g_5) was the best model with an Akaike weight of 72.5%. The average model was quite close to the best model, as the best model had a high Akaike weight (Figure 3).

Table 2. ***Example 2*: Summary of the parameterization of the candidate models g_i and of the Akaike Information Criterion (AIC) values, Akaike differences Δ_i, Akaike weights w_i, estimated probability of detection P_a and effective strip half-width □, with the corresponding standard errors. The model-averaged estimations of P_a and □ and the corresponding unconditional standard errors are also given.**

	Model	Number of parameters key	Number of parameters series expansion	AIC	Δ_i	w_i	P_a	$se(P_a)$	μ (cm)	$se(\mu)$ (cm)
g_1	uniform + cosine	0	3	1970.4	4.1	9.3%	0.442	0.041	176.9	16.4
g_2	uniform + simple polynomial	0	3	1974.5	8.2	1.2%	0.512	0.037	205.0	14.9
g_3	half normal + cosine	1	2	1969.3	3.1	15.7%	0.421	0.043	168.3	17.2
g_4	half normal + Hermite polynomial	1	0	1974.3	8.0	1.3%	0.568	0.034	227.0	13.4
g_5 (or g_6)	hazard rate + cosine (or simple polynomial)	2	0	1966.3	0.0	72.5%	0.356	0.066	142.3	26.4
model-averaged estimations							**0.379**	**0.071**	**151.5**	**28.6**

5.2. Multiple Covariate Distance Sampling

As stated before, detection probability and the shape of the detection function depend on several factors other than distance. Due to the 'pooling robustness' property of the detection function models (provided that animals at zero distance are detected with certainty), distance sampling estimators of population density and abundance are unbiased (or nearly unbiased), even though heterogeneity in the detection probabilities due to covariates other than distance is ignored (Burnham et al., 2008).

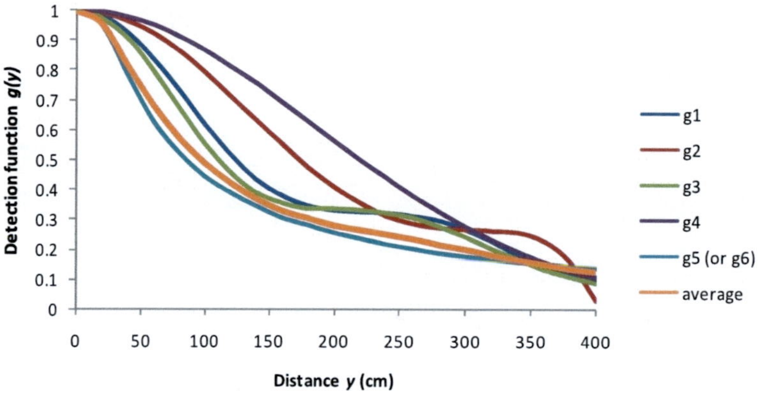

Figure 3. *Example 2*: The six candidate models and the average model of the detection function of the fan mussel *P. nobilis* in Souda Bay (NW Crete, Greece), as estimated with conventional distance sampling (CDS). Estimation of the average model was based on an information-theory approach.

However, inference might be improved in some cases by estimating a detection function $g(y,\mathbf{z})$, which apart from distance y from the centerline, also depends on a vector of covariates $\mathbf{z}$. This might be true when a large component of the variance of the abundance estimate is due to the estimation of the detection function and this variance can be 'explained' by variables other than distance or when detection probability changes across strata but there are inadequate detections in some strata to allow separate estimation of detection probability within each stratum (Borchers and Burnham, 2008; Marques and Buckland, 2003; 2008).

Marques and Buckland (2003; 2008) proposed that the covariates are incorporated into the estimation of the detection probabilities via the scale term σ (that appears in the half-normal and hazard-rate models), according to the relationship $\sigma = \exp\left(\beta_0 + \sum_{i=1}^{r} \beta_i z_i\right)$. In this formulation the covariates are assumed to affect the rate at which detectability changes as a function of distance. Abundance is estimated by the 'Horvitz-Thompson-like' estimator $\hat{N} = \sum_{i=1}^{n} \frac{1}{\hat{P}_a(\mathbf{z})}$.

Variance of the abundance estimator may be estimated either empirically (Marques and Buckland, 2008) or by using the bootstrap (Efron and Tibshirani, 1993), taking the line transects as the sampling unit. If model selection is carried out in each resample of the bootstrap, this approach has the advantage of incorporating model selection uncertainty into the precision estimate (Buckland et al., 1997; Burnham and Anderson, 2002).

Example 3: Modeling Detection Function with a Size Covariate

During the line transect survey described in *Example 2*, apart from the distance of each individual fan mussel from the line, the shell width (= s_i; the maximum dorso-ventral length) was also measured using vernier calipers.

The detection function of the fan mussel in the study area, $g(y)$, was estimated following an information-theory approach with multi-model inference. Specifically, the one-parameter half-normal function and the two-parameter hazard-rate function were considered as key functions, either with no series adjustment or with just one adjustment term. Twelve models were included in the set of candidate models (Table 3). In models $g_1 - g_6$, the scale parameter σ was considered constant, while in models $g_7 - g_{12}$ the size s of *P. nobilis* (as expressed by the shell width) was included as a covariate, because shell size might significantly affect detectability. Specifically, it was assumed that the covariate affects detectability via the scale term σ, according to the relationship $\sigma = \exp(\beta_0 + \beta_1 \cdot s)$ (Marques and Buckland 2008).

Table 3. *Example 3*: Summary of the parameterization of the candidate models g_i and of the Akaike Information Criterion (AIC) values, Akaike differences Δ_i, Akaike weights w_i, estimated probability of detection P_a and effective strip half-width □, with the corresponding standard errors. The model-averaged estimations of P_a and □ and the corresponding unconditional standard errors are also given.

	model key	model adjustment	covariate	number of parameters	AIC	Δ_i	w_i	P_a	$se(P_a)$	μ (cm)	$se(\mu)$ (cm)
g_1	Half-normal	-	-	1	1974.3	31.8	0.0%	0.568	0.034	227.0	13.4
g_2	Hazard-rate	-	-	2	1966.3	23.8	0.0%	0.356	0.066	142.3	26.4
g_3	Half-normal	cosine (1 term)	-	2	1969.7	27.2	0.0%	0.461	0.042	184.5	16.6
g_4	Half-normal	Hermite polynomial (1 term)	-	2	1976.2	33.7	0.0%	0.567	0.034	226.9	13.4
g_5	Hazard-rate	cosine (1 term)	-	3	1966.3	23.9	0.0%	0.326	0.074	130.5	29.7
g_6	Hazard-rate	simple polynomial (1 term)	-	3	1967.9	25.4	0.0%	0.367	0.069	147.0	27.4
g_7	Half-normal	-	size	2	1943.0	0.6	21.7%	0.504	0.031	201.5	12.5
g_8	Hazard-rate	-	size	3	1942.5	0.0	28.6%	0.447	0.032	178.8	12.8
g_9	Half-normal	cosine (1 term)	size	3	1943.5	1.0	17.7%	0.458	0.029	183.4	11.6
g_{10}	Half-normal	Hermite polynomial (1 term)	size	3	1945.0	2.5	8.0%	0.504	0.034	201.4	13.8
g_{11}	Hazard-rate	cosine (1 term)	size	4	1944.3	1.8	11.4%	0.441	0.032	176.6	12.9
g_{12}	Hazard-rate	simple polynomial (1 term)	size	4	1944.1	1.6	12.6%	0.446	0.032	178.3	12.7
model-averaged estimations								**0.465**	**0.040**	**186.0**	**16.0**

The shell widths of the recorded fan mussels varied between 2.1 cm and 21.4 cm, and the shell width distribution had two modes: the first at ~3 cm (corresponding to juveniles of the first age class) and the second at ~15 cm (Figure 4).

All models incorporating a size covariate ($g_7 - g_{12}$) had much higher support from the data than the models that assumed detectability was independent of shell size ($g_1 - g_6$) (Table 3). The best model was the hazard-rate model with no adjustment term and size as a covariate (g_8) with w_i = 28.6%, but models g_7, g_9, g_{10}, g_{11}, and g_{12} also had substantial support by the data with Δ_i between 0.6 and 2.5. The expression of model g_8 was:

$$g(y) = 1 - \exp\left(-\left(\frac{y}{\exp(\beta_0 + \beta_1 \cdot s)}\right)^{-b}\right) = 1 - \exp\left(-\left(\frac{y}{\exp(3.739 + 0.131 \cdot s)}\right)^{-1.995}\right).$$

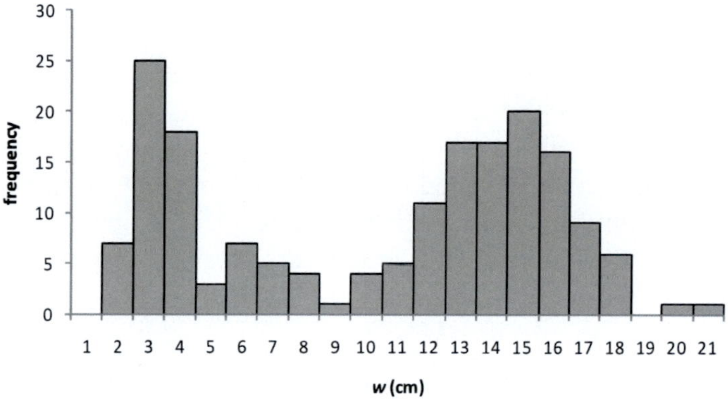

Figure 4. *Example 3*: Size-frequency distribution of the maximum width of fan mussel shells (N = 169), recorded in Souda Bay (NW Crete, Greece) during a line transect survey in August 2007.

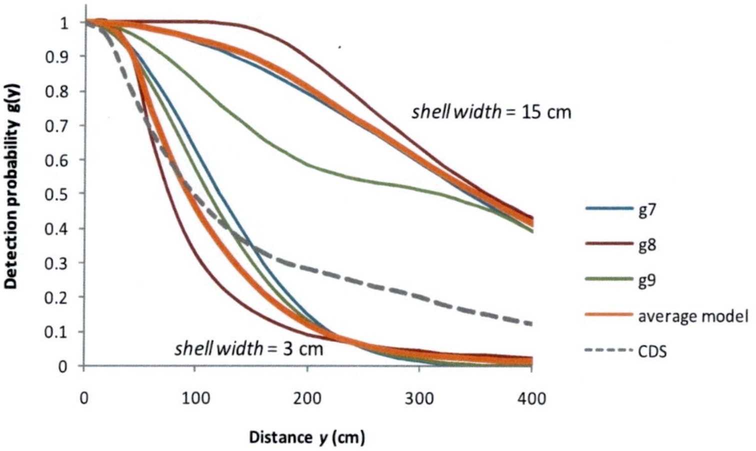

Figure 5. *Example 3*: The three best models (g_7, g_8, and g_9) and the average model (among the set of candidate models; Table 3) of the detection function of the fan mussel *P. nobilis* in Souda Bay (NW Crete, Greece), as estimated with covariate distance sampling (MCDS engine in DISTANCE); shell size was used as a covariate. Estimation of the average model was based on an information-theory approach. Detection functions were plotted for two values of shell width corresponding to the two modes of the size-frequency distribution of *P. nobilis* (Figure 4). The average model as estimated by conventional distance sampling (CDS; *Example 2*) is also plotted for comparison.

As no model was a ‘clear winner’ (e.g., with w_i > 90%), a multi-model inference approach was followed for more robust results. Model averaged estimates of P_a and μ were deduced, in the same way as in *Example 2* (Table 3), and the average model was estimated by model-averaging the response variable (Figure 5). In Figure 5, the detection function of the three ‘best’ models and of the average model is plotted for two values of shell size, corresponding to the two modes of shell size distribution. Clearly, detectability of small individuals is much lower than that of large individuals. The model-averaged probability of detection in the strips with half-width w = 400 cm, was P_a = 46.5 % ± 4.0 % and the effective strip half-width was μ = 186.0 ± 16.0 cm. It has to be noticed that the standard errors of P_a and μ are higher than those conditional on the best model, which are $se(\hat{P}_a \mid g_8) = 3.2\%$ and $se(\hat{\mu} \mid g_8) = 12.8$ cm, as model selection uncertainty has also been taken into account when following a MMI approach. Model selection uncertainty would have been ignored if only the best model had been used for inference, causing an overestimation of precision by approximately 20%.

It has to be emphasized that the results of an information-theoretic approach depend on the set of the candidate models. Using AIC or other similar methods, one just hopes to select the best model (or models) from the set of candidate models. However, if all the candidate models are poor, AIC will still select the best among them but even this "best" model will be poor in an absolute sense. If good models are missing from the set of candidate models, they cannot be discovered by any method of model selection. In this example, models incorporating shell size as a covariate proved to have much higher support by the data. When only conventional distance sampling was used (Example 2), the hazard rate with no adjustment was the best model with an Akaike weight of 72.5% (Table 2). However, when models that included shell size as a covariate were included in the set of candidate models, this same model had no support by the data (model g_2 of Table 3). It has also to be noticed that precision was noticeably improved by using a size covariate in the detection function; standard error of P_a was reduced from an estimated 7.1% in Example 2 to an estimated 4.0% in this example.

5.3. Density Surface Modeling (DSM)

A topic for which significant methodological advances are expected in the near future is the integration of modeling with Geographic Information Systems (GIS) and model-based inference from sample survey data (Buckland et al., 2000; Hedley et al., 2008). Wildlife managers increasingly wish to extract more than an abundance estimate from their surveys and frequently want to relate animal density to spatial variables, reflecting various factors like topography or habitat (Hedley et al., 2004). A first step towards this direction was made by Hedley (2000) and Hedley and Buckland (2004), who developed methods for improving abundance estimation of cetacean abundance, allowing heterogeneity in the spatial distribution of cetaceans to be modeled from standard line transect data. Two approaches were suggested that enable spatial variation in animal density to be modeled using standard generalized linear modeling (GLM; McCullagh and Nedler, 1989) or generalized additive modeling (GAM; Hastie and Tibshirani, 1990). In the first approach (count model), the transect lines were divided into smaller discrete units, and the expected number of detections in each unit was modeled using explanatory spatial covariates. In the second approach (waiting distance model), the response was derived from the observed waiting times (or distances) between detections (Hedley, 2000; Hedley and Buckland, 2004; Hedley et al., 2008). I will focus on the first approach hereafter.

According to the count model, each transect is divided up into small segments of length $l_{seg,i}$ and area $a_i = 2wl_{seg,i}$. The number of animals n_i detected in each segment i is recorded. Additionally, some spatial covariates (locational or environmental variables) are recorded for each segment (such as latitude, longitude, habitat type, depth). The total number of animals within segment i is estimated from the Horvitz-Thompson-like estimator $\hat{n}_i = \sum_{j=1}^{n_i} \frac{1}{\hat{p}_{ij}}$, where $\hat{p}_{ij}$ is the probability of detection of animal j in segment i. These probabilities are obtained from the detection function modeling. The expected values of n_i can be related to the spatial covariates using a GLM or GAM formulation. The general formulation for a GLM will be $f\left(\mathrm{E}[\hat{n}_i]\big/\alpha_i\right) = c + \sum_m \beta_m z_{mi}$, and for a GAM $f\left(\mathrm{E}[\hat{n}_i]\big/\alpha_i\right) = c + \sum_m s_m(z_{mi})$, where f is the link function, β_m is the coefficient for spatial covariate m, $s_m(\cdot)$ is the one-dimensional smooth function for spatial covariate m, z_{mi} is the value of spatial covariate m for segment i, and $a_i = 2wl_{seg,i}$ is the covered area of the segment. Using the selected model for n_i, predictions can be made for regions of the study area that were not surveyed (provided that there is a known distribution of the spatial covariates that were included in the model). If the whole study area is divided into a prediction grid of sufficiently small cells, the abundance of the target species in the study area may be estimated as the sum of $\mathrm{E}[\hat{n}_r]$ at each cell r of the prediction grid, i.e., $\hat{N} = \sum_r \mathrm{E}[\hat{n}_r]$. Based on the predictions $\mathrm{E}[\hat{n}_r]$, a distribution map of the target species in the study area may also be produced.

Density surface modeling (DSM) with GLMs or GAMs employs model-based inference for abundance and density estimation in the study area. With DSM, abundance is related to spatial covariates and the inferred relationships between abundance and ecologically meaningful covariates might have great biological significance and could be of more importance than simple abundance estimation. An example of using density surface modeling to estimate the abundance of *Pinna nobilis* in a marine lake is given in the case study of paragraph 7.

6. Underwater Line Transects

General guidelines for the design of a distance sampling survey and outlines of appropriate field methods are given in Buckland et al. (2001). Here, I focus on specific guidelines regarding underwater surveys of benthic populations with SCUBA.

A nylon line with distance marks that is deployed using a diving reel (Figure 6) seems the most efficient way to define the transect line. In this way, the transect line is well defined and its length is easily and accurately measured. Another option might be to not physically define the line but to move along an imaginary line using a compass. When no real line is deployed, there are difficulties in accurately estimating the length of the transect. An accompanying vessel with a GPS would probably be the easiest way to estimate the transect length by measured positions of the line end points (start point and end point of the dive) or by summing the lengths for a sequence of positions along the line (in which case, the divers could display their position e.g., by towing a buoy). The use of an underwater scooter is also an option, in which case the line length could be estimated as the product of the scooter speed and the operating time; caution will be needed both to accurately estimate the speed (better by experimentation) and to monitor the effective duration of movement, i.e., deduct the time needed for distance measurements of detected individuals from the total survey time). Using an underwater scooter would increase the length of the transect that could be surveyed within the time limits of a dive, which might be of importance for sparsely distributed species. A combination of an underwater scooter and an accompanying vessel for transect length estimation is also possible, with the advantages of both long transects and better accuracy in line length estimation than for estimates based on scooter speed.

Figure 6. A classic diving reel with a 200 m nylon line that is marked with a water-resistant paint marker every meter and labeled every 5 m with a distance sign. This reel was used to define the line transects in all the examples and the case study of this chapter.

Although not deploying a real line with a diving reel would save diving time (the extra time to deploy and reel back the line), a common problem would be that a large percentage of detected individuals are often recorded as on the line, i.e., at $y = 0$. The main reason for this is that the line is not sufficiently well defined and when the observer detects an object within a few cm from the (imaginary) line, he cannot accurately measure its distance and so records it as being on the line. Modeling of the distance data with so many zeros is problematic and will give unreliable estimations of density and abundance. When the line is not marked with the use of a diving reel, an effort should be made in the survey protocol to avoid bias due to heaping at zero distance. One option is to have an assistant diver swimming along the transect using a compass to follow the (imaginary) line and towing a rope. The observer could swim behind and measure the distance of any detected object from the moving rope.

Another reason for recording a large percentage of detected individuals as on the line is that animals themselves have dimensions, and when an object intersects with the line there is a tendency to record it as at zero distance, instead of measuring the distance of its 'center' from the line, which is the proper practice.

Underwater visibility varies a lot depending on the specific location and environmental conditions, and may vary from a few centimeters to many tenths of meters. Furthermore, diving masks constrain peripheral vision and restrict the field of vision of the observer to a narrow angle forward, and thus the underwater observer should not rely so much on his peripheral vision but rather try to scan a wide area around the line by turning his head intermittently left and right of the line. The most important assumption of distance sampling is that $g(0) = 1$ and detectability is nearly certain 'near' the line and falls off smoothly at greater distances. Thus, the observer must try to optimize the detection of individuals in the vicinity of the line. If there is a pair of divers/observers, each diver could search independently on one side of the line to increase overall efficiency.

When surveying sessile or slow-moving species, the best way to satisfy the '$g(0) = 1$' assumption, is by swimming slowly just above the line and preferably moving stepwise in small length increments than continuously. For every length increment, the observer should first make a thorough scan directly on the line and close to it and then search at greater distances on both sides of the line. Hence, for every length increment, the observer should first attempt to detect all individuals in an inner region around the line and only after thoroughly searching the inner region, check the outer region. The diver should avoid moving away from the line, except to measure the distance of a detected individual, and if he does so, he should return to the exact position where he left the line.

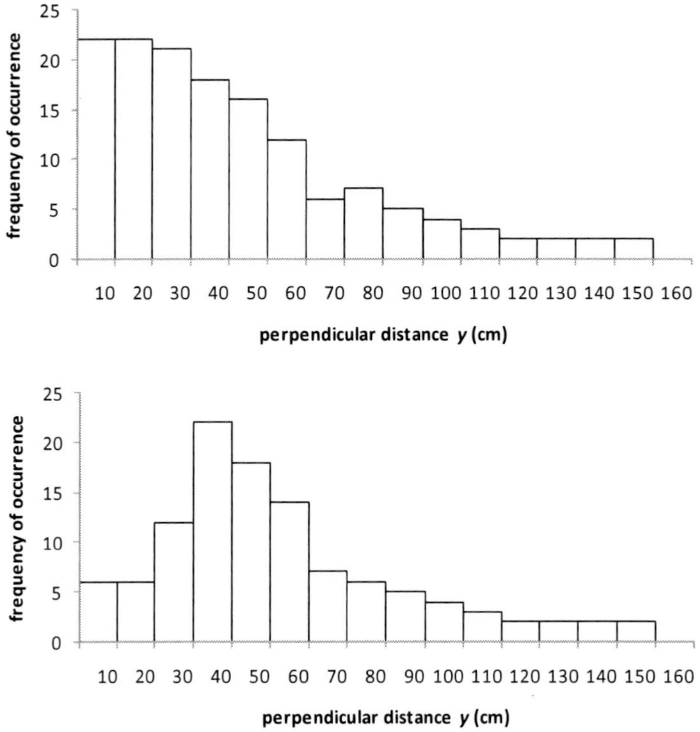

Figure 7. Histograms of perpendicular distance data, illustrating the effect of a response to the observer prior to detection. In the top histogram, no or very little movement away from the observer was experienced prior to detection, whereas in the bottom histogram, there was a striking response to the observer and most individuals that were at a distance < 30 cm from the line moved away prior to detection.

When surveying mobile species such as fish, the diver should be careful to satisfy the second important assumption of distance sampling: that individuals are detected at their original location, prior to any movement in response to the observer. To satisfy this assumption, the diver should move along the line but instead of searching below, he should search forward and near the line, trying both to detect individuals that are in front of him before they move and ensuring that $g(0) = 1$. He should also move fast (in comparison to surveys of sessile species), ideally faster than the speed of the target species. The observer should be careful to locate the point of first sighting of each individual and to measure the perpendicular distance from that point to the line. Depending on the conditions and the surveyed species, it might be useful to move at 1-2 m above the sea floor (and the line) in order to increase the field of view. To reduce the range over which individuals might respond to the observer, the use of a rebreather (closed-circuit SCUBA) instead of an open-circuit breathing set is beneficial. Rebreathers produce far fewer bubbles and make less noise, thus making it possible to reduce the distance beyond which marine animals respond to the observer. If a substantial portion of the detected individuals moves further from the line prior to detection, this will often be apparent in the histogram of distance data (Figure 7).

Accurate measurement of distance should be a principal goal of the sampling protocol. Biased distance measurements such as 'heaping', i.e., rounding to convenient values, will lead to biased estimates of density and abundance. Distances should be measured directly and ocular estimation should be avoided. Visual estimation of distances invites heaping of distances and/or biased estimates of distance. Underwater, the bias in visual estimates of distance is expected to be greater in relation to land surveys due to distance distortion. Visually perceived distortions of size and distance are produced by the diver's facemask, which introduces an air-water interface between the eye and the object of regard. The effect of this interface is that the diver sees a virtual image, which is optically located at about 3/4 of its physical distance, i.e., the object's apparent distance is decreased by about one-fourth. A negative bias in distance measurements will result in a positive bias in density.

Distances measured underwater are usually on the order of a few centimeters or a few meters. A meter rule or a measuring tape could be used to measure distances directly. In most cases, I have used a two-meter plastic rod bearing marks every 5 cm, which I found easy to use underwater without the need of an assistant.

7. Case Study: The Endangered Fan Mussel *Pinna nobilis* in a Marine Lake

7.1. Introduction

This case study focuses on an important and well-studied fan mussel population in the marine lake 'Vouliagmeni' in Greece (Katsanevakis 2006; 2007a; 2007b). Lake Vouliagmeni is located on the 'Perachora' Peninsula and is connected to the Korinthiakos Gulf through a narrow (18.7 m) and shallow (1.1 m maximum depth) channel (Figure 8). It has a maximum length (E-W) of 1881 m, width (N-S) of 931 m, depth of 49 m, and a total surface area of 150.4 ha. In the deep areas of the lake, the temperature is relatively constant (annual temperature range of 10 – 14°C), whereas surface temperatures may reach 30°C in the summer. A strong thermocline occurs at 10-20 m depth from mid spring until early autumn.

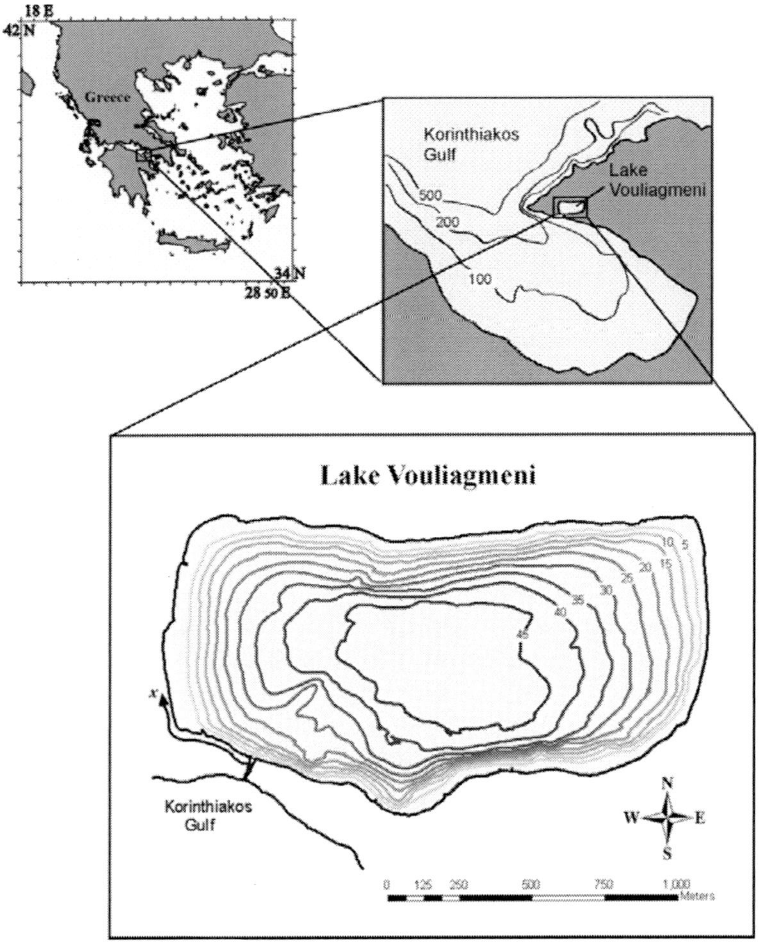

Figure 8. Map of Lake Vouliagmeni. The bathymetric contours of the lake (at 5-m intervals) are given.

The study area was defined as the part of the lake between the coastline and the 30 m depth contour. The fan mussel is mostly found at depths <16 m, and no individual has been recorded deeper than 22 m. Consequently, the study population (i.e, individuals living at depths <30 m) may be considered with high certainty to be the total fan mussel population in the lake. The abundance of this population was estimated with distance sampling techniques between 2004 and 2007; all surveys were conducted during the summer. During the first three years (2004 – 2006), classical distance sampling techniques were used. A detailed description of the survey design and analytical results for the first year (2004) are given in Katsanevakis (2006). In 2006, a new survey design appropriate for density surface modeling (DSM) was put forward; both designs were implemented that year (Katsanevakis 2007a). In 2007, the fan mussel population was surveyed only with the new design with some additional improvements.

7.2 Methods

In the initial survey design, at each of four randomly chosen different locations of the lake, 15 density measurements were conducted at the following depths: 2, 4, 6, ... , 28, 30 m. At each depth, a 200 m line transect was defined with a nylon line that was deployed using a diving reel while SCUBA diving. All *P. nobilis* individuals within 2 m (= w) of the line were counted. For each detected individual, the perpendicular distance y_i from the line and the maximum shell width (= s_i) were measured. The perpendicular distance from the line was measured with the use of a 2 m plastic rod bearing marks every 5 cm. The maximum shell width was measured *in situ* with vernier calipers. Population density was estimated separately in each depth stratum, and mean density was estimated as the mean of the stratum densities weighted by stratum area. Abundance was estimated as the product of the mean density and the area of the study region.

In the initial survey design, the detection function of the fan mussel in the lake was estimated separately for each year (2004 – 2006) following an information-theory approach. Specifically, the one-parameter half-normal function and the two-parameter hazard-rate function were considered as key functions, either with no series adjustment or with just one adjustment term. Eight models were included in the set of candidate models (Table 4). In models $g_1 - g_6$, the scale parameter σ was considered constant, while in models g_7 and g_8 the size s of *P. nobilis* (as expressed by the shell width) was included as a single covariate.

In the new survey design in 2006, eighteen line transects, perpendicular to the depth contours and extending from the shore (0 m depth) to a depth of 30 m, were defined randomly in the lake (nylon line deployed using a diving reel). The line was divided into 4-m segments, with water-resistant numbered signs. After deploying the line, all *P. nobilis* individuals within 2 m (= w) of the line were counted. For each detected individual, the corresponding segment in which it was found, the perpendicular distance from the line (= y_i), and the shell width (= s_i) were recorded. In addition, at the mid-point of each segment of the line transect, the exact depth was measured using the electronic depth meter of a diving computer (Suunto, Vyper). After evaluating the results of the 2006 survey, some improvements were implemented in the survey of the following year. In 2007, apart from the eighteen transects defined in 2006, two extra line transects were surveyed (i.e., a total of 20 transects), the strip half-width (w) was increased to 5 m in order to increase the sample size, and the segment length was increased to 5 m.

In the new survey design (2006 – 2007), the one-parameter half-normal function and the two-parameter hazard-rate function were considered as key-functions with no series adjustment (series adjustments are not yet implemented in the MRDS engine of DISTANCE, which is used to model the detection function in DSM projects). Four models were included in the set of candidate models (Table 5). In g_1 and g_2, the half normal and the hazard rate functions, respectively, were used and the scale parameter σ was considered constant. In g_3 and g_4, the half normal and the hazard rate function were again used and the size s of *P. nobilis* (as expressed by the shell width) was included as a covariate.

Table 4. ***Case study*****: Summary of the parameterization of the candidate models g_i for the years 2004, 2005, and 2006 (initial survey design) and of the Akaike Information Criterion (AIC) values, Akaike differences Δ_i, Akaike weights w_i, estimated probability of detection P_a and effective strip half-width □, with the corresponding standard errors. The model-averaged estimations of P_a and □ and the corresponding unconditional standard errors are also given.**

model			number of	AIC	Δ_i	w_i	P_a	$se(P_a)$	μ (cm)	$se(\mu)$
key	adjustment	covariate	parameters							(cm)
2004 (sample size = 437)										
g_1 Half-normal	-	-	1	596.6	11.4	0.2%	0.841	0.040	168.2	7.9
g_2 Hazard-rate	-	-	2	597.8	12.6	0.1%	0.800	0.065	160.0	13.0
g_3 Half-normal	cosine (1 term)	-	2	594.4	9.2	0.7%	0.731	0.057	146.2	11.4
g_4 Half-normal	Hermite polynomial (1 term)	-	2	594.7	9.5	0.6%	0.761	0.036	152.1	7.2
g_5 Hazard-rate	cosine (1 term)	-	3	597.1	11.9	0.2%	0.744	0.056	148.9	11.3
g_6 Hazard-rate	simple polynomial (1 term)	-	3	599.3	14.1	0.1%	0.795	0.070	158.9	14.0
g_7 Half-normal	-	size	2	586.7	1.5	31.2%	0.854	0.018	170.8	3.6
g_8 Hazard-rate	-	size	3	585.2	0.0	67.0%	0.747	0.024	149.4	4.8
model-averaged estimations							**0.781**	**0.052**	**156.1**	**10.5**
2005 (sample size = 468)										
g_1 Half-normal	-	-	1	650.8	0.0	31.2%	0.998	0.049	199.6	9.9
g_2 Hazard-rate	-	-	2	652.8	2.0	11.5%	1.000	0.003	200.0	0.1
g_3 Half-normal	cosine (1 term)	-	2	651.6	0.8	20.4%	0.914	0.082	182.7	16.5
g_4 Half-normal	Hermite polynomial (1 term)	-	2	652.8	2.0	11.6%	0.992	0.071	198.5	14.2
g_5 Hazard-rate	cosine (1 term)	-	3	654.8	4.0	4.2%	1.000	0.065	200.0	13.1
g_6 Hazard-rate	simple polynomial (1 term)	-	3	654.8	4.0	4.2%	1.000	0.033	200.0	6.5
g_7 Half-normal	-	size	2	652.6	1.8	12.4%	0.980	0.007	196.0	1.4
g_8 Hazard-rate	-	size	3	654.7	3.9	4.4%	1.000	0.001	200.0	0.3
model-averaged estimations							**0.978**	**0.055**	**195.7**	**11.1**
2006 (sample size = 491)										
g_1 Half-normal	-	-	1	665.1	14.4	0.0%	0.816	0.035	163.2	6.9
g_2 Hazard-rate	-	-	2	662.2	11.5	0.2%	0.746	0.063	149.1	12.5
g_3 Half-normal	cosine (1 term)	-	2	659.3	8.6	0.9%	0.686	0.051	137.2	10.1
g_4 Half-normal	Hermite polynomial (1 term)	-	2	666.9	16.2	0.0%	0.815	0.047	163.0	9.4
g_5 Hazard-rate	cosine (1 term)	-	3	659.9	9.2	0.6%	0.691	0.059	138.3	11.9
g_6 Hazard-rate	simple polynomial (1 term)	-	3	664.0	13.3	0.1%	0.747	0.066	149.3	13.1
g_7 Half-normal	-	size	2	650.7	0.0	62.9%	0.870	0.020	174.0	3.9
g_8 Hazard-rate	-	size	3	651.9	1.2	35.3%	0.797	0.029	159.4	5.7
model-averaged estimations							**0.841**	**0.043**	**168.2**	**8.7**

The number of *P. nobilis* individuals detected within each segment was denoted by n_i, $i = 1, ..., T$. The probability of detecting animal j on segment i was symbolized by $\hat{p}_{ij}$ and was obtained from the estimated detection function. The total number of individuals within segment i was obtained using the Horvitz-Thompson-like estimator $\hat{n}_i = \sum_{j=1}^{n_i} \frac{1}{\hat{p}_{ij}}$ (Hedley et al. 2008). In the current context, in all candidate models for the detection function, detectability was considered independent of any spatial covariates and thus the i subscript in $\hat{p}_{ij}$ may be eliminated, i.e., $\hat{p}_{ij} = \hat{p}_j$.

Two spatial covariates were used in modeling the density surface of *P. nobilis* in the lake: depth d and the variable x representing the distance from the channel connecting the lake with the open sea, when moving clockwise along the shoreline (Figure 8). The expected values of abundance in each segment $\hat{n}_i$ were related to the spatial covariates using GAMs (Hastie and Tibshirani 1990), according to the formulation $f\left(\mathrm{E}[\hat{n}_i]/a\right) = c + \sum_m s_m(z_{mi})$, where f is the link function, $s_m(\cdot)$ is the one-dimensional smooth function for spatial covariate m, z_{mi} is the value of spatial covariate m for segment i, and $a = 2wl$ is the covered area of the segment. The logarithmic link and a quasipoisson error distribution were used, and thus the above equation became $\ln(\mathrm{E}[\hat{n}_i]) = c + \sum_m s_m(z_{mi}) + \ln(a)$. The smooth function $s_m(\cdot)$ was represented using penalized regression splines (cubic splines with basis dimension $q = 10$), estimated by penalized iterative least squares (Wood 2006). The smooth for the spatial covariate x was a cyclic regression spline, meaning that the smooth function had both the same value and first and second derivatives at its upper and lower boundaries (because the shoreline of the lake is a closed loop). The optimum degree of smoothing was defined by generalized cross validation (GCV), increasing the amount that each model effective degree of freedom counts in the GCV score by a factor $\gamma = 1.4$. The GCV method is known to have some tendency for occasional overfitting, and it has been suggested that using $\gamma \approx 1.4$ can largely correct this without compromising model fit (Kim and Gu 2004).

Table 5. *Case study*: Summary of the parameterization of the candidate models g_i for the years 2006 and 2007 (new survey design) and of the Akaike Information Criterion (AIC) values, Akaike differences Δ_i, Akaike weights w_i, estimated probability of detection P_a and effective strip half-width μ, with the corresponding standard errors. The model-averaged estimations of P_a and μ and the corresponding unconditional standard errors are also given.

model			number of	AIC	Δ_i	w_i	P_a	$se(P_a)$	μ (cm)	$se(\mu)$
key	adjustment	covariate	parameters							(cm)
2006 (sample size = 74)										
g_1 Half-normal	-	-	1	100.9	0.0	37.1%	0.788	0.083	157.5	16.7
g_2 Hazard-rate	-	-	2	101.2	0.3	32.3%	0.647	0.149	129.4	29.8
g_3 Half-normal	-	size	2	102.3	1.4	18.3%	0.786	0.045	157.2	9.0
g_4 Hazard-rate	-	size	3	103.1	2.2	12.2%	0.636	0.050	127.2	10.0
model-averaged estimations							**0.723**	**0.120**	**144.7**	**23.9**
2007 (sample size = 166)										
g_1 Half-normal	-	-	1	2065.0	0.0	42.3%	0.954	0.079	477.2	39.7
g_2 Hazard-rate	-	-	2	2067.0	2.1	14.9%	0.966	0.096	482.9	48.1
g_3 Half-normal	-	size	2	2065.2	0.2	37.3%	0.938	0.025	469.2	12.5
g_4 Hazard-rate	-	size	3	2069.0	4.1	5.5%	0.966	0.017	482.9	8.4
model-averaged estimations							**0.951**	**0.060**	**475.3**	**29.9**

Three candidate GAMs h_i, $i = 1$ to 3, were fitted. In h_1, d was used as a single spatial covariate ($m = 1$, $z_{1i} = d_i$), in h_2 only x was used as a covariate ($m = 1$, $z_{1i} = x_i$), while in h_3 one-dimensional smooths of both d and x were included ($m = 2$, $z_{1i} = d_i$, $z_{2i} = x_i$). Model selection among the set of the three density surface models was conducted based on their

GCV score (Wood, 2006). For generalized additive modeling, the package *mgcv* (Wood 2000; 2006) was used in R v.2.5.1 (R Development Core Team 2007).

Using ArcMap 8.1 software (ESRI), a prediction grid was created on the map of the study area by dividing it to 8670 square cells of 88.5 m^2. The abundance of *P. nobilis* in the study area was estimated as the sum of $\mathrm{E}[\hat{n}_r]$ at each cell r of the prediction grid, i.e., $\hat{N} = \sum_r \mathrm{E}[\hat{n}_r]$, where $\mathrm{E}[\hat{n}_r]$ were predictions according to the selected spatial density model h_i (where in the offset term the covered area of the segment $a = 2wl$ was replaced by the surface of the prediction cell). Based on the predictions $\mathrm{E}[\hat{n}_r]$, a distribution map of *P. nobilis* in Lake Vouliagmeni was produced using ArcMap 8.1.

The delta method (Seber, 1982) was applied to estimate the variance of the abundance estimate, according to the relationship $[cv(\hat{N})]^2 = [cv(\hat{p})]^2 + [cv(\hat{N}_{DSM})]^2$, where $cv(\hat{p})$ is the coefficient of variation of the estimator of detection probability and $cv(\hat{N}_{DSM})$ is the coefficient of variation related to density surface modeling. The first component was obtained analytically according to Buckland et al. (2001). For the second component, a parametric bootstrap approach was followed (Efron and Tibshirani 1993), with sample size B = 999; details are given in Katsanevakis 2007a.

The CDS and MCDS analysis engines of Distance 6.0 (Thomas et al., 2006) were used for analyses of the line transect surveys that were based on the initial design, while the MRDS and DSM analysis engines were used for density surface modeling (new design).

7.3. Results and Discussion

Initial Design (2004–2006)

The best models of the detection function among candidate models was the hazard-rate with the shell size as a covariate for 2004, the half-normal with no covariate for 2005, and the half-normal with the shell size as a covariate for 2006 (Table 4). In Figure 9, a graph of the detection functions for the three years is given for two selected shell sizes (4.3 and 12.2 cm) corresponding to the modes of the first two age classes (Katsanevakis, 2006).

Detectability of individuals of the first age class was low, while the detection probability for individuals of the second and all other age classes was almost 1. Recruitment of *P. nobilis* is very variable and years with almost zero recruitment are not uncommon. Such was the case in 2005, when individuals of the first age class were almost completely absent. This explains why models having shell size as a covariate did not have substantial support by the data in the 2005 survey.

Abundance of *P. nobilis* in Lake Vouliagmeni in 2004, 2005, and 2006 (the initial design) were estimated to be (95% confidence intervals in parenthesis): 8144 (5236 – 12668), 6774 (4300 – 10671), and 8294 (5236 – 12668), respectively.

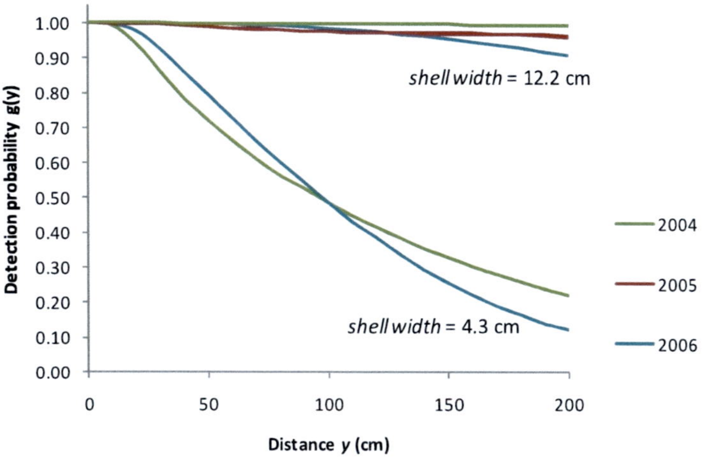

Figure 9. *Case Study*: The average models (among the set of candidate models; Table 4) of the detection function of the fan mussel *P. nobilis* in Lake Vouliagmeni, based on distance sampling data under the initial survey design, for years 2004, 2005, and 2006. Estimation of the average models was based on an information-theory approach. Detection functions were plotted for two values of shell width corresponding to the first ($s = 4.3$ cm) and the second ($s = 12.2$ cm) age classes of the fan mussel in the lake. For 2005, the two branches of the detection function (for the two sizes) largely overlap.

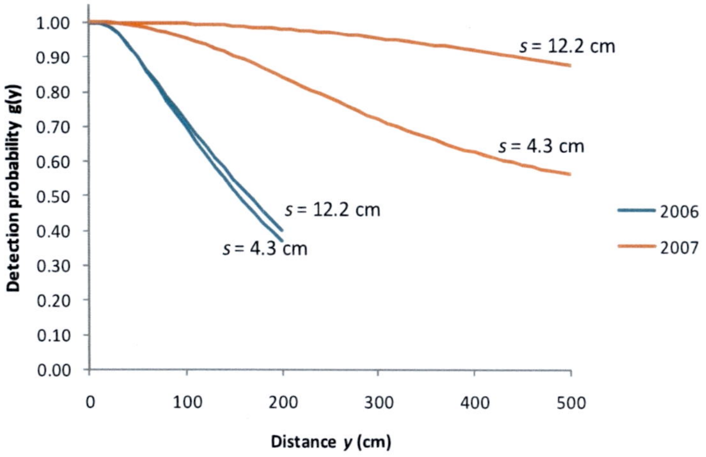

Figure 10. *Case Study*: The average models (among the set of candidate models; Table 5) of the detection function of the fan mussel *P. nobilis* in Lake Vouliagmeni, based on distance sampling data under the new survey design, for years 2006 and 2007. Estimation of the average models was based on an information-theory approach. Detection functions were plotted for two values of shell width corresponding to the first ($s = 4.3$ cm) and the second ($s = 12.2$ cm) age classes of the fan mussel in the lake.

New Design (2006–2007)

The best model of the detection function among the models tested was the half-normal function with constant scale parameter (i.e., no covariate) both in 2006 and 2007 (Table 5). However, in both years, models that included a size covariate were also supported by the data; in 2007, the half-normal model with a size covariate had almost the same support from the data as the half-normal function with no covariate. It is quite possible that the low sample size of 2006 and 2007 (especially in 2006) in relation to the sample sizes achieved with the initial survey design made it difficult for a model with a size covariate (i.e., with an extra parameter to estimate) to be selected as a best model. Actually, the low sample size of the 2006 survey was one of the reasons to extend the transect half-width to 5 m in 2007 from 2m in 2006. In 2007, recruitment was low and the small number of individuals of the first age class also contributed to the high support of models with no size covariate.

Although the transect half-width was increased in 2007, the probability of detection in 2007 was higher than in 2006 (Table 5). This might seem odd, as both the observer and the transects (apart from the two new transects) were the same for both two years. However, it should be apparent that detectability is a function of many factors that are temporally variable, such as visibility and the size distribution of the fan mussel in the lake. Water turbidity in the lake was very sensitive to environmental conditions and it is quite possible that visibility in the summer of 2006 was worse overall than in the following summer.

In both 2006 and 2007, the best density surface model was h_3, which included univariate smoothes of both d and x (Table 6). The expression of h_3 was $\ln(\mathrm{E}[\hat{n}_i]) = c + s_1(d) + s_2(x) + \ln(a)$, where a = 16 m^2 in 2006 and a = 50 m^2 in 2007. For the 2006 data c = -7.08 ± 0.53 (± SE), while for the 2007 data c = -10.98 ± 0.29 (± SE); the smooth functions s_i are given in Figure 11. The density of the *P. nobilis* population in Lake Vouliagmeni had a bimodal distribution in relation to depth; a major peak was found at depths between 12 and 13 m and a secondary peak at ~4 m depth. In relation to the x coordinate, there is a peak of *P. nobilis* density at $x \approx 2300 - 2500$ m.

Table 6. *Case study*: Evaluation of the three density surface models for the 2006 and 2007 surveys, based on their GCV (generalized cross validation) score. The percentage of deviance explained by the model and the corresponding estimated degrees of freedom (edf) are also given.

Model	GCV score	Deviance explained (%)	edf
		2006	
h_1	0.554	28.4	6.13
h_2	0.725	6.4	6.08
h_3	0.527	33.5	10.91
		2007	
h_1	1.0153	33.9	6.46
h_2	1.3524	11.5	5.79
h_3	0.8696	45.4	12.22

The abundance of *P. nobilis* in the study area was estimated to be $\hat{N} = 6770$ with a 95% confidence interval of 5460 – 8393 individuals in 2006, and $\hat{N} = 4232$ with a 95% confidence interval of 3524 – 5083 in 2007. The distribution maps of *P. nobilis* for 2006 and 2007, according to h_3, are given in Figure 12. There was a marked zonation of *P. nobilis*, which was restricted in the shallow peripheral zone of the lake, and most individuals were predicted to be in the strip between the 10 and 15 m contours. No individual was predicted to be at depths >22 m (hence limiting the study area at depths <30 m was sufficient to estimate *P. nobilis* abundance in the whole lake).

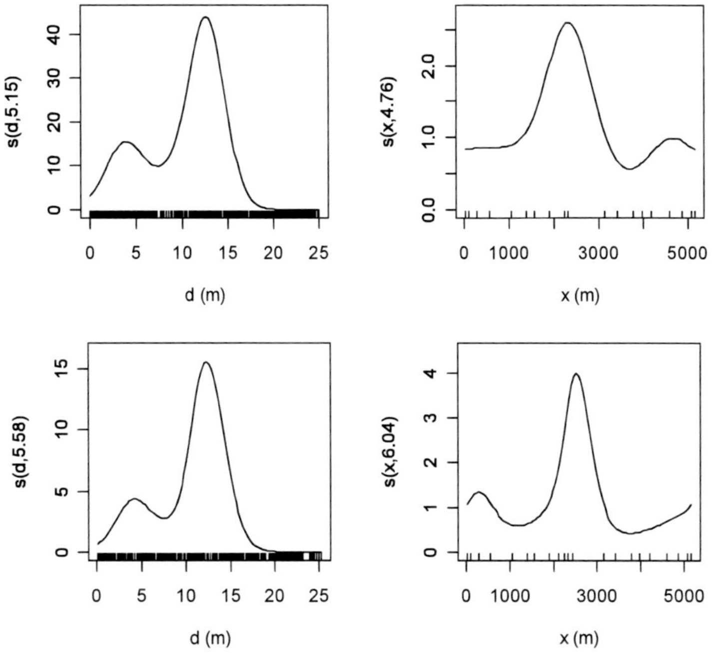

Figure 11. *Case study*: Estimated smooth terms for the h_3 model of *Pinna nobilis* abundance in Lake Vouliagmeni for the years 2006 (*top panel*) and 2007 (*bottom panel*). Smooth terms are given in the response scale (i.e., they were exp-transformed). The number *edf* in s(z_m, *edf*) is the estimated degrees of freedom of the smooth term. A one-dimensional scatterplot is given at the bottom of each graph, using a vertical bar as the plotting symbol, to illustrate the distribution of available data.

General Comments

An important benefit of DSM is that abundance is related to spatial covariates and the distribution of the species may be visually depicted. Abundance may be easily estimated in any subset of the study area by simply numerically integrating under the relevant section of the fitted density surface, whereas conventional distance sampling restricts abundance estimations to the whole study area or to predefined (at the design stage) strata (Hedley et al. 2008). Density surface modeling and the inferred relations to spatial covariates might provide insights and act as the starting point for further ecological investigations and manipulative experiments seeking causal relationships between abundance and environmental covariates (Katsanevakis, 2007a). The map of the density surface might be by itself a useful tool for wildlife managers. With a model-based approach like DSM, assuming that the line transects provide a good spatial coverage of the study area, the line transects are not required to be located according to a formal and restrictive survey sampling scheme. This is quite important, as in an underwater benthic survey like this one, it is not always easy or feasible to strictly follow a formal survey design. A good spatial model could offer more reliable estimation of abundance than traditional distance sampling, and DSM is expected to provide an improvement in the precision of the abundance estimate, as part of the spatial variability is actually modeled.

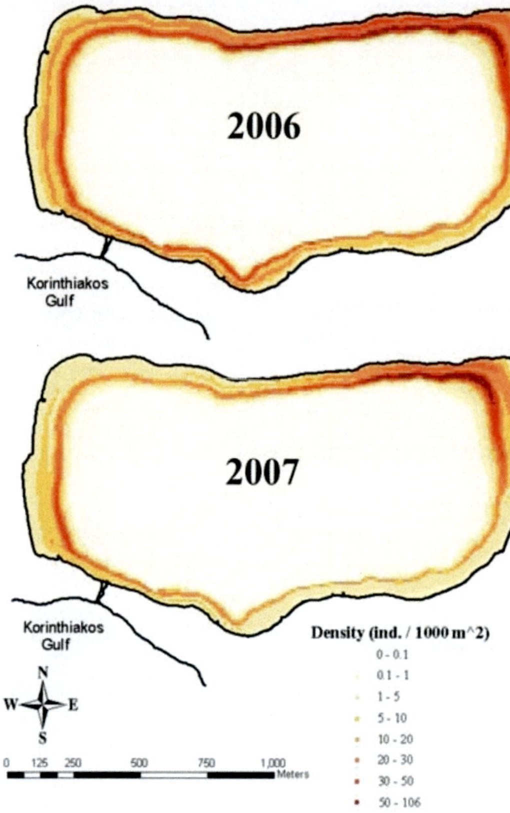

Figure 12. Distribution map of *Pinna nobilis* in Lake Vouliagmeni.

A marked zonation of *P. nobilis* was observed, with a bimodal distribution with depth. In a study of the fan mussel growth and mortality in Lake Vouliagmeni (Katsanevakis, 2007b), it was found that the survival of large individuals in shallow waters was strikingly low due to poaching, whilst at a depth of 12 m, large individuals did not suffer from illegal fishing. This is because poaching of *P. nobilis* in Lake Vouliagmeni is conducted exclusively by free-diving. Given the low visibility in the lake (usually much less than 10 m), skin divers are generally restricted to shallow depths. Because of these high fishing mortalities in the shallow areas, *P. nobilis* individuals do not have the chance to grow large and most of them are poached at a size $s < 18$ cm. This results in a size segregation, with small individuals having a peak density at a depth of ~4 m (which seems preferential to recruitment), while large individuals are mostly distributed at depths between 10 and 15 m. Thus, the observed bimodal distribution of *P. nobilis* in the lake is mainly an outcome of fishing mortality. If there were no fishing mortality in the shallow zone and because recruitment is more successful in the shallow zone of the lake, the spatial distribution and the density surface would probably be completely different, with higher densities in the shallow zone, declining with depth (Katsanevakis, 2007b).

From 2004 to 2006, no significant differences in abundance of *P. nobilis* were observed in the lake (Figure 13). However, in 2007, the abundance of the fan mussel declined in relation to the previous year (Figures 12 and 13). This was mostly due to poaching and to low recruitment that year.

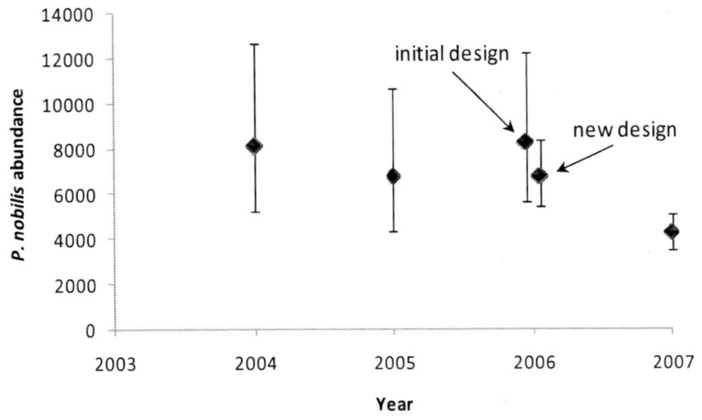

Figure 13. *Case study*: Time series (2004 – 2007) of the abundance of the fan mussel *P. nobilis* in Lake Vouliagmeni (Korinthiakos Gulf, Greece). For each estimate the corresponding 95% confidence intervals are given.

The confidence intervals of abundance estimates were rather large with the initial survey design (Figure 13) but substantially decreased when the new design was put forward in 2006, as the transects were defined as perpendicular to depth contours (and thus parallel to the main gradient in population density) and as part of the spatial variability of the fan mussel population was actually modeled. Precision was further improved in 2007 after the decision to increase the strip half-width from 2 m to 5 m (and thus increase the sample size) and to increase the number of transects from 18 to 20 (and thus increase both the sample size and the spatial coverage of the study area).

8. Conclusion

Distance sampling is widely used to estimate abundance and/or density of biological populations and is the standard method for abundance estimations of many endangered species. However, it has only rarely been used for underwater surveys of benthic fauna. As population assessment and monitoring is missing for most endangered marine benthic species, distance sampling through SCUBA diving may prove to be a valuable management tool, at least at depths where surveys with SCUBA diving are practically feasible. Regarding endangered benthic species, distance sampling is a much better alternative to fishery surveys using dredges or trawls, as it is a non-destructive method. In addition, estimates based on surveys that use commercial fishing gear are often unreliable due to low and variable efficiency. In comparison to strip transects (or general plot sampling), distance sampling is generally more reliable, efficient, and accurate. Strip transects may lead to negatively biased estimates of abundance, as they fail to properly account for detection probability and may give estimates with low precision due to small sample size if very narrow strips are surveyed in order to assure certain detectability. Distance sampling overcomes these issues. Density surface modeling with line transect sampling is beneficial in relation to conventional distance sampling, as apart from providing a more precise total abundance estimate, it relates the density of the species to spatial covariates of interest, gives a visual depiction of the species spatial distribution, and easily provides abundance estimates in any sub-region of the study area. Distance sampling with SCUBA diving has been successfully applied to monitor populations of the endangered fan mussel *P. nobilis* in Greece and is probably a good choice to estimate abundance for many other endangered benthic species.

REFERENCES

Ackerman, J.L. and Bellwood, D.R. (2000). Reef fish assemblages: a re-evaluation using enclosed rotenone stations. *Marine Ecology-Progress Series, 206*, 227-237.

Akaike, H. (1973). Information theory as an extension of the maximum likelihood principle. In: B.N. Petrov and F. Csaki (Eds.) *Proceedings of the second international symposium on information theory.* Budapest: Akademiai Kiado; pp. 267-281.

Akaike, H. (1983). Information measures and model selection. *Bulletin of the International Statistical Institute, 44*, 277-290.

Borchers, D.L. and Burnham, K.P. (2008). General formulation for distance sampling. In: S.T. Buckland, D.R. Anderson, K.P. Burnham, J.L. Laake, D.L. Borchers and L. Thomas (Eds.) *Advanced distance sampling: estimating abundance of biological populations.* New York: Oxford University Press; pp. 6-30.

Borchers, D.L., Buckland, S.T. and Zucchini, W. (2004). *Estimating animal abundance.* London: Springer-Verlag.

Buckland, S.T., Burnham, K.P. and Augustin, N.H. (1997). Model selection: An integral part of inference. *Biometrics, 53(2)*, 603-618.

Buckland, S.T., Goudie, I.B.J. and Borchers, D.L. (2000). Wildlife population assessment: Past developments and future directions. *Biometrics, 56(1)*, 1-12.

Buckland, S.T., Anderson, D.R., Burnham, K.P., Laake, J.L., Borchers, D.L. and Thomas, L. (2001). *Introduction to distance sampling: Estimating abundance of biological populations.* New York: Oxford University Press.

Buckland, S.T., Anderson, D.R., Burnham, K.P., Laake, J.L., Borchers, D.L. and Thomas, L. (2008). *Advanced distance sampling: Estimating abundance of biological populations.* New York: Oxford University Press.

Burnham, K.P. and Anderson, D.R. (1984). The need for distance data in transect counts. *Journal of Wildlife Management, 48(4)*, 1248-1254.

Burnham, K.P. and Anderson, D. (2002). *Model selection and multi-model inference.* Berlin: Springer.

Burnham, K.P., Buckland, S.T., Laake, J.L., Borchers, D.L., Marques, T.A., Bishop, J. R. B. and Thomas, L. (2008). Further topics in distance sampling. In: S.T. Buckland, D.R. Anderson, K.P. Burnham, J.L. Laake, D.L. Borchers and L. Thomas (Eds.) *Advanced distance sampling: estimating abundance of biological populations.* New York: Oxford University Press; pp. 307-392.

Caddy, J.F. (1968). Underwater observations on scallop (*Placopecten magellanicus*) behaviour and drag efficiency. *Journal of the Fisheries Research Board of Canada, 25(10)*, 2123-2141.

Caddy, J.F. (1989). A perspective on the population dynamics and assessment of scallop fisheries, with special reference to the sea scallop, *Placopecten magellanicus* Gmelin. In: J.F. Caddy (Ed.) *Marine Invertebrate Fisheries: Their Assessment and Management.* New York: Wiley; pp. 559–589.

Chabanet, P., Dufour, V. and Galzin, R. (1995). Disturbance impact on reef fish communities in reunion island (Indian Ocean). *Journal of Experimental Marine Biology and Ecology, 188(1)*, 29-48.

Chapman, C.J. (1980). Ecology of juvenile and adult nephrops. In: S. Cobb and B. Philips (Eds.) *The biology and management of lobsters, vol. II.* New York: Academic Press; pp. 143-178.

De Girolamo, M. and Mazzoldi, C. (2001). The application of visual census on Mediterranean rocky habitats. *Marine Environmental Research, 51(1)*, 1-16.

Denny, C.M. and Babcock, R.C. (2004). Do partial marine reserves protect reef fish assemblages? *Biological Conservation, 116(1)*, 119-129.

Edgar, G.J. and Barrett, N.S. (1997). Short term monitoring of biotic change in Tasmanian marine reserves. *Journal of Experimental Marine Biology and Ecology, 213(2)*, 261-279.

Efron, B. and Tibshirani, R.J. (1993). *An introduction to the bootstrap (Monographs on statistics and applied probability).* New York: Chapman & Hall/CRC.

Ensign, W.E., Angermeier, P.L. and Dolloff, C.A. (1995). Use of line transect methods to estimate abundance of benthic stream fishes. *Canadian Journal of Fisheries and Aquatic Sciences, 52(1)*, 213-222.

Galinou-Mitsoudi, S., Vlahavas, G. and Papoutsi, O. (2006). Population study of the protected bivalve *Pinna nobilis* (Linaeus, 1758) in Thermaikos Gulf (North Aegean Sea). *Journal of Biological Research, 5*, 47-53.

Giguere, M. and Brulotte, S. (1994). Comparison of sampling techniques, video and dredge, in estimating sea scallop (*Placopecten magellanicus*, Gmelin) populations. *Journal of Shellfish Research, 13(1)*, 25-30.

Guidetti, P., Fanelli, G., Fraschetti, S., Terlizzi, A. and Boero, F. (2002). Coastal fish indicate human-induced changes in the Mediterranean littoral. *Marine Environmental Research, 53(1)*, 77-94.

Hall-Spencer, J.M., Froglia, C., Atkinson, R.J.A. and Moore, P.G. (1999). The impact of Rapido trawling for scallops, *Pecten jacobaeus* (L.), on the benthos of the Gulf of Venice. *ICES Journal of Marine Science, 56(1)*, 111-124.

Hastie, T.J. and Tibshirani, R.J. (1990). *Generalized additive models (Monographs on statistics and applied probability).* London: Chapman & Hall/CRC.

Hedley, S.L. (2000). *Modelling heterogeneity in cetacean surveys,* PhD thesis, University of St Andrews, UK.

Hedley, S.L. and Buckland, S.T. (2004). Spatial models for line transect sampling. *Journal of Agricultural Biological and Environmental Statistics, 9(2)*, 181-199.

Hedley, S.L., Buckland, S.T. and Borchers, D.L. (2008). Spatial distance sampling models. In: S.T. Buckland, D.R. Anderson, K.P. Burnham, J.L. Laake, D.L. Borchers and L. Thomas (Eds.) *Advanced distance sampling: estimating abundance of biological populations.* New York: Oxford University Press; pp. 48-70.

Hilborn, R. and Walters, C.J. (1992). *Quantitative fisheries stock assessment: choice, dynamics and uncertainty*. New York: Chapman & Hall.

Hurvich, C.M. and Tsai, C.L. (1989). Regression and time-series model selection in small samples. *Biometrika, 76(2)*, 297-307.

Katsanevakis, S. (2005a). Habitat use by the pearly razorfish, *Xyrichtys novacula* (Pisces : Labridae). *Scientia Marina, 69(2)*, 223-229.

Katsanevakis, S. (2005b). Abundance and spatial distribution of the Mediterranean scallop, *Pecten jacobaeus*, in a marine lake. *Fisheries Research, 76(3)*, 417-429.

Katsanevakis, S. (2006). Population ecology of the endangered fan mussel *Pinna nobilis* in a marine lake. *Endangered Species Research, 1*, 51-59.

Katsanevakis, S. (2007a). Density surface modeling with line transect sampling as a tool for abundance estimation of marine benthic species: the *Pinna nobilis* example in a marine lake. *Marine Biology, 152(1)*, 77-85.

Katsanevakis, S. (2007b). Growth and mortality rates of the fan mussel *Pinna nobilis* in Lake Vouliagmeni (Korinthiakos Gulf, Greece): a generalized additive modeling approach. *Marine Biology, 152(6)*, 1319-1331.

Katsanevakis, S. and Verriopoulos, G. (2004a). Abundance of *Octopus vulgaris* on soft sediment. *Scientia Marina, 68(4)*, 553-560.

Katsanevakis, S. and Verriopoulos, G. (2004b). Den ecology of *Octopus vulgaris* Cuvier, 1797, on soft sediment: availability and types of shelter. *Scientia Marina, 68(1)*, 147-157.

Katsanevakis, S. and Thessalou-Legaki, M. (2007). First record of *Alicia mirabilis* (Anthozoa: Actiniaria) from the Aegean Sea and density assessment with distance sampling in a site of high abundance. *Marine Biology Research, 3(6)*, 468-472.

Kim, Y.J. and Gu, C. (2004). Smoothing spline Gaussian regression: more scalable computation via efficient approximation. *Journal of the Royal Statistical Society Series B-Statistical Methodology, 66*, 337-356.

Kinne, O. (2006). Protecting nature. *Endangered Species Research, 1*, 1-2.

Kulbicki, M. and Sarramegna, S. (1999). Comparison of density estimates derived from strip transect and distance sampling for underwater visual censuses: a case study of Chaetodontidae and Pomacanthidae. *Aquatic Living Resources, 12(5)*, 315-325.

Letourneur, Y., Kulbicki, M. and Labrosse, P. (1998). Spatial structure of commercial reef fish communities along a terrestrial runoff gradient in the northern lagoon of New Caledonia. *Environmental Biology of Fishes, 51(2)*, 141-159.

Marques, F.F.C. and Buckland, S.T. (2003). Incorporating covariates into standard line transect analyses. *Biometrics, 59(4)*, 924-935.

Marques, F. F. C. and Buckland, S.T. (2008). Covariate models for the detection function. In: S.T. Buckland, D.R. Anderson, K.P. Burnham, J.L. Laake, D.L. Borchers and L. Thomas (Eds.) *Advanced distance sampling: estimating abundance of biological populations*. New York: Oxford University Press; pp. 31-47.

McCullagh, P. and Nelder, J.A. (1989). *Generalized linear models, second edition (Monographs on statistics and applied probability)*. London: Chapman & Hall/CRC.

McLoughlin, R.J., Young, P.C., Martin, R.B. and Parslow, J. (1991). The Australian scallop dredge - estimates of catching efficiency and associated indirect fishing mortality. *Fisheries Research, 11(1)*, 1-24.

Pet-Soede, C., van Densen, W.L.T., Pet, J.S. and Machiels, M.A.M. (2001). Impact of Indonesian coral reef fisheries on fish community structure and the resultant catch composition. *Fisheries Research, 51(1)*, 35-51.

Pink, M., Pratt, T.C. and Fox, M.G. (2007). Use of underwater visual distance sampling for estimating habitat-specific population density. *North American Journal of Fisheries Management, 27(1)*, 246-255.

R Development Core Team. (2007). R: A language and environment for statistical computing. R Foundation for Statistical Computing: Vienna, Austria. ISBN 3-900051-07-0, http://www.R-project.org.

Seber, G.A.F. (1982). *The estimation of animal abundance and related parameters.* New York: Macmillan.

Shafee, M.S. (1979). Underwater observation to estimate the density and spatial distribution of black scallop, *Chlamys varia* (L.) in Lanveoc (Bay of Brest). *Bulletin Off. Natl. Pêches (Tunisie), 3*, 143-156.

Thomas, L., Laake, J.L., Rexstad, E., Strindberg, S., Marques, F.F.C., Buckland, S.T., Borchers, D.L., Anderson, D.R., Burnham, K.P., Burt, M.L., Hedley, S.L., Pollard, J.H., Bishop J.R.B. and Marques, T.A. (2006). Distance 6.0. Release Beta 3. Research Unit for Wildlife Population Assessment, University of St. Andrews: St. Andrews, UK. http://www.ruwpa.st-and.ac.uk/distance/.

Thompson, W.L. (2004). *Sampling rare or elusive species: concepts, designs, and techniques for estimating population parameters.* Washington: Island Press.

Thompson, W.L., White, G.C. and Gowan, C. (1998). *Monitoring vertebrate populations.* San Diego: Academic Press.

Thresher, R.E. and Gunn, J.S. (1986). Comparative-analysis of visual census techniques for highly mobile, reef-associated piscivores (Carangidae). *Environmental Biology of Fishes, 17(2)*, 93-116.

Tuck, I.D., Chapman, C.J., Atkinson, R.J.A., Bailey, N. and Smith, R.S.M. (1997). A comparison of methods for stock assessment of the Norway lobster, *Nephrops norvegicus*, in the Firth of Clyde. *Fisheries Research, 32(1)*, 89-100.

Tuya, F.C., Soboil, M.L. and Kido, J. (2000). An assessment of the effectiveness of Marine Protected Areas in the San Juan Islands, Washington, USA. *ICES Journal of Marine Science, 57(4)*, 1218-1226.

Williams, B.K., Nichols, J.D. and Conroy, M.J. (2002). *Analysis and management of animal populations.* San Diego: Academic Press.

Willis, T.J. (2001). Visual census methods underestimate density and diversity of cryptic reef fishes. *Journal of Fish Biology, 59(5)*, 1408-1411.

Wood, S.N. (2000). Modelling and smoothing parameter estimation with multiple quadratic penalties. *Journal of the Royal Statistical Society Series B-Statistical Methodology, 62*, 413-428.

Wood, S. (2006). *Generalized additive models: An introduction with R (Texts in Statistical Science).* Florida: Chapman & Hall/CRC.

In: Endangered Species: New Research
Editors: A. Columbus and L. Kuznetsov
ISBN 978-1-60692-241-5

Chapter 4

CURRENT STATUS AND CONSERVATION OF ENDANGERED MEDICINAL PLANTS IN THE MIDDLE EAST

Naima Bouhouche*
Faculty of Science, Department of Biology, UAE University, Al Ain, United Arab Emirates

ABSTRACT

The Middle East is characterized by a high diversity of flora including a large number of medicinal plants. This region has one of the oldest and richest traditions of medicinal plant use. However, these plants are becoming increasingly rare and facing extinction due to a number of threats. Agricultural expansion, extensive urbanization, desertification, unsustainable harvesting, destruction of natural habitat, overgrazing, increasing demands of drugs and climatic changes have resulted in the loss or the endangerment of many of these plant species.

In view of this alarming situation, many efforts have been attempted during the past few decades in the Middle East region to conserve these plants and the traditional knowledge related to them. Such efforts are conducted by governmental and non-governmental organizations, academic institutes and research centers.

This article will review the status and causes of medicinal species endangerment in the Middle East as well as conservation measures to protect and preserve them from extinction. Conservation strategies include protected areas, cultivation, tissue culture, seed banks and botanical gardens. Some suggestions will be put forward for the efficient protection of these valuable natural resources of the region.

* Email: naimabouhouche@gmail.com

Introduction

The use of plants for medicinal purposes has a long history in the Middle East and dates back to the ancient Mesopotamian period (beginning with Sumer 3,000 BC) (Price, 2001). The first written records detailing the use of herbs in the treatment of illness are the Mesopotamian clay tablets and the Egyptian papyrus, circa 2,000 B.C. Arab scholars in Baghdad in the 8th century, were the first to separate medicine from pharmacological science, leading to great advances in the field that included plant extract recipes. The first drug stores in the world were established in Baghdad in 754. The forms used in that period are still used in the therapy and some formulations of drugs can still be found in the pharmacopeias even today (Hadzović, 1997).

This rich cultural heritage together with a rich flora has resulted in the accumulation of a wealth of knowledge on traditional and folk medicine in the Middle East. This rich tradition of herbal medicine is still alive today with many people both in rural and urban areas. Unfortunately, these heritages and information are threatened by many factors.

The value and importance of traditional medicinal knowledge are now being increasingly acknowledged all over the world. The pharmaceutical industry continues to investigate and confirm the efficacy of many medicines and toxins used by traditional communities (Posey and Dutfield, 1996). Medicinal plants are in fact staging a comeback and herbal "renaissance" is happening all over the world.

Many of these medicinal plants are unfortunately facing several pressures that threaten their survival. Among the concerns surrounding the medicinal plants are the loss of biological diversity and the availability of resources. These concerns exist, mostly, because most species of medicinal plants are collected from the wild. It is estimated that above two thirds of the 50,000 medicinal plants used today are still harvested from the wild, from which 4,000 to 10,000 may now be endangered (Hamilton, 2003).

Many of the threats to medicinal plant species are similar to those causing endangerment to plant diversity in general. The most serious threats generally are habitat loss, habitat degradation and over-harvesting. One reason why medicinal plants have become increasingly threatened has been the weakening of customary laws that traditionally have regulated the use of natural resources. Such laws have proved often to be easily undermined by modern socio-economic forces (Pant, 2002). Concerns about loss of medicinal plants, considered as material resources, relate to worries about health care, livelihood security and financial income (Hamilton, 2003). It is estimated that about 80% of people worldwide rely mainly on traditional, largely herbal medicine to meet their primary health care needs although modern medicine has dominated most of the health care systems in the world. The global demand for herbal medicine is increasing (Srivastava, 2000). There is the risk that a growing herbal market and its great commercial benefit might pose a threat to biodiversity through the over-harvesting of the raw material for herbal medicines and other natural health care products. These practices, if not controlled, may lead to the extinction of endangered species and the destruction of natural habitats and resources.

In the Middle East, medicinal plants are becoming increasingly rare due to the ongoing destruction of their natural habitat, over-harvesting of wild species, and detrimental climatic and environmental changes. Land conversions for agriculture, overgrazing, water pollution, and conflict have exacerbated the degradation of natural ecosystems, resulting in desertification and the endangerment of many species. As a result, it is predicted that in semi-arid regions such as the Middle East, a number of species will disappear within the next 10 years, particularly in desert or dry areas where almost a third of native plants are found (Azaizeh *et al.*, 2006). This gives a sense of urgency to the task of recording the identity and uses of these medicinal plant species, and initiating programs of preservation of the genetic resource of medicinal plants of the region.

MIDDLE EAST: GEOGRAPHIC SETTING AND CLIMATIC OVERVIEW

The Middle East region is situated at the juncture of Eurasia and Africa and of the Mediterranean Sea and the Indian Ocean. The Middle East defines a geographical area, but does not have precisely defined borders. The modern definition of the region includes: Bahrain, Iran, Iraq, Israel, Jordan, Kuwait, Lebanon, Oman, Palestine, Qatar, Saudi Arabia, Syria, Turkey, the United Arab Emirates, and Yemen.

The climate of the Middle East is primarily arid and semi-arid, and can be subject to drought; however, there exists vast expanses of forests and fertile valleys. The region consists of grasslands, rangelands, deserts, and mountains. Water shortages are a problem in many parts of the Middle East, with rapidly growing populations increasing demands for water, while salinization and pollution threaten water supplies. Several major rivers provide sources for irrigation water to support agriculture in limited areas whereas some areas depend on the sea to get water through desalination.

The Middle East is well known for its wide variation in topography and climate that favored the formation of different habitat and vegetation zones, which created a wealth of species. While the Middle East mainly contains areas with low relief, portions of Turkey, Iran, and Yemen include mountainous terrain. A large lowland belt is located on the Arabian Peninsula, from central Iraq through Saudi Arabia, and to Oman and the Arabian Sea. The Euphrates and Tigris rivers cut through the lowland belt in Iraq and flow into the Persian Gulf forming a delta at its northern part. Rub'al KhāLī, one of the world's largest sand deserts, spans the southern third of the Arabian Peninsula in Saudi Arabia, parts of Oman, the United Arab Emirates and Yemen.

BIODIVERSITY, MEDICINAL PLANTS AND CONSERVATION

The Middle East is one of the richest biodiversity areas with a wide range of flora consisting of a large number of medicinal herbs, shrubs and trees. The Middle East is also one of the most water scarce regions in the world. These unique climatic conditions have given rise to a rich biodiversity characterized by species with high level of endemism, genetic diversity and a wide range of adaptations to this particular environment. A large number of medicinal plants are found in this region that has one of the oldest and richest traditions of medicinal plant use.

For the purpose of this review, the Middle East region will be divided into four regions depending on topography, climate and vegetation cover. These are: the Arabian Peninsula, the Levant (East Mediterranean), Iran and Turkey.

The Arabian Peninsula has a rich tradition of herbal medicine (Ghazanfar, 1994), which is still alive nowadays with many people. Surrounded by the Mediterranean Sea, the Near East, and the Abyssinian (Ethiopian) and Indian centers, the Arabian Peninsula is an important plant diversity center (Miller and Cope, 1996). The hostile desert environment, the extreme hot climate, and recurrent droughts have allowed particular kind of plant species to inhabit and adapt to this harsh environment. The desert eco-region of the Arabian Peninsula (located on the southern coast of the Peninsula and characterized by thick summer fogs) is characterized by a high diversity of flora. The fog brings the moisture necessary to sustain the many wildlife and plant species found there. It is a very species-rich habitat with over sixty endemic plants. Many of the plants have medicinal properties. However, many factors are threatening this unique and species-rich habitat. The causes of biodiversity loss are numerous, mostly related to human impact factors. Al-Eisawi (2003) has listed the most important causes in the dry ecosystems of the Arabian Peninsula. Urbanization is a major cause of destruction of flora and fauna. Agricultural expansion, overgrazing, destructive harvesting, increasing human population and urbanization, water over-pumping, camping activities, off-road driving are all factors that threaten the diversity of species. The cutting of wood for fodder, timber and firewood is also a serious problem.

The Eastern region of the Mediterranean, also called the Levant, is distinguished by a rich flora in which medicinal plants make up an important part. This region is covered with more than 2,600 plant species of which more than 700 are noted for their use as medicinal herbs or as botanical pesticides (Azaizeh *et al.*, 2006). Unfortunately, recent ethno-pharmacological surveys revealed that less than 200-250 plant species are still in use in Arab traditional medicine for the treatment of various diseases (Lev and Amar, 2000; 2002; Said *et al.*, 2002; Abu Irmaileh and Afifi, 2003). Many plant herbs used in traditional medicine are now rare or endangered species.

The flora of Iran is very rich, comprising some 8,000 species of seed plants of which about 1,800 are considered medicinal (American Botanical Council, 2007). Iran has also an impressive heritage of medico-pharmaceutical knowledge. However, Iran's environment is under a lot of pressure and faces many threats such as desertification, loss of traditional knowledge and over-grazing. It is estimated that 32% of plant species are vulnerable and endangered due to overgrazing and over-harvesting (Willis, 2001).

In Turkey, it is estimated that about 11,750 species are growing of which around 1,500 plant species are used as folk remedy (Yesilada, 2005). However, this traditional knowledge is rapidly being lost with the advance of development and modernization.

Although oil and gas activities are not cited among the major threats to biodiversity in the Middle East, a significant level of oil and gas activities are going on in this region. Biodiversity is becoming an increasingly important issue for the oil and gas industry operating in the Gulf countries such as Oman, Qatar and the United Arab Emirates.

Biodiversity loss leads to environmental degradation, which can have serious effects on human health. Biodiversity loss has direct effects on the discovery of potential medicines by diminishing the supplies of raw materials for drug discovery and biotechnology, and also threatens food production and water quality (Chivian, 2002). It leads to ecosystems that are less resilient, more vulnerable to shocks and disturbances, and less able to supply humans with needed services (Alves and Rosa, 2007).

Challenges for addressing these threats to biodiversity conservation include the weakness of institutions, lack of effective partnership and limited political support. Unless measures are taken to safeguard all species, then some of the relict populations could face extinction in the near future. In recognition of these threats and challenges, and the urgent need to challenge them, several actions are taken to reduce the current rate of biodiversity loss. Efforts are being directed towards bridging the gap between industry, government and academia, to identify potential opportunities for effective near and long-term action for the preservation of plant biodiversity in the Middle East.

Current Status of Medicinal Plants in the Middle East

For millennia, people in the Middle East were able to utilize their biological resources in a sustained fashion. In recent decades, however, the area of natural habitat has decreased or been degraded, through over-exploitation of natural resources, land conversion, poor agricultural practices and the pressures of an ever-expanding population. Plant populations have declined considerably. The centuries of old harmonious relationship of people and environment that has characterized the Middle East culture and history is rapidly disappearing. These alarming trends demand urgent conservation attention, to preserve this natural biotic wealth for future generations. An evaluation of the current status of medicinal flora in the Middle East is presented below.

The Arabian Peninsula

In the present context, the Arabian Peninsula will include the countries of Saudi Arabia, Yemen, Oman, UAE, Qatar, Bahrain, Kuwait and Iraq. Although there are some local variations, the region in general is characterized by relatively low relief and arid climate.

The flora of Saudi Arabia is one of the richest in the Arabian Peninsula and comprises very important genetic resources of crop and medicinal plants. In addition to its large number of endemic species, the components of the flora are the admixture of elements of Asia, Africa and the Mediterranean region. Approximately 2,250 native flowering plant species, in 142 families, are represented in the flora of Saudi Arabia (Collenette, 1998). Of these, 100 are endangered or of vulnerable status (NCWCD, 1998; Al Farhan, 2000). The existing and main potential threats to plant biodiversity include wood-cutting, over-grazing, off-road driving, agriculture, urbanization, and drought (El Sheikh *et al.,* 1989; NCWCD, 1998). Four endemic and 18 non-endemic species have been reported as extinct (Collenette, 1999). Approximately 319 species are commonly used in Saudi folk medicine (El-Shanwani, 1996). Investigation into the medicinally active compounds of these plants has shown a rich diversity in their pharmacological, phytochemical, antimicrobial and toxicological properties (Al-Yahya *et al.*, 1990).

A survey on the medicinal plant diversity in the flora of Saudi Arabia has been carried out recently with seven plant families: *Amaranthaceae, Apocynaceae, Capparidaceae, Euphorbiaceae, Labiatae, Polygonaceae* and *Solanaceae,* in order to assess their status in the wild for setting up conservation priorities and sustainable use and development (Rahman *et al.*, 2004). This study revealed that out of 254 species surveyed, 84 are medicinal and many of them are used by local and tribal people in the treatment of more than 150 ailments. Of these, 46 species are classified as rare or endangered in the wild (Table 1), 13 species among them are endemic to the Arabian Peninsula. According to Rahman *et al.* (2004), a complete inventory of the medicinal plant resources of Saudi Arabia is being developed. Two volumes of Medicinal Plants of Saudi Arabia were published by Mossa *et al.* (1987, 2000) with 300 species from the flora, representing 12% of the total species of this flora.

The flora of Yemen is very rich and heterogeneous. Over 3,000 plant species are found in the mainland. Approximately 850 plant species are found in Socotra Island, 254 (about 30%) of which are endemic. Precise data on the status and number of rare and endangered plants are not available. Some eight species (seven of these from Socotra) are included in the IUCN (the International Union for Conservation of Nature) Red Data Book as being endangered or rare, and an additional 19 species are considered to be endangered or rare at the national level in Yemen (UNDP/UNEP/GEF, 2001). The loss of biodiversity is the main specific issue of the habitat degradation problem in Yemen. A national biodiversity action plan was formulated for the conservation and sustainable use of Yemen's biodiversity (EPA, 2004).

Yemen has a large variety of medicinal herbs, which occupy a large size of the land and all over the country. Socotra Island is known as the medicinal plants Island as it is filled with medicinal plants like the Dragon's Blood tree, Frankincense trees, Socotra Aloe...etc. The island is distinguished by its unique collection of plants including medicinal plants. However, the medicinal flora in Yemen is not yet well documented, as research on this subject is still limited. A list of 224 medicinal and aromatic plants species along with their scientific names, families, vernacular names, distribution, active substances, medicinal part and medicinal use has been compiled. A similar study has concentrated on the use of medicinal plants endemic to Yemen (UNDP/UNEP/GEF, 2001).

According the Arabian Plant Specialist Group report (APSG, 2005), the total flora of Oman is about 1,100 species of which about 15% are endemic. The fog desert contains 150 species of which 10% are endemics. Many species are however data-deficient. Regional developments reports record concerns over loss of biodiversity as a result of overgrazing, road building and other developmental projects. Ghazanfar (1998) reported, in a study on the status of the flora and plant conservation in Oman, that the threatened flora constitutes 4.6% of the total species. 0.7% of the flora is critically endangered, 0.2% endangered, and 2% vulnerable.

Similarly, the APSG (2005) reported the occurence of approximately 600 species in the United Arab Emirates (UAE). Much of the flora is under threat from development, off-road driving, over-grazing, and a general lack of enforcement of conservation regulations. The harsh environment of the UAE (intense heat and limited water supplies) limits the biodiversity richness. Desertification is a growing problem and oil spills severely pollutes some areas. The UAE has established a national biodiversity strategy and action plan which aims to understand the country's environmental problems. It also includes instituting protected areas and a gene bank for traditional flora.

The plant diversity of Qatar consists of 371 species of flowering plants belonging to 236 genera in 61 families. A list of medicinal and poisonous plant species along with their scientific names, families, vernacular names, habitat, distribution, active constituents, and use has been compiled (Rizq and El-Ghazaly, 1995). However, no data are available on threatened species. The National Biodiversity Strategy and Action Plan report of the State of Qatar (NBSAP, 2004) states that there are few scientific studies in Qatar determining the threats to both terrestrial and marine flora and fauna. This lack of information seriously limits the ability of management authorities to conserve biodiversity and safeguard the environment. A complete review of species at risk occurring in Qatar is needed.

Table 1. Rare and endangered medicinal plants in the flora of Saudi Arabia*

Plant Species	Medicinal properties and uses
Achyranthes aspera	Astringent, diuretic and purgative
Amaranthus caudatus	Diuretic, strangury and blood purifier
Amaranthus spinosus	Antipyretic, diuretic and laxative
Celosia trigyna	Anthelmintic, diarrhoea, skin diseases
Adenium arabicum	Bone dislocations, painful joints, wound and skin infections
Carissa edulis	Anthelmintic, antiscorbutic, astringent, toothache
Nerium oleander	Diuretic, poisonous, skin diseases
Rhazya stricta	Antibacterial, bitter tonic, sore throat, fever
Cadaba farinose	Purgative, anthelmintic, antisiphilitic, emmena-gogue and aperient. Dysentery, fever, cough
Cleome arabica	Carminative, appetizer, tonic
Cleome brachycarpa	Appetizer, carminative, tonic
Cleome chrysantha	Anthelmintic, antiseptic
Acalypha indica	Expectorant, laxative, bronchitis, pneumonia, asthma
Chrozophora plicata	Depurative and purgative
Clutia lanceolata	Hypoglycaemic
Euphorbia arabica	Antibacterial, skin infections
Euphorbia cuneata	Sedative, antimicrobial
Euphorbia dracunculoides	Fruits are used to remove warts from the skin
Euphorbia schimperiana	Antiasthmatic, expectorant, coughs, ear pains, skin infections and snake bites
Euphorbia scordifoli	Carminative, febrifuge, laxative, fevers and constipation
Euphorbia terracina	Febrifuge. Remedy for fever and paralysis
Jatropha curcas	Antirheumatic, haemostatic, purgative. The leaf juice is used in wounds, eczyma and scabies
Lavandula dentata	Urine retention and removal of stones from kidney
Lavandula pubescens	Antimicrobial, headache and cold
Marrubium vulgare	Anthelmintic, alterative, expectorant, stimulant and resolvent. Coughs and chronic bronchitis, dyspepsia, jaundice amenorrhoea, rheumatism and hepatitis
Mentha lavendulacea	Analeptic, carminative
Mentha microphylla	Analeptic, appetizer, carminative
Nepeta deflersiana	Antimicrobial. Used as a tranquillizer
Ocimum americanum	Used in parasitic skin diseases
Ocimum tenuiflorum	Expectorant, stimulant. Used in cough and bronchitis
Origanum majorana	Antipasmodic, carminative, diaphoretic, diuretic. Used in asthma, cough, indigestion, rheumatism and headache
Otostegia fruticosa	Used as a remedy for sun-stroke
Plectranthus cylindraceus	Antibacterial. Used as a remedy for sore throat
Plectranthus tenuiflorus	Antimicrobial, used for the treatment of sore throat
Teucrium yemense	Anti-diabetic and in kidney problems
Thymus decussates	Aromatic, used for the treatment of nausea

Table 1.(Continued)

Plant Species	Medicinal properties and uses
Thymus vulgaris	Antiseptic, anthelmintic, expectorant, carminative, diuretic, emmenogogue and sedative. Used in whooping cough, bronchitis and colds
Calligonum comosum	Antimicrobial
Rumex nervosus	Used in skin diseases and skin burns
Rumex pictus	Sedative, spasmogenic and antimicrobial
Rumex steudelii	Purgative and astringent. Remedy for abdominal pains due to intestinal worms
Datura innoxia	Intoxicant, toxic and poisonous.
Datura metel	Astringent, anthelmintic, febrifuge, parasiticide, narcotic, emetic and poisonous. Used in fever, asthma, diarrhoea, skin diseases and cerebral complications
Hyoscyamus muticus	Antispasmodic, intoxicant and poisonous. Used as a remedy for asthma, toothache and sea sickness
Nicotiana rustica	Antispasmodic, sedative, emetic and purgative. Tobacco snuff is useful in nasal polyp, nasal catarrh, headache, chronic giddiness, fainting, rheumatic swellings and skin diseases
Physalis minima	Diuretic, purgative, tonic
Solanum surattense	Expectorant, febrifuge, toothache. Used in fever, asthma, cough, in sexual diseases and to promote female fertility

* Data from Rahman *et al.*, 2004.

About 357 species of wild plants have been recorded in the desert and cultivated areas in Bahrain. At least 20 different indigenous plant species have been recorded to have potential medicinal uses. However, the components of biodiversity have been subjected to increasing human-induced stresses, urbanization being the major threat. Because of the wide gaps in the available information, no assessment of the status of most species inhabiting Bahrain was undertaken. For the same reason also, no national lists of threatened and endemic species have been developed. There is essentially no information available about the status of genetic diversity in plant or animal species in Bahrain (GDEWP, 2006).

Approximately 234 plant species occur in Kuwait. However, no data are available on the number of threatened species. According the APSG (2005), the flora is under considerable pressure from over-use of land and off-road driving. It was even emphasized that accelerated development of the desert has subjected the fragile and vulnerable ecosystems to almost a non-restorable condition (Omar, 2007).

Iraq is considered a region of rich plants genetic resources and biodiversity. The country is central to the 'Fertile Crescent', one of the world's core areas of crop development and probably the first region to use crops and livestock in an integrated system of agricultural production, more than 10,000 years ago. Reflecting this heritage, Iraq has agricultural genetic resources of particular value in dry land farming, but the distribution of wild relatives and local varieties within the country is not well documented. There are no data available on the number of higher plants. Threats to biodiversity are currently mainly posed by conflict in the country. According to the United Nations Environment Program, World Conservation Monitoring Centre (http://www.unep-wcmc.org/latenews/Iraq_2003/biodiversity.htm), there appears to be no country-level assessment of the status of wild species of Iraq. About 35 species and subspecies are listed under Iraq by IUCN and assessed as globally threatened. Several of these appear to be extinct in Iraq. Overall, political instability is the major obstacle to biodiversity conservation in this country.

The Levant

The Levant is the Eastern Mediterranean region, which comprises Israel, Jordan, Lebanon, Palestine and Syria. The flora of this region is remarkably rich. Israel possesses almost 3,000 species of plants, of which at least one third are considered to be medicinal. Jordan has over 2,000 different species of plants. Recent studies investigating the medicinal uses of natural substances in the Levant revealed that 286 medicinal substances were in use as traditional compounds (Lev, 2002; Lev and Amar, 2000; 2002). However, this rich biodiversity is, in most cases, endangered by urbanization, poor land use, climatic changes, destruction of natural habitat, and population expansion. This has resulted in the decline and increasing rarity of many species. Table 2 lists some of the important rare and endangered plant species used traditionally in this region for treating human diseases or as botanical pesticides.

Table 2. Selected rare and endangered medicinal plants in the Eastern region of the Mediterranean, traditionally used for treating human diseases or as botanical pesticides*

Plant species	Uses	Red plant number**
Anchus negevensis	Anti-parasites, skin wounds and anti-coagulation	12
Anchus ovata	Anti-parasites, skin wounds and anti-coagulation	6
Eryngium barrelieri	Liver diseases and antitoxins	7
Eryngium maritimum	Liver diseases and antitoxins	6
Euphorbia dendroides	Botanical pesticides	9
Euphorbia hirsute	Anti-parasites	7
Ophioglossum lusitanicum	Anti-parasites, skin wounds and anti-coagulation	8
Ophioglossum polyphyllum	Anti-parasites, skin wounds and anti-coagulation	6
Teucrium procerum	Diabetes, liver diseases and wounds	12
Teucrium scordium	Chronic skin diseases, dyspepsia and hemorrhoids	7
Ziziphus nummularia	Diarrhea, lung inflammation and anti-congestion	8

*Data from Azaizeh *et al.*, 2006.

**The Red number is an additive index, summarizing values of four parameters: rarity, declining rate and habitat vulnerability, risk through attractivity and distribution type. The higher the number the more the plant is at risk.

Iran

There is a rich flora and extensive traditional medicinal knowledge in Iran. Iran's diverse climate produces some 8,200 species plant species, about 1,800 of which are considered medicinal (Convention Biological Diveristy; Iran, Status and trends of Biodiversity; http://www.cbd.int/countries/profile.shtml?country=ir). Iran's environment is under a lot of pressure and faces many threats such as desertification, soil erosion, over-grazing, loss of traditional knowledge, lack of awareness, population pressure, and unsustainable consumption. Many plants are facing considerable pressure from severe harvesting from the wild and overgrazing (Miraldi *et al.*, 2001; Ghorbani, 2005; Nadjafi *et al.*, 2007). About 32 % of plant species are classified under vulnerable or endangered status (Willis, 2001). A national inventory of medicinal plants is being developed. Iran's national biodiversity strategy action plan promotes the formation of biodiversity information systems, the sustainable use of biodiversity resources and the integrated conservation of biodiversity.

Turkey

The Turkish flora is estimated to contain more than 11,000 specific and infra-specific taxa of higher plants of which about 3,000 are endemic (Davis, 1965-1988, 1971; Guner *et al.*, 2000). The flora of Turkey is very rich in medicinal and aromatic plants where the rate of endemism is high. Some important genus that are used for medicinal and aromatic purposes are *Delphnium, Digitalis, Gypsophillia, Helychrysum, Leucojum, Linum, Liqiudambar, Malva, Matricaria, Mentha, Nigella, Orchidaceae* ssp*., Origanum, Pimpinella, Rosa, Salvia, Sideritis, Teucrium and Thymus* (M.E.F, 2007).

Nearly 100 % of the medicinal and aromatic plant material in trade in Turkey is wild collected – only c.25 is cultivated (Coskun and Ozkan, 2005). Many species such as *Gentiana lutea, Glycyrrhiza glabra, Gypsophila* sp., *Orchidaceae* sp., *Ruscus* sp., *Sideritis* sp., *Thymus* sp., *Origanum* sp.) were reported to be threatened as a result of over-collection from the wild (Ozhatay *et al.*, 1997). Unfortunately, trade of medicinal and aromatic plant species is largely unmonitored and levels of trade are unsustainable in many cases. The Red Data Book of Turkey containing the list of Endangered, Rare and Endemic Plant Species was published according to the IUCN (The World Conservation Union) criteria by Ekim *et al.* (2000).

Approaches to Medicinal Plants Conservation in the Middle East

The special significance of medicinal plants in conservation stems from the major cultural, livelihood and economic roles they play in many people's lives. Another important role for medicinal plant conservation is their use to achieve conservation of natural habitats more generally.

The Middle East harbors a rich diversity of valuable medicinal plants and attempts are being made at different levels for the conservation and sustainable utilization of this resource in order to conserve this biodiversity for future generations.

There are basically two types of conservation that can be undertaken in favor of the conservation and sustainable use of medicinal plants: *in situ* and *ex situ* conservation. *In situ* conservation strategies are measures taken at the places where the plants are growing, whereas *ex situ* conservation strategies refer to "distant" conservation measures at a far distance from the place where the plants naturally grow.

Successful conservation depends however on the existence of rules and regulations, and a reasonable degree of compliance to them. The WHO regulations (Akerele, 1993; WHO, IUCN, WWF, 1993) can be considered as a good basis for such regulations.

In situ Conservation

Over the past few years, conservation efforts of the Middle East biological resources have focused on the establishment of protected areas aiming at maintaining the diversity of the various components of biodiversity and their sustainable utilization. Cultivation projects were also initiated for the conservation of wild plants.

Protected Areas

Protected areas can be very useful for the conservation of medicinal plants in their natural environment. There are many types (national parks, forest reserves, strict nature reserves, etc.), generally serving various purposes in addition to biodiversity conservation, and with various rules applying to the conservation and collection of medicinal plants. The establishment of protected areas not only potentially preserves the natural ecological systems of the area, but it can also contribute positively to the region's ecological balance, scientific research and education, natural history preservation, recreational opportunities, and tourism. Protected areas are amongst the most effective tools used by countries to promote the *in-situ* conservation of biodiversity.

Steps are being taken in the Arabian Gulf countries to conserve and preserve the natural history of the ecosystems by setting aside areas of significant natural ecosystems or important ecological characteristics. Methods of conservation designed to suit the dry ecosystem of the Arabian Peninsula have been suggested. The most valuable method of conservation is the *in situ* conservation, in natural protected reserves, which in turn helps combat desertification (Al-Eisawi, 2003).

While some areas have been already established as protected reserves, more efforts are needed to manage resources and conserve species in their natural habitats.

Natural areas are being dedicated for the conservation and preservation of biological diversity in several countries. In Kuwait, for example, five protected areas have been established (Omar, 2007). Qatar has established 5 terrestrial protected areas accounting for about 18% of the total land area (http://www.cbd.int/countries/?country=qa). There are 91 designated protected areas in Oman, but protection is poorly implemented. No areas have been designated for the conservation of plant diversity. In Yemen, efforts have led to the identification of 15 areas throughout the country (including Socotra Island) that are of outstanding biodiversity/natural value and urgently need to be protected (EPA, 2004). There is only one terrestrial protected area in Bahrain (GDEWP, 2006). There are 131 protected areas in Iran, covering some 8% on the national land surface. Regulation implementation faces many problems, mostly due to inadequate size of protected areas, technical and administrative management inadequacies, and discouraging rigidity of protected area acts. Community-based natural management programs are used to implement and encourage the sustainable use of natural resources. Local communities are encouraged to manage their own environment. Although the current protection of traditional knowledge and local communities is very low, plans are under way to develop projects to support their culture and traditions through eco-tourism.

Many measures have been adopted to promote the conservation and sustainable use of biodiversity in the Middle East. Public awareness programs are implemented on regular basis, and the provisions of promoting the conservation and sustainable use of biodiversity have been incorporated into the national educational curricula.

Cultivation

Domestic cultivation is a viable alternative for the preservation of medicinal plants. Domestic cultivation of medicinal plants can be introduced as a measure to take the pressure off the wild populations, especially for the species collected in large quantities for commercial purpose. Introducing medicinal plants into farming systems also opens up the possibility of using biotechnology, and offers the possibility to optimize yield and achieve a uniform high quality herbal product (Canter *et al.*, 2005). Many countries of the Middle East are cultivating native medicinal plants for conservation as well as for commercial purposes. More than 20 plant species from the families of Asteraceae, Cucurbitaceae, Lamiaceae and Rosaceae are cultivated in Turkey (Uzun *et al.*, 2004; Kultur, 2007). In Iran, some of the native medicinal species are cultivated by private or state agricultural corporations. Cultivation programs also provide a sustainable source of raw plant material for scientific study.

Ex situ Conservation

The value of *ex situ* conservation is to serve biological conservation and developmental purposes. Today, there is a trend underway to preserve natural botanical resources through and increasing emphasis on conservation by way of seed banks, botanical gardens, herbariums, and tissue culture (Summer, 2000; Chaudhuri and Sarkar, 2002).

Seed Banks

Seed banks are an attractive way of storing the genetic diversity of many plants. The storage of material in the form of seeds is one of the most widespread and valuable *ex situ* approaches to conservation. Extensive expertise has been developed in this field by agencies and institutions involved with plant genetic resources over the past decades. Seed banking has considerable advantages over other methods of *ex situ* conservation such as ease of storage, economy of space, relatively low labor demands and consequently, the capacity to maintain large samples at an economically viable cost. However, medicinal plants are poorly represented in seed banks (Heywood, 2000).

Initiatives for the establishment of seed banks have been launched in different countries of the Middle East. Saudi Arabia has launched in 2002, the establishment of a national plant gene bank in which native medicinal herbs and endangered plant species will be included (Al Turki, 2002). Such gene bank will be important for the preservation of plant genetic diversity in Saudi Arabia. The initial work involved the collection of 83 samples of seeds of 52 plant species belonging to 35 genera and 19 families. Species collected include many endemic and endangered taxa. The seeds are stored at 5°C. Al-Turki (2002) noted that the absence of a gene bank in the Arabian Peninsula has hampered biotechnological progress and preservation of biodiversity.

Oman has initiated a collection of germplasm of medicinal plant species within a collaborative program between the Sultanate of Oman and ICARDA-APRP for the sustainable management of natural resources. Herbaria samples of 31 plant taxa of medicinal importance have been collected and preserved under cold storage in deep freezers (Nadaf *et al.,* 2003).

A seed bank for native species of Kuwait was established, and plans are to initiate large-scale seed production activities. Currently, the seed bank contains seed stock of 66 species of native plants (Omar, 2007).

Seeds of more than 2,000 endemic plant species in Turkey have been collected and transferred to a gene bank for *ex situ* conservation (Ekim, 1998).

Several countries in the Middle East are also involved in the Millenium Seed Bank Project based at the Kew Royal Botanic Gardens, in England (Kew Science Directory, 2006). The project is a massive plan to preserve seeds of native, endangered and economically important plants.

Botanical Gardens

There are many botanical gardens with collections of medicinal plants around the world. Botanic gardens can play major roles in medicinal plant conservation through developing propagation and cultivation protocols, and undertaking programmes of domestication and variety breeding (Hamilton, 2003).

Botanic gardens are burgeoning in the Arabian Peninsula. In the U.A.E, the Sharjah Botanic Gardens, founded in 1997, aim to include *ex situ* conservation of the flora of the entire Arabian Peninsula. This will comprise of halophytes and flora from the sand desert, gravel desert, mountains and coastal regions, totaling several thousand species (UNESCO, 2008). Plans are underway to establish botanic gardens in a number of countries such as Qatar, Kuwait that aim to conserve *ex situ* the flora of this region. The medicinal plants used in the local traditions will be included in the gardens. In Saudi Arabia, King Saud University Botanic Garden has started in 1994 within the university campus to protect the rare and endangered plants.

Among the botanic gardens already existing, special collections in rare and threatened medicinal plants are included along with conservation programs.

There are many botanical gardens in Israel, such as the Jerusalem Botanical Gardens at the Hebrew University with medicinal plant conservation programs and special collections of rare and threatened medicinal plants (http://www.bgci.org/garden.php?id=108). In Jordan, the Royal Botanic Garden is the first national botanic garden, founded in 2005 (http://www.bgci.org/eurasia/news/0022/). It aims to be a regional centre for native plant conservation, public education, and scientific research, and will include medicinal herbs.

There are many botanical gardens in Iran. The National Botanical Garden of Iran in Tehran, founded in 1968 (http://www.bgci.org/worldwide/article/174), and the University of Tehran Botanical Garden founded in 1931, both contain special collections of medicinal plants among others.

The botanical garden Nezahat Gokyigit Botanik Bahcesi, Turkey, founded in 2003, has a medicinal and aromatic plants garden under development.

Tissue Culture

Plant tissue culture is an alternative method of propagation, and is being used widely for the propagation of a large number of plant species. Tissue culture is also a powerful tool for the conservation and rapid multiplication of many threatened plant species (Fay, 1992). It has been particularly useful for the conservation and rapid propagation of valuable, rare and endangered medicinal species. Micropropagation protocols have been developed for many important medicinal plants such as *Limonium wrightii* (Huang *et al.*, 2000), *Adenophora triphylla* (Chen *et al*., 2001), *Thapsia gar-ganica* (Makunga *et al*., 2003), *Artemisia judaica* (Liu *et al*., 2003), *Rotula aquatica* (Martin, 2003), *Saussurea obvallata* (Joshi and Dhar, 2003), *Aconitum coreanum* (Xu *et al*., 2004), *Catharanthus roseus, Chlorophytum borivilianum, Datura metel* and *Bacopa monnieri* (Debnath *et al*., 2006), *Drosera indica* (Jayaram and Prasad, 2007).

An efficient *in vitro* plant regeneration protocol was established for the medicinal plant *Teucrium stocksianum,* which is a native plant to the U.A.E, Oman and Iran (Bouhouche and Ksiksi, 2007). This plant is under various stresses that threaten its survival. The development of such protocol offers a solution for the rehabilitation of the natural populations of this medicinal plant. Plants produced from this protocol can help reduce some of the pressure on the natural populations.

Conclusion

Over the last several decades, human activity has profoundly transformed the landscape and over-exploited available biological resources. This has resulted in the deterioration of many habitats and the endangerment/extinction of many plant species. Medicinal plants resources have seen a rapid decline all over the world including the Middle East. A unique tradition of herbal medicine in this region is being rapidly lost with the ongoing modernization. In response to this, initiatives for the documentation of traditional medicinal knowledge and the conservation of medicinal plants have been launched in different countries in the Middle East region.

The major causes of medicinal plants endangerment in the Middle East are habitat loss/degradation, unsustainable harvesting and extensive urbanization. Urgent measures must be undertaken in order to protect medicinal plants in the region from the ongoing destruction of their natural habitat as well as from over-harvesting wild species and detrimental environmental changes. The challenge of today, in the Middle East region, is to harmonize between progress, fast pace of development and environment protection. Different strategies for conservation are being set in many countries. Some of the actions taken to preserve these medicinal plants include: conservation of natural areas as gene banks; establishing seed banks and botanical gardens; enhancing the public awareness of wild species protection; developing the cultivation of traditional herbal medicinal plant; strengthening the investigation and study of endangered species; launching exchange and cooperation of conservation techniques on endangered species. Also, of most importance is the regulation on conservation addressing wild and cultivated medicinal plants, and enforcing the relative laws and rules for herbal resources protection.

All this requires coordinated conservation work involving conservation experts, specialized scientists, government, and also all aspects of trade. Trade monitoring, adjustments to legislation, regulation of *in situ* and *ex situ* conservation, improved management programs, public awareness initiatives, enhancement of cultivation efforts are all important issues to be considered in medicinal plants protection.

ACKNOWLEDGEMENT

This article is dedicated to Dr. F. N. Sadooni. I am deeply indebted to Dr. Sadooni for his unlimited support and encouragement, which were crucial in the preparation of this work. I would like hereby to express to him my deepest thanks and gratitude.

REFERENCES

Abu-Irmaileh, B. E & Afifi, F. U. (2003). Herbal medicine in Jordan with special emphasis on commonly used herbs. *J. Ethnopharmacol., 89*,193-7.

Al-Eisawi, D. (2003). Effect of biodiversity conservation on arid ecosystem with a special emphasis on Bahrain. *Journal of arid Environments, 54*, 81-90.

Al-Farhan, A. H. (2000). An evaluation of the current status of the flora of Saudi Arabia. *Country report presented at the Second Arabian Plants Subject Group Meeting, Abu Dhabi, May 2000.*

Al-Turki, T. A. (2002). An initiative in exploration and management of plant genetic diversity in Saudi Arabia. In J. M. M. Engels, V. Ramanatha Rao, A. H. D. Brown & M. T. Jackson (Eds.). *Managing Plant Genetic Diversity. IPGRI (International Plant Genetic Resources Institute*). pp: 339-349.

Alves, R. R. N. & Rosa, I. M. L. (2007). Biodiveristy, traditional medicine and public health: where do they meet? *J. Ethnobiology and Ethnomedicine, 3*,14.

Al-Yahya, M. A., Al-Meshal, I. A. R., Mossa, J. S., Al-Badar, A. A., & Tariq, M. (1990). Saudi plants: A phytochemical and biological approach. *GDRGP, KACST, Riyadh.*

American Botanical Council. (2007). Herbal medicine in Iran. *HerbalGram, 74*, 34-43. [online] Available from: URL: http://content.herbalgram.org/wholefoodsmarket/herbalgram/articleview.asp?a=3101&p=Y

APSG (Arabian Plants Specialist Group) (2005). Report on the Fourth Meeting of the Arabian Plants Specialist Group. [online] Available from: URL: http://www.iucnarabianpsg.org/Fourth%20Meeting.pdf.

Akerele, O. (1993). Nature's medicinal bounty: don't throw it away. *World Health Forum, 14 (4)*, 390-395.

Azaizeh, H., Saad, B., Khalil, K. & Said, O. (2006). The state of the art of traditional arab herbal medicine in the eastern region of the Mediterranean: a review. *eCAM, 3, (2)*, 229-235. DOI: 10.1093/ecam/nel034

Bouhouche, N. & Ksiksi, T. (2007). An efficient *in vitro* plant regeneration system for the medicinal plant *Teucrium stocksianum* Boiss. *Plant Biotechnol. Reports, 1*,179-184.

Canter, P. H., Thomas, H. & Ernst, E. (2005). Bringing medicinal into cultivation: opportunities and challenges for biotechnology. *Trends in Biotech. 23 (4)*, 180-185.

Chaudhuri, A. B. & Sarkar, D. D. (2002). Biodiveristy Endangered: India's Threatened Wildlife and Medicinal Plants. Jodhpur: Scientific Publishers.

Chen, C. C., Chen, S. J., Sagare, A. P. & Tsay, H.S. (2001). Adventitious shoot regeneration from stem internode explants of *Adenophora triphylla* (Thunb.) A. DC. (Campanulaceae)—an important medicinal herb. *Bot Bull Acad Sin 42*,1–7.

Chivian, E. (2002). Biodiversity: its importance to human health. Center fot health and the global environment. Harvard Medical School.
Collenette, S. (1998). Checklist of botanical species in Saudi Arabia. West Sussex (UK): *International Asclepiad Society*, p. 78.
Collenette, S. (1999). Wild flowers of Saudi Arabia. *National Commission for Wildlife Conservation and Development, Riyadh.*
Coşkun, M. & Özkan, A. M. G. (2005). Global phytochemistry: The Turkish frame. *Phytochemistry, 66, 9*, 956-960
Davis, P. H. (1971). Distribution Patterns in Anatolia with Particular Reference to Endemism. Plant Life of South-West Asia. *The Botanical Society of Edinburgh, UK*, 15–27.
Davis, P.H. (Ed.) (1965-1988). Flora of Turkey and the East Aegean Islands, vol. 1–10. Edinburgh Univ. Press, Edinburgh.
Debnath, M., Malik, C. P., Bisen, P. S. (2006) Micropropagation: a tool forthe production of high quality plant-based medicines. *Curr. Pharm Biotechnol* 7, 33–49.
Ekim, T. (1998). Project on Endemic Species of Turkey, TBAG/ DPT-C¸ .SEK-4, Ankara.
Ekim, T., Koyuncu, M., Vural, M., Duman, H., Aytac, Z. & Adıguzel, N. (2000). Red Data Book of Turkish Plants. Turkish Association for the Conservation of Nature and Van Centennial University, Ankara.
El-Shanwani, M. A. A. (1996). Al-nibatat al-moustakhdima fi al-ttib al-sha'abi al-Saudi (Plants used in Saudi folk medicine). General Directorate of Research Grants Program, KACST, Riyadh.
El-Sheikh, A. M., Chaudhary, S. A., Hassan, H. M., & Al Farraj, M. M. (1989). Endangered or rare plant species in Saudi Arabia. In: Abu Zinada, A.H., Goriup, P.D., and Nader, A. (eds) Wildlife Conservation and Development in Saudi Arabia. NCWCD, Riyadh, 193-199.
EPA (Environment Protection Authority) (2004). Ministry of Water and Environment. Republic of Yemen. Yemen First National Report on the Convention of Biological Diversity. 92p
Fay, M. F. (1992). Conservation of rare and endangered plants using *in vitro* methods. *In Vitro Cell Dev. Biol. Plant*, 28,1–4.
GDEWP (General Directorate for Environment and Wildlife Protection) (2006). Bahrain First National Report to the Convention on Biological Diversity. pp. 102. [online] Available from: URL: http://www.cbd.int/doc/world/bh/bh-nr-01-en.doc
Ghazanfar, S. A. (1994). Handbook of Arabian Medicinal Plants. CRC Press, Boca raton, Florida.
Ghazanfar, S. A. (1998). Status of the flora and plant conservation in the sultanate of Oman. *Biological Conservation, 85 (3)*, 287-295.
Ghorbani, A. (2005). Studies on pharmaceutical ethnobotany in the region of Turkmen Sahra, north of Iran (Part I): General results. *J. Ethnopharmacol. 102,* 58-68.
Guner, A., Ozhatay, N., Ekim, T. & Baser, K.H.C. (Eds.). (2000). Flora of Turkey and the East Aegean Islands (Suppl.), vol. 11. Edinburgh Univ. Press, Edinburgh.
Hadzović, S. (1997). Pharmacy and the great contribution of Arab-Islamic science to its development. *Med Arh. (Medicinski Arhiv), 51(1-2),* 47-50.
Hamilton, A. (2003). Medicinal Plants and Conservation: Issues and Approaches *WWF UK report.* pp. 50.

Heywood, V. (2000). Management and sustainability of the resource base for medicinal plants. In S. Honnef & R. Melisch (Eds.) *Medicinal utilization of wild species: challenge for man and nature in the new millennium.* WWF Germany /TRAFFIC Europe-Germany, EXPO 2000, Hannover, Germany.

Huang, C. L., Hsieh, M. T., Hsieh, W. C., Sagare, A. P. & Tsay, H. S. (2000) In vitro propagation of *Limonium wrightii* (Hance) Ktze. (Plumbaginaceae), an ethnomedicinal plant, from shoot tip, leaf- and inflorescence-node explants. *In Vitro Cell Dev Biol Plant 36*, 220–224.

Jayaram, K. & Prasad, M. N. V. (2007) Rapid in vitro multiplication of *Drosera indica* L.: a vulnerable, medicinally important insectivorous plant. *Plant Biotechnol Rep* 1, 79–84.

Joshi, M. & Dhar, U. (2003) In vitro propagation of *Saussurea obvallata* (DC.) Edgew.—an endangered ethnoreligious medicinal herb of Himalaya. *Plant Cell Rep 21,* 933–939.

Kew Science Directory. (2006). Millenium Seed Bank Project. [online] Available from: URL:
http://www.kew.org/science/directory/teams/MillenniumSeedBank/achievements.html

Kultur, S. (2007) Medicinal plants used in Kirklareli Province (Turkey). *J. Ethnopharmacol., 111 (2),* 341-364.

Lev, E. & Amar, Z. (2000). Ethnopharmacological survey of traditional drugs sold in Israel at the end of the 20th century. *J. Ethnopharmacol., 72,* 191-205.

Lev, E. & Amar, Z. (2002). Ethnopharmacological survey of traditional drugs sold in the Kingdom of Jordan. *J. Ethnopharmacol., 82,* 131-45.

Lev, E. (2002). Reconstructed materia medica of the Medieval and Ottoman al-Sham. *J. Ethnopharmacol., 80,* 167-79.

Liu, C. Z., Murch, S. J., El-Demerdash, M. & Saxena, P. K. (2003) Regeneration of the Egyptian medicinal plant *Artemisia judaica* L. *Plant Cell Rep 21*, 525–530.

Makunga, N. P., Jager, A. K.& Staden, J van (2003) Micropropagation of *Thapsia gargania*-a medicinal plant. *Plant Cell Rep 21,* 967–973.

Martin, K. P. (2003) Rapid in vitro multiplication and ex vitro rooting of *Rotula aquatica* Lour., a rare rhoeophytic woody medicinal plant. *Plant Cell Rep 21*,415–420.

MEF (Ministry of Environment and Forestry) (2007). Turkey's Biodiveristy. [online] Available from: URL: http://www.bcs.gov.tr/siteen/TurkeysBiodiversity/tabid/63/ Default.aspx.

Miller, A. G. & Cope, T. A. (1996). Flora of the Arabian Peninsula and Socotra. Edimburgh University Press, Edimburgh, UK.

Miraldi, E., Feri, S. & Mostaghimi, V. (2001). Botanical drugs and preparations in the traditional medicine of West Azerbaijan (Iran). *J. Ethnopharmacol., 75,* 77-87.

Mossa, J. S, Al-Yahya, M. A. & Al-Meshal, I. A. (1987). Medicinal plants of Saudi Arabia. Riyadh: King Saud University Press.

Mossa, J. S, Al-Yahya, M. A. & Al-Meshal, I. A. (2000). Medicinal plants of Saudi Arabia. Riyadh: King Saud University Press.

Nadaf, S. K., Al-Farsi, S. M. & Al-Hinai, S. A. (2003). Germplasm collection of rangeland forage and medicinal plant species in North Oman. *ICARDA-PRP Annual Report 2002-2003. Sustainable Management of Natural resources and improvement of major productions systems of Arabian Peninsula.*

Nadjafi, F., Koocheki, A., Moghaddam, P. R., Honermeier, B., & Asili, J. (2007). Autoecology, ethnobotanical and phytocehmical studies of *Nepeta binaludensis* Jamsad, a highly endangered medicinal plant of Iran. *Planta Med.* 73.

NBSAP (National Biodiversity Strategy Action Plan) (2004). National report – State of Qatar. [online] Available from: URL: http://www.cbd.int/doc/world/qa/qa-nbsap-01-en.doc

NCWCD (National Commission for Wildlife Conservation and Development) (1998). Species status and conservation strategy. B. Endangered, Vulnerable and rare plant taxa in the Kingdom of Saudi Arabia. Riyadh.

Omar, S. (2007). *In situ* and *ex situ* conservation of genetic diversity of desert plants in Kuwait. 3rd Global Botanic Gardens Congress, April 15-20, 2007, Wuhan, China.

Ozhatay, N., Koyuncu, M., Atay, S. & Byfield, A. J. (1997). The Wild Medicinal Plant Trade in Turkey. DHKD Publication, Istanbul, Turkey, ISBN 975-96081-9-7.

Pant, R. (2002). *Customs and conservation: cases of traditional and modern law in India and Nepal.* Kalpavriksh and International Institute of Environment and Development, Puni, India.

Posey, D. A. & Dutfield, G. (1996). Beyond Intellectual Property: Toward Traditional Resource Rights for Indigenous Peoples and Local Communities, Canada: International Development Research Centre. p. 303.

Price, M. (2001). History of ancient Medicine in Mesopotamia and Iran. [online] Available from: URL: http://www.iranchamber.com/history/articles/ancient_medicine_mesopotamia_iran.php 4/4/2008.

Rahman, M. A., Mossa, J. S., Al-Said, M. S. & Al-Yahya, M. A. (2004). Medicinal plant diversity in the flora of Saudi Arabia 1: a report on seven plant families. *Fitoterapia, 75,* 149-161.

Rizk, A. M. and El Ghazaly, G. A. (1995). Medicinal and Poisonous Plants of Qatar. Univeristy of Qatar, Scientific and Applied Research Center, Doha, Qatar. 306 pp.

Said, O., Khalil, K., Fulder, S. & Azaizeh, H. (2002). Ethnopharmacological survey of medicinal herbs in Israel, the Golan Heights and the West Bank region. *J. Ethnopharmacol., 83,* 251-65.

Srivastava, R. (2000). Studying the information needs of medicinal plant stakeholders in Europe. *TRAFFIC Dispatches* 15, 5.

Summer, J. (2000). The Natural History of Medicinal Plants. Portland, Oregon: Timber press.

UNDP/UNEP/GEF. (2001). The integration of Biodiversity into National Environmental Assessment Procedures. National Case Studies, Yemen, 20 p. [online] Available from: URL: http://www.unep.org/bpsp/EIA/Case%20Studies/Yemen%20(EIA).pdf

UNESCO. (2008). Quranic Botanic gardens. [online] Available from: URL: http://www.unesco.org/mab/biodiv/q_botanicgardens.shtml

Uzun, E., Sariyar, G., Adsersen, A., Karakok, B., Otuk, G., Oktayoglu, E. & Pririldar, S. (2004). Traditional medicine in Sakarya province (Turkey) and antimicrobial activities of selected species. *J. Ethnopharmacol., 95,* 287-296.

WHO, IUCN, WWF. (1993). *Guidelines on the Conservation of Medicinal Plants.* Published by The International Union for Conservation of Nature and Natural Resources (IUCN), Gland, Switzerland, in partnership with The World Health Organization (WHO), Geneva, Switzerland, and WWF-World Wide Fund for Nature, Gland, Switzerland.

Willis, A. J. (2001). Endangered plants in Iran. *New Phytologist, 149 (2),* pp. 165.

Xu , X., Yu, R. & Zhao, Y. (2004) Establishment of plantlet regeneration system of medicinal plant *Aconitum coreanum*. *Zhong Yao Cai 27*, 797–799.

Yesilada, E. (2005). Past and future contributions to traditional medicine in the health care system of the Middle-East. *J. Ethnopharmacol., 100 (1-2*), 135-137.

In: Endangered Species: New Research
Editors: A. Columbus and L. Kuznetsov
ISBN 978-1-60692-241-5

Chapter 5

THE CONSERVATION STATE OF PINE MARTEN (*MARTES MARTES*) IN EUROPE

Vercillo Francesca, Lucentini Livia, Panara Fausto and Ragni Bernardino
Dipartimento di Biologia Cellulare e Ambientale, Università degli Studi di Perugia, Via Elce di Sotto I-6123 Perugia - Italy

ABSTRACT

Pine marten (*Martes martes*) is a palaearctic species having a broad diffusion in central and north-eastern Europe, while it is localized or absent in southern and western Europe. British and Mediterranean insular populations are well developed and widespread. In Italy pine marten is diffused in the main islands, while it is rare and has a fragmented distribution in the peninsula. Its conservation state is poorly known; in addition, incidental killings, forest reduction and habitat fragmentation caused populations decrease in recent years. The conservation state of pine marten is defined by the III Appendix of Berna's International Convention and by the V Annexed of the Habitat Directive 92/43/CEE that defined this species as under risk.

One of the major criticisms concerning the management and conservation of this species is the difficulty to distinguish it from a "twin species", the beech marten (*Martes foina*); in several European regions the two species are in simpatry and seem to share the same trophic niche. Ecological competition between the two *Martes* species, with the supremacy of the more widespread and abundant beech marten, can be postulated. Thus the opportunity of a correct taxonomic identification of these congeneric species, and the status of genetic variability of pine marten, is fundamental for any management and future conservation program. Morphometric and molecular methodologies are an important tool for the study of wild fauna and, particularly, to distinguish pine and beech marten. The molecular approach, in fact, allows the unambiguous assignment of the studied samples, as well as phylogeographic and population genetics analyses. The application of molecular markers, furthermore, minimizes the impact on analyzed samples.

In fact, the animal manipulation is greatly reduced or absent when using non-invasive molecular methodologies for DNA extraction from hairs and faeces.

The aim of this chapter is to review the knowledge on molecular and morphological approaches that can be employed on this species in Europe, particularly concerning its conservation state.

INTRODUCTION

Pine marten is a species having a great scientific and conservation interest because it is poorly known, it has mainly a nocturnal way of life, it is a predator of poultry and game species and because, as in the past, it is a fur-bearing species (Broekhuizen, 2006). Furthermore, the increasing habitat fragmentation and the attendant isolation of European populations caused the decline of this species in several environments, with a consequent interest for both mainly scientific and conservation purposes. Another important aspects is the presence of a morphologically very similar species, beech marten (*Martes foina*), which is in sympatry with pine marten in most of Central Europe and shows a broad overlapping of the trophic niche. The very likely existence of an ecological competition between these two species underlines the importance of a clear and unambiguous species attribution and of researches specifically voted to study and manage these Mustelids in Europe. As a consequence, several researches were performed, since the beginning of the last century, first to analyze morphology and osteometric fields (Streuli, 1932; Rode & Didier, 1944; Anderson, 1970; Hartung, 1980; Gerasimov, 1985; Stubbe, 1993; Reig, 1992) and then to investigate the ecological aspects (Goszczynski, 1976 and 1986; Marchesi & Mermod, 1989; Marchesi *et al.*, 1989; Lode, 1994; Pulliainen & Ollinmaki, 1996; Bermejo & Guitian, 2000; Helldin, 2000; Ortega *et al.* 2002; Posłuszny *et al.*, 2007). In the last few years, a great increase of the application of molecular biology as a tool to investigate wild fauna was observed, particularly concerning pine marten (Hosoda *et al.*, 2000; Davison *et al.*, 2001; Domingo-Roura, 2002; Stone & Cook, 2002; Kyle *et al.*, 2003; Gomez-Moliner *et al.*, 2004; Marmi *et al.*, 2004; Sato *et al.*, 2004; Sommer & Benecke, 2004; Vercillo *et al.*, 2004; Colli *et al.*, 2005; Lucentini *et al.*, 2006; Pilot *et al.*, 2006; Sato *et al.*, 2006; Ruiz-Gonzales *et al.*, 2007; Pertoldi *et al.*, 2008; Rozhnov *et al.*, 2008).

TAXONOMY AND DISTRIBUTION

Pine marten (*Martes martes*, Linnaeus 1758) belongs of the family Mustelidae, the largest and most-diversified taxon of the order Carnivora. Mustelids are widely distributed in all geographical areas including Europe, Asia, Africa and America, indicating a great adaptive capability in different habitats from the arctic zone to tropical rainforests (Sato *et al.*, 2003). Mustelid phylogeny has been recently investigated by Sato and colleagues (2003) using nucleotide sequences of the nuclear interphoreceptor retinoid binding protein (IRBP) and mitochondrial cytochrome b genes. Their data support the monophyletic hypothesis for the genus *Martes,* although other investigators reported evidence supporting its paraphyly (Hosoda *et al.*, 2000). The genus *Martes* comprises 7 species: *M. americana* (American marten), *M. flavigula* (Yellow-Throated marten), *M. foina* (Beech or Stone marten), *M. martes* (Pine marten or European marten), *M. melampus* (Japanese marten), *M. pennanti* (Fisher) and *M. zibellina* (Sable) (Buskirk, 1994). Their distribution and abundance are strongly influenced by habitat change resulting from forestry and agricultural practices (Brainerd *et al.*, 1994; Kryštufek, 2000; Messenger & Birks, 2000; Proulx *et al.*, 2004), and the resiliency of populations to trapping and hunting pressure (Banci & Proulx, 1999). It is, therefore, important to regularly monitor the distribution of *Martes* species across their range to assess the effects of human activities on population changes, to recognize information gaps, to develop effective research programs, and to implement sound management programs that will ensure the future of these species. Among these seven species, pine marten can be distinguished on the basis of color pattern morphology and osteometric characters. Pine marten has a long body, a dark brown coat and a yellow-orange throat patch. Limbs are short and robust, semi-plantigrads, pentadactils and with semi-retractile nails. Furthermore, this species has a well developed tail representing circa half of the head-body length. The muzzle is elongated with little and rounded auricles (Macdonald & Barrett, 1995) (Fig. 1). The ethological characterization shows crepuscolar and nocturnal activities of this semi-arboricolar climber species (Stubbe, 1993), a facultative carnivorous characterized by a very large food spectrum spectrum. It is a solitary species and common dormitories were found just in rare cases. A separation between female and male home ranges was found, even though frequently such home ranges could be partially or completely super-imposable (Macdonald & Barrett, 1995; Stubbe, 1993).

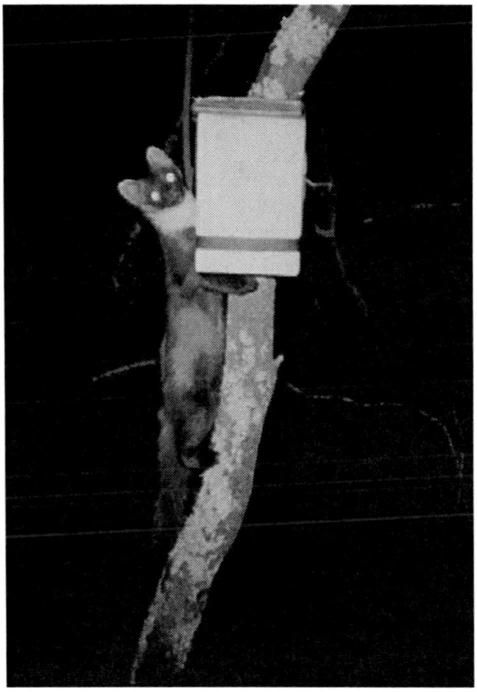

Figure 1. Pine marten.

Pine marten has a palaeartic distribution, with a broad diffusion in Western Europe (Mitchell-Jones *et al.*, 1999; Temple & Terry, 2007) (Fig. 2). It is found in a variety of habitat types including insular wooded areas and shrublands (Clevenger, 1993, De Marinis & Masseti, 1993), alpine shrublands with coniferous and broad-leaved stands (Fornasari *et al.*, 2000), lowland deciduous forests (Proulx *et al.*, 2004), mesic pine stands (Fedyk *et al.*, 1984,

Jedrzejewski *et al.,* 1993), and spruce-dominated forests (Pulliainen, 1984; Brainerd *et al.,* 1994).

Formerly widespread in Britain, pine marten declined because of habitat loss and persecution and is now mainly confined to northern Scotland, with small, relict populations surviving in parts of England and Wales. Elsewhere in Britain, populations remain isolated, vulnerable, and difficult to monitor (Messenger & Birks, 2000). In Belgium, pine marten is restricted to southern regions (Libois, 1983). In Finland, it is present in Lapland, at the northern limit of its range (Pulliainen, 1984) and in the central and southern forests of Norway (Helldin, 2000; Ryvarden, 2001). Pine marten is present throughout Sweden, Lithuania (Mickevicius & Baranauskas, 1992), Latvia (Ozolins & Pilats, 1995), the Czech Republic (Andera & Hanzal, 1996) and Poland, with no apparent change in distribution over the last 20 years. It occurs in northern Spain (Clevenger, 1993) and in France (Labrid, 1986) with the exception of the southwest. It is not yet considered a resident species of Portugal (Santos-Reis, 1983), while insular populations occur in the Balearic Islands of Minorca and Majorca (Clevenger, 1993). In Italy, the species is present in the forested areas of the peninsula, with a distribution that appears to be very fragmented; insular populations are also present in Sardinia, Sicily and Elba (De Marinis & Masseti, 1993; De Marinis *et al.,* 2000). In Switzerland, pine marten is believed to be widespread as well as throughout the forested regions of Germany, Austria and Hungary; it is present throughout Luxembourg and Corsica, its distribution in the Netherlands is patchy while in Denmark it is a rare species (Proulx *et al.*, 2004).

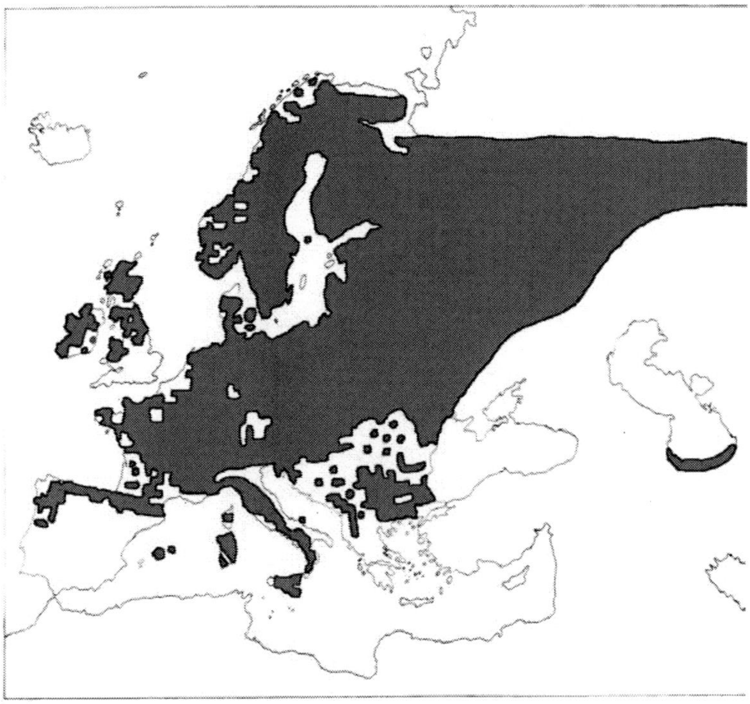

Figure 2. European distribution of pine marten (red).

It is likely that the marked difference between the high diffusion in the north-east and the decline of populations in the rest of Europe is due to deforestation, habitat fragmentation, trapping and accidental killing (Mitchell-Jones *et al.*, 1999; Temple & Terry, 2007). For these reasons the actual conservation state (see below) justifies the fact that pine marten is actually cited in the International Convention of Berna (Appendix III) and in the Habitat Directive 92/43/CEE (Annex V) and is considered a species under risk.

While information about pine marten populations is limited, few research and management programs are evaluating population monitoring techniques, distribution, reintroduction, reproduction, mortality and dispersal, and general ecology (Proulx et al., 2004). The reason for the lack of this type of data is mainly due to the fact that most common wild-biological methods, such as direct observations and telemetry, are not applicable to elusive nocturnal pine marten, therefore the collection of individual data are difficult to obtain as well as the exact determination of population size.

RELATIONSHIPS BETWEEN *MARTES MARTES* AND *MARTES FOINA*

In the genus *Martes*, five species (*M. americana*, *M. foina*, *M. martes*, *M. melampus* and *M. zibellina*) are morphologically very similar (Macdonald, 1984). Two of them, *M. foina* and *M. martes*, are sympatric in a vast part of Europe (Mitchell-Jones *et al.*, 1999; Temple & Terry, 2007).

One of the major criticisms concerning the management and conservation of this species is the difficulty to distinguish it from a "twin species", the beech marten (*M. foina*). These mustelids are usually very difficult to distinguish on the basis of qualitative external morphological characters (Anderson, 1970; Labrid, 1986; Reig, 1992), even though they are not the most closely related species within the genus *Martes* (Stone & Cook, 2002; Sato *et al.*, 2004; Marmi *et al.*, 2004).

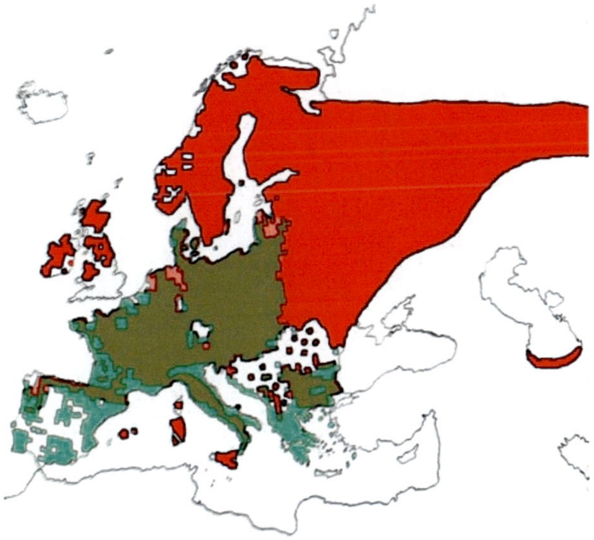

Figure 3. Superimposition of pine marten (red) and beech marten (light green) distributions (dark green).

These species exhibit differences in habitat use: pine marten is strictly associated with forest habitats and has a patchy, fragmented geographical distribution, whereas beech marten is more or less continuously distributed over a wide range of natural, semi-natural, and even urban habitats (Reig, 1992; Proulx *et al.*, 2004). Furthermore, in several European regions they share the same trophic niche (Bermejo & Guitian, 2000; Goszczynski, 1976 and 1986; Marchesi & Mermod, 1989; Marchesi *et al.*, 1989). It has been observed that beech marten is absent in northern Europe, while it is widespread and abundant in central and southern Europe, whereas pine marten is diffused in northern and central Europe and it is rare or absent in the south. Where they are both present, they are in sympatry (Mitchell-Jones *et al.*, 1999) (Fig. 3).

Several authors analyzed the alimentary behaviour of pine and beech martens in Europe (Bermejo & Guitian, 2000; Genovesi, Secchi & Boitani, 1996; Goszczynski, 1976 and 1986; Helldin, 2000; Lode, 1994; Marchesi & Mermod, 1989; Marchesi *et al.*, 1989; Ortega *et al.*, 2002; Posłuszny *et al.*, 2007; Pulliainen & Ollinmaki, 1996; Serafini & Lovari, 1993; Waechter, 1975). Collected data underlined that the diets of these two carnivores is constituted by several different food categories: mammals, birds, invertebrates, eggs, fruits and so on.

A detailed analysis of these data showed that in the Mediterranean area they prefer fruits (Bermejo & Guitian, 2000; Genovesi, Secchi & Boitani, 1996; Ortega *et al.*, 2002; Serafini & Lovari, 1993), while in continental areas the main food are mammals (Goszczynski, 1976 and 1986; Helldin, 2000; Lode, 1994; Marchesi & Mermod, 1989; Marchesi *et al.*, 1989; Pulliainen & Ollinmaki, 1996) (Tab. 1).

Table 1. Food categories of pine and beech marten in Continental and Mediterranean Europe

CONTINENTAL			
FINLAND	Pulliainen & Ollinmaki 1996	Pine marten	MAMMALS
SWEDEN	Helldin 2000	Pine marten	MAMMALS
POLAND	Goszczynski 1986	Martens	MAMMALS
SWITZERLAND	Marchesi & Mermod 1989	Pine marten	MAMMALS
	Marchesi *et al.* 1989	Beech marten	FRUITS
NORTH OF FRANCE	Lode 1994	Beech marten	MAMMALS
MEDITERRANEAN			
ITALY	Genovesi *et al.* 1996; Serafini & Lovari 1993	Beech marten	FRUITS
N-W SPAIN	Bermejo & Guitian 2000	Martens	FRUITS
BALEARICS (Minorca)	Clevenger 1993	Pine marten	MAMMALS
BALEARICS (Mallorca)	Ortega *et al.* 2002	Pine marten	FRUITS

Goszczynski (1976) shows that the two species feed equally on fruits and animals: in spring-summer mammals are preferred, particularly little rodents, while in autumn-winter the diet is composed mainly by fruits. A recent research conducted in Poland by Posłuszny *et al.* (2007) indicates a polyphagous character both of beech marten and pine marten. Both martens utilized a wide array of food, especially rodents, fruits, birds and insects. The food niche of both species of marten highly overlapped (O = 0.83 and O = 0.70 for percentage of occurrence and biomass, respectively). Such trophic niche superimposition between pine and beech marten is highly frequent. Nevertheless, an advantage of beech marten is the possibility to feed on food found in anthropic areas (Marchesi *et al.*, 1989).

In Europe several researches on pine and beech marten were performed (Anderson, 1970; Birks, 2002; Heptner & Naumov, 1974; Labrid, 1986; Libois & Waechter, 1991; Saint Girons, 1973; Streuli, 1932; Stubbe, 1993b,a; Waechter, 1975). One of the most studied aspects is the osteometry (Altuna, 1973; Gerasimov, 1985; Hartung, 1980; Reig, 1992; Rode & Didier, 1944). Furthermore, some characters, such as the throat patch and *baculum,* are considered diagnostic for species characterization (Anderson, 1970; Didier, 1947; Gerasimov, 1985; Labrid, 1986; Libois & Waechter, 1991; Reig, 1992; Streuli, 1932; Stubbe, 1993b,a).

As reported below, recently several molecular techniques to distinguish pine and beech martens were performed (Birks *et al.*, 2004; Broekhuizen, 2006; Davison *et al.*, 2002; Lucentini *et al.*, 2007).

On the basis of the reported consideration, in 2002 in our laboratory was started a research aiming to apply and compare the morphological and molecular species distinction techniques. To date, 122 *Martes* samples were analyzed: 92 *in carne* and 30 living individuals subdivided in 114 adults and 8 sub-adults.

The classification of individuals as pine or beech martens followed a 3-step procedure where animals were assigned to one species or the other on the basis of:

- Coat color and marking patterns;
- Relative *Baculum* Index (*B*I);
- PCR-RFLP mtDNA analysis.

Coat Color and Marking Patterns

Six characters diagnostic for the species-specific taxonomic discrimination between pine and beech marten were analysed:

1. color of *rhinarium* (hairless area of roughened skin at the tip of the snout) (Libois & Waechter 1991, Stubbe 1993a,b);
2. color and shape of throat patch (Anderson 1970, Labrid 1986, Libois & Waechter 1991, Stubbe 1993a,b);
3. muzzle and face color between nose and eyes, and between eyes and ears (Anderson 1970, Libois & Waechter 1991);
4. color of the *pinnae* (Libois & Waechter 1991);
5. color of the body sides (Anderson 1970, Libois & Waechter 1991, Stubbe 1993a,b);
6. color of the pads (Stubbe 1993a,b).

The analyses of such characters defined, for the Italian sample, 15 chromatic patterns, 3 more than those already known from the literature on the six discrimination points reported above. In particular, 2 new patterns were found for the *rhinarium* and 1 for the color of the pads.

Relative Length of the *baculum* (*B*I)

Furthermore, on the basis of data of several authors reporting that the *baculum* length can be used to distinguish pine from beech martens (Didier 1947, Saint Girons 1973, Heptner & Naumov 1974, Waechter 1975, Hartung 1980, Labrid 1986, Libois & Waechter 1991, Stubbe 1993a,b) the bacula of 54 adult males was analyzed.

Although 14 specimens had *baculum* lengths within the range described for pine martens (da 38.9 a 46.0 mm), and 23 for beech martens (range da 51.0 a 70.5 mm), the remaining 17 samples showed intermediate values and were difficult to assign to either species. We suggest that this value should be standardized with respect to body size, and thus that a *Baculum* Index be used.

The *Baculum* Index (*B*I) was calculated as (Head + Body length)/Length of the *Baculum*.

One group of marten specimens had a *B*I ranging from 9.52 to 11.17 mm (10.28±0.16 mm) whereas another group had values ranging from 6.24 to 8.10 mm (7.37±0.2 mm). These data permitted the separation of all the males into 2 distinct groups: 31 and 23 individuals (Fig. 4).

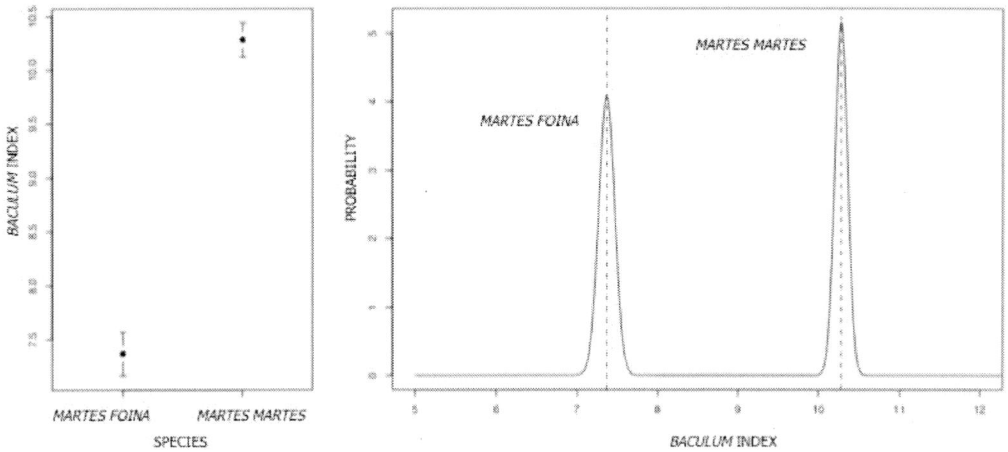

Figure 4. *Baculum* Index (*B*I) values for pine and beech marten.

PCR-RFLP mtDNA Analysis

The difficulty to distinguish these two species, due to the great morphological similarity reported above, was partially solved by a molecular approach based on PCR-RFLP performed by Vercillo and colleagues (2004). The entire sample was analyzed, extracting DNAs from muscle or hairs with a procedure performed in our laboratory for conservative samples

(Lucentini *et al.*, 2006 a,b and 2007). A 218bp Cytb fragment was digested by means of *Alu*I restriction enzyme, observing a cutting activity just for beech marten, for which two bands are clearly visible after separation on agarose gel (Fig. 5).

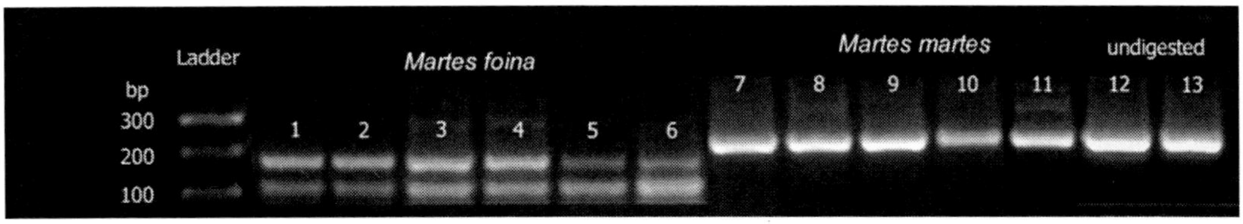

Figure 5. *Alu*I digestion patterns: Lanes 1–6, samples of *M. foina*; lanes 7–11, samples of *M. Martes*; lanes 12 and 13, undigested PCR products of samples 1 and 7, respectively.

The taxonomic attribution is currently performed in our laboratory using these three steps in the order in which they are shown (Fig. 6).

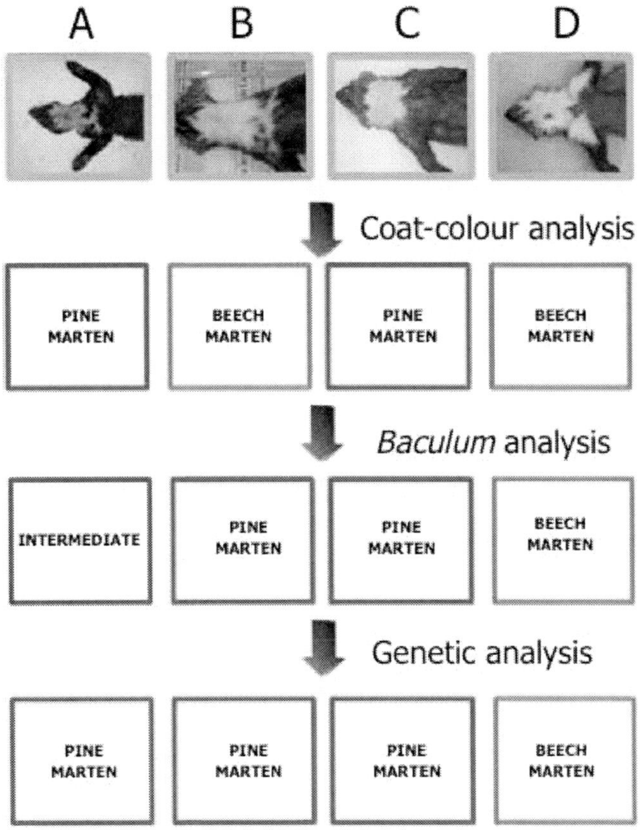

Figure 6. Three-point species attribution performed for pine and beech marten

This figure clearly shows that the species attribution based on coat color defined 48 samples as pine marten and 74 as beech marten. Two of these beech marten resulted, after the genetic characterization, pine marten; thus the coat color and marking patterns analysis may produce erroneous attribution ($p = 0.016$). On this basis an evaluation of the analysis of the six morphological characters was done, underlining that the most reliable are the throat patch color and shape (100% of correct attributions for beech marten and 96% for pine marten) and the color of the body sides (100% of correct attributions for beech marten and 86% for pine marten). The less reliable characters are the *rhinarium* color (10% of correct attributions for beech marten and 86% for pine marten) and the pads color (78% of correct attributions for beech marten and 70% for pine marten).

The subsequent RFLP analysis attributed 31 samples to pine martens and 23 samples to beech martens. In this study, this resulted in a 100% correct classification.

MOLECULAR ANALYSES

To date, there are several molecular methodologies specifically performed and currently used to distinguish pine from beech marten (Colli *et al.*, 2005; Domingo-Roura, 2002; Sato *et al.*, 2004; 2006; Pilot *et al.*, 2006; Fernandez *et al.*, 2007; Ruiz-Gonzales *et al.*, 2007; Rozhnov *et al.*, 2008). Some of them are similar to the one performed in our laboratory and are based on a PCR-RFLP approach (Colli *et al.*, 2005; Ruiz-Gonzalez *et al.*, 2007). Several authors, indeed, based genetic identification of species on direct comparison of particular sequences, as, for example, of APOB, IRBP, Cyt b or RAG1 gene sequences (Sato *et al.*, 2006; Rozhnov *et al.*, 2008). This approach is really sensible and accurate. Nevertheless, the already mentioned PCR-RFLP method has at least two advantages, as compared to the comparison of sequences: it is extremely rapid and very cheap; two aspects that are of primary importance for any extensive and evolutional study (Vercillo *et al.*, 2004; Colli *et al.*, 2005; Ruiz-Gonzalez *et al.*, 2007).

The use of fixate alleles in the genetic distinction of two or more species deserves a particular mention. Microsatellites are among the most powerful molecular markers and having several advantages: they are easy to analyse, highly variable, widespread in eukaryotic genomes and currently used for phylogenetic, phylogeographic and demographic purposes (Goldstein & Schlotterer, 1999; Domingo-Roura *et al.*, 2002; Lucentini *et al.*, 2006). Two researches were focused on the application of microsatellites in the genetic distinction of martens using the fixation of different alleles in different species (Domingo-Roura *et al.*, 2002; Pilot *et al.*, 2006). In particular, it was found that, for the locus *Mel*10, beech marten exhibits just the 128bp allele, while pine marten exhibits alleles in the range of 153-166bp (Domingo-Roura *et al.*, 2002; Pilot *et al.*, 2006). Analogously, Pilot and colleagues (2006) discovered that the *Ma*18 locus is characterized by alleles in the 146-152 range for pine marten and in the range 176-200 for beech marten. Microsatellites too have the advantage of being cheap and sensible, but they might present geographic variability. To avoid problems related to mutations in allele size related to the area of origin, the application of microsatellite must be preceded by a procedure validation based on samples of sure taxonomic attribution.

This short excursus underlined that there are, to date, several researches focuses on the application of molecular markers to the genetic identification of species or to phylogenetic and phylogeographic analyses. Nevertheless, just one recent record reports a spatial-temporal genetic population study in the Danish pine marten populations from the Jutland peninsula and from the island of Sealand; it was recently performed using 11 microsatellite markers applied to modern and historical samples (Pertoldi *et al.*, 2008). These authors found significant genetic divergence between the two sample groups, indicating changes in the genetic composition over time, and between two groups of modern samples, indicating genetic drift. It is particularly important that no deviations from the Hardy-Weinberg equilibrium were found, indicating no sub-structuring and, presumably, homogeneous and stabile populations. The scarcity of knowledge on martens could be partially ascribed to several aspects of samples drawing and recognition. It is likely that the development of methodologies ensuring the correct taxonomic attribution mentioned above will represent, in the future, a valid scientific basis for population genetic studies. These studies could be a key-tool to understand and define the real effective diffusion, population sizes and conservation state of pine marten in Europe.

CONCLUSION

The presence of pine marten in forested areas and, concurrently, their absence in treeless areas, raises concerns about the effects of the forest-cutting development in several countries. Data from Spain, France, Italy, Austria, Switzerland, Albania, Croatia, Bulgaria, Greece and Turkey have identified habitat loss resulting from forestry practices as a major concern for pine marten conservation (Proulx *et al.*, 2004; Temple & Terry, 2007).

Although many respondents were unable to describe marten-habitat relationships, it appears that forested areas continue to be the main strongholds of this species. In France, Switzerland, Austria, Hungary, Bulgaria, Yugoslavia, Italy, Sweden, Poland, Lithuania, Albania, and Croatia, marten populations reach higher densities in mature or old coniferous, deciduous or mixed forests (Proulx *et al.*, 2004; Temple & Terry, 2007).

Hunting or trapping of pine martens is permitted in 13 out of 25 countries. In most of them, forested regions still cover large areas, and most marten populations are considered stable. In most countries where pine marten is protected, population trends are either increasing due to habitat improvement, or are unknown. In the latter case, pine marten is so rare that respondents did not want to risk an assessment (Proulx et al., 2004; Temple & Terry, 2007). There is a need to develop cost-effective detection, survey, and monitoring methods for pine marten populations, particularly those at low densities. This should be done in parallel with the development of recovery programs for sparse populations inhabiting fragmented landscapes. The restoration and linkage of woodlands should be promoted to maximize the viability of populations. Management should also include measures to increase the availability of arboreal cavities suitable as natal dens (Proulx et al., 2004).

Owing the ongoing growth of the human population and the associated environmental impact, fragmentation of marten habitat and, as a result, the fragmentation of marten populations, will become an ever-growing important issue This means that genetic investigations can indicate whether changes in landscape management are urgently needed, especially when more primers are developed (Broekhuizen, 2006).

The future perspectives should be performed specifically to clarify the unknown aspects of pine marten's biology. First of all, it is fundamental to define whether pine and beech marten could produce hybrids. There is evidence about hybrids between Mustelids species (Amstislavsky & Ternovskaya, 2000), in particular there are documented hybrids between *M. zibellina* and *M. martes* (Grackov, 1994) and between *M. martes* and *M. americana* (Kyle et al., 2003). Our results on *baculum* length suggest that there might be anatomical difficulties for a pine marten male to fecundate a beech marten female. Furthermore, a recent perspective on Mustelids phylogenesis underlined that these two species are not the most similar across these animal family (Koepfli et al., 2008). Thus, the phylogenetic distance suggests that hybridization between pine and beech marten might be verified through *in vivo* tests and genetic analyses.

Other fundamental aspects that should be clarified are the population genetics and population dynamics of pine marten in Europe. The research begun by Pertoldi and colleagues (2008) should be absolutely extended to the whole of Europe, comparing actual and historical samples and defining gene flow across populations and their effective population sizes. Such data might represent a valid and useful tool to assess the effective conservation state and the effective species trend of pine marten in Europe.

REFERENCES

Altuna, J. (1973). Distincion craneal entre la marta (*Martes martes*) y la foina (*Martes foina*). *Mammalia, 25,* 33–38.

Amstislavsky, S., & Ternovskaya, Y. (2000). Reproduction in mustelids. *Animal Reproduction Science 60 – 61,* 571 – 581.

Andera, M., & Hanzal, V. (1996). Atlas of the mammals of the Czech Republic. II. Carnivores (*Carnivora*). Praha: National Museum.

Anderson, E. (1970). Quaternary evolution of the genus Martes (Carnivora, Mustelidae). *Acta Zoologica Fennica, 130,* 1–132.

Banci, V., & Proulx, G. (1999). Resiliency of furbearers to trapping in Canada. In G. Proulx (Ed.), *Mammal trapping* (175–203). Sherwood Park, Alberta: Alpha Wildlife Research & Management Ltd.

Bermejo, T., & Guitian, J. (2000). Fruit consumption by foxes and martens in NW Spain in autumn: a comparison of natural and agricultural areas. *Folia Zoologica, 49(2),* 89–92.

Birks, J. D. S. (2002). The Pine Marten. London: The Mammal Society.

Birks, J., Messenger, J., Braithwaite, T., Davison, A., Brookes, R., & Strachan, C. (2004). Are scat surveys a reliable method for assessing distribution and population status of pine marten?. In D.J., Harrison, A.K., Fuller, & G., Proulx, (Ed.). *Martens and fishers (Martes) in human-altered environments: an international perspective* (235-252). New York : Springer Science.

Brainerd, S. M., Helldin, J. O., Lindström, E., & Rolstad, J. (1994). Eurasian pine martens and old industrial forest in southern boreal Scandinavia. In S. W. Buskirk, A. S. Harestad, M. G. Raphael, & R. A. Powell (Ed.), *Martens, sables, and fishers: biology and conservation* (343–354). New York: Cornell University Press, Ithaca.

Broekhuizen, S. (2006). *Martes* issues in the 21ST Century: lessons to learn from Europe. In M. Santos-Reis, J. D. S. Birks, E. C. O'Doherty, & G. Proulx (Ed.), Martes in Carnivore Communities (3-19). Sherwood Park, Alberta: Alpha Wildlife Pubblications.

Buskirk, S. W. (1994). Introduction to the Genus *Martes.* In S. W. Buskirk, A. S. Harestad, M. G. Raphael, & R. A. Powell (Ed.), *Martens, sables, and fishers: biology and conservation* (1–10). New York: Cornell University Press, Ithaca.

Clevenger, A. P. (1993). The European pine marten *Martes martes* in the Balearic Islands, Spain. *Mammal Review, 23(2),* 65–72.

Colli, L., Cannas, R., Deiana, M. R., Gandolfi, G., & Tagliavini J. (2005). Identification of mustelids (*Carnivora*: *Mustelidae*) by mitochondrial DNA markers. *Mammalian Biology, 70(6),* 384-389.

Davison, A., Birks, J., Brookes, R.C., Messenger, J.E., & Griffiths, H.I. (2001). Mitochondrial philogeography and population history of pine martens (*Martes martes*) compared with polecats (*Mustela putorius*). *Molecular Ecology, 10,* 2479–2488.

De Marinis, A. M., & Masseti, M. (1993). Pine marten *Martes martes* on the Island of Elba. *Small Carnivore Conservation, 8,* 13.

De Marinis, A. M., Genovesi, P., & Spagnesi, M. (2000). Pine marten. In M. Spagnesi, S. Toso & A. M. De Marinis (Ed.), *Italian mammals* (158–159). Roma: Ministero dell'Ambiente, Servizio Conservazione della Natura and Istituto Nazionale per la Fauna Selvatica A. Ghigi.

Didier, R. (1947). Etude systématique de l'os pénien des mammiféres. Ordre des Carnivores II. Famille des mustélides (1). *Mammalia, 11,* 30–43.

Domingo-Roura, X. (2002). Genetic distinction of marten species by fixation of a microsatellite region. *Journal of Mammalogy, 83(3),* 907–912.

Fedyk, S., Gegczynska, Z., Pucek, M., Raczynski, J., & Sikorski M. D. (1984). Winter penetration by mammals of different habitats in the Biebrza Valley. *Acta Theriologica, 29,* 317–336.

Fernandes, C. A., Ginja, C., Pereira, I., Tenreiro, R., Bruford, M. W., & Santos-Reis, M. (2008). Species-specific mitochondrial DNA markers for identification of non-invasive samples from sympatric carnivores in the Iberian Peninsula. *Conservation Genetics, 9,* 681–690

Fornasari, L., Bani, L., Bonfanti, I., De Carli, E., & Massa R. (2000). A spatial analysis of mustelid distributions in northern Italy. In H. I. Griffiths (Ed.), *Management and conservation aspects of smallcarnivore: human interactions* (201–215). Leiden: Backhuys Publishers.

Genovesi, P., Secchi, M., & Boitani L. (1996). Diet of stone martes: an example of ecological flexibility. *Journal of Zoology (London), 238,* 545–555.

Gerasimov, S. (1985). Species and sex determination of *Martes martes* and *Martes foina* by use of systems of craniometrical indices developed by stepwise discriminant analysis. *Mammalia, 49,* 235–248.

Goldstein, D. B., & Schlotterer, C. (1999). Microsatellites: Evolution and Applications. Oxford: Oxford University Press.

Gòmez-Moliner, B.J., Cabria, M.T., Rubines, J., Garin, I., Madeira, M.J., Elejalde, A., Aihartza, J., Fournier, P. & Palazòn, S. (2004). PCR-RFLP identification of mustelid species: European mink (*Mustela lutreola*), American mink (*M. vison*) and polecat (*M. putorius*) by analysis of excremental DNA. *Journal of Zoology, 262(3),* 311–316.

Goszczynski, J. (1976). Composition of the Food of Martens. *Acta Theriologica, 21(36),* 527–534.

Goszczynski, J. (1986). Diet of Foxes and Martens in Central Poland. *Acta Theriologica, 31(36),* 491–506.

Grakov, N.N. (1994). Kidus - a hybrid of the sable and the pine marten. *Lutreola, 3,* 1–4.

Hartung, J. (1980). Zur Alterbestimmung bei den einheimischen jagdbaren Musteliden anhand des Penisknochen (On the age determination of authocthonous hunted Mustelids by the mean of Penic bone). *Beitr. Jagd. und Wildforsch, 11,* 350–359.

Helldin, J. (2000). Seasonal diet of pine marten *Martes martes* in southern boreal Sweden. *Acta Theriologica, 45(3),* 409–420.

Heptner, V., & Naumov, N. (1974). *Die Säugetiere der Sowjetunion (The mammals of the Soviet Union).* Volume II. Iena: Fischer Verlag.

Hosoda, T., Suzuki, H., Harada, M., Tsuchiya, K., Han, S.H., Zhang, Y., Kryukov, A.P., & Lin L.K. (2000). Evolutionary trends of the mitochondrial lineage differentiation in species of genera *Martes* and *Mustela*. *Genes & Genetic Systems, 75(5),* 259–267.

Koepfli, K. P., Deere, K. A., Slater, G. J., Begg, C., Begg, K., Grassman, L., Lucherini, M., Veron, G., & Wayne, R. K. (2008). Multigene phylogeny of the Mustelidae: resolving relationships, tempo and biogeographic history of a mammalian adaptive radiation. *BMC Biology, 6,* 10.

Kryštufek, B. (2000). Mustelids in the Balkans – small carnivores in the European biodiversity hot-spot. In H. I. Griffiths, (Ed). *Management and conservation aspects of small carnivore: human interactions* (281–294). Leiden: Backhuys Publishers.

Kyle, C.J., Davison, A., & Strobeck, C. (2003). Genetic structure of European pine martens (*Martes martes*), and evidence for introgression with *Martes americana* in England. *Conservation Genetics, 4,* 179–188.

Labrid, M. (1986). Encyclopedie des Carnivores de France: La martre (*Martes martes*). Puceul: S.F.E.P.M.

Libois, R. (1983). *Protégeons nos mammifères. Animaux menacés en Wallonie.* Gembloux: Editions Duculot.

Libois, R. & Waechter, A. (1991). Encyclopedie des Carnivores de France: La fouine (*Martes foina*). Puceul: S.F.E.P.M.

Lode, T. (1994). Feeding habits of the stone marten *Martes foina* and environmental factors in Western France. *Zeitschrift für Säugetierkunde, 59,* 189–191

Lucentini L., Caporali S., Palomba A., Lancioni H., Panara F. 2006. A comparison of conservative DNA extraction methods from fins and scales of freshwater fish: a useful tool for conservation genetics. *Conserv. Genet.* 6:1009-1012.

Lucentini L., Palomba A., Gigliarelli L., Lancioni H., Natali M., Panara F. 2006. Microsatellite polymorphism in Italian populations of northern pike (*Esox lucius* L.). *Fish. Res.* 80:251-262.

Lucentini, L., Vercillo, F., Palomba, A., Panara, F., & Ragni, B. (2007). A PCR-RFLP method on faecal samples to distinguish *Martes martes*, *Martes foina*, *Mustela putorius* and *Vulpes vulpes*. *Conservetion Genetics, 8,* 757–759.

Macdonald, D. (1984). Encyclopaedia of mammals. London: Allen & Unwin.

Macdonald, D., & Barrett, P. (1995). Guide complete des Mammifères de France et d'Europe. Lausanne: Delachaux et Niestlé.

Marchesi, P., Lachat, N., Lienhard, R., Debiéve, P., & Mermod, C. (1989). Comparaison des régime alimentaires de la fouine (*Martes foina* Erxl.) et de la martre (*Martes martes* L.) dans une région du Jura Suisse. *Revue Suisse de Zoologie, 96(2),* 281–296.

Marchesi, P., & Mermod, C. (1989). Régime alimentaire de la martre (*Martes martes* L.) dans le Jura Suisse (*Mammalia:Mustelidae*). *Revue Suisse de Zoologie, 96(1),* 127–146.

Marmi, J., Lopez-Giraldez, J.F., & Domingo-Roura, X. (2004). Phylogeny, evolutionary history and taxonomy of the *Mustelidae* based on sequences of the cytochrome b gene and a complex repetitive flanking region. *Zoologica Scripta, 33(6),* 481–499.

Messenger, J. E., & Birks, J. D. S. (2000). Monitoring the very rare: pine marten populations in England and Wales. In H. I. Griffiths (Ed.), *Management and conservation aspects of smallcarnivore: human interactions* (217–230). Leiden: Backhuys Publishers.

Mickevicius, E., & Baranauskas K. (1992). Status, abundance, and distribution of mustelids in Lithuania. *Small Carnivore Conservation, 6,* 11–14.

Mitchell-Jones, A., Amori, G., Bogdanowicz, W., Krystufek, B., Reinjnders, P., Spitzenberger, F., Stubbe, M., Thissen, J., Vohralik, V., & Zima J. (1999). Atlas of European Mammals. London: Academic Press.

Ortega, T., Seguí, B., Barceló, A., Pons, G. X., Bover, P., Palmer, M., & Manera, J. (2002). Estudi alimentari del mart (*Martes martes* L.) a Andratx (Mallorca, Illes Balears). *Bolletin Societat d'Història Natural de les Balears, 45,* 199-216.

Pertoldi, C., Barker, J.S.F., Madsen, A.B., Jørgensen, H., Randi, E., Muñoz, J., Baagoe, H.J. & Loeschcke, V. (2008). Spatio-temporal population genetics of the Danish pine marten (*Martes martes*). *Biological Journal of the Linnean Society, 93,* 457–464.

Pilot, M., Gralak, B., Goszczyński, J., & Posłuszny, M. (2007). A method of genetic identification of pine marten (*Martes martes*) and stone marten (*Martes foina*) and its application to faecal samples. *Journal of Zoology, 271 (2),* 140-147.

Posłuszny, M., Pilot, M., Goszczyński, J., & Gralak, B. (2007). Diet of sympatric pine marten (*Martes martes*) and stone marten (*Martes foina*) identified by genotyping of DNA from faeces. *Annales Zoologici Fennici, 44,* 269–284

Proulx, G., Aubry, K., Birks, J., Buskirk, S., Fortin, C., Frost, H., Krohn, W., Mayo, L., Monakhov, V., Payer, D., Saeki, M., Santos-Reis, M., Weir, R., & Zielinski, W. (2004). World Distribution and Status of the Genus Martes in 2000. In D. J. Harrison, A. K. Fuller, & G. Proulx (Ed.), *Martens and Fishers (Martes) in Human-Altered Environments* (21-76). Springer-Verlag

Pulliainen, E. (1984). Use of the home range by pine martens *(Martes martes* L.). *Acta Zoologica Fennica, 171,* 271–274.

Pulliainen, E., & Ollinmaki, P. (1996). A long-term study of the winter food niche of the pine marten *Martes martes* in northern boreal Finland. *Acta Theriologica, 41(4),* 337–352.

Reig, S. (1992). Geographic variation in pine marten (*Martes martes*) and beech marten (*Martes foina*) in Europe. *Journal of Mammology, 73,* 744–769.

Rode, P., & Didier, R. (1944). Difference entre la tete osseuse de la martre et celle de la fouine. *Mammalia, 8,*127–132.

Rozhnov, V. V., Morgulis, A. L., Kholodova, M. V., & Meshcherskii, I. G. (2008). The Use of Molecular Genetic Methods for Identification of Mustelid Species by Analyzing Feces. *Russian Journal of Ecology, 39,* 70–72.

Ruiz-González, A., Rubines, J., Berdión, O., & Gómez-Moliner, B. J. (2008). A non-invasive genetic method to identify the sympatric mustelids pine marten (*Martes martes*) and stone marten (*Martes foina*): preliminary distribution survey on the northern Iberian Peninsula. *European Journal of Wildlife Research, 54,* 253–261.

Ryvarden, L. (2001). La faune et la flore en Norvège. Oslo: Ministry of Foreign Affairs.

Saint Girons, M. (1973). Les mammifères de France et du Bènèlux. Paris: Ed. Doin.

Santos-Reis, M. (1983). Status and distribution of Portuguese mustelids. *Acta Zoologica Fennica, 172,* 213–216.

Sato, J. J., Hosoda, T., Wolsan, M., Tsuchiya, K., Yamamoto, M., & Suzuki, H. (2003). Phylogenetic relationships and divergence times among Mustelids (*Mammalia*: *Carnivora*) based on nucleotide sequences of the Nuclear Interphotoreceptor Retinoid Binding Protein and mitochondrial cytochrome b genes. *Zoological Sciencie 20,* 243–264

Sato, J. J., Hosoda, T., Wolsan, M., & Suzuki, H. (2004). Molecular Phylogeny of Arctoids (*Mammalia*: *Carnivora*) with Emphasis on Phylogenetic and Taxonomic Positions of the Ferret-badgers and Skunks. *Zoological Science, 21,* 111-118.

Sato, J. J., Wolsan, M., Suzuki, H., Hosoda, T., Yamaguchi, Y., Hiyama, K., Kobayashi, M., & Minami, S. (2006). Evidence from nuclear DNA sequences sheds light on the phylogenetic relationships of pinnipedia: singlc origin with affinity to *musteloidea, Zoological Sciencie, 23,* 125–146.

Serafini, P., & Lovari, S. (1993). Food habits and trophic niche overlap of the red fox and stone marten in a Mediterranean rural area. *Acta Theriologica, 38(3),* 233–244.

Sommer, R., & Benecke, N. (2004). Late- and Post-Glacial history of the *Mustelidae* in Europe. *Mammal Review, 34(4),* 249–284.

Stone, K.D., & Cook, J.A. (2002). Molecular evolution of holarctic martens (genus *Martes* and *Mammalia:Carnivora:Mustelidae*). *Molecular Phylogenetics and Evolution, 24,* 169–179.

Streuli, A. (1932). Zur Frage der Artmerkmale und der Bastardierung von Baum- und Steinmarder. *Zeitschr für Saugetierkunde, 7,* 58–72.

Stubbe, M. (1993)a. *Martes foina* (Erxleben, 1758). In M. Stubbe, & F. Krapp, (Eds.), *Handbuch der Säugetiere Europas (Handbook of the mammals of Europe)* (427–479). Wiesbadsen: Aula Verlag,.

Stubbe, M. (1993)b. *Martes martes* (Linneé, 1758). In M. Stubbe, & F. Krapp, (Eds.), *Handbuch der Säugetiere Europas (Handbook of the mammals of Europe)* (427–479). Wiesbadsen: Aula Verlag,.

Temple, H.J., & Terry, A. (2007). The Status and Distribution of European Mammals. Luxembourg: Office for Official Publications of the European Communities.

Vercillo, F., Lucentini, L., Mucci, N., Ragni, B., Randi, E., & Panara, F. (2004). A simple and rapid PCR-RFLP method to distinguishing *Martes martes* and *Martes foina. Conservation Genetics, 5,* 869–871.

Waechter, A. (1975). Ecologie de la fouine en Alsace. *Revue d'Ecologie, Terre et Vie, 29,* 399–457.

In: Endangered Species: New Research
Editors: A. Columbus and L. Kuznetsov
ISBN 978-1-60692-241-5

Chapter 6

NORTHERN PIKE: A SPECIES IN CRISIS?

Lucentini Livia, Palomba Antonella, Gigliarelli Lilia, Sgaravizzi Giada, Ricciolini Claudia, Puletti Maria Elena, Lancioni Hovirag, Lanfaloni Luisa and Panara Fausto
Dipartimento di Biologia Cellulare e Ambientale, Università degli Studi di Perugia
06123 Perugia Italy

ABSTRACT

The systematics of the family Esocidae is essentially based on morphological characters. It points to the existence of five species distributed in Eurasia and North America. Only northern pike (*Esox lucius* Linnaeus, 1758) is present in Europe with a broad geographical and environmental distribution, including most of the northern temperate zones, above 40° latitude up to the Arctic zone, and Italy, Greece and Turkey. Northern pike is one of the most important freshwater fish for recreational and commercial fisheries. In addition, being a big, edible, freshwater top predator, it is a key species for the conservation and management of lakes and rivers ecosystems. Although recent reports indicate a decline in most North American and European populations, northern pike is not yet considered an endangered species and does not appear in the IUNC Red List of Threatened Species (2007 IUNC: www.redlist.org). The effects of overfishing, habitat reduction and fragmentation, anthropic perturbations, climate changes and competition with newly introduced species, have a detrimental impact on northern pike. Furthermore, recent genetic investigations strongly indicate a very low polymorphism in all the populations studied, suggesting a high evolutionary risk for this species. With the aim to manage southern European population, in the last decades of the twentieth century this species was artificially repopulated using fries of unknown origin. This practice has probably introduced new genotypes which, besides polluting autochthonous populations, were not fully adaptable to the environment of destination. Furthermore a great effort should be spent to ensure that these genotypes are not used in artificial repopulation practice based on autochthonous breeders. This manuscript describes the actual conservation and management state of this species in Europe comparing genetic and molecular ecology data obtained for European and North American populations.

INTRODUCTION

Northern pike (*Esox lucius* Linnaeus, 1758), the most diffused Esocidae, is present in Europe with a broad geographical and environmental distribution, including most of the northern temperate zones above 40° latitude, and penetrating in the Arctic zone, and southern Europe, comprising Italy, Greece and Turkey. Northern pike is one of the most important species for recreational and commercial fisheries and for its role as top predator in freshwater ecosystems. As pointed out by Craig (2008), present records indicate this species at the same time as a problem for the management of natural ecosystems, and of which several populations are declining. North American and European populations show a very different conservationistic status. In Europe in particular, the effects of overfishing, habitat reduction and fragmentation, anthropic perturbations, climate changes and competition with newly introduced species, are having a detrimental impact on northern pike population. Furthermore, recent genetic investigations based on different molecular markers strongly indicate a very low polymorphism in all the populations studied, suggesting a high evolutionary risk for this species (Aguilar *et al.*, 2005; Jacobsen *et al.*, 2005; Laikre *et al.*, 2005; Larsen *et al.*, 2005; Lucentini *et al.*, 2006d). Nevertheless, northern pike is not yet considered an endangered species and does not appear in the IUNC Red List of Threatened Species (2007 IUNC: www.redlist.org).

Biodiversity conservation is the main objective of evolutionary and conservation biologists. Genetic variation is one out of three levels of biodiversity recommended by the World Conservation Union (IUNC) for conservation programs (Frankham *et al.*, 2004) and a number of studies demonstrated the importance of genetic analysis in finite wild populations and threatened species (Pinto *et al.*, 2002; Larsen *et al.*, 2005; Hansen *et al.*, 2006). Genetic diversity of species or populations is the result of their evolutionary history and its decrease may reduce their adaptability and surviving potential in a changing environment (Frankham *et al.*, 2004).

With the aim to partially manage southern European populations, in the last decades of the twentieth century this species was artificially repopulated using fries of unknown origin. This practice has probably introduced new genotypes which, besides polluting autochthonous populations, might not be completely adaptable to the environment of destination. Furthermore, a great effort should be spent to ensure that these genotypes are not used in artificial repopulation practice based on autochthonous breeders.

Moreover, genetic drift, inbreeding and gene flow reduction could damage the genetic diversity of small and isolated populations. In fact, conservation biologists attribute a great importance to the knowledge of population size, because small populations could be seriously affected by environmental instability, stochastic demographic change, loss of reproductive habitat, and inbreeding depression (Paschke *et al.*, 2002; Frankham *et al.*, 2004). In particular, inbreeding can affect demographic rates, thus increasing the probability of extinction, directly or through a magnification of non-genetic factors (Miller & Waits, 2003).

This manuscript briefly reviews the present conservation and management state of this species in Europe comparing genetic and molecular ecology data obtained for European and North American populations.

Taxonomy and Distribution

Northern pike (*Esox lucius* Linnaeus 1758) is the only European representative of Esocidae, a monogenetic family composed of only 5 species of freshwater fishes. Recently, the biological and morphological variability of this species raised the doubt that there could be more than one cryptic species, but is was concluded that just one species of northern pike exists (Craig, 2008). Nevertheless, this point underlined the great variability found by several pike researchers. As pointed out by Craig (2008), northern pike's evolution is peculiar from several points of view, including behaviour, ecology and physiology.

One of the aspects underlying this great variability is the environmental richness; northern pike inhabiting lakes and rivers with slow waters, is frequent also in light-briny waters, up to 7-10 in thousand parts, such as the Baltic Sea. Usually, it is a solitary and territorial species (Eklöv, 1995) that uses every part of the freshwater environment; it prefers deep waters in the winter, moving to the surface and to vegetable-rich backdrop during spring and summer. Its relationship with vegetation is very strong (Bry, 1996).

Its geographic distribution is extremely wide; it is present in temperate and temperate-cold zones of the northern hemisphere, in Europe, North America and Asia, from latitude 40° excluding the Arctic zone (Thienemann, 1950; McCarraher, 1961) (Figure 1).

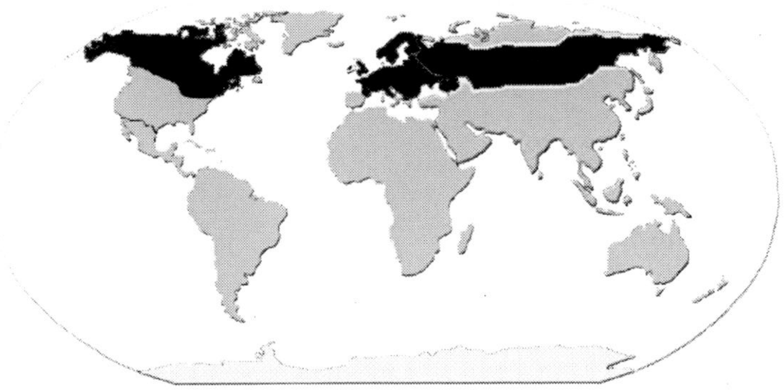

Figure 1. Northern pike wordwide distribution (black).

There are discordant opinions on the origin and distribution of this species; Wilson (1980) described esocid fossils in Paleocenic formation from Alberta and Saskatchenwam underlining the ancient origin of esocids, and suggesting a possible American origin. The analysis of these fossils suggests that *E. lucius* might be the most primitive Esocidae (Raat, 1988). Because of the balance between genetic drift and the origin from different glacial refuges, the analysis of modern northern pike population seems to be insufficient to define the evolutionary history of esocids (Raat, 1988; Nicod *et al.*, 2004; Lucentini *et al.*, 2006d).

Biology

Northern pike is highly variable in size, in relation to environmental conditions, such as water temperature and food availability. One trait of highest variability is the diet composition, mainly based on almost whatever prey is available. The foraging tactic may vary between individuals of similar-size and/or inhabiting similar-habitats, changing for each fish also on the basis of prey abundance or composition (Craig, 2008).

Water temperature and feeding possibility, together with the latitude, influence the sexual maturity (Heushmann, 1957; Toner & Lawler, 1969; Billard, 1996), for which several data, often discordant, are known. Our observations suggest that northern pike, in Central Italy, is sexually mature from the first year of age, while elsewhere just the four years old samples were mature (Nikoloski, 1957). Recorded data suggest that sexual maturity depends on the size of each sample, rather than on the age (see Billard, 1996 for a very interesting synthesis of bibliography about sexual maturity in northern pike). Eggs deposition takes place on aquatic or temporarily submerged plants, with temperature varying from 4° to 23°C (Willemsen, 1959), even though several records suggest that temperatures under 6°C and over 20°C cause death of embryos (Swift, 1965; Hassler, 1982; personal observations). Northern pike development depends on several environmental factors, such as water temperature and salinity and feeding quality and quantity. It was recently observed that larvae growing at lower salinity, other environmental factors being equal, are bigger than those developed in brackish water (Engström *et al.*, 2005). Data about water temperature during development are strongly divergent, even discordant, and several authors suggest that there are other environmental factors, such as water oxygenation, influencing the survival of eggs (Hassler, 1982).

POPULATION GENETICS

Population genetic studies on northern pike were first published using allozyme markers; subsequently nuclear and mitochondrial DNA markers were applied to investigate the genetic diversity of this species. In particular mtDNA analysis (Brzuzan *et al.*, 1998; Maes *et al.*, 2003; Nicod *et al.*, 2004), AFLP (Lucentini *et al.*, 2004; 2008) and microsatellites were used (Miller & Kapuscinski, 1996; 1997; Hansen *et al.*, 1999; Lucentini *et al.*, 2004, 2006d; Aguilar *et al.*, 2005; Jacobsen *et al.*, 2005; Laikre *et al.*, 2005; Larsen *et al.*, 2005). All these approaches underlined a very low genetic variability at both intra and inter-population levels, maybe one of the lowest ever recorded (Brzuzan *et al.*, 1998). Microsatellites appear to be the best way to analyse genetic diversity in northern pike, since values allow the analysis at inter-population or inter-stock levels with statistical significance (Aguilar *et al.*, 2005; Jacobsen *et al.*, 2005; Laikre *et al.*, 2005; Larsen *et al.*, 2005; Lucentini *et al.*, 2006d). Furthermore, microsatellites are a useful molecular approach to measure the effective population size (N_e) of northern pike populations, as verified for two North American (Miller & Kapuscinski 1997; Aguilar *et al.*, 2005) and one Danish (Larsen *et al.*, 2005) populations. The effective population size N_e refers to an ideal population showing the same homozygosity and genetic drift increase rate as the actual population considered (Rieman & Allendorf, 2001; Frankham *et al.*, 2004). Because managing genetic diversity is of the utmost importance in a conservation program, the N_e estimate becomes the key parameter to determine population structure, rates of genetic variation, fixation of deleterious alleles and inbreeding. Census population size (N) is very difficult to measure for most wild species and N_e is strongly affected by several parameters such as sex ratio, family size, number of individuals per generation and generations overlap (Frankham *et al.*, 2004; Nomura, 2005); all of these factors might determine marked deviations from the ideal conditions. To estimate N_e, several genetic methods have been suggested, usually classified as temporal methods since they are based on multiple comparisons across generations. For these reasons, according to the genetic property of interest, different concepts of N_e have been proposed such as the inbreeding effective size N_{ei} and the variance effective size N_{ev} (Wang, 2005). The former is the most widely used: it predicts the heterozygosity decrease rate or the homozygosity increase rate (inbreeding); the latter measures the change variance in gene frequency resulting from one generation of genetic sampling. They can differ deeply in particular populations not under equilibrium (Wang, 2005). There are two main computer-intensive approaches to statistical inference: the Markov chain Monte Carlo (MCMC) and the importance sampling (IS) analyses, both involving sampling of historical records (Beerli & Felsenstein, 2001; Nielsen & Wakeley, 2001; Xu & Fu, 2004).

Some recent researches showed a critical situation for several European populations (Kovács *et al.*, 2001; Lorenzoni *et al.*, 2002; Launey *et al.*, 2003; Jacobsen *et al.*, 2005; Laikre *et al.*, 2005; Larsen *et al.*, 2005; Lucentini *et al.*, 2006d; 2008). Evaluations of populations difficulties can be better understood if a genetic analysis is made. Genetic analysis of ichthyic stock is extremely important and, as underlined by the improvement of conservation and forensic animal genetics, it is fundamental for the evaluation and identification of genetic risks of anthropic or other origin (Shaklee & Currens, 2003).

In the last decade, genetic diversity of northern pike populations has been increasingly studied for several reasons:

- Northern pike is one of the biggest freshwater ecosystems predators of the holoarctic zone;
- It is a relevant resource for recreational and commercial fisheries;
- Some European populations are declining (Kovács *et al.*, 2001; Lorenzoni *et al.*, 2002);
- Different molecular approaches detect low genetic polymorphism (Healy and Mulchay, 1980; Seeb *et al.*, 1987; Brzuzan *et al.*, 1998; Hansen *et al.*, 1999; Nicod *et al.*, 2004; Laikre *et al.*, 2005);
- Effective population size and census population size show a low ratio (Miller & Kapuscinski, 1997).

All these aspects require controlled conservation programs, a management strategy and sustainability based on the knowledge of genetic differentiation of natural pike populations. Microsatellite markers are the most powerful and useful tools for the recognition of genetically distinctive pike populations. Up to now, results of microsatellite analyses were published for pike populations of North America (Miller & Kapuscinski, 1996, 1997; Senanan & Kapuscinski, 2000; Jacobsen *et al.*, 2005), North and Central Europe (Senanan & Kapuscinski, 2000; Launey *et al.*, 2003; Aguilar *et al.*, 2005; Jacobsen *et al.*, 2005; Laikre *et al.*, 2005; Larsen *et al.*, 2005) and Siberia (Senanan & Kapuscinski, 2000). In fact, until 2004 just a few articles about the genetic diversity of northern pike in Europe were published, but since then several articles have been published (Figure 2).

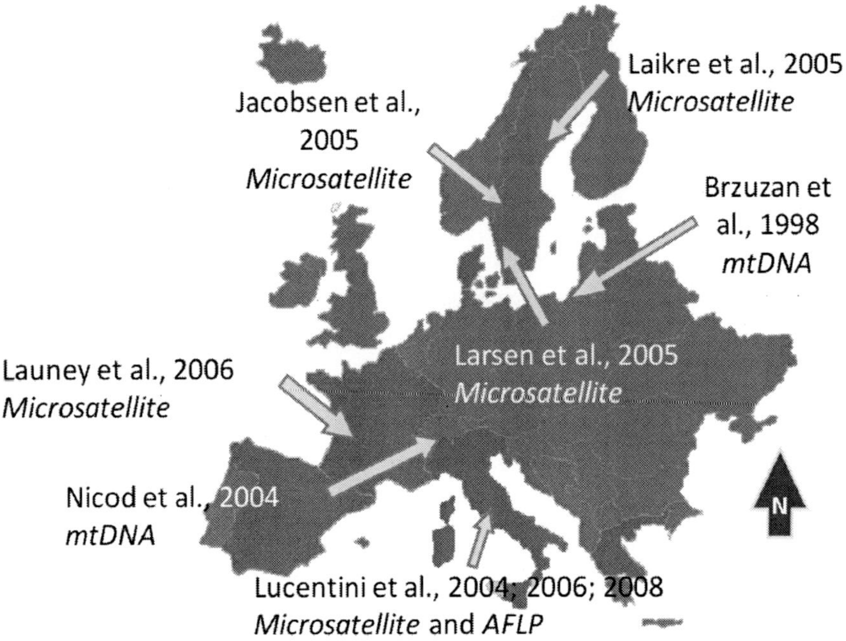

Figure 2. State-of-the art of publications concerning European northern pike.

Five of them estimate genetic diversity on the basis of microsatellites data, evaluating, by means of different statistical approaches, genetic introgression, spatial genetic structure, conservationistic state and conservative units as well as genetic structure and demographic history of the investigated populations.

Laikre and colleagues (2005), analysing seven sampling sites located along the Baltic coastal line, suggest the presence of isolation by distance pattern. According to these authors northern pike populations should be managed on a small scale in fisheries management units located respecting to the maximal dispersal distance and to the genetic patch size of 150 Km obtained the Moran's correlogram. Furthermore, they underline that, if conservationistic measures are to be applied in the future, they should primarily focus on the protection of the existing genetic variability. Habitats to protect should be as dispersed as possible, securing potential gene flow to avoid genetic isolation. Jacobsen and colleagues (2005), studying some north European populations compared with two from Greece and Canada, obtained strong evidence of a drastic decline of such a population on a time scale of a few thousand years, maybe due to both a glacial bottleneck and a post-glacial founder effect. According to Laikre *et alii* (2005), they suggest that microsatellites could allow the identification of major conservation units within this species in Europe and they assume the presence of distinct phylogeographical lineages in South-eastern Europe and North America (Senanan & Kapuscinski, 2000, Maes *et al.*, 2003).

Larsen and colleagues (2005) also applied microsatellites to the study of northern pike genetic characterization, particularly on stocking impact and temporal stability of a brackish population, analysing both historical and contemporary samples compared with other populations used for stocking. They found that, even though the effective population size (N_e) values were not particularly low, there were indications of bottlenecks in all samples and populations. These authors suggest that their data could be due to historical rather than recent bottlenecks and theorize founder events associated to postglacial recolonisation, as Jacobsen and colleagues do (2005).

Launey *et al.* (2006) analysed several northern European natural and stocked populations. In addition, because fish stocking with eastern European pike in French rivers is widespread, they have included these samples in their investigation. The results confirmed the low genetic variability within the French population, indicating an extensive introgression between wild and introduced stocks. Nevertheless, their data indicate that three genetically distinct evolutionary branches could be identified: continental Europe, Danube basin and south-western France. These finding agree with those obtained in our laboratory (Lucentini *et al.*, 2006d; 2008), underlining the genetic peculiarities of Italian populations. The importance of the genetic characterization of the Italian northern pike populations emerged on the basis of the reported evidence of glacial bottleneck and post-glacial recolonization (Nicod *et al.*, 2004; Jacobsen *et al.*, 2005; Larsen *et al.*, 2005) and because of the possible role of this geographical area as fish refugium during the last glaciation (Garcia-Marin *et al.*, 1999; Hewitt, 2000). For these reasons, in the Laboratory of Animal Biodiversity and Naturalistic Biotechnologies of the University of Perugia a research program was started aiming to characterize northern pike Italian populations by means of different molecular markers (PCR-RFLP, microsatellites and AFLP).

A scientific opportuntity was offered by Lake Trasimeno, a closed laminar lake of Central Italy having a surface of 128 Km^2. The inhabiting northern pike population is managed by the local administration (Centro Ittiogenico del Trasimeno – CIT, Provincia of Perugia), devoted to the artificial reproduction of pike and other freshwater fishes of Lake Trasimeno. Six hundred pike breeders are drawn every year from the lake, used for artificial reproduction and released in the lake. The physical characteristics of this lake, together with the self-stocking activity, make it a very good model-system for the analysis of genetic diversity of an isolated population of northern pike. The comparison with other nine non-isolated Italian and eastern European populations allows the definition of the genetic pattern of this species in Italy. The analysis was carried out using PCR-RFLP, microsatellites and AFLP as molecular markers which permit the definition of a genetic variability sufficient to investigate intra and inter-population relations (Lucentini *et al.*, 2004; Lucentini *et al.*, 2006a, d).

Sample locations were selected on the basis of Italian geomorphology, showing a clear geographic barrier, the Apennines, separating the peninsula into a central zone, where the Tiber hydrographic system is located, and in a northern zone, where the larger Po basin is located. In addition, Italian fish populations, including northern pike, were separated from Central Europe ones by the Alps barrier. In Italy, drainages are very small, if compared with the previously investigated ones of North Europe and North America (Miller & Kapuscinski, 1996, 1997; Senanan & Kapuscinski, 2000) and appear largely fragmented (i.e. the Tiber basin). In addition, the evidence indicates that, like other top predators, northern pike populations fluctuate yearly and tend to maintain a low effective population size, showing a metapopulation dynamics with frequent extinction and recolonization events on an evolutionary time scale (Gilpin, 1991; Miller & Kapuscinski, 1997). This condition is particularly significant for small and fragmented areas (see Miller & Kapuscinski, 1997 for a detailed discussion).

Furthermore, the presence of local mutation in the annealing primer zone could cause failure in the amplification procedure, producing an erroneous classification of heterozygotes as homozigotes. Taken together, all these factors could explain why three Italian populations (those from Chiusi, Piediluco and Bolsena Lakes) are out of the Hardy-Weinberg equilibrium.

The North Italian pike populations studied were located in the upstream trait of Po and Adda Rivers and in Maggiore and Segrino Lakes (Po drainage). Specimens from Central Italian populations were sampled from Trasimeno, Chiusi, Piediluco and Bolsena Lakes (Tiber drainage). The two Danube basin populations were sampled from the Danube River (Slovak Republic) and from its Hungarian tributary (Tisza River). Microsatellites were then applied on ten populations representative of central Italy, northern Italy and eastern Europe.

DNA was extracted from the distal portion of the caudal fin or from dried scales using a conservative protocol, providing a DNA whose quality and quantity had been already tested for the application of molecular markers (Lucentini *et al.*, 2006b, c, d). Such DNAs were analysed by means of seven microsatellite loci (Lucentini *et al.*, 2006d).

The procedure employed allowed the application of the microsatellite technique on a few fish scales to assess polymorphism pattern through an economic, rapid and non-invasive method and without quality loss in PCR products. In fact, results were compared with those obtained analysing tissues, confirming that microsatellites are completely applicable to conservative DNA (Lucentini *et al.*, 2006a, b, d). The possibility to apply molecular markers to conservative samples is a fundamental tool in forensic and conservation genetics because they allow a high quality research without damaging the analysed samples. This practice should be improved not only for endangered species, but also for every animal species, with the aim to maximize animal health and life quality.

Northern pike specimens, representative of eight Italian and two Danube populations, showed an appreciable heterogeneity as to allelic richness A, alleles size range, frequencies and other heterozygosity measures.

The pairwise t-test underlined the absence of significant differences ($p>>0.05$) between the distributions of Ho values and those already reported for the same microsatellite loci, showing that Ho values for the Po and Tiber drainages are well correlated to the ones reported for North America, Baltic area, North Europe and Siberia (Miller & Kapuscinski, 1996, 1997; Senanan & Kapuscinski, 2000; Jacobsen *et al.*, 2005; Larsen *et al.*, 2005) and Danube drainage (Launey *et al.*, 2006; Lucentini *et al.*, 2006d). The low genetic variability of both Italian and Danubian northern pike populations agrees with previous data indicating the allele size range and the allele number for pike populations from North America (Miller & Kapuscinski, 1996; 1997; Senanan & Kapuscinski, 2000) and North Europe (Hansen *et al.*, 1999; Senanan & Kapuscinski, 2000). Similar evidence about the low genetic variability emerged also from analyses carried out by means of other molecular markers (Healy & Mulchay, 1980; Seeb *et al.*, 1987; Brzuzan *et al.*, 1998; Nicod *et al.*, 2004). This finding seems to be species-specific: other fishes showed a large number of alleles for each locus in each of the studied populations (Balloux & Lugon-Moulin, 2002; Liu & Cordes, 2004), as, for example, brown trout, *Salmo trutta* (Hansen *et al.*, 2000), *Salvelinus fontinalis* (Wilson *et al.*, 2004) or *Thymmalus thymmalus* (Gum *et al.*, 2003). Nevertheless, deviation from the Hardy-Weinberg equilibrium is frequent in fish populations (Poteaux *et al.*, 1999; Bhassu *et al.*, 2004).

Our research (Lucentini *et al.*, 2006d) reported a Moran's I correlogram and the pairwise relationship between genetic and geographical distances that do not fully match the expectations based on the "isolation by distance" model and on the "long distance cline" (Diniz-Filho & Telles, 2002). This hypothesis agreed with the already found coexistence of low microsatellite variation and genetic differentiation among pikes populations (Senanan & Kapuscinski, 2000; Jacobsen *et al.*, 2005). The correlogram underlines a genetic correlation decreasing with the increase of geographical distances, and a positive correlation between pike collected at a distance of less than 110 Km, that agreed with data of Laikre and colleagues (2005). Nevertheless, the correlogram symmetry is not respected and, as highlighted also by the distances correlation, there were exceptions to the inverse correlation trend (Figure 3).

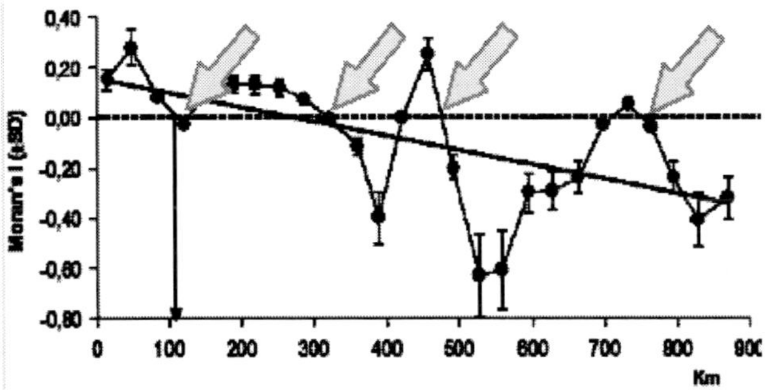

Figure 3. Moran's autocorrelogram. Modified by Lucentini *et al.*, 2006d.

Similar findings could agree with a natural population's differentiation whose patterns could be polluted by repopulation stocks. In fact, also Nicod *et alii* (2004) observed that a balance of two non-exclusive hypotheses could explain the present European distribution and the low genetic variation of northern pike: a post-glacial recolonization from few refuges and the extensive artificial transplants from a few source populations.

These findings, together with the hypotheses of Nicod *et alii* (2004) suggest the importance of Italian pike populations, since Italy was below the glacial limit and could have had a key role as a natural refuge for many species (see also Hewitt, 2000; Caputo *et al.*, 2004), including northern pike. Taking into account both the statistical information on population genetic and the literature on northern pike, it can be assumed that the genetic diversity and the populations structure of this species could be the result of a balance of gene flows and genetic drifts. Unfortunately, it is not possible to compare autochthonous and stocked specimens of pike, as reported for brown trout (Poteaux *et al.*, 1999), because stocking was practised in the last 100 years (Lorenz, 1868; Nicod *et al.*, 2004) and no information is now available on the specimens' typologies and their origin.

In addition, the presence of an appreciable number of regionally private alleles suggests the existence of endemic specimens in this area (Kalinowski, 2004); the particular geomorphological and hydrogeographical characteristics of Italy might have had an active role in preserving the local identity of some freshwater fish populations, including pike.

These data are of interest also because the knowledge of Italian population is scarce, fragmented, mostly old and regards growth, stomach contents, reproduction and parasitism (Calderoni, 1965; Tortonese, 1970; Alessio, 1975 a, b; Alessio, 1983). In the last few years several researches about feeding, growth and development of northern pike of Lake Trasimeno were carried out (Lorenzoni *et al.*, 2002; Lucentini *et al.*, 2006d).

Investigations of this kind are important because it is necessary to understand whether equilibrium between natural and anthropic factors may have genetically homogenized

European populations. Natural factors should be referred to the already mentioned glacial/post-glacial events, while the anthropic factor could be based on intra-basins stocking activity. It is known that Romans already practised stocking between basins for species of fisheries interest, such as Carp (*Cyprinus carpio*), but the great stocking effort was spent in the last three decades. The possible causes of the low genetic variability of northern pike are very interesting for evolutionary biology, and many speculative hypotheses were proposed such as the "isolation by distance" model of gene flow (Estoup *et al.*, 1998; Hansen & Mensberg, 1998) or the one known as "second contact" that could have homogenised divergent populations (Perez-Losada *et al.*, 1999; Østbye *et al.*, 2005). Other possible causes could be homoplasy, deriving from the deviation from the infinite allele mutation model (Rico *et al.*, 1997), which could "obscure" the phylogenetic signal (Petren *et al.*, 1999), and the Wahlund effect, based on the overlapping of different spatially and temporally separated breeding stocks (Poteaux *et al.*, 1999). Maes *et alii* (2003) suggest that only a young species or a severe bottleneck may justify the genetic characteristic of this species, particularly the low genetic differentiation, and Senanan and Kapuscinski (2000) discuss the possible applications of measures derived from models involving stepwise mutations and no constraint on allele size. Taken together, the limitation in allele size and the high mutation rate of microsatellite markers might have homogenized diverged groups (Nauta & Weissing, 1996). Furthermore, it was stressed that, human interference should also be taken into account (Grandjean *et al.*, 2001; Aguilar *et al.*, 2005) and the management activities of northern pike populations sometimes prevail over natural radiation from post-glacial refugium (Reist, 1983), although selection and recent or ancient historical events, as the presence of glacial refugia, might be relevant (Nicod *et al.*, 2004). In fact, the widespread transfer of a large number of samples between different sites might have eroded the historical levels of natural populations structures. These anthropic impacts may have affected the preservation of local adaptation patterns, which are the basis of an eco-compatible managing and an integrated approach to biodiversity conservation (Youngson *et al.*, 2003). Nevertheless, it is possible to find for this species a positive correlation between geographical and genetic distances (Laikre *et al.*, 2005 and this article), and the intermediate value of the Pearson Coefficient correlating the two parameters, could allow the possibility of a "second contact" either of anthropic or natural origin (Lucentini *et al.*, 2006d).

As mentioned above, the large distribution causes the existence of isolated populations and of samples with different morphological traits on the basis of which were hypothized the presence of several subspecies (Crossmann, 1970; 1977). One of the most debated morphological aspects is the colour pattern for which no scientific evidence was known. Fickling (1982) identified different types of colour patterns, in particular oval spots, rounded and stellate spots and longitudinal lines. Colour patterns are composed by a dark drawing on a white-yellow background. Different colour patterns might be referred to local ecotypes (Berg, 1962; Kulemin *et al.*, 1971). Data that we have recorded in the last years indicate the presence, in Italy, of at least five colour patterns one of which is referable to the Danube basin (Lucentini *et al.*, 2008): rounded and oval spots, longitudinal bands, marmorized pattern (stellate spots) and diagonal bands. This classification was performed analysing more than eight hundred northern pikes drawn in Italy and Eastern Europe. The genetic characterization of a subsample of 114 randomly chosen individuals was done by means of seven microsatellite and ten *Eco*RI/*Taq*I AFLP combinations (Lucentini *et al.*, 2008). This research underlined that AFLP, but not microsatellite, indicate a relationship between genotypes and colour patterns in northern pike. In particular, these ten AFLP combinations clearly distinguish a genotype strictly associated with rounded and oval spots, the phenotype classically attributed to Eastern Europe samples. In order to better characterize this phenotype, two new researches are currently in progress. As to the first, three couples of genetically phenotypically characterized breeders produced three F1 stocks that are presently fed with *Daphnia magna;* they will be analysed by means of molecular and phonotypical procedures when the development will be sufficient to allow the analysis of colour pattern. For the second research, the FAM marked hot amplification of each of the ten AFLP combinations are analysed, for 12 individuals representative of different phenotypes, by means of Genomix (Amersham Pharmacia), with the aim to excise and sequence the AFLP bands characterizing different genotype. This procedure will allow the identification of SNPs that distinguish the already found different phenotypes.

CONCLUSION

There are several ecosystems, especially in North America, where northern pike is an invasive species and where the spread of this species should be controlled (Aguilar *et al.*, 2005; Craig, 2008). The high fragmentation of the European populations, and the small size of several European environments, may have caused the decline of this species. There are several papers focusing the decline of particular northern pike populations, due to the recent introduction of invasive species (Lorenzoni *et al.*, 2002) or to the habitat, particularly spawning sites degradation (Lucentini *et al.*, 2006d). In general terms, many authors suggest that population decline might be attributed also to physiological tolerances and to the effect of climate change on this species, whose distribution is particularly interested by global warming and thus by warming of aquatic habitats. In fact, recent findings underlined that warming water could have an indirect effect on northern pike (Winfield *et al.*, 2008).

Molecular markers have simplified forensic genetics and are currently used for population analysis, for hybrid evaluation and geographic traceability, allowing the analysis of the effective influence of stocking activity on local populations. Furthermore, some molecular markers allowed the definition of genotype-phenotype relationships, with a great improvement of both conservation and management (Lucentini *et al.*, 2008). Also the knowledge of changes of a natural population is fundamental for such purposes but, on a time scale greater than a single generation, it is frequently very difficult to understand how and in which direction a population is changed. A very useful tool is represented by the study of historical samples that are frequently difficult to obtain for morphological and morphometric purposes, because of sample degradation or preservation, but that could be used for DNA analysis. Frequently just a little piece of the entire individual, such as scales for fishes, is available for modern analysis. It is possible to extract DNA from any kind of tissue, allowing the fascinating possibility to compare actual and historical samples without the risk of error induced by the experimental procedure and without damaging the historical sample. The comparison of actual and historical samples allowed the analysis of the allelic variation of particular codominant markers that permit the evaluation of population changes and the estimation of N_e, the effective population size. Such information could be of primary interest to define the indication for the artificial spawning programs, because it may have important influences on inbreeding and genetic flow (Caballero, 1994; Nomura, 2005). The importance of estimating population parameters, such as effective population size, is due also to its relationship with the genetic drift, particularly relevant in fragmented populations, such as most central European populations of northern pike (Hallerman, 2003).

The fine understanding of the genetic impact caused by stocking activity underlined the importance of such ecological problems. In fact, the compromission of the survival capability of local population is frequently managed with the introduction of fries or juveniles of allochthonous origin. This practice could introduce allochthonous species, pathogens and diseases that, particularly if reiterated, may damage the genetic characteristics of the local population (Launey *et al.*, 2003). The loss of genetic peculiarities of the autochthonous population could cause a cascade effect with consequences on the entire ichthyic stock and on the entire lake ecosystem. In fact, the characteristics of a particular population are the result of a unique local evolution defining, on a million years time scale, peculiar genotypic and phenotypic traits contributing to the ecosystem equilibrium. The introduction of different genotypes, and even phenotypes, might have deep influences on the food chain and, subsequently, on the quality and quantity of fisheries catches.

In Italy most freshwater basins are small and fragmented, particularly if compared with those described in other researches on the genetic variability of northern pike (Miller & Kapuscinski, 1996, 1997; Senanan & Kapuscinski, 2000). Furthermore, this species, being a great predator, tends to yearly fluctuations and shows metapopulation dynamics characterized by frequent extinctions and re-colonisations (Gilpin, 1991; Miller & Kapuscinski, 1997). Such aspects justify most biological characteristics of the Italian populations, in particular the genetic diversity values. The emerging factor is that, in spite of the high fragmentation, the small dimension and isolation of the Trasimeno's population, this is one of the best Italian populations, in terms of both heterozygosity values and health stat in general. It is already known that importing samples from Eastern Europe in Italy can have several negative consequences, for fisheries as well as for the biological integrity *per se*. These individuals, in fact, are frequently chosen for their morphological characteristics, such as the great size. Nevertheless, the greater growth could be due to a higher water temperature as compared to the one of origin and it could have several repercussions on the meat value and fat accumulation. A very interesting branch of this research is the analysis of the genotype dispersion underlining that in several populations genotypes typical of other population could be found. This could be due to both convergence or to the practice of repeated flow of samples across these environments. A particular case is that of Lake Trasimeno that shows a stable and well-structured population not showing genotypes assigned to other populations, while the genotypes typical of its population are dispersed all around Italy (Lucentini *et al.*, 2004; 2006d). This fact can refer to the possible glacial and post-glacial role of south-central Italy (Hewitt, 2000; Nicod *et al.,* 2004). Surely, a great impact is represented also by the stocking activity; in fact the three nearest lakes (Piediluco, Bolsena and Chiusi) present extremely problematic populations.

The reported data underline that, to date, a great effort is spent to define the northern pike health state, for the genetic diversity analysis and population genetics definition. Nevertheless, the lack of data characterizes the health state definition and the effective conservationistic state of this species. In fact, future researches should aim to the definition of key-parameters for the management of northern pike in different environments.

In conclusion, this brief review summarizes the recent knowledge of the genetic diversity of European northern pike populations and, particularly, of Italian pike populations, pointing out the existence of endemic groups that were partially polluted by anthropic activities, particularly by stocking practices. To date, northern pike shows several difficulties and look as a species in crisis, needing major attention and both conservative and management programs. We hope that our results will be relevant for fisheries, local authorities and all the researchers presently working on northern pike management and conservation programs in Europe.

ACKNOWLEDGMENTS

We are grateful to Mr. Romano Dolciami for helping us in the animal manipulation. This work was partially financed by grants of University of Perugia and by FISR-MICENA 2006-2009.

REFERENCES

Aguilar, A., Banks, J. D., Levine, K. F., & Wayne, R. K. (2005). Population genetics of northern pike (*Esox lucius*) introduced into Lake Davis, California. Canadian Journal of Fisheries and Aquatic Sciences, 62, 1589-1599.

Alessio, G. (1975a). Ricerche sulla biologia del luccio *Esox lucius* L. (Osteichthyes, Esocidae) in Lomellina occidentale ed in una valle "veneta". Bollettino di Pesca, Piscicoltura e Idrobiologia, 30, 235-256.

Alessio, G. (1975b). Accrescimento lineare e ponderale del luccio *Esox lucius* L. (Osteichthyes, Esocidae) in Lomellina occidentale ed in una valle "veneta". Bollettino di Pesca, Piscicoltura e Idrobiologia, 30, 257-275.

Alessio, G. (1983). Quelques aspects de la biologie et de l'élevage du brochet (*Esox lucius* L.) en Italie. In: Le Brochet: gestion dans le milieu naturel et élevage. Billard R. Ed., INRA, Parigi. 283-296 pp.

Balloux, F., & Lugon-Moulin, N. (2002). The estimation of population differentiation with microsatellite markers. Molecular Ecology, 11, 155-165.

Berg, L. S. (1962). Freshwater fishes of the USSR, and adjacent countries. Volume 1. Translated from Russian fourth, improved and augmented edition. Jerusalem, Israel Program for Scientific Translation, IPST Cat. No. 741. 504 p.

Bhassu, S., Yusoff, K., Panandam, J. M., Embong, W. K., Oyyan, S., Tan, S. G. (2004). The genetic structure of *Oreochromis* spp. (Tilapia) populations in Malaysia as revealed by microsatellite DNA analysis. Biochemical Genetics, 42, 217-229.

Billard, E. J. (1996). Reproduction of pike: gametogenesis, gamete biology and early development. In: Craig J. (Ed.), Pike: Biology and Exploitation. (Capitolo II). Nature.

Bry, C. (1996). Role of Vegetation in the life-cycle of pike. In: Craig J. (Ed.), Pike: Biology and Exploitation. (Capitolo III). Nature.

Brzuzan, P., Luczynski, M., & Kuzniar, P. A. (1998). Mitochondrial DNA variation in two samples of northern pike, *Esox lucius* L. Aquaculture Research, 29, 521-526.

Caballero, A. (1994). Developments in the prediction of effective population size. Heredity, 73, 657-679.

Calderoni, P. (1965). Contributo allo studio dell'accrescimento del luccio (*Esox lucius* L.) del lago Trasimeno. Rivista di Idrobiologia 4, 3-13.

Caputo, V., Giovannotti, M., Nisi Cerioni, P., & Caniglia, M. L. (2004). Genetic diversity of brown trout in central Italy. Journal of Fish Biology, 65, 403-418.

Craig, J. F. (2008). A short review of pike ecology. Hydrobiologia, 601, 5.

Crossmann, E. J., & Harington, C. R. (1970). Pleistocene pike, *Esox lucius* and *Esox* sp., from the Yukon Territory and Ontario. Canadian journal of earth sciences, 7, 1130-1138.

Crossman, E. J., & Meade, J. W. (1977). Artificial hybrids between Amur pike *Esox reicherti*, and North American esocids. Journal of the Fisheries Research Board of Canada, 34, 2338-2343.

Diniz-Filho, J. A. F., & Telles, M. P. C. (2002). Spatial autocorrelation analysis and the identification of operational units for conservation in continuous populations. Conservation Biology 16, 924-935.

Eklöv, P. (1995). Effects of habitat complexity and prey abundance on the spatial and temporal distribution of perch (*Perca fluviatilis*) and pike (*Esox lucius*). Canadian Journal of Fishieries and Aquatic Sciences, 4, 1520-1531.

Engström-Őst, J., Lethiniemi, M., Jónasdóttir, S. H., & Viitasalo, M. (2005). Growth of pike larvae (*Esox lucius*) under different conditions of food quality and salinity. Ecology of freshwater fish, 14, 385-393.

Estoup, A., Rousset, F., Michalakis, Y., Cornuet, J. M., Adrimanga, M., & Guyomard, R. (1998). Comparative analysis of microsatellite and allozyme markers: a case study investigating microgeographic differentiation in brown trout (*Salmo trutta*). Molecular Ecology 7, 339-353.

Fickling, N. J., 1982. The identification of pike by means of characteristic marks. Fisheries management and ecology, 13, 79-82.

Frankham, R., Ballou, J., Briscoe, D. & Mcinnes, K. H. (2004). A primer of conservation genetics. Cambridge, Cambridge University Press, 617p.

Garcia-Marin, J. L., Utter, F. M., & Pla, C. (1999). Postglacial colonization of brown trout in Europe based on distribution of allozyme variants. Heredity. 82, 46-56.

Gilpin, M. (1991). The genetic effective size of a metapopulation. Biological journal of the Linnean Society, 42, 165-175.

Grandjean, F., Gouin, N., Souty-Grosset, C., & Diéguez-Uribeondo, J. (2001). Drastic bottlenecks in the endangered crayfish species *Austropotamobius pallipes* in Spain and implications for its colonization history. Nature, 86, 431-438.

Gum, B., Gross, R., Rottmann, O., Schroder, W., & Kuhn, R. (2003). Microsatellite variation in Bavarian populations of European grayling (*Thymallus thymallus*): Implications for conservation. Conservation Genetics, 4, 659-672.

Hallerman, E. (2003). Random genetic drift. In: Hallerman E. (Ed.), Population genetics: principles and applications for fisheries scientist. (Capitolo IX). American Fisheries Society, Bethesda, USA.

Hansen, M. M., & Mensberg, K. L. D. (1998). Genetic differentiation and relationship between genetic and geographic distance in Danish sea trout (*Salmo trutta* L.) populations. Heredity, 81, 493-504.

Hansen, M. M., Taggart, J. B. & Meldrup, D. (1999). Development of new VNTR markers for pike and assessment of variability at di- and tetranucleotide repeat microsatellite loci. Journal of Fish Biology, 55, 183-188.

Hansen, M. M., Ruzzante, D. E., Nielsen, E. E., & Mensberg, K. D. (2000). Microsatellite and mitochondrial DNA polymorphism reveals life-history dependent interbreeding between hatchery and wild brown trout (*Salmo trutta* L.). Molecular Ecology, 9, 583-594.

Hansen, M. M., Bekkevold, D., Jensen, L. F., Mensberg, K. D., & Nielsen, E. E. (2006). Genetic restoration of a stocked brown trout *Salmo trutta* population using microsatellite DNA analysis of historical and contemporary samples. Journal of Applied Ecology, 43, 669-679.

Hassler, T. J. (1982). Effect of temperature on survival of northen pike embryos and yolk-sac larvae. Progressive Fish-Culturist, 44, 174-179.

Healy, J. A. & Mulcay, M. F. (1980). A biochemical genetic analysis of the northern pike, *Esox lucius* L., from Europe and North America. Journal of Fish Biology, 17, 317-324.

Heuschmann, O. (1957). Die Hechtartigen Ordung Haplomi (Esociformes). Handbuch der Binnenfischerei Mitteleuropas, 3, 1-22.

Hewitt, G. (2000). The Genetic Legacy of the Quaternary Ice Ages. Nature, 405, 907-913.

Jacobsen, B., Hansen, M. M., Loeschcke, V. (2005). Microsatellite DNA analysis of northern pike (*Esox lucius* L.) populations: insights into the genetic structure and demographic history of a genetically depauperate species. Biological journal of the Linnean Society, 84, 91-101.

Kalinowski, S. T. (2004). Counting alleles with rarefaction: Private alleles and hierarchical sampling designs. Conservation Genetics. 5, 1-12.

Kovàcs, B., Keresztùri, P., Kiss, K. M., Zsolt, G., Takòcs, P., & Lakatos, G. (2001). Ökològiai àllapotfelmérés alföldi mesterséges vìzfolyàsokon, különös tekintettel a halegyüttesek összetètelére. Hidrologiai közlöny, 81, 419-422.

Kulemin, A. A., Makkoveyeva, I. I., & Solopova, M. I. (1971). Age, composition growth rate and condition of the pike (*Esox lucius* L.) of Lake Pleshcheveyo. Journal of Ichthyology, 11, 1-36.

Laikre, L., Miller, L. M., Palmé, A., Palm, S., Kapuscinski, A. R., Thoresson, G., & Ryman, N. (2005). Spatial genetic structure of northern pike (*Esox lucius*) in the Baltic Sea. Molecular Ecology, 14, 1955-1964.

Larsen, P. F., Hansen, M. M., Nielsen, E. E., Jensen, L.F., & Loeschcke, L. (2005). Stocking impact and temporal stability of genetic composition in a brackish northern pike population (*Esox lucius* L.), assessed using microsatellite DNA analysis of historical and contemporary samples. Heredity, 95, 136-143.

Launey, S., Krieg, F., Morin, J., & Laroche, J. (2003). Five new microsatellite markers for Northern pike (*Esox lucius*). Molecular Ecology Notes, 3, 366-368.

Launey, S., Morin, J., Minery, S., & Laroche, J. (2006). Microsatellite genetic variation reveals extensive introgression between wild and introduced stocks, and a new evolutionary unit in French pike *Esox lucius* L. Journal of Fish Biology, 68, 193-216.

Liu, Z. J., & Cordes, J. F. (2004). DNA marker technologies and their applications in aquaculture genetics. Aquaculture, 238, 1-37.

Lorenz, P. (1868). Die Fishe des Kantons Graubünden (Schweiz). Schweizerische Fisherei-Zeitung, 41, 1-135.

Lorenzoni, M., Corboli, M., Dörr, A. J. M., Mearelli, M., & Giovinazzo, G. (2002). The growth of pike (*Esox lucius* Linnaeus, 1758) in Lake Trasimeno (Umbria, Italy). Fisheries Research, 59, 239-246.

Lucentini, L., Ricciolini, C., Lancioni, H., Baldoni, L., & Panara, F. (2004). Analisi della diversità genetica delle popolazioni di luccio (*Esox lucius* L.) del lago Trasimeno. Biologia Ambientale, 18, 15-18.

Lucentini, L., Palomba, A., Lancioni, H., Natali, M., & Panara, F. (2006a). A nondestructive, rapid, reliable and inexpensive method to sample, store and extract high-quality DNA from fish body mucus and buccal cells. Molecular Ecology Notes, 6, 257-260.

Lucentini, L., Caporali, S., Palomba, A., Lancioni, H., & Panara, F. (2006b). A comparison of conservative DNA extraction methods from fins and scales of freshwater fish: a useful tool for conservation genetics. Conservation Genetics, 7, 1009-1012.

Lucentini L., Palomba, A., Gigliarelli, L., Lancioni, H., Viali, P., & Panara, F. (2006c). Genetic characterization of a putative indigenous brown trout (*Salmo trutta* fario) population in a secondary stream of the Nera River Basin (Central Italy) assessed by means of three molecular markers. Italian Journal of Zoology, 73, 263-273.

Lucentini, L., Palomba, A., Gigliarelli, L., Lancioni, H., Natali, M., & Panara, F. (2006d). Microsatellite polymorphism in Italian populations of northern pike (*Esox lucius* L.). Fisheries Research, 80, 251-262.

Lucentini L., Ricciolini C., Palomba A., Gigliarelli L., Sgaravizzi G., Lancioni H., Puletti M. E., Lanfaloni L., Panara F. (2008). AFLP molecular markers - but not microsatellites - indicate a relationship between genotypes and colour patterns in northern pike (*Esox lucius L.)* XII AIIAD National Congress.

Maes, G. E., Van Houdt, J. K. J., De Charleroy, D., & Volckaert, M. (2003). Indications for a recent Holoartic expansion of pike based on a preliminary study of mtDNA variation. Journal of Fish Biology, 63, 254-259.

McCarraher, D. B. (1961). Extension range of the northern pike *Esox lucius.* Transactions of the American Fisheries Society, 90, 227-228.

Miller, L. M., & Kapuscinski, A. R. (1996). Microsatellite DNA markers reveal new levels of genetic variation in northern pike. Transactions of the American Fisheries Society, 125, 971-977.

Miller, L. M., & Kapuscinski, A. R. (1997). Historical analysis of genetic variation reveals low effective population size in a northern pike (*Esox lucius*) population. Genetics, 147, 1249-1258.

Miller, C. R., & Waits, L. P. (2003). The history of effective population size and genetic diversity in the Yellowstone grizzly (*Ursus arctos*): implications for conservation. Proceedings of the National Academy of Sciences of the USA, 100, 4334-4339.

Nauta, M.J., & Weissing, F.J. (1996). Constrains on allele size at microsatellite loci: implications for genetic differentiation, Genetics, 143, 1021-1032.

Nicod, J. C., Wang, Y. Z., Excoffier, L., & Largiader, C. R. (2004). Low levels of mitochondrial DNA variation among central and southern European *Esox lucius* populations. Journal of fish biology 64, 1442-1449.

Nielsen, R., & Wakeley J. (2001). Distinguishing migration from isolation: a Markov chain Monte Carlo approach. Genetics, 158, 885-896.

Nikoloski, G. W. (1957). Spezielle fischkunde. Berlin, VEB Deutscher Verlag der Wissenschafter, 632 pp.

Nomura, T. (2005). Developments in prediction theories of the effective size of population under selection. Animal Science Journal, 76, 87-96.

Østbye, K., Bernatchez, L., Naesje, T. F., Himberg, K. J. M., & Hindar, K. (2005). Evolutionary history of the European whitefish *Coregonus lavaretus* (L.) species complex as inferred from mtDNA phylogeography and gill-raker numbers. Molecular Ecology, 14, 4371-4387.

Paschke, M., Abs, C., & Schmid, B. (2002). Effects of population size and pollen diversity on reproductive success and offspring size in the narrow endemic *Cochlearia bavarica* (Brassicaceae), American Journal of Botany, 89, 1250-1259.

Pérez-Losada, M., Guerra, A., & Sanjuan, A. (1999). Allozyme differentiation in the cuttlefish *Sepia officinalis* (Mollusca: cephalopoda) from the NE Atlantic and Mediterranean. Heredity, 83, 280-289.

Petren, K., Grant, B. R., & Grant, P. R. (1999). Phylogeny of Darwin's Finches based on microsatellite DNA length variation. Proceedings of the Royal Society of London. Series B, 266, 321-329.

Pinto, J., Donnelly, M. J., Sousa, C. A., Gil, V., Ferreira, C., Elissa, N., do Rosário, V. E., Charlwood, J. D. (2002). Genetic structure of *Anopheles gambiae* (Diptera: Culicidae) in São Tomé and Príncipe (West Africa): implications for malaria control. Molecular Ecology, 11, 2183-2187.

In: Endangered Species: New Research
Editors: A. Columbus and L. Kuznetsov
ISBN 978-1-60692-241-5

Chapter 7

MANAGING PREDATORS TO PROTECT ENDANGERED SPECIES AND PROMOTE THEIR SUCCESSFUL REPRODUCTION

***Richard M. Engeman*[*,1], *Bernice U. Constantin*[2], *Kenneth S. Gruver*[3] and *Corey Rossi*[4]**

[1]USDA/Wildlife Services/National Wildlife Research Center, 4101 LaPorte Ave., Fort Collins, CO 80521-2154, USA

[2]USDA/Wildlife Services, 2820 East University Ave., Gainesville, FL 32641, USA

[3]USDA/Wildlife Services, 720 O'Leary Street NW, Olympia, WA 98502, USA

[4]USDA/Wildlife Services - Alaska District, 9001 East Frontage Road, Suite A, Palmer, AK 99645, USA

richard.m.enegman@aphis.usda.gov

ABSTRACT

Predation critically threatens many rare species, with the deleterious impacts of predation losses compounded by habitat loss. Predators of endangered species are frequently invasive species or artificially over-abundant native species. Often, predation is most damaging to a species' ability to reproduce. We use examples from the tropics to the tundra with which we have been involved to demonstrate how predator management can be a highly effective and economically efficient means to protect populations of rare species and enhance their reproduction.

Management of predators, like all wildlife management, must be carried out within finite fiscal and human resources. Examination of the predator populations in response to management actions only provides an indicator of success. The true measure of success is improvement of the endangered species as a result of the management action. Moreover, a vital means to establish the success of an endangered species protection program is to demonstrate that the benefits to the protected species exceed the cost of the program. To

* Correspondence: Richard Engeman Tel: (970) 266-6091 Fax: (970) 266-6089 email: richard.m.engeman@aphis.usda.gov

this end, methods to monetarily value rare species allow species improvement to be assessed in the same metric as the costs for the protection.

Predator management to aid conservation of rare species requires is much more likely to succeed if: 1) applied by skilled/trained personnel able to focus on the task, 2) management efforts are timed so the most favorable impact can be achieved, 3) the effort is applied with sufficient intensity that the desired effect can be achieved, 4) predator population information is used for optimizing the timing, distribution and intensity of management efforts, and 5) adaptive management strategies are applied to changing circumstances through time. If predator management is not being applied effectively, then predator management is not taking place. It would be a disservice to a species in need of protection to discount predator management as useful because it was ineffectively applied.

INTRODUCTION

Predation not only threatens many rare species (Hecht and Nickerson, 1999), but the deleterious impacts of predation losses are compounded by habitat loss (Reynolds and Tapper, 1996). Alien predators tend to be more dangerous than native predators to prey populations (Salo et al. 2007). In the USA, exotic species have played a role in the listing of 42% of the species protected by the Endangered Species Act (Stein and Flack 1996). Moreover, predators increase the risk of extinction of prey populations as a result of catastrophic events (Schoener et al. 2001). Therefore, rare species in a state such as Florida may be particularly vulnerable considering: extensive development has depleted many of the native habitats on which rare species depend: the state has one of the two most severe invasive species problems, with many of the exotic species being significant predators; and the state is subject to catastrophic hurricanes. While Florida offers a severe and broad example of the negative impacts of predation on rare species, countless other examples from diverse habitats, especially islands, demonstrate the negative impacts of predation, and the positive effects of predator management when appropriately applied.

Small or declining populations may benefit the most from reductions in predation if numbers are increased quickly and variability in productivity and survival rates are reduced (Hecht and Nickerson 1999). Reducing predation rates through predator control may be an essential component of a management plan to achieve recovery objectives for a species of concern (Bodenchuk and Hayes 2006). In many cases, if not most, seasonal control efforts may accomplish management goals while optimizing the efficiency of human and material resources, and funding. Application of predator control when a rare species is most vulnerable to predation may be as effective as year-round techniques. Moreover, in some instances compensatory mitigation for reducing predation during breeding may help compensate for losses in other life stages from a variety of mortality sources (Wilcox and Donlan 2007).

One of the complicating factors in the application of predator control for the benefit of a rare species is that removal of predators to conserve rare species sometimes places wildlife managers and the public in the uncomfortable position of choosing between removal of a charismatic predator species or conserving an endangered species, possibly allowing it to go extinct without sufficient predator management. While some significantly destructive predators of rare species receive little affection from the public, such as brown treesnakes or rats, many predators are held in high esteem in the public consciousness, especially predators such as raptors, wolves, or even raccoons, while other significant predators of rare species include feral domesticated animals commonly beloved pets such as cats and dogs. From a purely logical perspective, this would be an uncomplicated, straightforward decision. From an emotional point of view, it can be an unpleasant choice, especially when the public, usually without a full understanding of all ramifications and practical options, protests predator removal, especially lethal removal, even if the alternative would be significant harm or possibly extinction for a rare species in need of protection.

ECONOMIC ANALYSES OF CONSERVATION THROUGH PREDATOR MANAGEMENT

A key aspect in considering conservation approaches is the economics involved, especially the return on a conservation investment. Funding is finite for recovery and conservation of species and habitats, and must be carefully applied to maximize the positive impact on the protected resource. Economic analyses of management actions can provide managers with a logical working basis for selecting and implementing the most cost-effective conservation methodologies. While the direct costs for a conservation approach, such as predator management, may be relatively easy to identify and quantify because they can be measured by the budgetary outlay for implementation, the rewards from those budgetary allocations are measured in terms of resource improvements, such as population growth. To effectively evaluate the returns on the expenditures, they must be in the same metric as the expenditures. That is, the resource improvement must also be monetarily valued.

Determination of monetary values for rare species is not a straight-forward nor precise process. As an illustration, consider that values of endangered or threatened species have been deemed "incalculable" in U.S. Supreme Court case law (Tennessee Valley Authority vs. Hill, 1978), the opinion going so far as to say "it would be difficult for a court to balance the loss of a sum certain - even $100 million - against a congressionally declared 'incalculable' value, even assuming we had the power to engage in such a weighing process, which we emphatically do not." Nevertheless, infinite or astronomically high monetary species valuations would be unlikely to be widely viewed as credible. Credible monetary values for rare species can be estimated through the variety of means.

While contingent valuation, a method based on survey results, has been applied to create natural resource valuations (e.g., Loomis and Walsh 1997), the scenarios are hypothetical, the validity of the responses to a contingent valuation is unsure, and the results may not reflect the people's true willingness to pay (WTP), either because people do not have a realistic sense of how much they would pay, or because they have incentives to dishonestly report their WTP (Loomis and Walsh 1997). Nevertheless, we have found other methods of great use for defining societal values for rare species.

Legislatively designated values are a useful method for assigning societal values to resources (Engeman et. al 2004, Bodenchuk et al. 2002). Wildlife management agencies use estimates of economic values based on contributions to the economy by individual game species to derive their monetary values (Bodenchuk et al. 2002), and develop civil financial penalties for illegal kills (Bodenchuk et al. 2002). However, rare and endangered species do not have civil financial penalties assigned in relation to their contributions to the economy as "renewable" resources, because they are rarely, if ever, exploited in a financially measurable fashion such as through the sale of hunting or fishing licenses and sportsman equipment. Nevertheless, rare and endangered species are almost universally protected with civil penalties set forth legislatively. Such species likely will have more than one value available from multiple enabling legislations (e.g., United States federal and individual state laws). A conservative benefit-cost analysis is obtained when the minimal applicable value is employed. However, this could substantially under-value a species, especially when considering that all civil financial penalties from the different enabling legislations could apply simultaneously. Consider the example of predator depredations on marine turtle nests in Florida by Engeman et al. (2002). Their analyses chose the conservative route of applying a minimum legislative value of $100 from Florida statutes. However, the Florida Wildlife Code specified a value of $500 per life unit, and the federal Endangered Species Act (ESA) allows for civil penalties up to $25,000 per life unit. Thus, the monetary benefits accrued from the predator management approaches could have ranged by a factor of 250 (Engeman et al. 2002).

Captive Breeding costs provide an empirically observed measure of value actually paid to produce new individuals for a species. Captive breeding is not only a management strategy for assisting the recovery of a rare species, but it also provides data for placing a value on a species. The use of captive breeding costs as a means for monetarily valuing rare species is a simple concept, because those monies spent to produce animals in captivity are empirically explicit demonstrations of a willingness to pay for new animals. The costs of captive breeding divided by the number of healthy individuals produced defines a value for the species (e.g., Bodenchuk et al. 2002). Nevertheless, the valuing process is not quite as straight-forward as this seems. There may be multiple captive breeding facilities for the same species, each with its own budget (e.g., Engeman et al. 2003b). A facility may remain in operation year-in and year-out, but its temporal budget and animal production may fluctuate substantially, resulting in fluctuating species values. The most conservative analysis is obtained if the minimum cost per production of a healthy individual is used, whereas use of the maximum value provides the empirical peak expenditure to produce an individual of the species. Use of the median value for an individual provides an analysis representing the central tendency for valuing the species. A parallel concept to applying captive breeding costs to determine species values is to value species based on populations and budgetary outlay for refuges or preserves designated to protect and conserve a specific species. The population subject to budgetary outlay for its conservation thereby defines an empirically spent per-unit amount for the individuals.

Predator Management in Action for Rare Species Conservation

There are virtually countless examples in the literature demonstrating the value of predator management in conserving endangered species. Conversely, there are numerous examples where predator management did not appear to help the situation. Direct control can locally reduce predator populations, but the removal of animals does not always correlate well to the magnitude of damage reduction (e.g., Conner *et al.* 1998). Understanding the dynamics of the damaging species with the affected resource can lead to more efficient and effective strategies for protecting the resource (e.g., Knowlton et al. 1999; Ramsey and Wilson 2000). Just because a predator is identified as negatively impacting an endangered species does not guarantee that managing the predator will be an effective, efficient, or cost-effective means to help conserve the listed species. Predator management requires a thorough understanding of when and why predation takes place, and understanding the circumstances that make the endangered prey most vulnerable to predation. Optimizing predator management for application during the circumstances of greatest vulnerability of the endangered prey produces a great benefit for the endangered species while maximizing the benefit-cost ratio for expenditures of conservation funds.

We use a variety of situations from tropical rainforests to arctic tundra in which we have been involved to demonstrate how broadly effective predator management can be for conserving populations and/or bolstering reproduction of threatened and endangered species. In doing so, we also are demonstrating that predator management must be applied judiciously and effectively to obtain the desired positive effect for the endangered species. A haphazard application of predator management that consequently shows little conservation value may discourage a manager from its use in the future, when, in fact, it could be the essential tool for saving the species if applied prudently. Sometimes biological systems are viewed so complexly that a straight-forward application of predator management is overlooked as potentially solving a problem. On the other hand, the positive response to predator management is sometimes difficult to observe directly and its evaluation for efficacy is difficult without a thorough understanding of the techniques, which may include a combination of lethal control, predator harassment, and barriers (physical and behavioral). Throughout, if predators are removed, efficacy of predator removal is not judged by the number of predators removed, but rather by improvements in population or reproduction of the rare species to be conserved.

Protecting Sea Turtle Nests at a High Density Nesting Beach: An Informed Approach

The beach at Hobe Sound National Wildlife Refuge (HSNWR) on Florida's east coast is a high-density nesting beach (up to 1600 nests in 5.3 km) serving three species of threatened and endangered sea turtles: loggerhead (*Caretta caretta*), leatherback (*Dermochelys coriacea*), and green (*Chelonia mydas*) turtles. HSNWR is located in one of most important marine turtle nesting areas in Florida (Meylan et al. 1995), and is in the center of loggerhead nesting activity in the U.S. Historically, up to 95% of turtle nests at HSNWR were lost to predation (Bain *et al.* 1997) by raccoons (*Procyon lotor*), an over-abundant native species, and armadillos (*Dasypus novemcinctus*), an invasive species. Consequently, predator control was identified as the most important conservation tool at HSNWR (Bain *et al.* 1997; USFWS 2000).

Predator control had been carried out at HSNWR since 1972 (Bain *et al.* 1997). Through 1998, predator control had primarily been carried out by refuge staff in addition to their primary duties (Engeman et al. 2003a). Nest predation was reduced, but still was at an unacceptable level of 48.4% when the refuge developed a 1 person-month agreement with the US Department of Agriculture, Wildlife Services (USDA/WS) to have specialists carry out the predator control, resulting in a reduction in predation to 41.6% (Engeman et al. 2003a).

This was a step in the right direction, but greater reductions in predation were desired. For the 2000 nesting season, it was hoped that predator control in advance of the nesting season would eliminate the problem before it began. This was also the season that a passive tracking index (PTI) was applied to monitor the size and distribution of the predator populations along the beach (Engeman et al. 2003a).

The first result from incorporating the PTI information into control activities was to discover that the predators for the most part were not at the beach until the turtles began nesting in full force. Thus, the concept of applying predator control prior to turtle nesting would have resulted in expending the 1 person-month of control without effectively addressing the predators drawn to the beach during nesting, and probably would have resulted in very high levels of predation. The PTI methodology further indicated when the predators became active, where they were the greatest problem, and when their activity declined so that the control could be temporarily halted until needed later in the nesting season, thereby extending the timeframe of the 1 person-month agreement (Engeman et al. 2003a). Optimization of the timing and placement of predator control activities in this manner reduced predation to a remarkably (at that time) low 27.7% (Engeman et al. 2003a). To put these results in perspective, it was estimated this approach resulted in almost 84,000 more hatchlings into the ocean over historical high predation rates, over 62,000 more hatchlings than when the refuge was carrying out control, and nearly 54,000 more hatchlings than control specialists achieved prior optimizing their efforts with the population information from the PTI (Engeman et al. 2003a). Using conservative monetary valuations for sea turtles, The economic improvements over the previous predator control approaches ranged from $1.7 million to $8.4 million, depending on the approach used for comparison (Engeman et al. 2003a). These returns were achieved for a predator control agreement of approximately $10,000.

The success story does not end here. In 2002, the design of the PTI was improved so that armadillos could be better monitored, and therefore, more efficiently controlled. The outcome was another significant drop in predation to 9.4%, a level not believed achieved achievable (Engeman et al. 2005). Further increases in hatchling numbers and corresponding economic returns were produced beyond previous accomplishments (Engeman et al. 2005). Additional improvements appeared to be on the horizon initially in 2004, but predator control was removed midway through the nesting season due to budgetary shortfalls, and predation soared as a result (Engeman et al. 2006). The experience at HSNWR demonstrates that knowledge about the predator population can be shrewdly applied to maximize efficacy of predator management efforts while obtaining the greatest return for the conservation dollar, while halting a successful technique results in conservation reversals.

Conserving the Critically Endangered Puerto Rican Parrot

The Puerto Rican parrot (*Amazona vittata*) is one of the 10 most endangered birds in the world, and predation has been identified as one of the factors limiting Puerto Rican parrot productivity in the wild. The loss of a very few birds or a nest can have a great impact on the species. Management of red-tailed hawks (*Buteo jamaicensis*), and invasive mammals including black rats (*Rattus rattus*), feral cats (*Felis catus*) and small Indian mongooses (*Herpestes javanicus*) offers significant benefit to the parrot population. Each of these species is potentially a story unto itself and a key to conserving a bird this vulnerable and rare. For brevity, we only consider here lessons from the portion concerning black rats, but that does not imply a priority, as management of all predators is necessary for such a rare species (around 30-40 birds in the wild at the time of the described research).

Rats are primarily a threat to parrot nests. They may predate the eggs or chicks, or they may harass the parent birds sufficiently to deter adequate care of the nest, leading to its failure. Tracking plates, bait blocks, and trapping were applied to index black rats in the parrot nesting area. Although toxic baiting had been carried out to a degree around parrot nest sites, an extraordinary trap success for black rats at all sites in the parrot nesting area (42% all sites combined) demonstrated that the rat control strategy was insufficient to be effective for protecting parrot nests. Despite the existence of some control, the trapping index for rat abundance was among the highest reported in the literature anywhere in the world using live or snap traps (Engeman et al. 2006). Similarly, rat response to the nontoxic bait blocks for population monitoring purposes was universally high, regardless of ground or tree placement. Black rats appeared exceptionally abundant in the forest where the parrots nest. Most studies report <10% trap success for black rats (e.g., Dunlevy et al., 2000; Robinet et al., 1998; Tamarin and Malecha, 1972), but even those lower rat densities are well documented as causing insular avian extinctions or declines (e.g., Atkinson, 1985).

Wild parrot breeding success fluctuates considerably. A rat-induced nest failure was particularly unacceptable in a year (2002) when there were only three active nests, only one of which was successful and produced two fledglings. Nest success improved substantially in 2003 when rat control was intensified, with four of five active nests successful and eight fledglings produced (Engeman et al. 2006). Various factors may have influenced nesting success including weather conditions, natural fluctuations in breeding success, and enhanced rat control. Rat control is the only one of these factors that could be managed, and is highly cost-effective to apply (Engeman et al., 2003b).

As an illustration of control cost-efficacy, management of all predators as a general species enhancement method for the Puerto Rican parrot was analyzed from an economic perspective. A benefit-cost analysis was used to examine the potential improvements from predator management for protecting Puerto Rican parrots. Using median parrot values across five years from two captive breeding facilities demonstrated that saving only one parrot from predation every 2.6 years allows the combined predator management for all predator species to be cost-effective. Use of the maximal empirical per-parrot value during the same time period showed the combined application of all forms of predator management as cost-effective if only one parrot was saved from predation every 11.8 years.

The Puerto Rican parrot is another example of extreme cost-effectiveness for conserving an endangered species through predator management. The example of rats as nest predators is a demonstration that application of some level of predator control can lead to the belief that the predator species is being effectively managed when, in fact, that was not the case. Similar to the sea turtle situation at HSNWR, a better understanding and consequent management of the predator situation for the Puerto Rican parrot led to enhanced reproduction of the endangered species.

Steller's Eiders: The Simple Solution

Sometimes predation turns out to be the simplistic explanation for reproductive failure in a listed species and defies predictions from complex explanations of system dynamics pointing to a variety of other factors as playing more major roles in breeding success. The Alaska breeding population of Steller's eiders (*Polysticta stelleri*) is federally listed as threatened and state-listed as a species of concern. Steller's eiders are highly susceptible to predation during nesting season in late spring and early summer. Control of arctic fox (*Alopex lagopus*) on the Barrow Steller's Eider Conservation Planning Area (BSECPA) began in 2005 to protect the threatened Alaska-breeding population of Steller's eider, as well as other indigenous birds.

The nesting success of Steller's eiders at BSECPA has fluctuated greatly since 1991. Nest success averaged 16% from 1991-2004, prior to fox control. Since fox control from 2005-2007 nest success averaged 52% (Gilsdorf and Rossi 2008). Nest success for shorebirds at BSECPA also had a simultaneous dramatic increase, averaging about 29% for the years monitored pre-control (2003-2004), and averaging about 83% during the years with control (Gilsdorf and Rossi 2008). Prior to fox control, the eiders only nested successfully in less than half of the years where observations took place. During that time, they only nested successfully in two consecutive years twice, and they never successfully nested in three consecutive years. However, they successfully nested in all three consecutive years where fox control was applied. The positive influence from fox control on reproductive success for the Steller's eiders and the other shorebirds nesting in BSECPA has been dramatic and immediate (Gilsdorf and Rossi 2008).

Breeding by Steller's eiders and their consequent breeding success were considered dependent on a variety of factors, including predation. Predictions based on past breeding patterns in connection with other predator and prey species abundances and interactions suggested to some that the eiders would not breed in the third year that predator control was applied (Gilsdorf and Rossi 2008). If true, this would imply that application of predator control to protect breeding in a non-breeding year would be unproductive (and uneconomical). Fortunately, empirical evidence was sought, control was applied, and the eiders bred successfully contrary to predictions based on complex dynamics (Gilsdorf and Rossi 2008). Moreover, at this writing, preliminary results from 2008 indicate that this fourth year of predator management will be the fourth consecutive, and most outstanding, year of successful breeding by the Steller's eiders in BSECPA.

The average cost per year to apply the control has been less than $29,000. Detailed economic analyses of these results have been initiated at this writing, but it is clear from even a cursory scan of these results coupled with even minimum valuations for the Steller's eiders and shorebirds, that the monetarily valued returns in production (benefits) will be orders of magnitude greater than the costs. These returns, both biologically and economically, have the potential to be increased in the future. Arctic fox, while most harmful, are not the only eider predator on BSECPA. Red fox (*Vulpes vulpes*) was added to the predators managed in the 2008 breeding season. Jaegers (*Stercorarius groenlandicus*), snowy owls (*Nyctea scandiaca*), weasels (*Mustela* spp.), ravens (*Corvus corax*), and glaucous gulls (*Larus hyperboreus*) are also abundant and also prey on eiders, their eggs or young. Judicious management of these species may further enhance the returns from predator management for conserving Steller's eiders.

As demonstrated in other aspects of the examples presented earlier, hypothetical approaches for predator management should be tested by obtaining empirical results. Otherwise, the predator control would not have been applied for the third consecutive year, and breeding success for the eiders would likely have been lost for that year at BSECPA. This parallels the situation at HSNWR where predator control would have been expended prior to nest predators accumulating at the beach had not empirical information been obtained, and also the situation with the Puerto Rican parrot where population monitoring contradicted the belief that the originally applied level of rat control was sufficient to protect parrot nests.

Endangered Salmonids of the Columbia River Basin

A number of salmonid (*Onchyrhyncus spp*) Evolutionary Significant Units (ESUs), representing demographically independent groups of fish, within the Columbia River Basin in the northwestern U.S. have been designated as endangered (e.g., McClure et al. 2003). Salmon (*Onchyrhyncus spp*) and steelhead (*Onchyrhyncus mkkiss*) populations in the upper Columbia River cannot replace themselves due to the extensive series of hydroelectric dams and reservoirs, a problem which can only be resolved by reducing the mortalities caused by dams (USDA 2003, WDFW 1997). Therefore, hatchery-raised juvenile smolt are used to strengthen recovery efforts and supplement recreational and commercial harvest.

The dams pose several interrelated hazards for the migrating fish. The physiological condition of migrating juvenile salmonids may be altered by dam passage or transportation, increasing their vulnerability to predators (see USDA 2003 for citations and summary). Juvenile salmonids may be injured and also can experience various levels of gas bubble trauma in tailraces due to supersaturated water caused by air dissolved in water at pressures exceeding one atmosphere. The hydroelectric dams act as bottlenecks for juvenile salmonid migration, and the tailrace immediately below hydroelectric dams (approximately 300 m) is where smolt, especially the injured and disoriented, are most vulnerable to avian and piscine predators (Beamesderfer et al. 1996, USDA 2003). Reducing predation in the tailrace of each dam can allow smolt time to recover from the physiological effects of hydroelectric dam passage and to continue on their journey.

The challenge to protecting the smolt is that both avian and piscine predators accumulate at the tailraces of the dams to feed on the smolt. Not only do the piscivorous birds often feed in areas of high fish density, but their presence also attracts additional birds to feeding areas (see USDA 2003 for citations and summary). Juvenile salmonids are a major food source for avian predators on the Columbia River, and basin-wide losses to avian predators constitute a substantial proportion of the juvenile salmonid out-migration (Ruggerone 1986, USDA 2003). Because human-caused changes in the Columbia River Basin created situations with an excess of predators, these healthy predator populations may be controlled when the action is (1) part of a comprehensive recovery plan addressing all aspects of salmonid survival; and (2) as long as the predator population remains abundant (WDFW 1997).

An integrated management approach is used to thwart predation at dam tailraces. Northern pikeminnows (*Pytchocheilus oregonensis*), the primary piscine threat to the smolt, are captured and removed from the tailraces. Predation by piscivorous birds is reduced primarily by deterring birds from congregating and feeding at the tailraces where smolt are unnaturally exposed and susceptible to predation. Methods for reducing bird usage of these areas include overhead wiring systems to inhibit flight into the tailrace areas. Mylar tape, propane cannons, pyrotechnics, effigies and other harassment methods are also used to deter birds from the area (USDA 2003). While > 97% of the protective actions are nonlethal, some lethal removal is necessary for individual birds evading the nonlethal methods (R. Woodruff, USDA/WS, pers. comm.).

Despite reducing predation in discrete river segments of high smolt susceptibility (300 m of tailraces), it is difficult to directly observe the efficacy of predator management on the smolt population. The competing sources of mortality and an underwater population moving through an area make direct population impacts difficult to observe. Many studies have indicated tremendous smolt losses to predators (see Beamesderfer et al. 1996, USDA 2003). An application of bioenergetic modeling attempted to evaluate some aspects of predator management efficacy for protecting smolt (Weise et al. 2008). Recommendations based on the modeling results showed the key components for smolt protection were already in place (for a number of years) (Weise et al. 2008). However, there were also some recommendations contrary to practical management approaches in the wild. For example, the study recognized that the current low take of smolt by birds at tailraces is likely a result of the predator management programs in place for over a decade. Not surprisingly then, current smolt losses to birds in the reaches between the dams were indicated to be greater than at the tailraces, prompting the suggestion that bird management in these river segments that can be over 50 km-long would be an effective means to reduce smolt losses (Weise et al. 2008). This, of course, would be impractical due to the extreme costs that would be incurred for effective implementation. Similarly, it was suggested that lethal removal of birds actually results in greater smolt losses because those same birds would no longer also consume pikeminnow juveniles, thereby increasing predation by pikeminnows through larger populations (even though pikeminnows are also removed at tailraces) (Weise et al. 2008). While this makes for an interesting hypothesis, the number of birds lethally removed 2001 - 2007 has been insignificant. For example, during that time period < 6 birds/yr on average were removed from the dams in the Chelan Public Utility District (USDA/WS unpublished data). Lethal removals of birds across all dams in recent years have been too trivial to have such an impact to influence future adult pikeminnow populations, and the current removal numbers are also trivial in comparison to the (high-variance) mean figure of 3360 from 1997 to 2001 presented in Weise et al. (2008), the period when smolt protection from predators was in its initial phases and bird congregations at the dams were orders of magnitude higher than now (R. Woodruff, USDA/WS, pers. comm.). Moreover, the current low lethal take is highly necessary to handle some birds unaffected by the other deterrent methods. Those birds otherwise would not only consume smolt at will, but they would also serve as decoys for ever-increasing numbers of birds to also evade the deterrents, ultimately defeating or diminishing efficacy of the nonlethal measures in place (R. Woodruff, USDA/WS, pers. comm.). Thus, relative application of smolt protection methods has followed an adaptive management approach responding to induced and natural changes in populations and behaviors of the species preying on smolt.

Spotted Owls: The Brewing Concern

The northern spotted owl (*Strix occidentalis caurina*) was listed as federally endangered in Canada in 1986 (Campbell and Campbell 1984, Government of Canada 2002) and as federally threatened in the United States under the Endangered Species Act in 1990 (USFWS 1990). A land-based conservation strategy was devised for northern spotted owl recovery, with 3.01 million ha designated as Late-Successional Reserves to protect forests used by northern spotted owls, and another 1.06 million ha designated as riparian reserves, in large part to allow dispersal of northern spotted owls among Late-Successional Reserves, all in addition to existing protected areas such as national parks (USDA and USDI 1994; Marcot and Thomas 1997). Overall, "the federal forests in the Pacific Northwest underwent the largest shift in management focus since their creation" (Thomas et al. 2006), from timber production to protection of late-successional forests used by northern spotted owls and other species. As the basis of the Northwest Forest Plan, "no species in the United States has had a greater impact on land-use planning at the landscape scale" than the northern spotted owl (Noon and Blakesley 2006), resulting in significantly decreased timber harvest on federal lands within the range of the northern spotted owls (Charnley 2006, Thomas et al. 2006). Based on the value of the timber now unavailable for harvest and the numbers of owls potentially occupying the protected areas, an empirical valuation of northern spotted owls would probably show it to have one of the highest monetary values in the world.

This land-based conservation strategy is now being confounded by a species invasive to western North America. Barred owls (*Strix varia*) have invaded from eastern North America into the range of the northern spotted owl, where they are negatively affecting site occupancy, reproduction, and survival of northern spotted owls. Barred owls are larger than northern spotted owls, are physically aggressive toward them, can kill them, and use the same habitats and prey as they do. Moreover, barred owls negatively affect calling behavior, site occupancy, fecundity, and survival of northern spotted owls (see Livezey et al. 2007 for a summary of negative impacts). Therefore, the 2007 Draft Northern Spotted Owl Recovery Plan (USFWS 2007) identified Barred Owls as a very important threat to northern spotted owls.

As barred owls continue to expand their range and saturate the range of northern spotted owls, habitat preservation by itself will likely be insufficient to conserve northern spotted owls. Furthermore, barred owls are beginning to also invade the range of the California spotted owl (*Strix occidentalis occidentalis*). While not currently listed, subjecting California spotted owls to the same pressures that northern spotted owls are receiving from barred owls might well lead to their listing (Livezey et al. 2007). Thus, the threat posed by barred owls also may well lead to having to make a difficult choice: wide scale removal of barred owls or permit spotted owl populations to dwindle, possibly to extinction (Gutiérrez et al. 2004, Livezey et al. 2007). Such management of barred owls may eventually be required to save both northern spotted owls and California spotted owls. Even though the barred owl is an invasive species to the western U.S, and poses a substantial threat to a listed species, control of owls would still be an objectionable management choice to many wildlife professionals. Although raptor control is sometimes applied on a spot basis to protect endangered species such as black-footed ferrets or endangered ground squirrels, it has rarely been applied in the U.S. on a large scale to protect endangered species. The red-tailed hawk control to protect critically endangered Puerto Rican parrots would not compare in scale to what potentially would be needed to conserve northern spotted owls. More than likely, the difficult choice will need to be made if populations of northern spotted owls (and California spotted owls) are to remain viable.

Aleutian Cackling Goose: The Ultimate Success Story

The definitive assessment for predator management as a conservation tool would be delisting a species based primarily on this management approach. Such was the case for the Aleutian Cackling goose (*Branta canadensis leucopareia*), until recently known as the Aleutian Canada goose.

Over the course of nearly 200 years, arctic fox and red fox (*Vulpes vulpes*) were introduced for fur production to islands throughout the breeding range of the Aleutian Cackling goose. Aleutian Cackling geese were particularly easy targets for predators as they are ground nesters and flightless during molting in the summer, and only escaped extinction by persisting on three islands where foxes had not been established (Ebbert 2000), and the species became the third species overall to be listed under the U.S. Endangered Species Act.

Beginning in1949 and continuing into this century, foxes were targeted for elimination from the islands within the breeding range of the Aleutian Cackling goose by the U.S. Fish and Wildlife Service (USFWS), and in collaboration with USDA/WS. The island eradications involved a variety of methods and were highly successful. Coupled with natural and human translocations of geese to islands cleared of foxes, the removal of predators led to greatly improved breeding and rapid population increases (USFWS 2001). By 1999 the Aleutian Cackling goose population (~ 37,000) had reached nearly five times the population objective for delisting (USFWS 2001). The Aleutian Cackling goose was officially delisted in 2001 (USFWS 2001), and today's population exceeds 120,000. Thus, the Aleutian Cackling goose represents a significant conservation accomplishment for the recovery of an endangered species, and its recovery is largely a result of successful predator management.

Discussion

Through the use of a variety of example situations, the utility of predator management as a conservation tool for endangered species was demonstrated in the preceding section. However, most examples also demonstrated clear caveats concerning the application, or non-application, of predator management. We easily could have shown examples where applications of predator management did not appear to benefit the species intended to be protected. In fact, some of our examples showed predator management to be unsuccessful, or only marginally successful at assisting endangered species until it was applied in a fashion that allowed it to be successful. Predator management must be applied in an informed and skilled manner. The examples presented also illustrated a variety of application concepts enhancing the prospects for benefiting the species to be protected. Thus, key aspects for predator management to produce tangible benefits for protecting endangered species include:

- Application by skilled/trained personnel able to focus on the task.
- Timing of management efforts so the most favorable impact can be achieved.
- Applying the effort with sufficient intensity that the desired effect can be achieved.
- Use of predator population information for optimizing the timing, distribution and intensity of management efforts.
- Adapting management strategies to changing circumstances through time.

These concepts seem obvious, but they do not always seem to be recognized in practice. They are also interrelated. A specialist in the area is more likely to recognize the appropriate timing, intensity, and placement needed to achieve a desired outcome. Even so, empirical information can be invaluable for even an expert to carry out predator management most effectively. Placement of traps, baits or any management tools in the field might provide a sense that predator management is being carried out. However, just because tools are being applied in the field does not mean they are being applied effectively. If the methods are not being applied effectively, then predator management is not taking place. We saw this in the case of protecting sea turtle nests where predator management was originally assigned not to a specialist, but as an additional duty for refuge staff. Even when specialists were called in, efficacy was not maximized until empirical population observations were obtained and incorporated into method application strategies. The same was clearly true for protecting Puerto Rican parrot nests from rats. Rat baits were applied by staff without expertise in rat control, and as an adjunct to the other conservation activities for the parrot. Rat population information demonstrated the insufficient intensity in application and experts in rat control were able to apply control tools efficiently and effectively, and pass the information along (Engeman and Whisson 2004). It would be a disservice to the species in need of protection to discount predator management as useful because it was ineffectively applied. Fortunately, this was averted with the Puerto Rican parrot through empirical demonstration.

Sometimes empirical demonstrations serve to supersede a theoretical situation. Such was the case with the Steller's eiders where the hypothesized species interrelationships would have suggested the third consecutive year of predator control was unnecessary, because the eiders were unlikely to breed in that year. To the credit of all parties concerned with eider conservation, that hypothesis was evaluated through applying a third year of predator control, resulting in successful breeding. Similar empirical demonstrations likely may fortify strategies for protecting juvenile salmonids in the Columbia River Basin, and test cases may prove the advantage to northern spotted owls from managing barred owls.

There are rarely objections raised to managing rats for endangered species protection, or reclaiming land for endangered bird reintroduction by applying the highly effective control methods for brown treesnakes (*Boiga irregularis*) on Guam (e.g., Engeman and Vice 1999). However, when more popular species are targeted for management, we have seen important conservation aspects stymied. For example in Florida, objections frequently are raised to managing populations of highly abundant raccoons and feral cats for the protection of endangered prey species such as Key Largo woodrats (*Neotoma floridana smalli*), Lower Keys marsh rabbits (*Sylvilagus palustris hefneri*), or beach mice. Public buy-in is often difficult, but when permitted, monitored and appropriately applied, the positive impacts from predator management are usually incontrovertible. Initially, there was considerable resistance to managing red-tailed hawks to protect Puerto Rican parrots, but the necessity and logic were inescapable, and the approach has received acceptance. The spotted owl situation in all likelihood will draw a tight focus on having to make tough choices between managing a predator species and letting a listed species eventually disappear from the wild.

Monitoring populations, at least on the local management scale, has been a theme discussed in various contexts here. It has been our experience that monitoring populations greatly assists their successful management. We have discussed how monitoring predators can greatly aid in the optimal application of management techniques in terms of timing and placement. Efficacy in management also is indicated, but the true measure is in the benefits to the protected species. Thus, there also is a need to monitor the species requiring protection to demonstrate, or identify, efficacy of management methods. As espoused early on, the ability to monetarily value the protected species allows the returns on conservation expenditures to be evaluated, and compared in some circumstances. This also is highly beneficial to species conservation, as it provides a direct means to justify continued conservation expenditures.

REFERENCES

Atkinson, I.A.E. (1985). The spread of commensal species of Rattus to oceanic islands and their effects on avifaunas. In P.J. Moore (ed.) *Conservation of Island Birds. Case Studies for the Management of Threatened Island Species.* Pp. 35-81, International Council for Bird Preservation Technical Publication No. 3, International Council for Bird Preservation, Cambridge.

Bain, R.E., Jewell, S.D., Schwagerl, J., & Neely, B.S. Jr. (1997). *Sea turtle nesting and reproductive success at the Hobe Sound National Wildlife Refuge (Florida), 1972-1995.* Report to U.S. Fish and Wildlife Service, ARM Loxahatchee NWR.

Beamesderfer, R.C.P., D.L. Ward & A.A. Nigro. (1996). Evaluation of the biological basis for a predator control program on northern squawfish (*Pytchocheilus oregonensis*) in the Columbia and Snake Rivers. *Canadian Journal of Fisheries and Aquatic Sciences*, 53,2898-2908.

Bodenchuk, M.J. & Hayes, D.J. (2006). Predation impacts and management strategies for wildlife protection. In A.M.T. Elewa (ed): *Predation in organisms, a distinct phenomenon.* Pp 221-264. Springer-Verlag Berlin.

Bodenchuk, M.J., Mason, J.R. & Pitt, W.C. (2002) Economics of predation management in relation to agriculture, wildlife, and human health and safety. In L. Clark (ed.) *Proceedings of the 1st International Symposium on the Economics of Wildlife Damage Management.* Pp. 80-90 Colorado State University, Fort Collins, Colorado.

Campbell, E.C., & Campbell, R.W. (1984). *Status report on Spotted Owl in Canada, 1983.* Report to Committee on the Status of Endangered Wildlife in Canada, Ottawa, Ontario, Canada.

Charnley, S. (2006). The Northwest Forest Plan as a model for broad-scale ecosystem management: a social perspective. *Conservation Biology*, 20, 330-340.

Conner, M.M., Jaeger, M.M., Weller, T.J., & McCullough, D.R. (1998). Effect of coyote removal on sheep depredation in northern California. *Journal of Wildlife Management*, 62,690-699.

Dunlevy, P.A., Campbell, E.W. III & Lindsey, G.D. (2000). Broadcast application of a placebo rodenticide bait in a native Hawaiian forest. *International Biodeterioration and Biodegradation*, 45, 199-208.

Ebbert, S. (2000). Successful eradication of introduced arctic foxes from large Aleutian Islands. *Vertebrate Pest Conference*, 19, 127-132.

Engeman, R.M., Martin, R.E., Constantin, B., Noel, R., & Woolard, J. (2003a). Monitoring predators to optimize their management for marine turtle nest protection. *Biological Conservation,* 113,171-178.

Engeman, R.M., Martin, R.E., Smith, H.T., Woolard, J., Constantin, B. & Stahl, M. (2006). The impact on predation of sea turtle nests when predator control was removed midway through the nesting season. *Wildlife Research*, 33,187-192.

Engeman, R.M., Martin, R.E., Smith, H.T., Woolard, J., Crady, C.K., Shwiff, S.A., Constantin, B., Stahl, M. & Griner, J. (2005). Dramatic reduction in predation on sea turtle nests through improved predator monitoring and management. *The Oryx*. 39, 318-326.

Engeman, R.M., Shwiff, S.A., Cano, F., Constantin, B. (2003b). An economic assessment of the potential for predator management to benefit Puerto Rican parrots. *Ecological Economics*, 46,283-292.

Engeman, R.M., Shwiff, S.A., Constantin, B., Stahl, M., Smith, H.T. (2002). An Economic Analysis of Predator Removal Approaches for Protecting Marine Turtle Nests at Hobe Sound National Wildlife Refuge. *Ecological Economics*, 42, 469-478.

Engeman, R.M., Shwiff, S.A., Smith, H.T. & Constantin, B.U. (2004). Monetary valuation of rare species and imperiled habitats as a basis for economically evaluating conservation approaches. *Endangered Species Update,* 21, 66-73.

Engeman, R.M. & Vice, D.S. (2001) Objectives and integrated approaches for the control of brown tree snakes. *Integrated Pest Management Reviews*, 6, 59-76.

Engeman, R.M. & Whisson, D.A. (2004). *Costs of baiting and monitoring programs for rats and mongooses for protection of the Puerto Rican parrot.* Report to U.S. Fish and Wildlife Service. USDA/APHIS/WS Natioanl Wildlife Research Center, Fort Collins, Colorado.

Engeman, R.M., Whisson, D.A., Quinn, J., Cano, F. & White, T. Jr. (2006). Monitoring invasive mammalian predator populations sharing habitat with the critically endangered Puerto Rican parrot Amazona vittata. *The Oryx*. 40:95-102.

Gilsdorf, J. & Rossi, C.L. (2008). *Arctic fox control on the Barrow Steller's Eider Conservation Planning Area, 2005-2008 Report.* USDA/Wildlife Services, Olympia, WA.

Government Of Canada. (2002). *Species at Risk Act*. Government of Canada, Ottawa, Ontario, Canada.

Gutiérrez, R.J. (1994). Changes in the distribution and abundance of spotted owls during the past century. *Studies in Avian Biology*, 15, 293–300.

Hecht, A., & Nickerson, P.R. (1999). The need for predator management in conservation of some vulnerable species. *Endangered Species Update,* 16, 114-118.

Knowlton, F.F., Gese, E.M., Jaeger, M.M. (1999). Coyote depredation control: An interface between biology and management. *Journal of Range Management*. 52, 398-412.

Livesey, K., R.M. Engeman, D.F. Rock & D.A. Yasuda. (2007). Considering control of invasive barred owls to benefit California spotted owls: possible justification and draft methods. In G. Witmer, W. Pitt, K. Fagerstone, (eds.) *Managing Vertebrate Invasive Species: Proceedings of an International Symposium.* Pp 72-81 USDA/APHIS/WS, National Wildlife Research Center, Fort Collins, CO. (2007.

Loomis, J.B., & Walsh, R.G. (1997). *Recreation Economic Decisions: Comparing Benefits and Costs*, 2nd Edition, Venture Publishing, Inc. State College, Pennsylvania.

Marcot, B.G., & Thomas, J.W. (1997). *Of spotted owls, old growth, and new policies: a history since the Interagency Scientific Committee report.* Gen. Tech. Rep. PNW-GTR-408. U.S. Department of Agriculture Forest Service, Pacific Northwest Research Station, Portland, OR, USA.

McClure, M.M., Holmes, E.E., Sanderson, B.K., & Jordan, C.E. (2003). A large-scale multi-species status assessment: andromous salmonids in the Columbia River Basin. *Ecological Applications*, 13, 964-989.

Meylan, A., Schroeder, B., Mosier, A. (1995). *Sea turtle nesting activity in the state of Florida 1979-1992.* Florida Marine Research Publication No. 52. 51pp. Florida Marine Research Institute, St. Petersburg.

Noon, B.R., & Blakesley, J.A. (2006). Conservation of the Northern Spotted Owl under the Northwest Forest Plan. *Conservation Biology*, 20, 288–296.

Ramsey, D.S.L.,& Wilson, J.W. (2000). Towards ecologically based baiting strategies for rodents in agricultural systems. *International Biodeterioration and Biodegradation*, 45,183-197.

Reynolds, J.C., & Tapper, S.C. (1996). Control of mammalian predators in game management and conservation. *Mammal Review,* 26, 127-156.

Robinet, O., Craig, J.L. & Chardonnet, L. (1998). Impact of rat species in Ouvea and Lifou (Loyalty Islands) and their consequences for conserving the endangered Ouvea Parakeet. *Biological Conservation.* 86, 223-232.

Ruggerone, G.T. (1986). Consumption of migrating juvenile salmonids by gulls foraging below a Columbia River dam. *Transactions of the American Fisheries Society*, 115, 736-742.

Salo, P., Korpimäki, E., Banks, P.B., Nordström, M. & Dickman, C.R. (2007). Alien predators are more dangerous than native predators to prey populations. *Proc. Royal Society London B,* 274, 1237-1243.

Schoener, T.W., Spilier, D.A. & Losoa, J.B. (2001). Predators increase the risk of catastrophic extinction of prey populations. *Nature*, 412, 183-186.

Stein, B.A. & Flack, R.S., editors (1996). *America's least wanted: alien species invasions of U.S. ecosystems*. Arlington, Virginia, The Nature Conservancy.

Tamarin, R.H. & Malecha, S.R. (1972). Reproductive parameters in Rattus rattus and Rattus exulans of Hawaii, 1968 to 1970. *Journal of Mammalogy*, 53, 513-528.

Tennessee Valley Authority vs Hill. (1978). 437 U.S. 153.

Thomas, J.W., Franklin, J.F., Gordon, J. & Johnson, K.N. (2006). The Northwest Forest Plan: origins, components, implementation experience, and suggestions for change. *Conservation Biology*, 20, 277-287.

USDA. (U.S. Department of Agriculture). (2003). *Environmental assessment and finding of no significant impact on piscivorous bird damage management for the protection of juvenile salmonids on the mid-Columbia River*. USDA, Olympia, Washington, USA.

USDA and USDI (U.S. Department of Agriculture and U.S. Department of the Interior). (1994). *Record of Decision for amendments to Forest Service and Bureau of Land*

Management planning documents within the range of the northern spotted owl, and Standards and Guidelines for management of late-successional and old-growth forest related species within the range of the northern spotted owl. USDA Forest Service and USDI Bureau of Land Management. Portland, OR,USA.

USFWS (U.S. Fish and Wildlife Service). (1990). Endangered and threatened wildlife and plants; determination of threatened status for the northern spotted owl; final rule. *Federal Register*, 55, 26114–26194.

USFWS (U.S. Fish and Wildlife Service). (2000). Environmental Assessment for the Management of Predation Losses to Sea Turtle Nests at the Hobe Sound National Wildlife Refuge, Martin County, Florida. U.S. Fish and Wildlife Service.

USFWS (U.S. Fish and Wildlife Service). (2001). Endangered and threatened wildlife and plants: final rule to remove the Aleutian Canada goose from the federal list of endangered and threatened wildlife. *Federal Register*, 66:15643-15656.

USFWS (U.S. Fish and Wildlife Service). (2007). *2007 draft recovery plan for the Northern Spotted Owl (Strix occidentalis caurina): merged options 1 and 2.* U.S. Fish and Wildlife Service, Portland, OR, USA. 170 pp.

Waples, R. (1998). *Definition of a "species" under the Endangered Species Act: application to Pacific Salmon.* NOAA Technical Memo. National Marine Fisheries Service F/NWC-194. National Marine Fisheries Service, Portland, Oregon, USA.

WDFW (Washington Department of Fish and Wildlife). (1997*). Final Environmental Impact Statement for the Wild Salmonid Policy.* Washington Department of Fish and Wildlife, Olympia, Washington.

Wiese, F.K., Parrish, J.K., Thompson, C.W. & Maranto, C. (2008). Ecosystem-based management of predator-prey relationships: piscivorous birds and salmonids. *Ecological Applications*, 18, 681-700.

Wilcove, D.S., Rothstein, D, Dubow, J., Phillips, A. & Losos, E. (1998). Assessing the relative importance of habitat destruction, alien species, pollution, over-exploitation, and disease. *BioScience,* 48, 607-616.

Wilcox, C. & Donlan, J. (2007). Compensatory mitigation as a solution to fisheries bycatch-biodiversity conservation conflicts. *Frontiers in Ecology and Environment*, 5, 325-331.

In: Endangered Species: New Research
Editors: A. Columbus and L. Kuznetsov
ISBN 978-1-60692-241-5

Chapter 8

IN THE CYCLE OF LIFE: CRYOPRESERVATION OF POST-MORTEM SPERM AS A VALUABLE SOURCE IN RESTORATION OF RARE AND ENDANGERED SPECIES

***George Yu. Maksudov*[1], *Natalia V. Shishova*[2] *and Igor I. Katkov*[3]**

[1] Scientific Department, Moscow Zoo, Moscow 123242, Russian Federation
[2] Lab. Cryopreservation of Genetic Resources, Institute of Cell Biophysics RAS, Puschino 142290, Moscow region, Russian Federation
[3] CELLTRONIX (CTX), San Diego, California 92126. USA

ABSTRACT

The role of cryobanks in preservation of genetic material has been growing at an exponential rate. Practically all semen that is nowadays used in cattle industry in the developed countries is cryopreserved. However, collection (retrieval) of spermatozoa of wild animals has been a formidable task: it is expensive, time consuming and even sometime harmful both for the animal and for the collector. From this standpoint, collection of the mortem (cadaveric, posthumous) sperm of recently died animal (Postmortem Semen Cryopreservation, PMSCP) for rare and endangered species can be a substantial addition, and sometime the method of choice in preservation of reproductive cells, both in wild and at Zoos and & national parks.

This work addresses the cadaver sperm cryopreservation. A comprehensive review of the state of the art with the main emphasizes on the team's own achievements is presented and discussed in details. Special attention is given to the following aspects of PMSCP: 1) Epididymal sperm as the source for artificial insemination and *in vitro* fertilization in general. 2) Comparison of quality and viability of epididymal sperm *vs.* electroejaculated semen. 3) Brief summary of a 4-yr work in the Moscow Zoological Park (one of the largest Zoos in the World) in collaboration with ICB and Celltronix (CTX). The Chapter is focused on the use of mammalian post-mortem sperm; however, a similar approach can be applied to other higher terrestrial vertebrates.

Finally, in the Discussion underscores the importance of PMSCP, its achievements, pitfalls, ways of improvement and future directions.

Key Words: Rare and endangered species; post-mortem sperm; testicular sperm; epididymal sperm; cryopreservation; conservation of genetic resources; zoos.

INTRODUCTION

Implementation of methods of artificial insemination (ART), including genetic cryobanks for conservation and reproduction of rare and endangered species (RES) has been first suggested by Veprintsev and Rott (1979). Different aspects of this problem and the results that have been obtained by man scientists all over the World have been extensively discussed in books, reviews and at conferences. Currently, CP of genetic resources is recognized to be an important direction in conservation of RES (Comizzoli et al., 2000; Holt, Pickard, 1999; Leibo, Songsasen, 2002; Mazur et al., 2008, Wildt, 2000).

To this day, the research in the field of conservation of the genetic resources of RES by means of cryopreservation (CP) and assisted reproduction technique (ART) have been progressing very rapidly and involving many endangered taxons of mammals and other higher vertebrates. Beside substantial progress and achievements, a number of technical and organizational problems arise. Some of them are the cryobiological aspects of the genome CP, while the other address is of specific reproductive biology of different species. For instance, practical possibilities of ART use to reproduce the preserved genetic resources of a specific species. Some problems arise in regards to the use of genome resource banks to control genetic structures of rare species populations.

It is paradoxical though that the number of rare species genetic resources, available for research and preservation, are reducing with an essential progress achieved in this area. And the available to preservation genetic resources of those that are becoming extinct, the most endangered species, are negligible small. In other words, along with other factors, possibilities of preserving rare species genome by means of CP methods are also restrained by lack of the sufficient original source material.. Unlike oil, the humanity cannot rely on discovering new “birthplaces” of extinct or becoming extinct species (www.redlist.org), nor can it replace their genome.

Direct endanger of irrevocable extinction of rare species makes any operation with their biological material quite specific. First of all, experimental options are minimal in this case, and mass experiments are impossible. That restriction forces to use methods that have been already developed for allied domestic or other wild but not rare species analogs. Nevertheless, such species cannot be always found. Besides that, our knowledge of reproductive biology of RES has been very limited in the majority of cases.

For critically endangered species, it is strongly recommended to preserve any possible genetic material. It is advisable to preserve not only sperm samples, oocytes and embryos, but also fragments of sex glands, different organs and tissues, DNA samples, cell cultures and other available genetic material.

In other words, it is more possible to save these species using the “*total CP*” of their genetic resources. The main idea of such "total preservation" is to gather various genetic materials for future generations of biologists. Development of such ART methods as cloning, heterogenic transplanting of sex glands, intracellular sperm injection (ICSI) and others, will prospectively allow using this material to reproduce these species. Otherwise not preserved genetic resources will be lost irrevocably.

It has been getting more and more difficult to obtain genetic material from the wildlife resources due to both reduction of animals total population and their catching, collection and preserving of the samples. Besides, the legislative restrictions concerning handling rare species (SITES) are getting sricter.

Thus, the role of the zoos and breeding centers as sources of the genetic material for genome banks and ART is growing. "It is estimated that the thousand plus federated zoos of the world collectively house some 1,00,000 animals, predominantly higher vertebrates". (The World Zoo Conservation Strategy, 2003).

Even large zoos keep relatively low number of individuals from one species, usually up to 5, sometime 10 individuals. The number of animals usually provided for ART activities is even lower. Nevertheless, all leaving things are mortal, therefore even in ideal management conditions the animals die, often with no offspring produced or genetic samples obtained for genome banks.

Postmortem CP of the genome of rare species, *i.e.* from recently fallen animals, is a good combination of irrevocably lost genetic material, implementation of modern biotechnological methods, and absence of injuries possibility for researchers and objects. Valuable information in regard to reproductive peculiarities of species also could be obtained. It is important that a number of reproductive characteristics can be obtained only when gonads undergo histomorphological analysis.

Preservation and use of a postmortem sperm (and female gemetic germplasm) is the last chance to get a offspring from the dead male in case of unexpected loss of valuable individuals. It is comforting that this issue has attracted sufficiently more attention within last 6-8 years.

In this min-review, besides some background description, we will discuss available materials concerning collection of spermatozoa from postmortem testes of rare mammals and analyze a 5-year experience on collection and CP of postmortem sperm in the Moscow Zoological Park, one of the oldest of that kind in Europe and one of the largest and diverse zoos in the World (over 1000 animals, more than 600 species (2005) http://www.moscowzoo.ru/defengl.asp).

In this review, we will discuss the data on epididymal spermatozoa of *wild mammalian* species. Data on agricultural and laboratory species are given in case of existence of essential facts that clarify some general patterns, while description of important techniques, to demonstrate the possibilities of using postmortem spermatozoa, as well as in case when domestic animals can be used as models for their allied rare taxonomic units. We have not included the researches on human postmortem sperm in this review. Neither we discuss the post-mortem preservation of female germaplasm, particularly ovaries and ovarian tissues; this important avenue that will be discussed elsewhere.

Fundamentals of the Mammalian Sperm

The term sperm is derived from the Greek word (σπέρμα) *sperma* (meaning "seed") and refers to the male reproductive cells. A uniflagellar sperm cell that is motile is also referred to as **spermatozoon**, whereas a non-motile sperm cell is referred to as **spermatium** (http://en.wikipedia.org/wiki/Sperm). In contrast, the term **semen** constitutes both sperm and seminal fluids (http://en.wikipedia.org/wiki/Semen).

There are 3 distinctive subpopulations of sperm cells in the *mammalian* male genitalia: testicular, epididymal and ejaculate spermatozoa. Morphologically these groups are not very different, unlike their physiological characteristics. (Figure 1).

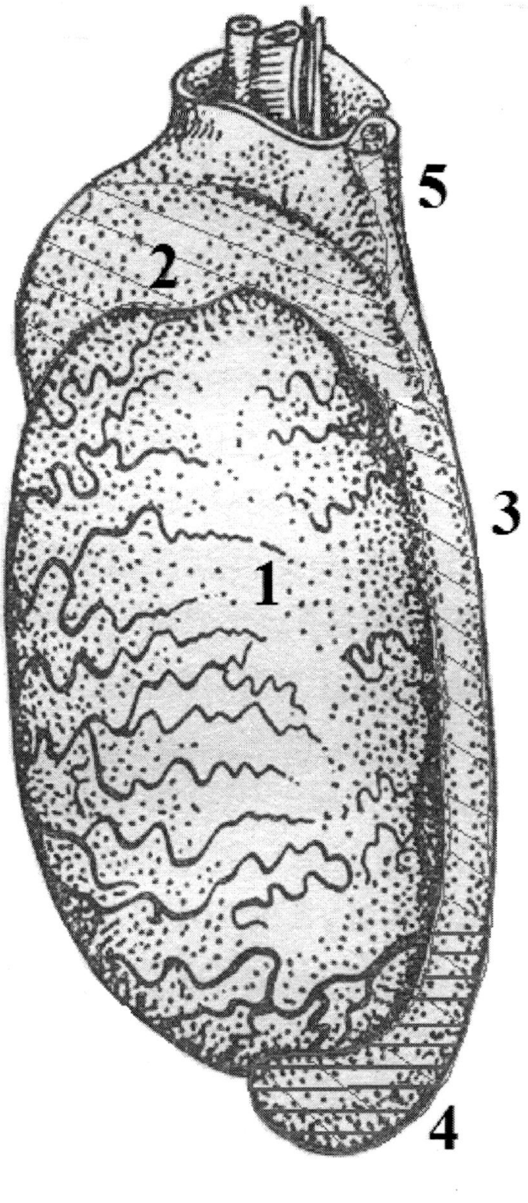

N. Shishova.

Figure 1. Scheme of mammalian testicle: 1. testis; 2. caput epididymides; 3. corpus epididymides; 4. cauda epididymides; 5. ductus deference.

Testicular Spermatozoa

Morphologically formed spermatozoa from male gonads (*testes)* are immovable. When put in activate mediums (diluents) they either stay motionless or gain weak oscillation motility. In case of artificial insemination or "*in vitro*" insemination testicular spermatozoa are not able to fertilize an ovum. However, injection of a testicular spermatozoa directly into ovoplasm (ICSI) allows fertilizing an ovum and get normal embryos (Wurfel et al., 1996). It is interesting that there are facts saying that the difference in human fertilization efficiency by ICSI method, testicle, epididymal or ejaculated spermatozoa is insufficient (Moghadam et al., 2005). It shows that testicular spermatozoa nuclei are already ready to the fusion with an ovum nucleus, and inability to be fertilized with other methods is connected with immaturity of a locomotion system and acrosome apparatus.

Epididymal Spermatozoa

Mammalian spermatozoa go from testes to epididymis, which consists of three parts: *caput, corpus* and *cauda epididymidis,* (Figure 1) through which spermatozoa go consecutively when matured. While this going through epididymis spermatozoa get their ability to progressive motility. Spermatozoa from *caput epididymidis* (Figure 1) have a limited movement potential. Activating mediums make them only oscillated or more seldom, circular movement. Spermatozoa from *cauda epididymidis* (Figure 1) when moved in activating mediums demonstrate active straightforward motility (Goldberg, 2000). The mechanisms involved in sperm storage in the epididymis of mammals in relation to the supply of energy substances, the regulation of motility and metabolism were reviewed by Goldberg, (2000); Jones and Murdoch, (1996); Milovanov, (1962); Verma, (2001). Here we provide a small piece of information contained in these works.

Despite spermatozoa from *caput epididymidis* are considered immature, they already can fertilize an ovum after their placement in female's reproductive tracts, with low efficiency level though (Tables 1 and, 2). During advance through epididymis, fertilizing ability of spermatozoa is increasing and the further the part of the epididymis is from a testis the higher is the sperm fertilizing ability (Goldberg, 2000).

Table 1. Fertility of spermatozoa of three mammalian species harvested from *caput* and *cauda epididymidis*. Artificial insemination in uterus or uterus horns

Species	*caput epididymidis*	*cauda epididymidis*
Rat	8%	93%
Guinea pig	33%	68%
Rabbit	36%	98%

Annotation: The % of fertilized eggs presented for rat and rabbit, for Guinea pig displayed pregnancy rate.

Blandau, Rumery, 1964.

Table 2. Fertility of rabbit spermatozoa from different parts of epididymis and in various diluents (Milovanov, 1962). Artificial insemination

Spermatozoa collection site	Dilution media	Pregnancy rate (%)
cauda epididymidis	glycin, sodium citrate, egg yolk	92
caput epididymidis	glycin, sodium citrate, egg yolk	25
caput epididymidis	rabbit blood serum	81

It is supposed that, spermatozoa from the most distal part of the *corpus epididymidis* and from the *cauda epididymidis* (Figure 1) are already fully functional (Abou-Haila et al., 2000). Note, that at the same time, freezeability of sperm *decreases* during its movement from *testes* to *cauda epididymidis* to *corpus* to *caputa* and towards ejaculation. It is believed to be attributed to the change in lipid content of the cell cytoplasmic membrane, particularly to the increase % of unsaturated acids and decrease in the cholesterol : phospholipids ratio during maturation in testicles through epididymis followed by ejaculation and sperm capacitation ("enabling"). . A comprehensive review of literature and original observation of modeling "*backward re-immaturation and decapacitation*" by treating ejaculated sperm with cholesterol-rich liposomes and egg yolk are summarized in (Katkov, 1985). Some additional data are updated in a recent review by Verma (Verma, 2001). Note that any data on fertilizing ability of epididymal spermatozoa are relative. In epididymis spermatozoa are immotile and cannot fertilize an ovum. Spermatozoa obtain their motility under the impact of accessory glands secretion during ejaculation or diluents in case ART collection.

When postmortem sperm is used, the cells are usually harvested from *cauda epididymidis*, sometimes spermatozoa contained in spermaducts (*ductus deferens*) (Figure 1) are used. This is the most efficient way as *cauda epididymidis* is a storage of ready to be ejaculated spermatozoa and contains not only the most functionally mature spermatozoa but also surpasses other parts of epididymis in respect to their number. The spermatozoa supply in epididymis is quite large and normally approximately ¾ of male's epididymal spermatozoa is contained in the tail part of epididymis (*cauda epididymidis*) (Milovanov, 1962). It is important that c*auda epididymidis* does not only stock, but also is responsible for elimination of aging spermatozoa when ejaculations are absent.

According to the abovementioned, testicular spermatozoa and spermatozoa from proximate epididymis parts can be used for genome conservation. Therefore, in case of death of very valuable individuals, we probably should not be limited by only CP of sperm from the tail part of epididymis (*cauda epididymidis*). Moreover, spermatozoa from the head of epididymis (*caput epididymides*) are less sensitive to cold shock as compared to spermatozoa from the tail of epididymis (*cauda epididymidis*) and evidently should better survive the CP process (see Katkov, 1985 and White, 1993 for references).

Ejaculated Spermatozoa

In a process of ejaculation, epididymal sperm is combined with secretions of accessory sex glands. Under their effect spermatozoa undergo through a number of physiological changes. Ejaculated spermatozoa are characterized by progressive motility and its highly active metabolic rate. Fertilizing ability of ejaculated spermatozoa is the best. The majority of CP methods and ART is developed to the ejaculated sperm, obtained with the help of an artificial vagina or by electroejaculation.

When stored for a long time, the fertilizing ability of ejaculated spermatozoa can be lowered due to the energetic exhaustion and starvation of active spermatozoa or a phenomenon of chromatin "overcondensation", existing under the effect of seminal plasma (Goldberg, 2000).

Mammalian Species Involved in Postmortem Sperm Collection and Preservation

First reports concerning preservation of fertile spermatozoa in animal epididymises after castration belong to the one of the founders of spermatology, and an inventor of artificial insemination and ART in general Ilya Ivanov (1899, summarized in Ivanov, 1907). He has observed forward motility of spermatozoa extracted from samples, stored for a long period at +2°C. Spermatozoa of a stallion were movable after 7 days after castration, male dogs – after 7.5 days and oxen' spermatozoa were movable within the period from 8 to 12 days. He was also an originator of an announcement on successful insemination of female rabbits with spermatozoa extracted from epididymises stored within 7 and 8 days at 1 - 2°C.

The number of similar reports has been increased recently. Blow is a brief summary of the reports grouped in taxons. Note that the predominant method preservation of postmortem spermatozoa is CP in liquid nitrogen and the most part of modern researches necessarily includes this element.

Perissodactyla

Odd-toed ungulates.

Equidae Horses

James et al 2002 worked with testes of a stallion and demonstrated that they have viable epididymal sperm up to 96 hours under storage at 4 degree C. Pregnancies were reported after using frozen-thawed equine epididymal sperm during hysteroscopic insemination (Morris et al., 2001). Spermatozoa, collected from the *cauda epididymidis* of stallion and Burchell.s zebra *Equus burchelli* males (Bruemmer, 2006; Bruemmer et al., 2002), cooled to 4 degree C, then cryopreserved and assessed at post-thaw for motility and membrane integrity. These sperm samples revealed decrease in motility but not in viability. Lubbe et al. (2000) freeze epididymal sperm collected from the domestic stallions, zebra and rhinoceros and compare two different diluents. There were no differences revealed between the post-thaw results of the two media for species. The quality of post-mortem sperm of of only one species, kiang (*Equus kiang*) (Figure2) was not satisfactory (Figure2A).

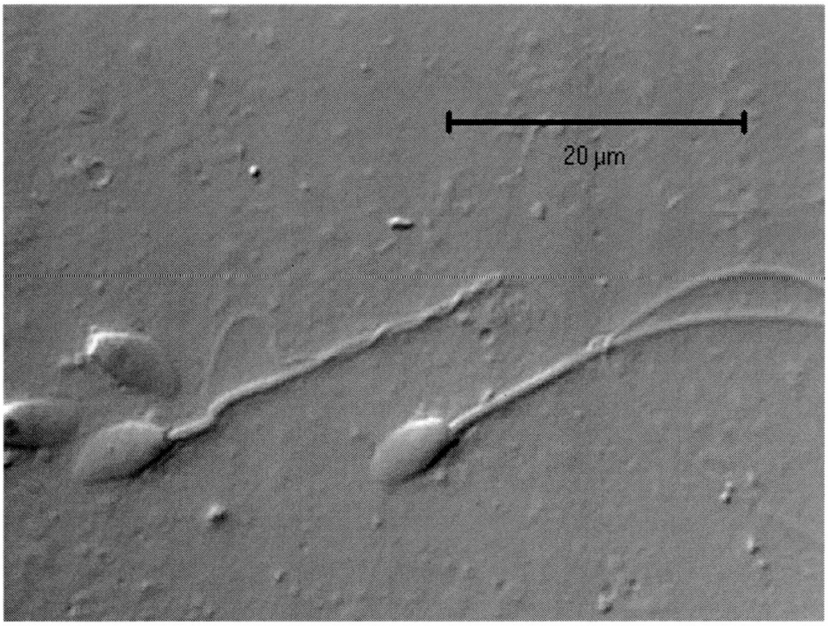

Figure 2. Kiang (*Equus kiang).* (A): Postmortem abnormal spermatozoa (DIC technique). Separate heads are in left, a spermatozoon with deformed tail in the center. Bar 20 μm.

Rhinocerotidae Rhinoceroses

Longevity in vitro and glycerol toxicity of epididymal sperm recovered from a white rhinoceros (*Ceratotherium simum*) were studied by Williams et al., 1995. O'Brien and Roth, (2000) cryopreserved epididymal spermatozoa of the African black rhinoceros (*Diceros bicornis*) 30 hours post-mortem. The testes were stored at +4°C in a fridge before sperm harvesting.

Artiodactyla

Even-hoofed ungulates.

Suidae True Pigs

We know only the fact of CP of domestic pig epididymal sperm. Kikuchi (Kikuchi et al., 1998) have demonstrated that motility and penetrating ability of boar spermatozoa *in vitro*, stored in epididymises at +4°C, gradually reduces while storing within 3 days. Still it was possible to fertilize ova *in vitro* with thawed spermatozoa after three days of storage.

Bovidae Horned Ungulates

Experiments conducted by Sipko (Sipko et al., 1993) have shown high quality of thawed epididymal spermatozoa of European bison *Bison bonasus* (30-50% of motile spermatozoa) after 3 years of storage in liquid nitrogen. Acroscopic test's data were: before freezing 80% of spermatozoa had intact acrosomes, after 1 month of storage – 67.5-55%, after 3 years of storage - 64-55%. Insemination of 8 cattle cows resulted in 4 hybrid calves.

A number of authors studied wild ungulate of Africa. Herold et al., (2006) indicates that epididymal sperm from African buffalo (*Syncerus caffer*) flushed in the field can be stored in freezing medium for up to 9 hours before being further processed. In other work were extracted and froze epididymal spermatozoa of bleshbock *Damaliscus dorcas*, African buffalo *Syncerus caffer*, springbuck, *Antidorcas marsupialis,* brindled gnu *Connochaetes gnou.* (Herrick et al., 2004). After thawing a range of parameters was established (motility, viability, acrosome status, capacitation *in vitro*). Spermatozoa of these species have shown in general 64% motility after unfreezing. For better results species specific methods adjustment is required. Loskutoff et al., 1996 froze epididymal spermatozoa of three species of African antelopes: bleshbock *Damaliscus dorcas*, impala *Aepyceros melampus*, and springbuck *Antidorcas marsupialis*. While studying cryoprotective characteristics and toxicity of glycerol, ethylene glycol, propylene glycol and dimethylsulfoxide (DMSO). Glycerol has proven to be least toxic for all species. However, motility of frozen-thawed spermatozoa of bleshbock and impala was the same when glycerol and ethylene glycol were used as cryoprotectors. For springbuck the most effective cryoprotector was DMSO. Winger (Winger et al., 1997) also reported the use of cryopreserved epididymal blesbok spermatozoa for *in vitro* fertilization.

Bartels et al., 1998 studied the morphological changes of caudal epididymal spermatozoa of African buffalo (*Syncerus caffer*) after storage at 6°C. According to Lambrechts (Lambrechts et al., 1999) CP significantly reduced the viability and motility of the epididymal African buffalo spermatozoa. Bezuidenhout et al. (1995) analyzed the motility of spermatozoa from four different species (African buffalo *Syncerus caffer*, red hartebeest *Alcelaphus bucelaphus*, eland *Tragelaphus oryx* and Burchell.s zebra *Equus burchelli*). Postmortem testicles were stored at 4°C.. The red hartebeest, eland and Burchell`s zebra exhibited a much shorter duration for motility of epididymal spermatozoa in compared with the African buffalo. Epididymal spermatozoa of gaur *Bos gaurus* were diluted and frozen in straws in 27 hours after animal's death (Hopkins et. al., 1989). The motility of thawed spermatozoa was mush lower, but pregnancy after insemination of cow was reported.

Fertilizing ability of ram spermatozoa extracted from epididymises stored at +5°C within 24 and 48 hours was the same as fresh epididymal spermatozoa (Kaabi et al., 2003). Saragusty et al., (2006) indicated that postmortem epididymal spermatozoa from endangered gazelle species (mountain gazelle *G. gazella* and desert gazelle *Gazella dorcas*) and one subspecies (*Gazella gazelle acaiae*) obtained after car accidents could be successfully frozen and cryobanking is achievable.

Spanish investigators study features of epididymal spermatozoa at Spanish ibex *Capra pyrenaica hispanica*. Santiago-Moreno et al. (Santiago-Moreno et al., Theryogenology, 2006) recovered and frozen epididymal sperm of Spanish ibex 2-24 hours after death. It was used for insemination of domestic goats. Only specimens frozen not later than 8 hours after an animal death provided successful fertilization, in spite of quite accepTable spermatozoa quality. They estimated effects of spermatozoa recovering techniques and of various diluents action on indices of frozen-thawed epididymal sperm (Santiago-Moreno, et al. Arch. Androl., 2007). There is a quite intriguing paper, in which correlation of semen quality with horn size and asymmetry in legally hunted 59 ibex males is analyzed (Santiago-Moreno et al., Anim.

Reprod. Sci. 2007). It was revealed that the horn quality was firstly associated with sperm motility.

Anel (Anel et al., 2000) recovered and frozen postmortem sperm of Spanish Cantabrian chamois (Rupicapra pyrenaica parva) over a 2-hours period after death of an animal. Graham (Graham et al., 1978) reports on 19% of alive spermatozoa of Dall's sheep (*Ovis dalli*) stored for 6 years and assayed by after-thawing filtration.

Cervidae Deers

Physiology and CP of postmortem spermatozoa of deers (*Cervus elaphus and Cervus nippon*) has now received the most study compared to other wild mammals.

Krzyvinski (Krzyvinski, 1981) firstly presented the results of freezing postmortem collected spermatozoa from moos *A. alces* and red deer *Cervus elaphus*. Epididymises of a sika deer *Cervus nippon*, recovered post-mortem at rut period were stored at +4° for up to 7 days. Epididymal spermatozoa motility decreased while storing becoming minimal at the 7th day. This did not affect on spermatozoa vitality. There were observed pycnosis of epithelial cells and their outgoing into epididymis lumen in epididymises under storing. Motility of fresh frozen-thawed spermatozoa was 58.1%, after a day storing it was 41.9%, and after 4 days storing 41.8% (Hishinuma et al., 2003).

After one to six days storing at +5°C of red deer (*Cervus elaphus*) (Figure 3) и sika deer (*Cervus nippon*) epididymises spermatozoa were recovered and frozen. Thawed gametes have from 10 to 25% motility. Amount of spermatozoa with intact acrosome was 55 to 57% (Sipko et al., 1997). In another work, (Comizzoli et al., 2001) conditions for *in vitro* maturation and fertilization of oocytes of red deer Cervus elaphus and the sika deer Cervus nippon, chosen for model objects for conservation of endangered species. Sperm of both species was recovered with electroejaculation and that of *Cervus elaphus* from epididymis either, and cryopreserved. After *in vitro* fertilization embryos were cultivated for 7 days, then fixed and examined under a microscope.

Study of red deer *Cervus elaphus* epididymal spermatozoa by two groups of Spanish investigators should be emphasized. They have studied comprehensively physiology of postmortem spermatozoa of several species of the deer (Martinez-Pastor et al., Theriogenology. 2006 ; v. 66, n. 5; Martinez-Pastor et al., Theriogenology, 2006; v. 66, n.3.; Martinez-Pastor et al., Theriogenology. 2005; Soler A. et al., Theriogenology, 2005; Soler A. et al., J. Exp. Zool.; 2003; Soler A., Garde. J Androl., 2003), features of postmortem spermatozoa of a deer recovered immediately after death were compared with those at long-term storage of gonads. In addition to detailed motional parameters of the deer sperm, the acrosomal status of and integrity of the cell membranes of freshly recovered and thawed spermatozoa were examined. Membrane potential of spermatozoa mitochondria was found to be practically unchangeable during 4 days of storage. Absence of changes in quality of the nuclear material of spermatozoa after 7 days storing of testicles is fact of prime importance for use of postmortem spermatozoa (Soler A., et al., Theriogenology. 2005). Thus, motility of spermatozoa recovered from epididymises of a red deer (*Cervus elaphus*) on the fourth day of storage at +5°C was 25% less than the initial one. At that, no changes of both parameters characterizing spermatozoa membranes integrity and amounts of morphologically normal spermatozoa were observed during this period. (Soler A. et al., J. Exp. Zool., 2003,).

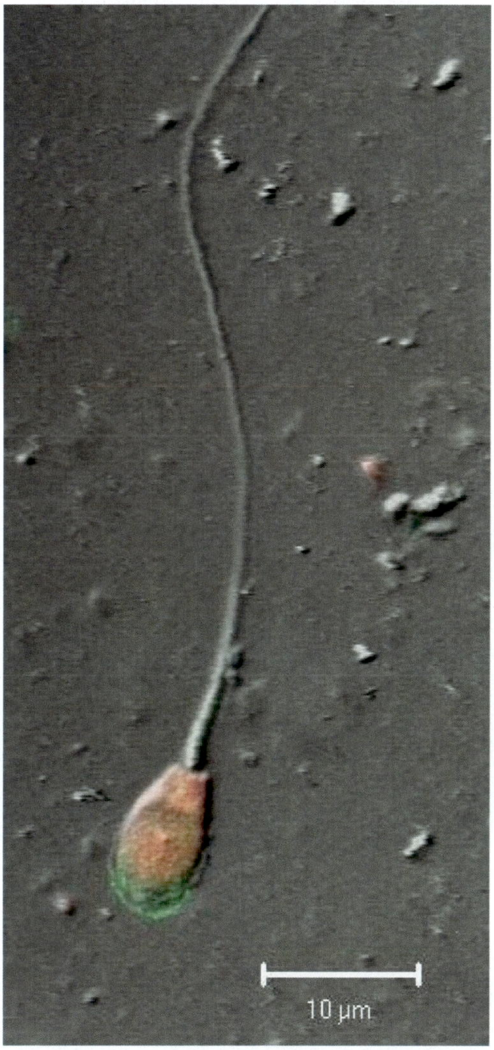

Figure 3. Red deer (*Cervus elaphus.)* postmortem spermatozoon. Bar 10 µm.

The same groups of authors has substantially contributed to development of techniques for CP of red deer epididymal spermatozoa, including: optimization of composition of diluting media, selection of cryoprotectors, adjustment of freezing schedules (Fernandez-Santos et al., J. Androl. 2007; Fernandez-Santos et al., Theriogenology. 2007; Fernández-Santos et al., Theriogenology, 2006; Fernández-Santos et al., Cryo Letters. 2005; Soler A. et al., J Androl. 2003). As a result Red deer is now one of a few wild species for which special CP techniques for not only ejaculated sperm are established but for epididymal one as well.

Our experience of postmortem sperm CP of even-hoofed ungulates includes markhor (*Capra falconeri*) (Figure 4, Fig 4A, Figure 4B), white-tailed gnu (*Connochaetes gnou*) (Figure 5, Fig 5A, Fig 5B, Figure5C), and East Caucasian tur (*Capra cylindricornis*) (Figure 6, Fig 6A, Figure6B, Figure 6C) (Shishova, Maksudov, *paper in preparation*). Spermatozoids of one of markhor (*Capra falconeri*) males were recovered and frozen 2 days after his death. Testicles of the other male were processed at the 3rd day after death of the animal. Mobility of spermatozoa before freezing was 20% and 50%, respectively. Mobility of thawed spermatozoa of the first male remained the same (20%), while motility of the second male's sperm decreased two-fold (25%), thus, showing remarkable individual variations in quality of fresh sperm and in the sperm cryotolerance ("freezeability"). Testicles of East Caucasian tur (*Capra cylindricornis*) were processed a day after death of the animal. Spermatozoids demonstrated satisfactory mobility (40%), being practically unchanged after thawing (35%). Testicles of white-tailed gnu (*Connochaetes gnou*) were processed with two-staged techniques: immediately after death of an animal (control) and in 7 days (experiment). Before freezing their mobility was 65% in control and 20% in experiment. After thawing it decreased to 45% (control) and 9% (experiment), respectively.

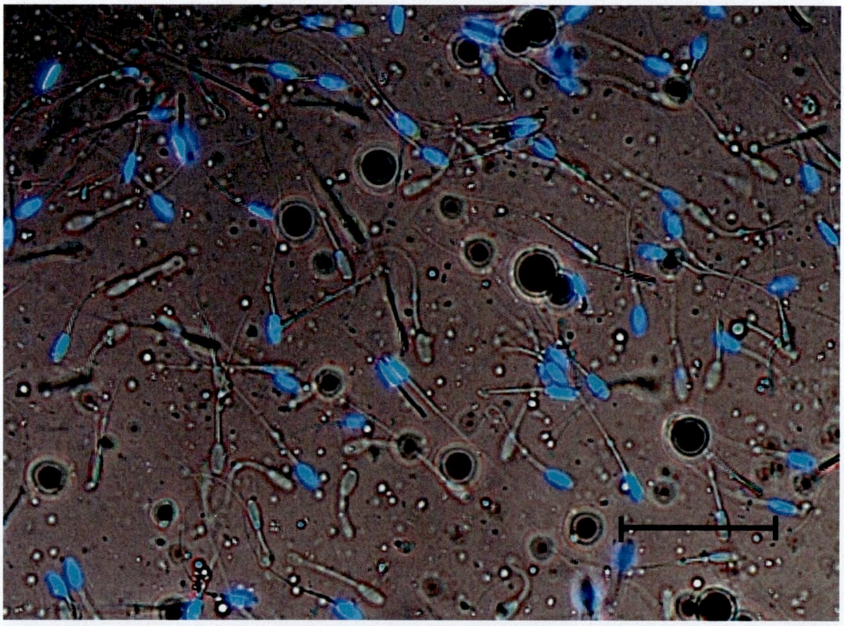

A

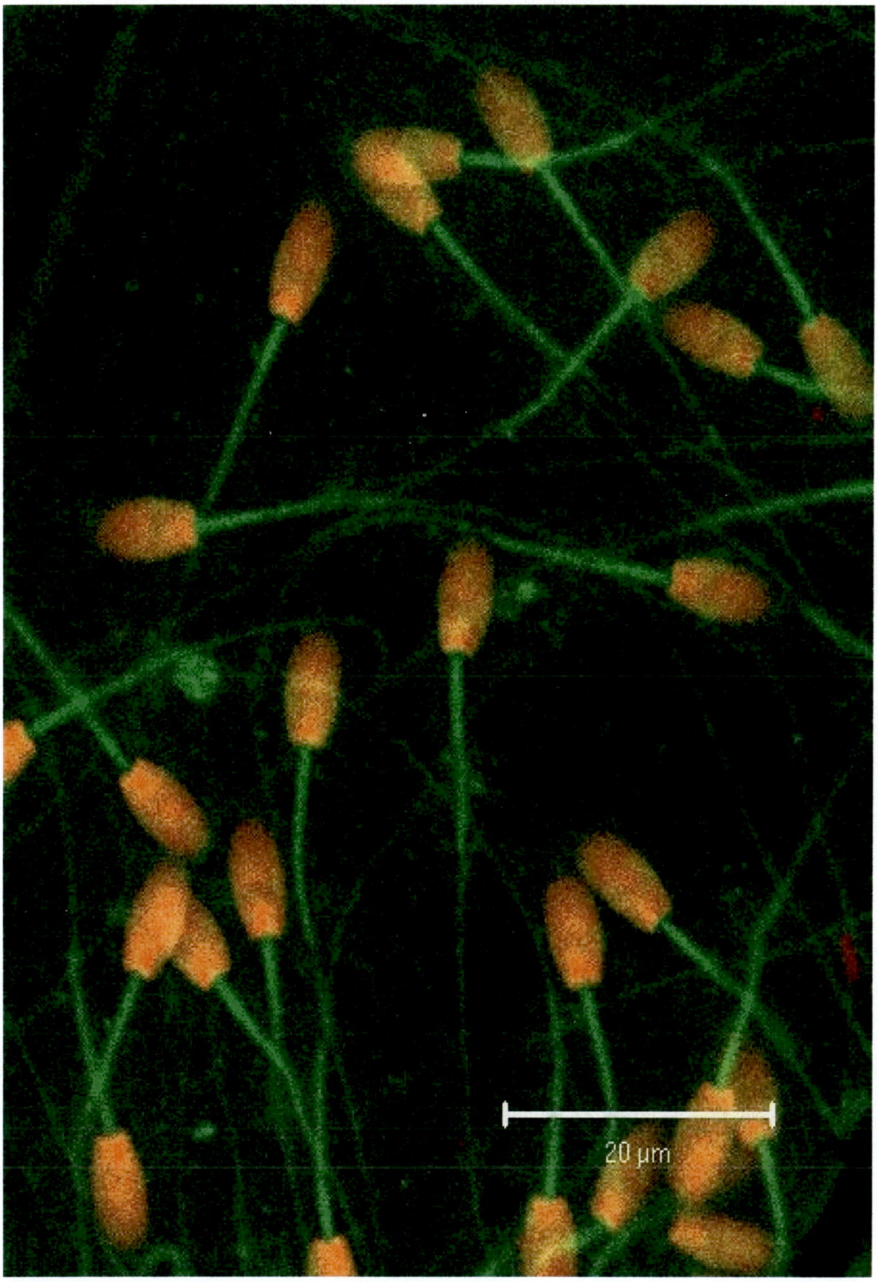

B

Figure 4. Markhor (*Capra falconeri*). (A, B): Postmortem spermatozoa . Viability fluorescence test (A). Dead sperm heads are blue, alive cells look as dark-brown contours. Bar 50 µm. Ethidium bromide and tetracycline staining (B). Bar 20 µm.

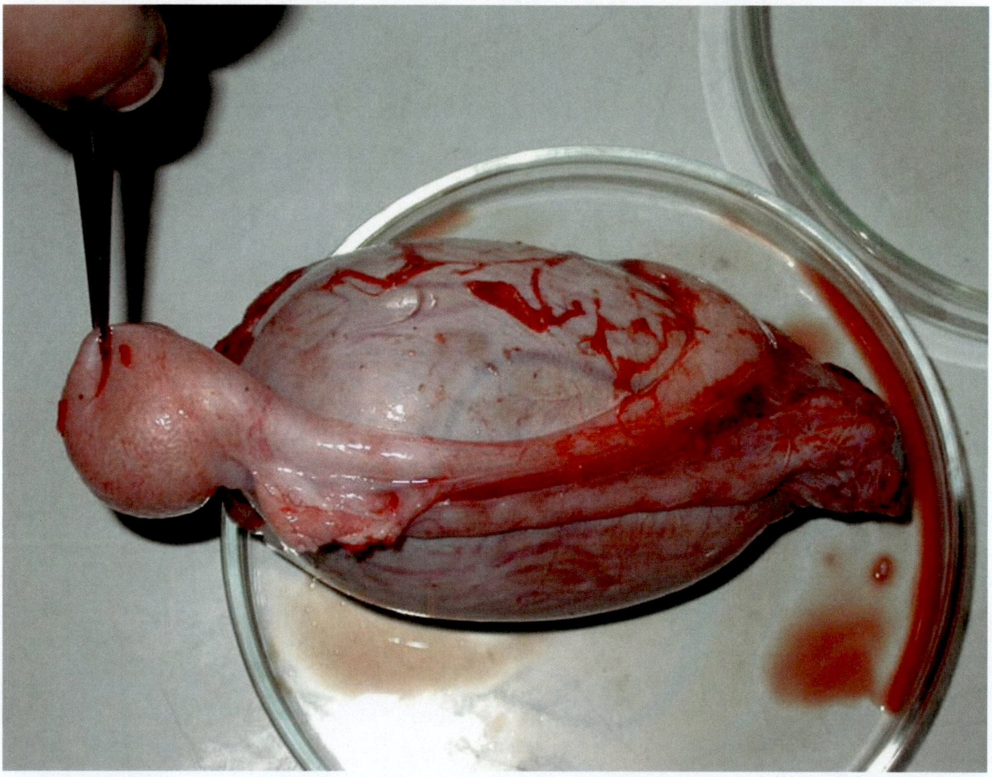

A

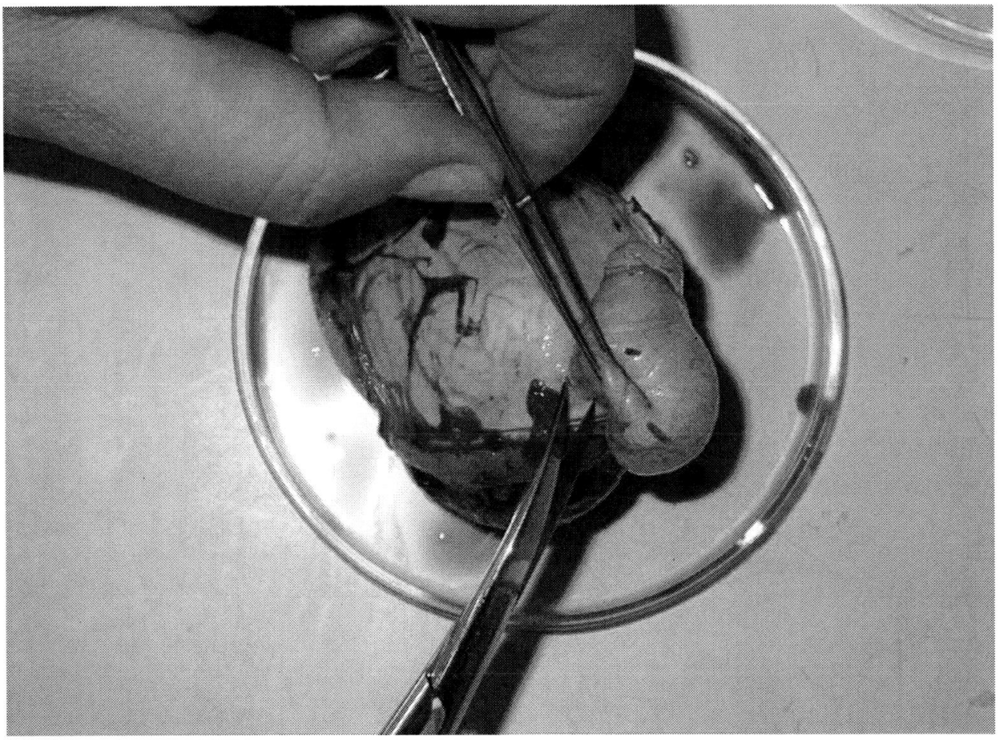

B

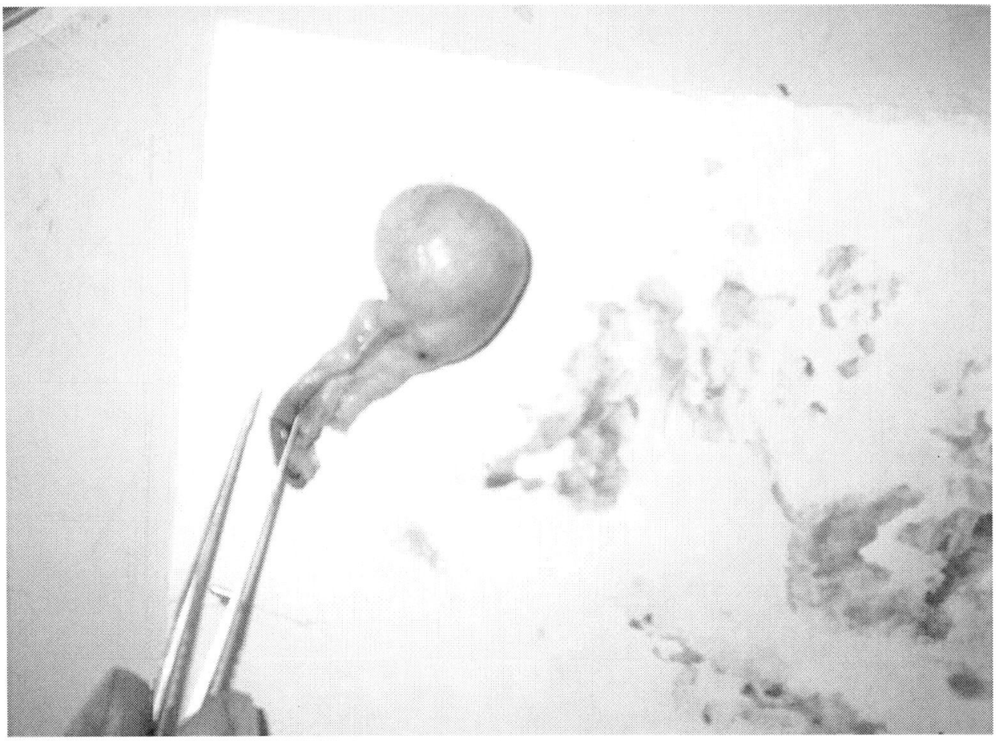

C

Figure 5. White-tailed gnu (*Connochaetes gnou*). (A): Testis, general view. (B). Testis under preparation. Separation of the epididymis from the testis. (C) Separated epididymis.

A

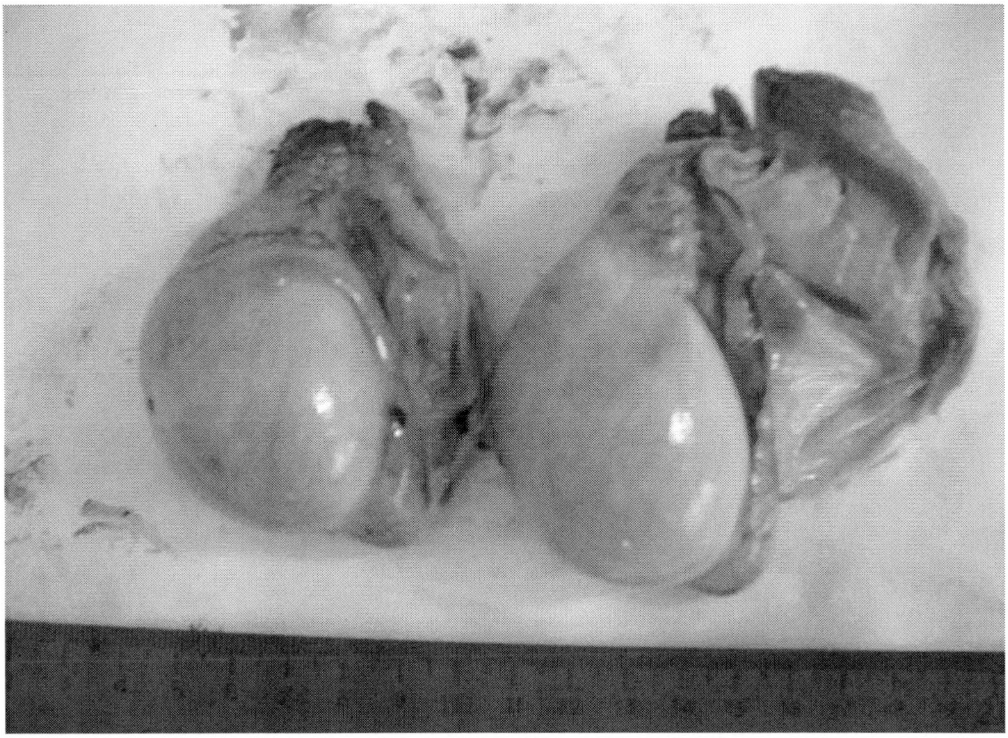

B

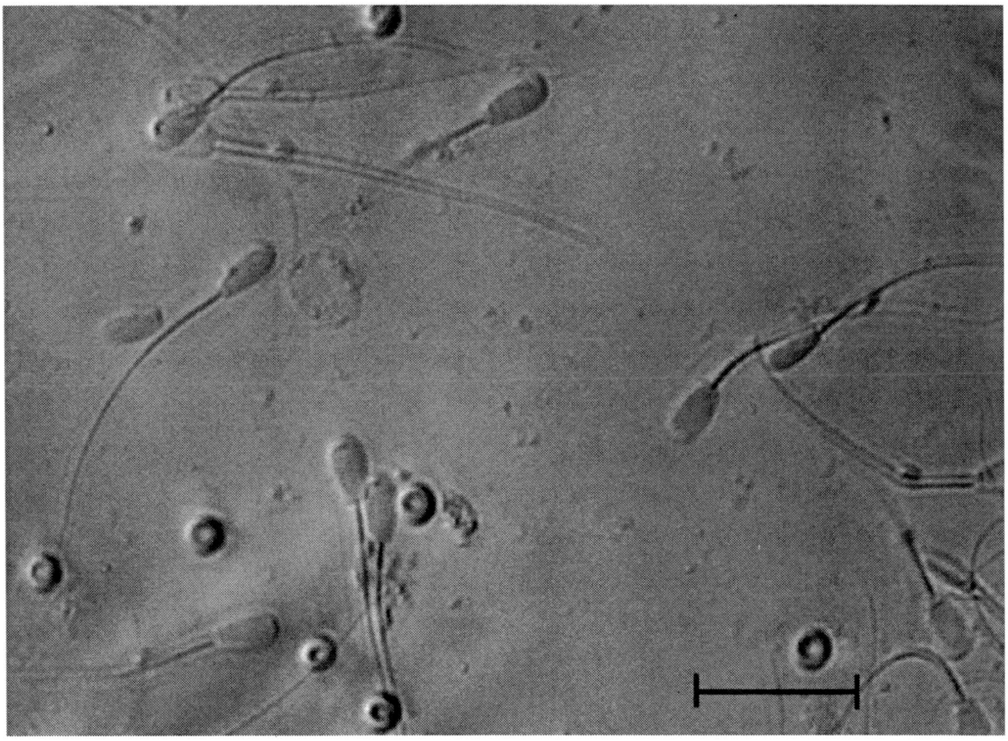

C

Figure 6. East Caucasian tur (*Capra cylindricornis*). (A): Testis in scrotum. (B): Teistis sperated from scrotum (C): Posmortem spermatozoa. Bar 20 μm.

Camelidae Camels

No mobile spermatozoa were found in testicles of guanacos *Lama guanicoe* after seven days of storage at low positive temperatures. Immature spermatozoa with drops of cytoplasm on bent necks were found in smears (Shishova, Maksudov, *paper in preparation*). (Figure 7, Figure 7A, Figure 7B) Morton (Morton et al, 2007) cryopreserved epididymal sperm of alpaca (*Vicugna pacos*), a close relative of llama, using various techniques. Note that dry ice instead of liquid nitrogen was used as the cooling agent for field freezing. It was concluded that CP of epididymal alpaca spermatozoa is feasible and freezing as pellets in a lactose-based diluent was recommended.

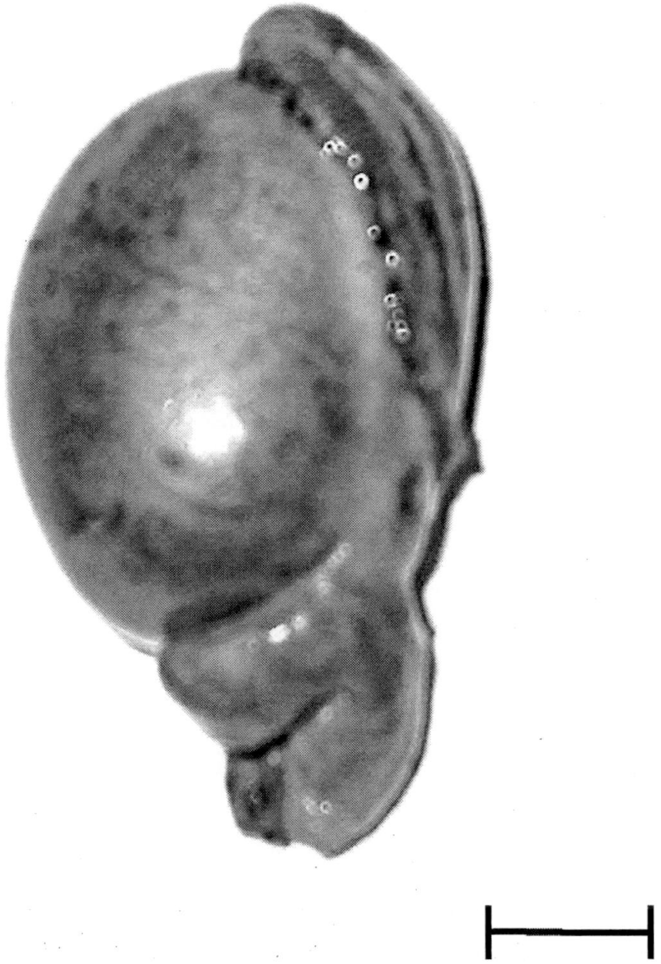

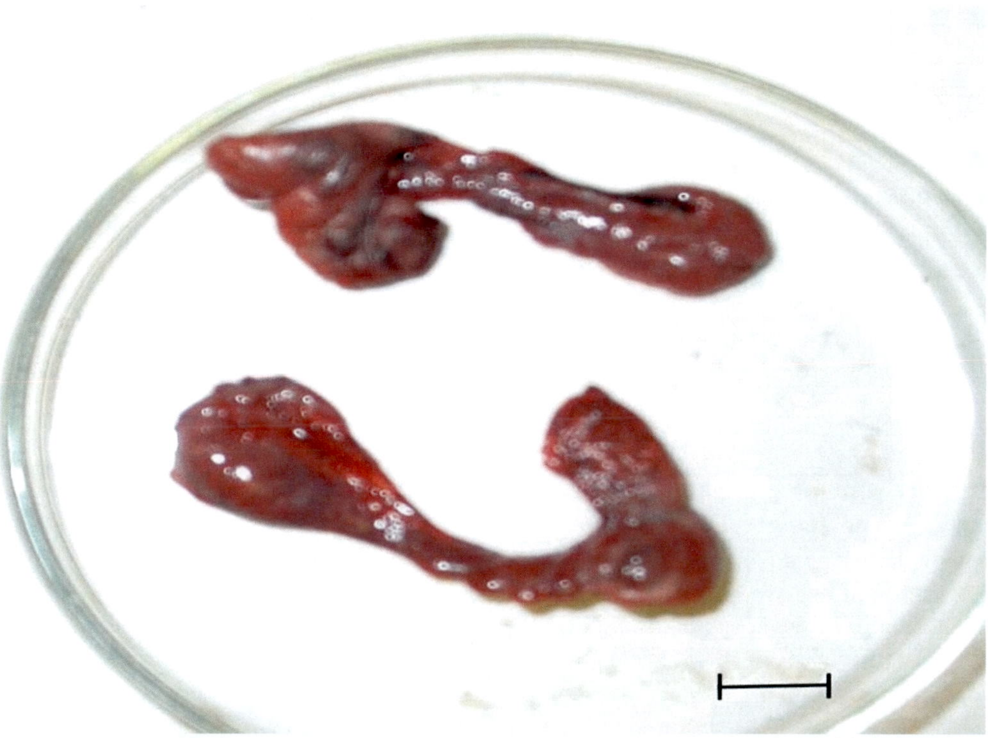

A

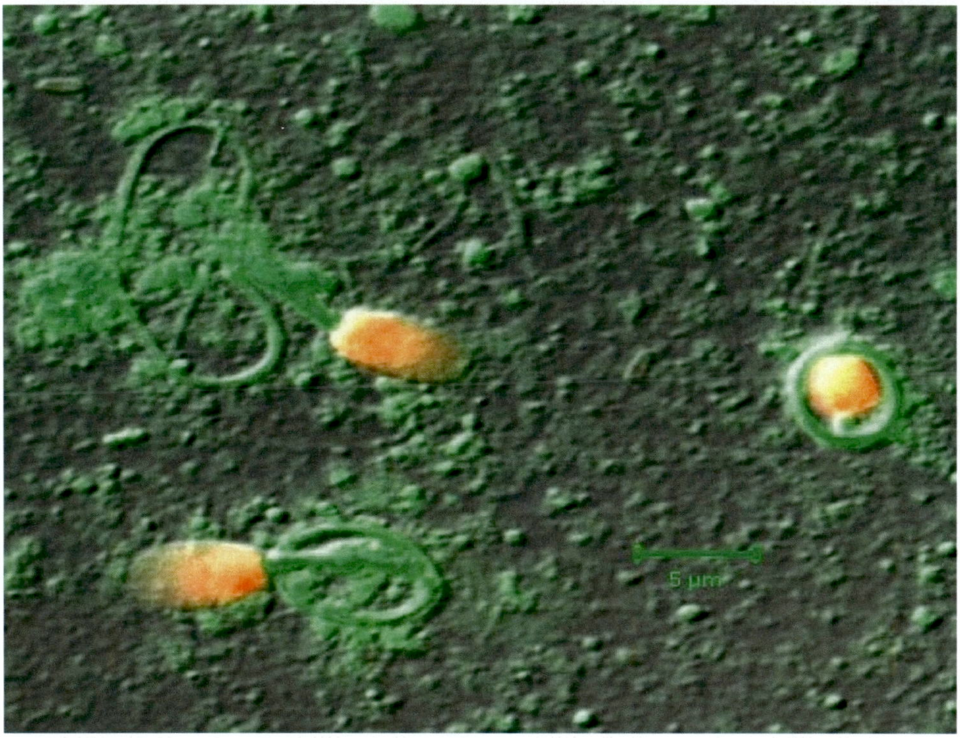

B

Figure 7. Guanaco (*Lama guanicoe*) testes. Bar 1 cm. (A): Separated epididymises. Bar 1 cm. (B): postmortem spermatozoa. Bar 5 µm.

Carnivora, the Carnivores

Felidae Cats

As to carnivores, there are felines for whom the most information on postmortem spermatozoa is available, thanks to the wide use of domestic cats as laboratory animals. Nevertheless reproductive biology of wild felines has unique features, demanding thereby great care in the use of results obtained with a domestic cat. Thus females of clouded leopard (*Felis nebulosa*) can ovulate not after copulation only, as domestic cats do, but spontaneously as well. Spermatozoa of ounce (*U. uncia*) are especially sensitive to pH of a sperm diluent, and spermatozoa motility decreases rapidly even at rather small increase of pH (Swanson, 2003). Graham (Graham et al., 1978) recovered epididymal spermatozoa from a leopard (*Panthera pardus*).

Jewgenow (Jewgenow *et al*, 1997) shows motility of frozen-thawed epididymal spermatozoa of lions (*Panthera leo*), tigers (*Panthera tigris*), leopards (*Panthera pardus*), pumas (*Felis concolor*), jaguar (*Panthera onca*). The use of cryopreserved epididymal sperm from puma, lion and leopard for IVF produced 18% embryos versus 26% in domestic cats.

Epididymises were collected from immobilized adult male lion by cauda epididymectomy, transported to the laboratory at 4°C and were punctured to retrieve epididymal sperm. Spermatozoa were cryopreserved and used for IVF of in vitro matured lioness ova. Post-thaw motility ranged from 55 to 65% and the percentage of fertilized ova was 12.7% for 30 hours of in vitro maturation and 11.5% for 36 hours of maturation (Bartels et al., 2000).

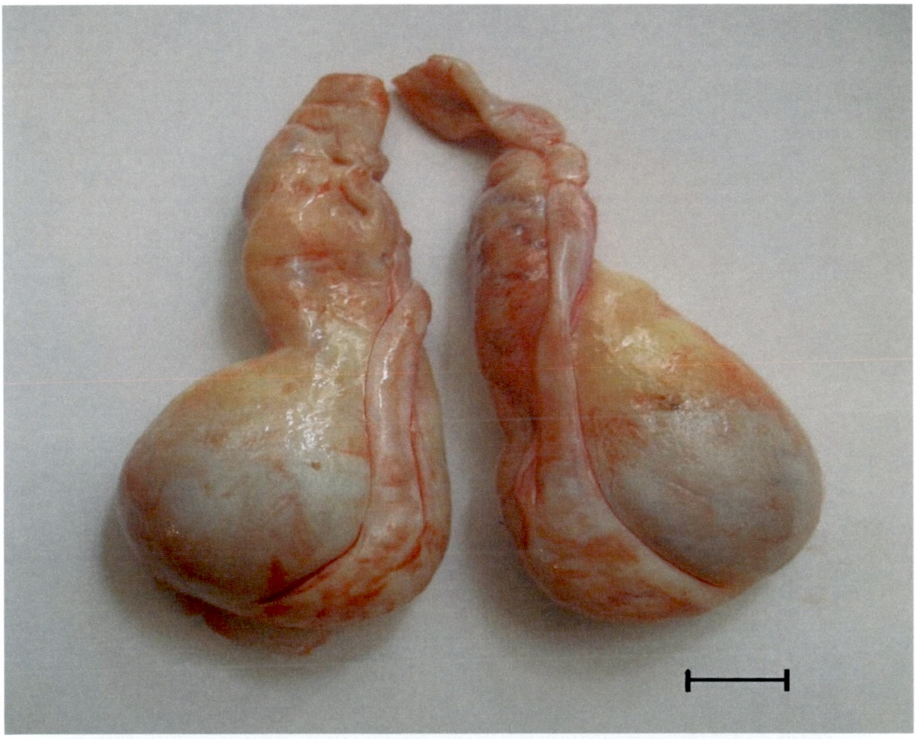

A

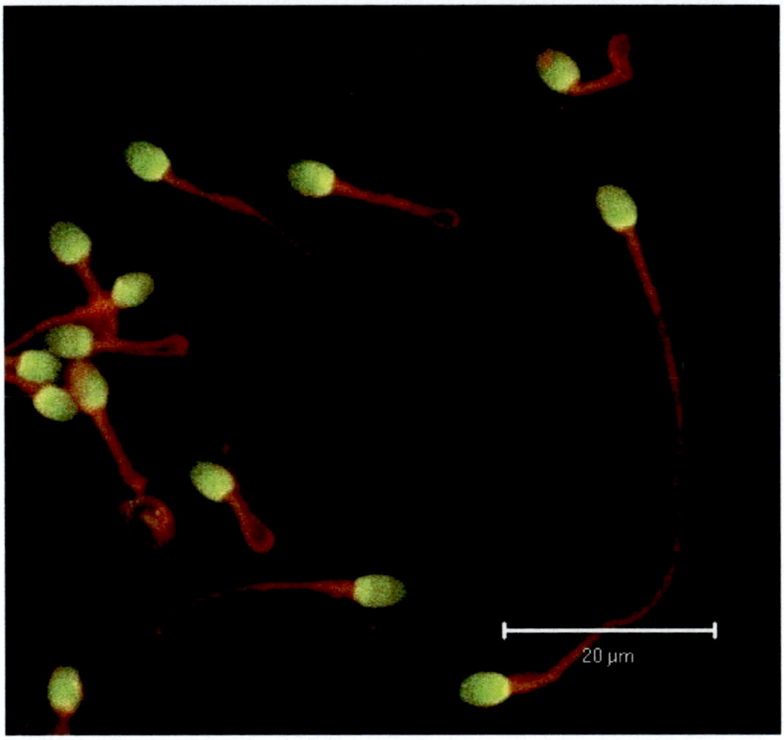

B

Figure 8. Amur leopard (*Panthera pardus orientalis*). (A): Testes. Bar 1 cm. (B): Postmortem spermatozoa. Bar 20 µm.

Canidae Canids

Experience in cryoconservation of postmortem semen of wild Canids is little. Though investigations in cryoconservation of epididymal spermatozoa of domestic dogs (Hori et al., 2005; Marks et al., 1994; Ponglowhapan et al., 2006; Stilley et al., 2000; Yu and Leibo, 2002) hold out a hope of application of the method with wild species.

Yu and Leibo (2002) preserved postmortem canine epididymal spermatozoa for up to 8 days at 4°C in the testicles. After 8 days storage, the sperm showed 50% progressive motility and 80% membrane integrity. Ponglowhapan et al., (2006) shows that canine epididymal spermatozoa could be stored at 5 degrees C for up to 4 days without a clear detrimental effect on post-thaw motility and acrosome integrity, but storage may have decreased post-thaw motility. Results were, however, generally low. Hori (Hori et al., 2005) described unilateral intrauterine insemination with cryopreserved caudal epididymal sperm recovered from refrigerated canine epididymides.

Stilley (Stilley et al., 2000) reported that canine epididymal spermatozoa could be frozen after being stored within the *cauda epididymidis* for up to 48 hours at 4°C.

Ursidae. Bears. Post-mortem recovery and freezing in a Cantabric brown bear (*Ursus arctos*) epididymal spermatozoa described by Anel et al. (1999). Spermatozoa were harvested no later than 70 minutes after death, assessed and cryopreserved. Pre-freeze and thawed spermatozoa had progressive motility 30 and 15%, intact acrosome 62 and 29%, accordingly.

The authors froze spermatozoa of Spectacled bear (*Tremarctos ornatus)* three days after death of an animal. Isolated spermatozoa of an aged (21 year) male showed only 20% of gametes with weak oscillating motion. Acrosome integrity was less than 80%. No motility was noticed after freezing-thawing. Nevertheless fluorescent vitality test revealed 40% of alive spermatozoa.

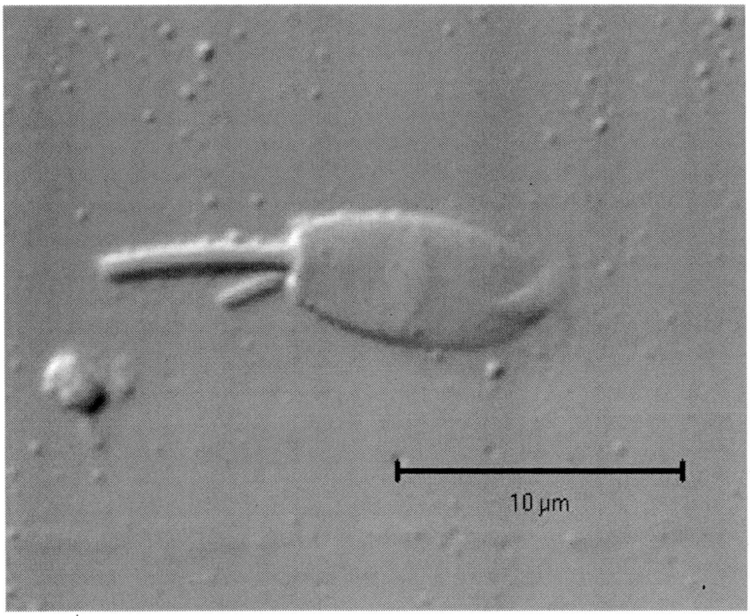

Figure 9. Maned wolf (*Chrysocyon bracyurus*). (A): Postmortem spermatozoa. Bar 10 µm. Abnormal cell with broken tail (DIC technique).

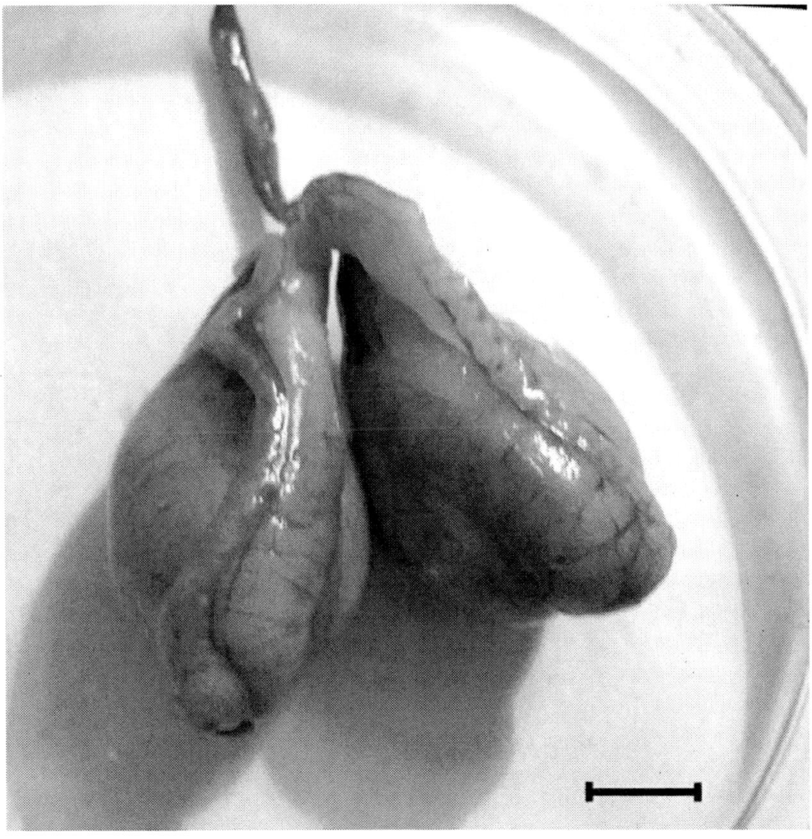

Figure 10. Dhole (*Cuon alpinus*) testes. Bar 1 cm.

Procyonidae. Raccoons

Perez-Garnelo (Perez-Garnelo et al., 2003) examined frozen postmortem sperm of a Giant panda (*Ailuropoda melanoleuca)*. 4 hours after death of male testicles were recovered, slashed with a razor-blade, and diluted with medium. Morphology of specimens frozen in liquid nitrogen and thawed was examined with computer image analyzing system.

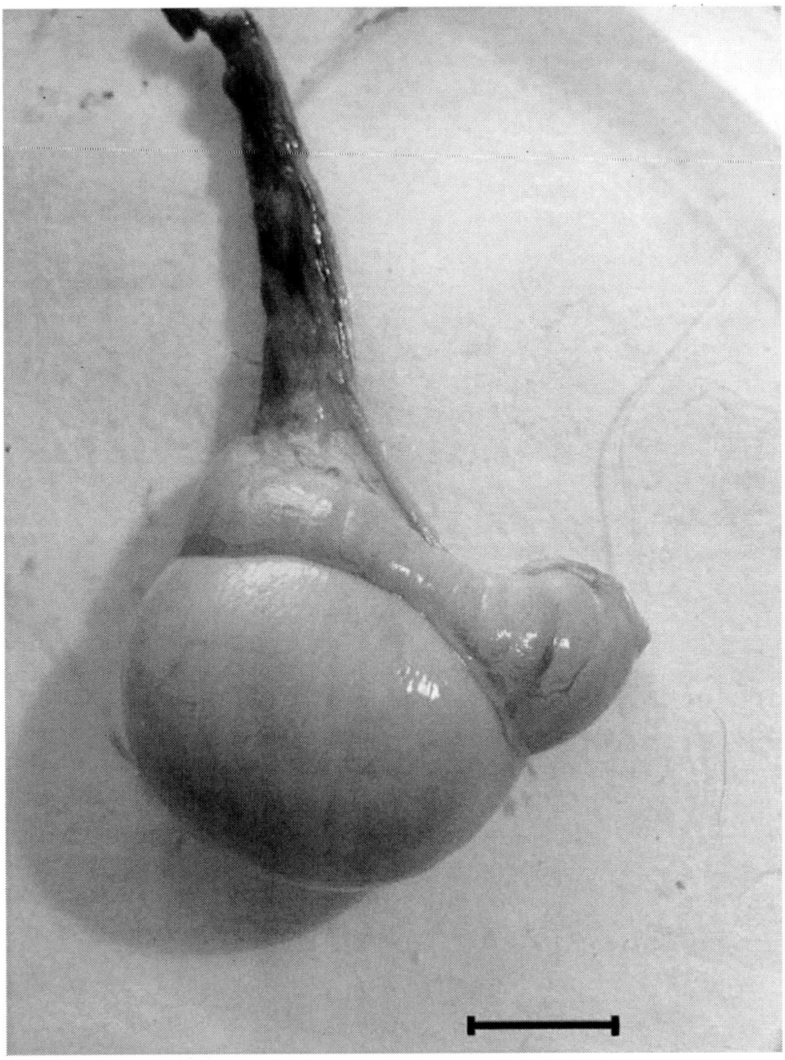

Figure 11. Raccoon (*Procyon lotor*) testes. Bar 1 cm.

Proboscidea, the Elephants

Jones (1973) examined methods of recovery and storing of African elephant (*Loxodonta Africana*) spermatozoa including those epididymal.

Primates, the Primates

Lemuridae Lemurs

Spermatozoa of ring-tailed lemur *Lemur catta* showed 70% of total mobility and 13% of progressive mobility 2 days after death. DAPI staining revealed 28% of damaged gametes, and a dark-field microscopy showed 86% of intact acrosomes. Spermatozoa were frozen with satisfactory results (Shishova, Maksudov, unpublished data). (Figure 12, Figure 12A, Figure 12B).

Epididymal spermatozoa of Pygmy chimpanzee, *Pan panistris*, lion-tailed macaque *Macaca silenus* and patas monkey *Erythrocebus patas*, frozen 12 hours after death of an animal, demonstrated accepTable after-thawing motility and capability to *in vitro* penetrating of a hamster oocyte (Durrant, 1997).

Morrell et al. (1997) stored epididymal spermatozoa harvested from common marmoset, *Callithrix jacchus* at 4 degree C for up to 48 hours after collection. Test yolk medium were used. Live births were achieved by AI with this cooled, non-frozen epididymal spermatozoa. Dong (Dong et al., 2008) studied the effect of prolonged storage (24 or 48 hours) of the *cauda epididymides* of rhesus monkey (*Macaca mulatta*) on the post thaw motility of epididymal spermatozoa. It was also investigated whether altering cryoprotectants and cooling methods could improve post-thaw motility after refrigerated storage. Epididymises stored at a higher temperature (4 degrees C-10 degrees C) yielded better results. Glycerol and ethylene glycol at 3% and 6% revealed similar post thaw motility. It was found that freezing at a higher rate of 220 degrees C/min to result better post thaw motility than the slower rate of 29 degrees C/min. Liow et al. (2002) reported the birth of two cynomolgus monkey (*Macaca fascicularis*) after ICSI with frozen-thawed epididymal sperm.

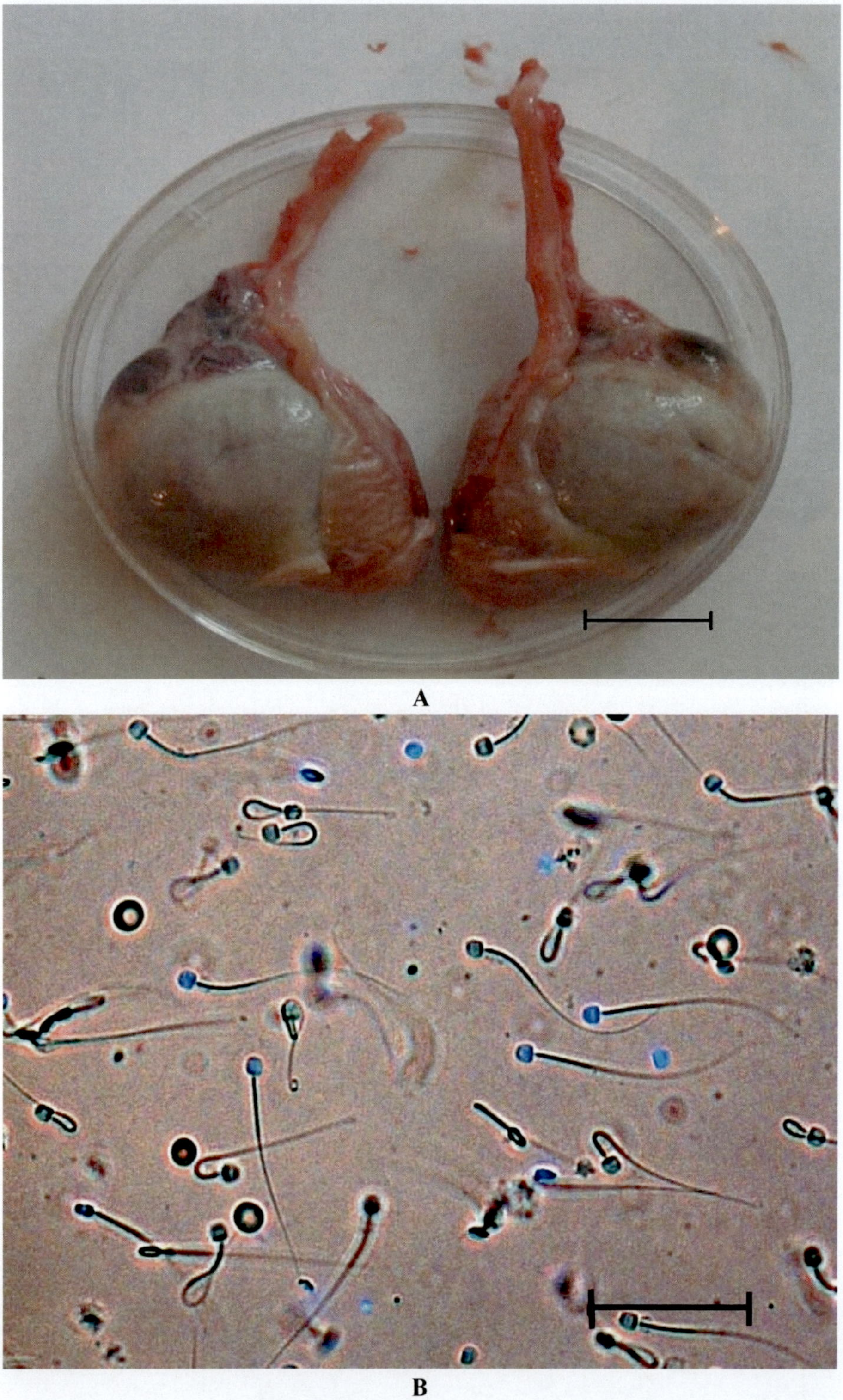

A

B

Figure 12. Ring-tailed lemur (*Lemur catta).* (A): Testes. (B): Postmortem spermatozoa. Viability fluorescence test. Dead sperm heads are blue, alive cells look as dark-brown contours. Bar 50 μm.

Rodentia, Rodents

Laboratory mice are long explored model for biological studies. Investigators of after-death survival rate of epididymal spermatozoa did not miss them either. Therefore survival rate and physiological characteristics of mouse postmortem sperm are rather thoroughly studied. Approach to use of information obtained at investigation of postmortem mice sperm is described above.

An (An et al., 1999) stored epididymal spermatozoa of killed mice *in situ* at +4°C. Fertilizing capacity of spermatozoa, recovered from mice bodies stored for 5 and 7 days at 0°C, appeared less than that of spermatozoa recovered from bodies stored for the same periods at +4 -6°C and 8 -10°C. After 5 days of storage 21% of ICR oocytes were fertilized, and 39% fertilizing after 7 days storage was reached at BDF1.

Sato (Sato et al., 2001) determined viability and fertility of isolated mouse epididymal spermatozoa stored at various temperatures (4 degrees C, 22 degrees C and 37 degrees C). Spermatozoa kept for 3 days at 22 degrees C were still active and can fertilize oocytes. Gametes kept at 4 degrees C or 37 degrees C exhibited great reduction in motility within 2 days after isolation. Six methods for short-term (up to 8 days), nonfrozen (5 to 20 degrees C) storage of mouse epididymides were compared (Sankai et al., 2001). A high percentage of progressively motile spermatozoa was obtained from epididymis stored for 8 days at 5 degrees C in mineral oil (78.3%), covered with body fat (80.0%), or stored in the intact body of the euthanized donor animal (77.5%). Fertilized eggs (6.4% fertilization rate) were obtained by IVF using spermatozoa that had been stored in mineral oil at 5 degrees C for at least 8 days, and offspring were obtained from 77.5% of transferred eggs that were fertilized by spermatozoa stored for 2 days. Success has also been reported on the production of live mouse pups using IVF and ICSI with epididymal sperm harvested as late as 20 days postmortem (Kishikawa et al., 1999).

Doronin (Doronin et al., 2004) studied the viability of spermatozoa in isolated mouse epididymides stored at 6 degrees C. In course of the whole experiment morphological indices, mobility and a number of biochemical indices, including ATP concentration, were fixed daily. 18 days after sacrifice the mobility of spermatozoa and presence of intracellular ATP in concentrations about 2.5 10^{-8} M/l per 10^{6} cells was registered.

Fertilizing capacity of epididymal spermatozoa recovered from mice bodies stored at +22°C after 6-, 12-, 18- and 24-hours storage was 81, 70, 64 и 19%, respectively (Songsasen et al., 1998). At storage of mice bodies at +4°C, progressive motility of epididymal sperm decreased reliably (Shishova et al., 2004). Nevertheless, such indices as total motility, integrity of cell membranes, and spermatozoa life-time at +37°C, did not undergo reliable changes for both native and frozen-thawed epididymal spermatozoa.

Few papers on cryoconservation of epididymal spermatozoa of wild rodents are available. We know study on Chinchilla (*Chinchilla laniger*) only (Ponce et al., 1998). We froze epididymal spermatozoa of arctic ground squirrel *Spermophilus undulatus* (Shishova, Ignat`ev, 2005) (Figure13). Nevertheless though cells and tissues of a ground squirrel have increased freezing tolerance, its spermatozoa appeared a very hard cryoconservation object. Despite good motility of initial material (35-60%), we managed to recover after freezing-thawing not more than 1-3% mobile spermatozoa.

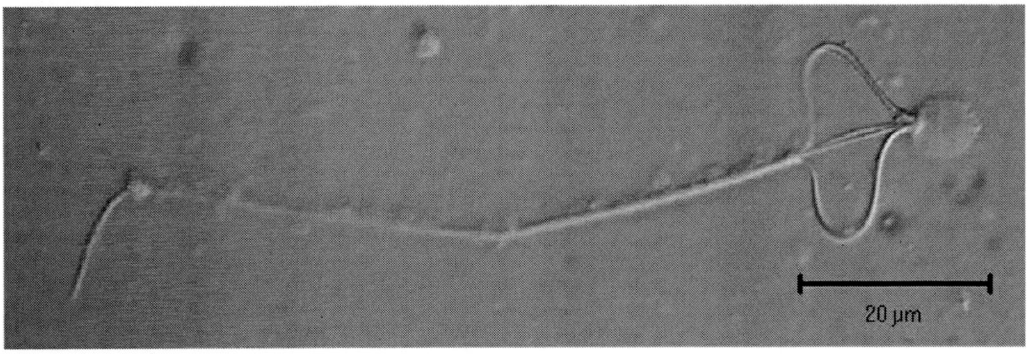

Figure 13. Ground squirrel (*Spermophilus undulates*) postmortem spermatozoa (DIC techique). Abnormal cells with the "fibrillary" type of damage: the major part of the tail is split into separate fibrillas. «Bar 20 µm.

As one can see, list of species for which cryoconservation of epididymal semen is realized is rather vast. But coverage of various taxons is very uneven. Approximately 20 orders of *Mammalia* are presented by 5 orders, for which data on postmortem spermatozoa are available, only. Considering our unpublished data the list extends up to 8 orders.

Prevalence of studies on Ungulates (*Ungulates*) is rather explainable. It's promoted by: availability of domesticated taxons close to many wild species; broad application of AI techniques in animal breeding practice and huge experience accumulated there; extremely important place of Ungulates both in earth ecosystems, and in humankind economics; availability of many really endangered species and subspecies of Ungulates; presence of numerous representatives of Ungulates in the most part of Zoos.

The same time such large taxons as bats (*Chiroptera*), insectivores (*Insectivora*), lagomorphs (*Lagomorpha*), whales (*Cetacea*), seals and walruses (*Pinnipedia*), marsupials (*Marsupalia*), not to mention small in numbers monotremes (*Monotremata*), edentates (*Edentata*), pangolines (*Pholidota*), flying lemurs (*Dermopthera*), earth hogs (*Tubulidentata*) and dugongs (*Sirenia*), stay uncovered. Meanwhile large number of representatives of listed taxons are enlisted in the Red Date List (www.redlist.org.)

Frozen Testicles and Epididymes

One of interesting research fields is attempts to freeze total testicles (Graff et al., 2000), testicles, separate epididymises, and even total bodies of small animals (Ogonuki et al., 2006). Not only liquid nitrogen (-196°C) was used, but low-temperature refrigerating chamber (-80°C) as well (Ogonuki et al., 2006). These techniques can be useful for urgent freezing of postmortem gonads of especially valuable animals in conditions of time-pressure and lack of experts. This way of cryoconservation besides offers a possibility (or a hope) for use such material for future genetic restoration.

COMPARISON OF EPIDIDYMAL AND EJACULATED SEMEN

The physiological conditions of spermatozoa changes dramatically after contact with accessory glands secrets during ejaculation. Their activity increases, their metabolism changes. Changes of composition and biophysical properties take place. These factors affect cryotolerance of spermatozoa (see Katkov, 1985 for references). Numerous physiological parameters of both epididymal and ejaculated spermatozoa of humans and domestic animals have been considered.

However, papers on the differences between epididymal spermatozoa and ejaculated sperm of wild animals_are very scarce. Important consideration is that data obtained at different taxons of wild mammals are not always comparable.

For example, Martinez-Pastor (Martinez-Pastor et al., Theriogenology. 2006, v. 66, n. 5), demonstrated that optimal osmolarity of a cryoprotective solution for epididymal sperm of a deer is much higher, then that for ejaculate. Optimal concentrations of the major cryoprotector (glycerol) for them are different as well.

Sperm motility, plasma membrane integrity and morphology of electroejaculated and epididymal spermatozoa were analyzed immediately after collection and after freezing and thawing. There were no significant differences between the fresh or frozen-thawed cat spermatozoa for any of the variables (Tebet et al., 2006). It was shown (Hermansson, Axner, 2007) that both epididymal and ejaculated cat spermatozoa are resistant to cold shock. The source of spermatozoa did not affect the susceptibility of spermatozoa to cooling and egg yolk promotes sperm longevity during cold storage at 4 degrees C.

ASSISITED REPRODUCTION TECHNIQUES AND POSTMORTEM SPERM

Embryologic researches bring staggering success last time. Techniques that seemed hypothetical just recently are implemented into practice. Among them there are: CP of single spermatozoa and use of them for *in vitro* fertilization; intra cytoplasmic sperm injection (ICSI), allowing use of both individual immobile spermatozoa and spermatozoa heads only for *in vitro* fertilization (Kuretake et al., 1996; Ogonuki et al., 2006); cloning (Loi et al., 2007).

Haploid nuclei of male gametes are strikingly resistant to obviously damaging factors. For example, mice spermatozoa were kept in 70% alcohol at -20°C for 24 hours and then injected into oocytes. In 20% of injection normal embryos developed and life cubs were received (Tateno et al., 1998). Ejaculates of mice and rabbits had been frozen in liquid nitrogen and dried (lyophilized); after storage at room temperature for 1.5 to 2 years sperm-heads were recovered from ejaculates and introduced into oocytes. As a result life cubs were received. (Wakayama, Yanagimachi, 1998; Kusakabe et al., 2001; Liu et al., 2004). Ogonuki (Ogonuki et al. 2006) reported that spermatozoa and spermatids retrieved from frozen reproductive organs or frozen whole bodies of male mice can produce normal offspring.

In practice this means that if 1 (one) spermatozoon of a last fallen male is available, one may, in principle, obtain his offspring. This will, certainly, demand for high-class experts, appropriate equipment and essential expenses.

Data of Swanson (2003) give additional evidence of ART techniques importance. 63 ejaculates of quality sufficient for CP that he recovered in Zoos of Latin America can potentially produce sperm for about 100 AI or several thousands of IVF. Thus preservation of postmortem spermatozoa is an important element of preservation of mammalian genetic diversity. But one must consider that realization of possibilities of the techniques demands for pertinacious and long-time efforts. Here are several instances of postmortem epididymal spermatozoa use in ART procedures.

Research of Zomborszky (Zomborszky et al., 1999) that froze postmortem spermatozoa of deer stags (*Cervus elaphus*), killed by hunters, is very interesting. Two years later (*Sic*!) the spermatozoa were thawed and used for AI of deer females. Embryos were recovered from reproductive tracts of the females and frozen as well. Another 2 years later two thawed embryos were transplanted to females-recipients. One kid was obtained.

Pregnancies were received after using frozen-thawed equine epididymal sperm during hysteroscopic insemination (Morris et al., 2001). Meintjes (Meintjes et al., 1997) reported the production of blastocysts after use of Burchell`s zebra *Equus burchelli* epididymal spermatozoa for IVF with both Burchell`s and Hartmann`s zebra oocytes.

The epididymides of African buffalo was collected from culled males and transported at 4°C for up to 24 hours. The sperm was extracted and processed for IVF. Fertilized ova resulting in 18 to 50% cleavage rates and 33 to 65% embryo developed to the morula stage (Shaw et al., 1995). Winger (Winger et al., 1997) applicated the standard bovine protocols for the maturation and fertilization of blesbok (*Damaliscus dorcas phillipsi*) oocytes using cryopreserved epididymal spermatozoa. Artificial insemination with postmortem epididymal spermatozoa of Spanish ibex (*Capra pyrenaica hispanica*) followed the life birth (Santiago-Moreno et al., 2006).

Postmortem epididymal sperm collected immediately at necropsy from a goat were successfully cryopreserved. Thawed sperm was used to produce one live kid by artificial insemination (Blash et al., 2000). Postmortem epididymal spermatozoa of goats stored at +5°C for 15 days fertilized oocytes in vitro by ICSI techniques. Nevertheless number of fertilized oocytes decreased remarkably during storage of testicles (Zhou et al., 2004). Bartels (Bartels et al., 2001) reported the birth of an eland *Tragelaphus orix* following AI with frozen-thawed epididymal spermatozoa.

Epididymal spermatozoa of adult male lion *Panthera leo* were cryopreserved and used for IVF of in vitro matured lioness ova. (Bartels et al., 2000). Jewgenow (Jewgenow et al., 1997) have also described the use of epididymal sperm for IVF in a few exotic felidae species. Pushett (Pushett et al., 2000) reported developmental rate to the blastocyst stage of 40% after successful IVF using feline frozen-thawed epididymal sperm.

Marks et al. (1994) noted the birth of a canine pup after AI with frozen-thawed epididymal sperm in spite of only a 5% progressive motility rate in thawed sperm. Morrell et al. (1997) used AI with cooled, non-frozen epididymal spermatozoa of common marmoset, *Callithrix jacchus* and achieved live births. Liow et al. (2002) used ICSI with frozen-thawed epididymal spermatozoa of cynomologous monkeys (*Macaca fascicularis*).

The total complex of development biology techniques (recovery of oocytes and sperm, including postmortem ones; *in vitro* maturation of oocytes; cryoconservation of sperm; *in vitro* fertilization of oocytes with cryoconserved sperm; cryoconservation of embryos; transplantation of embryos, and birth of offspring) is realized at two species: gaur *Bos gaurus*

(Godfrey et al., 1991; Hopkins et al., 1989; Johnston et al., 1994); mouflon *Ovis orientalis musimon* (Ptak et al., 2002.

SEMEN PROCESSING

Preface. On Necessity of Teaching and Explanatory Work

It is rather hard for ART specialists to trace independently death of animals even within one the same organization. And it is much harder to bring all postmortem material from other places. We receive research materials: mainly from veterinarians and, less frequently, from other Zoo staffers; sometimes these are delivered by colleagues from other Zoos, nurseries and some reservations of Russia. Most often these are ready-to-use testicles. Our acknowledgement to all these people for their help is enormous, but we are forced to mention the following. Despite detailed preliminary trainings and repeated distribution of study guides on techniques of isolation, storage and transportation of male genitals, meant for isolation of postmortem semen, not all follow these instructions.

Approximately at $1/7^{th}$ of cases, we received material unsuiTable for processing. This was especially frequent at the beginning of our work. The most often these were testicles, cooled up to essential negative temperatures in a freezing chamber (from -12 to -18°C). In two cases we received organs with deep cuts on testicles and epididymis. Unfortunately, in such damaged organs quick bacterial contamination of internal content takes place leading to damage or even total destroy of epididymal spermatozoa. Facts of misrecognizing of genitals and providing of other organs fragments as testicles took place, as well. Such cases are typical for species with intra-abdominal location of testicles. Once we got testicles freed up thoroughly and accurately of both scrotum and epididymises.

In no case we mean to be little merits of people that help us to get material. Nevertheless we would like to limelight the following fact: specialists tackling postmortem saving of animals' gametes are forced to fulfill active explanatory work.

Semen Harvesting

The sources of postmortem spermatozoa could be legally hunted mammals, animals killed in car accidents, males euthnazed after being injured or sick. In our case we receive testes from animals died of various reasons in the zoo

First step of spermatozoa harvesting is separation testes from the body of animal. Our experience shows that testicles should be separated together with scrotum (Figure 6A). This provides the better survival of postmortem spermatozoa. In such state testicles may be stored at room temperature for several hours depending on their state, air temperature and animal species. If long-term storage is necessary, a refrigerator should be used (from +4 to +6°C). Samples are placed into close container or plastic bag (paper) to prevent their drying. (Figure 14, Figure 14A) They should be transported to a processing site in a heat-insulated bag (thermos) with cold accumulators or hermetically packed ice. Contacts of testicle with ice, water or cold accumulators are undesirable. To meet storage conditions a thermometer allowing control of temperature changes during transportation must be placed inside.

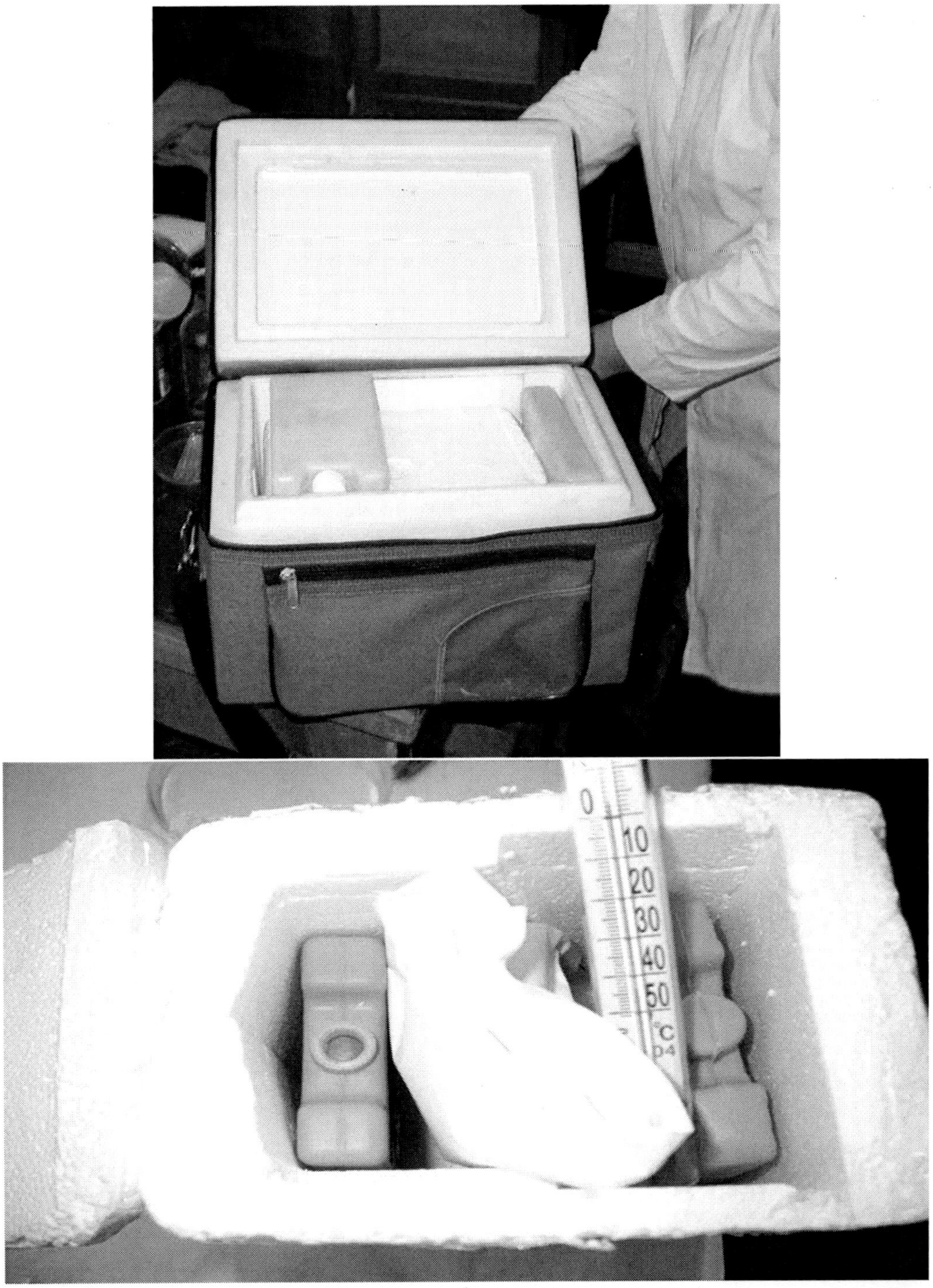

A

B

Figure 14. Thermal bag for collection of posmortem material. (A) Internal space of the thermal bag: cold plastic bags (accumulators) The testes are wrapped in plastics, placed between the bags and shipped from Novosibirsk to Moscow (3200 km). (B): Sample weighting.

To recover spermatozoa, testicles are withdrawn from scrotum and measured. (Figure 6A, Figure 6B, Figure 14B). Then *tunica albuginea*, covering testicle with *epididymis* is removed exposed *epididymis* is separated from testicle. (Figure 5B) And after that the main stock of spermatozoa being in *cauda epididymidis,* it is separated together with spermaduct from *corpus* and *caput epididymidis*. (Figure 5C, Figure 7A) This routine procedure may change a bit depending on specificity of testicles morphology. We observed essential differences in details of testicles structure at different species (Figure 5A, Figure 7, Figure 8A, Figure 10, Figure 11, Figure 12 Figure 15).

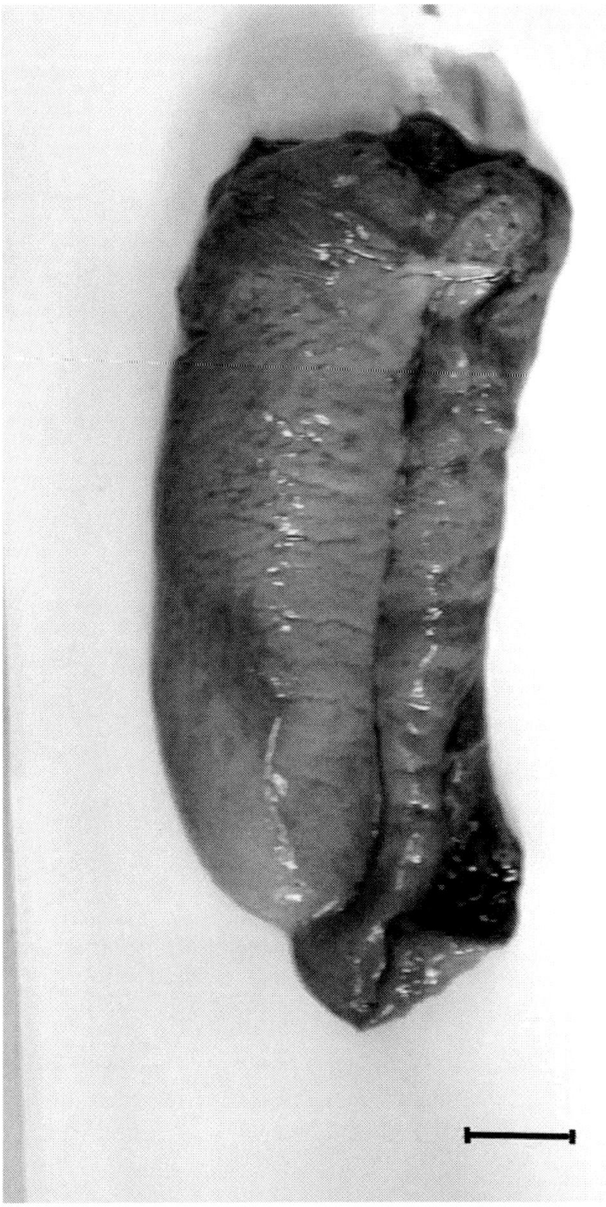

Figure 15. Walrus (*Odobenus rosmarus*) testis. Bar 2 cm.

Several techniques, described as far back as scientific proceeding of the beginning of the XX century, are applied to recover of just spermatozoa from *cauda epididymidis*. (Figure 1) The techniques were used by many authors for various species, so priority is hard to be determined. They come down to the following: cutting (homogenization) of total *cauda epididymidis*; washing out or aspirating (flushing) through sperm duct; making cuts (mincing) in the *cauda epididymidis* and squeezing of content; or just squeezing (pressing). Two first techniques are the most usable.

In our conditions homogenization techniques was more convenient one. After separation of *cauda epididymidis* with sperm duct placed in Petri dish, is cut (homogenized) to uniform suspension and a specified volume of a diluent is added to calculate resulting concentration of spermatozoa. The small amount of spermatozoa only is withdrawn mechanically; their main part comes into "spermatozoa-diluent" suspension by own motility just got. For total recovery of spermatozoa blended epididymis, deepened into a diluent is kept at room temperature for a while.

The cut (mincing) method is more practical on certain occasions but care must be taken to avoid contamination. The microperfused (flushed) method prevents contamination of sperm with extraneous cellular material and fluid components. Nevertheless it is less convenient at work with testicles of small species and samples after long storage. The number of recovered spermatozoa was similar for both methods. In case of severe contamination with blood, fat and particles of tissues a resulting suspension may be filtered through an appropriate filter or centrifuged. After spermatozoa are harvested their quality is assayed.

Quality Control (QC) of Postmortem Spermatozoa

Males' fertility is a complex phenomenon. It depends on heterogenic spermatozoa population that interacts with different parts of a female's reproductive tracts, ova and theirs membranes. In this regard, laboratory assessment of the sperm includes the analysis of a number of parameters. However, it should be mentioned that existence of many methods means that currently there is no universal spermatozoa fertility assessment criterion. The only completely valid criterion is producing of progeny. Rodriguez-Martinez (2003) has roughly assessed the methods of sperm fertility analysis. He assumes that it is an utopian idea to believe in discovering a laboratory method of sperm analysis, reliable enough to predict the potential fertility of a specific sample or a specific producer for AI, based on low correlations between the results, obtained while determination of fertility *in vitro* and data of laboratory analyses.

Though this criticism is true, other methods have not been invented yet. Usually postmortem spermatozoa are reported to have several standard parameters, which include different motility forms, morphological integrity of gametes and their acrosomes (Figure 2A, Figure 3, Figure 6C, Figure9A, Figure 13) and vitality. (Fig 4A, Figure 8B, Figure12B) Sometimes a number of specific tests are applied: penetration of cervical mucus; metabolic activity measurement; ability to pass through a density gradient; ability of sperm to bind to *zona pellucida*; penetrability into zona-free hamster ova (Soler A., Garde, J. Androl. 2003) response to hypo-osmotic swelling test, etc.

Postmortem spermatozoa have following specific parameters: time passed after an animal's death; storage conditions of testes before collection of spermatozoa; diluents and mediums used during sperm harvesting; microbial contamination of sperm suspension received; presence of blood and epididymis cells in suspension; amount of extracted spermatozoa usually expressed as the total spermatozoa store. Spermatozoa concentration is measured here in an artificially made suspension and it can vary depending on the research goals.

Typical parameters of semen: ejaculate volume, its pH, color and consistence are absent due to the known reasons. Microscopic analysis of a received suspension is the first and the most important thing that can be carried out with implementation of all achievements of modern microscopy. Use of different staining method, for example in (Soler C., et al., 2005), and laser confocal microscopy (Maksudov, Shishova, unpublished data) (Figure 2A, Figure 3, Figure 4B, Figure 6C, Figure 7B, Figure 8B, Figure 9A, Figure 13) to assess postmortem spermatozoa has been described. Dark-field microscopy is usually used to analyze the acrosome status.

Computer and Automated Systems Association (CASA) techniques as well as video-micrography related techniques are used extensively at investigation of post-mortal spermatozoa. CASA techniques is free from errors of an investigator but they, of course, require necessary hardware and conditions. Paper of Esteso (Esteso et al., 2006) is rather interesting in this respect. Computer-automated sperm head morphometry of epididymal samples was used to determine if measurements of sperm head area and shape are useful instruments for determination of sperm cryoresistance. It was shown that the lower is sperm head area in fresh samples, the greater is the sperm cryoresistance.

We often use a sperm analyzer by Biola Ltd. (www.biola.ru), convenient in field environment due to its small size, ability to work on batteries and use power, built-in microscope and digital video camera (Maksudov, Shishova, unpublished data).

We have information on only one case of postmortem spermatozoa intracellular ATP analysis conducted within the whole gonads storage process (Mohammadzadeh et al., 2008); at that, for postmortem spermatozoa, extracted in 24 or more hours after death this parameter is quite informative.

DISCUSSION

The issues regarding the fate of spermatozoa left in reproductive tracts of male mammals were first risen at the beginning of the XX century. It was already mentioned that Ivanov (Ivanov, 1907) has first documented cases of preservation of viable gametes in testes, without studying this phenomenon mechanisms though. According to Young (Young, 1929) spermatozoa proceed to from testis epididymis immature, so are maturating as they move along this structure. After full maturation, the cells age, as the author puts it, i.e. gradually lose their ability to fulfill a specific function and then they degenerate in *cauda epididymis* and *vas deferens*.

Now this scientific problem may be divided into several basic questions.

1. How long can spermatozoa survive in postmortem testicles?

Our work confirms the preservation of spermatozoa viability in isolated testicles from dead and castrated animals. For instance, we have found live spermatozoa in epididymises of *Capra hircus* 7 (Figure 14B) and 9 days after the animal's death and in testis of gnu *Connochaetes gnou* 7 days after castration. (Figure 5A) It is important to notice that cases of such long spermatozoa preservation periods we only registered for ungulates. For carnivores the period of isolated testicles storage never exceeded three days, notwithstanding the fact that in our experiments the quantity of observed carnivores` testicles was larger than that of ungulates. At the same time Ivanov (Ivanov, 1907) registered the long period of spermatozoa survival in dog's testicles (till 9 days). Yu and Leibo (2002) confirmed the case and described that after 7 days storage, spermatozoa of dog were not only live but also able to contact with *zona pellucida*. Evidently, comparative characteristics of postmortem spermatozoa from different mammalian species demand further researches.

Even longer periods are registered for laboratory animals. Kishikawa (Kishikawa et al. (1999). Injection (ICSI) of immobile spermatozoa, recovered from mice bodies stored postmortem for 20 days, in 80% of cases resulted in development of embryos. In our experiments mice spermatozoa were viable and kept sufficient level of ATP for 18 days while storing testicles at low positive temperatures (Mohammadzadeh et al., 2008; Doronin et al., 2004). Such data is the indirect evidence that time of spermatozoa death may differ from times of most tissue degradation. For example, irreversible alterations in kidney cells appear in 40 to 60 minutes at room temperature and in 2 to 4 hours at low positive temperatures (Shumakov, 1983).

Long viability preservation of postmortem epididymidal mice spermatozoa may be connected with their difference from ejaculated gametes. It is well-known, that in ejaculation process the contact of spermatozoa with accessory gland secretions leads to activation of their motility. It is noticed that the prolongation of periods between animals death and spermatozoa collection more influenced on acrosome preservation than on spermatozoa motility after CP (Sipko, Shishova et al. 1994; 1997).

This may prove to become important during the realization of programs on rare and endangered species preservation, animal sperm cryobanks foundation. (Maksudov, 1997, Jewgenov et al., 1997).

Thus, maximum period of viability preservation of mammalian postmortem spermatozoa is significantly longer than it was supposed to be.

2. **What are the mechanisms of postmortem spermatozoa degradation and fertility loss *in situ* и *ex situ*?**

The question has no definitive answer yet.

3. **Optimal methods of storage of testicles as the whole and spermatozoa, cell handling and preservation.**

A greater number of viable sperm provided when gametes stored in the epididymis at +4 to +5°C prior to collection compared with testicles stored at an elevated temperature.

It is appeared to be more effective to store separated testicles without significant freezing for several hours after the animal death. At prolonged testicles storage (for at least 24 hours) before processing, for example, at transportation, the best conditions is the storage at low positive temperatures. It allows for long samples transportation before the harvesting of spermatozoa. In our practice this distance was 3,191 km from Novosibirsk to Moscow. (Figure 14, Figure 14A)

As a rule, the methods developed for ejaculates with slight modifications are used for epididymidal spermatozoa CP. For rare and endangered species the techniques developed for other species ejaculated sperm, usually taxonomically close, are used. At absence of such, the methods for more distantly related species are used.

Methods developed for ejaculated sperm can hardly be considered optimal for epididymidal spermatozoa, especially for postmortem obtained after 24 hour and more after the animal death. But this practice results in convenient outcome. About half of the live gametes are survived after postmortem spermatozoa freezing. The survival rate of thawed spermatozoa is species specific and evidently depends on source quality.

Our experience shows that postmortem samples with high spermatozoa motility, as a rule, have lesser loses at CP compared to the samples having originally low mobility. At the same time, the luminescent viability tests show that even at totally immovable samples froze the significant quantity of live immovable spermatozoa is found after thawing (Figure 4A, Figure 12B) (Shishova, Maksudov, *paper in preparation*).

Characteristics of Postmortem Animal Sperm Processing in Zoos

There were few articles in regards to postmortem spermatozoa CP in zoos prior to 2000; however, the interest towards postmortem preservation of genetic material has been significantly increased recently (O`Brien, Rott, 2000, Maksudov, Shishova, 2006; Maksudov, 2005, 1997). Meanwhile, a number of problems *should be addressed in the future*. It includes but is not limited by the following:

1. The testicles brought to the laboratory very often belong to different animal species. As a rule they are from single naturally died animals.
2. Sample delivery is irregular and unpredicTable.
3. Testicles belong to animals of different age, physiological state and independent of specific species reproductive cycles. Usually it happens in one to three days from animal death.
4. Testicles storage condition and preliminary processing may be incorrectly executed.
5. The immediate spermatozoa separation, quick evaluation and CP in case of satisfactory quality are the most important tasks.
6. Data collection in regards to differential testicle morphology, microfilming, sample preparation for different microscope researches (luminescent, confocal) are also possible. Thawed straws or pellets allow for conclusions about convenience of CP type for the sperm of the given wild species.

One of the key strategic questions necessity of collection of postmortem animal material in zoos. One of the main purposes of a zoo nowadays is breeding, or transferring the genetic data by natural way. But this question can only appear in areas distant from wild animals keeping in captivity. Experts understand the difficulty of this task and know how often animals die without breeding.

Let us give the following example: Amur leopard *Panthera pardus orientalis.* **(Figure 8)** According taxon report for this species, Moscow Zoo has five adult males. By different reasons only one male (16th years old) breed for last 4 years. One male died in November 2007 (16th years old) and another one did in May 2008 (18th years old). Testes of both dead males were investigated and in one case we found spermatozoa accepTable for CP. Thus, half of existing males died in half a year, but we managed to save the genetic material by CP of postmortem spermatozoa for only one of them.

We can state that postmortem samples of most died animals became precious. And even if the male species had bred before or had been subject to semen collection, postmortem sperm samples are important for future breeding as well as for the research purposes.

What is the possibility of finding the valuable spermatozoa in dead animals' testicles? Postmortem material that can be obtained in zoos usually belongs to the aged animals with different diseases. Moreover, some species have seasonal breeding. All these factors can influence on the spermatozoa presence and quality in epididymis at accidental moment.

However, our experience shows that such skepticism has no actual ground. We studied 39 died mammalian testicles samples belonging to 27 species and 9 orders. They all were studied regadless the reason of death and season of a year (Maksudov, Shishova, 2006; Shishova et al. 2007). Only small rodents, juvenile animals and samples with signs of decomposition and mummification were rejected.

The total picture, without counting testicles damaged due to incorrect storage or at preliminary processing (see corresponding section) is the following. Morphologically standard spermatozoa were found in 80% of epididymis samples (26 samples of 32). In 78% of total samples (25 animals) spermatozoa quantity in two *cauda epididymis* exceeded 100 M/ml. In 38% of total samples (12 animals of 32) spermatozoa quantity exceeded even 1 billion of gametes at 1 ml of epididymal suspension.

Analysis of different factors showed that the concurrency of death with breeding season has the strongest affect on spermatozoa content in testicles of dead animals. In species without the distinct breeding season or died during that season we found spermatozoa in 90% of samples. Otherwise, in species died in no breeding period the spermatozoa were found only in 33% of samples. The spermatozoa quantity was significantly less that in the prior group (see Tables 3 and 4). It is important to note, though, that spermatogenesis peak and breeding period do not always coincide (Bronson, 1988).

The effect of the case of death and disease on gametes content is not as significant as we can suspect. The spermatozoa were found in animals died in different accidents (stresses, fights, etc) with the same frequency as in died of cancer or chronic cardiovascular or excretory systems disorders. Spermatozoa content and quality were almost the same in animals died of sickness and in males died in accidents.

Among the surveyed animals were several that were in age equal or exceeding the average lifetime of the given species (Table 5). It was a surprise to find spermatozoa in their testicles too. But spermatozoa content and quality parameters in *cauda epididymis* of aged males were, as a rule, lower.

Table 3. Postmortem epididymal semen quality of males dead during breeding season and males from non-seasonal breeding species

Order	Males, total	Species, total	Males				
			With spermatozoa	With stock of sperm in *cauda epididymides*		Motility	
				<10 M	>1 B	Total	Progressive
Primates	3	3	3 (100%)	0	1 (33%)	3 (100%)	2 (66%)
Carnivora	4	4	4	2 (50%)	1 (25%)	1 (25%)	1 (25%)
Artiodactyla	8	4	7 (87%)	0	7 (87%)	6 (65%)	4 (50%)
Rodenta	1	1	1	0	1	1	1
Total	16	12	15 (93%)	2 (13%)	10 (62%)	11 (69%)	8 (50%)

Table 4. Postmortem epididymal semen quality of males dead outside breeding season

Order	Males, total	Species, total	Males				
			With spermatozoa	With stock of sperm in *cauda epididymides*		With motile spermatozoa	
				<10 billions	>1 billion	Total motility	Progressive motility
Carnivora	7	5	4 (57%)	3 (43%)	0	2 (28%)	0
Pinnipedia	3	2	1 (33%)	0	0	0	0
Perissodactyla	1	1	1	1	0	0	0
Artiodactyla	3	2	2 (66%)	0	2 (66%)	2 (66%)	0
Total	14	10	8 (57%)	4 (29%)	2 (14%)	4 (28%)	0

Note. Data on species inhabitant to Southern hemisphere are not included in the Tables, because the breeding seasons in our conditions often differ from natural ones.

Table 5. Post mortem semen quality of aged mammalian males died in Moscow Zoo since January 2005 to May 2008.

Species	Age, years	The median life time of species, years.	Duration between death and testes processing, days.	A stock of sperm in *cauda epididymides*, billion cells.	Spermatozoa motility	Acrosome integrity	Vitality test (PI)
Anubis baboon *Papio anubis*	21	20-25	2	0,22	10%	55%	No data
ring-tailed lemur *Lemur catta*	22	20-22	2	0,34	13%	86%	73%
Manned wolf *Chrysocyon brachyurus*	16	12-15	7	<0,01	0	No data	No data
polar fox *Alopex lagopus*	12	8-10	3	<0,1	0	No data	No data
Spectacled bear *Tremarctos ornatus*	21	20-25	3	0,61	19%	80%	62%
Amur leopard *Panthera pardus orientalis*	18	15-18	1	Absent	-	-	-
Amur leopard *Panthera pardus orientalis*	19	15-18	2	0,05	3%	66%	70%
Kiang *Equus hemionus kiang*	27	20-25	4	<0,1	0	83%	No data

Postmortem spermatozoa quality of the animals from zoos is, unfortunately, lower compared to samples obtained after shooting wild animals. Literary data (Soler A. *et al.*, 2003 J. Androl.; Soler A. *et al.*, 2003 J. Exp.Zool.; Martinez-Pastor *et al.*, 2005), and our experience (Sipko *et al.*,1993) prove this. Interesting, though, that the quality of postmortem spermatozoa in these animals stays on the convenient level even if they are separated 3 to 4 days after shooting.

On the other side, viability test by propidium iodide staining shows that at mice samples after 18 days of testicles storage at +6 C quantity of live spermatozoa is 50-80%. By the way these samples do not contain moving spermatozoa. (Mohammadzadeh et al., 2008: Doronin et al., 2004). Apparently, we can only count on semen from animals died in zoos sufficiency for standard artificial insemination in rare specific cases. Other samples are usable only for other ART methods. Nevertheless, we assume that in case of rare and endangered species deaths it is necessary to save semen samples of any quality. Considering contemporary tendencies in biological diversity decrease and ART methods development such samples can be of much value in 10-20 years.

Any animal death is more or less unexpected. It often takes time to deliver postmortem material to the laboratory and process it. In zoos such conditions are often complicated by requirements to follow corresponding veterinary instructions that influence the delivery periods of postmortem material.

Additional peculiarity of zoo animals postmortem spermatozoa collection is a wide variety of species. (Figure 2, Figure 4, Figure 5, Figure 6, Figure 7, Figure 8, Figure 9, Figure 12, Figure 15) It is impossible to concentrate on several species or a couple of taxons. We need to have data on different species reproductive system features, or CP techniques. We must be ready to the situations when we have samples from species not yet described or surveyed in the literature. Such varieties of sample material and small amounts of every species animals make it difficult to analyze the obtained data and improve the CP methods. But there are also unbeatable advantages that make it worth. We have several rare samples that are difficult to obtain otherwise. Our experience is limited still but we have some semen samples of species that is very seldom presented in some other cryobanks, namely *Panthera pardus orientalis, Cuon alpinus, East Caucasian tur, Tremarctos ornatus, Lemur catta* an some others species.

7. We do not presume the necessity of immediate usage of our samples for artificial insemination. We, on the contrary, assume that the genetic value of these samples will only rise in the future!

FUTURE DIRECTIONS

A large amount of data is collected on the subject of postmortem semen usage. The increase of postmortem genetic material value for rare species preservation is obvious, and we need to develop and enhance the methods connected with it. Among the great variety of tasks and questions we would like to point out the most important ones to our opinion.

It is shown on the several species that methods developed for ejaculated sperm are effective for epididymidal spermatozoa freezing. But ejaculated and epididymidal spermatozoa physiologies are different and we can assume that optimum methods of freezing and thawing may be different. At CP of spermatozoa obtained several days postmortem the methods can also be different from those developed for gametes obtained immediately after death. The features of physiological and biophysical properties of ejaculated and epididymidal spermatozoa are also waiting do be thoroughly researched.

To date, our knowledge of the epididymal sperm metabolism of RES animals is limited and further research for taxonomic groups will contribute to the solution and development of optimized cryoprotective media customized to the specific animal species and even to particular anatomic subpopulations (testicular, from *caput* and *cauda epididymis* or electroejaculated sperm). It will also allow to use a quiescent state of epididymidal spermatozoa and will be important at development of methods of compensation of gametes' energy depletion at their storage before CP. We do not have comparative data on cryostability of epididymidal spermatozoa membranes of different species besides domestic husbandry ungulates (see Katkov, 1985 for literature synopsis). The immaturity of lipid content of the cell membranes of epididymidal spermatozoa can be compensated by modification of the cryoprotective medium specifically tailored to this type of sperm.

The study of mechanisms of the sperm cell death in testicles of dead animal for different species and understanding the factors responsible for long viability of mammalian postmortem spermatozoa is also an important task. **(Figure 2A, Figure 7B, Figure 9A, Figure 13)** Such data can help in search of postmortem storage negative effects compensation and widen the method application area. The process of spermatozoa ageing is not studied at all apparently their ageing in storage inside epididymis.

The destructive role of lipid peroxidation is also a vector of damage, both in process of PMSCP and during storage in genitalia prior to CP. We can assume that postmortem spermatozoa require more sufficient protection from active oxygen radicals than ejaculated sperm.

The study of postmortem spermatozoa nucleus integrity and all nuclear material is also a principal matter. Modern ART methods allow for insemination by motionless spermatozoa with destroyed acrosomes and damaged cell membrane. But the destruction of the nuclear material sterilizes the spermatozoa. We know that mammals' spermatozoa nuclear material is inert and compacted. We can assume that during the postmortem storage of mammalian spermatozoa DNA will not be significantly damaged. There is some data that proves our point of view (Fernandez-Santos et al., 2007). But its importance is high and we need to continue studies.

The problem of long-term testicles storage before postmortem spermatozoa CP effect on both their cryoresistence and on resulting offspring is quite uninvestigated.

CONCLUSION

The following are the basic conclusions made on the collected data.

1. Postmortem epididymidal spermatozoa can be viable for several days after the animal death. This period depends on the species, the storage conditions of testes and the sperm collection methods.

2. Processing the animal's testicles in several hours after death it proved to be more effective to store them in the separated organs without deep freezing. At prolonged testicles storage before processing, for instance, in need of transportation, the best conditions for gonads storage proved to be low positive temperatures. It allows carrying the postmortem material on sufficient distances. In our practice the distance was 3,191 km from Novosibirsk to Moscow.
3. Postmortem epididymidal spermatozoa can withstand the freezing in liquid nitrogen well, which made the method suitable for genetic banking. The methods developed for ejaculates can be used also for postmortem spermatozoa CP. In most cases, CP provides salvage of about ½ of the alive spermatozoa after thawing. But at the same time these methods cannot be considered perfect for the postmortem spermatozoa. Several physical and biochemical parameters of ejaculated and epididymidal spermatozoa are different. We would advise development of specific methods of CP intended for postmortem spermatozoa especially after their storage *ex situ*.
4. Our experience with animals died in zoos shows that the quality their postmortem semen of naturally died animals is worse than that of shot or accidentally died animals. Quite often, the postmortem semen does not have enough live spermatozoa for routine artificial insemination after long storage. But acceptable results are achieved when it is used in ART methods like *in vitro* insemination or ICSI.
5. Further research in areas of sperm collection, storage and ART may significantly improve efficacy of of postmortem semen as a viable source of genetic material, and can make substantial contribution in sustaining biological diversity.

ACKNOWLEDGEMENTS

This work was partially supported by RFBR grant 06-04-49268-a (Russian Federation) for *G.Yu.M.* and *N.V.Sh.* and by internal funding provided by CELTRONIX, USA (*I.I.K*).

We are very thankful to A. Yashina for help in microphotography (Figures 2, 3 4B, 7B, and 13) and M. Kuznetsova and I. Ivannikov for participation in postmortem biopsy.

REFERENCES

Abou-Haila A. and Tulsiani D.R. Mammalian sperm acrosome: formation, contents and function. *Arch Biochem Biophys* 2000, v. 379, n. 2, pp.173-82

An T.Z., Wada S., Edashige K., Sakurai T., Kasai M. Viable spermatozoa can be recovered from refrigerated mice up to 7 days after death. *Cryobiology*, 1999, v. 38, n. 1, pp. 27-34.

Anel L., Guerra C., Alvarez M., Kaabi M., Anel E., Boixo J.C., Paz P., Martinez F., and Herraez P. Basic parameters in spermatozoa recovered post-mortem from the Spanish Cantabrian Chamois (*Rupicapra pyrenaica parva*). *Theriogenology*, 2000, v. 53, n. 1, p. 323

Anel L., Martinez F., Alvarez M., Anel E., Boixo J.C., Kaabi M., and Paz P., Chamorro C., Herraez P. Post-mortem recovery and freezing in a Cantabric brown bear (*Ursus arctos*): A preliminary report. *Theriogenology*, 1999, v. 51, n. 1, p. 277.

Bartels P., Friedmann Y., Lubbe K., Mortimer D., Rasmussen L.A., and Godke R.A. The live birth of an eland (*Taurotragus oryx*) calf following estrous synchronization and artificial insemination using frozen thawed epididymal sperm. *Theriogenology*, 2001, v. 55, n.1, p. 381.

Bartels P., Lubbe K., Kilian I., Friedmann Y., van Dyk G., and Mortimer D. In vitro maturation and fertilization of lion (*Panthera leo*) oocytes using frozen-thawed epididymal spermatozoa recovered by cauda epididymectomy of an immobilized lion. *Theriogenology*, 2000, v. 53, n. 1, p. 325.

Bartels P., Lubbe K., Smith R.L., and Godke R.A. Morphological changes of caudal epididymal spermatozoa of African buffalo (*Syncerus caffer*) after storage at 6°C. *Theriogenology*, 1998, v. 55, n. 1, pp. 279.

Bezuidenhout C., le R. Fourie F., Meintjes M., Borman M.S., Bartels P., and Godke R.A. Comparative epididymal sperm cell motility of African ungulate and equid game species stored at 4°C. *Theriogenology*, 1995, v. 43, n. 1, p. 167.

Blandau R. J. and Rumery R. E.. The relationship of swimming movements of epididimal spermatozoa to their fertilizing capasity. *Fertil. Steril.*, 1964, v..15, n. 6, pp.571-579.

Blash S., Melican D. and Gavin W. CP of epididymal sperm obtained at necropsy from goats. *Theriogenology*. 2000, v. 54, n. 6, pp. 899-905.

Bronson F.H. Seasonal regulation of reproduction in mammals. In: The Physiology of reproduction, ed. E. Knobil, J. Neill et al., Raven Press, N.Y., 1988, P.1831-1871.

Bruemmer J.E. Collection and freezing of epididymal stallion sperm Vet. Clin. North. Am. Equine Pract. , 2006, v. 22, n. 3, pp. 677-682.

Bruemmer J.E., Reger H., Zibinski G., and Squires E.L. Effect of storage at 5 degree C on the motility and CP of stallion epididymal spermatozoa. *Theriogenology*, 2002, v. 58, n. 4, pp. 405-407.

Comizzoli P., Mermillod P., Cognié Y., Chai N., Legendre X., and Mauge R. Successful in vitro production of embryos in the red deer (Cervus elaphus) and the sika deer (Cervus nippon). *Theriogenology*, 2001, v. 55, n. 2, pp. 649-659.

Comizzoli P., Mermillod P. and Mauget R. Reproductive biotechnologies for endangered mammalian species. *Reprod Nutr Dev.* 2000, v. 40, n. 5, pp. 493-504.

Dong Q, Rodenburg S.E. and Vandevoort C.A. CP of rhesus monkey (Macaca mulatta) epididymal spermatozoa before and after refrigerated storage. *J. Androl.,* 2008, v. 29, n. 3, pp. 283-292.

Doronin Yu.K. and Maksudov G.Yu., Mohammadzadeh S.M Prolonged preservation of viability of postmortem epididymal mammalian spermatozoa. [Russian] *Cytologia,* 2004, v.46, n 9, pp. 786-787.

Durrant B.S. Penetration of humster ova by non-human primate spermatozoa. J.Androl., 1997, v.8, n.1, p. 27

Esteso M.C., Soler A.J., Fernández-Santos M.R., Quintero-Moreno A.A., and Garde J.J. Functional significance of the sperm head morphometric size and shape for determining freezability in iberian red deer (Cervus elaphus hispanicus) epididymal sperm samples. *J Androl.* 2006, v. 27, n. 5, pp. 662-670.

Fernandez-Santos M.R., Martinez-Pastor F, Garcia-Macias V, Esteso M.C., Soler A.J., de Paz P., Anel L., and Garde J.J. Extender osmolality and sugar supplementation exert a complex effect on the CP of Iberian red deer (Cervus elaphus hispanicus) epididymal spermatozoa. Theriogenology, 2007, v. 67, n. 4, pp. 738-753.

Fernandez-Santos M.R., Martinez-Pastor F, Garcia-Macias V, Esteso M.C., Soler A.J., de Paz P., Anel L., and Garde J.J. Sperm characteristics and DNA integrity of Iberian red deer (Cervus elaphus hispanicus) epididymal spermatozoa frozen in the presence of enzymatic and nonenzymatic antioxodants. J. Androl. 2007, v.28, n. 2, pp. 294-305.

Fernández-Santos M.R., Esteso M.C., Montoro V., Soler A.J., and Garde J.J. CP of Iberian red deer (Cervus elaphus hispanicus) epididymal spermatozoa: effects of egg yolk, glycerol and cooling rate. *Theriogenology,* 2006 v. 66, n. 8, pp. 1931-1942.

Fernández-Santos M.R., Esteso M.C., Soler A.J., Montoro V., and Garde J.J. The effects of different cryoprotectants and the temperature of addition on the survival of red deer epididymal spermatozoa. *Cryo Letters*. 2005; v. 26, n. 1, pp. 25-32.

Godfrey R.W., Lunstra D.D., French J.A., Schwartz J., Armstrong D.L., and Simmons L.G. Estrus synchronization ib the Gaur (*Bos gaurus*): behavior and fertility to artificial insemination after prostaglandin treatment. *Zoo Biology*, 1991, v. 10, pp. 35-41.

Goldberg, Erwin (Ed.) The Testis. From Stem Cell to Sperm Function Series: Serono Symposia USA 2000, XVII, 265 p. 33 illus.,

Graff K.J., Paccamonti D., Leibo S.P., and Godke R.A.. A simple method for storing spermatozoa in frozen excised canine testes for use in assisted reproductive technologies. Proc. 14th Int. Congr. Anim. Reprod., 2000, Stockholm, p. 160

Graham E.F.,Schmehl M.K.L.,Evensen B.K., and Nelson D.V. Sperm preservation in Non-Domestic Animals. in: Artificial Breeding of Non-Domestic Animals, London, Acad.Press,1978, pp. 153-173

Hermansson U. and Axner E. Epididymal and ejaculated cat spermatozoa are resistant to cold shock but egg yolk promotes sperm longevity during cold storage at 4 degrees C. Theriogenology, 2007, v. 67, n. 7, pp. 1239-1248.

Herold F.C., de Haas K., Colenbrander B., and Gerber D. Comparison of equilibration times when freezing epididymal sperm from African buffalo (Syncerus caffer) using Tryadyl or AndroMed. *Theriogenology,* 2006; v. 66, n. 5, pp. 1123-1130.

Herrick J.R., Bartels P. and Krisher R.L. Postthaw evaluation of in vitro function of epididymal spermatozoa from four species of free-ranging African bovids. *Biol Reprod.,* 2004, v. 71, n. 3, pp. 948-958.

Hishinuma A., Suzuki K. and Sekine J. Recovery and CP of sika-deer (Cervus nippon) spermatozoa from epididymides stored at 4- degrees-C. *Theriogenology*, 2003, v. 59, n. 3-4, pp 813-820

Holt W.V and Pickard A.R. Role of reproductive technologies and genetic resource banks in animal conservation. *Rev. Reprod.*, 1999, v. 4, n. 3, pp. 143-150.

Hopkins S.M., Armstrong D.L.,Hummel S.K.C., and Junior S. Successful CP of gaur (Bos gaurus) epididimal spermatozoa. *J.of Zoo Wildl. Med.*, 1989, v.19, n.4, pp. 195-201

Hori T., Haguida K., Endo S., Havama A., Kawakami E., and Tsutsui T. Unilateral intrauterine insemination with cryopreserved caudal epididymal sperm recovered from refrigerated canine epididymides. *J. Vet. Med. Sci.*, 2005, v. 67, n. 11, pp. 1141-1147

Ivanov I.I. Artififcial fertilization in mammals. [Russian] St Petersburg, 1907, 135 P.

James, A.N., Green H., Hoffman S., and Godke R.A. Preservation of equine cauda epididymal sperm stored in the cauda epididymidis of testes at 4°C for 24, 48, 72 and 96 hours. *Theriogenology*, 2002, v. 58, n. 2-4, pp. 401-404.

Jewgenow K., Blottner S., Lengwinat T., and Meyer H.H.D. New methods for gamete rescue from gonads of nondomestic felids. *J. Reprod. Fertil. Suppl.*,1997. v. 51, pp. 33-39.

Jones R.C. and Murdoch R.N. Regulation of the motility and metabolism of spermatozoa for storage in the epididymis of eutherian and marsupial mammals. *Reproduction, Fertility and Development*. 1996, v. 8, n. 4, pp. 553-568.

Jones R.C. Collection, motility and storage of spermatozoa from the African elephant Loxodonta africana. *Nature*, 1973, v. 243, n. 5401, pp. 38-39.

Johnston S.D., Parrish J.J., Monson R., Leibfried-Rutledge L., Susko-Parrish J.L., Northey D.L., Rutledge J.J., and Simmons L.J. Oocyte maturation, fertilization and embryo development *in vitro* and *in vivo* in the gaur (*Bos gaurus*). *Journ. Repr. Fert.* 1994, v. 100, n. 1, pp. 131-136.

Kaabi M., Paz P., Alvarez M., Anel E., Boixo J.C., Rouissi H., Herraez P., and Anel L. Effect of epididymis handling conditions on the quality of ram spermatozoa recovered post-mortem. Theriogenology, 2003, v. 60, n. 7, pp. 1249-1259.

Katkov I. Correlation Between Parameters of Spermatozoon Membranes Before Cryopreservation and Physiological Status of the Sperm After Thawing. Theses Ph.D. Degree Dissertation, 1985, Institute of Animal Breeding, Kharkov, Ukraine.

Kikuchi K., Nagai T., Kashiwazaki N., Ikeda H., Noguchi J., Shimada A., Soloy E., and Kaneko H. CP and ensuing in vitro fertilization ability of boar spermatozoa from epididymides stored at 4 degrees C. *Theriogenology*, 1998. v. 50, n 4, pp. 615-623.

Kilian I., Lubbe K., Bartels P., Friedmann Y., and Denniston R.S. Evaluating epididymal sperm of African wild ruminants: Longevity when stored at 4 degree C and viability following CP. *Theriogenology*, 2000, v. 53, n. 1, p. 336.

Kishikawa H., Tateno H. and Yanagimachi R. Fertility of mouse spermatozoa retrieved from cadavers and maintained at 4 degrees C. *J Reprod Fertil.* 1999. v. 116, n. 2. pp. 217-222.

Krzyvinski A. Freezing of post mortem collected semen from Moos and Red Deer. *Acta Theriologica*, 1981, 26, 28: 424-426.

Kuretake S., Kimura Y., Hoshi K., and Yanagimachi R. Fertilization and development of mouse oocytes injected with isolated sperm heads. *Biol. Repr.*, 1996, v. 55, n. 4, pp. 789-795.

Kusakabe H, Szczygiel M.A., Whittingham D.G., and Yanagimachi R. 2001. Maintenance of genetic integrity in frozen and freeze-dried mouse spermatozoa *Proc. Natl. Acad. Sci. USA*, 2001, v. 98, n. 24. 13501-13506.

Lambrechts H., van Niekerk F. E., Coetzer W. A., Cloete S. W., van der and Horst G. The effect of CP on the survivability, viability and motility of epididymal African buffalo (*Syncerus caffer*) spermatozoa. *Theriogenology*, 1999. v. 52, n 7.pp. 1241-1249.

Leibo S.P. and Songsasen N. CP of gametes and embryos of non-domestic species. *Theriogenology,* 2002, v. 57, n. 1, pp. 303-326.

Liow S.L., Martelli P., Herbert S., Oh S.H., Tan L.G., and Ng S.C. Intracytoplasmic injection of frozen-thawed epididymal spermatozoa in a non-human primate model, the cynomolgus monkey (*Macaca fascicularis*). Proc. 2nd Int. Symp. Assist. Reprod. Tech. (ART) for the Conservation and Genet. Mgmt. of Wildl. 2002, (September), Omaha, NE. p. 232.

Liu J.L., Kusakabe H., Chang C.C., Suzuki H., Schmidt D.W., Julian M., Pfeffer R., Bormann C.L., Tian X.C., Yanagimachi R., and Yang X. Freeze-dried sperm fertilization leads to term development in rabbits. *Biol Reprod.*, 2004, v. 70, n. 6, pp. 1776-1781.

Loi, P, Galli C. and Ptak, G. Cloning of endangered mammalian species: any progress? *Trends Biotechnol.* 2007, v. 25, n. 5, pp. 195-200.

Loskutoff N.M., Simmons H.A., Goulding M., Thompson G., Dejongh T., and Simmons L.G. Species and individual variations in cryoprotectant toxicities and freezing resistances of epididymal sperm from African antelope. 1996, *Anim. Reprod. Sci.,* v. 42, n. 1-4, pp. 527-535

Lubbe K., Bartels P., Kilian I., Friedmann Y.,. and Godke R. A. Comparing motility and morphology of horse, zebra and rhinoceros epididymal spermatozoa when cryopreserved with two different cryodiluents or stored at 4°C. *Theriogenology*, 2000, v. 53, n. 1., p. 338.

Maksudov G. Yu. and Shishova N. V. CP of post-mortal epididymal semen in Moscow Zoo. 1st European Congress of Conservation Biology. 22-26 August, 2006, Eger, Hungary. Book of Abstracts. A 578, p.135

Maksudov G.Yu. Vitality of postmortem epididymal goat spermatozoa after long time testes storage. [Russian] Scientific research in Zoological parks, Moscow, 2005, v. 18. pp. 100-104

Maksudov G.Yu. Storage and transportation of deceased animal testes for post-mortem harvesting of spermatozoa. [Russian]. Informational issue of Eurasian association of zoos and aquariums, 1997, Moscow, v. 16, pp.226-227

Marks S.L., Dupuis J., Mickelsen W.D., Memon M.A., and Platz C.C. Conception by use of postmortem epididymal semen extraction in a dog. *J. Amer. Vet. Med. Ass.* 1994, v. 204, n. 10, pp. 1639-1640

Martinez-Pastor F., Garcia-Macias V., Alvarez M., Chamorro C., Herraes P., de Paz P., and Anel L. Comparison of two methods for obtaining spermatozoa from the cauda epididymis of Iberian red deer. *Theriogenology*, 2006; v. 66, n.3, pp. 471-485.

Martinez-Pastor F., Garcia-Macias V., Esteso M. C., Anel E., Fernandez-Santos M.R., Soler A.J., de Paz P., Garde J.J., and Anel L. A pilot study on post-thawing quality of Iberian red deer spermatozoa (epididymal and electroejaculated) depending on glycerol concentration and extender osmolarity. *Theriogenology*, 2006, v. 66, n. 5, pp. 1165-1172.

Martinez-Pastor F., Diaz-Corujo A.R., Anel E., Herraes P., and Anel L., de Paz P. Post mortem time and season alter subpopulation characteristics of Iberian red deer epididymal sperm. Theriogenology, 2005, v. 64, n. 4, pp. 958-974.

Mazur P., Leibo S.P. and Seidel G.E., Jr. CP of the germplasm of animals used in biological and medical research: importance, impact, status, and future directions. *Biol Reprod.* 2008, v. 78, n. 1, pp. 2-12.

Meintjes M., Bezuidenhout C., Bartels P., Visser D.S., Meintjes J., Loskutoff N.M., Fourie F.L., Barry D.M., and Godke R.A. In vitro maturation and fertilization of oocytes recovered from free-ranging Burchell's zebra (Equus burchelli) and Hartmann's zebra (Equus zebra hartmannae). *J Zoo Wildl Med.* 1997, v. 28, n. 3, pp. 251-259.

Milovanov V.K. Biology of reproduction and artificial insemination of animals. [Russian] Moscow, Selhozgiz,1962. 696 P.

Moghadam K.K., Nett R., Robins J.C., Thomas M.A., Awadalla S.G., Scheiber M.D., and Williams D.B The motility of epididymal or testicular spermatozoa does not directly affect IVF/ICSI pregnancy outcomes. *J. Androl.*, 2005, v. 26, n. 5, pp. 619-623

Mohammadzadeh S., Maksudov G.Yu., Frunjan V.G., Kalistratova E.N., and Doronin Yu.K. Functional alterations of mouse spermatozoa under in viro storage conditions. Vestnik Moscow State Univ., Ser. XVI. *Biology,* 2008, v. 2, pp. 7-10

Morrell J.M., Nowshari M., Rosenbusch J., Nayudu P.L., and Hodges J.K. 1997. Birth of offspring following artificial insemination in the common marmoset, *Callithrix jacchus. Am. J. Primat.* v. 41, n. 1, pp. 37-43.

Morris, L.H.A., Tiplady C. and Allen W.R. Hysteroscopic insemination of mares with frozen-thawed epididymal spermatozoa. Proc. Havemeyer Foundation Workshop From Epididymis to Embryo., 2001, October, New Orleans, LA.

Morton K.M., Bathgate R., Evans G., and Maxwell W.M. CP of epididymal alpaca (Vicugna pacos) sperm: a comparison of citrate-, Tris- and lactose-based diluents and pellets and straws. *Reprod Fertil Dev.* 2007; v. 19, n. 7, pp. 792-796.

O'Brien J.K. and Roth T.L. Post-coital sperm recovery and CP in the Sumatran rhinoceros (Dicerorhinus sumatrensis) and application to gamete rescue in the African black rhinoceros (Diceros bicornis). *J Reprod Fertil*. 2000, v. 118, n. 2, pp. 263-71.

Ogonuki N, Mochida K, Miki H, Inoue K, Fray M, Iwaki T, Moriwaki K, Obata Y, Morozumi K, Yanagimachi R, and Ogura A. Spermatozoa and spermatids retrieved from frozen reproductive organs or frozen whole bodies of male mice can produce normal offspring. *Proc. Natl. Acad. Sci. U S A.* 2006, v. 103, n. 35, pp. 13098-13103.

Perez-Garnelo S.S., Delclaux M., Talavera C., Lopez M., and Delafuente J. Use of computerized image-analysis in the morphometric characterization of Giant Panda (Ailuropoda melanoleica) spermatozoa obtained from the epididymis 4 hours postmortem. *Zoo Biology*, 2003, v.22, n.4, pp. 355-364

Ponce A. A., Aires V.A., Carrascosa R., Fiol de Guneo M., Ruiz R.D., and Lacuara J.L. Functional activity of epididymal Chinchilla laniger spermatozoa cryopreserved in different extenders. *Res Vet Sci.* 1998. v. 64. n 3, pp. 239-43.

Ponglowhapan S., Chatdarong K., Sirivaidyapong S., and Lohachit C. Freezing of epididymal spermatozoa from dogs after cool storage for 2 or 4 days. *Theriogenology,* 2006, v. 66, n. 6-7, pp. 1633-1636.

Ptak G., Clinton M., Barboni B., Muzzeddu M., Cappai P., Tischner M., and Loi P. Preservation of the wild European mouflon: the first example of genetic management using a complete program of reproductive biotechnologies. *Biol Reprod.*, 2002, v. 66, n. 3, pp. 796-801.

Pushett D.A., Lacham-Kapln O. and Gunn I.M., Trounson A.O. Intracytoplasmic sperm injection (ICSI) using epididymal sperm and in vitro-matured oocytes in domestic cats: A model for endangered species. 2000, *Theriogenology*, v. 53, n. 1, p. 400

Rodriguez-Martinez H. Laboratory Semen Assessment and Prediction of Fertility - Still Utopia. Reprod. in Domestic Anim., 2003, v. 38, n. 4, pp 312-318

Sankai T., Tsuchiya H. and Ogonuki N. Short-term nonfrozen storage of mouse epididymal spermatozoa. *Theriogenology*, 2001, v. 55, n. 8, pp.1759-1768.

Santiago-Moreno J., Tolenado-Diaz A., Pulido-Pastor A., Gomez-Brunet A., and Lopez-Sebastian A. Horn quality and postmortem sperm parameters in Spanish ibex (Capra pyrenaica hispanica). *Anim Reprod Sci.* 2007, v. 99, n. 3-4, pp. 354-362.

Santiago-Moreno J., Toledano-Diaz A., Dorado J., Pulido-Pastor A., Coloma M.A., Lopez-Sebastian A. Recovery and CP of Spanish ibex epididymal spermatozoa. Arch. Androl., 2007, v. 53, n. 6, pp. 309-316

Santiago-Moreno J., Toledano-Diaz A., Pulido-Pastor A., Gomez-Brunet A., and Lopez-Sebastian A. Birth of life Spanish ibex (*Capra pyrenaica hispanica*) derived from artificial insemination with epididymal spermatozoa retrieved after death. *Theriogenology,* 2006, v. 66, n. 2, pp. 283-291.

Saragusty J., Gaciyua H., King R., and Arav A. Post-mortem semen CP and characterization in two different endangered gazelle species (Gazella gazella and Gazella dorcas) and one subspecies (Gazella gazelle acaiae). *Theriogenology*, 2006; v. 66, n. 4, pp. 775-784.

Sato M., Ishikawa A., Nagashima A., Watanabe T., Tada N., and Kimura M. Prolonged survival of mouse epididymal spermatozoa stored at room temperature. *Genesis* , 2001, v. 31, n. 4., pp. 147-155.

Shaw D.G., Kidson A., van Schalkwyk J.O., Bartels P., Loskutoff N.M., Bezuidenhout C., Rogers P., Barry D.M., and Lishman A.W. In-vitro production of African Buffalo (*Syncerus caffer*) embryos derived from follicular oocytes and epididymal sperm. 1995, *Theriogenology*,v. 43, p. 322.

Shishova N.V., Abilov A.I., Gakhova E.N., and Maksudov G.Y. Problems and perspectives of use of mammalian post mortem epidydimal semen for genome cryobank. [Russian] Veterinarnaja patologia, 2007, n. 1 (20), pp.34-36.

Shishova N.V. and Ignat`ev D.A. Reproductive cycles of arctic ground squirrel (Spermophilus undulatus) and its breeding in captivity. [Russian], Proc Conf. "Zooculture and biological resources", Moscow, 2005, pp. 263-265.

Shishova N.V., Melnikova E,V. and Gakhova E.N., The longivety of viability preservation of postmortem epididimal mice spermatozoa and the possibility of their CP. [Russian] *Cytology,* 2004, v. 46, n. 10, pp. 886-887

Shumakov V.I. Organ transplantation and artificial organs--a new direction in reconstructive surgery. [Russian] Vestn. Akad. Med. Nauk SSSR. 1983, n. 1, pp. 83-87

Sipko T.P., Rott N.N., Abilov A.I, Prisiazhniuk V.E, Shishova N.V., and Kombarova N.A. The conservation of the genetic resources of deer (Cervidae) by the CP of their germ cells [Russian] Izv. Akad. Nauk Ser. Biol., 1997, n. 5, pp. 546-555

Sipko T.P., Abilov A.I, Shurhal A.B., and Rott N.N. Creation of European bison sperm cryobank as a method of conservation of species genetic polymorphism. [Russian], Genetika, 1993, v. 29, n.12, pp 2051 -2056

Soler A.J., Esteso M.C, Fernandez-Santor M.R., and Garde J.J. Characteristics of Iberian red deer (Cervus elaphus hispanicus) spermatozoa cryopreserved after storage at 5 degrees C in the epididymis for several days. *Theriogenology,* 2005, v. 64, n. 7, pp. 1503-1517

Soler A.J. and Garde J.J. Relationship between the characteristics of epididymal red deer spermatozoa and penetrability into zona-free hamster ova. *J. Androl.* 2003, v. 24, n. 3, pp. 393-400.

Soler A.J., Perez-Guzman M.D. and Garde J.J. Storage of red deer epididymides for four days at 5-degrees-C - effects on sperm motility, viability, and morphological integrity. *J. Exp. Zool.*, 2003, v. 295A, n. 2, pp 188-199

Soler A.J., García A.J., Fernández-Santos M.R., Esteso M.C., and Garde J.J. Effects of thawing procedure on postthawed in vitro viability and in vivo fertility of red deer epididymal spermatozoa cryopreserved at -196 degrees C. J. Androl. 2003, v. 24, n. 5, pp. 746-756.

Soler C., Gadea B., Soler A.J., Fernández-Santos M.R., Esteso M.C., Núñez J., Moreira P.N., Núñez M., Gutiérrez R., Sancho M., and Garde J.J. Comparison of three different staining methods for the assessment of epididymal red deer sperm morphometry by computerized analysis with ISAS.*Theriogenology,* 2005, v. 64, n. 5, pp. 1236-1243.

Songsasen N., Tong J. and Leibo S.P. Birth of mice derived by in vitro fertilization with spermatozoa retrieved up to the twenty-four hours after death. *J Exp Zool.* 1998, v. 280, n. 2, pp. 189-196.

Stilley, K., Pope C.E. and Leibo S.P., Denniston R.S., Godke R.A. Survival of canine epididymal sperm stored at 4°C in the testicles. *Theriogenology*, 2000. v. 53, n. 1, p. 489

Swanson W.F. Research in nondomestic species: Experiences in reproductive physiology research for conservation of endangered felids. *ILAR J.,* 2003, v. 44, n. 4, pp.307-316

Tateno H., Wakayama T., Ward W.S., and Yanagimachi R. Can alcohol retain the reproductive and genetic potential of sperm nuclei? Chromosome analysis of mouse spermatozoa stored in alcohol. *Zygote*, 1998, v. 6, n. 3, pp. 233 – 238.

Tebet J.M., Martins M.I., Chirinea V.H., Souza F.F., Campagnol D., and Lopes N.D. CP effects on domestic cat epididymal versus electroejaculated spermatozoa. *Theriogenology,* 2006, v. 66, n. 6-7, pp.1629-1632.

Verma R.J. Sperm quiescence in cauda epididymis: a mini-review. *Asian J. Androl.,* 2001, v 3, n. 3, pp. 181-183

Veprintsev B.N. and Rott N.N. Conserving genetic resources of animal species .- *Nature*, 1979, v. 280, n. 5724, pp. 633-634.

Wakayama T., Yanagimachi R. Development of normal mice from oocytes injected with freeze-dried spermatozoa. Nat Biotechnol. 1998, 16. v. 7, pp. 639-641.

Wildt D.E. Genome resource banking for wildlife research, management, and conservation. *ILAR J.* 2000; v. 41, n. 4, pp. 228-234.

Williams K.R., Dyche W., Brinders J., Molteno F., van der Lanken M., Armstrong D.L., and Simmons L.G. Longevity in vitro and glycerol toxicity of epididymal sperm recovered from a white rhinoceros (Ceratotherium simum). *Theriogenology*, 1995, v. 43, p. 353

Winger Q., Damiani P. and Loskutoff N.M. The application of standard bovine protocols for the maturation and fertilization of Blesbok (*Damaliscus dorcas phillipsi*) oocytes using epididymal sperm cryopreserved in glycerol or dimethyl sulfoxide. *Theriogenology*, 1997, v. 47, n. 1, p. 412 (Abstr.).

White, I.G. Lipids and calcium uptake of sperm in relation to cold shock and preservation: A review. *Reprod. Fertil. Develop.* 1993. v. 5, n. 6, pp. 639-658.

Wurfel W., Krusmann G., Fiedler K, von Hertwig I., and Schwarzer U. [Pregnancies after in vitro fertilization (IVF) and intracytoplasmic sperm injection (ICSI) of testicular spermatozoa (TESE) from frozen semen] [German] Zentralbl Gynakol., 1996, V. 118, V. 12, pp.. 665-668

Young W.C. A study of the function of the epididymis. I. Is the attainment of full spermatozoon maturity attribuTable to some specific action of the epididymal secretion? *J. Morph. Physiol.* 1929, v. 47. pp. 479 – 495.

Yu I. and Leibo S.P. Recovery of motile, membrane-intact spermatozoa from canine epididymides stored for 8 days at 4 degrees C. *Theriogenology*, 2002. v. 57. n. 3. pp.. 1179-1190.

Zomborszky Z., Zubor T., Toth J., Horn P. Sperm collection from shot deer stags (Cervus elaphus) and the utilization of sperm frozen and subsequently thawed. Acta Vet. Hung., 1999, v.47, n.2, pp. 263-270.

Zhou J.B., Wu Y.G., Han D., Liu L.Q., Tan X.W., Liu N., Luo M.J., Chang Z.L., Tan J.H. Effects of sperm and oocyte quality control on intracytoplasmic sperm injection (ICSI) in goats. Shi Yan Sheng Wu Xue Bao. 2004, v. 37, n. 5, pp. 367-374.

In: Endangered Species: New Research
Editors: A. Columbus and L. Kuznetsov

ISBN 978-1-60692-241-5

Chapter 9

NON-INVASIVE APPROACHES TO SEX IDENTIFICATION IN AVIAN SPECIES

R. Rasero and P. Sacchi
Dipartimento di Produzioni Animali Epidemiologia Ecologia
Università degli Studi di Torino, Italy

ABSTRACT

During the last centuries, many wild avian species have suffered a steep decline in numbers and range. They are now rare and steel decreasing due to human activities affecting natural habitats and food supplies. In some species immatures and juveniles do not show sex-linked morphology and Authors do not agree upon the development of an unambiguous sexual dimorphism. Nevertheless, a discrimination between male and female is possible based on some discernible plumage traits. However, the knowledge of the sex of young individuals in a population greatly facilitates the study of behaviour, evolutionary ecology, conservation strategies, breeding system, and genetics. Therefore, the development of an objective test would undoubtedly facilitate the species management. In recent years, DNA-based tests have became available and have been applied for the detection of sex in some species of birds. In these tests the determination sex chromosomes specific markers have been used. A crucial point in any kind of studies of free ranging animals is sampling, that must be sample, not stressing, and non-invasive. In this respect, hair and faecies have been proved to be suitable materials in mammals, wile bird feathers increasingly used. Different approaches are compared and discussed.

INTRODUCTION

Sex identification is a task of the highest importance for management and conservation of endangered species, for captive management, and for basic research such as studies of evolutionary ecology, behaviour, and population structure.

During the last centuries, many wild avian species have suffered a steep decline in numbers and range. They are now rare and steel decreasing due to human activities affecting natural habitats and food supplies. In 2007, 1217 bird species out of 9956 evaluated were classified as threatened by the IUNC (IUNC, 2007). Knowledge of sex of individuals greatly facilitates the set up and the working-out of conservation plans. This is especially true when potential reintroduction programs are being considered. Moreover, when survival of these species depends on the establishment of breeding programs in captivity, it becomes important to determine the bird sex in order to maximize the success of the reproduction and to separate the couples that can produce the largest amounts of fertile eggs.

A full understanding of the ecology and biology of any sexually reproducing species depends on the ability to recognize males and females. Indeed, the males and the females are behaviourally and physiologically disparate and are subject to distinct evolutionary pressures (Hörnfeldt *et al.*, 2000; Hipkiss & Ellegren, 2002; Potti *et al.*, 2002). It has been widely speculated that parent could select the sex of their offspring in response to a range of social and environmental conditions (West & Sheldon, 2002), therefore the studies on the primary sex ratio and its variation among the nestlings need unambiguous and early distinction between the genders (Arnold *et al.*, 2003).

At a more applied level, our ability to identify the sex is pivotal to design breeding programs, whether for industrial or conservation purposes. The rapid sex identification would allows early and accurate trade, so the bird could settle into its new environment more quickly.

Whatever aim is pursues, management of endangered species, scientific research, or breeding, the problem of the sex identification is often encountered in the study of birds.

In contrast to mammals, birds do not possess external genital organs, thus secondary sexual characteristics such as plumage colour or body size have to be used for the gender discrimination. Unfortunately, it has been estimated that the sex of about half of all avian species cannot be identified by their external appearance in adult individuals (Griffith *et al.*, 1998).

If a distinct sexual dimorphism is missing, ethological parameters such as mating behaviour or acoustic signals can provide further information in sexual active birds (Eda-Fujiwara *et al.*, 2004). The gender identification is more difficult with immature forms. Indeed, in nestlings and juveniles, sex specific markers have not yet appeared, therefore in these stages sexual monomorphism is prevalent.

A method to identify sex in all bird species, at any stage of development, would find wide application. Many different approaches have been proposed to solve this problem.

Laparotomy and laparoscopy are surgical techniques already in use (Risser, 1971; Richner, 1989). Based on direct visualisation of the gonads, these techniques offer an immediate response for the sex identification in many species and, in the same time, they give the opportunity to diagnose anatomical abnormalities or pathological processes.

However, the surgical sexing is often impractical to use. In non breeding birds, the gonads regress and are consequently hard to identify. In small sized birds and in chicks, the task is yet more difficult because of the scale of surgery. Finally, need of anaesthesia involves a further risk. If carried out by an experienced professional, the laparotomy and laparoscopy allow rapid diagnosis with no apparent increase in mortality rate. Nevertheless, these two techniques require heavy handling and, undoubtedly, can result in a severe stress for animals, therefore they are inadequate for rare and/or elusive wildlife species.

Visual examination of *cloaca* proved to be a comparatively simple and accurate method for identifying the sex in many species. In *Galliformes*, *Anseriformes*, and ratites, the males have a phallus, which can be visualized by examining (chicks) or palpating (adults) the cranial wall of the *cloaca*. In *Columbiformes* and *Passeriformes*, the males have a prominent *papilla* of the *ductus deferens* that can be visualized on the cranial wall of the *cloaca*. Nevertheless, the vent sexing is not easy to apply in most bird species because of the lack of differences in the *cloaca* morphology. Despite its good reliability (95% accuracy), the method is stressful for the birds and should be avoided in terms of animal welfare (Bramwell, 2003; Van Krey, 2003).

Measurement of the oestrogen and testosterone levels in plasma or excrements has been used to identify the sex of some birds. However, the level of steroid hormones varies according the age, breeding season and sexual activity, therefore the interpretation of the oestrogen/testosterone ratio is difficult.

In birds, sex chromosome system is the opposite of that in mammals. The avian sex chromosomes are designed Z and W. Since the male birds have two identical sex chromosomes (ZZ) whereas the females are heterogametic (ZW), the sex identification can be made by detection of the W chromosome (Smith *et al*., 2007). Based on such a difference, cytogenetic approaches like karyotyping or flow cytometry have been used.

The avian kariotyping presents several difficulties, which make it a laborious and time-consuming process. Avian species possess a large number of chromosomes ranging from 40 in the Stone Curlew (*Burhinus oedicnemus*) to 126 in the Hoopoe (*Upupa epops*) (Shields, 1982). Seven to ten pairs are macrochromosomes including the Z chromosome, the others, characteristics of birds, have a significantly reduced size and are termed microchromosomes. In *Neognathae*, the W chromosome belongs to this latter group. The development of C-banding techniques that stain such a DNA was a major step in the avian sex identification (Bitgood & Shoffner, 2003).

A recent and effective approach to the avian sexing makes use of differing amounts of nuclear DNA that occur in the avian Z and W chromosomes. Since W chromosome is usually small, filled with repetitive arrays, and rich in heterocromatin (Yamada *et al*., 2006), cells from the females birds have a lower DNA content than cells from the males of the same species. The DNA content of the cells can be measured by means of flow cytometry or by UV-resonance Raman spectroscopy (Nakamura *et al*., 1990; De Vita *et al*. 1994; Canon *et al*., 2000; Hartz *et al*., 2008).

On the other hand, *Struthioniformes* are once more difficult to sex by means of approaches based on chromosome morphology, since the Z and W chromosomes are very similar in size and structure (Ansari *et al*., 1988).

On the whole, all the above-mentioned techniques are invasive, stressful, or laborious. Progress in molecular genetics has largely overcome these constraints, therefore sex identification using molecular methods has proven to be a valuable tool in wildlife conservation as well as in basic research and breeding programs.

Molecular Methods

DNA technologies have provided versatile, fast, and reliable approaches to identify the sex of birds using molecular markers (Cerit & Avanus, 2007). The source of discrimination has obviously been looked for on the W chromosome, since it occurs in the females but not in the males. Information on the Chicken (*Gallus gallus*) genome and comparative genomics have opened the way to expand our knowledge to potentially all avian species (International Chicken Genome Sequencing Consortium, 2004).

The most attractive technique is PCR (polymerase chain reaction). Ideally, a unique ('universal') primer set for the gender identification in all avian species should be designed.

A phylogenetic analysis indicated that the avian sex chromosome evolution initiated from an autosomal pair following an invertion on the proto-W and the consequent cessation of recombination (Fridolfsson *et al.* 1998; Lawson Handley *et al.* 2004). In *Neognathae*, the recombination stopped in a stratum on Zq 102-170 million years ago whereas a second stratum on Zp ceased to recombine 58-85 million years ago due to a series of independent events in different lineages. The oldest stratum includes CHD1 (chromodomain helicase DNA binding protein 1), ASW/HINT1 (avian sex-specific W-linked/histidine triad nucleotide binding protein 1), and SPIN (spindlin) genes, the second stratum includes UBAP2 (ubiquitin associated protein 2) and ATP5A1 (ATP synthase α-subunit) genes.

When the recombination stopped, the Z and W copies of a gene started to evolve independently (de Kloet & de Kloet, 2003; Agate & Arnold, 2004; Mank & Ellegren 2007; Stiglec *et al.*, 2007). Many genes on the non-recombining chromosome decayed to pseudogenes and eventually got lost and, in fact, a large portion of the W chromosome was enriched with heterochromatin containing non-coding repetitive sequences (Itoh *et al.*, 2006; Yamada *et al.*, 2006). These regions are rapidly evolving, so differences tend to broaden even among closely related species.

A 'universal' molecular protocol for the sex identification has to use a W-specific gene, which is expected to be more conserved among different species than non-coding sequences.

In mammals, SRY gene (sex-determining region on Y chromosome) has been discovered, which is highly conserved on the Y sex chromosome across the class (Sinclair *et al.*, 1990). Unfortunately, no widely conserved W-specific genes have been described in birds. The few genes identified on the W chromosome so far have their counterparts on the Z chromosome, FET-1 (female expressed transcript 1) possibly excluded (Reed & Sinclair 2002). The two copies of a Z-W gene pair are said gametologs and they share sufficient homology to prove the common ancestry (Garcia Moreno & Mindell 2000).

The CHD1 genes. CHD1 codes for proteins composed of three domains, *i.e.* chromo, helicase, and DNA-binding, from which its acronym came. It modifies chromatin structure and regulates gene expression (Delmas *et al.* 1993).

CHD1W was the first gene to be isolated from the W chromosome. Sequence comparison and Southern blot analysis proved the unusually high conservation of CHD1W across different bird species and, moreover, its high homology with both the gametolog CHD1Z and the mammalian CHD1 (Griffiths & Tiwari, 1993; Ellegren, 1996; Griffiths *et al.* 1996; Ellegren & Fridolfsson 1997; Griffiths & Korn 1997; Fridolfsson & Ellegren 2000).

These strict similarities allowed use of exonic sequences in order to design primers suitable in a wide range of bird species, but they still give rise to some drawback.

Firstly, the PCR primers could amplify foreign DNA (human included) if contamination occurred. Large size difference between contaminant products and fragments expected for the species of interest provides a guard against cross-species contamination, otherwise precautions should be taken (Griffiths *et al.* 1998).

Secondly, the primers usually amplify both gametologous fragments at the same time. In practice, this is not a serious constraint, since the simultaneous amplification of two different products may be an advantage. The females show a unique sex-specific fragment whereas the fragment provided by the Z gene is amplified in any bird, irrespective of its gender. A positive control is obtained with the same primer pair and, if PCR failed, no female may be misclassified as a male (Griffiths *et al.*, 1996).

The actual problem is discrimination of the sex-specific products. Some main strategies have been developed according to distinctive features of individual species, usually based on electrophoretic techniques (Tables 1 and 2) (Ellegren & Sheldom 1997).

Table 1. Methods for discriminating the difference between gametologous products

Type of approach	Type of difference	Technique
The primer pair yields two gametologous fragments different in length	large size difference	AGE
	small size difference	PAGE, SSCP
The primer pair yields two gametologous fragments equal in length	no size difference (difference exists at sequence level)	SSCP, RFLP
The gametologous fragments are produced by means of two distinct primer pairs	size difference is planned during the primer designing	AGE, real-time PCR +melting curve analysis

Table 2. Advantages and disadvantages of the common primer sets used for avian sexing

Primer set	Advantage	Disadvantage
P2-P8	is efficient in most species	may amplify gametologous products difficult to discriminate (small size difference)
		preferential amplification
		differential amplification
1237L-1271H	is efficient in most species	is potentially subject to the same limitations of P2-P8
		amplification of spurious products
2550F-2718R	amplifies products easy to separate on AGE (large size difference)	ineffective in some taxa (e.g., in Passeriformes)
		preferential amplification
		has been tested in fewer species than P2-P8

The most direct discrimination technique takes advantage of length difference that may exist between two gametologous PCR products.

Large length difference between highly conserved exonic sequences is not very frequent. P2-P3 primers, for instance, designed on the same exon (Figure 1), usually amplify a unique 110 bp fragment in both sexes (Griffiths & Tiwari, 1995; Jarvi & Farias, 2006). The choice of primers, which anneal to sequences of two different exons and amplify across an intervening intron, has proved to be a valuable solution. The introns are less conserved than the exons and their length is often different between gamelogs as a result of deletion/insertion events.

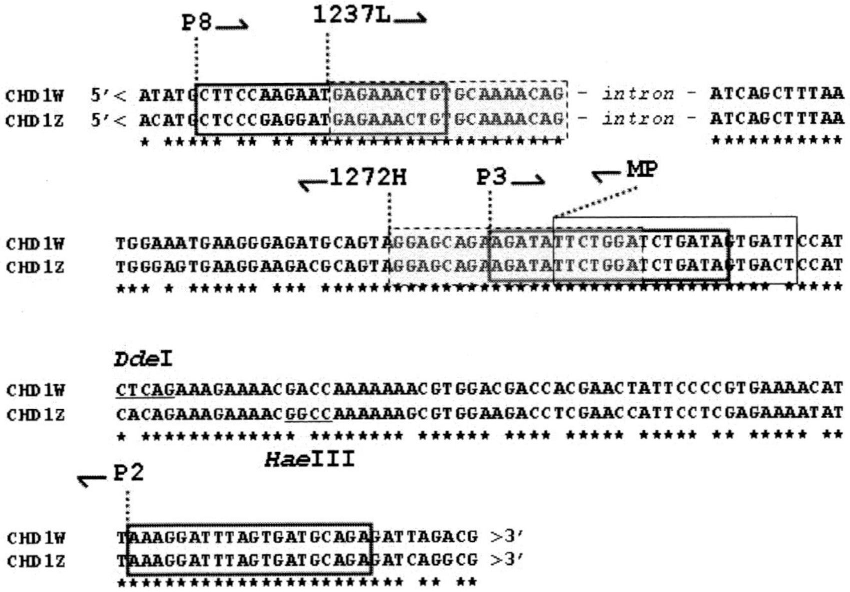

The two sequences are derived from the GenBank AF004397 and AF181826, *i.e.* Chicken CHD1Z and CHD1W, respectively. The *Dde*I and *Hae*III restriction sites are underlined.

Figure 1. The portion of the CHD1 genes commonly used as a target for the sex identification.

Based on such an approach, the primer sets P2-P8 (Griffiths *et al.*, 1998), 1237L-1272H (Kahn *et al.*, 1998), and 2550F-2718R (Fridolfsson & Ellegren, 1999) have allowed to successfully identify gender in several avian lineages, with the exception of the ratites.

The P2-P8 and 1237L-1272H primers span the same intron and so they yield gametologous fragments with equal difference in size (Figure 1). The P2-P8 products are 320-420 bp and 310-440 bp long for the Z and W genes, respectively, the 1237L-1272H set amplifies fragments 100 bp shorter. These two primer sets have shown to be efficient for sexing a very wide range of species (Birkhead *et al.*, 2001; Russello & Amato, 2001; Jensen *et al.*, 2003; Jarvi & Farias, 2006; An *et al.*, 2007; Weatherhead *et al.*, 2007; Chang *et al.*, 2008).

The 2550F-2718R primers amplify across an intron different from the target of the two foregoing sets and usually provides larger fragments. They yield fragments of 400-475 bp from CHD1W and 600-675 bp from CHD1Z, excepted many *Passeriformes* in which identical products in both sexes are amplified (Fridolfsson & Ellegren, 1999; Dawson *et al.*, 2001; Jensen *et al.*, 2003; Donohue & Dufty, 2006; Jarvi & Farias, 2006; Fukui *et al.*, 2008).

If the intervening intron of one gametolog is smaller than that of its counterpart, it may be preferentially amplified (Fridolfsson & Ellegren, 1999; Dawson *et al.*, 2001).

The 2550F-2718R Z intron is usually longer (150-250 bp) than the corresponding W intron. In some species, the primer set only amplifies the W product in the females whereas the Z is regularly amplified in the males. In such cases, birds may still be reliably sexed on the basis of the large size difference existing between these two gametologous fragments.

On the other hand, the P2-P8 W intron is larger than the Z intron in most species. These primers have the disadvantage that the CHD1Z could be preferentially amplified in both sexes, consequently females may be misclassified lacking the sex-specific marker.

In addition, non-specific products may appear (Jensen *et al.*, 2003; Harvey *et al.*, 2006). Although different in size than the CHD1 targets, these spurious fragments confound the Z-W pattern and may cause some bird to be misclassified, especially in the absence of reference samples. The 1237L-1272H primers yield more spurious products than the P2-P8 pair on most species.

AGE (agarose gel electrophoresis) is the most simple, quick, and cheap discrimination technique. It is powerful enough if length differences of at least 15-20 bp exist. A 3-7% AGE, depending on the size of the fragments, is usually effective. In those cases, two distinct bands are easily scored in all females whereas only one of them is present in the males.

The size difference between the 2550F-2718R gametologous fragments is usually larger than that of the P2-P8 and 1237L-1272H fragments (150-250 vs. 10-80 bp) so it is easier to discriminate on AGE.

The AGE is practically ineffective if small size difference is present, sometimes restricted to a few bp. In some species, the P2-P8 and 1237L-1272H products showed such a constraint (Griffiths *et al.*, 1998; Kahn *et al.*, 1998; Dawson *et al.*, 2001; Sacchi *et al.*, 2004).

If the primers match the two CHD1 templates with different efficiency, two bands very different in brightness and difficult to score on AGE are produced, especially if the amplification is weak. Adjustments of PCR conditions (*e.g.*, annealing temperature, magnesium chloride concentration) may solve this problem (Griffiths *et al.*, 1998; Soderstrom *et al.*, 2007).

If the AGE failed to discriminate, the high sensitivity of PAGE (polyacrylamide gel electrophoresis) still ensures good separation even though it is slightly more laborious and potentially hazardous (acrylamide is very toxic). The PAGE may help to overcome the differential amplification effects, if lowering the annealing temperature has not solved the problem (Griffiths *et al.*, 1998).

In some species analysed by Dawson *et al.* (2001), a unique CHD1W product and two CHD1Z alleles, Z and Z', different in length were separated on PAGE as a result of genetic variation in the P2-P8 intervening intron. In presence of polymorphism, the size difference between the allelic bands may be very similar to that observed for the Z-W pattern. As a consequence, the correct sex assignment needs the careful analysis of the actual sizes of the PCR products because two bands are also present in the heterozygous ZZ' males.

As an alternative to the standard PAGE, SSCP (single strand conformation polymorphism) analysis is more powerful. The SSCP is a non-denaturing PAGE and separates single strand DNA fragments very similar in size or even identical but different for at least one point mutation (substitution). This approach was successfully used to discriminate P2-P3 products (Ellegren, 1996; Ellegren *et al.*, 1996; Cortés *et al.*, 1999).

Ellegren (1996) obtained two different products using a sort of allele-specific PCR. In *Falconiformes*, Ito *et al.* (2003) developed a similar method, the ARMS (amplification refractory mutation system). A P2-1237F primer combination amplified two gametologous products very similar in size, so a new primer, MP, was designed annealing to a point mutation only present on the W template. A duplex PCR reaction was then arranged. The P2-1237F pair amplified a nearly unique 380-390 bp fragment working as a positive control, the 1237F-MP pair provided a female-specific fragment 85 bp shorter, easy to separate on AGE.

As an alternative to the direct discrimination of PCR products, a PCR-RFLP-like protocol performs well, if the site of a restriction enzyme is only present on one of the two gametologous templates.

In the Chicken, *Hae*III and *Dde*I restriction sites are present on the P2-P3 Z and W products, respectively (Figure 1) (Griffiths *et al*., 1996). The *Hae*III site showed to be highly conserved on the Z fragment across bird species whereas it is absent on the W homolog. *Hae*III cuts the Z fragment (45 and 65 bp), so only the females have an additional, uncut fragment (110 bp). Since small digestion products falling into the size range of primer dimers are not easy to score on AGE, some confusion could arise.

The real problem is that the scoring of the restriction pattern of some individual is prone to mistakes, if a portion of undigested fragments is present in males. Identification of W-specific restriction sites overcomes this drawback.

After digestion with *Dde*I, for instance, the male P2-P3 product provides a unique, uncut fragment (110 bp) while female pattern is resolved into three fragments (110, 80, and 30 bp). No ambiguity is possible in the case of an incomplete reaction because the Z product cannot be cut.

In general, restriction sites present on CHD1W and absent on CHD1Z should be preferred when an approach based on the restriction enzyme analysis is selected.

It should be noted that a restriction site may be open to mutation and its discrimination power is unlikely to be conserved across many different taxa (Griffiths *et al*., 1996; Bermudez-Humaran *et al*., 2002; Jarvi *et al*., 2006). If a protocol failed to discriminate sex-specific products in some species, the PCR fragments have to be cloned and sequenced in order to discover other more informative (even not necessarily 'universal') sites at individual species level.

In the Short-toed Eagle (*Circaetus gallicus*), Sacchi et al. (2004) amplified two gametologous fragments 9 bp different in length using the P2-P8 primers, so the AGE was ineffective. In addition, the *Dde*I site was present on both gametologous templates.

The identification of a W-specific *Asp*700I restriction site in proximity of the *Dde*I site overcame this drawback. After digestion, the male uncut product provided a unique band (378 bp) on AGE while the female pattern was resolved into three bands (378, 280, and 107 bp). Alignment of sequences from different *Falconiformes* species indicated that the *Asp*700I W site is well conserved in this order.

Very recently, Wang *et al.* (2008) proposed an innovative approach based on oligonucleotide microarrays. In some *Strigidae* species, the gender identification using intron length differences often produces ambiguous results. On sequences of the 1237F-1272H and 2550F-2718R fragments from three owl species, both W-specific probes and ZW-common probes (positive controls) were designed. The probes showed to be suitable in sexing eight different owl species. Since the W probes were designed on intron sequences in order to select high female-specific markers, they are expected to restrict its efficiency to closely related species.

Chang *et al.* (2008) combined real-time PCR with melting curve analysis (PCR/MCA) in order to identify the gender in *Spilornis cheela hoya*. Since the P2-P8 gametologous products showed to have very similar size on AGE, new sex-specific primers were designed. This method holds a great potential for high throughput sexing and it is useful if other approaches failed.

In synthesis, the confident sex assignment using the CHD1 genes as markers is a reliable task, still all protocols require to be optimised for any new species of interest (Harvey *et al.*, 2006).

In individual species, a particular primer set may fail to provide strong amplification or its gametologous products may be very similar in size or even identical. In order to identify the most suitable tool, comparative tests of the different primer sets must be preliminary carried out on a panel of known-sex individuals. Obviously, many reference samples are not available for threatened species. Sequencing and comparison of results with phylogenetically related species may allow to identify the most accurate molecular test (Jarvi *et al.*, 2006).

The selected PCR protocol must be optimised by means of adjustments of the reaction conditions. Differences in equipments of individual laboratories could impose further refinements.

All tests should include both reference samples and samples with no DNA added as negative controls to identify the presence of contamination.

As far as the discrimination of the sex-specific product is concerned, the AGE is the most simple and direct technique. The standard PAGE and the SSCP are more laborious.

The analysis of restriction products requires an additional step for discriminating the female-specific product by means of enzyme digestion.

More innovative approaches are powerful, nevertheless they seem to be useful if other techniques consistently failed in individual species.

Other W-specific genes. Other sex chromosome genes have been exploited as markers to perform the sex identification, *i.e.* ATP5A1 and SPIN (Carmichael *et al.*, 2000; Itoh *et al.*, 2001a; de Kloet & de Kloet, 2003).

ASW (alias HINTW) and FET-1 have been mapped on the W chromosome, both showing expression profiles consistent with a role in gender determination. FET-1, in particular, appears to have no Z gametolog and no clear homology to any known gene (Hori *et al.*, 2000; Reed and Sinclair, 2002; Smith, 2007).

In spite of this, the early discovery of CHD1W provided an efficient marker for sexing several avian species and, consequently, most methods have been improved based on differences with its Z-linked counterpart.

The EE0.6 sequence. A non-repetitive region, called EE0.6, has been cloned from the W chromosome of the Chicken. It shows to be widely conserved across both *Neognathae* and *Palaeognathae* and is likely a part of a pseudogene. A gametologous region is present on the Z chromosome, still significant divergences are expected to be found because these sequences seem to have no functions (Itoh *et al.*, 1997; Ogawa *et al.*, 1997).

Itoh et al. (2001b) designed different sets of PCR primers on the W-linked EE0.6 sequences of the Chicken and other species. The length of the sex-specific fragments was easy to predict because the primers did not amplify across an intron. The gender of different non-ratites species was clearly identified (Cortés *et al.*, 1999; Pitzer *et al.*, 2008).

Other markers and analytical approaches. The sex identification has also been performed through the detection of W-specific anonymous or repetitive sequences using different techniques. Most of these markers were used when no widely conserved sex-specific genes had yet been discovered (Cerit & Avanus, 2007).

RAPD (random amplified polymorphic DNA) technique, in itself, is very easy and low cost (Welsh & McClelland, 1990; Williams *et al.*, 1990). It requires no preliminary sequence information. Many short primers of arbitrary sequences are designed and screened for their ability to amplify fragments under low stringency conditions. As the primer length decreases, a greater number of target sites should be encountered around the genome and the chance of obtaining female-specific fragments from at least one primer increases. Usually, 5-10 different fragments per single primer are produced (Griffiths & Tiwari, 1993; Griffiths and Tiwari, 1995; Ellegren & Sheldon, 1997; Lessells & Mateman, 1998).

Similar to the RAPD, AFLP (amplified fragment length polymorphism) provides a means to identify sex markers with no information on specific sequences. The technique is based on the selective amplification of restriction fragments from an overall digest of genomic DNA (Vos *et al*., 1995).

The restriction fragments are ligated to oligonucleotide adapters of defined sequences and used as templates for PCR. Primers are designed to be complementary to the adapters but, in addition, they carry three randomly chosen nucleotides at their 3' end as an elongation. This short tail anneals only if it falls in with its exact complementary sequence on the restriction fragment, immediately beyond the adapter. As a consequence, a reduced number of PCR products is obtained on the whole and individual differences due to substitutions or insertions/deletions are punctually revealed. Several primers may be devised with different elongations.

The AFLP is more powerful than the RAPD because 50-100 different fragments per primer pair combination are provided, so the high number of alternative primer combinations maximizes the probability of revealing a W-specific product.

Most RAPD and AFLP markers appear to be monomorphic in all birds whereas some fragments are polymorphic, i.e. present or absent among individuals, irrespective of their gender. Sometimes, a W-specific fragment amplifies, unique to the females (Griffiths & Orr, 1999; Questiau *et al.*, 2000).

The RAPD markers have been shown to offer questionable reliability, low reproducibility, and high sensitivity to reaction conditions, therefore the analyses may become laborious and time-consuming. Even if more complex and expensive, the AFLP is more reliable than the RAPD.

Using these techniques, the recovery of a female-specific product is due to chance. It is more likely that the very abundant non-coding sequences of the W chromosome are amplified rather than a gene. Since these regions evolve quickly and are more or less species-specific, consequently the sex marker isolated from one species seldom succeeds outside the cluster of phylogenetically closest species.

These approaches have shown to be useful to find sex-specific markers when no prior sequence information are available (Griffiths & Tiwari, 1993). Once a female-specific fragment is found, it can be isolated, cloned, and sequenced and a locus-specific PCR protocol is arranged. This removes the burden of useless fragments and makes the analyses simple, reliable, and inexpensive (Duan & Fuerst, 2001; Horng *et al.*, 2006; Soderstrom *et al.*, 2007; Wu *et al.*, 2007).

Microsatellite loci, or short tandem repeats, have been successfully used as markers in genus *Falco* (Nesje & Røed, 2000). If a product is amplified only in the females, as for the Peregrine Falcon (*F. peregrinus*), Gyrfalcon (*F. rusticolus*), and Hobby (*F. subbuteo*), some subject could be misclassified as a consequence of PCR failure. The successful cross-species transfer of the primers depends on conservation of the flanking sequences, it is unevenly distributed across *taxa* and more frequent among species within *genus* (Barbará *et al.*, 2007).

The special case of Palaeognathae. In contrast to the *Neognathae* birds, *Palaeognathae* ratite species like the Ostrich (*Struthio camelus*), Cossowary (*Casuarus casuarus*), and Emu (*Dromaius novaehollandiae*), show primitive forms of avian sex chromosomes, which are largely homomorphic. The W chromosome still retains large euchromatic regions.

Palaeognathae tinamous species, or *Tinamiformes*, are classified as a sister group to the ratites even though their W chromosome is considered to be an intermediated stage between the highly euchromatic W of the ratites and the highly heterochromatic W of *Neognathae* (Tsuda *et al.*, 2007).

In the Ostrich and Tataupa Tinamous (*Crypturellus tataupa*), the 2550F-2718R primer set provided no female-specific patterns (Fridolfsson & Ellegren, 1999).

In the ratites, the P2-P8 and 1237L-1272H primer sets yielded only single fragments for both sexes. Sequence analyses consistently revealed no sex-specific difference (Griffiths *et al.*, 1998; Kahn *et al.*, 1998).

On the other hand, sequence comparison of the P2-P8 fragments from New Zealand Kiwi (*Apterix sp.*) showed the existence of a W-specific $(C)_{12}$ tract (Huynen *et al.*, 2006). A primer was designed on this sequence, which in conjunction with P2 amplified a female-specific product.

Although it has been shown that EE0.6 sequences exist on the sex chromosomes of the ratites, no difference recognisable with the standard molecular methods has took place during the evolution of this *taxon* (Itoh *et al.*, 2001b).

As expected, the RAPD and AFLP techniques allowed to identify female-specific fragments (Bello & Sánchez, 1999; Griffiths & Orr, 1999). Some markers were cloned and sequenced, and simple, fast, and accurate protocols were established for sexing of Ostrich, Cassowari, and Emu (de Kloet, 2001a; Malagó *et al.*, 2002; Wu *et al.*, 2006).

These protocols are basically species-specific. On the other hand, a female-specific marker was identified in the North Island Brown Kiwi (*Apteryx australis manteui*), and a PCR protocol was designed for efficiently sexing different ratite species (Huynen *et al.*, 2002; Rossi-Fraire & Martella, 2006).

In tinamous species, the molecular sex identification based on CHD1, ATP5A1, PKCI, and EE0.6 sequences failed using both the PCR and Sourthern blotting (de Kloet & de Kloet, 2003). On the contrary, the SPIN gene has different copies on the two sex chromosomes providing a sensitive and accurate tool (de Kloet, 2001b).

NON-INVASIVE SAMPLING METHODS

The molecular sexing is one of the simplest and most widely used methods applied to wild birds but it entirely relies on the availability of genetic material. To date, the most common sampling method for obtaining material for sexing involves acquiring blood samples during banding or from nestlings. Blood is relatively easy to obtain from captured animals and the nucleated erythrocytes of birds make avian blood an unusually rich source of nuclear DNA. On the other hand, feather samples are an appealing, alternative tissue type.

Use of feathers instead of blood as genomic DNA source minimizes the stress on the bird, simplifies sampling, and requires simpler storage procedures. Moreover, in juvenile and small-sized birds, the calibre of the blood vessels makes blood extraction very difficult.

Over the last several years, non-invasive sampling of hairs or faeces has become an important tool for providing information on both rare and elusive wildlife species difficult to sample otherwise. Although several studies demonstrate the usefulness of these methods in mammals, non-invasive large scale studies in birds remain infrequent. If more destructive sampling would conflict with research goals, the collection of feathers or even faeces (Idaghdour *et al.*, 2003), urine (Nota & Takenaka, 1999), and nest materials (Pearce *et al.*, 1996) could be a simple, non-invasive strategy for obtaining genetic material, and, finally, it is strongly recommended in endangered species.

However, the use of non-invasive sampling often does not provide reliable results because of low quantity and quality of the extracted DNA. DNA in feather samples is typically present in much lower copy number than that from blood or tissue sample, therefore DNA yields from extractions of feather material are correspondingly low. In addition, DNA from feathers may be somehow degraded, if it originates from died cells as the feather matures.

The amount and the integrity of the isolated DNA are essential for the successful optimisation of PCR protocols. Degradation of genomic DNA does not necessarily inhibit PCR amplification, particularly when small regions (100-200 bp) are amplified, but usually leads to non-specific amplification.

A study undertaken with the aim to compare feathers *versus* blood samples as a DNA source demonstrated that, although feather sampling provides lower DNA yields, both type of samples provided adequate DNA template for the molecular sexing reactions. Being the initial template concentration lower in the feather extracts, more PCR cycles were needed to achieve reliable results. As far as the DNA quality is concerned, feather-derived DNA was not associated with substantially higher PCR failure or scoring error rate, if compared with blood-derived DNA (Harvey *et al.*, 2006).

Another matter is the choice of procedure for feather collecting. Some studies have successfully used feathers plucked from living birds whereas only few investigations concerned moulted feathers collected in field. In detail, these two approaches were classified by Taberlet *et al.* (1999) as non-destructive and non-invasive, respectively.

Segelbacher (2002), testing feathers as sources of DNA for genotyping microsatellite loci, demonstrated that DNA quantity in larger flight feathers (remiges and rectrices) is higher than that in smaller feathers, and PCR amplification success is higher from extracts of plucked feathers than moulted feathers. In contrast, Rudnick *et al.* (2005) demonstrated that single, naturally shed eagle feathers yields sufficient quantities of DNA for both genetic sexing and microsatellite genotyping.

In most investigations using feathers samples, the DNA was extracted from the basal tip of the *calamus* (Bello *et al.*, 2001). A blood clot embedded in the shaft was proposed by Horváth *et al.* (2005) as an alternative source of DNA. In the developing feather, mesenchymal pulp contains an axial artery. Once the feather is completely developed, the vessel is completely reabsorbed and a keratinised pulp cap remains. If only the feather tip is used, the pulp cap and the feather follicle cells, attached to the outer surface of the *calamus*, are the main DNA source. However, when the reabsorbing pulp crosses the *calamus* wall in a narrow channel during feather development, the superior *umbilicus* typically contains a visible blood clot, which is the relict of the axial artery. The blood clot found in the superior *umbilicus* of moulded feathers provides more and better quality DNA than the basal tip of the *calamus*. The higher DNA concentration of clot samples consistently resulted in more efficient molecular sexing and microsatellite genotyping.

When a non-invasive sampling is used, a considerable task is the risk of contamination with exogenous DNA, especially if moulted feathers are collected in field. As a consequence, all sets of samples should include reference controls, as mentioned above.

CONCLUSION

Most traditional techniques for bird sexing are invasive, stressful, or laborious. The progress in molecular genetics has largely overcome these constraints. The sex identification using molecular methods has proven to be a valuable approach in wildlife conservation as well as in basic research and breeding programs. The best method for sexing birds belonging to threatened species must be non-invasive, applicable at any stage of development, simple, quick, and inexpensive. In addition, it would be suitable for as many species as possible.

Although non-invasive sampling in birds exhibits limitation similar to those shown in mammals, the use of feathers seems to be an important genetic tool. Taking into account its possible limitation, non-invasive sampling and its use for conservation genetics looks quite promising.

REFERENCES

Agate, R. J. & Arnold, A.P. (2004). Sex differences in structure and expression of the sex chromosome genes CHD1Z and CHD1W in Zebra Finches. *Molecular Biology and Evolution, 21,* 384-396.

An, J., Lee, M.-y., Min, M.-S., Lee, M.-H. & Lee, H. (2007). A molecular genetic approach for species identification of mammals and sex determination of birds in a forensic case of poaching from South Korea. *Forensic Science International, 167*, 59-61.

Ansari, H.A., Takagi, N. & Sasaki, M. (1988). Morphological differentiation of sex chromosomes in three species of ratite birds. *Citogenetics and Cell Genetics, 47*, 185-188.

Arnnold, K. E., Orr, K.J & Griffiths, R. (2003). Primary sex ratios in birds: problems with molecular sex identification of undeveloped eggs. *Molecular Ecology, 12*, 3451-3458.

Babará, T., Palma-Silva, C., Paggi, G.M., Bered, F., Fay, M. & Lexer, C. (2007). Cross-species transfer of nuclear microsatellite markers: potential and limitations. *Molecular Ecology, 16*, 3759-3767.

Bello, N. & Sánchez, A. (1999). The identification of a sex-specific DNA marker in the ostrich using a random amplified polymorphic DNA (RAPD) assay. *Molecular Ecology, 8*, 667-669.

Bello N., Francino, O. & Sánchez, A. (2001). Isolation of genomic DNA from feathers. *Journal of Veterinary Diagnostic Investigation, 13,* 162-164.

Bermúdez-Humarán, L.G., García-García, A., Leal-Garza, C.H., Riojas-Valdes, V.M., Jamarillo-Rangel, G. & Montes-de-Oca-Luna, R. (2002). Molecular sexing of monomorphic endangered *Ara* birds. *Journal of Experimental Zoology, 292*, 677-680.

Birkhead, T.R., Hatchwell, B.J., Lindner, R., Blonqvist, D., Pellatt, E.J., Griffiths, R. & Lifjeld, J.T. (2001). Extra-pair paternity in the Common Murre. *The Condor, 103*, 158-162.

Bitgood, J.J., & Shoffner, R.N. (2003). Cytology and Cytogenetics. In : Crawford R.D., (Ed). *Poultry breeding and genetics* (2003, pp. 401-427). Amsterdam, The Netherlands: Elsevier.

Bramwell, R.K. (2003). Sexing chicks in the backyard flok. *Avian Advice, 5*, 4-5.

Canon, N.R., Tell, L.A., Needham, M.L. & Gardner, I.A. (2000). Flow cytometric analysis of nuclear DNA for sex identification in three psittacine species. *American Journal of Veterinary Research, 61,* 847-850.

Carmichael, A.N., Fridolfsson, A.K., Halverson, J. & Ellegren, H. (2000). Male-biased mutation rates revealed from Z and W chromosome-linked ATP synthase α-subunit (ATP5A1) sequences in birds. *Journal of Molecular Evolution, 50*, 443-447.

Cerit, H. & Avanus, K. (2007). Sex identification in avian species using DNA typing methods. *World's Poultry Science Journal, 63,* 91-99.

Chang, H.-W., Cheng C.-A., Gu, D.-L., Chang, C.-C., Su, S.-H., Wen, C.-H., Chou, Y.-C., Chou, T.-C., Yao, C.-T., Tsai, C.-L. & Cheng, C.-C. (2008). High-throughput avian molecular sexing by SYBR green-based real-time PCR combined with melting curve analysis. *BioMed Central Biotechnology*, 8:12. doi:10.1186/1472-6750-8-12.

Cortés, O., Barroso, A. & Dunner, S. (1999). Avian sexing: an optimized protocol using polymerase chain reaction–single-strand conformation polymorphism. *Journal of Veterinary Diagnostic Investigation, 11*, 297-299.

Dawson, D.H., Darby, S.,, Hunter, S.M., Krupa, A.P., Jones, I.L. & Burke, T. (2001). A critique of avian *CHD*-based molecular sexing protocols illustrated by a Z-chromosome polymorphism detected in auklets. *Molecular Ecology Notes, 1*, 201-204.

de Kloet, S.R. (2001a). Development of a CAPS (cleaved amplified polymorphics sequence) assay for sex identification of the emu (*Dromaius novaehollandiae*). *Molecular Ecology Notes, 1*, 273-275.

de Kloet, S.R. (2001b). Molecular sex identification of tinamous with PCR using primers derived from the spindling gene. *Molecular Ecology Notes, 2*, 465-466.

de Kloet, R.S. & de Kloet, S.R. (2003). Evolution of the spindlin gene in birds : independent cessation of the recombination of sex chromosomes at the spindlin locus in neognathous birds and tinamous, a palaeognathous avian family. *Genetics, 119,* 333-342.

Delmas, V., Stokes, D.G. & Perry, R.P. (1993). A mammalian DNA-binding protein that contains a chromodomain and an SNF2/SWI2-like helicase domain. *Proceedings of the National Academy of Sciences of the United States of America, 90,* 2414-2418.

De Vita, R., Cavallo, D., Eleuteri, P. & Dell'Olmo, G. (1994). Evaluation of interspecific DNA content variation and sex identification in *Falconiformes* and *Strigiformes* by flow cytometric analysis. *Cytometry, 16,* 346-350.

Donohue, K.C. & Dufty, A.M. (2006). Sex determination of Red-tailed Hawks (*Buteo jamaicensis calurus*) using DNA analysis and morphometrics. *Journal of Field Ornithology, 77*, 74-79.

Duan, W. & Fuerst, P.A. (2001). Isolation of a Sex-Linked DNA Sequence in Cranes. *Journal of Heredity, 92*, 392-397.

Eda-Fujiwara, H., Yamamoto, A., Sugita, H., Takahashi, Y., Kojima, Y., Sakashita, R., Ogawa, H., Miyamoto, T. & Kimura T. (2004). Sexual dimorphism of acoustic signal in the oriental white stork: non-invasive identification of sex in birds. *Zoological Science, 21,* 817-821.

Ellegren, H. (1996). First gene on the avian W chromosome (CHD) provides a tag for universal sexing of non-ratite birds. *Proceedings of the Royal Society of London B, 263,* 1635-1641.

Ellegren, H. & Fridolfsson, A.-K. (1997). Male-driven evolution of DNA sequences in birds. *Nature Genetics, 17,* 182-184.

Ellegren, H. & Sheldon, B.C. (1997). New tools for sex identification and the study of sex allocation in birds. *Trends in Ecology and Evolution, 12,* 255-259.

Ellegren, H., Gustafsson, L. & Sheldon, B.C. (1996). Sex ratio adjustment in relation to paternal attractiveness in a wild bird population. *Proceedings of the National Academy of Sciences of the United States of America, 93,* 11723-11728.

Fridolfsson, A.-K. & Ellegren, H. (1999). A simple and universal method for molecular sexing non-ratite birds. *Journal of Avian Biology, 30,* 116-121.

Fridolfsson, A.-K. & Ellegren, H. (2000). Molecular evolution of the avian *CHD1* genes on the Z and W sex chromosomes. *Genetics, 155,* 1903-1912.

Fridolfsson, A.-K., Cheng, H., Copeland, N.G., Jenkins, N.A., Liu, H.-C., Raudsepp, T., Woodages, T., Chowdhary, B., Halverson, J & Ellegren, H. (1998). Evolution of the avian sex chromosomes from an ancestral pair of autosomes. *Proceedings of the National Academy of Sciences of the United States of America, 95,* 8147-8152.

Fukui, E., Sugita, S. & Yoshizawa, M. (2008). Molecular sexing of Jungle crow (*Corvus macrorhynchos japonensis*) and Carrion crow (*Corvus corone corone*) using a feather. *Animal Science Journal, 79,* 158-162.

Garcia Moreno, J. & Mindell, D.P. (2000). Rooting a phylogeny with homologous genes on opposite sex chromosomes (Gemetologs): a case study using avian *CHD. Molecular Biology and Evolution, 17,* 1826-1832.

Griffiths, R. & Korn, R.M. (1997). A *CHD1* gene is Z chromosome linked in the chicken *Gallus domesticus. Gene, 197,* 225-229.

Griffiths, R. & Orr, K. (1999). The use of amplified fragment length polymorphism (AFLP) in the isolation of sex-specific markers. *Molecular Ecology, 8,* 671-674.

Griffiths, R. & Tiwari, B. (1993). The isolation of molecular genetic markers for the identification of sex. *Proceedings of the National Academy of Sciences of the United States of America, 90,* 8324-8326.

Griffiths, R. & Tiwari, B. (1995). Sex of the last wild Spix's macaw. *Nature, 375,* 454.

Griffiths, R., Daan, S. & Dijkstra, C. (1996). Sex identification in birds using two CHD genes. *Proceedings of the Royal Society of London B, 263, 1*1251-1256.

Griffiths, R., Double, M., Orr, K. & Dawson, R.J.G. (1998). A DNA test to sex most birds *Molecular Ecology, 7,* 1071-1075.

Harvey, M.G., Bonter, D.N., Stenzler, L.M. & Lovette, I.J. (2006). A comparison of plucked feathers versus blood samples as DNA sources for molecular sexing. *Journal of field ornithology, 77,* 136-140.

Harz, M., Krause M., Bartels, T., Cramer, K., Rösch, P., & Popp, J. (2008). Minimal invasive gender determination of birds by means of UV-resonance Raman spectroscopy. *Analytical Chemistry, 80,* 1080-1086.

Hipkiss, T. & Ellegren, H. (2002). Sex ratio and age structure of nomadic Tengmalm's owls: a molecular approach. *Journal of avian biology, 33,* 107-110.

Hori, T., Asakawa, S., Itoh, Y., Shimizu, N. & Mizuno, S. (2000). *Wpkci*, encoding an altered form of *PKCI*, is conserved widely on the avian W chromosome and expressed in early female embryos: implication of its role in female sex determination. *Molecular Biology of the Cell, 11*, 3645-3660.

Hörnfeldt, B., Hipkiss, T., Fridolfsson, A.-K, Eklund, U. & Ellegren, H. (2000). Sex ratio ad fledging success of supplementary-fed Tengmalm's owls broods. *Molecular Ecology, 9*, 187-192.

Horng, Y.-M., Wu, C.-P., Wang, Y.-C. & Huang, M.-C. (2006). A novel molecular genetic marker for gender determination of pigeons. *Theriogenology, 65*, 1759-1768.

Horváth, M.B., Martínez-Cruz, B., Negro, J.J., Kalmár, L. & Godoy, J.A. (2005). An overlooked DNA source for non-invasive genetic analysis in birds. *Journal of Avian Biology, 36,* 84-88.

Huynen, L., Miles, J. & Lambert, D. (2006). Unusual electrophoretic mobility of a DNA fragment of the universal 'non-ratite' sexing marker *CHD* allows sexing of New Zealand's endangered kiwi ratite Apteryx spp. *Ibis, 148*, 167-168.

Huynen, L.,, Millar, C.D. & Lambert, D.M. (2002). A DNA test to sex ratite birds. *Molecular Ecology, 11*, 851-856.

Idaghdour, Y., Broderick, D. & Korrida A. (2003). Faeces as a source of DNA for molecular studies in a threatened population of Great Bustards. *Conservation Genetics, 4,* 789-792.

International Chicken Genome Sequencing Consortium (2004). Sequence and comparative analysis of the chicken genome provide unique perspectives on vertebrate evolution. *Nature*, *432*, 695-716.

Itoh, H., Sudo-Yamaji, A., Abe, M., Murase, T. & Tsubota, T. (2003). Sex identification by alternative polymerase chain reaction methods in Falconiformes. *Zoological Science, 20*, 339-344.

Itoh, Y., Kampf, K. & Arnold, A.P. (2006). Comparison of the chicken and zebra finch Z chromosomes shows evolutionary rearrangements. *Chromosome Research, 14*, 805-815.

Itoh, Y., Hori, T., Saitoh, H. & Mizuno S. (2001a). Chicken spindling genes on W and Z chromosomes: transcriptional expression of both genes and dynamic behaviour of spinclin in interphase and mitotic cells. *Chromosome Research, 9*, 283-289 (*erratum ibidem*, 519).

Itoh, Y., Ogawa A., Murata, K., Hosoda, T. & Mizuno, S. (1997). Identification of the sex of Oriental white stork, *Ciconia boyciana*, by the polymerase chain reaction based on its sex chromosome-specific DNA sequences. *Genes and Genetic Systems, 72,* 51-56.

Itoh, Y., Suzuki, M., Ogawa, A., Munechika, I., Murata, K. & Mizuno, S. (2001b). Identification of the sex of a wide range of Carinatae birds by PCR using primer sets selected from chicken EE0.6 and its related sequences. *Journal of Heredity, 92*, 315-321.

IUCN 2007, 2007 IUCN Red List of Threatened Species <www.iucnredlist.org>

Jarvi, S.I. & Farias, M.E.M. (2006). Molecular sexing and sources of CHD1-Z/W sequence variation in Hawaiian birds. *Molecular Ecology Notes, 6*, 1003-1005.

Jensen, T., Pernasetti, F.M. & Durrant, B. (2003). Conditions for rapid sex determination in 47 avian species by PCR of genomic DNA from blood, shell-membrane blood vessels, and feathers. *Zoo Biology, 22*, 561-571.

Kahn, N.K., St.John, J. & Quinn, T.W. (1998). Chomosome-specific intron size differences in the avian CHD gene provide an efficient method for sex identification in birds. *The Auk, 115*, 1074-1078

Lawson Handley, L.-J., Ceplitis, H. & Ellegren, H. (2004). Evolutionary strata on the chicken chromosome: Implications for sex chromosome evolution. *Genetics, 167,* 367-376.

Lessells, C.M. & Mateman, A.C. (1998). Sexing birds using random amplified polymorphic DNA (RAPD) markers. *Molecular Ecology, 7*, 187–195.

Malagó, W., Franco, H.M., Matheucci, E., Medaglia, A. & Henrique-Silva, F. (2002). Large scale sex typing of ostriches using DNA extracted from feathers. *BioMed Central Biotechnology*, 2:19. http://www.biomedcentral.com/1472-6750/2/19.

Mank, J.E. & Ellegren, H. (2007). Parallel divergence and degradation of the avian W sex chromosome. *Trends in Ecology and Evolution, 22,* 389-391.

Nakamura, D., Tiersch, T.D., Douglass, M., & Chandler, R.W. (1990). Rapid identification of sex in birds by cytometry. *Cytogenetics and Cell Genetics, 53,* 201-205.

Nesje, M. & Røed, K.H. (2000). Sex identification in falcons using microsatellite DNA markers. *Hereditas, 132*, 261-263.

Nota ,Y. & Takenaka, O. (1999). DNA extraction from urine and sex identification of birds. *Molecular Ecology, 8,* 1237-1238.

Ogawa, A., Solovei, I., Hutchison, N., Saitoh, Y., Ikeda, J.-E, Macgregor, H. & Mizuno, S. (1997). Molecular characterization and cytological mapping of a non-repetitive DNA sequence region from the W chromosome of chicken and its use as a universal probe for sexing Carinatae birds. *Chromosome Research, 5*, 93-101.

Pearce, J.M. , Fields, R.L. & Scribner K.T. (1996). Nest materials as a source of genetic data for avian ecological studies. *Journal of Field Ornithology, 68,* 471-481.

Pitzer, S., Hull, J., Ernest, H.B. & Hull, A.C. (2008). Sex determination of three raptor species using morphology and molecular techniques. *Journal of Field Ornithology, 79,* 71-79.

Potti, J., Dávila, J. A., Tella, J. L., Frías, Ó. & Villar, S. (2002). Gender and viability selection on morphology in fledgling pied flycatchers. *Molecular Ecology, 11*, 1317-1326.

Questiau, S., Escaravage, N., Eybert, M.-C. & Taberlet, P. (2000). Nestling sex ratios in a population of Bluethroats Luscinia svecica inferred from AFLP™ analysis. *Journal of Avian Biology, 31*, 8-14.

Reed, K.J. & Sinclair, A.H (2002). FET-1: a novel W-linked, female specific gene up-regulated in the embryonic chicken ovary. *Mechanisms of Development, 119S,* S-87-S90.

Richner, H. (1989) Avian laparoscopy as a field technique for sexing birds and an assessment of its effects on wild birds. *Journal of Field Ornithology, 60*, 137-142.

Risser , A.C. (1971) A technique for performing laparotomy on small birds. *Condor, 73,* 376-379.

Rossi Fraire, H.J., & Martella M. B. (2006). DNA test to sex the lesser rhea (Rhea pennata pennata). *British Poultry Science, 47*, 375-377.

Rudnick, J.A., Katzner, T.E., Bragin, E.A., Rhodes, O.E & Dewoody, J.A. (2005). Using naturally shed feathers for individual identification, genetic parentage analyses, and population monitoring in an endangered Eastern imperial eagle (*Aquila heliaca*) population from Kazakhstan. *Molecular Ecology, 14,* 2950-2967.

Russello, M.A. & Amato, G. (2001). Application of noninvasive, PCR-based test for sex identification in an endangered parroe, *Amazona Guildingii. Zoo Biology, 20*, 41-45.

Sacchi, P., Soglia, D., Maione S., Meneguz, G., Campora, M. & Rasero, R. (2004). A non-invasive test for sex identification in Short-toed Eagle (*Circaetus gallicus*). *Molecular and Cellular Probes, 18*, 193-196.

Segelbacher, G. (2002). Noninvasive genetic analysis in birds: testing reliability of feather samples. *Molecular Ecology Notes, 2,* 367-369.

Shields, G.F. (1982). Comparative avian cytogenetics: a review. *Condor, 84*, 45-58.

Sinclair, A.H., Berta, P., Palmer, M.S., Hawkins, J.R. Griffiths, B.L., Smith, M.J., Frischauf, A.-M., Lovell-Badge, R. & Goodfellow, P.N. (1990). A gene from the human sex-determining region encodes a protein with homology to a conserved DNA-binding motif. *Nature, 364,* 240-244.

Smith, C.A. (2007). Sex determination in birds: HINTs from the W sex chromosome? *Sexual Development, 1,* 279-285.

Smith, C.A., Roeszler, K.N., Hudson, Q.J. & Sinclair, A.H. (2007). Avian sex determination: what, when and where? *Cytogenetic and Genome Research, 117,* 165-173.

Soderstrom, K., Qin, W. & Leggett, H. (2007). A minimally invasive procedure for sexing young zebra finches. *Journal of Neuroscience Methods, 164*, 16-119.

Stiglec, R., Ezaz, T. & Graves, J.A. (2007). A new look at the evolution of avian sex chromosomes. *Cytogenetic and Genome Research, 117*, 103-109.

Taberlet, P., Waits, L.P. & Luikart, G. (1999). Noninvasive genetic sampling: look before you leap. *Trends in Ecology and Evolution, 14,* 323-327.

Tsuda, Y, Nishida-Umehara, C., Ishijima, J., Yamada, K. & Matsuda, Y. (2007). Comparison of the Z and W sex chromosomal architectures in elegant crested tinamou (*Eudromia elegans*) and ostrich (*Struthio camelus*) and the process of sex chromosome differentiation in palaeognathous birds. *Chromosoma, 116*, 159-173.

Van Krey H.P. (2003). Reproductive biology in relation to breeding and genetics. In: Crawford R.D., (Ed). *Poultry breeding and genetics* (2003, pp. 61-90). Amsterdam, The Netherlands: Elsevier.

Vos, P., Hogers, R., Bleeker, M., Reijans, M., van de Lee, T., Hornes, M., Frijters, A., Pot, J., Peleman, P. & Kuiper, M. (1995). AFLP: a new technique for DNA fingerprinting. *Nucleic Acids Research, 23*, 4407-4414.

Wang, L.C., Severinghaus, L.L., Chen, C.T., Liu, L.Y., Pan, C.H., Huang, D., Lee, H.Y., Lir, J.T., Chin, S.C., Pu, C.E. & Wang, C.H. (2008). Sex identification of owls (family Strigidae) using oligonucleotide microarrays. *Journal of Heredity, 99*, 187-192.

Weatherhead, P.J., Muma, K.E., Maddox, J.D., Knox, J.M. & Dufour, K.W. (2007). Morphology versus molecules: sexing Red-winged Blackbird nestlings. *Journal of Field Ornithology, 78*, 428-435.

Welsh, J. & McClelland, M. (1990). Fingerprinting genomes using PCR with arbitrary primers. *Nucleic Acids Research, 18*, 7213–7218.

West, S. A. & Sheldon B.C. (2002) Constraints in the evolution of sex ratio adjustment. *Science, 295,* 1685-1688.

Williams, J.G., Kubelik, A.R., Livak, K.J., Rafalski, J.A. & Tingey, S.V. (1990). DNA polymorphisms amplified by arbitrary primers are useful as genetic markers. *Nucleic Acids Research, 18*, 6531–6535.

Wu, C.-P., Horng, Y.-M., Yang, K.-T., Huang, C.-W. & Huang, M.C. (2006). Female-specific DNA sequences in ostriches. *Molecular and Cellular Probes, 20*, 307-310.

Wu, C.-P., Horng, Y.-M., Wang, R.-T., Yang, K.-T. & Huang, M.-C. (2007). A novel sex-specific DNA marker in Columbidae birds. *Theriogenology, 67*, 328-333.

Yamada, K., Nishida-Umehara, C., Ishijima, J., Murakami, T., Shibusawa, M., Tsuchiya, K., Tsudzuki, M. & Matsuda, Y. (2006). A novel family of repetitive DNA sequences amplified site-specifically on the W chromosomes in Neognathous birds. *Chromosome Research, 14*, 613-627.

In: Endangered Species: New Research
Editors: A. Columbus and L. Kuznetsov

ISBN 978-1-60692-241-5

Chapter 10

SELECTION OF RESTORATION AND CONSERVATION AREAS USING SPECIES ECOLOGICAL NICHE MODELING: A CASE STUDY OF THE NEOTROPICAL RIVER OTTER *LONTRA LONGICAUDIS ANNECTENS* IN CENTRAL MEXICO

Verónica Cirelli and Víctor Sánchez-Cordero
Departamento de Zoología, Instituto de Biología,
Universidad Nacional Autónoma de México
Apartado postal 70-153, México D.F. 04510. México

ABSTRACT

We used ecological niche modeling and place prioritization procedures to identify areas for conservation and restoration for the Neotropical river otter, *Lontra longicaudis annectens* Major 1897, in central Mexico. This species is highly sensible to fluvial ecosystem degradation, and large areas of the Apatlaco-Tembembe basin fluvial ecosystems have been highly transformed. We selected ecological indicators (EI) from literature and own field work to determine variables best describing the fluvial ecosystem degradation, relating them to the species' presence or absence. Field data of EI, species records, and digital thematic information of hydrology, geomorphology and climate were used in ResNet Place Prioritization algorithm for the selection of potential conservation and restoration areas. We generated a spatial model considering a hierarchy of key areas based on river otter's ecological niche requirements and habitat *ad hoc* conditions for the species permanence. This allowed identifying areas to be included in landscape management plans for conservation and restoration. The sequential integration of species′ potential distribution and place prioritization modeling allows merging biodiversity conservation and ecological restoration strategies at different ecological scales, helping adaptive management in land planning to be more flexible and feasible.

Key words: Conservation, ecological niche modeling, ecological restoration, fluvial ecosystems, GARP, Mexico, potential distribution, river otter *Lontra longicaudis annectens* (Major, 1897), ResNet place prioritization algorithm.

INTRODUCTION

A major challenge in conserving biological diversity is the proper selection of priority areas for conservation and restoration where land use changes, and social and economic constraints are incorporated (Virolainen et al., 1999; Brown and Lugo, 1994; NRC, 1992; Dobson et al., 1997; Meffe and Carroll, 1997; Margules and Pressey, 2000; SER 2002). Selection of these areas should involve structural and functional ecosystem attributes for assessing degrees of transformed habitats to reverse and prevent further habitat degradation (Sanderson et al., 2002; Sarkar and Margules, 2002; Sarkar, 2004).

A promising approach for prioritizing conservation and restoration areas is combining species' ecological niche modeling projected as potential distribution (Stockwell and Peters, 1999), and optimization algorithms for place prioritization using biodiversity surrogates (Aggarwal et al., 2002; Fuller et al., 2006,2007; Garson et al., 2002; Sánchez-Cordero et al., 2005a,b; Sarkar et al., 2004). Ecological niche modeling projected as species' potential distributions provides robust hypotheses for coarse-grained predictions of species presence in particular habitats (Pressey et al., 1997; Stockwell and Peters, 1999; Phillips et al., 2006), and has been widely used for different taxa worldwide (Cabeza and Moilanen, 2001; Peterson, 2001; Sarakinos et al., 2001; Anderson, et al., 2002; Feria and Peterson, 2002; Ortega-Huerta and Peterson, 2004; Peterson et al., 2002; Sarkar et al., 2002; Stockwell and Peterson, 2002; Illoldi et al., 2004, 2008). These predictions can be further refined by incorporating transformed and untransformed habitats into the modeling approach, projecting potential habitat for restoration and conservation within the species' distributions, and disregarding areas highly transformed which may be unsuitable for the target species (Cirelli, 2005; Sánchez-Cordero et al., 2004, 2005a,b; Illoldi et al., 2008).

In addition, place prioritization procedures are becoming increasingly relevant for conserving biodiversity (Margules et al., 1988; Nicholls and Margules, 1993; Margules and Pressey, 2000; Tognelli et al., 2005). These optimization computer algorithms incorporate basic distributional information of biotic and abiotic attributes as biodiversity surrogates into a rarity-complementarity procedure for prioritizing site selection (Garson et al., 2002; Kerley et al., 2003; Sarkar, 2004; Sánchez-Cordero, et al., 2005b; Moffet and Sarkar, 2006). One such algorithms is ResNet Place Prioritization (free download at http://uts.cc.utexas.edu/~consbio/Cons/ResNet.html), which has been widely used for a number of taxa in different regions worldwide (Sarakinos et al., 2001; Garson et al., 2002; Kelley et al., 2002a; Sánchez-Cordero et al., 2005a; Fuller et al., 2006, 2007; Illoldi et al., 2008). Despite that ResNet was originally designed for conservation purposes (Sarkar, 2004), we explored the idea for its applicability on restoration, given that both conservation and restoration pursue similar goals: selection of areas suitable for restoration will ultimately contribute to species long-term conservation (Sarkar, 2004).

We used the Neotropical river otter (*Lontra longicaudis annectens*), a charismatic species highly sensitive to aquatic and riparian habitat degradation (Gallo, 1989; Hanski, 1999;

Bifolchi and Lodé, 2005) as a case study. This species is included in CITES Appendix I, under extinction risk (US Endangered Species Act), vulnerable (IUCN; www.iucn.org), threatened in Mexico (NOM 059-2001; www.semarnat.gob.mx), and protected in Argentina, Bolivia, Brazil, and the United States of America (Larivière, 1999). Identifying river otter habitat and ecological niche requirements will address riparian ecosystem restoration with concrete objectives including fragmentation analysis as well as its biogeographic and evolutionary implications (Gallo-Reynoso, 1989; Peres and Terborgh, 1995; Hanski, 1999; Holl and Cairns, 2002; Barbosa et a., 2003; Cirelli, 2005).

Figure 1. Study area in the Apatlaco-Tembembe river basin, State of Morelos, located in central Mexico. Gray areas indicate the decreed natural protected areas (protected) Reserva de la Biósfera Corredor Biológico del Chichinautzin to the north, and the Reserva de la Biósfera Sierra de Huautla to the south; white areas (non-protected) indicate mostly secondary vegetation and transformed areas into agrosystems and urban settlements.

Here, we combined ecological niche modeling and place prioritization, both heuristic and spatially explicit algorithms, for identifying the Neotropical river otter potential areas for conservation and restoration in heterogeneous landscapes of a highly transformed region in central Mexico. Our specific aims were (1) prioritize potential conservation and restoration areas for the Neotropical river otter by combing ecological niche modeling and a diagnosis of habitat degradation, and (2) provide baseline landscape and local information for launching conservation, restoration and management programs for this species. Specifically, we identified and allocated riparian priority areas susceptible for Neotropical river otter and ecosystem restoration and conservation.

METHODS

Study Area

The Apatlaco-Tembembe fluvial basin is located in the Balsas river hydrological region in the State of Morelos in central Mexico, running through a geomorphologic system north to south (Arriaga-Cabrera et al., 1998) (Fig. 1). The study area was restricted to the river and its riparian ecosystem. This fluvial basin is surrounded by the biosphere reserves Reserva de la Biósfera Corredor Biológico del Chichinautzin and Reserva de la Biósfera Sierra de Huautla (Fig. 1). Temperature varies from temperate mesothermic (mean annual temperature 12-18°C) to warm (mean annual temperature >22°C); rainy season occurs from late May to early November. This region holds a high biodiversity of ecosystems, species, and endemicity (Contreras-MacBeath and Urbina-Torres, 1995; Sánchez-Cordero et al., 2004). Pine, oak, and mesophyl forests occur in the north, while pastures, xerophytic shrubs, riparian forests and low dry forests occur in the south (Contreras-MacBeath and Urbina-Torres, 1995).

The region is considered of conservation priority, serving as a biological corridor and holding a high number of flora and fauna species under local extirpation risk (NOM 059-2001 México). The Apatlaco-Tembembe fluvial basin is important for fresh water supply in the highlands of central Mexico, but has suffered high habitat degradation strongly affecting aquatic communities and populations of several species (Aguilar-Benítez, 1990; Trimble and Mendel, 1995; Belsky et al., 1999; CONABIO, 1999a,b; INEGI, 2002; Rutherford et al., 1999). River otters have suffered population declines in the last two decades (Gallo, 1989).

Ecological Indicators

Ecological indicators (EI) were used as indirect surrogates of biodiversity content as they reflect the riparian ecosystem degradation (NRC, 1992; Kondolf and Micheli, 1995; Guisan and Zimmermann, 2000; Wiens, 2002; Sarkar, 2004; EMAP, 2005). The comparison between areas for potential restoration and conservation is viable since biodiversity content is presumably linked to habitat degradation. We used EI values strongly related to the Neotropical river otter ecology as estimator surrogates of species presence, resulting in an empiric habitat and ecological niche model (hereafter *empiric* ecological niche) (Cirelli, 2005), assuming that the spatial and temporal natural stability of the physical environment (temperature, altitude, geology, etc.) was pertinent for long term conservation and restoration. However, once the physical variables are altered by human-induced actions, natural recovery is considered practically impossible. EI defining the physical structure of the environment and which are hardly changed by human-induced actions were considered as "structural"; EI reflecting human-induced actions with a consequent degradation but restorable, were considered "instrumental". Thus, it was assessed a threshold for an arbitrary desirable non modified scenario considered as a reference ecosystem (Margules and Pressey, 2000; Mc Donald, 2000; Young et al., 2005). This allowed a specific selection of areas for restoration facilitating the detection of structural characteristics, linking functional relationships among areas for restoration and/or conservation objectives. We used ResNet to generate these groups of areas along a 200 m buffer riparian zone adjacent to water courses (approximately 114,072 ha), and a 50 m buffer layer was produced to minimize georeference differences among digital data while including riparian ecosystem.

Selection of Attributes

An attribute (surrogate) and its categories defining the species' habitat were identified for each EI. A unique attribute number was assigned to each defined category to be identified by ResNet (http://uts.cc.utexas.edu/~consbio/Cons/ResNet.html; Sarakinos et al., 2001; Garson et al., 2002; Sarkar et al., 2002; Sarkar, 2004). EI reflecting suitable conditions of Neotropical river otter ecological niche were used for selecting conservation areas. When selecting areas for restoration, EI reflected habitat degradation conditions (Table 1). Attributes were selected *ad hoc* considering their importance for restoration objectives, and based on an ecological niche model for this species (Cirelli, 2005). Conservation and restoration categories are not mutually exclusive, but rather complementary (Fig. 2).

Ecological Niche Modeling

We used the genetic algorithm for rule-set prediction, GARP (Stockwell and Peters, 1999; http://wwg.lifemapper.org/desktopgarp/) for modeling the river otter's ecological niche, projected as a potential distribution hypothesis (hereafter *raw* PDH). GARP generates ecological niche models based on point occurrences, environmental thematic maps, and a GIS platform. Its geographic projection to the landscape produces species′ potential distributions depicting areas where the species is predicted present (Stockwell and Peters, 1999; Anderson, 2002; Anderson et al., 2003). Solution is reached through an iterative random process applied on a set of training data, generating a set of potential solutions to a problem (rules), and iteratively modifying the data set until an optimal solution is found. GARP builds an ecological niche model (training phase) with the 50% of the records randomly chosen as training points to generate the models, and afterwards tested using the remaining 50% as testing points (see Stockwell and Peters, 1999 for details). We run 100 models and selected 10 holding the lowest omission errors; further refinement consisted of selecting the best-subsets with the median commission errors following published recommendations (Anderson et al., 2003). The best-subsets were superimposed to produce a consensus map representing a consistent combination of all species' presence likelihood from ecological niche models (Anderson et al., 2003). Further methodological details as well as environmental thematic maps used herein are described elsewhere (Illoldi et al., 2004; Sánchez-Cordero et al., 2005a,b). We further refined the potential distribution hypothesis by restricting the modeled ecological niche exclusively to riparian habitat incorporating hydrological detailed variables into the modeling (hereafter *detailed* DPH), as the Neotropical river otter is ecologically confined to such ecosystem in the region (Gallo, 1989) (Figs. 2 and 3).

Table 1. Instrumental (*) and structural (**) ecological indicators (EI) and their categories indicative of (a) non-degraded riparian ecosystem conditions used for modeling potential conservation areas prioritized with ResNet algorithm, and (b) degraded riparian ecosystem conditions used for modeling potential restoration areas prioritized with ResNet algorithm; (+), Morelos State thematic layers (1:50,000 INEGI, 2002); (++), field data (Cirelli 2005); (+++), layers obtained from River Tools expert system

Attribute	Ecological Indicator (EI)	(a) Conservation attributes and categories Non-degraded conditions	(b) Restoration attributes and categories Degraded conditions
1	% Primary and secondary riparian vegetation (*)(++)	> 50	< 50
2	Dominant riparian vegetation type (*)(++)	Primary and secondary riparian vegetation	agriculture, human induced pastures, livestock, urban settlements.
3	Vegetation type and surrounding land use (*)(++)	low dry forest, 1° riparian vegetation	agriculture, human induced pastures, livestock, urban, secondary riparian vegetation
4	River permanence (**)(+)	permanent	permanent
5	Presence of deep river parts (*)(+)	yes	yes (medium to deep)
6	Estimated river depth (cm) (*)(+)	> = 50	> = 50
7	Min. abs. temp. (°C) (**)(+)	> = 10	> = 10
8	River width (m) (**)(+)	> 7	> 7
9	Strahler Order (RiverTools) (**)(+++)	3-4-5-6-7	1-2-3
10	Both banks characteristics (**)(++)	boulder, root, muddy ravine, beach	boulder, root, muddy ravine, beach, dam, plane
11	Both banks slope (**)(++)	high-high, high-medium, medium-medium	null-null, null-low, low-low
12	Protected natural areas (*)(+)	yes	no
13	2000 Vegetation type and land use map (*)(+)	forests, low dry forest	agriculture, no vegetation, human induced pasture, urban, secondary vegetation

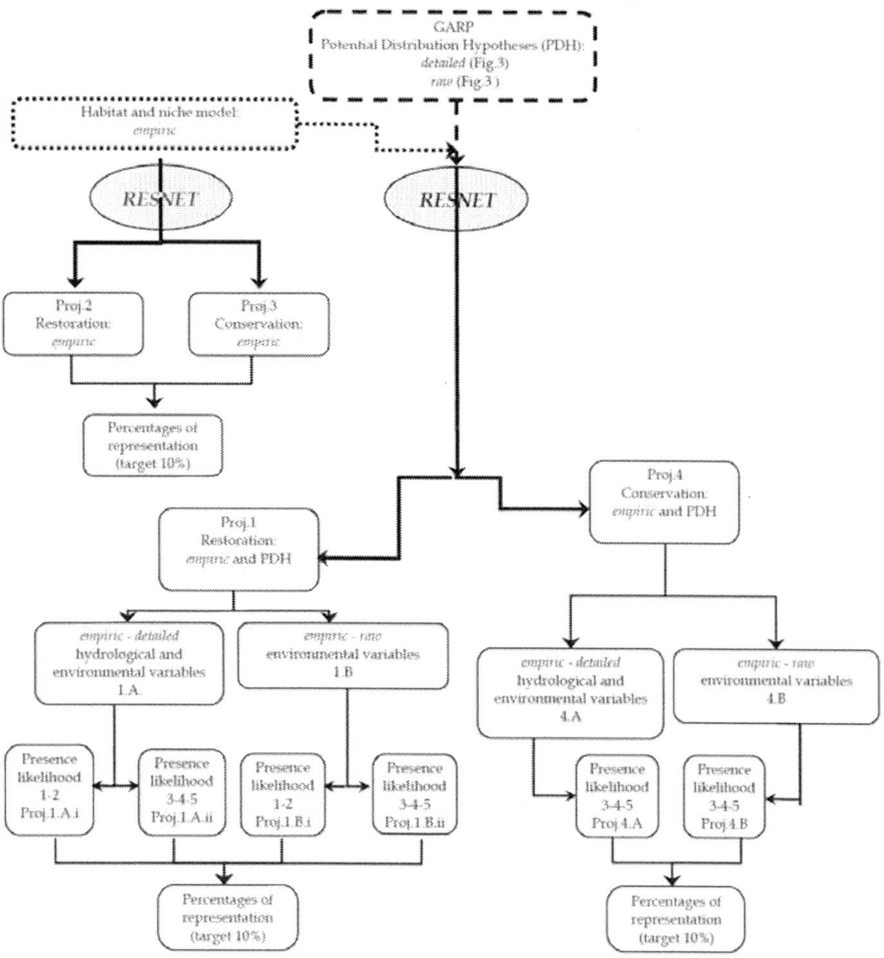

Figure 2. Flow chart depicting methods included for modeling species' ecological niche projected as potential distributions and selection of priority restoration and conservation areas for the Neotropical river otter *Lontra longicaudis annectens* in the study region. Three ecological niche models of the river otter were produced; *empiric*, based exclusively on ecological indicators of habitat and ecological niche (top left); *raw* PDH, based on point localities, environmental thematic layers, the genetic computer algorithm GARP, and a GIS platform, projected as a potential distribution hypothesis; *detailed* PDH, based on the raw model, but refined by restricting potential distribution hypothesis to the riparian ecosystem (top right). The ResNet Place Prioritization algorithm was applied to all ecological niche models as follows; Projections 2 for restoration areas (Proj. 2) and projection 3 for conservation areas (Proj. 3) show the individual influence of ecological indicators (EI) of habitat/niche *empiric* model. The influence of species presence likelihood was evaluated in projection 1 for restoration areas (Proj. 1), and projection 4 for conservation areas (Proj. 4). For conservation and restoration areas, we incorporated the influence of (1) total hydrological and general environmental layers- *detailed* PDH (Proj. 1.A), and (2) general environmental layers- *raw* PDH (Proj. 1.B). For hierarchical restoration area prioritization analyses, PDH species' presence likelihood was subdivided in two categories (low: 1-2 and high: 3-4-5), depicted in projections 1.A.i, 1.B.i, and 1.A.ii, 1.B.ii, respectively. High species' presence likelihood was included exclusively for conservation areas (Proj. 4.A, 4.B). A 10% target of total area was set for site prioritization selection of conservation and restoration areas, respectively. See text for more details.

Place Prioritization

The flexibility of this algorithm allowed the simultaneous manipulation and spatial representation of multiple criteria (EI as surrogates, see below; Aggarwal et al., 2002; Kelley et al., 2002b) combined with the river otter's modeled ecological niche. To select groups of cells maximizing the attribute EI number, the routine MESCP (Maximal expected surrogate covering problem) was used. Each cell contained the maximum number of attributes (richness) that could be selected for a specific spatial target (%) of the total study area. This basic selection can be spatially aggregated by incorporating an adjacency condition. ResNet maximizes the number of habitat and ecological niche characteristics with the corresponding values defining the ecological niche. The model was initialized using richness and avoiding existent conservation areas; adjacency was incorporated in a second stage. A 10% target was arbitrarily set as we felt that this area meets the ecological requirement of the Neotropical river otter (Gallo, 1989).

Several ResNet models were produced for prioritizing restoration and conservation areas (Figs. 2 and 3). A first group excluded information on river otter's presence to support the selection on habitat conditions (Projections 2 and 3); a second group included the categories of presence likelihood of the river otter's potential distribution (Projections 1 and 4) (Fig. 2). Comparisons were performed as follows: (1) including all set of attributes (general environmental and hydrological), and the river otter potential distribution (Projection1.A, *detailed* PDH), and (2) general environmental variables avoiding the detailed hydrological attributes (Projection1.B, *raw* PDH). For restoration analyses, presence likelihood was differentiated in low (1-2) *vs.* high (3-4-5) (Projections 1.A.i, 1.B.i and 1.A.ii, 1.B.ii, respectively) (Figs. 2 and 3). These comparisons produced different restoration priorities, assuming a direct relationship between presence likelihood and restoration or conservation importance (Barbosa et al., 2003). For conservation, only higher categories (3-4-5) were included. Pseudo-absence categories (cero) were not included in any case, as they are irrelevant in selecting areas neither for conservation nor restoration. A 10% target of total area was set for prioritization in each case.

The selection of EI for prioritization of areas allowed comparisons of their respective contribution, and were incorporated *a posteriori* as independent layers, differing from those incorporated *a priori* during the modeled ecological niche, using environmental and hydrological layers (Table 1). Different ResNet prioritized area solutions were compared as follows: EI alone (*empiric*) *vs.* both EI and potential distributions prioritized solutions for restoration (Projection 2 *vs.* Projection 1.A.ii *vs.* Projection 1.B.ii) (Fig. 3A), and conservation (Projection3 *vs.* Projection 4.B) (Fig. 3B); *raw* PDH vs. *detailed* PDH (incorporating hydrological detailed variables into the modeling) potential distributions; only high presence likelihood categories were included in these comparisons for both restoration (Projection 1.A.ii *vs.* Projection 1.B.ii), and conservation (Projection 4.A *vs.* Projection 4.B) (Fig. 3B); differences produced by a hierarchy of presence likelihood for restoration (low *vs.* high; Projection 1.A.i *vs.* Projection 1.A.ii, and Projection 1.B.i *vs.* Projection 1.B.ii) (Fig. 3C,D); modeled conservation and restoration areas (Projection 1.A.ii *vs.* Projection 4.A and, Projection 1.B.ii *vs.* Projection 4.B) (Fig. 3A,B). For visual simplicity, we plotted the *empiric* (EI alone) restoration and conservation models (Projection 2 and Projection 3, respectively) over *raw* PDH, although the latter were not considered during empiric modeling (Figs. 2 and 3).

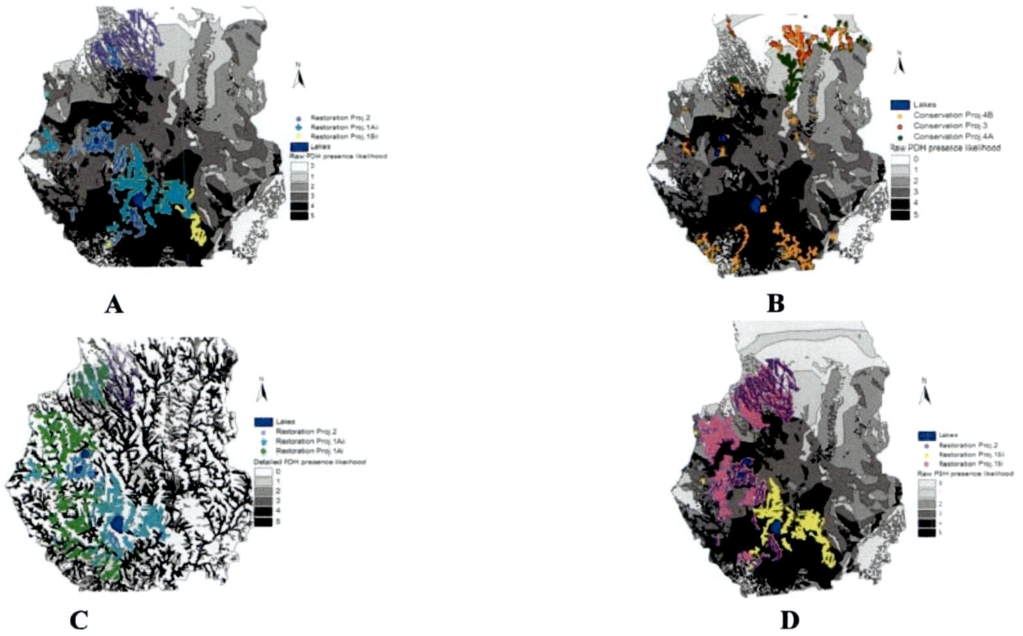

Figure 3. Site prioritization for river otter restoration and conservation areas in the Apatlaco-Tembembe river basin in central Mexico, based on influence of EI *vs*. both EI and *raw* PDH combined, and the differential influence of *raw* PDH on (**A**) Restoration areas; *empiric* (Proj. 2) *vs. empiric - detailed* PDH high species' presence likelihood (Proj. 1.A.ii) *vs. empiric - raw* PDH high species' presence likelihood (Proj. 1.B.ii). A high overlap is observed between selected areas. Areas were drawn over *detailed* PDH for visual clarity although this information was not used in Proj.2. *Raw* PDH produced more extended areas which widely overlaid to the other two models; (**B**) Conservation areas; *empiric* (Proj. 3) *vs. empiric - detailed* PDH high species' presence likelihood (Proj. 4A) *vs. empiric/raw* high species' presence likelihood (Proj. 4B). Both models selected areas geographically coincident with decreed natural protected areas; (**C** and **D**) Comparison of species' presence likelihood in selected restoration areas; *empiric - detailed* PDH low species' presence likelihood (Proj. 1.A.i) *vs. empiric - detailed* PDH high species' presence likelihood (Proj. 1.A.ii). In many cases, species' likelihood categories (1-2 vs. 3-4-5) produced spatial differences among prioritized selected areas for restoration; *empiric - raw* PDH low species' presence likelihood (Proj. 1.B.i) *vs. empiric - raw* PDH high species' presence likelihood (Proj. 1.B.ii). Differences of selected conservation and restoration areas are clearly distinguished based on their respective attributes in this figure, by comparing Conservation: *empiric - raw* PDH high species' presence likelihood (Proj. 4.B) *vs*. Restoration: *empiric - raw* PDH high species' presence likelihood (Proj. 1.B.ii), and Conservation: *empiric - raw* high species' presence likelihood (Proj. 4.A) *vs*. Restoration: *empiric - detailed* PDH high species' presence likelihood (Proj. 1.A.ii), respectively.

RESULTS

Potential areas for restoration and conservation were identified at both landscape and local scales, based on the Neotropical river otter niche requirements and habitat conditions (conserved or degraded). Conservation areas coincided with decreed natural protected areas as well as low degraded areas. Conversely, restoration areas coincided with highly degraded areas and land use (Figs. 1 and 3). In both cases, the Neotropical river otter potential distribution showed high geographic coincidence to the "core" of prioritized areas (Fig. 3); adjacency restoration and conservation solutions produced the most consistent and smaller spatial models.

Species' *raw* PDH resulted in larger areas than *detailed* PDH, and both produced larger areas than areas produced by the *empiric* habitat/ecological niche model. For all species' potential distributions, we observed geographic overlap with core areas. Hierarchies of presence likelihood (low, 1-2; high, 3-4-5) also produced significant spatial differences. Surprisingly, for models generated with highest presence likelihood categories (3-4-5), we observed prioritized areas in places corresponding to low categories (1-2). Restoration and conservation areas were significantly different according to habitat conditions (Fig. 3).

DISCUSSION

A conceptual challenge of biodiversity conservation is to identify true surrogates (abiotic and biotic) for place prioritization. Several authors (Inhaber, 1976; Prendergast et al., 1993; Erasmus et al., 1999; Lindenmayer et al., 2000; Sarakinos et al., 2001; Garson et al., 2002; Sarkar and Margules, 2002; Sarkar, 2004) have proposed biotic and abiotic variables as estimator surrogates (EI) as substitutes of true surrogates (species). Modeling the spatial distribution of estimate surrogates or some related pattern can be used to predict spatial distributions of true surrogates or related patterns (Faith and Walker, 1996; Ferrier and Watson, 1997; Ferrier, 2002). Our approach allowed identification of priority areas based on EI attributes or estimate surrogates, representing the minimum requirements for true surrogates. By combining species' ecological niche modeling and place prioritization procedures, we identified potential conservation and restoration areas for the river otter in the Apatlaco-Tembembe basin in central Mexico. Priority areas were hierarchically chosen for both objectives as they showed a wide spectrum of habitat degradation resulting in different ecological attributes. This allowed delineating a set of conditions sketching a hierarchy of priorities that can be readily set as a robust framework for decision planning (Ferrier et al., 2000; Cabeza and Moilanen, 2001, 2003). ResNet considers all the attributes as equivalent, allowing the selection of indicator attributes of degradation, although it was not specifically designed for establishing their relative weight in area selection (Sarkar et al., 2002; Sarkar and Garson, 2004). Nonetheless, our approach is flexible for refinement as we improve our knowledge of the Neotropical river otter ecology. *A priori* selection of EI was used to reflect differences in degree of habitat degradation.

Selected priority areas showed geographic coincidence in all cases. Although *raw* PDH depicts the species' fundamental ecological niche (Soberón and Peterson, 2005), the incorporation of detailed EI, ecological requirements and actual species' records produced a refined model resembling a realized ecological niche (Grinnell, 1917; Hutchinson, 1957), or *detailed* PDH. The geographic coincidence among modeled areas from diverse environmental variables could highlight some ecological niche characteristics of primary importance present in all cases. Coincident areas can be ranked first as priorities for restoration and conservation. Moreover, adjacent and close areas containing additional untransformed habitat can be incorporated as buffer zones at larger scales (Figs. 2 and 3). We arbitrarily set a 10% target for place prioritization in our modeling approach. Although the amount of percentage for place prioritization is hotly debated (Sarkar, 2004) it is desirable to compare our results with higher and lower targets in selecting conservation and restoration areas for this region.

Raw and Detailed PDH Models and Site Prioritization

Based on the Neotropical river otter minimum habitat and ecological niche requirements, untransformed and degraded habitat of riparian ecosystem for restoration and conservation were identified. Incorporating species' potential distribution to site prioritization resulted in spatial refinement according to presence likelihood. Likewise, *raw, detailed* and *empiric* distribution models constrained each other, highlighting specific areas of priority interest for restoration and conservation (Fig. 3). Specifically, the fact that *raw* PDH based prioritized areas broaden to the south (Fig. 3B) probably resulted from general environmental variables influencing river otter potential distribution, while *empiric* models referred mainly to actual riparian ecosystem conditions of habitat degradation located in the central and northern study region (Fig. 1). Despite that larger areas of *detailed* PDH than *empiric* models were due to highest PDHs′ categories of species' presence likelihood (Fig. 3), most of the spatial differences were observed for *raw* PDH models (Fig. 3A,B). Hydrological and riparian ecosystem variables restricted the *empiric* models; nonetheless, both *empiric* and *detailed* PDH models coincided extensively when analyzed simultaneously (Fig. 3).

The *detailed* PDH model (Fig. 3C) is quite conservative as it includes the whole data set: hydrological plus environmental variables, and historical (1986-87) and actual (1996-2002 and 2003-04) species records (Cirelli, 2005; Sierra-Huelsz and Vargas-Contreras, 2002; Gallo, pers. comm.). Hence, larger prioritized areas resulting from *raw* PDH suggests that these were likely over-predictions (Fig. 3). Conversely, *empiric* models produced larger prioritized areas than models combined with PDH (Fig. 3B). Thus, more detailed EI describing ecosystem conditions linked to conservation or restoration goals are relevant for selecting areas related to species′ ecological requirements. Interestingly, the inverse scenario was also feasible: *raw* PDH models produced smaller areas during prioritization processes than those generated by *empiric* based models (Fig. 3A). Perhaps this was due to high omission or commission errors creating an artificial effect on PDH, or to an under-representation of records and/or layers used in the *empiric* model, resulting in omission errors on PDH. In *empiric* models, EI are by their own generating areas that partially coincided with those obtained when *raw* models were included. Two questions emerge: over-predictions may result in overestimating restoration efforts, while under-predictions of the selected area likely impact the species ecology (dispersion, reproduction, etc.). Both errors will probably diminish successful restoration or conservation programs. As expected, prioritized areas based solely on ecological niche and habitat models (*empiric*) can include low presence likelihood areas (Figs. 3A-D).

Our study showed that EI are strongly related to the river otter ecological requirement and can be used to further refine place prioritization of areas under different habitat transformation scenarios. The incorporation of detailed ecological information into place prioritization algorithms can be used as a robust tool for identifying priority areas for restoration. A future challenge is to identify critical EI (surrogates) that could incorporate additional areas for other species as well. The differences resulting by incorporating EI, *a priori* (in GARP) or *a posteriori* (in ResNet) can be effective for conservation, restoration and adaptive management plans (Cirelli, 2005). In the latter case, areas were already classified because of their need to be restored. High spatial coincidence among ResNet prioritized areas for different environmental scenarios (Fig. 2) could compose a subsequent and important hierarchy than using exclusively distribution hypotheses (Fig. 3).

Ecological Niche Modeling Influence Area Prioritization

Hydrological and riparian ecosystem data refined suitable habitat resulting in smaller areas of *detailed* than *raw* PDH models (Fig. 3). However, spatial differences among prioritized areas based on *raw* and *detailed* PDH models evidence suboptimal habitat suited for river otter dispersion promoting natural recolonization or restoration; superimposed areas can be selected as first priority based on ecological factors. Surprisingly, areas corresponding to low species' likelihood presence (1-2) were prioritized when only high species' likelihood presence categories (3-4-5) were considered. Thus, selected priority areas did not correspond with selected attributes (Fig. 3D; Proj. 1Bi vs. 1Bii), likely resulting as consequence of an over-prediction associated to the *raw* PDH models. Given that landscape fragmentation is a main problem for species conservation (Andrén, 1994; Margules et al., 1994; Keymer et al., 2000; Ricketts, 2001; Fischer and Lindenmayer, 2006), selected areas for restoration within fragmented landscapes will improve connectivity of remnant natural areas (Gonzalez del Tánago and García de Jalón, 2001; Marzluff and Ewing, 2001; Tewksbury et al., 2002; Holl and Crone, 2004; Sarkar, 2004; Fuller et al., 2006). Remnant habitat with specific conditions could be extremely important as source-sink areas (Cabeza and Moilanen, 2001).

Complementing Conservation and Restoration Areas

Restoration and conservation objectives are tightly integrated for ecosystems recovery (Dobson et al., 1997). As restoration implies human intervention to recover functional and/or structural attributes of an ecosystem, specific human actions need to be identified. ResNet provided selection of conservation and restoration areas upon dissimilarities on their degradation status. In our study, degradation conditions limited conservation areas (Table 1; Figs. 2 and 3), and thus, areas requiring restoration needs could be identified. Selected areas proposed for conservation coincided with decreed natural protected areas, and prioritized restoration areas strongly fitted human-induced landscapes (Figs. 1 and 3). When selected conservation and restoration areas coincided, the attributes of shared cell-groups should be used to interpret each particular case upon field validation.

Prioritized areas can be further refined by reducing the number of selected sites using similar criteria (Sarkar, 2004). Our results were not optimal but spatial differences among suboptimal modeled solutions appear small (Fig. 3). Suboptimal solutions generated from heuristic algorithms (Peterson and Cohoon, 1999; Stockwell, 1999; Stockwell and Peters, 1999; Anderson et al., 2002; Anderson et al., 2003) are clearly advantageous as their flexibility facilitates incorporation into adaptive management plans and the assessment of priority hierarchies (Margules and Pressey, 2000). We contend that the sequential implementation of methods combining species' ecological niche modeling with place prioritization, can lead to robust spatially explicit models for identifying and hierarchically assessing areas for Neotropical river otter conservation and restoration in this region. The fact that conservation and restoration areas can be assessed simultaneously facilitates the analysis of their viability. We see our approach as a venue for integrating conservation and restoration areas in strategic conservation planning (Margules and Sarkar, 2007).

ACKNOWLEDGMENTS

We acknowledge funding from UNAM Program "Maestría en Ciencias Biológicas, Orientación Restauración Ecológica", UNAM Postgraduate Program, and Packard Foundation. VS-C thanks the Secretaría de Educación Pública and the Consejo Nacional de Ciencias y Tecnología for partial funding (Project SEP-CONACyT 51562). We gratefully thank S. Sarkar and collaborators, at the Biodiversity and Biocultural Conservation Lab., Univ. of Texas in Austin, for their great help with ResNet program. V. Sorani and collaborators provided digital thematic maps of Morelos, and J.P. Gallo and J.A. Sierra-Huelz helped with historical records of river otters.

REFERENCES

Aguilar-Benítez., 1990. Dimensiones ecológicas del estado de Morelos. UNAM-Centro Regional de Investigaciones Multidisciplinarias (CRIM). Morelos, 221 pp.

Aggarwal A., Garson, J., Sarkar, S., 2002. ResNet Ver.1.2., Manual report. Austin: Biodiversity and Biocultural Conservation Laboratory, University of Texas at Austin.

Anderson, R.P., Gómez-Laverde, M., Peterson, A.T., 2002. Geographical distributions of spiny pocket mice in South America: insights from predictive models. Global Ecology and Biogeography, 11:131-141.

Anderson, R.P., Lew, D., Peterson, A.T., 2003. Evaluating predictive models of species' distributions: criteria for selecting optimal models. Ecological Modelling, 162:211-232.

Andrén, H., 1994. Effects of habitat fragmentation on birds and mammals in landscapes with different proportions of suitable habitat. Oikos, 71:355-366.

Arriaga-Cabrera, L. V., Aguilar Sierra, J., Durand, A., Jiménez Rosenberg, R., Muñoz López, E., Vázquez Domínguez, E. (Coords.)., 1998. Regiones hidrológicas prioritarias. Escala de trabajo 1:4 000 000. 2ª, edición. Comisión Nacional para el Conocimiento y Uso de la Biodiversidad. México.

Barbosa, A.M, Real R., Olivero J., & J.M. Vargas. 2003. Otter (Lutra lutra) distribution modelling at two resolution scales suited to conservation planning in the Iberian Peninsula. Biological Conservation, 114:377-387.

Belsky, A., Matzke, A., Uselman, S., 1999. Survey livestock influences on stream and riparian ecosystems in the western United Sates. Journal of Soil and Water Conservation, 54:419-431.

Bifolchi, A., Lodé, T., 2005. Efficiency of conservation shortcuts: an investigation with otters as umbrella species. Biological Conservation, 126:523-527.

Brown, S., Lugo, A., 1994. Rehabilitation of tropical lands: a key to sustaining development. Restoration Ecology, 2(2):97-111.

Cabeza, M., Moilanen, A., 2001. Design of reserve networks and the persistence of biodiversity. Review, Trends in ecology and evolution, 16(5):242-248.

Cabeza, M., Moilanen, A., 2003. Site-selection algorithms and habitat loss. Conservation Biology, 17:1402-1413.

Cirelli, V., 2005. Restauración ecológica en la Cuenca Apatlaco-Tembembe. Estudio de caso: Modelado de la distribución de la nutria de río, Lontra longicaudis annectens. Tesis de maestría, Instituto de Biología, UNAM, México.

CONABIO (Comisión Nacional para el Conocimiento y Uso de la Biodiversidad), 1999a. Uso de suelo y vegetación modificado por CONABIO. Escala 1: 1 000 000. Comisión Nacional para el Conocimiento y Uso de la Biodiversidad. México.

CONABIO (Comisión Nacional para el Conocimiento y Uso de la Biodiversidad). 1999b. Regiones hidrológicas prioritarias. URL: http://www.conabio.gob.mx

Contreras-MacBeath, T., Urbina-Torres, U., 1995. Historia natural del área de protección de Flora y fauna silvestre Corredor Biológico Chichinautzin. CIBUAEM. Centro de Investigaciones Biológicas de la Universidad Autónoma del Estado de Morelos.

Dobson, A.P., Bradshaw, A.D., Baker, A.J.M., 1997. Hopes for the future: restoration ecology and conservation biology. Science, 277:515-522.

EMAP, 2005. Environmental Monitoring and Assessment Program for Ecological Indicators. Environmental Protection Agency, [URL]: http://www.epa.gov/emap/.

Erasmus, B.F.N., Freitag S., Gaston K.J., Erasmus B.H., van Jaarsveld, A.S., 1999. Scale and conservation planning in the real world. Proceedings of the Royal Society of London, 266:315-319.

Faith, D.P., Walker, P.A., 1996. How do indicator groups provide information about the relative biodiversity of different sets of areas? : on hot spots complementarity and pattern-based approaches. Biodiversity Letters, 3:18-25.

Feria, T.P., Peterson, A.T., 2002. Prediction of bird community composition on point-occurrence data and inferential algorithms: a valuable tool in biodiversity assessments. Diversity and Distributions, 8:49-56.

Ferrier, S., 2002. Mapping Spatial Pattern in Biodiversity for Regional Conservation Planning: Where to from Here? Systematic Biology, 51(2):331-363.

Ferrier, S., Watson, G., 1997. An evaluation of the effectiveness of environmental surrogates and modelling techniques in predicting the distribution of biological diversity. Consultancy report to the Biodiversity Convention and Strategy Section of the Biodiversity Group, Environment Australia (New South Wales: Environment Australia).

Ferrier, S., Pressey, R.L., Barrett, T.W., 2000. A new predictor of the irreplaceability of areas for achieving a conservation goal, its application to real-world planning, and a research agenda for further refinement. Biological Conservation, 93:303-325.

Fischer, J., Lindenmayer, D.B., 2006. Beyond fragmentation: the continuum model for fauna research and conservation in human-modified landscapes. Oikos, 112(2):473-480.

Fuller, T., Munguía, M., Mayfield, M., Sánchez-Cordero, V., Sarkar, S., 2006. Incorporating connectivity into conservation planning: a multi-criteria case study from central Mexico. Biological Conservation, 133(2):131-142.

Fuller, T. M., V. Sánchez-Cordero, P. Illoldi-Rangel, M. Linaje & S. Sarkar, 2007. The cost of postponing biodiversity conservation. *Biological Conservation,* 134(4):593-600.

Gallo Reynoso, J.P., 1989. Distribución y estado actual de la nutria o perro de agua (Lutra longicaudis annectens Major, 1897) en la Sierra Madre del Sur, México. Facultad de Ciencias, UNAM. Tesis de Grado de Maestro en Ciencias, 196 pp.

Garson, J., Aggarwal, A., Sarkar, S., 2002. Bird as surrogates for biodiversity: an analysis of a data set from southern Québec. Journal of Bioscience, 27(4)2:347-360.

Godown, M.E., Peterson, A.T., 2000. Preliminary distributional analysis of US endangered bird species. Biodiversity and Conservation, 9:1313-1322.

González del Tánago, M., García de Jalón, D., (Editors), 2001. Restauración de ríos y riberas. Fundación Conde del Valle de Salazar - Ediciones Mundi - Prensa. Madrid. 319 pp.

Grinnell, J., 1917. Field tests on theories concerning distributional control. Am.Nat.51:115-128.

Guisan, A., Zimmermann, N.E., 2000. Predictive habitat distribution models in ecology. Ecological Modelling, 135:147-186.

Hanski, I., 1999. Metapopulation ecology. Oxford University Press, 313 pp.

Holl, K.D., Cairns Jr., J., 2002. Monitoring and appraisal. In: M.R. Perrow and. A.J. Davy (Editors), Handbook of ecological restoration. Cambridge University Press, Part 5, Chpt.21.

Holl, K.D., Crone, E.E., 2004. Applicability of landscape and island biogeography theory to restoration of riparian understorey plants. Journal of Applied Ecology, 41(5):922-933.

Hutchinson, G.E., 1957. Concluding remarks. Cold Spring Harbor Symp. Quant. Biol., 22,415-427.

Illoldi-Rangel, P., V. Sánchez-Cordero & A. T. Peterson. 2004. Predicting distributions of Mexican mammals using ecological niche modeling. Journal of Mammalogy. 85(4): 658-662.

Illoldi-Rangel, P., T. Fuller, M. Linaje, V. Sánchez-Cordero & S. Sarkar. 2008. Solving the maximum representation problem to prioritize areas for the conservation of terrestrial mammals at risk in Oaxaca. Diversity and Distributions, 14(3): 493-508.

INEGI, 2002. Centro de Investigaciones Biológicas "J. Félix Frías Sánchez". Univ. Autónoma del Estado de Morelos (CIBUAEM). Página del Corredor Biológico Chichinautzin. México. [URL]:http//www.inegi.gob.mx

Inhaber, H., 1976. Environmental indices. John Wiley and Sons. New York. 178 pp.

Kelley, Ch., Garson, J., Aggarwal, A., Sarkar, S., 2002a. Place prioritization for biodiversity reserve network design: a comparison of the SITES and ResNet software packages for coverage and efficiency. Diversity & Distributions, 8(5):297-306.

Kelley, C., Garson, J., Sarkar, S., 2002b. ResNet Graphics User Interface (GUI) Manual Ver.2.1. The Biodiversity and Biocultural Conservation Laboratory, Section of Integrative Biology, University of Texas in Austin, USA., 19 pp.

Kerley, G.I.H., Pressey, R.L., Cowling, R.M., Boshoff, A.F., Sims-Castley, R., 2003. Options for the conservation of large and medium-sized mammals in the Cape Floristic Region hotspot, South Africa. Biological Conservation, 112:169-190.

Keymer, J.E., Marquet, P.A., Velasco-Hernández, J.X., Levin, S.A., 2000. Extinction thresholds and metapopulation persistence in dynamic landscapes. The American Naturalist, 156(5):478-494.

Kondolf, G.M., Micheli, E.R., 1995. Evaluating stream restoration projects. Environmental Management, 19(1):1-15.

Lindenmayer, D.B., Margules, Ch.R., Botkin, D.B., 2000. Indicators of Biodiversity for Ecologically Sustainable Forest Management. Conservation Biology, 14(4):941-950.

Margules, C.R., Nicholls, A.O., Pressey, R.L., 1988. Selecting networks of reserves to maximize biological diversity. Biological Conservation, 43:63-76.

Margules, C.R., Nicholls, A.O., Usher, M.B., 1994. Apparent species turnover, probability of extinction and the selection of nature reserves: a case study of the Ingleborough limestone pavements. Conservation Biology, 8:398-409.

Margules, C.R., Pressey, R.L., 2000. Systematic conservation planning. Nature, 405:243-253.

Margules, C. R., and S. Sarkar. 2007. Systematic Conservation Planning. Cambridge University Press. 270 p.

Marzluff, J.M., Ewing, K., 2001. Restoration of Fragmented Landscapes for the Conservation of Birds: A General Framework and Specific Recommendations for Urbanizing Landscapes. Restoration Ecology, 9(3):280-292.

Mc Donald, T., 2000. Resilience, recovery, and the practice of restoration. Ecological restoration, 18(1):10-20.

Meffe, G.K., Carroll, C.R., 1997. Principles of conservation biology. Second Edition, Sinauer Associates, Inc., 729 pp.

Moffett, A., Sarkar, S. 2006. Incorporating multiple criteria into the design of conservation area networks: a minireview with recommendations. Diversity and Distributions, 12:125-137.

NRC, 1992. Restoration of aquatic ecosystems: science, technology and public policy. Water Science and Technology Board, Commission of Geosciences, Environment and Resources, National Research Council. National Academy of Sciences, Washington, D.C., 522 pp.

Ortega-Huerta, M.A., Peterson, A.T., 2004. Modelling spatial patterns of biodiversity for conservation prioritization in north-eastern Mexico. Diversity and Distributions, 10:39-54.

Peres, C.A., Terborgh, J.W., 1995. Amazonian nature reserves: an analysis of the defensibility status of existing conservation units an design criteria for the future. Conservation Biology, 9(1):34-46.

Peterson, A.T., Cohoon, K.P., 1999. Sensitivity of distributional prediction algorithms to geographic data completeness. Ecological Modelling, 117:159-164.

Peterson, A.T., Ortega-Huerta, M.A., Bartley, J., Sánchez-Cordero, V., Soberón, J., Buddemeier, R.H., Stockwell, D.R.B., 2002a. Future projections for Mexican faunas under global climate change scenarios. Nature, 416:626-628.

Phillips, S.J., Anderson, R.P., Schapired, R.E., 2006. Maximum entropy modeling of species geographic distributions. Ecological Modelling, 190:231–259

Prendergast, J.R., Quinn, R.M., Lawton, J.H., Eversham, B.C., Gibbons,D.W., 1993. Rare species, the coincidence of biodiversity hot spots and conservation strategies. Nature (London), 365:335-337.

Pressey, R.L., Possingham, H.P., Day, J.R., 1997. Effectiveness of alternative heuristic algorithms for identifying indicative minimum requirements for conservation reserves. Biological Conservation, 80:207-219.

Ricketts, T. H., 2001. The matrix matters: effective isolation in fragmented landscapes. The American Naturalist, 158:87-99.

Rutherford, J.C, Davies-Colley, R.J., Quinn, J.M., Stroud, M.J., Cooper, A.B., 1999. Stream shade: towards a restoration strategy. Department of conservation, Wellington, New Zealand.

Sánchez-Cordero, V., Munguía, M., Peterson, A.T., 2004. GIS-based predictive biogeography in the context of conservation. In: M.V. Lomolino and L. Heaney (Editors), Frontiers in Biogeography. New directions in the geography of nature. Sinauer Associates, Inc. Publishers, pp. 311-322.

Sánchez-Cordero, V., Illoldi-Rangel, P., Linaje, M., Sarkar, S., Peterson, A.T., 2005a. Deforestation and extant distributions of Mexican endemic mammals. Biological Conservation, 126:465-473.

Sánchez-Cordero, V., Cirelli, V., Munguía, M., Sarkar, S., 2005b. Place prioritization for biodiversity representation using species′ ecological niche modeling. Biodiversity Informatics, 2:11-23.

Sanderson, E.W., Redford, K.H., Vedder, A., Coppolillo, P.B., Ward, S.E., 2002. A conceptual model for conservation planning based on landscape species requirements. Landscape and Urban Planning, 58:41-56.

Sarakinos, H., Nicholls, A.O., Tubert, A., Aggarwal, A., Margules, C.R., Sarkar, S., 2001. Area prioritization for biodiversity conservation in Québec on the basis of species distributions: a preliminary analysis. Biodiversity and conservation, 10:1419-1472.

Sarkar, S., 2004. Conservation Biology. The Stanford Encyclopedia of Philosophy. E.N. Zalta (Ed.), [URL]: http://plato.stanford.edu/archives/win2004/entries/conservation-biology/.

Sarkar, S., Margules, C., 2002. Operationalizing biodiversity for conservation planning. Journal of Bioscience, 27(4)2:299-308.

Sarkar, S., Garson, J., 2004. Multiple Criterion Synchronization (MCS) for Conservation Area Network Design: The use of Non-Dominated Alternative Sets. Preliminary draft, [URL]: http:\www.sarkar@mail.utexas.edu.

Sarkar, S., Aggarwal, A., Garson, J., Margules, Ch.R., Zeidler, J., 2002. Place priotitization for biodiversity content. Journal of Bioscience, 27(4)2:339-346.

Sarkar, S., Pappas, Ch., Garson, J., Aggarwal, A., Cameron, S., 2004. Place prioritization for biodiversity conservation using probabilistic surrogate distribution data. Diversity and Distributions, 10(2):125-133.

SER, 2002. The SER primer on ecological restoration. Society for Ecological Restoration Science and Policy Working Group, First Edition, 9 pp. [URL]: http:\www.ser.org

Sierra-Huelsz, J. A., Vargas-Contreras, J.A., 2002. Registros notables de Lontra longicaudis annectens (Carnivora: Mustelidae) en el Río Amacuzac en Morelos y Guerrero. Revista Mexicana de Mastozoología, 6:83-89.

Soberón, J., Peterson, A.T. 2005. Interpretation of models of fundamental ecological niches and species' distributional areas. Biodiversity Informatics, 2:1-10.

Stockwell, D.R.B., 1999. Genetic algorithms II: species distribution modelling. In: A.H. Fielding (Editor), Machine learning methods for ecological applications. Kluwer Academic Publishers.

Stockwell, D., Peters, D., 1999. The GARP modelling system: problems and solutions to automated spatial prediction. International Journal of Geographical Information Service, 13(2):143-158.

Stockwell, D.R.B., Peterson, A.T., 2002. Effects of sample size on accuracy of species distribution models. Ecological Modelling, 148:1-13.

Tewksbury, J.J., Levey, D.J., Haddad, N.M., Sargent, S., Orrock, J.L., Weldon, A., Danielson, B.J., Brinkerhoff, J., Damschen, E.I., Townsend, P., 2002. Corridors affect plants, animals, and their interactions in fragmented landscapes. PNAS, 99(20):12923-12926.

Tognelli, M.F., Silva-García, C., Labra,F.A., Marquet, P.A., 2005. Priority areas for the conservation of coastal marine vertebrates in Chile. Biological conservation, 126:420-428.

Trimble, S.W., Mendel, A.C., 1995. The cow as a geomorphic agent. A critical review. Geomorphology, 13:233-253.

Virolainen, K.M., Virola, T., Suhonen, J., Kuitunen, M., Lammie, A., Siikamaki, P., 1999. Selecting networks of nature reserves: methods do affect the long term outcome. Proceedings of the Royal Society of London Series B. Biological Sciences, 266:1141-1146.

Wiens, J.A., 2002. Riverine landscapes: taking landscape ecology into the water. Freshwater Biology, 47: 501-515.

Young, T.P., Petersen D.A., Clary, J.J., 2005. The ecology of restoration: historical links, emerging issues and unexplored realms. Ecology Letters, 8:662-673.

In: Endangered Species: New Research
Editors: A. Columbus and L. Kuznetsov
ISBN 978-1-60692-241-5

Chapter 11

Deforestation and Biodiversity Conservation in Mexico

Víctor Sánchez-Cordero[1], Patricia Illoldi-Rangel[1,4], Tania Escalante[2], Fernanda Figueroa[1], Gerardo Rodríguez[3], Miguel Linaje[1], Trevon Fuller[4] and Sahotra Sarkar[4]

[1] Departamento de Zoología, Instituto de Biología,
Universidad Nacional Autónoma de México
Apartado Postal 70-153, México, D.F. México 04510
[2] Museo de Zoología "Alfonso L. Herrera", Departamento de Biología Evolutiva,
Facultad de Ciencias, Universidad Nacional Autónoma de México
Apartado Postal 70-399, México, D. F. México 04510
[3] Laboratorio de Macroecología, Departamento de Ecología de la Biodiversidad,
Instituto de Ecología, Universidad Nacional Autónoma de México
Apartado Postal 70-275, México, D.F. México 04510
[4] Biodiversity and Biocultural Conservation Laboratory, Section of Integrative Biology,
University of Texas at Austin, Austin, TX 78712-1180, USA

Abstract

Deforestation is one of the main factors negatively affecting the conservation of biological diversity. We assess the impact of deforestation on biodiversity in Mexico by quantifying its effect on (1) mammal species' distributions, (2) delineation of biogeographical regionalization, (3) the effectiveness of conservation area networks to prevent biologically deleterious land use/land cover change, and (4) area prioritization for biodiversity conservation. Deforestation has a significant impact on species' distributions with habitat loss ranging from 10-90%, leading in some cases to high risks of extinction. Significant changes also occur in the delineation of biogeographical provinces (bioregionalization) due to deforestation because several areas with unique fauna show high rates of natural habitat reduction, leading to potential ecological and biogeographical changes in species interactions and distributions. A variety of decreed natural protected areas now show increasing pressures due to potential land use conversion from natural habitat to agriculture and urban settlements which threatens their biodiversity content. Area prioritization for biodiversity conservation is seriously negatively affected by deforestation because a significantly increased total area is required to conserve endemic mammals as compared to what would have been adequate 30 years ago before significant loss of forest cover. These trends urge immediate collaborative actions between academic, governmental, and NGO sectors to prevent and reduce further deforestation nationwide.

INTRODUCTION

High rates of deforestation threaten biodiversity conservation worldwide (Dale *et al.*, 1994, Lidlaw, 2000; Sala *et al.*, 2000; Kinnard *et al.*, 2003), causing land degradation (Riezebos and Loerts, 1998; Islam and Weil, 2000), local, regional, and global climatic changes (Houghton *et al.*, 1999; Chase *et al.*, 2000), and loss of ecosystem services (Vitousek *et al.*, 1997). Of major concern are impacts of deforestation on individual species' distributions and, consequently, their conservation status (Wilson, 1988; Reaka-Kudla *et al.*, 1997; Mace *et al.*, 1998; Sánchez-Cordero *et al.*, 2005), as well as on natural protected areas (NPAs) which form the foundation of most strategies of environmental conservation. Although international forums have proposed that the global network of Natural Protected Areas (NPAs) should reach 10% of the Earth's surface (IUCN 2005), conservation of this area is not guaranteed because many NPA networks face a variety of threats and suffer from a variety of degradation processes worldwide (Carey *et al.* 2000).

One approach for evaluating the impact of deforestation on biodiversity conservation is to quantify land use-land cover changes (LULCC) in dominant vegetation types because of habitat loss and the accompanying loss of biodiversity. Several studies have identified vegetation types with high species richness and endemicity suffering considerable deforestation; such hotspots occur primarily in tropical and montane regions (Wilson, 1988; Laurance and Bierregaard, 1997; Mittermeier *et al.*, 1998; Myers, 1998; Kinnaird *et al.*, 2003; Rodrigues *et al.*, 2004), especially in tropical rainforests, of which over 70% has been deforested (Myers, 1998; Laurance and Bierregaard, 1997; Heaney *et al.*, 1999).

Mexico is a megadiverse country showing high rates of deforestation posing threats to its biological conservation. Annual rates of deforestation are over 1.2% (Masera *et al.*, 1997; Arriaga *et al.*, 2001; Mas *et al.*, 2004; United Nations Food and Agriculture Organization, 2007). Further, an estimated 90% of the original humid tropical forest has been converted into agrosystems or urban settlements, presumably resulting in significant biodiversity loss (Toledo *et al.*, 1989; Dirzo and García, 1992; Mittermeier *et al.*, 1998; Arriaga *et al.*, 2001).

Recent developments in ecological niche modelling provide the possibility of insight into these challenges (Soberón & Peterson, 2005); by integrating known occurrences with digital maps of relevant environmental parameters, areas suitable for species can be characterized and projected as potential geographic distributions (Soberón & Peterson, 2005; Soberón, 2007). Terrestrial mammals have been extensively used as a model group in different ecological, biogeographical and conservation studies. Some of the reasons for this are that there exists an extensive tradition of their study, their individual distributional areas are more or less well-known, and their phylogenetic relations are typically well-understood. Mammals in México are well represented in biological collections: there are 28 national collections which compile 162,288 specimens (Espinoza *et al.*, 2006), and there are collections in Canada and the USA in which there exist approximately 242,420 specimens (López-Wilchis, 2006). Also, for the majority of biological collections, specimen data are accessible online (e. g., http://manisnet.org/, http://unibio.ibiologia.unam.mx/ http://www.gbif.org/, http://www.conabio.gob.mx/remib/doctos/remib_esp.html), which facilitates their use and analysis.

We address diverse negative impacts of deforestation on biodiversity conservation in Mexico using terrestrial mammals as a case study. Specifically, we (1) analyze changes in estimated range loss due to deforestation by determining the remnant untransformed habitats within species' potential distributions based on ecological niche modeling, and identify regions of potentially high species' endangerment and extinction risk; (2) delineate the impact of deforestation on biogeographic region delineation based on patterns of endemism by contrasting species' potential and extant distributions; (3) evaluate the extent of change of areas in which the original vegetation was completely transformed to human settlements, and agricultural and grazing lands in federal NPAs, as a measure of the impact of deforestation on conservation policies; and (4) carry out area prioritization for biodiversity conservation targeted to conserve endemic mammals, comparing what is required now to what would have been adequate 30 years ago (before significant loss of forest cover).

DEFORESTATION AND BIODIVERSITY LOSS

Many previous studies have linked deforestation of predominant vegetation types with biodiversity loss (Dirzo and García, 1992; Laurance and Bierregaard, 1997; Heaney *et al.*, 1999). Although these studies are relevant insofar as they correlate general trends of deforestation and biodiversity loss, these approaches were limited insofar that they did not assess the impact of deforestation on individual species. Recently developed methodologies for modeling species' distributions are based on the modeling of species' ecological niches (*sensu* Grinnell [1917]) – the suite of environmental conditions within which a species can maintain its population without immigration (MacArthur, 1972). These methodologies use occurrence data, environmental layers, and a GIS platform to predict species' distributions. Coarse-grained ecological niche models can identify geographic areas potentially suitable for each species (Peterson *et al.*, 1999; Stockwell and Peters, 1999; Peterson, 2001; Anderson *et al.*, 2003). We believe that such geographical predictions of niches can provide a framework for understanding how habitat loss impacts distribution patterns of individual species and hence, their conservation status (Sánchez-Cordero *et al.*, 2001, 2004).

We modeled ecological niches for the continental endemic Mexican mammals, and estimated range loss due to deforestation using the 2000 land use and vegetation map by determining the remnant untransformed habitats within species' potential distributions. We only included endemics to ensure that the modeled ecological niches projected as species' potential distributions remained within México (for which we had all the relevant data). To overcome geographic biases in delimiting species' distributions, we generated models of ecological niche for each species, using the Genetic Algorithm for Rule-set Prediction (GARP; Stockwell and Peters 1999; available for download at www.lifemapper.org/desktopgarp), which has proven to be quite robust for predicting mammal distributions in México (Illoldi *et al.*, 2004). Our main results indicate that more than one-fourth of the endemics (23 out of 85 species) have lost >50% of untransformed habitat within their potential distributions. Two endemics showed a particularly drastic distributional loss of >90%, and another two showed losses of >80%; only 10 endemics retained >80% of untransformed habitat within their distributional areas (Sánchez-Cordero *et al.*, 2005). Overall, 35% of untransformed habitat has been lost nationwide, with major losses occurring mostly in tropical habitats. Most endemics (61 of 85 species, 72%) showed a higher proportion of transformed habitat within their potential distributions compared to the overall proportion of transformed habitat at the national level. Endemics showing significant areal reductions with low remnant untransformed habitat coverage within their potential distribution can be interpreted as posing an extinction threat. Nearly all endemics with large ranges lost a large proportion of their potential habitats, whereas species with small ranges showed both high and low loss, indicating that a broad distribution does not preclude a high extinction risk. Endemic species can be particularly vulnerable to extirpation in certain parts of their ranges, in which only small fragments of untransformed habitat remain.

No significant correlation existed between the proportion of untransformed area and the original distributional area ($r = 0.07$, $p > 0.1$); rather, the proportional area of untransformed habitat appeared more dependent on geographic location. For example, 25 out of 37 (68%) endemic species retaining <60% of untransformed habitat in their distributions occurred in eastern Mexico and central Mexico. Conversely, 45 out of 48 (94%) endemic species retaining >60% of untransformed habitat in their potential distributions occurred in other regions (Sánchez-Cordero *et al.*, 2005). Historically, the eastern and central regions in Mexico have seen deforestation and urbanization increases since the 1960s, converting 70% of untransformed habitat into agrosystems and rural or urban settlements (Toledo *et al.*, 1989; Challenger, 1998; Arriaga *et al.*, 2001) (Fig. 1). Extinction risk for endemics in these regions appears higher compared with other regions of the country. Nearly 40% of Mexican endemics are restricted to these regions (Hall, 1981; Ceballos *et al.*, 1998; Sánchez-Cordero *et al.*, 2005). If habitat loss across the landscape is assumed to occur at random, we expect more variability in the loss rates of potential habitat for species with small rather than large distributional ranges. Interestingly, most endemics restricted to these regions have small distributions (Hall, 1981), showing high variability in their proportion of untransformed distribution (Sánchez-Cordero *et al.*, 2005). These results suggest that populations face different extirpation risks depending on geographic location, thus providing a geographic context for designing regional and local conservation plans. This criterion can be extrapolated generally to other faunistic groups as a useful tool for defining conservation priorities (Ceballos and Rodríguez, 1993; Mace *et al.*, 1998; Hilton-Taylor, 2000; Kinnaird *et al.*, 2003; Sánchez-Cordero *et al.*, 2004, 2005; Fuller *et al.*, 2006). However, while habitat loss is recognized as a critical factor for extinction risk, other factors, such as hunting pressure, and species' biological properties are also important when considering conservation status (Laurance *et al.* 2006; see also www.conabio.gob.mx and www.ine.gob.mx).

Our distribution models are based on the assumption that coarse-scale conversion of natural habitats into agrosystems or human habitation (rural or urban settlements) results in non-viable conditions for species (Egbert *et al.*, 1999; Peterson *et al.*, 2000; Ortega-Huerta and Peterson, 2004; Sánchez-Cordero *et al.*, 2004). Ecological support for this idea comes from the hypothesis of general niche conservatism which has been tested for a diverse range of fauna in México and elsewhere (Peterson *et al.*, 1999; Peterson and Vieglais, 2001; Peterson and Holt, 2003). Theoretically, rapid adaptation to new environments produced by anthropogenic habitat transformation is unlikely, and populations may not be able to persist without significant immigration from adjacent natural habitats (Peterson and Holt, 2003). This effect reinforces claims of the importance of conserving untransformed habitats. These factors are likely to hold for locally-adapted endemic species.

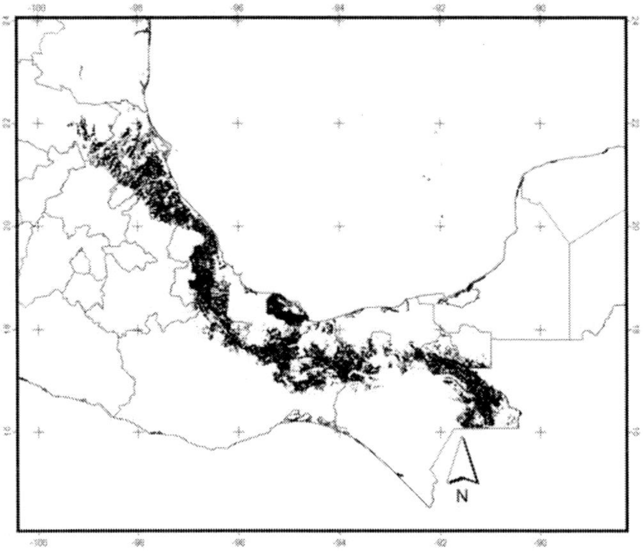

A

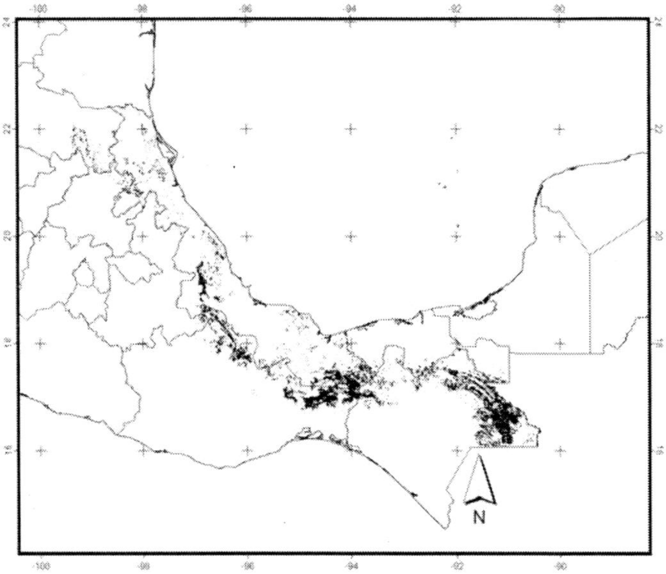

B

Figure 1. Effect of land conversion on endemic mammal distributions in Mexico. Black areas include the habitat of the Mexican agouti (*Dasyprocta mexicana*), a charismatic and economically important mammal typically inhabiting rainforest. The modeled distribution of *D. mexicana* showed a reduction of 33.5% from 1970 (A) to 2000 (B).

Our model does not specifically predict which endemics may be tolerant to transformed habitat, as is known to be the case for some mammals (see Fisher *et al.*, 2003; Sánchez-Cordero and Zepeda, 2003; Isaac and Cowlishaw, 2004). Moreover, because we used a coarse forest pixel resolution, the areas assumed to be suitable habitat may include portions of transformed habitat. This would lead to an underestimation of the loss for species' potential distributions. Other factors not included in our model may also contribute to population extirpation, such as illegal hunting, and biological attributes of species, home range, fecundity rate, and rarity in fragmented habitats (Mace *et al.*, 1998). These methodological limitations do not affect our main conclusions based on the observed patterns of reductions in species' suitable niches due to anthropogenic habitat transformation. From the perspective of biodiversity conservation, our approach satisfies the precautionary principle: even where it requires subsequent refinement and modification, it is conservative about what constitutes viable habitat for species; as such, it will have done no harm to conservation aims (Sarakinos *et al.*, 2001; Cooney & Dickson 2005). If some areas are selected for conservation, but other areas also allow the persistence of species, the use of our model will not result in detriment of potential suitable habitat for conserving species (Sarkar, 2004). We propose to expand our analyses more broadly to other taxa in order to identify areas of potential general extinction risk, in which conservation investment or habitat restoration would have a strong impact in preventing biodiversity loss. A clear result of these analyses is that a regional, rather than taxonomic, focus should guide mammal conservation assessment and planning in México (Sánchez-Cordero *et al.*, 2004, 2005; Fuller et al., 2006, 2007).

On a broader scale, our approach can be incorporated into current methodologies for assigning species' global conservation status (Hilton-Taylor, 2000), providing quantitative estimates of likely extent of the loss of the geographic distributions of individual species. Increasing efforts supported by universities and governmental agencies are leading to compilation of large databases of georeferenced species point occurrences. These developments will facilitate conducting analyses similar to ours for a wide range of biotic groups anywhere in the world.

DEFORESTATION AND BIOGEOGRAPHICAL REGIONALIZATION

Deforestation affecting species' distributions has an impact on biogeographic region delineation, because deforestation induces changes in historical patterns of species' distributions (Escalante *et al.*, 2007a,b). Biogeographic regionalization consists of delineating a hierarchy of geographic areas derived from successively nested areas of endemism, in which the province is the smallest area of endemism to be identified, followed by dominions, regions, and realms. Because areas of endemism are delineated using individual species' distributions, we have good reason to believe that distributional patterns derived from individual distributions change with deforestation.

Hierarchical biogeographic regionalizations are inferred from historical patterns of endemism but these may be modified by transformation of natural habitats. We analyzed the impact of deforestation on patterns of endemism by contrasting potential and extant distributions using terrestrial mammals in Mexico as a case study. Specifically, we showed changes in distributional patterns of terrestrial mammal under two scenarios: by modelling species' ecological niches projected as potential distributions using the original natural vegetation map (t_1), and projected as extant distributions using the 2000 land use and vegetation map (t_2). We generated models of ecological niche for 429 species, using GARP (see above) and built two matrices to develop the regionalization: matrix-t_1, using species' distributions t_1, and matrix-t_2, using species' distributions t_2. Both matrices were used in a Parsimony Analysis of Endemicity (PAE; Morrone, 1994) for 248 quadrats nationwide. For t_1 and t_2, characteristic and endemic species were mapped and these species and the cladograms obtained were used for biogeographic regionalizations.

We observed significant changes between the t_1 and t_2 cladograms resulting in dramatic changes in biogeographical patterns at major scales. We found an obvious delineation of regions in t_1, but not in t_2, suggesting a change in historical distributional patterns by which the boundary between Nearctic and Neotropical regions virtually disappears; thus such biogeographic transitional zones which were formed in historical times have suffered dramatic changes as a consequence of deforestation. Surprisingly, the Sierra Madre Occidental province was not identified under the t_2 scenario (Fig. 2). Species may respond to deforestation by (1) reducing their distributional area only to remnant suitable habitats, (2) modifying their distributional area using perturbed habitats, and/or (3) moving to other remnant suitable habitats (Holt, 1990). If each species responds in different ways to drastic ecological changes, then shared distributional patterns are modified and, in that sense, lost.

Figure 2. Area cladogram showing the final biogeographic regionalization based on extant mammals distributions in Mexico. Deforestation significantly reduced the distribution of many mammals which affected historical biogeographic region delineation. See text for further details.

Changes in biogeographic regionalizations should be expected over ecological or evolutionary times, produced by unique geologic, geographic, and climatic changes at a global scale. We showed that changes in species' distributions attributable to deforestation can result in significant changes in biogeographical regionalization using terrestrial mammals as a case study. If further deforestation continues, it is likely that additional regions holding unique patterns of species' distributions may disappear with unknown consequences for ecological-evolutionary processes (Wilson, 1988). Similarly, deforestation and climate change can also act in concert to produce rapid changes in species' distributions thus affecting biogeographic regionalization as well (Peterson *et al.*, 2002). Studies incorporating biogeographic regionalization of areas of endemism and transition zones can help identify conservation priorities.

Deforestation and Natural Protected Areas

Networks of Natural Protected Areas (NPAs) constitute the foundation of policies for maintaining biological diversity, the livelihood of local communities, and the provision of ecosystems services (Ervin, 2003; IUCN 2005). Notwithstanding, NPAs face several threats worldwide, such as deforestation and other land use-land cover changes (LULCC) such as other forms of land degradation, exotic species invasions, illegal logging, hunting and extraction of resources, among others (Carey *et al.*, 2000). Recent trends of high natural landscape transformation due to human activity jeopardize the integrity and health of ecological systems, posing a threat to NPAs which frequently consist of the only remaining natural habitat of many species.

Deforestation poses a critical threat to biodiversity conservation in megadiverse México, and this challenge is further exacerbated by the existence of a growing and highly dispersed rural population increasingly demanding direct use of natural resources (Sarukhán *et al.*, 1996). Conservation strategies in Mexico rely heavily on NPAs. In 2003, there were 160 officially decreed NPAs to protect terrestrial and marine ecosystems, varying in size and management category, and covering approximately 9% of the nation (CONANP, 2003; http://www.conanp.gob.mx/anp/anp.php). As in most developing countries, NPAs in Mexico have been historically inhabited by local communities, many of which have been living in these areas for centuries. An estimated 1,404,516 people were living in 4,485 localities inside NPAs in 2000 (CONANP, 2003). Many factors influence the NPAs' degradation by human activities including demographic dynamics, local and non-local economic interests and activities, poverty, market demand and prices of local products, governmental policies, and conflicts among different social groups over the control and use of natural resources (Barbier and Burgess, 1996; Ghimire and Pimbert, 1997; Barbier and Burgess, 2001; Lambin *et al.*, 2001; Geist and Lambin, 2002). Consequently, there is an increasing concern over the NPAs' capacity to fulfill their conservation goals (Hockings, 1998; 2003).

An evaluation of degradation processes within NPAs is essential for conservation planning, especially for detecting areas of particular concern, and for designing strategies to prevent biodiversity loss (Sánchez-Cordero and Figueroa, 2007; Sánchez-Cordero *et al.*, 2007). We evaluated land use - land cover change (LULCC) processes in Mexican NPAs from 1993 to 2002, assuming a correlation between natural vegetation cover reduction and the loss of biological diversity and the ability to provide ecosystem services. We used the extent and rate of change of highly transformed areas inside NPAs as a surrogate of LULCC. These included areas transformed due to agriculture, induced and cultivated pastures, forestry plantations, and human settlements. We estimated the extent and rate of change of transformed areas using land use and vegetation maps produced by the Instituto Nacional de Estadística, Geografía e Informática for 1993 and 2002 (INEGI, 1993; 2005), the map of the decreed federal NPAs of Mexico (CONANP, 2003), and a GIS platform (Figs. 3 and 4). We estimated LULCC rate as the annual percentage of change of transformed areas relative to the total evaluated area, as follows:

$$LULCCR = \frac{S_2 - S_1}{S_t} \times \frac{100}{N}$$

where *LULCCR* = change rate, S_1 = initial transformed surface area, S_2 = final transformed area, S_t = total evaluated area, and N = time difference in years.

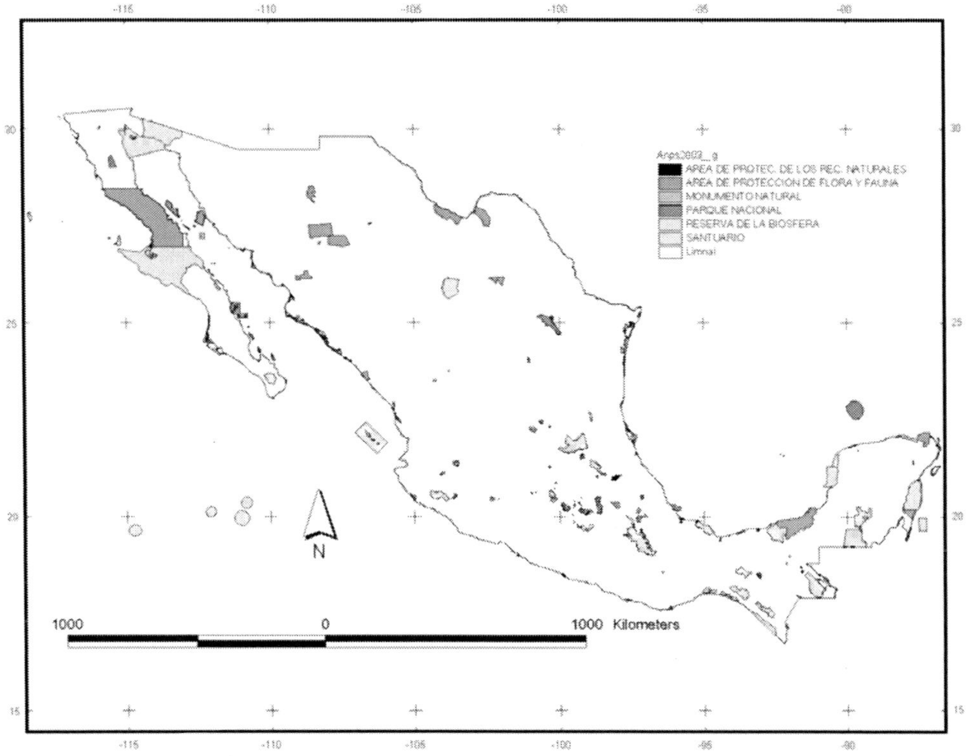

Figure 3. Map depicting the decreed terrestrial federal Natural Protected Areas of Mexico (CONANP 2003), covering approximately 9% of the nation (see www.conanp.gob.mx).

The extent of transformed area was estimated for 89 terrestrial federal NPAs decreed before 2003, and larger than 1,000 ha (CONANP, 2003); the rate of change was estimated for 69 of these areas decreed before 1997. The main results showed that approximately one-fourth of Mexico had been converted to highly transformed areas by 2002 (Fig. 2) reflecting a history of inadequate land use and management policies for the conservation of natural resources. Most NPAs suffered less habitat transformation (mean of 16% of their area), showing smaller percentages of transformed area than nationwide. Fifty percent of NPAs showed less than 10% of transformed area, but one third showed more than 30% of transformed area; 8% showed more than 50% of transformed area. These trends indicate high threats to biodiversity conservation in these NPAs and should be viewed with concern.

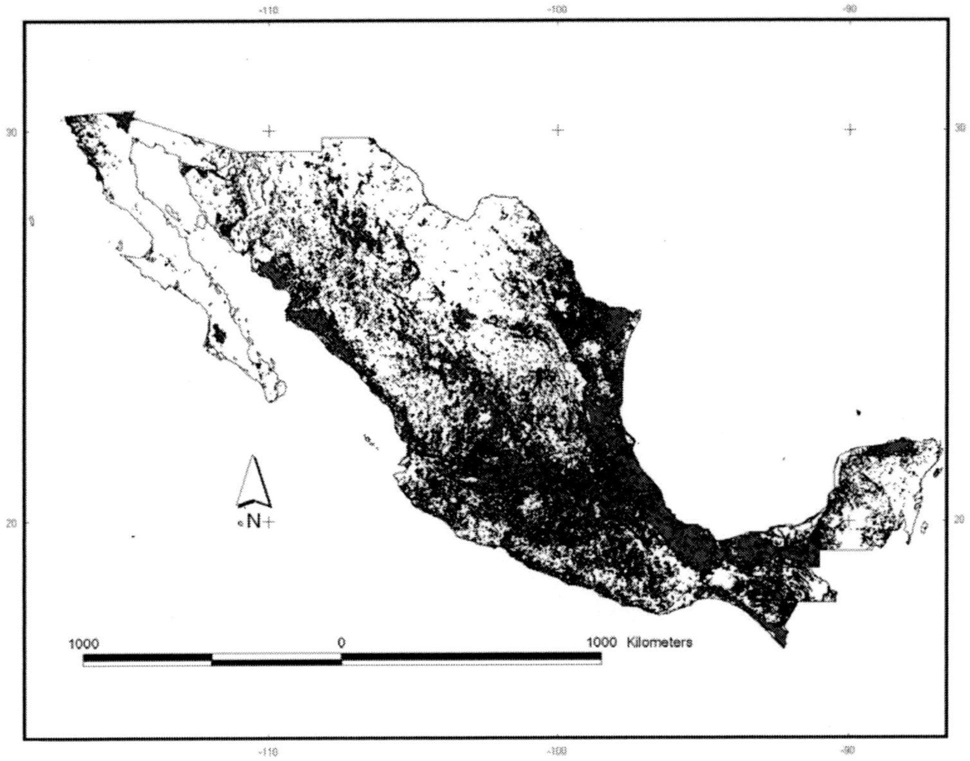

Figure 4. The 2002 transformed areas of Mexico including agriculture fields, induced and cultivated pastures, and urban settlements (black area). Large portions of deforested regions occur predominantly in central, eastern and south of Mexico (see www.inegi.gob.mx).

The growth rate of transformed areas nationwide was 0.2% annually; this rate means that roughly 2% of Mexico is anthropogenically transformed each decade. The mean annual rate of change in NPAs was of 0.03%, with more than half of NPAs (57%) showing a reduction of transformed areas (rates ranging 0 to -1.5); in these NPAs, natural vegetation is either not being reduced spatially, or is recovering. Somewhat less than half (43%) of NPAs showed increments in transformed area (Fig. 5), although with lower rates than the national level. However, as many as 20% of NPAs showed rates of change higher than nationwide.

We expected lower estimates for transformed areas and rates of LULCC in NPAs. The lower rate change in NPAs may result from the combination of environmental policies and resources, along with the fact that many of these areas show conditions that result in lower suitability for economic activities, such as greater isolation due to less access to roads, or because soil types and topographic characteristics compromise potential agricultural productivity (Pressey *et al.,* 2002, Brandon *et al.,* 2005, Mas, 2005). This trend is expected in a country such as México because of its long history of intensive human occupation, because of which the best suitable areas for agricultural production have been under use for a long time with the consequence that decreed NPAs are usually located in areas that are less suitable for such economic activities (Cantú *et al.*, 2004; Sánchez-Cordero and Figueroa, 2007; Sánchez-Cordero *et al.*, 2007).

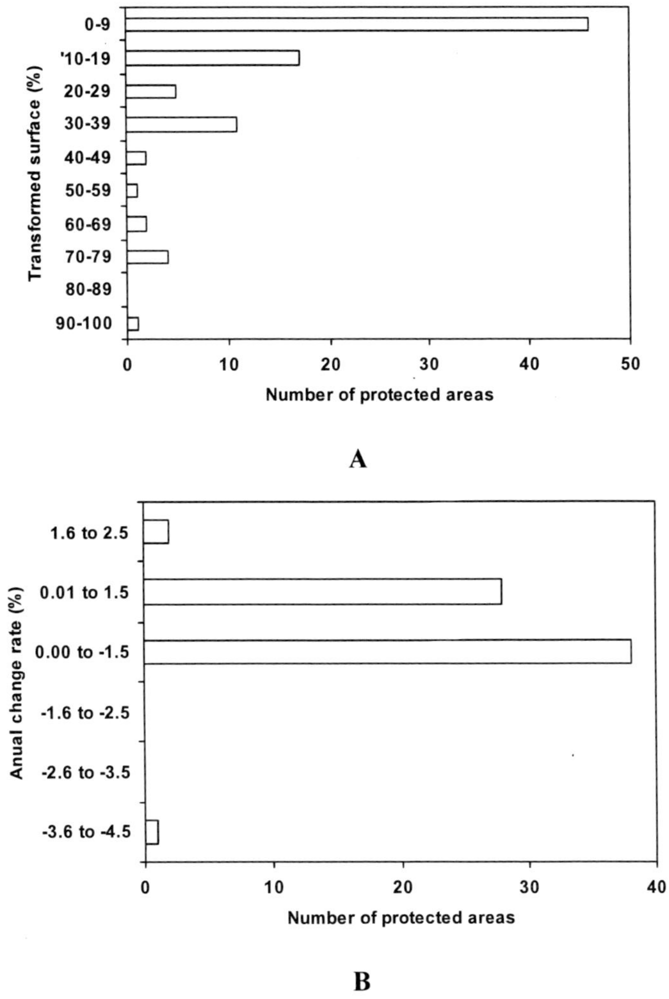

Figure 5. (A) Range (%) of transformed areas in 89 NPAs in Mexico; national mean value is 26%. (B) Annual rate of change of transformed area in 69 NPAs in Mexico; national mean value is 0.2%.

Most NPAs showed a reduction or slight increment in transformed areas, but many had processes of LULCC that nevertheless constitute a threat to conservation. The design and implementation of strategies of vegetation recovery such as ecological restoration in areas of particular concern is urgently needed, along with research focusing on causal factors underlying LULCC processes. Policies aimed at sound economic activities based on the sustainable use of natural resources by local people should be supported by government agencies, both in communities living inside and surrounding NPAs. This is particularly important, as many of these rural communities show conditions of high marginalization

(Nadal, 2003). Future work should link spatial overlapping of priority areas for conservation and biogeographic regionalization with location of NPAs in which transformed areas are both decreasing and increasing. Such analyses are important inputs for systematic conservation planning of the biological diversity in Mexico.

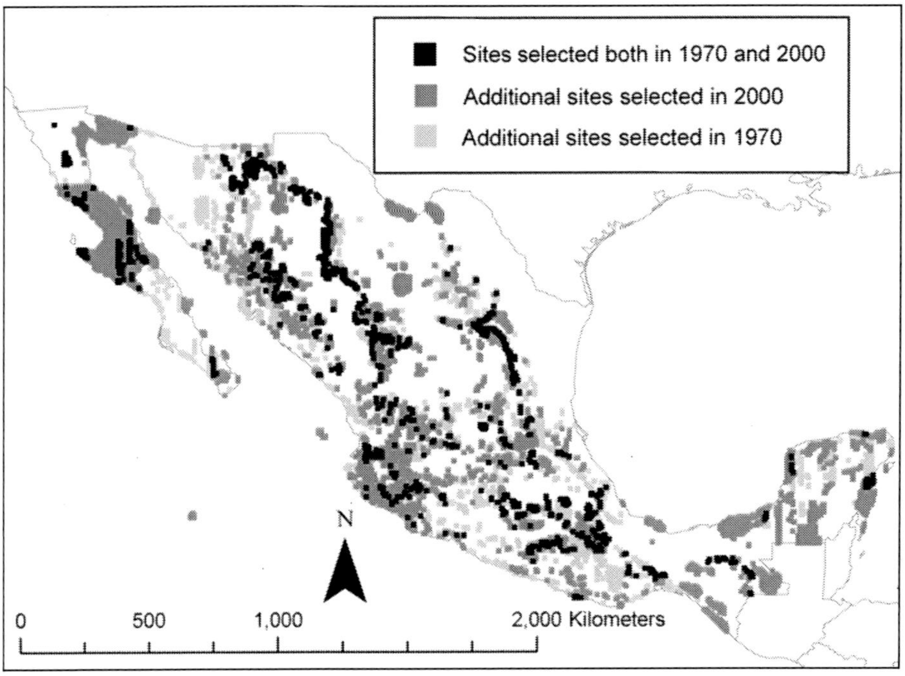

Figure 6. Optimal conservation areas for Mexican endemic mammals in 1970 and 2000 obtained by including 10% of each species' potential distribution. The optimization was initialized with the natural protected areas. Note the large amount of additional conservation area required to conserve the same number of endemics in 2000 (dark gray) compared to 1970 (light gray). Taken from Fuller *et al.* (2007).

Deforestation and the Cost of Postponing Biodiversity Conservation

As in many other developing countries, land conversion in México during the last thirty years has been extensive. Tropical and temperate forests in México are disappearing at high annual rates (Masera *et al.*, 1997; Mendoza *et al.*, 1999) with increasing agricultural lands, shrubs, and pastures for cattle (Bocco *et al.*, 2001). These reductions of natural habitat can extirpate many vertebrates such as mammals from regions severely affected by deforestation (Peterson *et al.*, 2006). Conversion to agricultural use creates habitat that is typically unsuitable for at-risk mammal species (Ceballos *et al.*, 2005; Sánchez-Cordero *et al.*, 2005; Stoleson *et al.*, 2005), which is particularly critical, as Mexico's mammal fauna ranks second in richness worldwide, and of which 30% is endemic (Fa and Morales, 1993). Moreover, Mexican endemic mammals are of special conservation concern because they are underrepresented in international treaties about at-risk species (Ceballos *et al.*, 2002).

Recently, a database with remote-sensed data was created for the extent and rate of LULCC in Mexico, which includes nationwide land use and vegetation maps since the 1970s (Sorani and Alvarez, 1996; Mas *et al.*, 2004; see www.igeograf.unam.mx, and www.conabio.gob.mx). However, such data do not indicate how land conversion affects strategies for the conservation of biodiversity (Kinnaird *et al.*, 2003). In particular, the effects of land use change on the required size of adequate biodiversity conservation area networks were largely unknown. We combined the database on land conversion with ecological niche modeling of 86 Mexican endemic mammals projected as species' distributions, and (1) analyzed distributional shifts in the recent past by quantifying the impact of land use patterns on species' distributions from 1970 to 2000, and (2) assessed how shifts in species' ranges affect the design of optimal conservation area networks. We hypothesized that deforestation resulting in reduction and fragmentation of natural habitats has a cost in the amount of land that must be placed under protection to represent mammalian biodiversity today. We predicted that a greater area of land would be required today compared to the area that would have been required to protect endemic mammals at equivalent levels thirty years ago using the same target level of representation of the species in both cases (Fuller *et al.*, 2007).

Our main results verify this prediction and indicate that significantly more land is required to represent mammal habitat in 2000 than when sites are selected with the 1970 distribution (41 *vs* 89 %, respectively), and > 60 % of the optimal conservation areas that would have been selected in 1970 had been transformed by 2000. Moreover, for 90% of the endemic mammals, the potential distributions in 2000 comprised fewer sites than the potential distribution in 1970. If a conservation area network had been implemented even as late as 1970, mammal habitat could have been protected in a considerably smaller set of sites than what is required today owing to land degradation and concomitant thinning of species' ranges. Consequently, area prioritization for biodiversity conservation is negatively affected by deforestation because a significantly increased area is required to conserve these endemics compared to what would have been adequate 30 years ago before significant loss of forest cover.

CONCLUSION

In sum, deforestation has dramatic negative effects on species' distributions, biogeographic regionalization, the performance of NPAs, and the design of conservation area networks. All these factors emphasize the threat to biodiversity conservation posed by deforestation. These trends urge immediate collaborative actions involving academic, governmental, and NGO sectors to prevent and reduce further deforestation nationwide. These conclusions are hardly new but the methods we have developed allowed us to quantify all these effects. This quantification required the systematic use of remote-sensed data, GIS platforms, and a variety of algorithms and other computer-aided techniques. Moreover, our analyses can be linked with recent theoretical framework in conservation as systematic conservation planning (Margules and Sarkar, 2007) to facilitate implementation at regional and local scales requiring immediate conservation actions. Though our analyses were all performed in the context of México, the methodologies developed were fully general and can be exported unchanged to any other (terrestrial) context. Other biodiversity hotspots that are experiencing deforestation at a rate at least as high as that of Mexico include Burma, Ecuador, Indonesia, the Phillipines, and Sri Lanka (Myers *et al.*, 2000; United Nations Food and Agriculture Association, 2007). The findings presented here on the cost of postponing biodiversity conservation in Mexico may also apply to those other hotspots. Testing this hypothesis will require the construction of a multidate database on LULCC, which are not presently available for most developing countries.

REFERENCES

Anderson, R. P., Lew, D. & Peterson, A.T. (2003). Evaluating predictive models of species distributions: criteria for selecting optimal models. Ecological Modelling, 162, 211–232.

Arriaga, L., Espinosa-Rodríguez, J. M., Aguilar-Zúñiga, C., Martínez-Romero, E., Gómez-Mendoza, L. & Loa Loza, E. (2001). Regiones Prioritarias Terrestres de México. Comisión Nacional para el Conocimiento y Uso de la Biodiversidad. México, D. F.

D. F.Barbier, E. B. & Burgess, J. C. (1996). Economic analysis of deforestation in Mexico. Environment and Development Economics, 1, 203-239.

Barbier, E. B. & Burgess, J. C. (2001). The economics of tropical deforestation. Journal of Economic Surveys, 15, 413-433.

Bocco, G., Mendoza, M., & Velázquez, A. (2001). Remote sensing and GIS-based regional geomorphological mapping – a tool for land use planning in developing countries. Geomorphology 39, 211–219.

Brandon, K., Gorenflo, L. J., Rodrigues, A. S. L. & Waller, R. W. (2005). Reconciling biodiversity conservation, people, protected areas, and agricultural suitability. World Development, 33, 1403-1418.

Cantú, C., Wright, R. G., Scott, J. M. & Strand, E. (2004). Assessment of current and proposed nature reserves of Mexico based on their capacity to protect geophysical features and biodiversity. Biological Conservation, 115, 411-417.

Carey, C., Dudley, N. & Stolton, S. (2000). Squandering paradise? WWF, Gland.

Ceballos, G. & Rodríguez, P. (1993). Diversidad y conservación de los mamíferos de México. II. Patrones de endemicidad. In: Ceballos, G. & Medellín, R.A. (Eds.), Avances en el Estudio de los Mamíferos de México. Publicaciones Especiales No. 1. Asociación Mexicana de Mastozoología, A.C., México D. F. pp. 87–108.

Ceballos, G., Rodríguez, P. & Medellin, R. A. (1998). Assessing conservation priorities in megadiverse Mexico: mammalian diversity, endemicity, and endangerment. Ecological Applications, 8, 8-17.

Ceballos, G., Arroyo-Cabrales, J. & Medellín, R.A. (2002). The mammals of México: composition, distribution, and conservation status. Occasional Papers, Museum of Texas Tech University 218, 1–27.

Ceballos, G., List, R., Pacheco, J., Manzano-Fischer, P., Santos, G. & Royo, M. (2005). Prarie dogs, cattle, and crops: diversity and conservation of the grassland-shrubland habitat mosaic in Northwestern Chihuahua. In: Cartron, J.-L.E., Ceballos, G. & Felger, R.S. (Eds.), Biodiversity, Ecosystems, and Conservation in Northern Mexico. Oxford University Press, New York, pp. 425-438.

Challenger, A. (1998). Utilización y conservación de los ecosistemas terrestres de México: Pasado, presente y futuro. Comisión Nacional para el Conocimiento y Uso de la Biodiversidad, Instituto de Biología, Universidad Nacional Autónoma de México. México D. F.

Chase, T. N., Pielke, R. A., Kittel, T. G. F., Nemani, R. R. & Running, S.W. (2000). Simulated impacts of historical land cover changes on global climate in northern winter. Climate Dynamics, 16, 93-105.

CONANP. Comisión Nacional de Áreas Naturales Protegidas. (2003). Mapa de Áreas Naturales Protegidas Federales de México, 1:250,000. Secretaría de Medio Ambiente, Recursos Naturales y Pesca, México, D. F.

Cooney, R. & Dickson, R. (2005). Biodiversity and the Precautionary Principle: Risk and Uncertainty Analysis in Conservation and Sustainable Use. Earthscan, London.

Dale, V. H., Pearson, S. M., Offerman, H. L. & O'Neill, R. V. (1994). Relating patterns of land-use change to faunal biodiversity in the Central Amazon. Conservation Biology, 8, 1024-1036.

Dirzo, R. & García, M. C. (1992). Rates of deforestation in Los Tuxtlas, a Neotropical area in southeast Mexico. Conservation Biology, 6, 84–90.

Egbert, S. L., Peterson, A. T., Sánchez-Cordero, V. & Price, K. (1999). Modeling conservation priorities in Veracruz, Mexico. In: Morain, S. (Ed.), GIS Solutions in Natural Resource Management. OnWord Press, Santa Fe, New Mexico. pp. 141–150.

Escalante, T., Sánchez-Cordero, V., Morrone, J. J. & Linaje, M. (2007a). Areas of endemism of Mexican terrestrial mammals: A case study using species' ecological niche modeling, Parsimony Analysis of Endemicity and Goloboff fit. Interciencia, 32, 151-159.

Escalante, T., Sánchez-Cordero, V., Morrone, J. J. & Linaje, M. (2007b). Deforestation affects biogeographical regionalization: A case study contrasting potential and extant distributions of Mexican terrestrial mammals. Journal of Natural History, 41, 965-984.

Ervin, J. (2003). Protected Area Assessments in Perspective. Bioscience, 53, 819-822. Fa, J. & Morales, L. (1993). Patterns of mammalian diversity in Mexico. In: Ramamoorthy, T., Bye, R., Lot, A. & Fa, J. (Eds.), Biological Diversity of Mexico: Origins and Distribution. Oxford University Press, Oxford, pp. 319–364.

Fa, J. & Morales, L. (1993). Patterns of mammalian diversity in Mexico. In: Ramamoorthy, T., Bye, R., Lot, A. & Fa, J. (Eds.), Biological Diversity of Mexico: Origins and Distribution. Oxford University Press, Oxford. pp. 319–364.

Fuller, T., Mayfield, M., Munguía, M., Sánchez-Cordero, V. & Sarkar, S. (2006). Incorporating connectivity into conservation planning: A multi-criteria case study from Central Mexico. Biological Conservation, 133,131-142.

Fuller, T., Sánchez-Cordero, V., Illoldi-Rangel, P., Linaje, M. & Sarkar, S. (2007). The cost of postponing biodiversity conservation. Biological Conservation, 134,593-600.

Geist, H. J. & Lambin, E. F. (2002). Proximate and underlying driving forces of tropical deforestation. Biosicience, 52, 143-150.

Ghimire, K. B. & Pimbert, M. P. (1997). Social change and conservation: an overview of issues and concepts. In: Ghimire, K. B. & Pimbert, M. P. (Eds.), Social Change & Conservation. Earthscan Publications, London, pp. 1-45.

Grinnell, J. (1917). The niche-relationship of the California thrasher. Auk, 43, 427–433.

Hall, E. R. (1981). The Mammals of North America, vols. 1 and 2. Ronald Press, New York.

Heaney, L. R., Balete, D. S., Rickart, E., Utzurrum, R. C. B. & Gonzalez, P.C. (1999). Mammalian diversity on Mount Isarog: a threatened center of endemism on southern Luzon Island, Phillippines. Fieldiana Zoology, 95, 1–62.

Hilton-Taylor, C. (Ed.), 2000. 2000 IUCN Red List of Threatened Species. IUCN Gland, Switerland.

Hockings, M. (1998). Evaluating management of protected areas: integrating planning and evaluation. Environmental Management, 22, 3, 337-345.

Hockings, M. (2003). Systems for assessing the effectiveness of management in protected areas. Bioscience, 53, 823-832.

Holt, R. D. (1990). The microevolutionary consequences of climate change. Trends in Ecology and Evolution, 5, 311-315.

Houghton, R. A., Hackler, J. L. & Lawrence, K. T. (1999). The U. S. carbon budget: contributions from land-use change. Science, 285, 574-578.

Illoldi-Rangel, P., Sánchez-Cordero, V. & Peterson, A. T. (2004). Predicting distributions of Mexican mammals using ecological niche modeling. Journal of Mammalogy 85, 658–662.

INEGI. (1993). Carta II de uso del suelo y vegetación, serie II, 1:250,000. Instituto Nacional de Estadística, Geografía e Informática, Dirección General de Geografía, Aguascalientes.

INEGI. (2005). Conjunto de datos vectoriales de uso de suelo y vegetación. 1:250,000, serie 3 (continuo nacional). Instituto Nacional de Estadística Geografía e Informática, Aguascalientes.

Isaac, N. J. B. & Cowlishaw, G. (2004). How species respond to multiple extinctions threats. Proceedings of the Royal Society of London B, 271, 1135–1141.

Islam, K. R. & Weil, R. R. (2000). Land use effects on soil quality in a tropical forest ecosystem of Bangladesh. Agriculture, Ecosystems & Environment, 79, 9-16.

IUCN. World Conservation Union. (2005). Benefits Beyond Boundaries: Proceedings of the Vth IUCN World Parks Congress. Durban: Vth IUCN World Parks Congress.

Kinnaird, M. F., Sanderson, E. W., O'Brien, T. G., Wibisono, H. T. & Woolmer, G. (2003). Deforestation trends in a tropical landscape and implications for endangered large mammals. Conservation Biology, 17, 245-257.

Lambin, E. F., Turner, B. L., Helmut, J. G., Agbola, S. B., Angelsen, A., Bruce, J. W., Coomes, O. T., Dirzo, R., Fischer, G., Folke, C., George, P. S., Homewood, K., Imbernon, J., Leemans, R., Li, X., Moran, E. F., Mortimore, M., Ramakrishnan, P. S., Richards, J. F., Skanes, H., Steffen, W., Stone, G. D., Svedin, U., Veldkamp, T. A., Vogel, C. & Xu, J. (2001). The causes of land-use and land-cover change: moving beyond the myths. Global Environmental Change, 11, 261-269.

Laurance, W. F. & Bierregaard, R. O. (1997). Tropical Forest Remnants: Ecology, Management, and Conservation of Fragmented Communities. University of Chicago Press, Chicago.

Laurance, W. F., Croes, B. M., Tchignoumba, L., Lahm, S. A., Alonso, A., Lee, M. E., Campbell, P., & Ondzeano, C. (2006). Impacts of roads and hunting on Central African rainforest mammals. Conservation Biology, 20, 1251-1261.

Lidlaw, R. K. (2000). Effects of habitat disturbance and protected areas of mammals of peninsular Malaysia. Conservation Biology, 14, 1639-1648.

MacArthur, R. H. (1972). Geographical Ecology: Patterns in the Distribution of Species. Princeton University Press, Princeton, New Jersey.

Mace, G. M., Balmford, A. & Ginsberg, J. R. (1998). Conservation in a Changing World. Oxford University Press, New York.

Mas, J.-F., Velazquez, A., Diaz-Gallegos, J.-R., Mayorga-Saucedo, R., Alcantara, C., Bocco, G., Castro, R., Fernandez, T. & Pérez-Vega, A. (2004). Assessing land use/cover changes: a nationwide multidate spatial database for Mexico. International Journal of Applied Earth Observation and Geoinformation, 5, 249-261.

Mas, J. (2005). Assessing protected area effectiveness using surrounding (buffer) areas environmentally similar to the target area. Environmental Monitoring and Assessment, 105, 69-80.

Masera, O.R., Ordóñez, M.J., & Dirzo, R. (1997). Carbon emissions from Mexican forests: current situation and long-term scenarios. Climatic Change, 35, 265-295.

Margules, C., & S. Sarkar. (2007). Systematic Conservation Planning. Camridge University Press. 270 pp.

Mendoza, E., Fay, J. & Dirzo, R. (1999). Deforestation in Lacandonia (southeast Mexico): evidence for the declaration of the northernmost tropical hot-spot. Biodiversity and Conservation, 8, 1621-1641.

Mittermeier, R. A., Myers, N., Thomsen, J. B., da Fonseca, G. A. B. & Olivieri, S. (1998). Biodiversity hotspots and major tropical wilderness areas: approaches to setting conservation priorities. Conservation Biology 12: 516-520.

Morrone, J. J. (1994). On the identification of areas of endemism. Systematic Biology, 43,438-441.

Myers, N. (1998). Global biodiversity priorities and expanded conservation policies. In: Mace, G. M., Balmford, A. & Ginsberg, J. R. (Eds.) Conservation in a Changing World. Oxford University Press, New York. pp. 273-286.

Myers, N., Mittermeier, R.A., Mittermeier, C.G., da Fonseca, G.A.B. & Kent, J. (2000). Biodiversity hotspots for conservation priorities. Nature 403, 853-858.

Nadal, A. (2003). Natural protected areas and social marginalization in Mexico. CEESP Occasional Papers, 1, 1-28.

Ortega-Huerta, M. & Peterson, A. T. (2004). Modeling spatial patterns of biodiversity for conservation prioritization in North-eastern Mexico. Diversity and Distributions 10, 39–54.

Peterson, A. T., Egbert, S. L., Sánchez-Cordero, V. & Price, K. P. (2000). Geographic analysis of conservation priority: endemic birds and mammals in Veracruz, Mexico. Biological Conservation, 93, 85-94.

Peterson, A. T. (2001). Predicting species geographic distributions based on ecological niche modeling. Condor, 103, 599-605.

Peterson, A. T. & Vieglais, D. A. (2001). Predicting species invasions using ecological niche modeling. BioScience, 51, 363–371.

Peterson, A. T., Soberón, J., & Sánchez-Cordero, V. (1999). Conservatism of ecological niches in evolutionary time. Science 285,1265-1267.

Peterson A. T, Ball L. G, & Cohoon K. P. (2002). Predicting distributions of Mexican birds using ecological niche modelling methods. Ibis [online]144, E27-E32.

Peterson, A. T. & Holt, R. D. (2003). Niche differentiation in Mexican birds: using point occurrences to detect ecological innovation. Ecology Letters, 6, 774–782.

Peterson, A. T., Sánchez-Cordero, V., Martínez-Meyer, E. & Navarro-Siguenza, A. (2006). Tracking population extirpations via melding ecological niche modeling with land-cover information. Ecological Modeling, 195,229-236.

Pressey, R. L., Wish, G. L., Barret, T. W. & Watts, M. E. (2002). Effectiveness of protected areas in north-eastern New South Wales: recent trends in six measures. Biological Conservation, 106, 57-69.

Reaka-Kudla, M. L., Wilson, D. E. & Wilson, E. O. (1997). Biodiversity II: Understanding and Protecting Our Biological Resources. Joseph Henry Press, Washington, D.C.

Riezebos, H. T. & Loerts A. C. (1998). Influence of land use change and tillage practice on soil organic matter. Soil & Tillage Research, 49, 271-275.

Rodrigues, A. S. L., Andelman, S. J., Bakarr, M. I., Boitani, L., Brooks, T. M., Cowling, R. M., Fishpool, L. D. C., da Fonseca, G. A. B., Gaston, K. J., Hoffmann, M., Long, J. S., Marquet, P. A., Pilgrim, J. D., Pressey, R. L., Schipper, J., Sechrest, W., Stuart, S. N., Underhill, L. G., Waller, R. W., Watts, M. E. J., Yan, X. (2004). Effectiveness of the global protected area network in representing species diversity. Nature, 428, 640-643.

Sala, O. E., Chapin III, F. S., Armeso, J. J., Berlow, E., Bloomfield, J., Dirzo, R., Huber-Sanwald, E., Huenneke, L. F., Jackson, R. B., Kinzig, A., Leemans, R., Lodge, D. M., Mooney, H. A., Oesterheld, M., LeRoy Poff, N., Sykes, M. T., Walker, B. H., Walker, M. & Wall, D. H. (2000). Global biodiversity scenarios for the year 2100. Science, 287, 1770-1774.

Sánchez-Cordero, V., Peterson, A. T. & Escalante-Pliego, P. (2001). El modelado de la distribución de especies y la conservación de la diversidad biológica. In: Hernández, H. M., García-Aldrete, A. N., Alvarez, F. & Ulloa, M. (Eds.), Enfoques contemporáneos para el estudio de la biodiversidad. Ediciones Científicas Universitarias Fondo de Cultura Económica, Academia Mexicana de Ciencias, A.C., Instituto de Biología, Universidad Nacional Autónoma de México. México, D. F. México, pp. 359–379.

Sánchez-Cordero, V. & García-Zepeda, S. (2003). Modeling rodent pests distributions in Mexico. In: Singleton, G. R., Hinds, I. A., Krebs, C. J. & Spratt, D. M. (Eds.), Rats, Mice, and People: Rodent Biology and Management. Australian Centre for International Agricultural Research, Canberra, Australia. pp. 526–528.

Sánchez-Cordero, V., Munguía, M. & Peterson, A. T. (2004). GIS-based predictive biogeography in the context of conservation. In: Lomolino, M. & Heaney, L. R. (Eds.), Frontiers in Biogeography. Sinauer Assocaites, Sunderland, Massachusetts, USA, pp. 311–323.

Sánchez-Cordero, V., Illoldi-Rangel, P., Linaje, M., Sarkar, S. & Peterson, A.T. (2005). Deforestation and extant distributions of Mexican endemic mammals. Biological Conservation 126, 465-473.

Sánchez-Cordero, V. & Figueroa, F. 2007. La efectividad de las reservas de la biosfera en MÉXICO para contener procesos de cambio en el uso del suelo y la vegetación. In: Halffter, G. & Guevara, S. (Eds.), Hacia una Cultura de Conservación de la Diversidad Biológica, Sociedad Entomológica Aragonesa, CONABIO, CONANP, CONACyT, Instituto de Ecología, A. C., MAB-UNESCO, Ministerio de Medio Ambiente-Gobierno de España, Zaragoza, España. pp. 161-171.

Sánchez-Cordero, V., Figueroa, F., Illoldi-Rangel, P. & Linaje, M. 2007. Efectividad de una selección de áreas protegidas para conservar la vegetación primaria y evitar el incremento de las áreas transformadas. In: CONABIO-CONANP-TNC-PRONATURA, FCF &

UANL (Eds.), Análisis de vacíos y omisiones en conservación de la biodiversidad terrestres de México: espacios y especies. Comisión Nacional para la Conservación y Uso de la Biodiversidad, Comisión Nacional de Areas Naturales Protegidas, The Nature Conservancy-Programa México, Probatura, A.C., Facultad de Ciencias Forestales, Universidad Autónoma de Nuevo León, México. pp. 53-56.

Sarakinos, H., Nicholls, A. O., Tubert, A., Aggarwal, A., Margules, C. R. & Sarkar, S. (2001). Area prioritization for biodiversity conservation in Québec on the basis of species distributions: a preliminary analysis. Biodiversity and Conservation, 10, 1419 -1472.

Sarkar, S. (2004). Conservation Biology. In Zalta, E. N., (ed.), Stanford Encyclopedia of Philosophy. Winter 2004 ed.http://plato.stanford.edu/archives/win2004/entries/ conservation-biology/

Sarukhán, J., Soberón, J. & Larson, J. (1996). Biological conservation in a high beta-diversity country. In: di Castri, F. & Younes, T. (Eds.), Biodiversity, Science and Development. Towards a new partnership. CAB International / IUBS, Paris. pp. 246-263.

Soberón, J. & Peterson, A. T. (2005) Interpretation of models of fundamental ecological niches and species' distributional areas. Biodiversity Informatics, 2, 1-10.

Soberón, J. (2007) Grinnellian and Eltonian niches and geographic distributions of species. Ecology Letters, 10, 1115-1123.

Sorani, V. & Alvarez, R. (1996). Hybrid maps: a solution for updating of forest cartography with satellite images and existing information. Geocarto International 11, 17-23.

Stockwell, D.R.B. & Peters, D. (1999). The GARP modelling system: problems and solutions to automated spatial prediction. International Journal of Geographical Information Science, 13, 143-158.

Stoleson, S.H., Felger, R.S., Ceballos, G., Raish, C., Wilson, M.F. & Búrquez, A. (2005). Recent history of natural resource use and population growth in Northern Mexico. In: Cartron, J.-L.E., Ceballos, G. & Felger, R.S. (Eds.), Biodiversity, Ecosystems, and Conservation in Northern Mexico. Oxford University Press, New York, pp. 52–86.

Toledo, V. M., Carabias, J. & González-Pacheco, C. (1989). La Producción Rural en México. Alternativas Ecológicas. Ed. Universo Siglo 21, México, D. F.

United Nations Food and Agriculture Organization (2007). State of the World's Forests. United Nations Food and Agriculture Association, Rome, Italy.

Vitousek, P. M., Mooney, H. A., Lubchenco, J. & Melillo, J. M. (1997). Human domination of earth's ecosystems. Science, 277, 494-499.

Wilson, E. O. (1988). Biodiversity. National Academy Press, Washington, D.C.

In: Endangered Species: New Research
Editors: A. Columbus and L. Kuznetsov
ISBN 978-1-60692-241-5

Chapter 12

ARE ANIMALS IN ZOOS RATHER CONSPICUOUS THAN ENDANGERED?

D.Frynta, J. Marešová, E. Landová, S. Lišková, O. Šimková, I. Tichá, M. Zelenková, and R. Fuchs

Ecology and Ethology Group, Department of Zoology, Faculty of Science, Charles University, Viničná 7, CZ-128 44 Praha 2, Czech Republic;
e-mail: frynta@centrum.cz

ABSTRACT

The chapter challenges the assumption that humans generally treat all animal species equally according to their need of conservation. We reviewed recent studies suggesting that humans show strong preferences toward particular animal species/taxa and are willing to protect them more than others. Such understanding of human preferences is an important part of conservation strategies.

The main body of the chapter is based on original data analyses performed separately for main reptile, bird and mammalian taxa. The representation of animal taxa in zoos and sizes of zoo populations are reviewed. Human preferences to particular species and/or families were examined directly by presenting their picture to the respondents. The results showed that factors affecting human aesthetic preferences toward particular species differ among higher taxonomic groups. We concluded that animal attractiveness (both body size and beauty itself) influences human effort devoted to ex situ breeding projects more than inclusion in Red book lists. Special attention has to be paid to less preferred, but endangered species. Fortunately, the highly preferred species are present in almost every family and also among threatened species. Thus, the zoos can replace preferred but common species by endangered one that reaches both, conservation as well as visitor's aesthetic criteria.

1. INTRODUCTION

Captive breeding has enabled survival of numerous species facing extinction. The stories of such species as California condor (*Gymnogyps californianus*), Hawaiian goose (*Branta sandvicensis*), black-footed ferret (*Mustela nigripes*), Guam rail (*Gallirallus owstoni*), Lord Howe Island woodhen (*Gallirallus sylvestris*), golden lion tamarin (*Leonthopithecus rosalia*), European bison (*Bos bonasus*), addax (*Addax naomaculatus*), scimitar-horned oryx (*Oryx dammah*), Arabian oryx (*Oryx leocoryx*), southern white rhino (*Ceratotherium simum simum*) or Przewalski's horse (*Equus przewalskii*) are well-known textbook examples (cf. Frankham et al. 2002, Frankham 2008). Many of these species were saved owing to few individuals unintentionally kept in various zoos, private farms and circuses. At the time of the crisis, these animals became founders of rescue breeding programs. Nowadays the proportion of potentially endangered species is rapidly increasing and in fact no species is actually safe from possible disaster (Wilson et al. 2002). Thus the maintenance of captive populations is a form of survival insurance.

Some reintroduction programs were fairly successful (e.g., Denton et al. 1997, Brighsmith et al. 2005, White et al.2005, Bertolero et al. 2007, Brown et al. 2007, but see Price and Fa 2007). Nevertheless, the value of zoo populations as a source for future reintroduction may be questioned (e.g., Jule et al. 2008). Captive populations are affected by unintended behavioral (McDougall et al. 2006), morphological (O'Regan and Kitchener 2005, Connolly and Cree 2008) and genetic adaptations (Frankham 2008) to captivity. Most damaging are usually the loose of genetic variation and inbreeding (for review see Frankham et al. 2002). However, these problems as well as those associated with obtaining enough individuals for successful reintroduction event may be avoided by keeping source populations of sufficient size (i.e., hundreds or thousands specimens).

It is, however, not self-evident that any endangered species will be kept in sufficient numbers. Zoos are luxury hotels in the world full of animal refugees. Consequently, there is an excess of species in need and accommodation capacity is strictly limited (Soulé 1986, Wilson 1992, Tudge 1995). Moreover, new zoo exhibits tend to be larger and support markedly fewer individuals than the older ones (Baker 2007) as legal standards of welfare and veterinary care become more and more strict. As a result of these requirements the costs of keeping animals tend to gradually rise. This further escalates competition among animal species for ex situ breeding programs and increases the role of human decision making (Cohn 1992). The winners may be the species that satisfy human aesthetic and emotional requirements, rather than those most vulnerable. Moreover, fashon may further enhance risky fluctuations in captive populations of endangered species in a similar manner as reported in breeds of domestic dogs (Herzog et al. 2004).

Thorough analysis of reintroduction projects (Seddon et al. 2005) demonstrated apparent taxonomic bias, e.g., some attractive vertebrate taxa as mammals (especially artiodactyls and carnivores) and birds (anseriforms, falconiforms, gruiforms and galliforms) are overrepresented. As a result, species composition of future biota is more and more affected by an artificial species selection.

Animals have been an integral component of the human environment and culture from the very beginning of our species. Even illiterate hunter-gatherers were able to name and categorize animal species in a very similar way as contemporary scientists (Berlin 1992). Evolutionary psychologists suggest that our mind is evolutionarily prepared to respond to animal stimuli (Barkow et al. 1992). There is an innate predisposition to easily learn fear of snakes and spiders (Davey et al. 1998), and on the other hand, people experience positive emotions toward other taxa. It is not accidental that large herbivores, domestic animals and birds frequently occurred in paintings since the Pleistocene (Lewis-Williams 2002, Guthrie

2005) up to the Modern Age (Baenninger 1988, Barkow et al. 1992). Both positive and negative emotions raise human interest in the particular species. It should be emphasized that the vast majority of species are inevitably neglected by us. Anthropologists and ethnobiologists demonstrated in tribal societies that the number of generic names, each representing an independent concept of an animal, usually do not exceed 500 units (for a review see Berlin 1992). Thus our mental capacity devoted to animals is scant in view of the worldwide diversity of the vertebrate genera. Consequently, the endangered species compete with one another for our attention that may help them by providing financial and political support for conservation projects.

As a rule, distribution of any conservation effort and willingness to support varies greatly from species to species. Funding decisions by FWS (Federal Wildlife Service) are not related to a species recovery priority rank (Simon et al. 1995). The U.S. federal government's protection and spending decisions concerning individual species are based more on "visceral" characteristics of the species (i.e. physical size and the degree to which the species is considered to be a "higher form of life") than on "scientific" ones (i.e. degree of endangerment and "taxonomic uniqueness") (Metrick & Weitzman 1996). Incredibly, a 10% increase in body length is associated with an 8.6% rise in funding. Sometimes, human willingness to protect a species may even negatively correlate with the degree of endangerment. Metrick and Weitzman (1998) reported this phenomenon in public comments on the changes in the Red List. There is more public support for saving species perceived as attractive, larger in size (Gunnthorsdottir 2001) and resembling humans (Samples et al. 1986).

Animal taxa differ also in its social construction and political power (expressed as, e.g., number of NGOs supporting particular animals). Birds receive the highest public support among vertebrates; however, mammals and fish also belong to "advantaged" taxa. In contrast, amphibians and reptiles (except turtles and tortoises) receive almost no support (Czech et al. 1998, see also Kellert 1985).

Humans are able to differentiate between attractive and unattractive animals, e.g., cat or tiger faces from early childhod (Quinn et al. 2008). Interestingly, nearly all species reported by respondents as most preferred are mammals (Morris 1967). Although, human-animal relationships in zoos are more complex phenomenon (Hosey 2008), popularity of zoo animals may be successfully explained by simple traits as body size (Ward et al. 1998). Plethora additional hypotheses were proposed (e.g., Morris 1967) to explain differential attractiveness of animal species for humans: most studied were the effects of juvenile body proportions (Gould 1979, Pittenger 1990), form close to average (Halberstadt and Rhodes 2003) and conspicuous coloration (e.g., Van Hook 1997, Stokes 2007).

Although perceived attractiveness of animal species is easy to quantify and its potential consequences for conservation practice are fundamental, little attention has been paid to these issues so far. Moreover, existing studies usually suffer from comparisons among unrelated groups of animals and small number of compared species. Quantitative studies carried out on a finer taxonomic scale are therefore needed.

Recently we studied the influence of factors putatively enhancing sensory stimulation of human observers (i.e., zoo visitors and/or keepers) on ex-situ conservation efforts. We analyzed worldwide zoo populations of boas and pythons; we have found strong positive effects of perceived attractiveness on the zoo population size of the species worldwide (Marešová and Frynta 2008).

Although, we are conscious that local culture may affect human preferences toward animal species, an elementary cross-cultural agreement could be reasonably expected. This assumption derived from evolutionary psychological theory (Barkow et al. 1992) should, however, be subjected to further testing. Our preliminary data reveal surprisingly close correspondence between rankings of snake species by people from so different cultures as are those in Europe and Papua New Guinea (Marešová, Krása and Frynta, unpublished results).

In this chapter we examine population sizes of animals in zoos worldwide. We focus on three classes of terrestrial vertebrates (Amniota): reptiles, birds and mammals, and analyze factors affecting representation of these animals in zoos. Besides taxonomic bias (uneven representation of particular taxa) and representation of endangered species, we paid special attention to body size and perceived attractiveness of zoo animals.

2. Data Sources and Testing Procedures

To avoid problems with uncertain nomenclature and taxonomy, we used the following species lists which are nowadays widely accepted by vertebrate zoologists: Wilson and Reeder (2005, available on http://nmnhgoph.si.edu/msw/) for mammals, Masi (1996, available on http://www.scricciolo.com/classificazione/sibley's_index.htm) and The BirdLife Checklist (The BirdLife Taxonomic Working Group (BTWG), 2008; based mainly on Sibley and Monroe (1990, 1993); available on http://www.birdlife.org/datazone/species/taxonomy.html) for birds and The TIGR Reptile Database for reptiles (Uetz et al. 2008; available on http://www.reptile-database.org). The extinct and domestic animals (dog, cat, cow, horse, goat, sheep, camels, lamas, pig, laboratory mouse, rat, guinea pig, hen, turkey, goose and duck) were excluded, although some of them may be viewed as endangered (Taberlet et al. 2008). The IUCN status of all species was obtained from the official IUCN website (IUCN 2008; http://www.iucnredlist.org). The above species lists do not match one another exactly and also their agreement with taxonomies used by zoos is limited. To avoid mistakes we resolved these disparities ad hoc, and therefore the total numbers of species in particular taxa may a bit deviate from that found in the original databases.

The population size of each species in worldwide zoo collections was obtained from The International Species Information System database (ISIS, http:// www.isis.org, downloaded on 1 January 2008). It seems to be the only relevant public source covering approximately 650 zoos and aquaria all over the world.

It may be argued that the database does not include all keepers as some local zoos as well as private breeders are not comprised. However, we consider the institutions participating in ISIS to be the most important since they support a much larger number of animals, at least in the case of some larger species, compared with that kept by the other breeders. Last but not least, breeding programs of these credible institutions are well coordinated and attract the attention of the general public and the media, thus helping the selected species gain additional support. The number of individuals kept in zoos provides therefore a good estimate of the conservation efforts.

To assess human preferences towards animal species, we asked our respondents (mostly students from various faculties of the Charles University in Prague) to sort particular sets of pictures and rank the animals according to the perceived aesthetic attractiveness (beauty) following method of Marešova and Frynta (2008).

We carried out these analyses at two different levels: (1) Species, by comparing particular species within a family (pythons and boas – Boidae, pheasants – Phasianidae, antelopes and allies – Bovidae) or an order (turtles – Testudines); (2) higher taxa, by comparing families or sufamilies, each represented by a randomly selected species (see under Effects of perceived attractiveness and body size on higher taxonomic scale; Table 3).

For statistical analyses we used STATISTICA 6.0, StatSoft Inc. (2001). Prior the statistical analyses, the data were normalized when necessary; population and body sizes were log-transformed, while relative ranks of pictures were square-root arcsin transformed. Either GLM models or Multiple Linear Regression were applied. The agreement in ranking the pictures was visualized by Principal Component Analysis (PCA). The percentage of explained variability by the first principle component (PC1) was used to quantify the congruence among the respondents.

3. Representation of Vertebrate Classes in Zoos

It has been previously demonstrated that the vertebrate species kept in zoos are unequally distributed among higher taxa. Mammals and birds are obviously overrepresented while amphibians and fishes tend to be underrepresented (e.g., Price and Fa 2007, Leader-Williams 2007). Nevertheless, the differential representation of vertebrate taxa in the worldwide zoo population is worth further analyses. This is an obligatory step towards understanding the underlying processes that control the efficiency of ex situ conservation.

Even a first glance at the data (Table 1) is eloquent. The numbers of species kept in zoos are surprisingly high. As many as 1154 reptile, 2337 bird, and 990 mammalian species, representing 13.4%, 24.3%, and 18.5% of non-extinct species of these groups, respectively are listed among the zoo population.

The total numbers of individuals kept in zoos are about the same for birds and mammals (200 and 152 thousand, respectively), while the corresponding figure is nearly three times lower for reptiles (67 thousands). When the number of individuals kept in zoos was scaled to the total number of living species of the given class, the difference was even more evident. In zoos, there are just 7.80 reptiles, but 20.74 birds and even 28.45 mammals per living species. Only a small portion of this difference may be attributed to the fact that reptiles (as well as amphibians and fishes) are more frequently kept in small zoos and private collections which are not covered by the ISIS database. As mammals and birds are in general more active, possess higher metabolism (Schmidt-Nielsen 1984), need larger spaces and more keeper's care than reptiles and other cold-blooded vertebrates, their clear overrepresentation in zoos is in a strong contradiction to the elevated costs of their keeping (see also Balmford 2000). Obviously, this phenomenon reflects some kind of human preference in favor of these warm-blooded animals.

Table 1. Representation of reptiles, birds and mammals in zoos

Class:	Reptiles	Birds	Mammals
number of living species	8602	9627	5353
number of individuals in zoos	67073	199686	152314
number of species kept in zoos	1154	2337	990
number of species with zoo population size over 50	247	634	416
number of species with zoo population size over 500	28	80	79
number of zoo individuals per living species	7.8	20.7	28.5
% zoo species out of all living species	13.4	24.3	18.5
% species with zoo population size over 50 out of all living species	2.9	6.6	7.8
% species with zoo population size over 500 out of all living species	0.3	0.8	1.5
% zoo species with population size over 50 out of all zoo species	21.4	27.1	42.0
% zoo species with population size over 500 out of all zoo species	2.4	3.4	8.0
number of individuals in zoos/ n of species kept in zoos	58.1	85.5	153.9
mean size of zoo population computed from log-transformed data	12.6	14.5	30.3
median	12	13	34.5
lower quartile	3	3	6
upper quartile	39	57	141
H' (Index of diversity, Shannon and Wiener 1963)	5.543	6.152	5.671
J' (Index of equitability, Sheldon 1969)	0.786	0.793	0.822
H'/H'max (real biodiversity in zoos/maximal possible biodiversity)	0.612	0.671	0.660

We understand the network of zoos (cf. Field and Dickie 2007) as a specific habitat supporting specific synusy of the animals that may be studied by the methods adopted from the ecology of communities. We applied the standard indices of species diversity (H'; Shannon 1963; natural logarithms were used for the computations) and equitability (J'; Pielou 1966, Sheldon 1969). The former index increases with increasing number of species as well as with increasing equitability of their representation in the synusy (worldwide zoo network in our case). The latter one (ranging from 0 to 1) quantifies only the equitability component of diversity and is thus independent of on the number of species. It is the ratio between the observed H' and maximum theoretical value of H' computed for the observed number of species in a given sample. As the equitability assessed by J' omits the species which are not present in zoos by at least one individual, we computed an additional modified index of equitability (I) as the ratio between H' and the maximum theoretical H' computed for the total number of species in the taxon (class).

In general, the values of all the three indices were fairly similar among the studied classes of vertebrates. From this it follows that zoos are not extremely selective with respect to the vertebrate classes. There are, however, some remarkable differences. Birds as a specious group with the highest number of zoo species have a higher index of diversity (H'=6.15) than less specious mammals (5.67) and reptiles less represented in zoos (5.54). Surprisingly, our modified index of equitability also suggests that zoos support higher species diversity in the case of birds (I=0.671) and mammals (0.660), than in reptiles (0.612). In contrast, the standard index of equitability was somewhat higher in mammals (J'=0.822) than in birds (0.793) and reptiles (0.786). Thus, the biodiversity of warm bloodied vertebrates is better represented in zoos than that of reptiles, but the main reasons clearly differ between birds and mammals. These are high number of bird species kept in zoos, while fairly equal size of captive populations in the case of mammals.

4. SIZE OF CAPTIVE POPULATIONS

The worldwide zoo populations of most vertebrate species are extremely small (Table 1). Zoos keep on average 58, 85 and 154 individuals per one reptile, bird and mammalian species occurred in zoos, respectively. These figures are, however, much higher than those typical for zoo species of these taxa. It is due to log-normal distribution of zoo population sizes. When this statistical distribution is taken into account, the respective means decrease to 12.6, 14.5 and 30.3. One half of the reptile, bird and mammalian species have the worldwide zoo population smaller than median values 12, 13, and 34.5, respectively. Populations of such sizes are obviously not sustainable and stochastic demographic and genetic processes lead to their extinction or genetic degradation within a few generations nearly inevitably (Frankham et al. 2002) even in such improbable case that all kept animals take part in reproduction. It is really doubtful whether perpetuation of such small populations in captivity may play any beneficial role in ex situ conservation except attracting the public and providing an opportunity for zoo staff training and accumulation of skills in how to keep and breed a given species (for the role of zoos in conservation education see Sterling et al. 2007).

On the other hand, some successful rescue breeding projects started with only handful captive specimens. Sometimes, small number of founders was enough even for reestablishment of free-ranging population (e.g., Taylor et al. 2005). This is in accord with population genetic theory suggesting a few (>10) unrelated individuals of diploid species contain vast majority of the overall genetic variation of the large source population. Therefore, from purely genetic perspective even narrow bottlenecks followed by a rapid restoration of the population size are not as risky as prolonged maintenance of low or moderate population size (Frankham et al. 2002). Thus presence of just a few unrelated individuals in zoos may occasionally save the species if captive population is immediately expanded when necessary, e.g., after unexpected crisis of the wild populations (but see Hale and Briskie 2007 for negative effects of bottlenecking). The prerequisite that the founding animals have to be unrelated says in another words either obtained from nature or from another large captive population. This, however, requires blurring boundaries between captive and wild populations (Dickie et al. 2007).

Fundamental theory of population ecology suggests that removal of handful individuals have usually no deleterious effect on wild populations. In steady-state or increasing populations, the removed individuals are easily replaced by those born and/or survived due to relaxation of density dependent factors. Even in most declining populations, loose of few individuals does not matter. In spite of this, it is increasingly difficult to source animals from wild (Dickie et al. 2007). Administrative obstacles, usually resulting from misinterpretation and/or bureaucratic abuse of conservation legislation (Holst and Dickie 2007) prevent zoos to exchange the blood and captive populations of small size become inbred or extinct.

Population size is without any doubt the most important factor of population viability (Raup 1991, Wilson 1992, Frankham et al. 2002). Small populations are prone to rapid extinction especially due to stochastic demographic factors (Lande 1999) and negative effects of accumulation of deleterious mutations via genetic drift and/or inbreeding (Kimura 1983, Lande 1999, Rodrígez-Clarc1999, Frankham et al. 2002). Both these processes decrease sharply with increasing population size and thus large populations are much safer than the smaller ones. As the theory of population viability is complex and many parameters necessary for its estimates are usually not easily available for particular species, we adopted straightforward arbitrary criteria based solely on the size of the zoo population worldwide. Our approach was based on empirical experience that the minimum population size necessary for short-time captive maintenance of animal species/breed under controlled conditions is about 50 (Soulé 1980), and populations over about 500 individuals are not affected by inbreeding depression (Reed et al. 2007). Nevertheless, we keep in mind that the theory suggests rather continuous increase of the risks as well as its dependence on population history, generation time, and many other parameters (for review see Frankham et al. 2002). Moreover, estimates of minimum viable population are much larger: amphibian and reptiles 5,409, birds 3,742 and mammals 3,876 individuals (Traill et al. 2007).

We focused on the species whose zoo populations exceeded these arbitrary criteria and found 247 (28) reptiles, 634 (80) birds, and 416 (79) mammals with zoo populations over 50 and 500 (given in parentheses) individuals. Although, one might perceive these values as small and invaluable, we consider the support of 2.9% (0.3%) of reptile, 6.6% (0.8%) of bird and 7.8% (1.5%) of mammalian species relevant enough to justify funding of the zoos.

5. Relative Representation of Endangered Species

Not all vertebrate species are currently at risk of extinction; therefore the beneficial role of captive breeding in conservation of global species diversity may be enhanced by selective keeping of endangered species. We analyze here the representation of the species listed by IUCN in the categories "nearly threatened" or higher. Among the studied vertebrate classes, there are 481 reptiles (5.6% of extant species), 1869 birds (19.4%), and 1145 mammals (21.4%) of these categories (further referred as IUCN species). Thus, reptiles seem to be nearly four times less endangered than birds or mammals. Otherwise, they may be just less frequently listed in IUCN categories as members of the group attracting less human attention.

Zoos keep 167 IUCN species of reptiles, 364 IUCN species of birds and 250 IUCN species of mammals (Table 2). Interestingly enough, the IUCN species are nearly three times more represented among the zoo species of reptiles (34.7%) than among those absent in zoos (12.7%; χ^2=198.7, df=1, P<0.0001). The corresponding difference was much smaller for mammals (25.3 versus 20.6%, χ^2=10.4, df=1, P<0.0012). For birds we found an inverse relationship with the IUCN species being underrepresented in zoos: 15.6 versus 20.6% (χ^2=29.1, df=1, P<0.0001).

Besides the presence or absence of the IUCN species in zoos, there is an even more important issue: the population size of these species supported by the global network of zoos. Fortunately, mean zoo populations of the IUCN species are as a rule somewhat larger than those of less endangered. This difference was higher in reptiles (27.5 versus 11.1 individuals;

t-test: t=6.51, df=1152, P<0.0001) than in birds (23.7 versus 13.3; t=5.50, df=2334, P<0.0001) and mammals (48.0 versus 28.4; t=4.07, P=0.0001; see Table 2). More illustrative are plots comparing distribution of population sizes among the IUCN and non-IUCN species (Figures 1-3). In addition to overrepresentation of the IUCN taxa, it is clearly visible that within each analyzed class, a handful percent of the species with the largest population sizes in zoos are apparently overrepresented as their data points deviates from the strait line characterizing the remaining species.

Table 2. Representation of endangered species in zoo collections

Class:	Reptiles	Birds	Mammals
number of living IUCN species (degree of "nearly threatened" or more)	481	1869	1148
number of IUCN species kept in zoos	167	364	250
IUCN species with zoo population size over 50	70	141	130
IUCN species with zoo population size over 500	6	20	23
mean size of zoo population of IUCN species*	11.1	23.7	26.4
number of living non-IUCN species	8121	7758	4205
number of non-IUCN species kept in zoos	988	1973	740
non-IUCN species with zoo population size over 50	177	492	286
non-IUCN species with zoo population size over 500	22	60	56
mean size of zoo population of non-IUCN species*	27.5	13.3	48

*Computed from log transformed data.

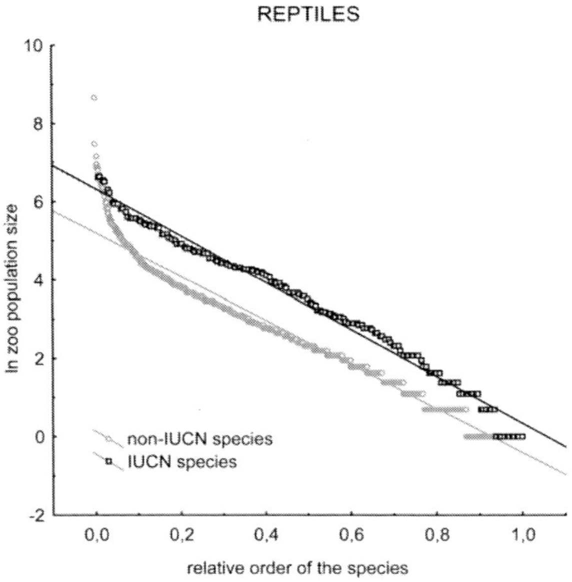

Figure 1. Size distribution of worldwide zoo populations of reptiles: a comparison of endangered species (IUCN category NT-nearly threatened or higher) with the remaining ones (non-IUCN). ln population size = log transformed number of individuals of a given species kept in zoos worldwide. Population sizes are sorted in descending order on the x axis. Order of each species was scaled to the total number of IUCN or non-IUCN species.

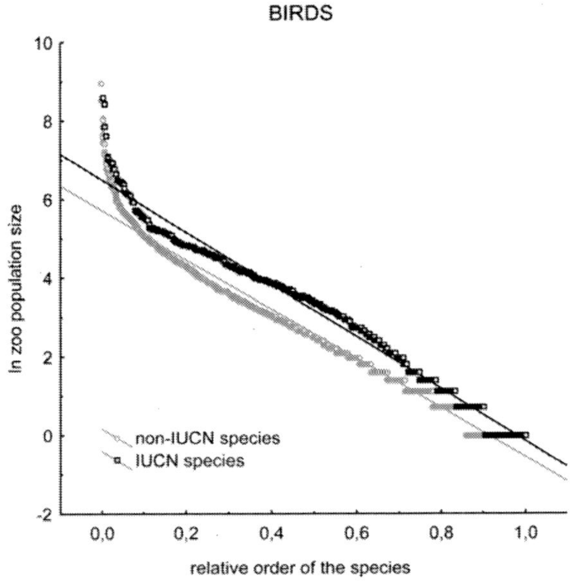

Figure 2. Size distribution of zoo populations of birds: a comparison of endangered species (IUCN category NT-nearly threatened or higher) with the remaining ones (non-IUCN). ln population size = log transformed number of individuals of a given species kept in zoos worldwide. Population sizes are sorted in descending order on the x axis. Order of each species was scaled to the total number of IUCN or non-IUCN species.

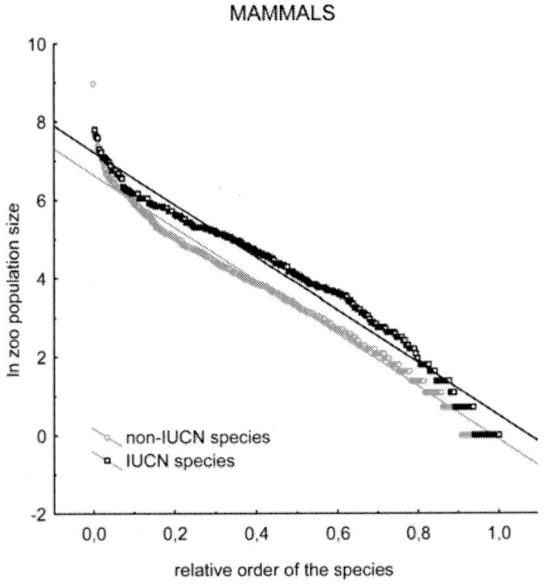

Figure 3. Size distribution of zoo populations of mammals: a comparison of endangered species (IUCN category NT-nearly threatened or higher) with the remaining ones (non-IUCN). ln population size = log transformed number of individuals of a given species kept in zoos worldwide. Population sizes are sorted in descending order on the x axis. Order of each species was scaled to the total number of IUCN or non-IUCN species.

That is why we paid special attention to the species whose zoo populations are large enough to secure short-term survival in captivity.

6. Effects of Perceived Attractiveness and Body Size among Related Species

Pythons and Boas

Recently, we studied human preferences towards a representative sample of 56 species of pythons and boas of the family Boidae. Colorful and patterned species such as the rainbow boa (*Epicrates cenchria cenchria*), ball python (*Python regius*), Burmese python (*Python molurus bivittatus*), red blood python (*P. brongesmai*), Emerald tree boa (*Corallus caninus*) were most preferred, while brownish Hispaniola boa (*Epicrates gracilis*), Puerto Rican boa (*E.inornatus*), olive python (*Liasis olivaceus*), Indian sand boa (*Eryx johni*), ringed tree boa (*Corallus annulatus*) were least preferred. We clearly demonstrated that the sizes of the worldwide zoo populations of individual boid species are closely correlated with both body size and human preferences (β=0.39 and -0.39; Marešová and Frynta 2008). The question was whether such a close dependence of the zoo population on factors reflecting sensory and/or emotional stimulation of the visitors/keepers is universal or is confined to the specific taxa such as snakes evoking arousal in most human beings. To answer this question we also performed similar experiments also in turtles as well as in one bird and one mammalian group.

Turtles

Captive breeding programs are really fundamental for survival of several species of turtles and tortoises (Testudines) which are heavily exploited or even extinct in the wild. Thus zoos may play an important role in conservation of these animals. Currently, ISIS reports in zoos 31,078 individuals belonging to 221 species (of about 298 extant species of chelonians). Since zoo visitors perceive turtles as a very homogenous group, we had to include the species representing all turtle subfamilies to increase both taxonomic and morphological variation. In this analysis we selected the most abundant zoo species and the subfamilies exceeding 20 extant species were represented by two most abundant species kept in zoos. There was a fairly good agreement among the 25 respondents; PC1 explained 57% of the total variation in species ranks.

Next, we excluded three obligatory marine species that are difficult to keep in zoos and carried out the GLM analysis. The size of the zoo population was significantly predicted by human aesthetic preferences ($F_{(1,23)}$=6.3, P=0.0197), but not by body size ($F_{(1,23)}$=3.8, P=0.0647) or IUCN listing ($F_{(1,23)}$=1.7, P=0.2081). The correlation between human aesthetic preference and size of zoo populations (Figure 4) was only moderate (r=-0.492), but highly significant (P<0.0107). The most deviating point from this relationship represents the common snapping turtle (*Chelydra serpentina*). Although the zoo population of this species is the largest, it was not preferred by our respondents. Nevertheless, this discrepancy may be easily explained by emotional arousal induced by the dangerous species.

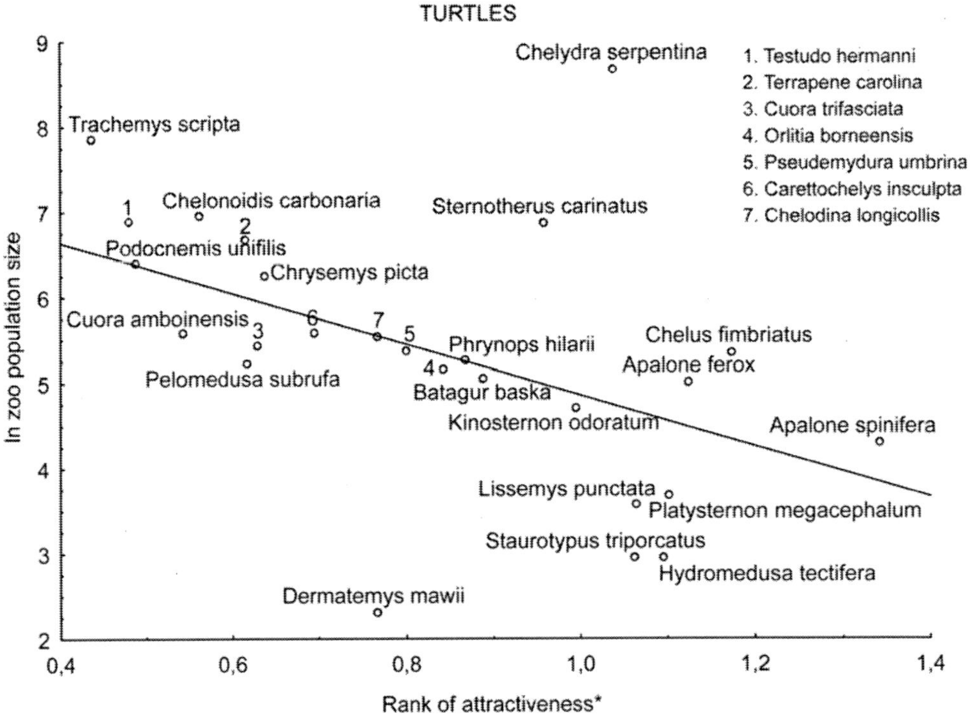

*Please note that the higher value of mean rank, the less attractive animal.

Figure 4. Relationship between size of zoo populations and human preferences in turtles (Testudines). Rank of attractiveness = mean square-root arcsin transformed rank. ln zoo population size = log transformed number of individuals of a given species kept in zoos worldwide. $R^2 = 24.2\%$, $P = 0.0107$, $y = 7.83 * x - 2.97$.

Pheasants

Pheasants and allies of the family Phasianidae (sensu del Hoyo 1992-2002, i.e., excluding Tetraonidae and Meleagridae) are frequently kept and bred in zoos; in total 9,731 individuals belonging to 79 species are reported by ISIS. We sorted these species according to size of zoo populations, and selected every even for further analysis. Next we tested human aesthetic preferences towards these 40 species and found a good agreement among respondents; the first principal component explained 35.2% of the total variation. Species exhibiting elaborated tail feathers and/or loud colours such as Indian peafowl (*Pavo cristatus*), Lady Amherst's pheasant (*Chrysolophus amherstiae*), Reeve's pheasant (*Syrmaticus reevesii*), silver pheasant (*Lophura nycthemera*), Swinhoe's pheasant (*Lophura swinhoii*) were most preferred while short-tailed dull ones such as Cabot's tragopan (*Tragopan caboti*), Salwadori's pheasant (*Lophura inornata*), brown quail (*Coturnix ypsilophora*), Hildebrandt's francolin (*Francolinus* hildebrandti), Natal francolin (*F. natalensis*) were least preferred.

The GLM analysis revealed the human aesthetic preference ($F_{(1,36)}$=16.6, P=0.0002), but not body size ($F_{(1,36)}$=2.6, P=0.1119) or IUCN listing ($F_{(1,36)}$=0.02, P=0.8882), to be a relevant predictor of the zoo population size. The correlation between human aesthetic preference and size of zoo populations was high enough (r=-0.601; P<0.0001) to be worth of conservationists' attention (Figure 5).

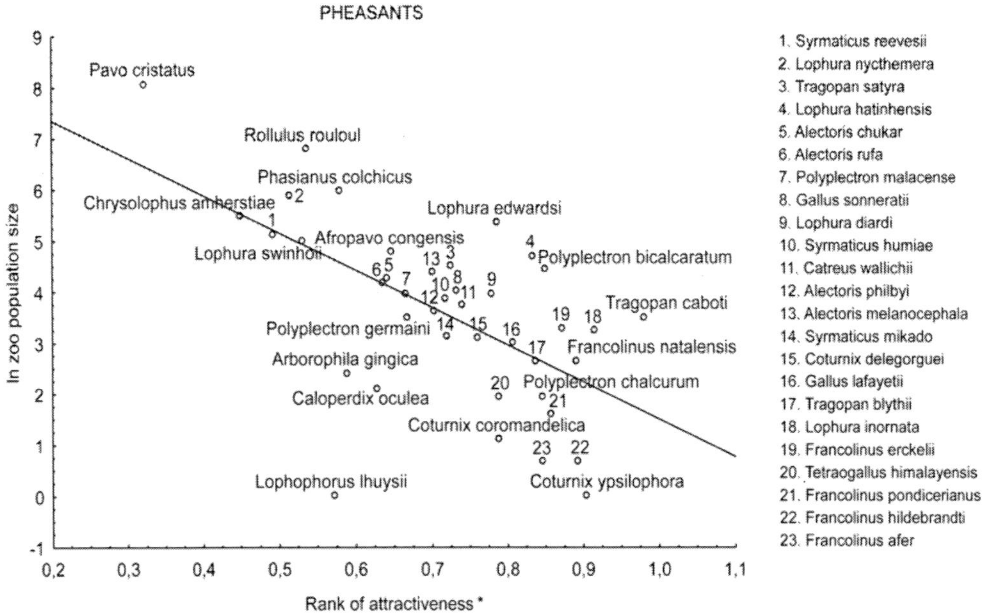

*Please note that the higher value of mean rank, the less attractive animal.

Figure 5. Relationship between size of zoo populations and human preferences in pheasants (Phasianidae). Rank of attractiveness = mean square-root arcsin transformed rank. ln zoo population size = log transformed number of individuals of a given species kept in zoos worldwide. R^2 = 36.1%, P < 0.0001, y = -8.81 * x -7.29.

Antelopes and Allies

The family Bovidae comprising 138 extant species of antelopes, goats, sheep and buffaloes belong to the hard core of the zoo animals. ISIS recorded 26,794 individuals in zoos belonging to 96 species. Similarly as in the case of pheasants we sorted the species according to the zoo population size and selected a set of 45 species (every even one represented in zoos by more than 12 individuals) for further analysis. The first principal component explained only 26% of the total variance, thus the agreement among the respondents was poorer than in the case of pheasants. Consequently, the GLM analyses revealed that size of zoo populations can be explained neither by human aesthetic preferences ($F_{(1,44)}$=0.31, P=0.5793) nor by IUCN listing ($F_{(1,44)}$=1.87, P=0.1782). Body size has remained the only significant predictor of the zoo population size ($F_{(1,44)}$=5.23, P=0.0270, Figure 6).

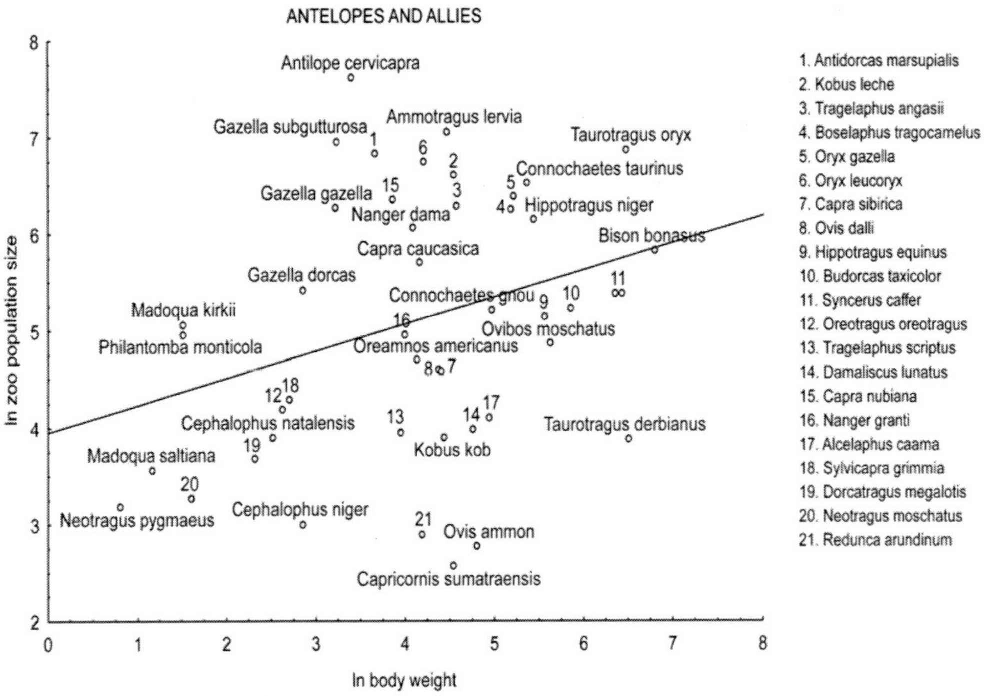

Figure 6. Relationship between size of zoo populations and body size in antelopes and allies (Bovidae). ln zoo population size = log transformed number of individuals of a given species kept in zoos worldwide. R^2 = 10.3%, P = 0.0261, y = 3.91 * x +0.29.

Although antelopes and allies vary in their body form and/or in the presence and shape of their horns (Caro et al. 2003), their coloration is rather uniform as in most mammalian taxa. Therefore, body size is the only other stimulus that may influence decision making of zoo visitors and keepers.

7. Effects of Perceived Attractiveness and Body Size on Higher Taxonomic Scale

The results provided in the previous paragraphs suggest that aesthetic preferences towards particular species are correlated with zoo population size in several vertebrate taxa. Nevertheless, not only the extinction of individual species, but also the extinction of higher taxa poses a major threat to global biodiversity. Therefore, we also carried out similar analyses for presumably monophyletic groups on the family and/or subfamily scale.

For this purpose we split the studied classes of vertebrates into eleven more homogenous groups, each consisting of two or three dozens of families/subfamilies or other monophyletic taxa of comparable level (or more detailed in the case of primates, in accord with Goodman et al.1998). Reptiles were split into three morphologically (for recent phylogenies see Towsend et al 2004, Vidal and Hedges 2005, Uetz et al. 2008) distinct groups: snakes (Ophidia), lizards (tuataras and squamates except snakes) and turtles (Testudines). Birds are a morphologically most homogenous class of terrestrial vertebrates. Moreover, phylogeny (Sibley and Ahlquist

1990, Ericson et al. 2006, Hackett et al. 2008) does not reflect the variability in appearance properly. We analyzed the following groups defined by a combination of the phylogenetic (Ericson et al. 2006) and ecomorphological features: "basal birds" (Paleognathae, Galloanserae and Columbidae belonging to Metaves), "aquatic birds" (belonging to Neoaves and Metaves), "terrestrial birds" (selected Neoaves) and "passerines" (Passeriformes: Passerida; Barker et al. 2004). Mammals were split based on the purely phylogenetic criteria (Murphy et al. 2001, Bininda-Emonds 2007) into following four groups: "basal mammals" (Monotremata, Metatheria, Xenarthra, Afrotheria), "Glires" (Rodentia and Lagomorpha), "Euarchonta" (Scandentia, Dermoptera and Primates), and finally "Laurasiatheria" (Eulipotyphla, Artiodactyla, Perissodactyla, Pholidota and Carnivora; Cetacea and Chiroptera were omitted because of their specific requirements and deviation of typical mammalian life style).

Each of these families/subfamilies was characterized by the total number of individuals kept in zoos worldwide, the number of extant species, the typical body size (i.e., weight for birds and mammals, and length for reptiles) and estimated of human preference. To assess the last variable we randomly selected one (or more) species of each family/subfamily from the complete species list and included them into the set of pictures presented to our respondents (for more details see Data sources and testing procedures). When a relevant picture was not available for the particular species, we repeated random selection once again. When pictures of more than one species belonging to the group were included in the test, the data were pooled to avoid pseudoreplication.

Multiple regression in which log-transformed number of individuals per species (i.e., mean population size) was given as a dependent variable, and log-transformed body size and human preference as independent (explanatory) variables was computed for each studied vertebrate group. All these eleven models computed for particular vertebrate groups except one (turtles) were significant and explained enough variation to be considered in conservation biology (see Table 3).

Table 3. Results of multiple regression explaining zoo population per species (log-transformed) by body size (log-transformed) and human preferences (square root arcsin transformed ranks)

	Body size - median for particular family/subfamily			Rank of perceived attractiveness			Explained variance by PC1	number of respondents	summary of regression model
Higher taxonomic groups	**β**	**t**	**p <**	**β**	**t**	**p <**	**PC1**	**N**	
Reptiles									
Snakes	0.721	5.76	**0.0001**	-0.024	-0.19	0.8497	**48.0%**	32	R2=0.5289; $F_{(2.32)}$=18.0; **p<.0001**
Lepidosauria except snakes	0.536	3.85	**0.0001**	-0.203	-1.46	0.1548	**38.5%**	50	R2=0.3429; $F_{(2.34)}$=8.9; **p<.0008**
Turtles	-0.214	-1.00	0.3319	-0.389	-1.81	0.0868	**47.5%**	53	R2=0.1788; $F_{(2.18)}$=2.0; p<.1697
Birds									
Basal birds	0.638	4.20	**0.0003**	-0.273	-1.80	0.0826	**24.1%**	36	R2=0.3939; $F_{(2.28)}$=9.1; **p<.0009**
Aquatic birds	0.463	2.86	**0.0084**	-0.306	-1.89	0.0704	**31.6%**	36	R2=0.4144; $F_{(2.26)}$=9.2; **p<.0010**
Terrestrial birds	0.541	3.22	**0.0039**	-0.353	-2.10	**0.0473**	**32.4%**	36	R2=0.3277; $F_{(2.22)}$=6.8; **p<.0049**
Passerines	0.525	3.20	**0.0035**	-0.284	-1.74	0.0940	**17.2%**	36	R2=0.3006; $F_{(2.27)}$=5.8; **p<.0080**
Mammals									
Bassal mammals	0.260	1.70	0.0986	-0.417	-2.73	**0.0102**	**28.3%**	45	R2=0.2885; $F_{(2.32)}$=6.5; **p<.0043**
Glires	0.397	2.38	**0.0238**	-0.242	-1.45	0.1577	**42.4%**	52	R2=0.1863; $F_{(2.30)}$=3.4; **p<.0454**
Euarchonta	0.482	2.71	**0.0110**	-0.150	-0.84	0.4055	**21.5%**	51	R2=0.1979; $F_{(2.30)}$=3.7; **p<.0366**
Laurasiatheria	0.663348	5.29177	**0.000010**	-0.277793	-2.21605	**0.034418**	**20.4%**	42	R2=0.5291; $F_{(2.30)}$=16.9; **p<.0001**

In accord with expectations, body size was the best predictor of the number of individuals per species. Its effect was positive in ten out of eleven analyzed groups (except turtles); nine of these effects were significant (P<0.05) and one (group of "basal mammals") approached significance (P<0.1). The larger the typical species of the family/subfamily is, the more individuals per species are kept in zoos. This relationship was really strong within most studied groups, in particular snakes and Laurasiatheria (Figures 7-8, 10-12, 14, 16-18). The only exception were turtles exhibiting even an inverse relationship, which was, however, statistically insignificant.

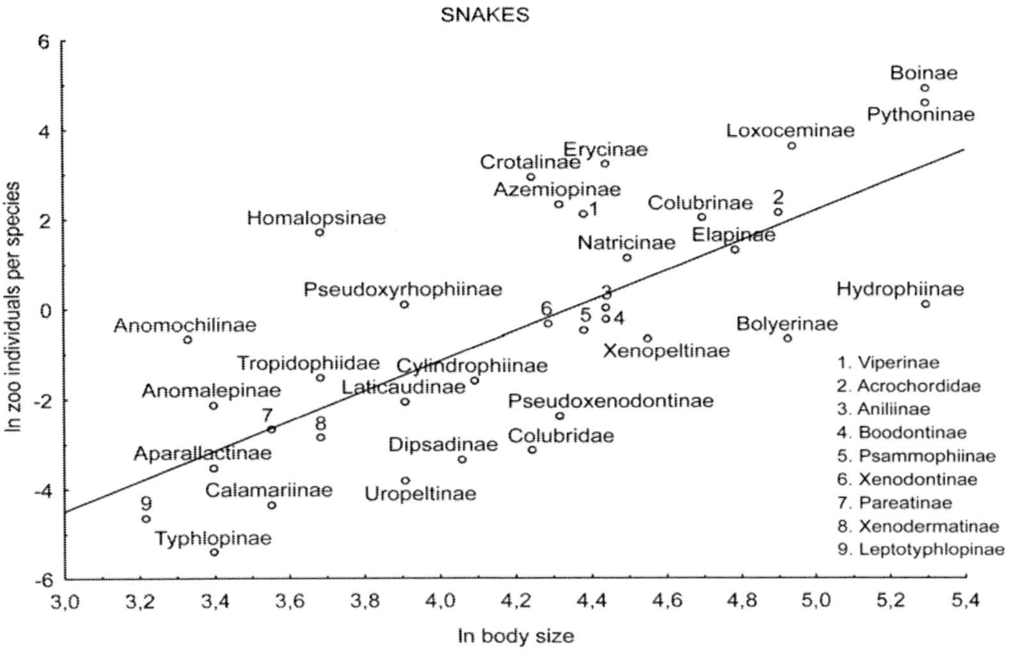

Specimen species representing the taxa sorted according to rank of attractiveness in descending order: *Parias flavomaculatus* (Crotalinae), *Geophis semidoliatus* (Dipsadinae), Anilius scytale (Aniliinae), *Laticauda colubrina* (Laticaudinae), *Cercaspis carinata* (Colubridae incertae sedis), *Atractaspis bibronii* (Aparallactinae, Atractaspidinae), *Xenopeltis unicolor* (Xenopeltinae), *Azemiops feae* (Azemiopinae), *Acrantophis madagascariensis* (Boinae), *Hydrophis cyanocinctus* (Hydrophiinae), *Cylindrophis maculatus* (Cylindrophiinae), *Tropidophis greenwayi* (Tropidophiidae, Ungaliophiidae), *Vipera ursinii* (Viperinae), *Acrochordus granulatus* (Acrochordidae), *Pseudoxenodon macrops* (Pseudoxenodontinae), *Boulengerina annulata stormsi* (Elapinae), *Enhydris enhydris* (Homalopsinae), *Achalinus spinalis* (Xenodermatinae), *Ialtris dorsalis* (Xenodontinae), *Anomochilus weberi* (Anomochilinae), *Pareas monticola* (Pareatinae), *Psammophis schokari* (Psammophiinae), *Calmaria schmidti* (Calamariinae), *Amphiesma platyceps* (Natricinae), *Antaresia maculosa* (Pythoninae), *Ithycyphus miniatus* (Pseudoxyrhophiinae), *Eryx colubrinus* (Erycinae), *Lycodomorphus bicolor* (Boodontinae), *Loxocemus bicolor* (Loxoceminae), *Tantilla coronata* (Colubrinae), *Rhinophis pillippinus* (Uropeltinae), *Casarea dussumieri* (Bolyerinae), *Leptotyphlops humilis* (Leptotyphlopinae), *Liotyphlops beui* (Anomalepinae), *Typhlops brongersmianus* (Typhlopinae).

Figure 7. Relationship between size of zoo populations per species and body size in snakes. Ln zoo individuals per species = log-transformed number of individuals belonging to a given family/subfamily kept in zoos worldwide per the total number of living species in this group. ln body size = log-transformed length. $R^2 = 52.8\%$; $P < 0.0001$, $y = -14.53 * x + 3.35$.

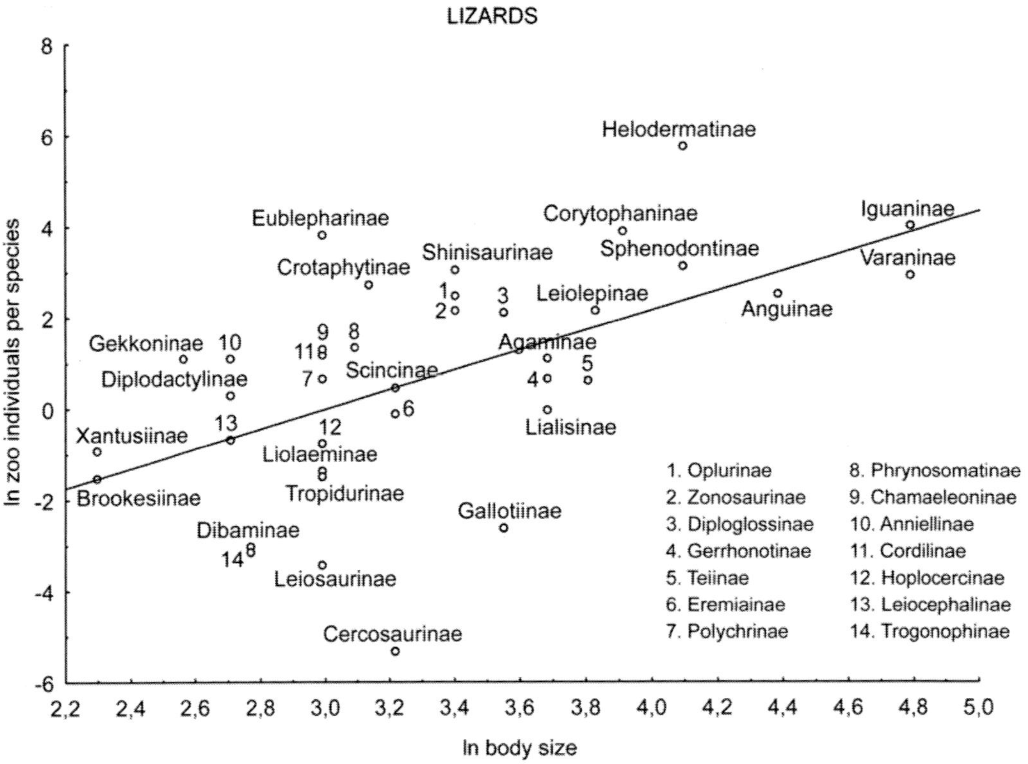

Specimen species representing the taxa sorted according to rank of attractiveness in descending order: *Chamaeleo rudis* (Chamaeleoninae), *Oplurus fierinensis* (Oplurinae), *Microlophus thoracicus* (Tropidurinae), *Abronia vasconcelosii* (Gerrhonotinae), *Cnemidophorus gularis* (Teiinae), *Heloderma suspectum* (Helodermatinae), *Leiocephalus l. lunatus* (Leiocephalinae), *Lepidophyma sylvaticum* (Xantusiinae), *Liolaemus chiliensis* (Liolaeminae), *Heliobolus spekii* (Eremiainae), *Ctenophorus fordi* (Agaminae), *Eublepharis hardwickii* (Eublepharinae), *Cordylus tropidosternum* (Cordilinae), *Varanus niloticus* (Varaninae), *Zonosaurus quadrilineatus* (Zonosaurinae), *Heteronotia binolei* (Gekkoninae), *Crotaphytus antiquus* (Crotaphytinae), *Pristidactylus torquatus* (Leiosaurinae), *Anolis wattsi* (Polychrinae), *Corytophanes hernandesii* (Corytophaninae), *Schinisaurus crocodylurus* (Shinisaurinae), *Galotia galloti* (Galotiinae), *Hoplocercus spinosus* (Hoplocercinae), *Dipsosaurus dorsalis* (Iguaninae), *Sphenodon punctatus* (Sphenodontinae), *Saltuarius cornutus* (Diplodactylinae), *Potamites apodemus* (Cercosaurinae), *Lankascincus deraniyagalai* (Scincinae), *Celestus stenurus* (Diploglossinae), *Sceloporus spinosus* (Phrynosomatinae), *Rhampholeon boulengeri* (Brookesiinae), *Ophisaurus atennuatus* (Anguinae), *Uromastyx aegyptia* (Leiolepinae or Leiolepidinae), *Trogonophis wiegmani* (Trogonophinae), *Aprasia rostrata* (Lialisinae or Pygopodinae), *Dibamus bogadeki* (Dibaminae), *Anniella pulchra* (Anniellinae).

Figure 8. Relationship between size of zoo populations per species and body size in lizards (including tuataras). ln zoo individuals per species = log-transformed number of individuals belonging to a given family/subfamily kept in zoos worldwide per the total number of living species in this group. ln body size = log-transformed snout-vent length. R = 30.5%, P= 0.0004, y = -6,52 * x +2,17.

Human preference contributed less apparently to the models explaining the number of individuals per species. Interestingly enough, the effects of ranking were always negative, i.e., the higher the human preference, the better the representation of the given family/subfamily in zoos. However, this factor reached formal statistical significance (P<0.05) only in two mamamlian ("basal mammals" and Laurasiatheria) and one bird ("terrestrial birds") groups (see Figures 15, 13). In additional one reptile (turtles; Figure 9) and three bird groups ("basal birds", "aquatic birds" and "passerines") this factor approached significance (P<0.1).

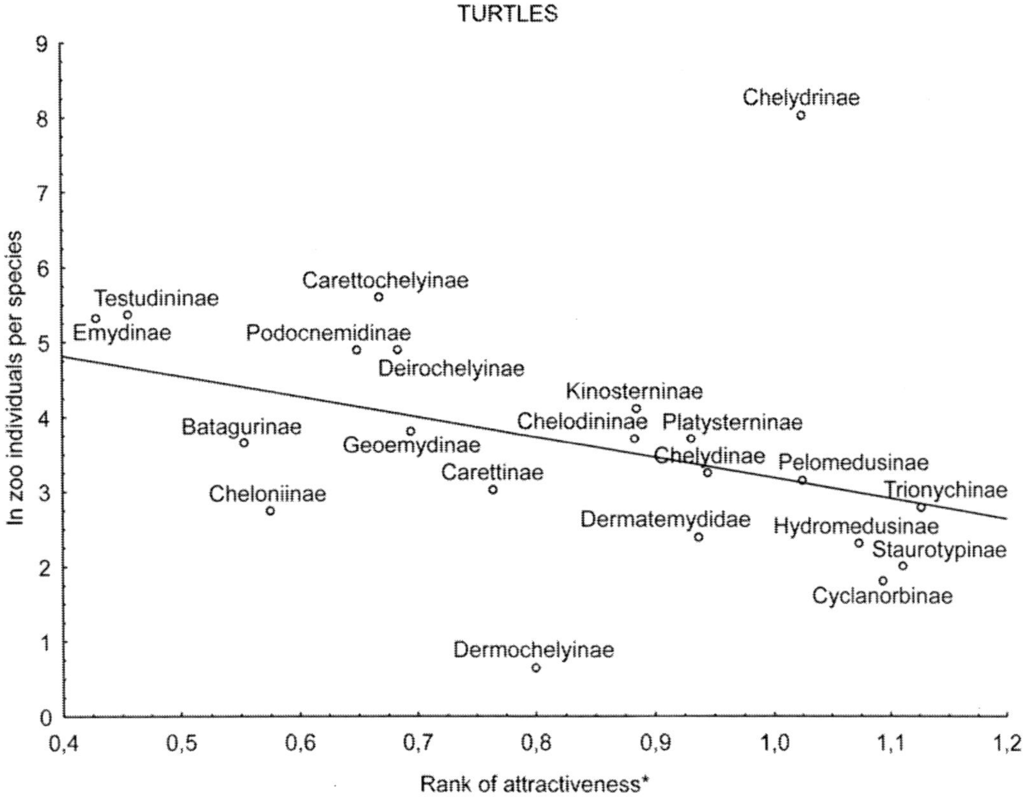

*Please note that the higher value of mean rank, the less attractive animal.

Specimen species representing the taxa sorted according to rank of attractiveness in descending order: Clemmys guttata (Emydinae), Astrochelys yniphora (Testudininae), Malayemys subrijuga (Batagurinae), Chelonia mydas (Cheloniinae), Podocnemis erythrocephala (Podocnemidinae), Carettochelys insculpta (Caretochelynae), Pseudemys nelsoni (Deirochelyinae), Cuora trifasciata (Geoemydinae), Lepidochelys olivacea (Carettinae), Dermochelys coriacea (Dermochelyinae), Elseya albagula (Chelodininae), Kinosternon flavescens (Kinosterninae), Platysternon megacephalum (Platysterninae), Dermatemys mawii (Dermatemydidae), Phrynops hilari (Chelidinae), Chelydra serpentina (Chelydrinae), Pelusios castanoides (Pelomedusinae), Hydromedusa tectifera (Hydromedusinae), Lissemys punctata (Cyclanorbinae), Staurotypus triporcatus (Staurotypinae), Apalone ferox (Trionychinae).

Figure 9. Relationship between size of zoo populations per species and attractiveness in turtles. ln zoo individuals per species = log-transformed number of individuals belonging to a given family/subfamily kept in zoos worldwide per the total number of living species in this group. Rank of attractiveness = mean square-root arcsin transformed rank. $R^2 = 13.35\%$, $P = 0.1034$, $y = 59.0 * x - 2.71$.

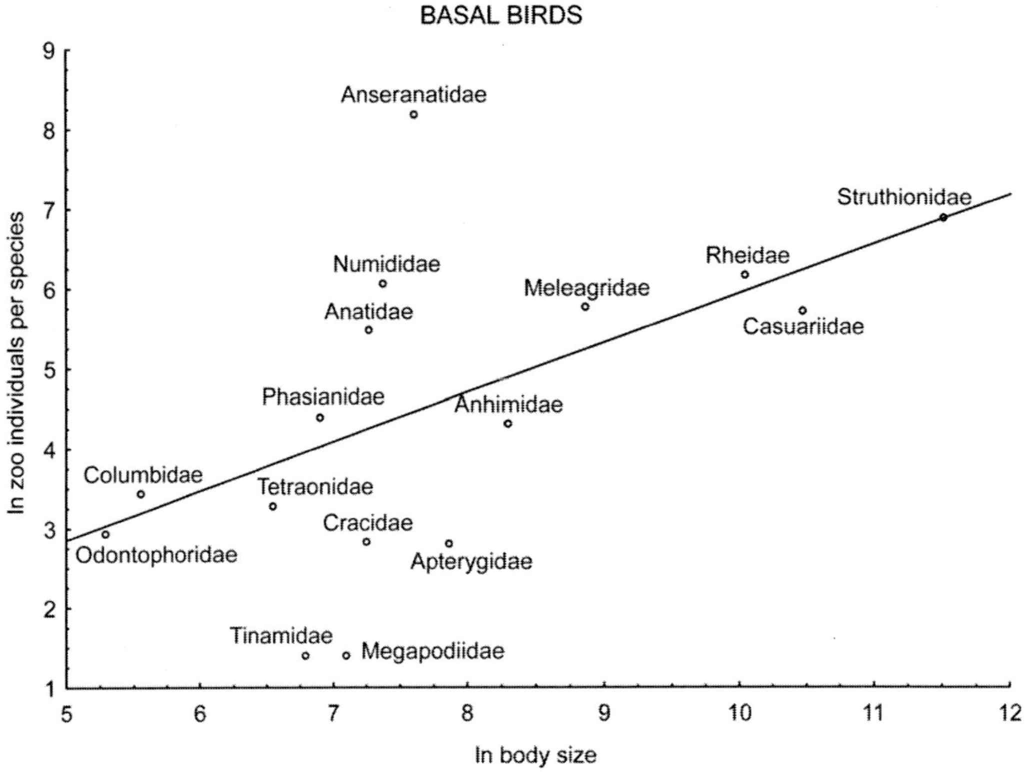

Specimen species representing the taxa sorted according to rank of attractiveness in descending order: *Apteryx australis* (Apterygidae); *Chalcophaps stephani, Ptilinopus arcanus, Treron oxyura, Geophaps scripta, Columba delegorguei, Zenaida aurita* (Columbidae), *Bonasa bonasia* (Tetraonidae); *Chloephaga poliocephala, Anas undulata, Oxyura maccoa,Tadorna radjah* (Anatidae); *Rhea pennata* (Rheidae); *Struthio camelus* (Struthionidae); *Callipepla squamata, Odontophorus hyperythrus* (Odontophoridae); *Margaroperdix madagarensis, Tetraogallus caucasicus, Argusianus argus, Gallus sonneratii, Francolinus rufopictus* (Phasianidae); *Chauna chavaria* (Anhimidae); *Casuarius casuarius* (Casuariidae); *Guttera plumifera* (Numididae); *Ortalis erythroptera, Penelope ortoni* (Cracidae); *Anseranas semipalmata* (Anseranatidae); *Nothocercus julius, Tinamus tao* (Tinamidae); *Meleagris gallopavo* (Meleagridae); *Megapodius laperouse* (Megapodiidae).

Figure 10. Relationship between size of zoo populations per species and body size in basal birds. ln zoo individuals per species = log-transformed number of individuals belonging to a given family/subfamily kept in zoos worldwide per the total number of living species in this group. ln body size = log-transformed weight. $R^2 = 32.4\%$, $P = 0.0008$; $y = -0.24 * x + 0.62$.

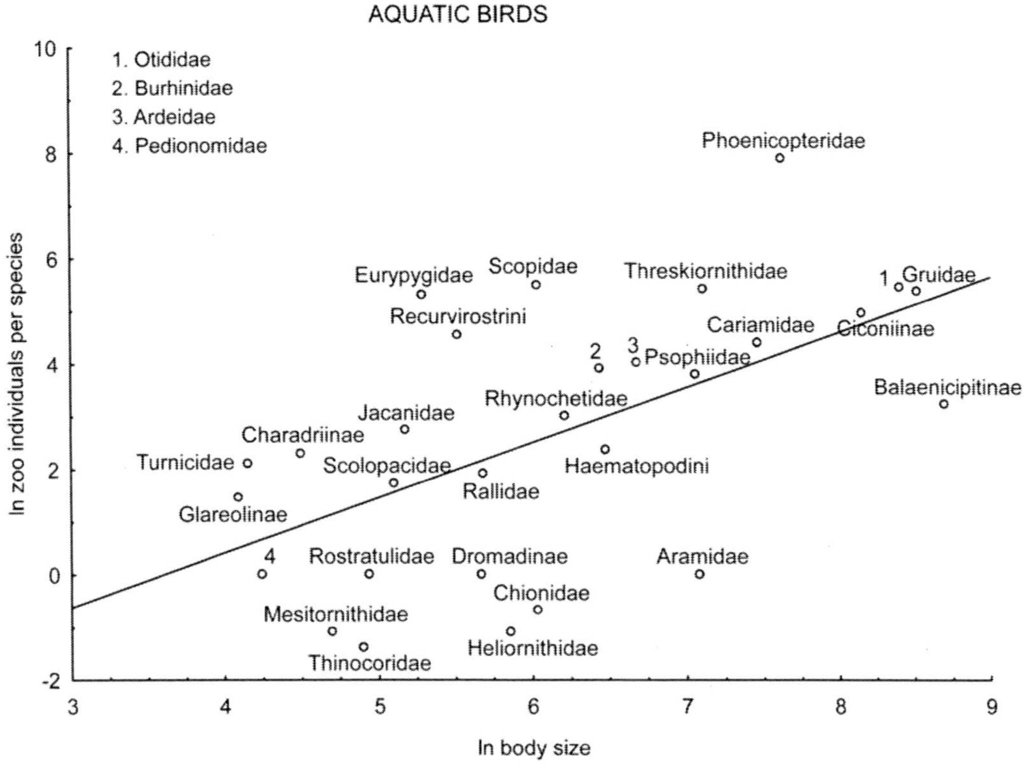

Specimen species representing the taxa sorted according to rank of attractiveness in descending order: *Phoenicopterus ruber* (Phoenicopteridae), *Balearica pavonina* (Gruidae), *Himantopus mexicanus* (Recurvirostrini), *Aramus guarauna* (Aramidae), *Ardea humbloti* (Ardeidae), *Ciconia nigra* (Ciconiinae), *Dromas ardeola* (Dromadinae), *Jacana jacana* (Jacanidae), *Eupodotis caerulescens* (Otididae), *Eurypyga helias* (Eurypygidae), *Theristicus melanopis* (Threskiornithidae), *Balaeniceps rex* (Balaenicipitinae), *Vanellus melanocephalus* (Charadriinae), *Rostratula semicollaris* (Rostratulidae), *Scopus umbretta* (Scopidae), *Glareola ocularis* (Glareolinae), *Tringa incana* (Scolopacidae), *Psophia leucoptera* (Psophiidae), *Heliopais personata* (Heliornithidae), *Pedionomus torquatus* (Pedionomidae), *Burhinus recurvirostris* (Burhinidae), *Haematopus moquini* (Haematopodini), *Monias benschi* (Mesitornithidae), *Thinocorus orbignyianus* (Thinocoridae), *Amaurolimnas concolor* (Rallidae), *Rhynochetos jubatus* (Rhynochetidae), *Turnix velox* (Turnicidae), *Chunga burmeisteri* (Cariamidae), *Chionis alba* (Chionidae).

Figure 11. Relationship between size of zoo populations per species and body size in aquatic birds. ln zoo individuals per species = log-transformed number of individuals belonging to a given family/subfamily kept in zoos worldwide per the total number of living species in this group. ln body size = log-transformed weight. $R^2 = 33.4\%$, $P = 0.0010$, $y = -3.76 * x + 1.05$.

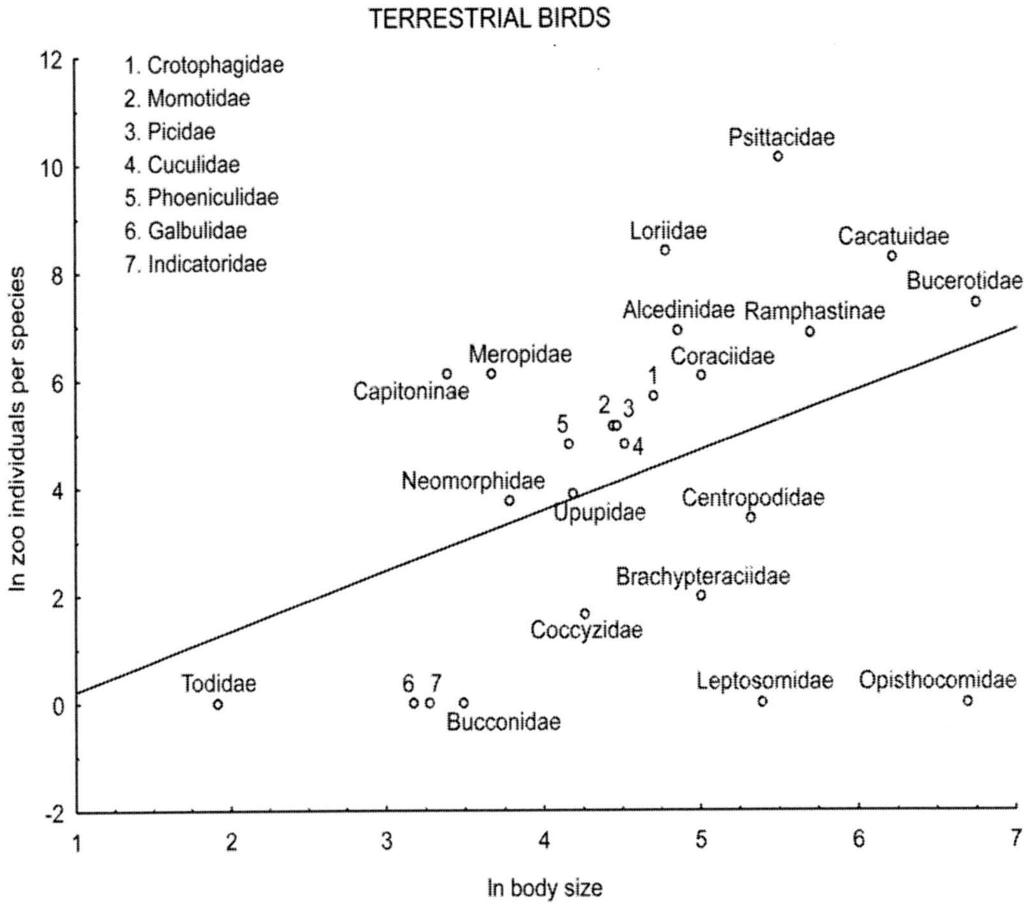

Specimen species representing the taxa sorted according to rank of attractiveness in descending order: *Alcedo cyanopecta, Halcyon smyrnensis, Megaceryle alcyon* (Alcedinidae); *Momotus mexicanus* (Momotidae); *Upupa epops* (Upupidae); *Merops boehmi* (Meropidae); *Aulacorhynchus prasinus* (Ramphastinae); *Ara chloropterus, Bolborhynchus ferrugineifrons* (Psittacidae); *Jacamerops aureus* (Galbulidae); *Todus multicolor* (Todidae); *Charmosyna rubronotata* (Loriidae); *Phoeniculus staneiceps* (Phoeniculidae); *Coracias naevia* (Coraciidae); *Opisthocomus hoazin* (Opisthocomidae); *Dryocopus pileatus, Picumnus pygmaeus* (Picidae); *Uratelornis chimaera* (Brachypteraciidae); *Cacatua alba* (Cacatuidae); *Tricholaema frontata, Semnornis ramphastinus* (Capitoninae); *Anorrhinus galeritus* (Bucerotidae); *Leptosomus discolor* (Leptosomidae); *Neomorphus geoffroyi* (Neomorphidae); *Coccyzus lansbergi* (Coccyzidae); *Eudynamys scolopacea* (Cuculidae); *Malacoptila rufa* (Bucconidae); *Centropus violaceus* (Centropodidae); *Crotophaga sulcirostris* (Crotophagidae); *Indicator willcocksi* (Indicatoridae).

Figure 12. Relationship between size of zoo populations per species and body size in terrestrial birds. ln zoo individuals per species = log-transformed number of individuals belonging to a given family/subfamily kept in zoos worldwide per the total number of living species in this group. ln body size = log-transformed weight. R^2 = 17.1%; P = 0.0399, y = -0,89 * x + 1,12.

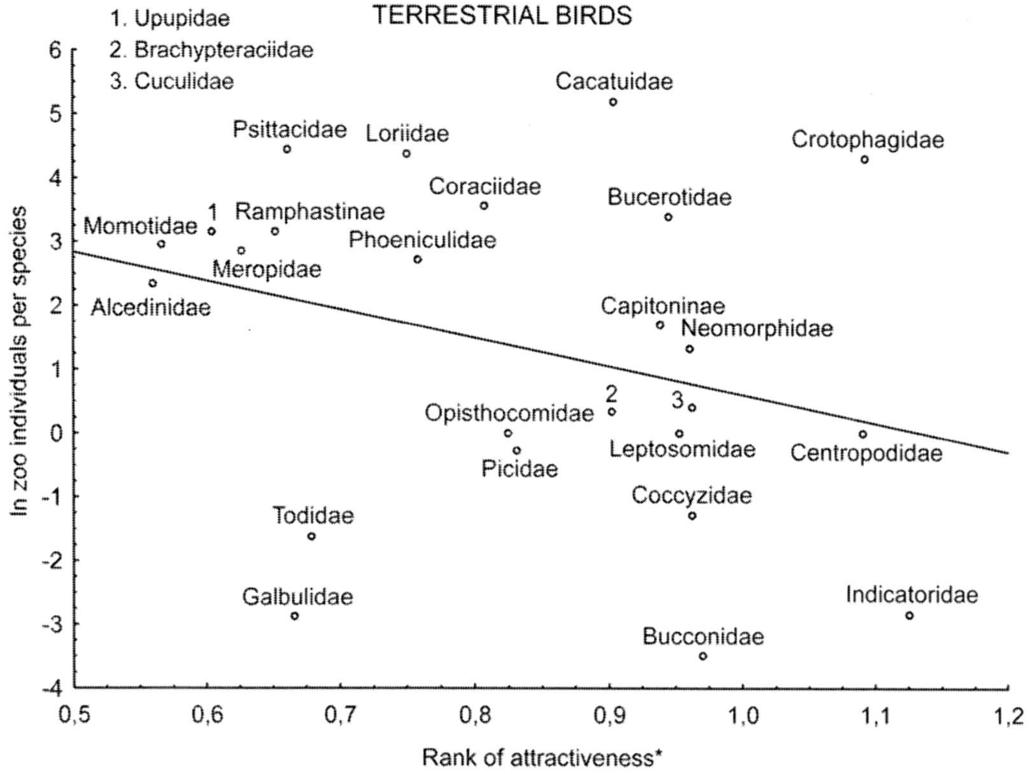

*Please note that the higher value of mean rank, the less attractive animal.

Specimen species representing the taxa sorted according to rank of attractiveness in descending order: *Alcedo cyanopecta, Halcyon smyrnensis, Megaceryle alcyon* (Alcedinidae); *Momotus mexicanus* (Momotidae); *Upupa epops* (Upupidae); *Merops boehmi* (Meropidae); *Aulacorhynchus prasinus* (Ramphastinae); *Ara chloropterus, Bolborhynchus ferrugineifrons* (Psittacidae); *Jacamerops aureus* (Galbulidae); *Todus multicolor* (Todidae); *Charmosyna rubronotata* (Loriidae); *Phoeniculus staneiceps* (Phoeniculidae); *Coracias naevia* (Coraciidae); *Opisthocomus hoazin* (Opisthocomidae); *Dryocopus pileatus, Picumnus pygmaeus* (Picidae); *Uratelornis chimaera* (Brachypteraciidae); *Cacatua alba* (Cacatuidae); *Tricholaema frontata, Semnornis ramphastinus* (Capitoninae); *Anorrhinus galeritus* (Bucerotidae); *Leptosomus discolor* (Leptosomidae); *Neomorphus geoffroyi* (Neomorphidae); *Coccyzus lansbergi* (Coccyzidae); *Eudynamys scolopacea* (Cuculidae); *Malacoptila rufa* (Bucconidae); *Centropus violaceus* (Centropodidae); *Crotophaga sulcirostris* (Crotophagidae); *Indicator willcocksi* (Indicatoridae).

Figure 13. Relationship between size of zoo populations per species and attractiveness in terrestrial birds. ln zoo individuals per species = log-transformed number of individuals belonging to a given family/subfamily kept in zoos worldwide per the total number of living species in this group. Rank of attractiveness = mean square-root arcsin transformed rank. R^2 = 09.3%, P = 0.14, y = 5.07 * x - 4.47.

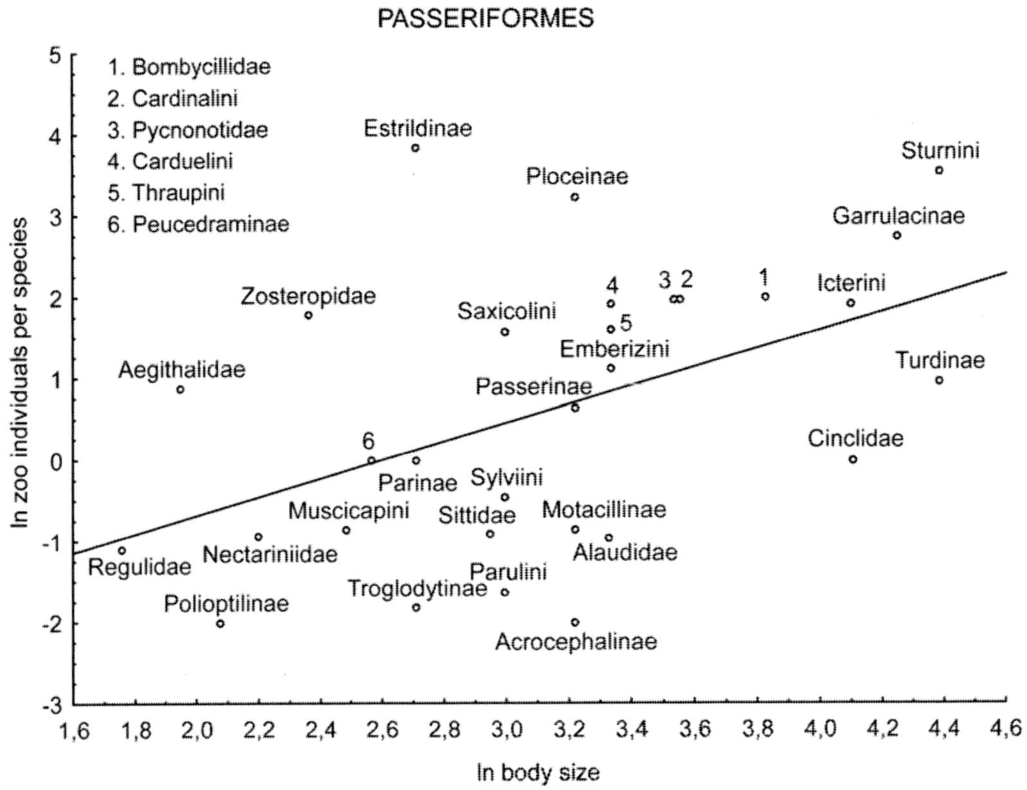

Specimen species representing the taxa sorted according to rank of attractiveness in descending order: *Cyanoptila cyanomelaena* (Muscicapini), *Parus caeruleus* (Parinae), *Peucedramus taeniatus* (Peucedraminae), *Parula americana* (Parulini), *Aethopyga siparaja* (Nectariniidae), *Passerina ciris* (Cardinalini), *Uraeginthus angolensis* (Estrildinae), *Ploceus cucullatus* (Ploceinae), *Regulus teneriffae* (Regulidae), *Pycnonotus jocosus* (Pycnonotidae), *Passer Melanurus* (Passerinae), *Garrulax pectoralis* (Garrulacinae), *Phoenicurus auroreus* (Saxicolini), *Loxia curvirostra* (Carduelini), *Gracula religiosa* (Sturnini), *Bombycilla cedrorum* (Bombycillidae), *Sitta europaea* (Sittidae), *Zosterops palpebrosus* (Zosteropidae), *Emberiza citrinella* (Emberizini), *Bradypterus seebohmi* (Acrocephalinae), *Cinclus cinclus* (Cinclidae), *Thryothorus ludovicianus* (Troglodytinae), *Polioptila caerulea* (Polioptilinae), *Molothrus ater* (Icterini), *Catharus guttatus* (Turdinae), *Anthus campestris* (Motacillinae), *Sylvia melanocephala* (Sylviini) *Mirafra erythroptera* (Alaudidae), *Aegithalos caudatus* (Aegithalidae), *Coereba flaveola* (Thraupini).

Figure 14. Relationship between size of zoo populations per species and body size in passerines. ln zoo individuals per species = log-transformed number of individuals belonging to a given family/subfamily kept in zoos worldwide per the total number of living species in this group. ln body size = log-transformed weight. $R^2 = 22.3\%$, $P = 0.0085$, $y = -2.96 * x + 1,14$.

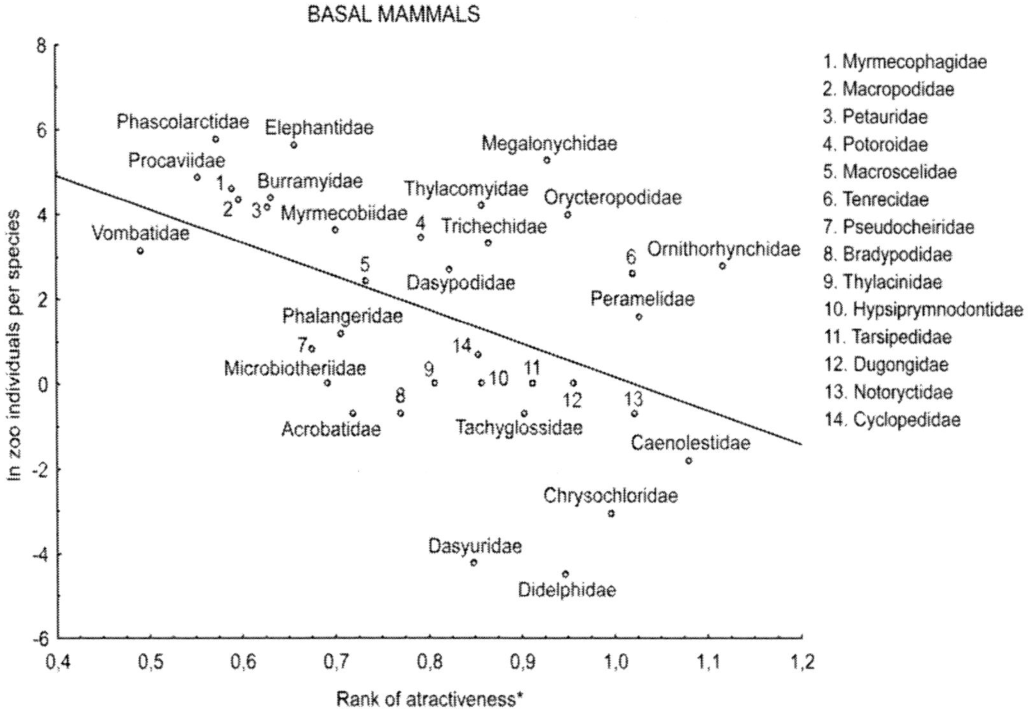

*Please note that the higher value of mean rank, the less attractive animal.

Specimen species representing the taxa sorted according to rank of attractiveness in descending order: *Lasiorhinus krefftii* (Vombatidae), *Dendrohyrax arboreus* (Procaviidae), *Phascolarctos cinereus* (Phascolarctidae), *Tamandua mexicana* (Myrmecophagidae), *Petrogale xanthopus* (Macropodidae), *Petaurus norfolcensis* (Petauridae), *Cercartetus nanus* (Burramyidae), *Loxodonta africana* (Elephantidae), *Pseudocheirus peregrinus* (Pseudocheiridae), *Dromiciops gliroides* (Microbiotheriidae), *Myrmecobius fasciatus* (Myrmecobiidae), *Trichosurus caninus* (Phalangeridae), *Distoechurus pennatus* (Acrobatidae), *Macroscelides proboscideus* (Macroscelidae), *Bradypus tridactylus* (Bradypodidae), *Aepyprymnus rufescens* (Potoroidae), *Thylacinus cynocephalus* (Thylacinidae), *Chaetophractus vellerosus* (Dasypodidae), *Sminthopsis murina* (Dasyuridae), *Cyclopes didactylus* (Cyclopedidae), *Hypsiprymnodon moschatus* (Hypsiprymnodontidae), *Macrotis lagotis* (Thylacomyidae), *Trichechus manatus* (Trichechidae), *Zaglossus bruini* (Tachyglossidae), *Tarsipes rostratus* (Tarsipedidae) *Choloepus didactylus* (Megalonychidae), *Marmosa murina* (Didelphidae), *Orycteropus afer* (Orycteropodidae), *Dugong dugong* (Dugongidae), *Cryptochloris asiatica* (Chrysochloridae), *Microgale taiva* (Tenrecidae), *Notoryctes caurinus* (Notoryctidae), *Perameles unnii,* (Peramelidae), *Lestoros inca* (Caenolestidae), *Ornithorhynchus anatinus* (Ornithorhynchidae).

Figure 15. Relationship between size of zoo populations per species and attractiveness in basal mammals including Prototheria, Methatheria, Xenarthra and Afrotheria. ln zoo individuals per species = log-transformed number of individuals belonging to a given family/subfamily kept in zoos worldwide per the total number of living species in this group. Rank of attractiveness = mean square-root arcsin transformed rank. R^2 = 22.4%, P = 0.0041, y = 8.09 * x – 7.92.

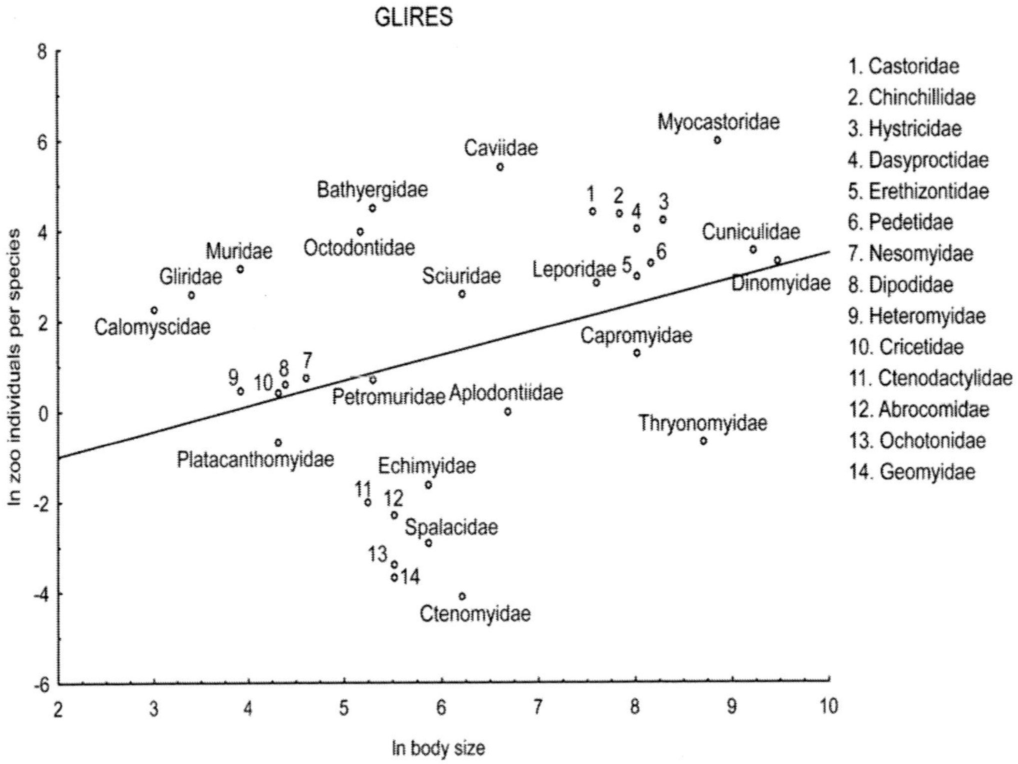

Specimen species representing the taxa sorted according to rank of attractiveness in descending order: *Ochotona alpina* (Ochotonidae), *Petromus typicus* (Petromuridae), *Octodon degu* (Octodontidae), *Macrotarsomys bastardi* (Nesomyidae), *Graphiurus kelleni* (Gliridae), *Sylvilagus obscurus* (Leporidae), *Dolichotis patagonum* (Caviidae), *Spermophilus columbianus* (Sciuridae), *Chaetodipus baileyi* (Heteromyidae), *Pedetes capensis* (Pedetidae), *Dasyprocta leporina* (Dasyproctidae), *Calomyscus* (Calomyscidae), *Dinomys branickii* (Dinomyidae), *Platacanthomys lasiurus* (Platacanthomyidae), *Allactaga elater* (Dipodidae), *Massoutiera mzabi* (Echimyidae), *Lagostomus maximus* (Chinchillidae), *Cuniculus paca* (Cuniculidae), *Apodemus agrarius* (Muridae), *Atherurus africanus* (Hystricidae), *Castor canadensis* (Castoridae), *Capromys pilorides* (Capromyidae), *Proechimys guarirae* (Ctenodactylidae), *Myocastor coypus* (Myocastoridae), *Ctenomys* (Ctenomyidae), *Thryonomys winderianus* (Thryonomyidae), *Geomys* (Geomyidae), *Aplodontia rufa* (Aplodontiidae), *Melanomys caliginosus* (Cricetidae), *Abrocoma benetti* (Abrocomidae), *Cryptomys mechowi* (Bathyergidae), *Coendou prehensilis* (Erethizontidae), *Spalax leucodon* (Spalacidae).

Figure 16. Relationship between size of zoo populations per species and body size in Glires. ln zoo individuals per species = log-transformed number of individuals belonging to a given family/subfamily kept in zoos worldwide per the total number of living species in this group. ln body size = log-transformed weight. $R^2 = 12.9\%$, $P = 0.0398$, $y = -2.12 * x + 0.56$.

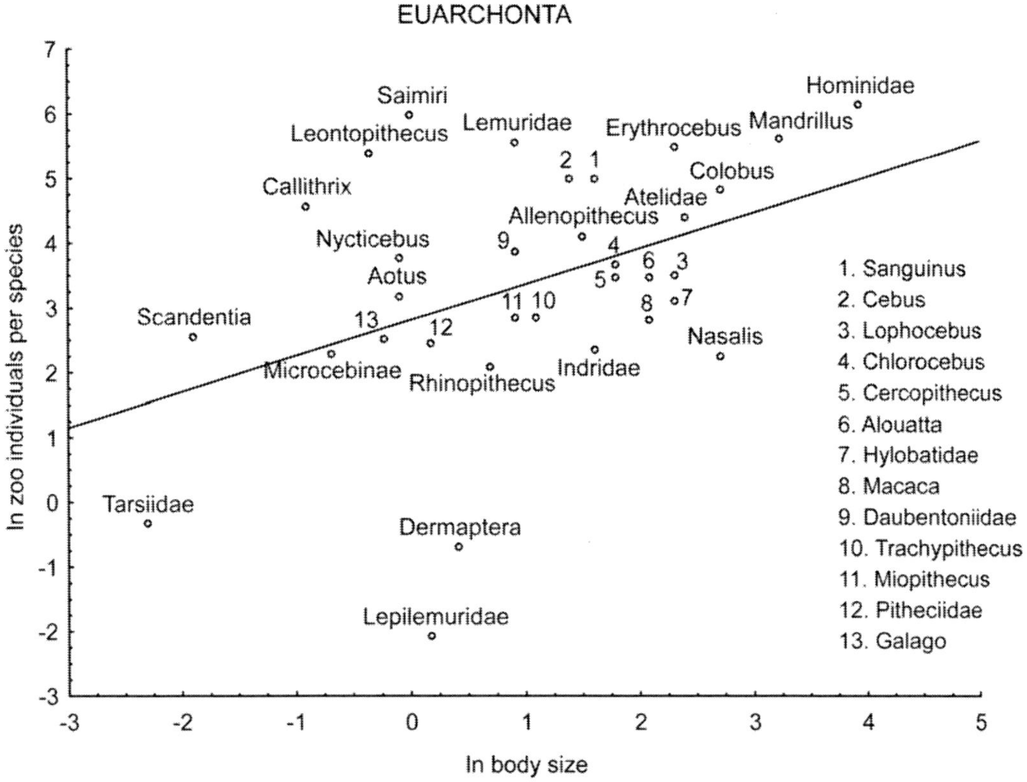

Specimen species representing the taxa sorted according to rank of attractiveness in descending order: *Galago rondoensis* (Galagidae: *Galago, Euoticus, Otolemur*); *Microcebus ravelobensis* (Microcebinae); *Lemur catta* (Lemuridae); *Nycticebus coucang* (Lorisidae: *Arctocebus, Loris, Perodicticus, Nycticebus, Pseudopotto*); *Propithecus edwardsi* (Indridae); *Leontopithecus rosalia* (Leontopithecina: *Leontopithecus*); *Miopithecus talapoin* (Cercopithecina II: *Miopithecus*); *Callicebus torquatus* (Pitheciidae); *Cebus olivaceus* (Cebinae: *Cebus*); *Saguinus oedipus* (Sanguina: *Sanguinus, Callimico*); *Macaca sylvanus* (Macaca); *Trachypithecus francoisi* (Colobinae: *Semnopithecus, Trachypithecus, Presbytis*); *Pongo abelii* (Hominidae); *Aotus trivirgatus* (Aotidae: *Aotus*); *Alouatta caraya* (Atelidae: *Alouatta*); *Tarsius syrichta* (Tarsiidae); *Nomascus concolor* (Hylobatidae); *Lepilemur septentrionalis* (Lepilemuridae); *Saimiri oerstedii* (Saimirinae: *Saimiri*); *Lophocebus albigena* (*Lophocebus, Cercocebus*); *Callithrix pygmaea* (Callithrichina: *Callithrix*); *Daubentonia madagascariensis* (Daubentoniidae); *Mandrillus leucophaeus* (*Mandrillus, Papio, Theropithecus*); *Colobus guereza* (Colobina: *Colobus, Procolobus*); *Galeopterus variegates* (Cynocephalidae: *Dermaptera*); *Cercopithecus diana* (Cercopithecina V: *Cercopithecus*); *Chlorocebus aethiops* (Cercopithecina IV: *Chlorocebus*); *Allenopithecus nigrovirridis* (Cercopithecina I: *Allenopithecus*); *Brachyteles arachnoides* (Atelidae: Atelidae except *Alouatta*); *Erythrocebus patas* (Cercopithecina III: *Erythrocebus*); *Ptilocercus lowii* (Ptilocercidae: *Scandentia*); *Nasalis larvatus* (odd-nosed II: *Nasalis, Simias*) *Rhinopithecus roxellana;* (odd-nosed I: *Rhinopithecus*).

Figure 17. Relationship between size of zoo populations per species and body size in Euarchonta. ln zoo individuals per species = log-transformed number of individuals belonging to a given family/subfamily kept in zoos worldwide per the total number of living species in this group. ln body size = log-transformed weight. R^2 = 17.9%, P = 0.0142, y = 2.81 * x + 0.55.

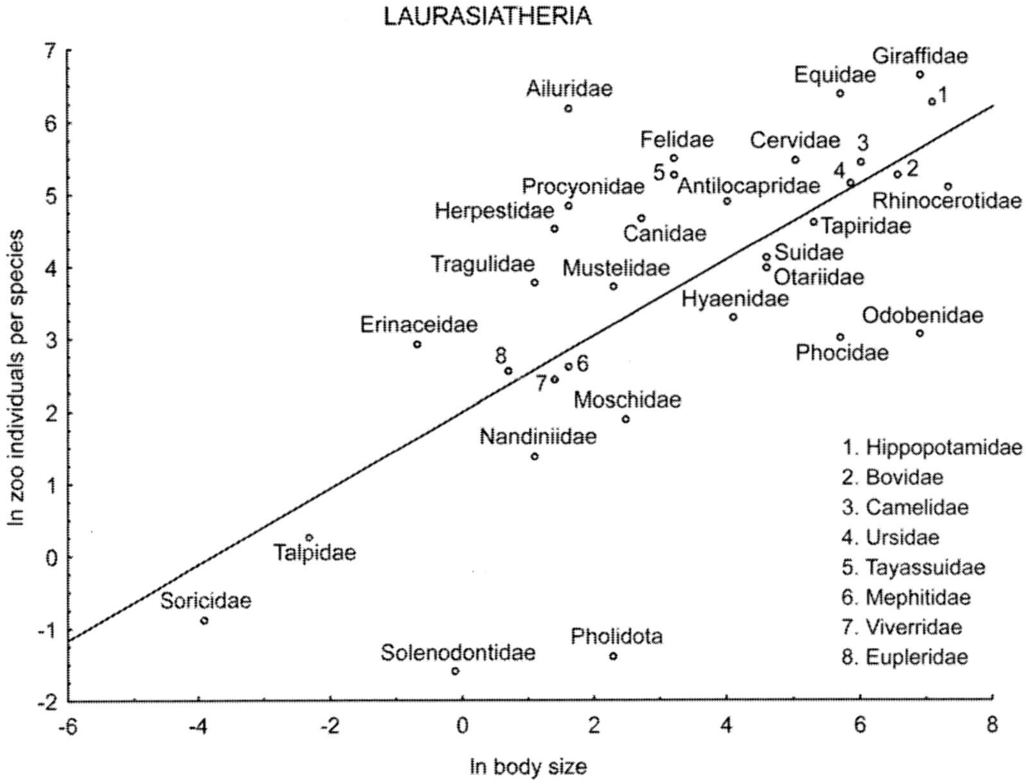

Specimen species representing the taxa sorted according to rank of attractiveness in descending order: *Ailurus fulgens* (Ailuridae), *Hemiechinus auritus* (Erinaceidae), *Ursus arctos* (Ursidae), *Leopardus pardalis* (Felidae), *Giraffa camelopardalis* (Giraffidae), *Vicugna vicugna* (Camelidae), *Galidictis fasciata* (Eupleridae), *Manis culionensis* (Pholidota), *Crocuta crocuta* (Hyaenidae), *Moschus moschiferus* (Moschidae), *Erignathus barbatus* (Phocidae), *Conepatus semistriatus* (Mephitidae), *Tragulus javanicus* (Tragulidae), *Rangifer tarandus* (Cervidae), *Nasua narcia* (Procyonidae), *Hexaprotodon liberiensis* (Hippopotamidae), *Diceros bicornis* (Rhinocerotidae), *Equus grevyi* (Equidae), *Nyctereutes procyonoides* (Canidae), *Tayassu pecari* (Tayassuidae), *Arctocephalus gazella* (Otariidae), *Genetta genetta* (Viverridae), *Mungos mungo* (Herpestidae), *Antilocapra americana* (Antilocapridae), *Nandinia binotata* (Nandiniidae), *Sorex minutus* (Soricidae), *Mellivora capensis* (Mustelidae), *Odobenus rosmarus* (Odobenidae), *Talpa europaea* (Talpidae), *Tapirus bairdii* (Tapiridae), *Phacochoerus africanus* (Suidae), *Bos sauveli* (Bovidae), *Solenodon cubanus* (Solenodontidae).

Figure 18. Relationship between size of zoo populations per species and body size in Laurasiatheria. ln zoo individuals per species = log-transformed number of individuals belonging to a given family/subfamily kept in zoos worldwide per the total number of living species in this group. ln body size = log-transformed weight. $R^2 = 45.2\%$, $P = 0.00002$ $y = 1.99 * x + 0.53$.

In conclusion, the relationship between human preference and mean size of zoo population was less apparent, but still detectable, when the analyzed units were the families/subfamilies instead of individual species. Obviously, when comparing families/subfamilies several additional differences in their biological features may mask the relationship. Moreover, decreased strength of the relationship may also be attributed to the fact that not all families/subfamilies are homogenous enough to be reliably represented by a picture of the randomly selected species. This is an especially important factor in the case of morphologically highly homogenous groups (e.g. passerines) in which human preferences are highly determined by coloration, i.e., the character sometimes exhibiting considerable variation even among related species as well as parallel evolution of the same patterns (Chiari et al. 2004). The analysis of 54 published datasets carried out by Areekul and Quicke 2006 confirmed that most color characters (except aposematic or mimetic ones) do not provide good phylogenetic signal and suffer from frequent homoplasies.

8. Preferred Species and Characters

The assessment of human preferences among representatives of families or subfamilies provided us also with additional information.

First, the agreement between the respondents was surprisingly higher for the animal groups least known by the respondent and/or inducing in humans negative rather than positive emotions. The first principal component explained the highest proportion of total variation in such groups as are snakes (48.0%), turtles (47.5%), Glires (= rodents and lagomorphs; 42.4%) and lizards (38.5%). On the other hand, the lowest agreement among the respondents was recorded in such popular groups as passerines (17.2%), Laurasiatheria (=ungulates, carnivors, pangolins and insectivores; 20.4%) and Euarchonta (primates and allies; 21.5%). Possibly, knowledge or positive attitude towards the animal species may obscure the relationship; while the pictures of unknown animals are ranked solely according to aesthetic rules which are more or less universal (see above).

It is worth of interest, which animals within each particular analyzed group of vertebrates were preferred by our respondents. Top ranking species of each group are listed at the Table 4 and some of them depicted in Figures 19-24. To figure out what taxa/species are perceived by

Table 4. Top ranking species according to human preferences

Group	The most attractive species	Species perceived as ugly
Snakes	1. Philippine pitviper	35. Brongersma's Worm Snake
	Parias flavomaculatus (Crotalinae)	*Typhlops brongersmianus* (Typhlopinae)
	2. Coral Earth Snake	34. Beu's Dawn Blind Snake
	Geophis semidoliatus (Dipsadinae)	*Liotyphlops beui* (Anomalepinae)
	3. Coral Cylinder Snakes	33. Western Threadsnake
	Anilius scytale (Aniliinae)	*Leptotyphlops humilis* (Leptotyphlopinae)
Lizards	1. Coarse Chameleon	37. California legless lizard
	Chamaeleo rudis (Chamaeleoninae)	*Anniella pulchra* (Anniellinae)
	2. Anzamala Madagascar Swift	36. Blind Lizard
	Oplurus fierinensis (Oplurinae)	*Dibamus bogadeki* (Dibaminae)
	3. Tschudi's Pacific Iguana	35. Exmouth Worm-lizard
	Microlophus thoracicus (Tropidurinae)	*Aprasia rostrata* (Lialisinae or Pygopodinae)

Table 4. (Continued)

Group	The most attractive species	Species perceived as ugly
Turtles	1. Spotted Turtle *Clemmys guttata* (Emydinae) 2. Madagascan Tortoise *Astrochelys yniphora* (Testudininae) 3. Snail-eating Turtle *Malayemys subtrijuga* (Batagurinae)	21. Florida Softshell Turtle *Apalone ferox* (Trionychinae) 20. Mexican Giant Musk Turtle *Staurotypus triporcatus* (Staurotypinae) 19. Indian Soft-shelled Turtle *Lissemys punctata* (Cyclanorbinae)
Basal birds	1.Brown Kiwi *Apteryx australis* (Apterigidae) 2. Stephan's Dove *Chalcophaps stephani* (Columbidae) 3. Hazel Grouse *Bonasa bonasia* (Tetraonidae)	16. Micronesian Scrubfowl *Megapodius laperouse* (Megapodiidae) 15. Wild Turkey *Meleagris gallopavo* (Meleagridae) 14. Grey Tinamou *Tinamus tao* (Tinamidae)
Aquatic birds	1. Greater Flamingo *Phoenicopterus ruber* (Phoenicopteridae) 2. Crowned Crane *Balearica pavonina* (Gruidae) 3. Black-Necked Stilt *Himantopus mexicanus* (Recurvirostrini)	29. Snowy Sheathbill *Chionis alba* (Chionidae) 28. Black-Legged Seriema *Chunga burmeisteri* (Cariamidae) 27. Little Buttonquail *Turnix velox* (Turnicidae)
Terrestrial birds	1. Indigo-banded Kingfisher *Alcedo cyanopecta (Alcedinidae)* 2. Russet-Crowned Motmot *Momotus mexicanus* (Momotidae) 3. Common Hoopoe *Upupa epops* (Upupidae)	25. Willcock's Honeyguide *Indicator willcocksi* (Indicatoridae) 24. Groove-Billed Ani *Crotophaga sulcirostris* (Crotophagidae) 23. Violaceous Coucal *Centropus violaceus* (Centropodidae)
Passerines	1. Blue-and-White Flycatcher *Cyanoptila cyanomelana* (Muscicapini) 2. Blue-Tit *Parus caeruleus* (Parinae) 3. Olive Warbler *Peucedramus taeniatus* (Peucedraminae)	30. Common bananaquit *Coereba flaveola* (Thraupini) 29. Long-Tailed Tit *Aegithalos caudatus* (Aegithalidae) 28. Indian Lark *Mirafra erythroptera* (Alaudidae)
Bassal mammals	1. Northern Hairy-nosed Wombat *Lasiorhinus krefftii* (Vombatidae) 2. Southern Tree Hyrax *Dendrohyrax arboreus* (Procaviidae) 3. Koala *Phascolarctos cinereus* (Phascolarctidae)	35. Duck-billed Platypus *Ornithorhynchus anatinus* (Ornithorhynchidae) 34. Incan Caenolestid *Lestoros inca* (Caenolestidae) 33. Eastern Barred Bandicoot *Perameles gunnii* (Peramelidae)
Glires	1. Alpine Pika *Ochotona alpina* (Ochotonidae) 2. Dassie Rat *Petromus typicus* (Petromuridae) 3. Degu *Octodon degu* (Octodontidae)	33. Lesser Blind Mole Rat *Spalax leucodon* (Spalacidae) 32. Brazilian Porcupine *Coendou prehensilis* (Erethizontidae) 31. Giant Mole-rat *Cryptomys mechowi* (Bathyergidae)
Euarchonta	1. Rondo Bushbaby *Galago rondoensis* (Galagidae) 2. Ravelobe Mouse Lemur *Microcebus ravelobensis* (Microcebinae) 3. Ring-tailed Lemur *Lemur catta* (Lemuridae)	33. Golden Snub-nosed Monkey *Rhinopithecus roxellana* (odd-nosed I former Colobinae*) 32. Proboscis Monkey *Nasalis larvatus* (odd-nosed II, Colobinae*) 31. Pen-tailed Treeshrew *Ptilocercus lowii* (Ptilocercidae)
Laurasiatheria	1. Red Panda *Ailurus fulgens* (Ailuridae) 2. Long-eared Hedgehog *Hemiechinus auritus* (Erinaceidae) 3. Brown Bear *Ursus arctos* (Ursidae)	33. Cuban Solenodon *Solenodon cubanus* (Solenodontidae) 32. Kouprey *Bos sauveli* (Bovidae) 31. Common Warthog *Phacochoerus africanus* (Suidae)

*Colobinae were split into three separate groups according to Sterner et al. 2006.

humans as beautiful, indifferent or disgusting, we aligned the set of the pictures according the human's mean ranking in ascending order and tried to interpret the features linked with current position of the picture in whole sequence. Supplementary information was extracted also from remarks of our respondents during the testing.

Figure 19. Examples of most preferred species within particular higher taxa according to our respondents. Blue-and-White Flycatcher (*Cyanoptila cyanomelana*); Passeriformes: Muscicapini. Original painting by Silvie Lišková.

Figure 20. Examples of most preferred species within particular higher taxa according to our respondents. Indigo-banded kingfisher (*Alcedo cyanopecta*); Terrestrial birds: Alcedinidae. Original painting by Silvie Lišková.

Figure 21. Examples of most preferred species within particular higher taxa according to our respondents. Spotted turtle (*Clemmys guttata*); Turtles: Emydinae. Original painting by Silvie Lišková.

Figure 22. Examples of most preferred species within particular higher taxa according to our respondents. Royal antelope (*Neotragus pygmaeus*); Antelopes and allies (Bovidae). Original painting by Silvie Lišková.

Figure 23. Examples of most preferred species within particular higher taxa according to our respondents. Red panda (*Ailurus fulgens*); Laurasiatheria: Ailuridae. Original painting by Silvie Lišková.

Figure 24. Examples of most preferred species within particular higher taxa according to our respondents. Common wombat (*Vombatus ursinus*); Basal mammals: Vombatidae. Original painting by Silvie Lišková.

The preferred traits varied greatly from set to set. Obviously, contribution of coloration on human preferences was important among birds (see Bennett & Owens 2002 for evolution of bird coloration) and reptiles, while it was only marginal among mammals characterized by limited variance in this character (for evolution of mammalian coloration see Caro 2005). We further discuss the observed patterns group by group.

Snakes

The preferred snakes were those with bright background colors: green as Philippine pitviper (*Parias flavomaculatus*, Crotalinae), red as coral earth snake (*Geophis semidoliatus*, Dipsadinae) and coral cylinder snakes *Anilius scytale* (Aniliinae), and bluish as colubrine *Laticauda colubrina* (Laticaudinae). Also stripes or disruptive pattern contributed to beauty. The plain grey or brownish species with snake-typical body plan were placed in the middle of preference scale. Species without clearly differed head and tail were perceived as unattractive: Brongersma's worm snake (*Typhlops brongersmianus,* Typhlopinae), *Liotyphlops beuii* (Anomalepinae), western threadsnake (*Leptotyphlos humilis*, Leptotyphlopinae), Peters' Philippine earth snake(*Rhinophis pillippinus*, Uropeltinae) or southeastern crowned snake (*Tantilla coronata*, Colubrinae).

Lizards and Tuataras

Our respondents preferred green species irrespective to their morphology: coarse chameleon (*Chameleo rudis,* Chameleonidae), Anzamala Madagascar Shift (*Oplurus fierinensis*, Oplurinae), and terrestrial arboreal alligator lizard (*Abronia graminea*, Gerrhonotinae). Species exhibiting whatever distinct color pattern in combination with lizards-typical body plan as were also preferred. Interestingly, those labeled by respondents as "strange" or "fanciful" were perceived as less attractive, e.g. tuatara (*Sphenodon punctatus,* Sphenodontidae), northern leaf-tail gecko (*Saltuarius cornutus,* Diplodactylinae), Egyptian mastigure (*Uromastyx aegyptia,* Leiolepinae) or Boulenger's pygmy chameleon (*Rhampholeon boulengeri*, Brookesiinae). The animals with reduced limbs as Deraniyagala's tree skink (*Lankascincus deraniyagalai,* Scincinae), Cope's galliwasp (*Celestus stenurus,* Diploglossinae), slender glass lizard (*Ophisaurus atennuatus*, Anguinae) or even worm-like body plan as checkerboard worm lizard (*Trogonophis wiegmani,* Trogonophidae), exmouth worm-lizard (*Aprasia rostrata,* Pygopodinae), blind lizard (*Dibamus bogadeki*, Dibaminae) and California legless lizard *(Anniella pulchra*, Annielinae) were perceived as unattractive or ugly.

Testudines

The most preferred were turtles and tortoises with yellow or red pattern on carapax and/or on the head: .spotted turtle (*Clemmys guttata*, Emydinae), Madagascan tortoise (*Astrochelys yniphora*, Testudininae), snail-eating turtle (*Malayemys subrijuga,* Batagurinae), red-headed Amazon side-necked turtle (*Podocnemis erythrocephala*, Podocnemidinae), Florida redbelly turtle (*Pseudemys nelsoni,* Deirochelyinae), three-banded box turtle (*Cuora trifasciata*, Geoemydinae). The list of top ten includes also marine turtles and pig-nosed turtle (*Carettochelis insculpta*, Caretochelinae) with similar appearance. The species placed at the end of the preference scale were labeled by most respondents as "strange" as South-American snake-headed turtle (*Hydromedusa tectifera,* Hydromedusinae) and soft-shelled turtles or "dangerous" and "hostile" as big-headed turtle (*Platysternon megacephalum,* Platysterninae), common snapping turtle (*Chelydra serpentina*, Chelidrinae), or *Staurotypus triporcatus* (Staurotypinae). This feeling of potential danger corresponds also with opinion of many proficient breeders (Figure 9.).

Basal Birds

Favorites of this set were: kiwi (Apteryx australis, Apterygidae), pigeons especially the species with green feathers e.g. Stephan's dove Chalcophaps stephani, negros fruit-dove Ptilinopus arcanus, Sumatran green pigeon Treron oxyura (Columbidae). The species belonging to families Tetraonidae and Anatidae were highly preferred to. The lengths of legs e.g. in lesser rhea (Rhea pennata, Rheidae), ostrich (Struthio camelus, Struthionidae), , northern screamer (Chauna chavaria, Anhimidae) and long tail, e.g., in great argus (Argusianus argus, Phasianidae) or crest as in scaled quail (Callipepla squamata, Odontophoridae) and cassowary (Casuarius casuarius, Casuariidae), are the other observable features increasing the attractiveness of the species/family for humans.

Aquatic Birds

Elegance of shape and length of neck, legs and prominent beaks are the traits of species/families ranked as the most beautiful. Species with short neck, relatively shorter legs and beaks were perceived as unattractive. In this set of pictures, coloration had no marked effect on human ranking.

Terrestrial Birds

For human aesthetic preference is coloration of birds most important features. Brightly colored (blue, red, and green) species from different families were perceived as most beautiful: e.g. indigo-banded kingfisher *Alcedo cyanopecta,* white-throated kingfisher *Halcyon smyrnensis* (Alcedinidae), russet-crowned motmot (*Momotus mexicanus*, Momotidae) or red-and-green macaw (*Ara chloropterus*, Psittacidae). Also prominent beak (in e.g. Boehm's bee-eater (*Merops boehmi,* Meropidae), Emerald toucanet (*Aulacorhynchus prasinus*, Ramphastinae), great jacamar (*Jacamerops aureus*, Galbulidae) and/or crest e.g. in common hoopoe (*Upupa epops*,Upupidae,) shift the species upwards on the preference scale (Figure 12.). The combination of bright coloration with prominent beak and crest evoke positive emotions reliably. The lengths of the legs or tail are not important.

Passerines

Brightly colored birds with blue e.g. blue waxbill (*Uraeginthus angolensis* Estrildinae), blue-tit (*Parus caerules,* Parinae), blue-and-white flycatcher (*Cyanoptila cyanomelana,* Muscicapini), red e.g. Crimson sunbird (*Aethopyga siparaja,* Nectariniidae), green and yellow or orange colures are perceived as the most beautiful. The black mask on a head e.g. in olive warbler (*Peucedramus taeniatus,* Peucedraminae), village weaver (*Ploceus cucullatus*, Ploceinae) also enhances preferences to the holder. However, the congruence among respondents is low. Probably, human's cognitive abilities are not adjusted to recognize and classify passerines with such uniform morphology.

Basal Mammals

Characterization of three most preferred basal mammals, i.e., northern hairy-nosed wombat (*Lasiorhinus krefftii,* Vombatidae), southern tree hyrax (*Dendrohyrax arboreus,* Procaviidae) and *Phascolarctos cinereus* (Phascolarctidae) is quite simple – they all have appearance of lovely Teddy bears with dense fur, shaggy round ears and relatively big eyes. The animals possessing long and shaggy tail as northern tamandua (*Tamandua mexicana,* Myrmecophagidae), yellow-footed rock-wallaby *Petrogale xanthopus* (Macropodidae), squirrel glider *Petaurus norfolcensis* (Petauridae).are preferred too. Interestingly, elephant (*Loxodonta africana*) occupies just the eighth position on the scale of preferences. Subterranean, mouse-like animals and duck-billed platypus are placed on the tail of humans' preferences.

Glires

This set of the pictures was unpopular among our respondents. Some students even tried to avoid evaluation of this set and expressed wisdom to arrange sets consisting of other animals. Most preferred species resemble approximately "Mickey Mouse" body scheme e.g. Alpine pika (*Ochotona alpina*, Ochotonidae), degu (*Octodon degu*, Octodontidae) or lesser big-footed mouse (*Macrotarsomys bastardi*, Nesomyidae). The length shaggy tail, big ears and bigger body size are preferred traits in this group. As in the previous group, the subterranean species e.g. giant mole-rat (*Cryptomys mechowi*, Bathyergidae) or lesser blind mole rat (*Spalax leucodon,* Spalacidae) and those resembling rat were unequivocally perceived as ugly.

Euarchonta

It is obvious that respondents prefers small nocturnal species with big eyes and ears e.g. rondo bush baby (*Galago rondoensis*, Galagidae), ravelobe mouse lemur (*Microcebus ravelobensis*, Microcebinae) or slow lori (*Nycticebus coucang,* Lorisidae). The primates with long and shaggy tail, e.g., ring-tailed lemur (*Lemur catta*, Lemuridae), Milne-Edwards's

(*Propithecus edwardsi,* Indridae), golden lion tamarin (*Leontopithecus rosalia,* Leontopithecina, Calitrichidae) or collared titi (*Callicebus torquatus,* Pitheciidae) are highly preferred too, similarly as in other groups (see above Basal mammals and Glires). Surprisingly, great apes represented by orang-outan (*Pongo abelii,* Hominidae) were placed to thirteenth position only on preference scale. The species placed at the end of the preference scale were in some aspect different from apish typical appearance e.g. pen-tailed tree-shrew *Ptilocercus lowii* (Ptilocercidae), proboscis monkey (*Nasalis larvatus,* Colobinae).

Laurasiatheria

In these set again bear-like animals as red panda (*Ailurus fulgens*, Ailuridae) or really bears brown bear (*Ursus arctos*, Ursidae) were preferred. Again species with dense fur, shaggy round ears animals long-eared hedgehog (*Hemiechinus auritus*, Erinaceidae) and/or apparent color pattern e.g. leopard (*Leopardus pardalis,* Felidae) or giraffe (*Giraffa camelopardalis*, Giraffidae) were perceived as charming or beautiful. For the list of unattractive species see Table 4.

9. Conclusion

Worldwide net of zoos supports considerable proportions of living species, at least in the case of terrestrial vertebrates as mammals, birds and reptiles. This collection may play a role of valuable Noah's Ark providing that following conditions are fullfilled.

1) It is reasonable selection of species to keep that may help to cover all major clades and species/taxa under most apparent risk of extinction. This requires application of both phylogenetic approach and actual information on conservation status of concerned species.
2) It is necessary to reflect the fact that economics and space limit invevitably the size of zoo populations. We clearly demonstrated that zoo populations of most species (including those actually going to extinction in nature) are too small to be sustainable even in the short-time perspecive. Thus management of these insufficient populations should be promptly acommodated to this alarming situation. This especially requires blurring boundaries between captive and wild populations (cf. Dickie et al. 2007) as well as those between zoo animals and populations kept by other respectable breeders (including private and NGO collections). Surplus animals from zoos should not be further castrated or killed as dictated by defenders of animal rights and wellfare ethics, but preferably moved from hard core of studbook populations kept in zoos and professional breeders into its periphery, e.g., private breeders, NGOs, reintroduction programs, etc. Simultaneously, priming, coordination and methodical role of zoos and their breeding programs should be extended. Conservation ethics (Hutchins 2007) evaluating survival of the species as moral priority have to be used to overcome administrative barriers and popular preconceptions.

3) Decisions, which species to keep and breed in great numbers, have to follow conservation needs rather that popularity of the species. Only 187 out of 23,582 living species of higher vertebrates have worldwide zoo population exceeding 500 specimens. Even more alarming is that only 49 out of these 187 species are those actually endangered.

We confirmed that zoo collections are biased in favor of the birds (higher numer of captive species) and mammals (larger population sizes), while reptiles are underepresented. Thorough analyses of zoo population sizes suggest that body size is without any doubt the most prominent factor increasing the representation of given species or higher taxon in zoos. Although large animals are disproportionally more expensive to keep they are frequently elected, probably due to visitor's preferrence.

In addition to body size, there is appearance of the animal per se. Some animals are perceived as more attractive than the others. Our respondents were exposed to the sets of pictures depicting different animal species and asked to rank the species according to their beauty. We were surprised by the high degree of congruence among the responses of different persons. Nevertheless, the characters contributing to human preferences varied greatly among studied sets of pictures. Conspicuous coloration was prominent factor in some birds and reptiles taxa, while preferred body proportions varied among studied taxa. Most comparisons carried out among related species showed the strong effects of beauty on size of zoo populations. In contrast, when not species, but families/subfamilies were compared this effect has remained significant within particular animal tax only (basal mammals, Laurasiatheria, terrestrial birds). Obviously, characters matching human aethetic criteria are distributted across different animal taxa. Thus, human preferences towards particular species belonging to the same family/subfamily may sometimes differ considerably. This may help zoos to find the species satistfying aesthetic criteria of the visitors and keepers in almost every clade of animals worth of ex situ conservation effort.

REFERENCES

Areekul, B. & Quicke, D. L. J. (2006). The use of colour characters in phylogenetic reconstruction. *Biological Journal of Linnean Society, 88,* 193-202.

Baenninger, R. (1988). Animals in Art: Some Trends Across Three Millennia. *The Journal of psychology, 122,* 183-191.

Baker, A. (2007). Animal ambassadors: an analysis of the effectiveness and conservation impact of ex situ breeding efforts. In Zimmermann, & M. Hatchwell, & A. D. Lesley, & C. West (Eds.), *Zoos in the 21st Century. Catalysts for Conservation?* (pp. 139-155). New York, NY: Cambridge University Press.

Balmford, A. (2000). Separating fact from artfact in analyses of zoo visitor preferences. *Conservation Biology, 14(4),* 1193-1195.

Barker, F. K. & Cibois, A. & Schikler, P. & Einstein, J. & Cracraft, J. (2004). Phylogeny and diversification of the largest avian radiation. *Proceedings of the National Academy of Science, 101(30),* 11040-11045.

Barkow, J. H., & Cosmides, L., & Tooby, J., (1992). *The Adapted Mind.* New York, NY: Oxford University Press.

Bennett, P. M., & Owens, I. P. F. (2002). Evolutionary Ecology of Birds. New York, NY: Oxford University Press.

Berlin, B. (1992). *Ethnobiological classification: principles of categorization of plants and animals in traditional societies*. Princeton, NJ: Princeton University Press.

Bertolero, A. & Oro, D. & Besnard, A. (2007). Assessing the efficacy of reintroduction programmes by modelling adult survival: the example of Hermann's tortoise. *Animal Conservation, 10,* 360-368.

Bininda-Emonds, O. R. P. & Cardillo, M. & Jones, K. E. & MacPhee, R. D. E. & Beck, R. M. D. & Grenyer, R. & Price, S. A., & Vos, R.A. & Gittleman, J. L. & Purvis, A. (2007). The delayed rise of present-day mammals. *Nature, 446,* 507-512.

Brighsmith, D. & Hilburn, J. & Campo, A. & Boyd, J. & Frisius, R. & Janik, D. & Guilen (2005). The use of hand-raised psittacines for reintroduction: a case study of scarlet macaws (*Ara macao*) in Peru and Costa Rica. *Biological Conservation, 121,* 465-472.

Brown, M. & Perrin, M. & Hoffman, B. (2007). Reintroduction of captive-bred African Grass-Owls *Tyto capensis* into natural habitat. *Ostrich, 78(1),* 75-79.

Caro, T. M. & Graham, C. M. & Stoner, C. J. & Flores, M. M. (2003). Correlates of horn and antler shape in bovids and cervids. *Behavioral Ecology and Sociobiology, 55,* 32-41.

Caro, T. M. (2005). The adaptive significance of coloration in mammals. *Bioscience, 55(2),* 125-136.

Chiari, Y. & Vences, M. & Vieites, D. R. & Rabemananjara, F. & Bora, P. & Ramilijaona Ravoahanangimalala, O. & Meyer, A. (2004). New evidence for parallel evolution of colour patterns in Malagasy poison frogs. (Mantella). *Molecular Ecology, 13,* 3763-3774.

Cohn, J. P. (1992). Decisions at the zoo: Ethics, politics and animal rights concerns affect the process of balancing conservation goals and the public interests. *BioScience, 42(9),* 654-659.

Connolly, J. D. & Cree, A. (2008). Risks of a late start to captive management for conservation: Phenotypic differences between wild and captive individuals of a viviparous endangered scink (*Oligosoma otagense*). *Biological Conservation, 141,* 1283-1292.

Czech, B. & Krausman, P. R. & Borkhataria, R. (1998). Social Construction, Political Power, and Allocation of Benefits to Endangered Species. *Conservation Biology, 12(5),* 1103-1112.

Davey, G. C. L. & McDonald, A. S. & Hrisave, U. & Prabhu, G. G. & Iwawaki, S. & Jim, C. I. & Merckelbach, H. & de Jong, P. J. & Leung, P. W. L. & Reimann, B. C. (1998). A cross-cultural study of animal fears. *Behaviour Research and Therapy, 36,* 735-750.

del Hoyo, J., & Elliot, A., & Sargatal, J. (Eds.) (1992-2002). *Handbook of the Birds of the World (Volumes 1-7)*. Barcelona, Spain: Lynx Edicions.

Denton, J.S. & Hitchings, P. S. & Beebee, T. J. C. & Gent, A. (1997). A recovery program for the natterjack toad (*Bufo calamita*). *Conservation biology, 11(6),* 1329-1338.

Dickie, L. A., & Bonner, J.P., & West, C. (2007). In situ conservation and ex situ conservation: blurring the boundaries between zoos and the wild. In Zimmermann, & M. Hatchwell, & A. D. Lesley, & C. West (Eds.), *Zoos in the 21st Century. Catalysts for Conservation?* (pp. 220-236). New York, NY: Cambridge University Press.

Ericson, P. G. P. & Anderson, C. L. & Britton, T. & Elzanowski, A. & Johansson, U. S. & Källersjo, M. & Ohlson, J. I. & Parson, J. T. & Zuccon, D. & Mayer, G. (2006). Diversification of Neoaves: integration of molecular sequence data and fossils. *Biology Letters, 2,* 543-547.

Field, D.A., & Dickie, L.A. (2007). Zoo coalitions for conservations. In Zimmermann, & M. Hatchwell, & A. D. Lesley, & C. West (Eds.), *Zoos in the 21st Century. Catalysts for Conservation?* (pp. 287-303). New York, NY: Cambridge University Press.

Frankham, R., & Ballou, J. D., & Briscoe, D. A. (2002). *Introduction to conservation genetics.* Cambridge, UK: Cambridge University Press.

Frankham, R. (2008). Genetic adaptation to captivity in species conservation programs. *Molecular Ecology, 17,* 325-333.

Goodman, M. & Porter, C. A. & Czelusniak, J. & Page, L. C. & Schneider, H. & Shoshani, J. & Gunnell, G. & Groves, C. P. (1998). Toward a phylogenetic classification of primates based on DNA evidence complemented by fossil evidence. *Molecular Phylogenetics and Evolution, 9(3),* 585-598.

Gould, S. J. (1979). Mickey Mouse meets Konrad Lorenz. *Natural History, 88(5),* 30-34.

Gunnthorsdottir, A. (2001). Physical attractiveness of an animal species as a decision factor for its preservation. *Anthrozoos, 14(4)*, 204-215.

Guthrie, R. D. (2005). *The nature of Paleolithic art.* Chicago, IL: University of Chicago Press.

Hackett, S. J., & Kimball, R. T. & Reddi, S. & Bowie, R. C. K. & Braun, E. L. & Braun, M. J. & Chojnowski, J. L. & Cox, A. W. & Han, K. L. & Harshman, J. & Huddleston, C. J. & Marks, B. D. & Miglia, K. J. & Moore, W. S. & Sheldon, F. H. & Steadman, D. W. & Witt, C. C. & Yuri, T. (2008). Phylogenomic study of birds reveals their evolutionary history. *Science, 320(27*), 1763-1768.

Halberstadt, J. & Rhodes, G. (2003). It's not just average faces that are attractive: Computer-manipulated averageness makes birds, fish and automobiles attractive. *Psychonomic Bulletin and Review, 10(1),* 149-156.

Hale, K. A. & Briskie, J. V. (2007). Challenges to understanding the consequences of population bottlenecks for the conservation of endangered wildlife. *Animal Conservation, 10,* 19-21.

Herzog, H.A. & Bentley, A. & Hahn, M. W. (2004). Random drift and large shifts in popularity of dog breeds. *Proceedings of Royal Society Series B Biology, 271,* S353-S356.

Holst, B., & Dickie L.A. (2007). How do national and international regulations and policies influence the role of zoos and aquariums in conservation? In A. Zimmermann, & M. Hatchwell, & A. D. Lesley, & C. West (Eds.), *Zoos in the 21st Century. Catalysts for Conservation?* (pp. 22-37). New York, NY: Cambridge University Press.

Hosey, G. (2008). A preliminary model of human-animal relationships in zoos. *Applied Animal Behaviour Science, 109,* 105-127.

Hutchins, M. (2007). The animal rights-conservation debate: can zoos and aquariums play a role? In In A. Zimmermann, & M. Hatchwell, & A. D. Lesley, & C. West (Eds.), *Zoos in the 21st Century. Catalysts for Conservation?* (pp. 92-110). New York, NY: Cambridge University Press.

International Species Information System (ISIS) database (2008). URL: http://www.isis.org

IUCN (2008). IUCN Red List of Threatened Species. World Conservation Union, URL: http://www.iucnredlist.org

Jule, K. L. & Leaver, L. A. & Lea, S. E. G. (2008). The effects of captive experience on reintroduction survival in carnivores: A review and analysis. *Biological Conservation, 141,* 355-363.

Kellert, S. R. (1985): Social and Perceptual Factors in the Preservation of Animal Species. *Journal of Wildlife Management, 49(2),* 528-536.

Kimura, M. (1983). *The neutral theory of molecular evolution.* Cambridge, UK: Cambridge University Press.

Lande, R. (1999). Extinction risks from anthropogenic, ecological, and genetics factors. In Landweber, L. F. & Dobson, A. P. (Eds.), *Genetics and the extinction of species: DNA and the conservation of biodiversity.* (pp. 1-23) Princeton, NJ: Princeton University Press.

Leader-Williams, N., & Balmford, A., & Linkie, M., & Mace, G.M., & Smith, R.J., & Stevenson, M., & Walter, O., & West, C. & Zimmerman,A. (2007). Beyond the ark: conservation biologists' views of the achievements of zoos in conservation. In Zimmermann, & M. Hatchwell, & A. D. Lesley, & C. West (Eds.), *Zoos in the 21st Century. Catalysts for Conservation?* (pp. 236-257). New York, NY: Cambridge University Press.

Lewis-Williams, J. D. (2002). *The Mind in the Cave: Consciousness and the Origins of Art.* London, UK: Thames & Hudson.

Marešová, J. & Frynta, D. (2008). Noah's Ark is full of common species attractive to humans: the case of boid snakes in Zoos. *Ecological Economics, 64,* 554-558.

Masi, A. (1996). Birds: DNA Sibley's Sequence. URL: http://www.scricciolo.com/classificazione/sibley's_index.htm

McDougall, P. T. & Réale, D. & Sol, D. & Reader, S. M. (2006). Wildlife conservation and animal temperament: causes and consequences of evolutionary change for captive, reintroduced, and wild populations. *Animal Conservation, 9,* 39-48.

Metrick, A. & Weitzman, M. L. (1996). Patterns of behaviour in endangered species preservation. *Land Economics, 72(1),* 1-16.

Metrick, A. & Weitzman, M. L. (1998). Conflict and choices in biodiversity preservations. *Journal of Economic Perspectives, 12(3),* 21-35.

Morris, D. (1967). *The naked ape.* New York, NY: McGraw-Hill.

Murphy, W. J. & Eizirik, E. & Johnson, W. E. & Zhang, Y. P. & Ryder, O. A. & O'Brien, S. J. (2001). Molecular phylogenetics and the origin of placental mammals. *Nature, 409,* 614-618.

O'Regan, H. J. & Kitchener, A. C. (2005). The effects of captivity on morphology of captive, domesticated and feral mammals. *Mammal Review, 35(3-4),* 215-230.

Pielou, E. C., (1966). The measurement of diversity in different types of biological collections. *Journal of Theoretical Biology, 13,* 131–144.

Pittenger, J. B. (1990). Body proportions as information for age and cuteness: Animals in illustrated childrens books. *Perception and Psychophysics, 42(2),* 124-130.

Price, M. R. S., & Fa J. E. (2007). Reintroductions from zoos: a conservation guiding light or a shooting star? In Zimmermann, & M. Hatchwell, & A. D. Lesley, & C. West (Eds.), *Zoos in the 21st Century. Catalysts for Conservation?* (pp. 155-178). New York, NY: Cambridge University Press.

Quinn, P. C. & Kelly, D. J. & Lee, K. & Pascalis, O. & Slater, A. M (2008). Preference for attractive faces in human infants extends beyond conspecifics. *Developmental Science, 11(1),* 76-83.

Raup, D. M. (1991). *Extinction: Bad genes or bad luck?* New York, NY: W.W. Norton and Company.

Reed, D. H. & Nicholas, A. C. & Stratton, G. E. (2007). Genetic quality of individuals impacts population dynamics. *Animal Conservation, 10,* 275-283.

Rodrígez-Clarc, K. M. (1999). Genetic theory and evidence supporting current practices in captive breeding for conservation. In Landweber, L. F. & Dobson, A. P. (Eds.), *Genetics and the extinction of species: DNA and the conservation of biodiversity.* (pp. 47–73) Princeton, NJ: Princeton University Press.

Samples, K. C. & Dixon, J. A. & Gowen, M. M. (1986). Information Disclosure and Endangered Species Valuation. *Land Economics, 62(3),* 306-312.

Schmidt-Nielsen, K. (1984). *Scaling: Why Is Animal Size So Important?* Cambridge, UK: Cambridge University Press.

Seddon, P. J. & Soorae, P. S. & Launay, F. (2005). Taxonomic bias in reintroduction projects. *Animal Conservation, 8,* 51-58.

Shannon, C. D. (1963): *The mathematical theory of communication.* Urbana/Chicago, IL: University of Illinois Press.

Sheldon, A.L. (1969). Equitability indices: dependence on the species count. *Ecology, 50,* 466-467.

Sibley, C. G., & Alquist, J. E. (1990). *Phylogeny and classification of birds: a study in molecular evolution.* New Haven, CT: Yale University Press.

Sibley, C. G. & Monroe, B. L. (1990). *Distribution and taxonomy of birds of the world.* New Haven, CT: Yale University Press.

Sibley, C. G. & Monroe, B. L. (1993). *A supplement to 'Distribution and taxonomy of birds of the world'.* New Haven, CT: Yale University Press.

Simon, B. M. & Leff, C. S. & Doerksen, H. (1995). Allocating scarce resources for endangered species recovery. *Journal of Policy Analysis and Management, 14(3),* 415-432.

Soulé, M. E. (1980). Thresholds for survival: maintaining fitness and evolutionary potential. In: Soulé, M. E. & Wilcox, B. A. (Eds.), *Conservation Biology: An evolutionary-ecological perspective* (pp. 151-169). Sunderland, MA: Sinauer.

Soulé, M. E. & Gilpin, M. & Conway, W. & Foose, T. (1986). The millennium ark: how long a voyage, how many staterooms, how many passengers? *Zoo Biology, 5,* 101-113.

StatSoft Inc. (2001). *STATISTICA* (data analysis software system), vers.6.0., URL: http://www.statsoft.com.

Sterling, E., & Lee, J., & Wood, T. (2007). Conservation education in zoos: an emphasis on behavioral change. In A. Zimmermann, & M. Hatchwell, & A. D. Lesley, & C. West (Eds.), *Zoos in the 21st Century. Catalysts for Conservation?* (pp. 37-51). New York, NY: Cambridge University Press.

Sterner, K. N. & Raaum, R. L. & Zhang Y. P. & Steward, C. B. & Disotell, T. D. (2006). Mitochondrial data support and odd-nosed colobine clade. *Molecular Phylogenetics and Evolution, 40,* 1-7.

Stokes, D. L. (2007). Things We Like: Human Preferences among Similar Organisms and Implications for Conservation. *Human Ecology, 35,* 361-369.

Taberlet, P. & Valentini, A. & Rezaei, H. R. & Naderi, S. & Pompanon, F. & Negrini, R. & Ajmone-Marsan, P. (2008). Are cattle, sheep, and goats endangered species? *Molecular Ecology, 17,* 275-284.

Taylor, S. S. & Jamieson, I. G. & Armstrong, D. P. (2005). Successful island reintroductions of New Zealand robins and saddlebacks with small number of founders. *Animal Conservation, 8,* 415-420.

The BirdLife Taxonomic Working Group (BTWG) (2008). The BirdLife Checklist, May 2008, mainly based on Sibley and Monroe (1990, 1993) and others taxonomic sources. URL: http://www.birdlife.org/datazone/species/taxonomy.html

Towsend, T. M. & Larson, A. & Louis, E. & Macey, J. (2004). Molecular phylogenetics of Squamata: The position of snakes, amphisbaenians and dibamids, and roots of squamale tree. *Systematic Biology, 53,* 737-757.

Traill, L. W. & Bradshaw, C. J. A. & Brook, B. W. (2007). Minimum viable population size: A meta-analysis of 30 years of published estimates. *Biological Conservation, 139,* 159-166.

Tudge, C. (1995). Captive audiences for future conservation. *New Scientist, 145(1962),* 51-52.

Uetz, P. et al (2008). The TIGR Reptile Database, URL: http://www.reptile-database.org. Peter Uetz and German Herpetological Society (DGHT), Heidelberg, Germany, accesed May 23, 2006

Van Hook, T. (1997). Insect coloration and implication for conservation. *Florida Entomologist, 80(2),* 193-210.

Vidal, N. & Hedges, B. S. (2005). The phylogeny of squamate reptiles (lizards, snakes and amphisbaenians) inferred from nine nuclear protein-coding genes. *C. R. Biologies, 328,* 1001-1008.

Ward, P. I. & Mosberger, N. & Kistler, C. & Fischer, O. (1998). The relationship between popularity and body size in zoo animals. *Conservation Biology, 12,* 1408-1411.

White, T. H. Jr. & Collazo, J. A. & Viella, J. F. (2005). Survival of captive-reared puerto rican parrots released in the caribbean national forest. *Condor, 107,* 424-432.

Wilson, D. E., & Reeder, D. A. M. (Eds.) (2005). *Mammal species of the world: A taxonomic and geographic reference (3rd ed).* Johns Hopkins, University Press, 2,142 pp. Checklist available on: http://nmnhgoph.si.edu/msw/

Wilson, E. O. (1992). *The diversity of life*. Cambridge, MA: Harvard University Press.

Wilson, E. O. (2002). *The future of life.* New York, NY: Alfred A. Knopf.

In: Endangered Species: New Research
Editors: A. Columbus and L. Kuznetsov
ISBN 978-1-60692-241-5

Chapter 13

ENDANGERED FELIDAE USED IN TRADITIONAL MEDICINES

***Rômulo Romeu da Nóbrega Alves*[1], *Raynner Rilke Duarte Barboza*[2] and *Wedson de Medeiros Silva Souto*[3]**

[1] Departamento de Biologia, Universidade Estadual da Paraíba, Avenida das Baraúnas, Campina Grande, Paraíba 58109-753, Brazil

[2] Pós-Graduação em Ciência e Tecnologia Ambiental, Universidade Estadual da Paraíba, Avenida das Baraúnas, Campina Grande, Paraíba 58109-753, Brazil

[3] Programa Regional de Pós-Graduação em Desenvolvimento e Meio Ambiente (PRODEMA), Universidade Estadual da Paraíba, Avenida das Baraúnas, Campina Grande, Paraíba 58109-753, Brazil

ABSTRACT

Felidae have had long and uneasy relationships with humans. Many of the world's wild cats are or becoming endangered species and one of the reasons is the use for traditional medicinal purposes. The present work provides an overview of the global usage of felines in traditional folk medicine around the world and the implications for its conservation. The results demonstrated that at least 27 felines are used in traditional medicine worldwide. Of the felines recorded, 24 are included on the IUCN Red List of Threatened Species (with 7 species classified as vulnerable and 3 as endangered) and all is listed in the CITES. This evidenciates the importance of understanding such medicinal uses regarding animal conservation as well as the need for considering socio-cultural factors when establishing management plans concerning the sustainable use of these mammals.

Keywords: Felidae, traditional medicine, animal conservation

INTRODUCTION

Traditional medicinal systems set a key role in health care around the world. Millions of people relied partially or completely of natural products collected from ecosystems for medicinal purposes [1]. Many animals and plants species are used as remedies in traditional medical practices, by far, discussions of the links between Traditional medicine and biodiversity, therefore, are imperative [2, 3].

Since ancient times animals and products derived from different body parts have constituted element of the inventory of medicinal substances used in many cultures, and such uses still exist in ethnic folk medicine [4]. Currently, examples of animal-derived remedies can be found in many urban, semi-urban and more remote localities spread out the world (e.g., Almeida and Albuquerque [5], Alves and Pereira-Filho [6], Alves and Rosa [7, 8], Apaza et al. [9], Pieroni et al. [10], Silva et al. [11], Sodeinde and Soewu [12], Vázquez et al. [13]). Despite the use of medicinal animals being practice marked both by a broad geographical distribution and very deep historical origins, studies on the therapeutic use of animals and animal products have been neglected, when compared to plants [14].

Ingredients sourced from wild plants and animals are not only widely used in traditional medicines, but are also increasingly valued as raw materials in the preparation of modern medicines and herbal preparations. The trade in wildlife body parts and products includes traditional medicine, and it is well known that the annual global trade in animal-based medicinal products accounts for billions of dollars per year. Greater demand and maximized human populations are leading to increased and often unsustainable rates of exploitation of wild sourced ingredients, with some wild species already threatened with extinction [15, 16].

Unsustainable use of plants and animals in traditional medicine is recognized as one menace to wildlife conservation. The linkage between species endangerment and demand from traditional medicine has arrested much concern of conservation community of the world [3, 17-22]. A large number of mammals are used in traditional folk medicine and many of these are of relevant to conservation [23]. The case of large, terrestrial mammals (e.g. tigers, rhinoceros, bears) threatened by trade for traditional medicine, especially traditional Chinese medicine, is well-known. Nevertheless, the list of wild animals believed to have medicinal and curative properties is long and is unknown the real number of mammal's species used in traditional medicine.

Felidae have had long and uneasy relationships with humans. Some cats present a danger to domestic animals, even to humans in the case of the big cats. For such reasons, as well as for sport and fur, cats have been a target of hunters and trappers. In addition, Felines are among the animal species most frequently used in traditional folk medicine. Because of such hunting, combined with loss of suitable habitat and other causes, most species are now considered to be endangered in the wild and one of the reasons is the use for traditional medicinal purposes. This chapter has focused on the global use of felines in traditional folk medicine around the world and the implications for its conservation. We hope this chapter will serve as stimulus for further research about this use of biodiversity and its implications for feline's conservation.

METHODS

In order to examine the diversity of felines used in traditional medicine, all available references or reports about folk remedies based on feline sources were examined. Only taxa that could be identified to species level were included in the database. Scientific names provided in publications were updated according to the ITIS Catalogue of Life: 2007 Annual Checklist [24] and Wilson and Reeder [25]. The conservation status of the Felidae species follows IUCN [23] and CITES [26]. The sources analyzed were: Apaza et al. [9], Baker et al. [27], Begossi et al. [28], CITES [29-32], Costa-Neto [33-35], Duckworth et al. [36], El-Kamali [37], Ezemvelo KZN Wildlife [38], Hanazaki [39], Isichei [40], Justina et al. [41], Khalid et al. [42], Lee and Miththapala [43], Lev and Amar [44], Morris [45], Negi and Palyal [46], Nilsson [47], Nowell and Jackson [48], Solanki and Chutia [49], Taylor and Dunstone [50], Tejada et al. [51], TRAFFIC [52], TRAFFIC/WWF [53], Tratado de Cooperación Amazonica [54], Vargas [55], Vázquez et al. [13], Winter [56], Wu [57], Yates [58], Yi-Ming [59].

RESULTS AND DISCUSSION

Felidae have had a profound effect on human sensibilities since the ancient of time. The lion, leopard, tiger, jaguar and puma have evoked a diversity of cultural responses across the world and throughout history. In art, myth, ideology and religious belief, many societies have employed feline icons as metaphors to express human qualities and symbolize human relations [60]. In the primordial Egypt the Sphinx for example is a representation of a lion, and is one of the earliest works of Egyptian art. The sphinx has the head of the pharaoh, and the body of a lion, showing the pharaoh's power and importance [61].

The role of the felines in folk practices related to the healing and/or prevention of illnesses has been recorded in different social-cultural contexts throughout the world (e.g. Alves et al. [62], Apaza et al. [9], Dexel [63], Mills and Jackson [64], Vázquez et al. [13], Nowell [65]). Despite the fact that technical studies recording the use of felines in traditional medicine are all relatively recent, some authors indicated that feline have been used in traditional medicines since ancient times. For example, a historical revision of the therapeutic uses of animals as described in medieval manuscripts from Azerbaijan revealed that during the Middle Ages, the medicinal use of animals such as lions, tigers, leopards and other small carnivores were widespread in Azerbaijan [66]. Various organs (meat, skin, etc.) of these animals were used in the medieval Azerbaijan medicine. In China, the first references to use of tiger (*Panthera tigris*) bone in traditional medicines date back more than 1500 years. In the herbal compendium, *Mingyi Bielu*, or *Records of Famous Physicians* (Tao Hongjing, circa 500 AD), Tiger bone was said to have the properties of "warding off harmful air, killing evil pathogens, stopping convulsions, and curing carbuncles and ulcerative scrofula." Subsequent herbals have instead emphasized its anti-inflammatory, strengthening and pain-relieving properties for rheumatoid pain, tendonitis and muscular paralysis. Before its removal by the government from the official Pharmacopoeia of the Peoples Republic of China in 1993, Tiger bone was listed for "strengthening tendons and bones, dispelling rheumatism, and relieving pain" and used to treat "pain in joints, tendons and bones, and asthenia in loins and legs" [67].

The results of our review demonstrated that at least 27 felines are used in traditional medicine worldwide. Considering that there are 40 known species of felids in the world today (Wilson and Reeder, 2005), 67.5% of the species know is used in traditional medicines. Some species are used in different countries. For instance, *Panthera onca* (in Bolivia, Mexico and Brazil) [9, 13, 62], *Puma concolor* in Brazil and Bolívia [28, 68], *Panthera tigris* in India, China, Vietnam, Sumatra, Cambodia, Nigeria [12, 65, 69-71]. In Bolivia the species *Panthera onca* contributes with its "fat" for the cure of human illnesses as fatigue, fever and bone pain. [51, 55]. The second and third largest Asian forest felids, the leopard (*Panthera pardus*) and clouded leopard (*Neofelis nebulosa*), are both also hunted for their skins and body parts [72, 73], as well as are many of the smaller species [74]. This evidenciates that the utilization of some species is widespread and the importance of understanding such uses in the context of biodiversity conservation.

Some species are handled for treatment of a single disease, for example, in Sudan *Panthera leo* fat is smeared on the chest to relieve pain and *Panthera pardus* fat is applied externally in cases of paralysis [37], on the other hand, others felines often has multiple medicinal uses and can be employed to treat several ailments, for instance, some Asian cultures imbue tiger (*Panthera tigris*) with enormous healing qualities, and use various tiger parts - especially bone, but also hair, teeth, skin, penis and many other parts - as a cure for dozens of ailments [32]. In China, tiger bones have long been used in the treatment of a variety of diseases, including hemiplegia and joint sprains. Tiger urine was said to be a sovereign remedy for rheumatism [75]. In Brazil, *Panthera onça* and *Puma concolor* is used in treatment of the wounds and leishmaniosis [28].

Besides their role in healing, natural products often have magical-religious significance, reflecting the different views of health and disease that exist within different cultures [76]. In this context, animal parts are used to prepare clinical remedies as well as to make amulets or charms used in magical/religious diagnoses. Popular beliefs usually affect the way species are used in zootherapy [7]. One form of spiritual treatment involves the use of amulets containing feline parts to protect the user diseases [65]. An example is tiger in Traditional Asian medicine Skin is made into magical amulets and novelties, as are teeth and claws [65]. Skin and teeth of *Panthera onca* were historically used as ornaments. Teeth amulets are believed to protect the wearer against snakebites [77]. In the Ancient Egypt, the Egyptian cat (*Felis silvestris*) was held in high esteem in the Nile Valley and still today has a large numbers of admires and its role in antiquity has a religious significance by covering the Pharaohs with their skins giving them supernatural gifts and protections [78].

Of the felines recorded, 24 (88.8 %) are included on the IUCN Red List of Threatened Species (with 7 species classified as vulnerable and 3 are endangered) and all is listed in the CITES (see Table 1). For some of those species the medicinal usage represents an additional pressure that added by other issues has been contributing to the decline of the natural populations, for other, however, the medicinal use has been pointed as one of the main threats to the conservation. For instance, the utilization of tiger products in traditional Chinese Medicine has certainly contributed to the decline of South China tiger and is considered by some authorities to be most serious risk to the Tiger's survival, eclipsing habitat loss [64, 79]. Although almost all tigers' products, from whiskers to faeces, are used in age-old medicines, tiger bone is most valued as treatment for various conditions such as rheumatism [64, 80]. Consumption of tiger bone has increased in recent years and continues today as both human population and per capita expendable income have increased dramatically in East Asia in concert with a resurgence of interest in traditional cures [64, 79].

Table 1 - Felidae used in the wordwide traditional medicine

Species	IUCN Red List	CITES Appendices
Acinonyx jubatus (Schreber, 1775)	VU	I
Caracal caracal (Schreber, 1776)	LC	I, II
Catopuma temminckii (Vigors and Horsfield, 1827)	VU	I
Felis manul Pallas, 1776	-	II
Felis silvestris Schreber, 1775	LC	II
Herpailurus yaguarondi (Lacépède, 1809)	LC	II
Leopardus colocolo (Molina, 1782)	-	II
Leopardus jacobitus (Cornalia, 1865)	-	I
Leopardus pardalis (Linnaeus, 1758)	LC	I
Leopardus tigrinus (Schreber, 1775)	NT	I
Leopardus wiedii (Schinz, 1821)	LC	I
Leptailurus serval (Schreber, 1776)	LC	II
Lynx canadensis Kerr, 1792	LC	II
Lynx lynx (Linnaeus, 1758)	NT	II
Lynx rufus (Schreber, 1777)	LC	II
Neofelis nebulosa (Griffith, 1821)	VU	I
Oncifelis guigna (Molina, 1782)	VU	II
Oreailurus jacobita (Cornalia, 1865)	EN	II
Panthera leo (Linnaeus, 1758)	VU	I
Panthera onca (Linnaeus, 1758)	NT	I
Panthera pardus (Linnaeus, 1758)	LC	I
Panthera tigris (Linnaeus, 1758)	EN	I
Pardofelis marmorata (Martin, 1837)	VU	I
Prionailurus bengalensis (Kerr, 1792)	LC	I, II
Prionailurus planiceps (Vigors and Horsfield, 1827)	VU	I
Puma concolor (Linnaeus, 1771)	NT	I
Uncia uncia (Schreber, 1775)	EN	I

Legend: IUCN Red List of Threatened Species Categories – CR (Critically Endangered), DD (Data Deficient), EN (Endangered), EX (Extinct), EW (Extinct in the Wild), LR/cd (Lower risk: *Conservation dependent*), LR/lc or LC (Least Concern), LR/nt or NT (Near Threatened), VU (Vulnerable). CITES Appendices – I, II or III

In the early 1990s, it became evident that medicinal trade in Tiger bone threatened to drive the already endangered tiger *Panthera tigris* to extinction in the wild. Consumer demand for and trade in their parts and derivatives supply luxury markets as well as markets for cultural and medicinal needs. One of the most complex and far-reaching of these demands is for use in traditional medicines. Traditional Chinese medicine (TCM) uses these animal derivatives to prepare medications in two forms-as individually prepared prescriptions and as over-the-counter medicines. Most of these latter medicines are labelled as having been manufactured in China and are sold in markets worldwide. Since 1994 there has been increased national and international investment in tiger conservation and trade control and promotion of substitutes for tiger bone. But what progress there has been has brought new challenges and some old problems remain to be tackled. Traditional Asian medicine uses tiger bone in a number of different formulae. Skin is made into magical amulets and novelties, as are teeth and claws, while tiger penis is an ingredient of allegedly powerful sexual tonics. However, many of these parts and products are fake tiger, made from the parts of other, more common animals. It is not clear what effect the plethora of fakes has on wild tiger populations. Fakes may satisfy some consumer demand which would otherwise have an impact on wild tigers, or they may stimulate increased demand for genuine tiger parts.

Ironically, analyses conducted by the National Forensics Laboratory of US Fish and Wildlife Service have not yet found any detectable levels of bone in samples of tiger based pharmaceuticals but have revealed high levels of toxic metals, particularly arsenic [81]. This example reinforce the observation of Alves and Rosa [14] that emphasizes the need for implementation of sanitary measures to the trade of animal or their parts for medicinal purposes. Schnurrenberger and Hubbert [82] drew attention to the possibility of transmission of other serious and widespread zoonoses such as tuberculosis or rabies, an aspect that should be considered whenever animal tissues from unknown sources are handled and used as remedies. Traditional drugs and traditional medicine in general represent a still poorly explored field of research in terms of therapeutic potential or clinical evaluation [83], and little research has been done so far to prove the claimed clinical efficacy of animal products for medicinal purposes [84].

The commercialization of animals for medicinal purposes is a widespread phenomenon, with significant implications for their conservation and sustainable use [14]. In various cities parts or products derived of felidae is commercialized, mainly in Africa and Asia. For example, bones claiming to be of Tiger *Panthera tigris* and Leopard *Panthera pardus,* Clouded Leopard *Neofelis nebulosa* (bones or fur) were frequently commercialized in markets in Nigeria [12].

In Cambodia *Panthera pardus* is among the marketed species in local markets. China is not only a consumer, but also the world's largest exporter of tiger bone and other tiger derivatives, exploring over 27 million units' tiger medicines and wine to 26 countries and territories in 1990-92 [64]. Most of the Tiger parts sourced in Cambodia were being exported, while remedies in the domestic marketplace usually contained the bones of other animals and herbal substitutes. The reason given for this was that prices of medicine containing Tiger bone were too high for locals [85]. The male's penis is made into soup, said to give potency, for rich Asian businessmen who pay as much as US$18,000 for a dinner featuring it [86].

Today the Felidae are among the most threatened groups of mammals. The IUCN/SSC Cat Specialist Group's review of felid status for the 2002 *IUCN Red List of Threatened Animals* includes almost half of the family Felidae. Five species are included in the categories Critically Endangered and Endangered. In general, the felids categorized as Threatened fall into two groups: those that appear to be naturally rare, with a limited distribution; and those that have become threatened due to human factors. The Critically Endangered Iberian Lynx fits both criteria, and is near to becoming the first cat species to go extinct in modern times. Considering that most of the felidae species is handled in traditional medicine, such uses should be considered according to an establishment of conservation measures and handling manners.

By 1969, the fur industry had pushed many species of felines to the verge of extinction. The animals declined because they were rare in the wild, had large territories, were trophy hunted, were persecuted by livestock farmers, or pushed from their territories as a result of habitat destruction. Protests and publicity began to mount to ban sale of their fur. In 1969, the U.S. Congress enacted the Endangered Species Conservation Act, which included prohibitions on the importation for commercial purposes of many foreign species [47].

The therapeutic indications of wild animals and plants and domestic or cultivated species also overlapped in many cases. This aspect opens the possibility of, where suitable, replacing the use of threatened species with others in traditional medicine recipes. Such replacement of products is of interest from a conservationist perspective, in the context of reducing the pressure on overexploited populations, or legally protected species [3]. Many of the animal products are intended to increase male potency, and a recent drug marketed in the West, Viagra, may reduce demand for wildlife products such as Tiger and seal penises that have been sold at high prices for this purpose in the past [47].

However, replacement of ingredients in natural remedies should be done with caution, because as pointed by Sodeinde and Soewu [12], substitutes may not always be feasible because recipes using different species may not have the same efficacy, nor may it be advisable without a thorough examination into the sustainability of utilizing substitute species to ensure the viability of any such exploitation. Additionally, consumers sometimes prefer wild versions.

Precaution should also be taken when suggesting the replacement of animal products [3]. The snow leopard (*Uncia uncia*) subject is emblematic. There is demand for snow leopard bones for use as a substitute for Tiger Bone in traditional Asian medicines. In China, snow leopard bones are much in demand for their medicinal use, and probably represent their primary indigenous value today [87, 88]. Leopard bone has been used for some time as a substitute for tiger bone in the manufacture of drug wine which sells far and wide in China and Southeast Asia. The poaching of snow leopards in China is therefore closely connected with this business [88].

The widespread and growing popularity of Traditional Medicine threatens the survival of some species of felines and others animals such as rhinoceroses, bears, seahorses and other/additionally endangered species historically used in these traditional formulations [89]. It must be emphasized, however, that many factors affect feline's populations in the world, and the use of these animals for medicinal purposes is only part of the problem. As such, the medicinal use of felines must be considered together with other/extra anthropogenic pressures. Feline's populations are being seriously reduced throughout the world. As predators, wild cat populations need relatively large blocks of habitat and sufficient quantities of suitable wild prey. With the increasing pace of human population growth and development over the last century, both habitat and prey for cats have declined widely. The big cats have been heavily persecuted because they are a danger to humans and livestock, and for their skins, and some small cat species have been subject to heavy offtakes for the fur trade. All species have declined in range and number, but the situation is illustrated most acutely by the decline of the big cats over the last century [90].

For many Asian cultures, and indeed to cultures around the world, plants and animals are seen as objects to serve human needs. Prohibiting the utilization of natural resources simply does not make sense to many people. Therefore, the concept of wildlife conservation can be alien to them. If the need for conservation is to be accepted by people who make their livelihoods from wildlife or use wildlife for necessities such as food and medicine, then care should be taken to avoid what may be seen as ideological or culturally imperialistic approaches. It is important to accept and respect differing views of the value of wildlife, while, at the same time, explaining the necessity of conservation measures [89].

Some traditional medicinal systems, like the Chinese Traditional Medicine, is recognized by the World Health Organization (WHO) and accepted by one-fourth of the world human population [14], and the reliance on traditional medicinal uses of animals by communities around the world should be addressed when designing strategies to conserve biodiversity. There is a growing recognition of the need to consider the socio-cultural aspects in all discussions on sustainable development (e.g., Alves and Nishida [91], Morin-Labatut and Akhtar [92], Posey [93]), a view that encompasses people's perception, utilization, allocation, transference and management of their natural resources [94]. In that context, Nations [95] emphasizes the utilitarian value of species' protection, and the perspective of long term use of biological diversity, while Soejarto [96] remarks that conservation permits the continuing use of the resources in ways that are non-destructive and sustainable, while from the pharmaceutical point of view, it provides time to eventually demonstrate fully the potentially medicinal value of the resources.

Conclusion

The collection of felidae from the wild for medicinal purposes has been invoked as a factor contributing to the decline of certain species. As pointed by Almeida and Albuquerque [5], the popularity of folk medicine certainly places pressure on these natural resources. The trade of medicinal felines represents an important factor for their over-exploitation. Of the species cataloged in this study, all are included in one or two CITES Appendices, although the reasons for their inclusion are not necessarily related to medicinal use. These results demonstrate the need to assess the implications of the use and trade of felidae parts used in traditional medicines on their wild populations, and the need for including such uses in discussions of Felidae conservation.

References

[1] WHO – World Health Organization. Millennium Ecosystem Assessment. Ecosystems and Human Well-being: Synthesis. 1st ed. Geneva, Switzerland: WHO, 2005.

[2] Anyinam, C. Ecology and ethnomedicine: exploring links between current environmental crisis and indigenous medical practices. *Social Science & Medicine*, 1995 40, 321–329.

[3] Alves, RRN; Rosa, IL. Zootherapeutic practices among fishing communities in North and Northeast Brazil: A comparison. *J Ethnopharmacol*, 2007 111(1), 82-103.

[4] Lev, E. Traditional healing with animals (zootherapy): medieval to present-day Levantine practice. *J Ethnopharmacol*, 2003 86, 107-118.

[5] Almeida, CFCBR; Albuquerque, UP. Uso de plantas e animais medicinais no Estado de Pernambuco (Nordeste do Brasil): Um estudo de caso. *Interciencia*, 2002 27(6), 276-284.

[6] Alves, RRN; Pereira-Filho, GA. Commercialization and use of snakes on North and Northeastern Brazil: implications for conservation and management. *Biodivers. Conserv*, 2007 16, 969-985.

[7] Alves, RRN; Rosa, IL. From cnidarians to mammals: The use of animals as remedies in fishing communities in NE Brazil. *J Ethnopharmacol*, 2006 107, 259-276.

[8] Alves, RRN; Rosa, IL. Zootherapy goes to town: The use of animal-based remedies in urban areas of NE and N Brazil. *J Ethnopharmacol*, 2007b 113, 541-555.

[9] Apaza, L; Godoy, R; Wilkie, D; Byron, E; Huanca, O; Leonard, WL; Peréz, E; Reyes-García, V; Vadez, V. Markets and the use of wild animals for traditional medicine: a case study among the Tsimane' Amerindians of the Bolivian rain forest. *J Ethnobiol*, 2003 23, 47–64.

[10] Pieroni, A; Giusti, ME; Grazzini, A. Animal remedies in the folk medicinal practices of the Lucca and Pistoia Provinces, Central Italy. In: Fleurentin J, Pelt JM, Mazars G editors. *Des sources du savoir aux médicaments du futur/from the sources of knowledge to the medicines of the future*. Paris, France: IRD Editions; 2002, 371-375.

[11] Silva, MLV; Alves, AGC; Almeida, AV. A zooterapia no Recife (Pernambuco): uma articulação entre as práticas e a história. *Biotemas*, 2004 17(1), 95-116.

[12] Sodeinde, OA; Soewu, DA. Pilot study of the traditional medicine trade in Nigeria. *Traffic Bull*, 1999 18(1), 35-40.

[13] Vázquez, PE; Méndez, RM; Guiascón, OGR; Piñera, EJN. Uso medicinal de la fauna silvestre en los Altos de Chiapas, México. *Interciencia*, 2006 31(7), 491-499.

[14] Alves, RRN; Rosa, IL. Why study the use of animal products in traditional medicines?. *J Ethnobiol Ethnomed*, 2005 1, 1-5.

[15] Kang, S; Phipps, M. A question of attitude: South Korea's Traditional Medicine Practitioners and Wildlife Conservation. 1st ed. Hong Kong: TRAFFIC East Asia, 2003.

[16] Lee, S; Hoover, C; Gaski, A; Mills, J. A world apart? Attitudes Toward Traditional Chinese Medicine and Endangered Species in Hong Kong and the United States. 1 st ed. Washington, D.C., USA: TRAFFIC East Asia, TRAFFIC North America and World Wildlife Fund, 1998.

[17] Anon. Medicines from the Wild: TRAFFIC examines impact on North American Wildlife. *TRAFFIC USA*, 1996 15(3), 1.

[18] Brautigam, AJ; Howes, T; Hutton, H; Hutton, J. Analysis of the Market for Tigers, Bears and Musk Deer in the Russian Far East. *TRAFFIC Bull*, 1994 15(1), 23-30

[19] Reed, H. Saiga Antelope Threatened by Massive Trade. *TRAFFIC USA*, 1995 14(2), 1-2.

[20] Biodiversity Working Group. Fourth Annual Report of the BWG/CCICED. In: MacKinnon J, Sung W, Yan X, Smith A editors. *Conserving China's Biodiversity*. Beijing, China: China Environmental Science Press; 1996; 47-66.

[21] Wang, S. Sustainable Development of Traditional Chinese Medicine in Harmony with Wildlife Conservation.

[22] Mills, J. Why Traditional Chinese Medicine is a Wildlife Conservation Concern to be Reckoned with. Presentation at Workshop Stream 1, World Conservation Congress, Montreal, Canada: 1996.

[23] IUCN-The World Conservation Union. 2007 IUCN Red List of Threatened Species [online]. 2007 [cited 2007 December]. Available from: http://www.iucnredlist.org/

[24] ITIS-Integrated Taxonomic Information System. Catalogue of Life: 2007 Annual Checklist. 2007 [cited 2007 December]. Available from: http://www.catalogueoflife.org/search.php.

[25] Wilson, DE; Reeder, DM editors. Mammal Species of the World. 3rd ed. Baltimore, USA: Johns Hopkins University Press; 2005

[26] CITES-Convention on International Trade in Endangered Species of Wild Fauna and Flora. The CITES Appendices. 2007 [cited 2007 November]. Available from: http://www.cites.org/eng/resources/species.html

[27] Baker, MA; Nassar, K; Rifai, L; Qarqaz, M; Al-Melhim, W; Amr, Z. On the current status and distribution of the Jungle Cat, Felis chaus, in Jordan (Mammalia: Carnivora). *Zoology in the Middle East*, 2003 30, 5-10.

[28] Begossi, A; Silvano, RAM; Amaral, BD; Oyakawa, OT. Uses of Fish and Game by Inhabitants of an Extractive Reserve (Upper Juruá, Acre, Brazil). *Environment, Development and Sustainability*, 1999, 1, 73-93.

[29] CITES-Convention on International Trade in Endangered Species of Wild Fauna and Flora. Summary of the status of wild populations of species listed on CITES Appendix I and the difficulty of keeping or breeding specimens of these species in captivity [online]. 2000 [cited 2007 September]. Available from: URL: http://www.cites.org/common/com/AC/16/E16-Inf-15.pdf.

[30] CITES- Convention on International Trade in Endangered Species of Wild Fauna and Flora. List of animal species used in traditional medicine [online]. 2001 [cited 2008 January]. Available from: URL: http://www.cites.org/eng/com/AC/17/E17i-05Rev.doc

[31] CITES-Convention on International Trade in Endangered Species of Wild Fauna and Flora. Trade in products, possibly used as medicinals, of the species listed in document AC18 Doc. 13.1 [online]. 2002 [cited 2007 November]. Available from: URL: http://www.cites.org/common/com/ac/18/E18i-08.doc.

[32] CITES. List of species traded for medicinal purposes [online]. 2002b [cited 2008 January]. Available from: URL: http://www.cites.org/eng/com/ac/18/E18-13-1.pdf

[33] Costa-Neto, EM. Barata é um santo remédio: introdução a zooterapia popular no Estado da Bahia. 1st ed. Feira de Santana, Brazil: Editora Universitária da UEFS; 1999b

[34] Costa-Neto, EM. Recursos animais utilizados na medicina tradicional dos índios Pankararés, que habitam no Nordeste do Estado da Bahia, Brasil. *Actualidades Biologicas*, 1999c 21, 69-79.

[35] Costa-Neto, EM. Animal-based medicines: biological prospection and the sustainable use of zootherapeutic resources. *Anais da Academia Brasileira de Ciências*, 2005 77(1), 33-43.

[36] Duckworth, JW; Salter, RE; Khounboline, K. Wildlife in Lao PDR: 1999 Status Report. 1st ed. Gland, Switzerland: IUCN; 1999.

[37] El-Kamali, HH. Folk medicinal use of some animal products in Central Sudan. *Journal of Ethnopharmacology* 2000 (72), 279-282.

[38] Ezemvelo KZN Wildlife. Felis lybica-African wildcat [online]. 2007 [cited 2007 December 12]. Available from: URL: http://www.kznwildlife.com/site/conservation/wildlife/fauna/African_Wildcat.html
[39] Hanazaki, N. Ecologia de Caiçaras: Uso de recursos e dieta. 1st ed. Campinas, Brazil: Universidade Estadual de Campinas, 2001.
[40] Isichei, AO. Omo Biosphere Reserve, current status, utilization of biological resources and sustainable management: Nigeria. 1st ed. Paris, France: UNESCO; 1995.
[41] Justina, C; Hunter, L; Zigouris, J. Setting Conservation and Research Priorities for Larger African Carnivores. *WCS Working Paper,* 2005 December (24), 77 pp.
[42] Khalid, HS; Elkamali, HH; Elmanan, AMA. Trade of Sudanese Natural Medicinals and their role in Human and Wildlife Health Care [online]. 2007 [cited 2007 November]. Available from: URL: http://www.cropwatch.org/Trade%20of%20Sudanese%20Natural%20Medicinals%20(2).pdf
[43] Lee, SKH; Miththapala, S. An overview of the use of wild animals and plants as medicine [online]. 2006 [cited 2007 December]. Available from URL: http://www.sur.iucn.org/listaroja/biodiversity06/medicinals/Lee%20final.pdf
[44] Lev, E; Amar, Z. Ethnopharmacological survey of traditional drugs sold in the Kingdom of Jordan. *Journal of Ethnopharmacology* 2002 82, 131-145.
[45] Morris, B. The Power of Animals: An Ethnography. 1st ed. New York: Berg; 1998.
[46] Negi, CS; Palyal, VS. Traditional Uses of Animal and Animal Products in Medicine and Rituals by the Shoka Tribes of District Pithoragarh, Uttaranchal, India. *Ethno-Med* 2007 1(1), 47-54.
[47] Nilsson, G. Endangered Species Handbook –Trade [online]. 2005 [cited 2007 Dec.]. Available from: URL: http://www.endangeredspecieshandbook.org/pdfslive/esh_chapter10.pdf
[48] Nowell, K; Jackson, P. Wild Cats: Status Survey and Conservation Action Plan. 2nd ed. Gland, Switzerland: IUCN, 1996.
[49] Solanki, GS; Chutia, P. Ethno Zoological and Socio-cultural Aspects of Monpas of Arunachal Pradesh. *J Hum Ecol* 2004 15(4), 251-254.
[50] Taylor, VJ; Dunstone, N. The Exploitation of Mammal Populations. 1st ed. New York: Springer; 1996.
[51] Tejada, R; Chao, E; Gómez, H; Painter, REL; Wallace, RB. Evaluación sobre el uso de la fauna silvestre en la Tierra Comunitaria de Origen Tacana, Bolivia. *Ecología en Bolivia,* 2006 October 41(2), 138-148.
[52] TRAFFIC. A survey of wildlife trade in Russia [online]. 1998 [cited 2007 December]. Available from: URL: http://www.traffic.org/general-reports/traffic_pub_trade11.pdf
[53] TRAFFIC/WWF. A CITES Priority: Conservation of Tigers and other Asian big cats. CoP12 briefing document. 2002 [cited 2007 November]. Available from URL: http://www.traffic.org/cop12/ABC_CoP12.pdf.
[54] Tratado de Cooperación Amazonica. Conservación y uso de la fauna silvestre en areas protegidas de la Amazonia [online]. 1999 [cited 2008 January]. Available from: URL: http://www.otca.org.br/publicacao/SPT-TCA-VEN-69.pdf
[55] Vargas, LMA. Estudio comparativo de la caza y uso de mamíferos en dos Comunidades Tsimane. 1st ed. La Paz, Bolívia: Universidad Mayor de San Andrés; 2002.

[56] Winter, KA. Subsistence use of terrestrial and aquatic animal resources in the Tierra Comunitaria de origen Itonama of lowland Bolivia. 1st ed. Athens, Georgia: University of Georgia; 2002.

[57] Wu, J. World Without Borders: Wildlife Trade on the Chinese-language Internet. *TRAFFIC Bulletin*, 2007 21(2), 75-84.

[58] Yates, BC. Distinguishing Real vs Fake Tiger Penises. Identification Guides for Wildlife Law Enforcement No. 6. USFWS, National Fish and Wildlife Forensics Laboratory, Ashland, OR [online]. 2005 [cited 2008 January]. Available from URL: http://www.lab.fws.gov/idnotes/TigerPenisIDN6.pdf

[59] Yi-Ming, L; Zenxiang, G; Xinhai, L; Sung, W; Niemelä, J. Illegal wildlife trade in the Himalayan region of China. *Biodiversity and Conservation*, 2000 9, 901-918.

[60] Saunders, NJ. Icons of Power: Feline Symbolism in the Americas. 1st ed. London: Routledge, 1998.

[61] Lattimore, DN. The Winged Cat: A Tale of Ancient Egypt. 1 st ed. New York: HarperCollins, 1992.

[62] Alves, RRN; Rosa, IL; Santana, G. The Role of Animal-derived Remedies as Complementary Medicine in Brazil. *BioScience*, 2007 57(11), 1-7.

[63] Dexel, B. The illegal trade in snow leopards – A global perspective [online]. 2003 [cited 2007 December]. Available from URL: http://www.nabu.de/schneeleopard/report.pdf

[64] Mills, JA; Jackson, P. Killed for a Cure: A Review of the Worldwide Trade in Tiger Bone [online]. 1994 [cited 2008 January]. Available from URL: http://www.traffic.org/species-reports/traffic_species_mammals14.pdf

[65] Nowell, K. Far from a cure: The Tiger trade revisited [online]. 2000 [cited 2007 December]. Available from URL: http://www.traffic.org/species-reports/traffic_species_mammals13.pdf

[66] Alakbarli, F. Medical manuscripts of Azerbaijan. 1st ed. Baku, Azerbaijan: Heydar Aliyev Foundation, 2006.

[67] But, P. Conservation of tigers and bears for sustainable use in Chinese medicine. Paper presented at the International Symposium on Traditional Chinese Medicine and Wildlife Conservation, TRAFFIC/WWF and the Government of Hong Kong, Hong Kong: TRAFFIC, 1995.

[68] Barbarán, FR. Usos mágicos, medicinales y rituales de la fauna en la Puna del Noroeste Argentino y Sur de Bolivia. *Contribuciones al Manejo de Vida Silvestre en Latinoamérica*, 2004 1(1), 1-26.

[69] Patil, SH. Ethno-medico-zoological studies on Nandurbar district of Maharashtra.Indian. *Journal of Traditional Knowledge*, 2003 2(3), 297-299.

[70] Long, B. Tiger conservation and survey training for the Central Vietnam Tiger corridor [online]. 2001 [cited 2007 November]. Available from URL: http://assets.panda.org/downloads/tiger_training_report.pdf

[71] Ng, J.; Nemora. Tiger trade revisited in Sumatra, Indonesia [online]. 2007 [cited 2008 January]. Available from URL: http://www.traffic.org/species-reports/traffic_species_mammals37.pdf

[72] Shepherd, CR. Observations on wildlife trade at Golden Rock, Myanmar. *TRAFFIC Bulletin*, 2001 19, 7–10.

[73] EIA. The tiger skin trail. London: Environmental Investigation Agency, 2004.

[74] Corlett, RT. The Impact of Hunting on the Mammalian Fauna of Tropical Asian Forests. *Biotropica*, 2007 39(3), 292-303.

[75] Laider, L; Laider, K. China's threatened wildlife. 1st ed. London: Blandford A. Cassell Imprint, 1996.

[76] Alves, RRN; Vieira, WLS; Santana, GG. Reptiles used in traditional folk medicine: conservation implications. *Biodiversity and Conservation*, 2008, 13 pp.

[77] Iwokrama. Jaguar, King of the South American Jungle [online]. 2004 [cited 2007 November]. Available from URL: http://www.iwokrama.org/forest/animals/jaguar.htm

[78] Bothmer, BV. Ptolemaic reliefs: A Votive Tablet. *Bulletin of the Museum of fine arts*, 1953 51(286), 80-84.

[79] Henley, G; Mills, J. The tiger in trade: How much and what to do about it? In: Seidensticker J, Jackson P, Christie S editors. *Tigers 2000*. Cambridge, UK: Cambridge University Press; 1997.

[80] Mainka, SA; Mills JA. Wildlife and Traditional Chinese Medicine-Supply and Demand for Wildlife Species. *Journal of Zoo Wildlife Medicine*, 1995 26(2), 193-200.

[81] Espinoza, EP; Mann, MJ; Yates, B; Elliot, L. Preliminary forensic analysis of the wildlife content of patented Asian medicines. In: Gaski AL, Johnson, KA editors. *Prescription for Extinction: Endangered Species and Patented Oriental Medicines in Trade*. Washington DC, USA: TRAFFIC USA; 1994; 94-132.

[82] Schnurrenberger, PR; Hubbert, WT. An Outline of the Zoonoses. 1st ed. Ames, IA, USA: Iowa State University Press, 1981

[83] De Smet, PAGM. Is there any danger in using traditional remedies? *Journal of Ethnopharmacology*, 1991 32, 43-50.

[84] Still, J. Use of animal products in traditional Chinese medicine: environmental impact and health hazards. *Complement Ther Med*, 2003 11, 118-122.

[85] Heng, K. Interviews with Traditional Medicine Pharmacists and Traders in Cambodia. Cat Action Treasury, Los Gatos, California, USA: Unpublished report, 1999.

[86] Highley, K; Highley, SC. Bear Farming and Trade in China and Taiwan. Washington, DC: Humane Society of the United States, 1994.

[87] Schell, J. The Fate of the Earth. 1st ed. New York: Knopf; 1982.

[88] Yanfa, L; Bangjie, T. A Preliminary Study on the Geographical Distribution of Snow Leopards in China. Proceedings of the fifth Iinternational Snow Leopard Symposium. Seattle, USA: ISLT; 1988.

[89] Lee, SKH. Trade in traditional medicine using endangered species: an international context. Proceedings of the second Australian Symposium on traditional medicine and wildlife conservation. Melbourne, Australia: Environment Australia; 1999.

[90] Nowell, K. Status and conservation of the Felidae. *Handbook of the Mammals of the World*. Madrid, Spain: Lynx Edicions; 2001.

[91] Alves, RRN; Nishida, AK. A ecdise do caranguejo-uçá, *Ucides cordatus* L. (Decapoda, Brachyura) na visão do caranguejeiros. *Interciencia*, 2002 27(3), 110-117.

[92] Morin-Labatut, G; Akhtar, S. Traditional environmental knowledge: a resource to manage and share. *Development*, 1992 4, 24-30.

[93] Posey, DA. Exploração da biodiversidade e do conhecimento indígena na América Latina: desafios à soberania e a velha ordem. In: Cavalcanti C, editor. *Meio Ambiente, desenvolvimento sustentável e políticas públicas*. São Paulo, Brazil: Cortez, 1997; 436 pp.

[94] Johannes, RE. Integrating traditional ecological knowledge and management with environmental impact assessment. In: Inglis JT, editor. *Traditional Ecological Knowledge: Concepts and Cases*. Ottawa, Canada: International Program on Traditional Ecological Knowledge and International Development Research Centre, 1993, 142 pp.

[95] Nations, JD. A ecologia profunda encontra o mundo em desenvolvimento. In: Wilson EO, editor. *Biodiversidade*. Rio de Janeiro: Nova Fronteira, 1997, 657 pp.

[96] Soejarto, DD. Biodiversity prospecting and benefit-sharing: perspectives from the field. *Journal of Ethnopharmacology*, 1996 51, 1-15..

INDEX

A

B

C

D

E

F

G

H

J

K

L

M

P

Q

R

S

T

U

V

W

Y

Z